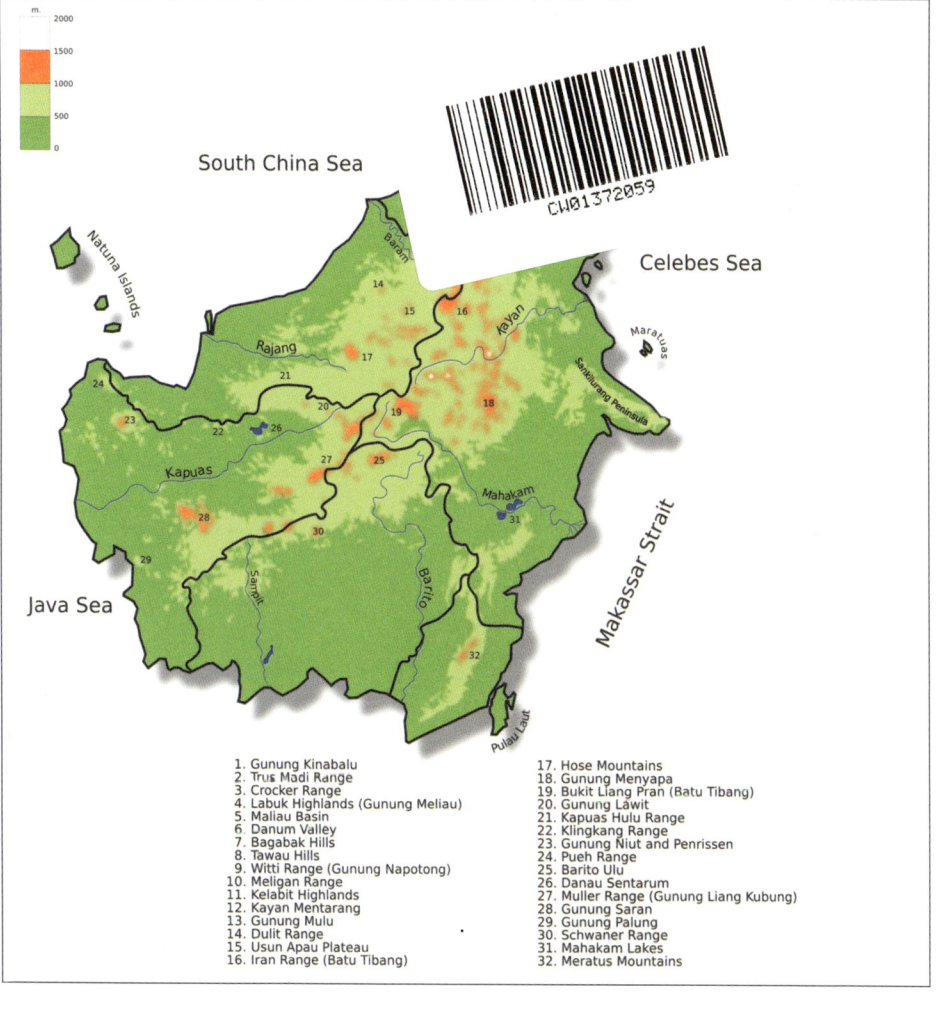

A FIELD GUIDE TO THE
BIRDS
OF
BORNEO

A FIELD GUIDE TO THE
BIRDS
OF
BORNEO

SUSAN MYERS

Illustrated by Richard Allen, Hilary Burn, Clive Byers, Daniel Cole, John Cox,
Anthony Disley, Martin Elliott, Alan Harris, Szabolcs Kokay, Mike Langman,
Ian Lewington, Andrew Mackay, Stephen Message, Christopher Schmidt,
Jan Wilczur and Tim Worfolk

First published in 2009 by New Holland Publishers
London • Cape Town • Sydney • Auckland

www.newhollandpublishers.com

Garfield House, 86-88 Edgware Road, London W2 2EA, United Kingdom
80 McKenzie Street, Cape Town, 8001, South Africa
Unit 1, 66 Gibbes Street, Chatswood, NSW 2067, Australia
218 Lake Road, Northcote, Auckland, New Zealand

10 9 8 7 6 5 4 3 2 1

Copyright © 2009 in text: Susan Myers
Copyright © 2009 in cartography: Susan Myers
Copyright © 2009 in plates: Richard Allen, Hilary Burn, Clive Byers,
　Daniel Cole, John Cox, Anthony Disley, Martin Elliott, Alan Harris,
　Szabolcs Kokay, Mike Langman, Ian Lewington, Andrew Mackay,
　Stephen Message, Christopher Schmidt, Jan Wilczur and Tim Worfolk
Copyright © 2009 in avian topography: Richard Allen
Copyright © 2009 New Holland Publishers (UK) Ltd

All rights reserved. No part of this publication may be reproduced, stored
in a retrieval system or transmitted, in any form or by any means, electronic,
mechanical, photocopying, recording or otherwise, without the prior written
permission of the publishers and the copyright holders.

A CIP catalogue record for this book is available from the British Library.

ISBN 978 1 84773 381 8

Publisher: Simon Papps
Editors: Simon Papps and Nigel Collar
Designer: Alan Marshall
Index: Jennifer Lunsford
Production: Melanie Dowland
Publishing Director: Rosemary Wilkinson

Reproduction by Modern Age Repro Co. Ltd, Hong Kong
Printed and bound in Singapore by Tien Wah Press (Pte) Ltd

CONTENTS

Visual index	Frontpapers	
INTRODUCTION	7	
Climate	7	
Habitats	7	
Birds	8	
Geological history	9	
Taxonomy	9	
Range & status	9	
Explanation of species accounts	10	
Abbreviations	11	
Endemic birds of Borneo	11	
Avian topography	12	
Glossary	13	
Map key	14	
Useful addresses	15	
Acknowledgements	15	

SPECIES ACCOUNTS

Megapodiidae: Scrubfowl	16
Phasianidae: Partridges, quail & pheasants	16
Anatidae: Ducks, geese & swans	22
Procellariidae: Petrels & shearwaters	27
Hydrobatidae: Storm-petrels	27
Podicipedidae: Grebes	28
Ciconiidae: Storks	28
Threskiornithidae: Ibises & spoonbills	29
Ardeidae: Herons	30
Phaethontidae: Tropicbirds	38
Fregatidae: Frigatebirds	38
Sulidae: Gannets & boobies	40
Phalacrocoracidae: Cormorants	41
Anhingidae: Darters	42
Falconidae: Falcons	42
Pandionidae: Osprey	45
Accipitridae: Hawks, eagles & allies	45
Rallidae: Rails, gallinules & coots	57
Burhinidae: Thick-knees	61
Recurvirostridae: Avocets & stilts	62
Vanellidae: Lapwings & allies	63
Pluvialidae: *Pluvialis* plovers	64
Charadriidae: *Charadrius* plovers & allies	64
Jacanidae: Jacanas	68
Rostratulidae: Painted-snipe	69
Scolopacidae: Snipe, sandpipers & allies	69
Glareolidae: Pratincoles & coursers	84
Stercorariidae: Skuas & jaegers	85
Sternidae: Terns	86
Laridae: Gulls	91
Columbidae: Pigeons & doves	91
Psittacidae: Parrots & parakeets	100
Cuculidae: Cuckoos	102
Tytonidae: Barn-owls, grass-owls & bay owls	113
Strigidae: Typical owls	114
Podargidae: Frogmouths	119
Caprimulgidae: Nightjars	122
Apodidae: Swifts	124
Trogonidae: Trogons	128
Coraciidae: Rollers	131
Alcedinidae: Kingfishers	131
Meropidae: Bee-eaters	136
Upupidae: Hoopoes	137
Bucerotidae: Hornbills	137
Ramphastidae: Barbets	142
Indicatoridae: Honeyguides	145
Picidae: Woodpeckers	145
Eurylaimidae: Broadbills	154
Pittidae: Pittas	158
Vireonidae: Vireos, shrike-babblers, epornis & allies	163
Acanthizidae: Thornbills & allies	164
Eupetidae: Rail-babbler & allies	164
Pachycephalidae: Whistlers & allies	165
Campephagidae: Cuckooshrikes, trillers & minivets	166
Oriolidae: Old World orioles	169
Genera incertae sedis: Woodshrikes, flycatcher-shrikes & philentomas	171
Artamidae: Woodswallows	172
Aegithinidae: Ioras	173
Rhipiduridae: Fantails	173

Monarchidae: Monarchs, paradise-flycatchers & allies	174	**Alaudidae:** Larks	227
		Pycnonotidae: Bulbuls	227
Dicruridae: Drongos	176	**Hirundinidae:** Swallows & martins	236
Corvidae: Crows, jays, magpies & treepies	178	**Cettiidae:** *Abroscopus* warblers, Mountain Tailorbird, *Cettia* bush-warblers, stubtails & allies	238
Pityriaseidae: Bristlehead	181		
Laniidae: Shrikes	181	**Phylloscopidae:** *Seicercus* & *Phylloscopus* warblers	239
Nectariniidae: Sunbirds & spiderhunters	183		
		Timaliidae: Babblers	241
Dicaeidae: Flowerpeckers	189	**Acrocephalidae:** *Acrocephalus* warblers & allies	257
Chloropseidae: Leafbirds	194		
Irenidae: Fairy-bluebirds	195	**Megaluridae:** Grasshopper warblers, *Bradypterus* bush-warblers, grassbird & allies	258
Sittidae: Nuthatches	196		
Estrildidae: Avadavats, parrotfinches, munias & allies	196		
		Cisticolidae: Cisticolas, tailorbirds, prinias & allies	260
Passeridae: Old World sparrows	198		
Emberizidae: Buntings & allies	199		
Motacillidae: Pipits & wagtails	200		
Sturnidae: Starlings	204		
Turdidae: Thrushes & allies	207		
Muscicapidae: Old World flycatchers including chats, forktails & allies	210		
Stenostiridae: Canary-flycatchers & allies	226	**References**	262
		Index	266
Paridae: Tits	226	**Maps**	**Endpapers**

INTRODUCTION

The island of Borneo straddles the equator in a key position on the edge of the South-East Asian region next to the interchange zone ('Wallacea') with the Australasian region. It is divided into three countries—Brunei, Malaysia and Indonesia. The region of Kalimantan, Indonesia, occupies the major portion of the surface area of the island, while the states of Sabah and Sarawak belong to Malaysia. The South-East Asia region consists of Indochina and the Thai-Malay Peninsula on the mainland and the Indo-Malayan Archipelago extending south and east of the mainland. Geologically, the Thai-Malay Peninsula and much of the Indo-Malayan Archipelago lies on the Sunda Shelf, an extension of the continental shelf of South-East Asia. The term 'Sundaland' refers to the Thai-Malay Peninsula, and the islands of Sumatra, Java, Bali, Borneo, Palawan and many smaller islands that lie on the Sunda Shelf. Sundaland is distinct from most of the Philippine islands, which are largely oceanic and of volcanic origin, and from the islands of Wallacea (Sulawesi, the Moluccas, and the Lesser Sundas), which lie east of Wallace's Line on the Sahul (Australian) continental shelf.

While much of Borneo is low-lying, with well over half of its area under 150 m, a central mountain range extends from Sabah in a south-westerly orientation down the border between Sarawak and Kalimantan with extensions to the south-west, south and south-east.

The central range extends from Gunung Kinabalu to roughly the centre of Borneo on the border between Sarawak and Kalimantan. This range incorporates the Crocker and Tama Abu Ranges, the Kelabit Highlands including Gunung Murud, and Iran Range. From there the western chain extends to the Kapuas Hulu and the somewhat more isolated Pueh Ranges in West Sarawak. A south-western chain extends from the centre at the Kapuas–Mahakam Rivers divide to the Muller and Schwaner ranges in West and Central Kalimantan. A south-eastern chain extends from the centre around Barito Ulu to the rather isolated Meratus Mountains and an eastern chain to the Sambaliung Mountains on the Sangkulirang Peninsula. There are further outlying ranges including the Brassey Range, Tawau Hills, Trus Madi Range, Gunung Mulu and the Dulit Range.

The central ranges and outliers are generally relatively low. At 4,010 m, Gunung Kinabalu is the highest peak between West Papua and the Himalayas but few other peaks in Borneo exceed 2,000 m. The highest mountains occur in Sabah. These mountains also have the largest number of endemic species, and they feature several bird species with odd distributions. Throughout Borneo a vast network of rivers rise from the interior mountains and fan down to the coast.

Climate

Borneo lies between the latitudes 7ºN and 4ºS. The climate can be classified as moist tropical with the equator passing roughly through the centre of the island. Temperatures average 25º–35ºC in the lowlands throughout the year, and humidity is always high.

Borneo is influenced by two monsoonal systems. The north-west monsoon from November to April is wetter than the so-called dry south-east monsoon from May to October. Monthly rainfall generally exceeds 200 mm but peaks in November, with a second peak in April. June to August are the driest months, but even then rainfall is never less than 100 mm a month. Rainfall is generally higher in North Borneo (defined below under 'Range & status') and lowest on the east coast where the influence of the north-west monsoon is weaker, as most of the rain has fallen in the central mountain ranges. The mountain ranges also influence climate locally. In the lowlands the warm, everwet climate supports large expanses of rich lowland evergreen rainforest.

Habitats

The main forest types in Borneo are mangroves, coastal woodlands, peatswamp forest, kerangas (heath forest), lowland dipterocarp forest, hill forest and montane forest. There is an exceptionally high floral diversity comparable to that of New Guinea or the Amazon, with up to 15,000 species of flowering plant. Floristic richness and forest type are largely dependent on soil type and elevation. The lowland dipterocarp forests support the greatest biological diversity and are very important commercially. Borneo's lowland dipterocarp forests (rainforest) are the most extensive in the region but they have been much exploited for timber in the last few decades and are rapidly being replaced by plantations, in particular oil palm. Much of the canopy of these forests is 60 m or more tall. These forests display a marked stratification and the layers of the forest can roughly be categorised as emergent, upper, middle and lower storeys and forest floor. The emergents and upper storey are dominated by commercially valuable dipterocarp trees. Rainforest birds in particular also show a clear vertical stratification, with a number of groups specific to the canopy, middle and lower storeys and the forest floor, respectively.

Mangroves A number of bird species in Borneo are largely dependent on mangroves but few are restricted to this habitat type. Frugivores are rare in the mangroves but this forest type is valuable for passage migrants and for roosting sites for a number of species.

Peatswamp forest This forest type is largely absent from Sabah but there are large expanses of it further south, mostly near the coast, particularly in Central Kalimantan. Species diversity is lower than that of the lowland dipterocarp forest, but a handful of species are commoner in peatswamp forest.

Kerangas Kerangas, a local Iban name for heath forest (literally 'land which cannot grow rice'), is characterised by poor soils and low plant diversity. As with peatswamp forest, many of the plants have toxic leaves. The low plant diversity is reflected by a low diversity of birds, generally less than half that of lowland dipterocarp forests.

Lowland dipterocarp forest Here bird diversity reaches its peak. Over 60% of species on Borneo are confined to this forest type, while almost 80% are dependent to some degree. The great structural and floristic diversity combined with the stable conditions exhibited by the lowland dipterocarp forest has contributed to the development of this bird diversity. A single family of massive flowering trees, the dipterocarps, dominate this forest. They are so named for their two-winged fruits (actually many have three to five wings) and they are supported by huge buttresses that are needed to stabilise them in the shallow soils of the rainforest.

Dipterocarps are most abundant in South-East Asia and especially in Borneo, where the biologically diverse forests contain upward of twelve hundred tree species. Dipterocarps often account for half of all canopy trees. They do not depend on animals or the wind to disperse their seeds. The winged seeds are heavy and helicopter to the ground close to the parent tree. Mature trees may not reproduce for three to ten years and then suddenly blanket the forest floor with their seeds in a cyclical mode of reproduction known as masting.

Many species of dipterocarp flower and fruit synchronously. Within the forest these trees all begin to flower over the same two-month period, requiring a further four months for the fruits to mature. Then, within four to five weeks, all the fruits drop. Once on the forest floor, they immediately begin to germinate. A number of species, including the hornbills, rarely breed during non-masting years. In Borneo some animals such as parakeets, pigs and orang-utans even migrate in search of masting forests.

Hill and montane forest The mountain ranges of Borneo are or were like islands in a sea of lowland forest. The isolation of numerous peaks has led to the evolution of many unique species. Over 60% of the island's endemic birds are montane residents and many more species are dependent on the hill and montane forests. However, species diversity decreases with altitude. The upper montane avifauna has largely Himalayan affinities and it is thought that these arrived in Borneo during a period of mainland landbridge connection during the glacial periods of the Pleistocene. Gunung Kinabalu is of particular importance with 64% of Bornean endemics found here alone.

(Elevations for these forest types are given under 'Habitat' below.)

Birds

The birds of Borneo are essentially Asian in origin, showing many similarities with the Thai-Malay Peninsula and Sumatra, and to a lesser extent Java and Bali. Of the 633 species described in this book, 430 are resident. Of particular interest are the 50 endemic species, most of which are montane residents and are restricted to Sabah and Sarawak, with some only just occurring in Brunei and Kalimantan (although the situation is sure to change as we come to understand the avifauna of Kalimantan better). The highest rate of endemism in the Sundaic islands is here in Borneo. Additionally, more than 200 endemic subspecies are found on the island.

The distribution of birds in Borneo is not uniform and is influenced by habitat, altitude and geological history. There are seven major biogeographical zones on the island: (1) the interior mountain ranges of central Borneo (from north-west Sabah extending along the Sarawak–Kalimantan border), (2) the north-west coast (Brunei and east Sarawak), (3) the north-east (Sabah and north-east East Kalimantan), (4) the seasonally drier east coast (eastern East Kalimantan), (5) the Meratus Mountains (South Kalimantan), (6) the southern lowland plains (the extensive swamp forests of Central Kalimantan), and (7) the hills of the north-west coast (western Sarawak and West Kalimantan).

Geological history
The make-up and distribution of the avifauna of Borneo has been largely determined by the geological history of the Sundaic Region. The Sundaic Region consists of the Thai-Malay Peninsula, Sumatra, Borneo, Palawan, Java and Bali. During the Tertiary and Quaternary Periods sea-levels rose and subsided owing to tectonic activity, and later as a result of long periods of alternation between glacial and interglacial periods. Bornean biogeography has been heavily influenced by changes in sea-levels during this prolonged period of Pleistocene glaciation. At this time the climate was also markedly more seasonal than that of today. During the Pleistocene the glacial periods were considerably longer than the interglacial periods and for the last two million years or so the Sunda Shelf has been exposed above sea-level. These factors all allowed immigration from the Asian mainland. When the sea-levels were at their lowest, the land linkages between the mainland and the Sundaic islands were formed and broken many times. Java, Bali and Palawan were connected less often to the other islands on the Sunda Shelf. Lower sea-levels allowed movements of bird populations to and from the island and the mainland. Mainland Asia thus became a conduit for the process of speciation as fluctuations in sea-level allowed a series of colonisation and isolation events promoting increased diversity on the land mass.

Sea-level changes are also thought to have played a particularly important role in the evolution of endemic species on Borneo. Thirty-five (70%) of Borneo's 50 endemic species (see list below) have montane distributions. It is thought that during periods of elevated sea-level, mountains offered refuge for otherwise lowland populations. These populations diverged genetically while isolated on peaks, and when sea-levels subsided, were displaced from the lowlands by invading congeneric competitors. At times of glacial maxima, temperatures were lower than today, leading to lower montane zones and the spread of many montane species throughout the island.

In the north-east, particularly in Sabah, there are several endemic species and subspecies of lowland birds which are distinct from their more widespread, lowland sister taxa. These include White-fronted Falconet *Falco latifrons* and Black-thighed Falconet *F. fringillarius*, and Black-and-crimson Pitta *Pitta ussheri* and Garnet Pitta *P. granatina*. A faunal divide in the vicinity of the border between Sabah on the one hand and Sarawak and E Kalimantan on the other has long been recognised. And recently evidence of genetic differentiation across the faunal divide in several groups of species that exhibit no obvious morphological differences has been recognised. This cryptic differentiation has been found in other groups including bats and tree shrews. North-eastern Borneo was never directly connected to the mainland or to the major Sundaic islands, so birds colonising Borneo filtered more slowly north-eastward through the island to reach modern Sabah. In other words, the populations of these species in Sarawak are recent Pleistocene invaders from the mainland or Sumatra, whereas the populations of sister taxa in Sabah represent older Bornean lineages.

Taxonomy
The entire continent of Asia has long been neglected when it comes to the study of the taxonomy of the avifauna. Happily, in recent years there has been more attention paid to the birdlife of the region and a number of important publications have sought to correct this unfortunate situation. Of particular interest are a number of taxa that have been relatively recently recognised as endemic to Borneo. These are Bornean Frogmouth *Batrachostomus mixtus*, Bornean Leafbird *Chloropsis kinabaluensis*, Bornean Bulbul *Pycnonotus montis*, Pale-faced Bulbul *Pycnonotus leucops*, Cinereous Bulbul *Hemixos cinereus*, Bornean Whistling-thrush *Myophonus borneensis*, Bornean Forktail *Enicurus borneensis*, Bare-headed Laughingthrush *Melanocichla calva*, and Chestnut-hooded Laughingthrush *Rhinocichla treacheri*. One taxon has lost its endemic status: Bornean Spiderhunter *Arachnothera everetti* is now recognised as a subspecies of Streaky-breasted Spiderhunter *Arachnothera affinis*.

In general the taxonomy and nomenclature follows that of Robson's 2008 edition of the *A Field Guide to the Birds of South-East Asia*.

Range & status
Brunei is the smallest political unit on Borneo, consisting of two parts located on the north-west coast surrounded by the Malaysian state of Sarawak. The Malaysian state of Sabah occupies the entire northern portion of the island to approximately 7°N. It shares a border with Sarawak and East Kalimantan and can be roughly divided west and east by the northern mountain ranges. Sarawak occupies most of the north-central and west coastal area, sharing a border with East and West Kalimantan. The border straddles the central and west mountain ranges. Sarawak can be roughly divided into east, central and west. The Indonesian region of Kalimantan is the largest political unit on Borneo and is divided into four

provinces—East Kalimantan, Central Kalimantan, South Kalimantan and West Kalimantan. Kalimantan remains very poorly known ornithologically.

A number of offshore islands are politically and biogeographically part of Borneo. Some of the most important islands include Mantanani, Banggi and Sipidan (Sabah), Labuan (a Malaysian federal territory), the Maratuas (East Kalimantan), the Karimata Islands (West Kalimantan), the Anambas and North and South Natunas (politically part of Sumatra but closest to West Kalimantan).

Explanation of species accounts
I have largely followed Robson's lead from *A Field Guide to the Birds of South-East Asia* (New Holland, 2008) in the presentation of the species accounts, with some differences.

Identification The overall length of the species is given at the beginning of each account, followed in many cases by a brief general description. Differing from Robson (2008), a full description of each species then follows. Where not monotypic the subspecies is identified and the **Adult male** is described first, followed by the **Adult female** and, the **First winter**, the **Immature** and the **Juvenile** where appropriate. In most cases the breeding plumage is described first except in cases on non-breeding visitors. Where more than one subspecies occurs the taxon most likely to be encountered by birders is described first. In many cases, there then follows a brief summation of differences between **similar species**.

Habitat Generally, habitat types are defined as follows: primary forest has had little or no human disturbance; secondary forest is forest in which large trees have been removed but there has been some regeneration. Lowland forest is roughly defined as forest from 0–400 m, hill forest 400–950 m, lower montane forest 950–1,400 m and upper montane forest >1,400 m. In most cases altitudinal ranges known from Borneo are given. Habitat types in Borneo are discussed briefly above. Also mentioned are a number of anthropogenic habitats such as paddyfields, plantations, parks and gardens.

Behaviour Notes on the behaviour of most regularly occurring species are given under this heading. Many behaviours provide important identification tools for the observer.

Voice Calls and songs are notoriously difficult to describe in words and can only be rendered in a subjective manner. In most cases, where possible, recordings of vocalisations made in Borneo were analysed. The tone and timbre, pitch and frequency, and rhythm and timing are described with adjectives and often with measurements. Increasingly, birders are becoming familiar with sonagrams, and descriptions of the frequency in kiloHertz (sound wave cycles per second) are comprehensible and useful. In many cases the timing is given in terms of notes per second. This is less subjective than some other methods of describing vocalisations.

Range & status The extralimital range is given followed by the range and status within Borneo. Where South-East Asia is referred to this generally means Indochina and the Thai-Malay Peninsula. If the species occurs in South-East Asia but not in Indochina the Thai-Malay Peninsula is specified. The term Indian Subcontinent refers in general to Pakistan, India, Nepal, Bhutan, Bangladesh and Sri Lanka.

Definition of terms used to describe the status of species in Borneo: **abundant** – a conspicuous species that occurs in very large numbers; **common** – a species that occurs in large numbers; **fairly common** – a species that occurs in fair to moderate numbers; **uncommon** – a species that is found in low numbers; **rare** – a species that is recorded in very low numbers. Additionally the terms 'local' or 'locally common/uncommon' may be used for species that are found in restricted areas but where they occur are common or uncommon as the case may be.

Definition of terms used to describe the status of species in Borneo are: **resident** – a breeding species present throughout the year; **non-breeding visitor** – usually absent from Borneo at least a few months of the year (usually during the northern hemisphere summer – June, July, August – but in most cases the time period is given); **passage migrant** – occurs on passage to breeding or non-breeding areas; **vagrant** – rare and unexpected, does not occur annually.

The term North Borneo refers to Sabah, Brunei, Sarawak, northern East Kalimantan, and far north Central and West Kalimantan, while South Borneo is South Kalimantan, and southern East, Central and West Kalimantan. The divide can be thought of as occurring roughly at the equator. Generally, the distributions within Borneo are given in detail according to state and province, and divisions within those units (E and W Sabah; Brunei; E, C and W Sarawak; E, C, W and S Kalimantan).

Breeding A great deal is still unknown about Bornean birds, especially with regard to breeding biology, so breeding dates are merely those recorded so far. Generally speaking, rainforest birds in Borneo tend to breed towards and following the end of the north-west 'wet' monsoon from November to April, as insects reach their peak abundance and conditions are drier. Where known, descriptions of the eggs and nest are summarised.

Abbreviations In the species accounts, points of the compass are given as N, S, E and W. Gunung (mountain) is shortened to G., kiloHertz to kHz and seconds to s.

Endemic birds of Borneo
Dulit Partridge *Rhizothera dulitensis* *
Red-breasted Partridge *Arborophila hyperythra* *
Crimson-headed Partridge
   Haematortyx sanguiniceps * ‡
Bulwer's Pheasant *Lophura bulweri*
Bornean Peacock-pheasant
   Polyplectron schleiermacheri
White-fronted Falconet *Microhierax latifrons*
Mountain Serpent-eagle *Spilornis kinabaluensis* *
Bornean Ground-cuckoo *Carpococcyx radiatus*
Dulit Frogmouth *Batrachostomus harterti* *
Bornean Frogmouth *Batrachostomus mixtus* *
Bornean Swiftlet *Collocalia dodgei* *
Whitehead's Trogon *Harpactes whiteheadi* *
Mountain Barbet *Megalaima monticola* *
Golden-naped Barbet *Megalaima pulcherrima* *
Bornean Barbet *Megalaima eximia* *
Hose's Broadbill *Calyptomena hosii* *
Whitehead's Broadbill *Calyptomena whiteheadi* *
Blue-headed Pitta *Pitta baudii*
Blue-banded Pitta *Pitta arquata* *
Black-and-crimson Pitta *Pitta ussheri*
Bornean Whistler *Pachycephala hypoxantha* *
Black Oriole *Oriolus hosii* *
Bornean Treepie *Dendrocitta cinerascens* *
Bornean Bristlehead *Pityriasis gymnocephala* †
Whitehead's Spiderhunter *Arachnothera juliae* *
Yellow-rumped Flowerpecker
   Prionochilus xanthopygius
Black-sided Flowerpecker *Dicaeum monticolum* *
Bornean Leafbird *Chloropsis kinabaluensis* *
Dusky Munia *Lonchura fuscans*
Fruit-hunter *Chlamydochaera jefferyi* * ‡
Everett's Thrush *Zoothera everetti* *
Bornean Whistling-thrush *Myophonus borneensis* *
White-crowned Shama *Copsychus stricklandii*
Bornean Forktail *Enicurus borneensis* *
Bornean Blue Flycatcher *Cyornis superbus*
Eyebrowed Jungle-flycatcher *Rhinomyias gularis* *
Bornean Bulbul *Pycnonotus montis* *
Pale-faced Bulbul *Pycnonotus leucops* *
Cinereous Bulbul *Hemixos cinereus* *
Bornean Stubtail *Urosphena whiteheadi* *
Pygmy White-eye *Oculocincta squamifrons* ‡
Mountain Blackeye *Chlorocharis emiliae* * ‡
Chestnut-crested Yuhina *Staphida everetti* *
Black-browed Babbler *Malacocincla perspicillata*
Bornean Ground-babbler
   Ptilocichla leucogrammica
Black-throated Wren-babbler *Turdinus atrigularis*
Mountain Wren-babbler *Napothera crassa* *
Bare-headed Laughingthrush *Melanocichla calva* *
Chestnut-hooded Laughingthrush
   Rhinocichla treacheri *
Friendly Bush-warbler *Bradypterus accentor* *

* lower and upper montane species
‡ endemic genus
† endemic family

AVIAN TOPOGRAPHY

The figures below illustrate the main plumage tracts and bare-part features. This terminology for bird topography has been used extensively in the species descriptions, and a full understanding of these terms is important if the reader is to make full use of this book; they are a starting point in putting together a description.

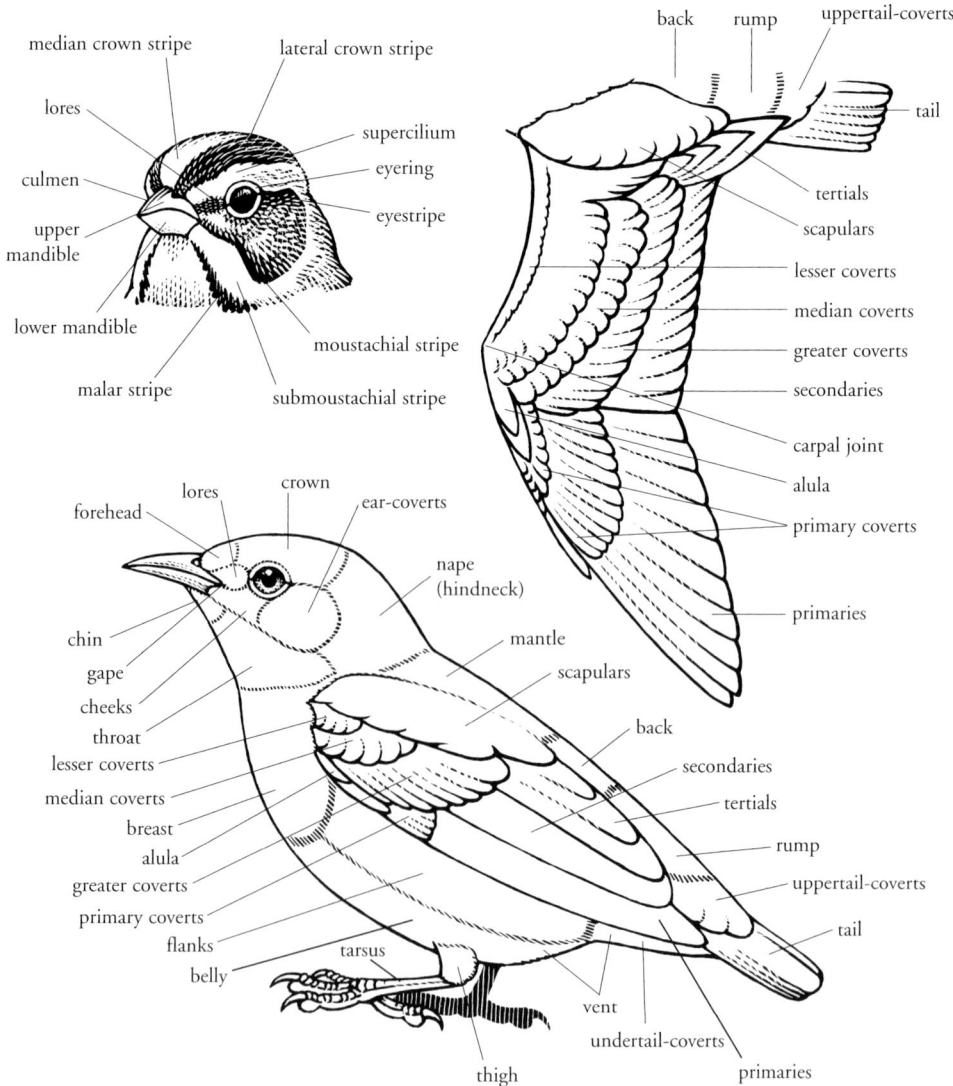

GLOSSARY

Arboreal: tree-dwelling.

Axillaries: the feathers at the base of the underwing.

Bare parts: collective term for bill, legs and feet, eyering, exposed facial skin, etc.

Cap: well-defined patch of colour or bare skin on top of the head

Casque: an enlargement of the upper mandible, as in many hornbill species.

Cere: a fleshy structure at the base of the bill, which contains the nostrils.

Colony: an aggregation of birds that nest or roost usually in close proximity.

Comb: erect unfeathered fleshy growth, situated lengthwise on crown.

Coverts: short contour feathers that overlay the wing and tail feathers on the upper and lower surfaces.

Crepuscular: active at dawn and dusk.

Crest: tuft of feathers on crown of head, sometimes erectile.

Crown: the upper part of the head.

Dihedral: the upward angle of the wings from the horizontal when a bird is in flight.

Eclipse: a dull short-term post-nuptial plumage.

Endemic: restricted or confined to a specific country or region (Borneo in this book).

Eye-stripe: a line of feathers in front of and behind the eye.

Eye-ring: feathers or skin surrounding the eye.

Face: informal term for the front part of the head, usually including the forehead, lores, cheeks and often the chin.

Facial disc: a rounded, rather concave and well defined part of the face, notably seen in owls.

Flight feathers: In this work, a space-saving collective term for primaries and secondaries.

Fringe: complete feather margin.

Frugivorous: fruit-eating.

Graduated tail: tail on which each feather, starting outermost, is shorter than the adjacent inner feather.

Gregarious: living in flocks or communities.

Gular: pertaining to the throat.

Gunung: Malay and Indonesia word for mountain.

Hackles: long, pointed neck feathers.

Hepatic: brownish-red (applied to the rufous morph of some cuckoos).

Iban: one of the largest groups of Dayak or indigenous peoples of Borneo.

Immature: a non-specific term for pre-adult stages.

Indian Subcontinent: a large section of the Asian continent that includes India, Pakistan, Bangladesh, Nepal, Bhutan and Sri Lanka.

Iris: the coloured part of the eye.

Juvenile: an immature bird immediately after leaving the nest, most birds lose this plumage soon after leaving the nest.

Kilohertz (kHz): a measure of sound frequency or pitch, equal to 1,000 hertz, measuring the number of sound waves per second.

Knob: a fleshy protrusion on the upper mandible of the bill.

Lateral: on or along the side.

Leading edge: the front edge (usually of the forewing in flight).

Local: occurring or relatively common within a small or restricted area.

Mask: informal term for the area of the head around the eye, often extending back from the bill and covering (part of) the ear-coverts.

Mesial: down the middle (applied to streak on chin/throat, mostly of raptors); interchangeable with gular.

Monotypic: a taxonomic group with only one type, for example a monotypic species has no subspecies, a monotypic genus has only one species.

Morph: a permanent alternative plumage exhibited by a species, having no taxonomic standing and usually involving base colour, not pattern.

Morphology: the physiological attributes of a bird.

Nomadic: prone to wandering, or occurring erratically, with no fixed territory outside breeding season.

Nuchal: pertaining to the nape and hindneck.

Ocelli: eye-like spots, often iridescent.

Orbital: surrounding the eye.

Palearctic: a terrestrial ecoregion that includes Europe, parts of northern Africa and Asia north of the Himalayas.

Pelagic: of the open sea.

Phase: a temporary alternative plumage exhibited by a species.

Polyandrous: mating with more than one male (usually associated with sex-role reversal).

Post-ocular: behind the eye.

Pre-ocular: in front of the eye.

Primary projection: the distance between the longest primary feathers and the longest secondaries or tertials in the folded wing.

Pulau: Malay and Indonesia word for island.

Race: see subspecies.

Sexually dimorphic: where the sexes exist in two forms, differing in morphology.

Shaft-streak: a pale or dark line in the plumage produced by the feather shaft.

Speculum: a panel of iridescent feathers on the secondaries of some ducks.

Spur: a bony outgrowth from the tarsus with a sharp point, often found in partridges and pheasants.

Subspecies: a geographical population whose members collectively show constant differences, usually in morphology, from those of other populations of the same species.

Subterminal: immediately before the tip or edge.

Supercilium: a line of feathers above the eye, sometimes referred to as an eyebrow.

Tarsi: plural of tarsus

Tarsus/Tarsal: the lower leg – the part of the leg between the reverse 'knee' and the foot.

Terminal: at the tip.

Terrestrial: living or occurring mainly on the ground.

Thai-Malay Peninsula: the southern extremity of continental Asia encompassing the geographic region from southern Tenasserim in peninsular Burma, the peninsular Thailand (the Kra Peninsula), the Malay Peninsula to Singapore.

Tibia: upper half of often visible avian leg (above the reverse 'knee').

Trailing edge: the rear edge (usually of the wing in flight).

Underparts: the lower parts of the body (loosely applied).

Upperparts: the upper parts of the body, usually excluding the head, tail and wings (loosely applied).

Vagrant: a status for a species when it is accidental (rare and irregular) in occurrence.

Vermiculated: marked with narrow wavy lines, often only visible at close range.

Wing-bar: a line across a closed wing formed by different-coloured tips to the greater or median coverts, or both.

Wing-panel: a lengthwise strip on closed wing formed by coloured fringes (usually on flight feathers).

Zygodactyl: arrangement of feet in which two toes point forward, two backward.

MAP KEY

 Resident

 Non-breeding visitor

 Passage migrant

 Rare resident/isolated records

 Vagrant or non-breeding visitor with isolated records

? Uncertain record

USEFUL ADDRESSES

SABAH

Malaysian Nature Society (Sabah Branch)
Lot F- 4-18, BLKF, 4th Floor
Plaza Tanjung Aru
Jalan Mat Salleh
Tanjung Aru
88100 Kota Kinabalu
Sabah
Malaysia
Email mns_sabah@yahoo.com

WWF Malaysia (Sabah Office)
Suite 1 - 6 - W11
6th Floor CPS Tower
1 Jalan Centrepoint
88800 Kota Kinabalu
Sabah
Malaysia
Email http://www.wwfmalaysia.org

Borneo Bird Club (BoBC)
Website http://borneobirdclub.blogspot.com/

SARAWAK

Malaysian Nature Society (Kuching Branch)
P.O.Box A144 Kenyalan Park
93824 Kuching
Sarawak
Malaysia
Email mnskuching@gmail.com

WWF Malaysia (Sarawak Office)
Suite -01, Level 6 Menara MAA
Lot 86 Section 53
Jalan Ban Hock
93100 Kuching
Sarawak
Malaysia
Email www.wwfmalaysia.org

Wildlife Conservation Society
7 Jalan Ridgeway
93200 Kuching
Sarawak
Malaysia
Email mgumal@wcs.org

BRUNEI

Penaga Natural History Society
Penaga Club
KB 3534
Seria
Brunei Darussalam
Email PNHS.brunei@gmail.com

EAST KALIMANTAN

Conservation Foundation for Rare Aquatic Species of
   Indonesia (Yayasan Konservasi RASI)
Komplek Pandan Harum Indah Blok D No. 87
Samarinda, East Kalimantan
Indonesia
Email yk.rasi@gmail.com or yk-rasi@samarinda.org

ACKNOWLEDGEMENTS

I would first like to thank the artists for their immensely important contributions. I am grateful to Simon Papps and Alan Marshall at New Holland for their patience and assistance. Marianne Taylor made many digital amendments to the artworks. In particular, I appreciate the useful comments and advice of Nigel Collar who reviewed the text. Many people provided valuable assistance in the production of this book. I'd like to thank Per Alström, Bas van Balen, David Bakewell, Chris Bradshaw, Nick Brickle, Jason Bugay Reyes, Bill Clark, Nigel Cleere, Stuart Dashper, Lincoln Fishpool, Christian Gonner, Peter Hosner, David Johnson, Haw-Chuan Lim, Hafidzi Mohn Noor, Ronald Orenstein, Frank Rheindt, Craig Robson, Ken Scriven, Frederick H Sheldon, Andrew Siani, Mano Tharmalingan, Lisa Thurston, Joseph Tobias and Dennis Yong.

ARTWORK ACKNOWLEDGEMENTS

(a=above, b = below, l = left, r = right, c = centre).

Richard Allen: pages 16-19, 22b-42a, 57-61c, 100-101, 131a, 137b, 154-157, 163b, 169-170, 173a, 173c, 176-177, 181b-196a, 226b, 236-237, 241a, 241c.
Hilary Burn: pages 113-114, 116a, 117, 118a, 118b.
Clive Byers: pages 158a, 159, 240.
Daniel Cole: pages 20-22a.
John Cox: pages 45b, 49c, 49b, 52c, 54a, 91b-99, 106a, 108a, 109b, 110a, 111b.
Anthony Disley: pages 56b, 208a, 209b, 211-215.
Martin Elliott: pages 164b, 178, 180a.
Alan Harris: pages 43a, 43b, 115, 116b, 118c, 179, 180c, 180b, 255b-256.

Szabolcs Kokay: pages 160-163.
Mike Langman: pages 102-105, 106c-107, 108c-109a, 110c-111a, 112.
Ian Lewington: pages 42b, 43c, 44, 46b, 50-51.
Andrew Mackay: pages 45a, 47-49a, 52a, 52b, 53, 56a, 56c.
Stephen Message: pages 46a, 48, 163a, 238a, 239b, 241b-255c.
Christopher Schmidt: pages 164a, 207c, 208c-209c, 210, 216-226a, 238c, 238b, 239a, 257-261.
Jan Wilczur: pages 128-130, 131b-137a, 138-141, 165-168, 171, 172a, 172c, 173b-175.
Tim Worfolk: pages 61b-91a, 119-127, 142-153, 172b, 181a, 196c-207a, 227-235.

MEGAPODIIDAE: Scrubfowl

Worldwide c.22 species, 1 in Borneo. Robust, chicken-like terrestrial birds with strong legs and very large feet. Most incubate eggs using an extraneous source of heat such as thermal energy or rotting vegetation; many species build a mound of vegetation. Males construct the mound in which the females lay large batches of eggs. The chicks receive no parental care and are totally independent upon hatching.

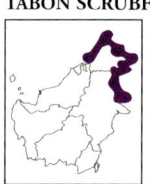

TABON SCRUBFOWL *Megapodius cumingii* **Identification** 32–38 cm. **Adult *cumingii*** Crown olive-brown with small inconspicuous crest, bare skin around sides of head conspicuous reddish-pink, upperparts olive-brown, underparts blue-grey, tail short, feet very large and strong; iris brown, bill yellow, legs greyish. **Juvenile** Like adult but more extensive feathering around eye. **Habitat** Beach forest and coastal scrub of small offshore islands and mainland, at sea-level. **Behaviour** Feeds on insects, worms, snails; usually encountered singly or in pairs; escapes from danger by running rapidly into thick undergrowth; chicks are independent on hatching and capable of making short flights. **Voice** An ethereal, drawn-out whistle, rising then falling in pitch (4.7 s, 0.73–1.3 kHz), often uttered in late evening. Described by Whitehead (1893) as 'like a cat in distress'. **Range & status** Philippines, Sulawesi. **Borneo** Formerly very common, now uncommon resident on off-shore islands and some mainland sites of N Borneo from Labuan (Sabah) to the Maratuas (E Kalimantan); not recorded from Sarawak or Brunei. **Breeding** Eggs are incubated in large mound of sand or decaying vegetation constructed in coastal forests and maintained by one or many pairs of bird. The whitish eggs are rough and oval-shaped, and left untended by adults during incubation and after hatching; eggs are probably laid throughout year.

PHASIANIDAE: Partridges, quail & pheasants

Worldwide c.160 species, 14 in Borneo. A large family of ground-dwellers with small head, stout decurved bill, heavy body and short rounded wings. Usually exhibit pronounced sexual dimorphism, the males often being highly coloured with modified tail feathers while the females are typically cryptic. In many species males perform elaborate courtship displays. The diet is varied and includes fruit, seeds, leaves, insects and other small invertebrates usually taken from the ground. Occupy a wide variety of habitats. Often highly vocal.

LONG-BILLED PARTRIDGE *Rhizothera longirostris* **Identification** 37 cm. Monotypic. Large partridge with distinctive large, long decurved black bill. **Adult male** Crown chestnut-brown, thin line above orange-chestnut supercilium and black eye-line, sides of head and throat rusty-brown, upperparts mottled brown and black with buffish fringes, grey breast band and sides of neck, rest of underparts bright rufous-buff with white lower belly; iris light brown, bill black, legs and feet yellow with tarsal spur. **Adult female** Like male but grey breast-band absent, underparts all rich rufous, tarsal spur smaller. **Juvenile** Like female but throat, breast, neck and back streaked buff; dark spots and barring on flanks and breast. **Habitat** Extreme lowland specialist found in primary lowland dipterocarp forest; possibly favours areas with limestone hills. **Behaviour** Very shy and secretive ground-dweller, usually solitary or in pairs. Feeds on berries, seeds, insects, possibly using unusual large bill to dig for food. **Voice** Antiphonal duetting performed by pairs. A prolonged loud, piping call and response *kan king* or *kan kan king* (1.6 kHz) (hence Malay name *Kanking*). Pairs advertise early morning and late evening. Contact call a single soft whistle. **Range & status** Thai-Malay Peninsula, Sumatra. **Borneo** Very rare resident Sabah (two confirmed records), W Sarawak (no recent records), Kalimantan (few recent records). Not recorded from Brunei. **Breeding** One nest containing two eggs has been found on ground in bamboo thicket.

DULIT PARTRIDGE *Rhizothera dulitensis*

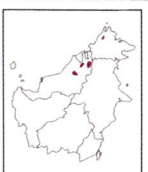

Identification 37 cm. Monotypic. **Adult male** As Long-billed Partridge but throat and upper breast grey in broader band, rest of underparts buffish-white to white. **Adult female** As adult female Long-billed Partridge. **Immature female** Broken dark brown supercilium with buff streaks, buff streaks on sides of throat and breast to hind neck, chin and throat light chestnut, orange-buff on flanks, no grey on underparts, dark brown vermiculations on sides of breast, centre of lower breast, abdomen and flanks creamy buff; bill rosy with pale tip. **Immature male** As immature female but chin and throat duller and greyer, grey vermiculations on sides of breast; pale, breast dull orange-buff; flanks, belly and vent pale smoky-grey. **Habitat** Hill and lower montane forest, from 900 to 1,200 m. **Behaviour** Not described but presumably similar to Long-billed Partridge. **Voice** Not described. **Range & status** Endemic, very rare resident known only from G. Dulit, G. Murud and G. Batu Song (E Sarawak) and G. Kinabalu (Sabah). **Breeding** Undescribed.

BLACK PARTRIDGE *Melanoperdix nigra*

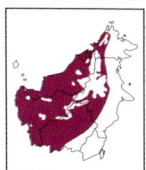

Identification 24–27 cm. **Adult male *borneensis*** (endemic subspecies) Plumage entirely glossy black with brownish tinge to wings; iris dark brown, distinctive stout, thick bill black, legs and feet pale slaty-grey. **Adult female** Rich chestnut, throat and lower belly paler, black bars on inner secondaries. **Juvenile** Upperparts brown speckled with buff, underparts from lower breast brown with blackish vermiculations and large white spots; juvenile male acquires scattering of black feathers. **Habitat** Primary lowland dipterocarp, peatswamp and kerangas forest, to 1,000 m in Kelabit Highlands. **Behaviour** Little known; runs when disturbed; very shy and secretive. **Voice** Poorly known but said to be a double whistle similar to Crested Partridge. **Range & status** Thai-Malay Peninsula, Sumatra. **Borneo** Few records since 1980, all from Kalimantan. Formerly described as 'not uncommon', this species has declined markedly throughout its range in recent decades. **Breeding** September–May; nest is simple depression on ground lined with dead leaves; lays 2–5 elliptical, dull white eggs; downy chicks are rufous.

BLUE-BREASTED QUAIL *Coturnix chinensis*

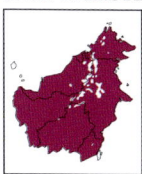

Identification 12–15 cm. Small, dark quail. **Adult male *lineata*** Crown and nape dark brown blotched with black, forehead and face greyish-blue, chin and throat black with broad white malar stripe, a broad crescent-shaped band below black throat on foreneck bordered by thin black line below, breast and flanks greyish-blue, belly to undertail-coverts rich rufous-chestnut, upperparts dark olive-brown vermiculated and blotched with black and streaked buffish; iris reddish-brown, bill dark grey, legs and feet orange; in flight upperwing greyish-brown, underwing pale greyish-white. **Adult female** Crown and nape dark brown blotched with black, broad buffish supercilium, dark brown eyestripe and buffish-orange sides of head and throat; upperparts as male but with bolder whitish shaft-streaks, underparts buff barred black, centre of belly buffish-white and unbarred; iris dark brown, legs and feet pale orange. **Juvenile** Male like adult female but upperparts with more conspicuous black and buff markings, underparts diffusely mottled brown; female like adult but underparts more spotted than barred. **Habitat** Swamp edges, scrubby vegetation, grassland, paddyfields, plantations, to 1,500 m. **Behaviour** Feeds on grass seeds (including rice), small insects. Secretive. Forages on ground, gleaning and scratching in litter. Explodes at feet, flying straight with rapidly whirring wings, dropping back into dense cover. Will rapidly colonise recently cleared areas. **Voice** A throaty, low-pitched long growl, increasing in volume (1.2 kHz, c.2 s) and a short, piercing descending crow *keeer* (3–2.2 kHz, 0.6 s). **Range & status** Indian Subcontinent, SE China, Taiwan, SE Asia, Indonesia, Philippines, New Guinea, Australia. **Borneo** Common resident throughout. **Breeding** November–March; lays 5–6 olive-brown eggs with black and brown speckles; nest is shallow scrape in soil lined with grass.

17

Male
erythrophrys

Female
erythrophrys

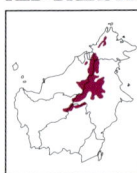

RED-BREASTED PARTRIDGE *Arborophila hyperythra*
Identification 25 cm. **Adult male *erythrophrys*** Crown and nape blackish with brown spots, broad chesnut supercilium above prominent dark eye-line from lores to sides of neck, upperparts olive-brown barred black with bold black spots on wing-coverts, throat and breast rusty-red, belly whitish, flanks with broad black band distinctively marked with large white spots; iris grey with broad dark red eye-ring, bill black, legs and feet salmon-pink. **Adult male *hyperythra*** Darker breast, grey supercilium sometimes extending onto cheek. **Adult female** Smaller black spots on wing-coverts and smaller spots on flanks. **Juvenile** Undescribed. **Habitat** Primary and secondary hill to upper montane forest from 600 to 3,050 m. Favours bamboo stands and thickets. **Behaviour** Terrestrial; feeds on insects, small fruits, seeds; roosts in low bushes; secretive, more often heard than seen; usually in pairs or coveys. **Voice** Strident, repetitive and steady duetting call becoming louder and faster *pyu-pyu-pyu-pyu-*... (c.55 notes in 19–20 s, 1.3 kHz). **Range & status** Endemic, uncommon resident confined to north-central mountain ranges from G. Kinabalu south to Barito Ulu in north C Kalimantan (Sabah, E Sarawak, C and E Kalimantan). *A. h. erythrophrys* is restricted to Crocker Range in Sabah including G. Kinabalu and G. Trus Madi. *A. h. hyperethra* in Sarawak and Kalimantan. Not recorded in Brunei. **Breeding** Undescribed.

CHESTNUT-NECKLACED PARTRIDGE
Arborophila charltonii
Identification 28–30 cm. **Adult *graydoni*** (endemic subspecies) Crown and nape brown, indistinct whitish supercilium and lores flecked black, sides of neck and lower throat spotted black and white; chin and upper throat white, small buffish-white patch on ear-coverts, wide chestnut band on upper breast around neck, rest of underparts indistinctly barred tawny and black, undertail-coverts whitish, upperparts mottled brown and dark brown; iris brown, bill dark grey, legs and feet greenish-yellow. **Immature** Duller with more barring on upperparts. **Habitat** A lowland specialist found in primary lowland dipterocarp forest, to 800 m. **Behaviour** Terrestrial; feeds on insects, seeds and berries, foraging in pairs or coveys; very vocal and more often seen than heard. **Voice** A continuous duetting song *pi pi pi pi-*

Adult

pyu pi-pyu pi-pyu (call sequence lasting c.18 s, 1.4 kHz) delivered in rather flat tone; call is a tremulous, evenly paced, repeated *hyuuu-hyuuu-hyuu-*... (c.1 note/1 s, 0.9–1.2 kHz). **Range & status** Thai-Malay Peninsula, Sumatra. **Borneo** Locally common resident in Sabah; may occur but not yet confirmed from northern E Kalimantan. **Breeding** Undescribed in Borneo.

FERRUGINOUS PARTRIDGE *Caloperdix oculea*
Identification 23–27 cm. Small, distinctively plumaged partridge scalloped orange, black and white. **Adult *borneensis*** (endemic subspecies) Head bright orange-rufous, blackish post-ocular stripe, underparts orange-rufous, flanks and mantle scaled black and white, rump and uppertail-coverts black with orange-rufous arrows, wings olive-brown with large black spots; iris dark brown, bill black, legs and feet greenish-olive, male with one or two spurs, female without spur. **Immature** Black markings on nape and breast. **Habitat** Primary and secondary hill and lower montane forests, favouring lower to middle slopes, mostly recorded from 1,000 to 1,200 m in Borneo. **Behaviour** Feeds on fallen figs, berries, insects, seeds. **Voice** A series of ascending notes running together to crescendo (reminiscent of *Eurylaimus* broadbills) ending with two explosive notes *pi-*

Adult

pi-pi pi pi pi pi pyuwit pyuwit (call sequence lasting c.7 s, 1.2–1.9 kHz); quiet, paced contact calls *pyuu pyuu* (1.3 kHz). **Range & status** Thai-Malay Peninsula, Sumatra. **Borneo** Uncommon resident E Sarawak and E Kalimantan, not confirmed for Sabah (unconfirmed reports from G. Magdelena, SE Sabah). **Breeding** December–January.

CRIMSON-HEADED PARTRIDGE
Haematortyx sanguiniceps

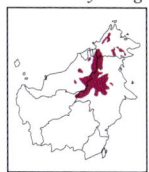

Identification 25 cm. Monotypic. **Adult male** Head and breast crimson, rest of plumage dark blackish-brown, vent crimson; iris brown, bill bright orange-yellow, legs and feet greyish-black with one to three spurs. **Adult female** Head and breast orangey-red, rest of plumage olive-brown, vent orangey-red; bill brown. **Immature** Like female but crimson limited to crown. **Habitat** Kerangas and primary lower and upper montane forests, from 1,000 to 3,050 m (with records from 500 m); favours sandy forest valley floors of montane areas. **Behaviour** Feeds on berries, insects, small crustaceans. Shy, usually in pairs and encountered on forest trails. **Voice** A ringing, loud two-note song, often perfomed in antiphonal duet, *kong-krrang... kong-krrang...* (1 s, 1.3–3 kHz), hence probably its Dusun name *mabparang*. **Range & status** Endemic, formerly common resident, now uncommon in north-central ranges from G. Kinabalu to G. Menyapa (Sabah, E Sarawak, E Kalimantan) and outlying mountains in SE Sabah. **Breeding** January–April; eggs are coffee-coloured with umber smears.

CRESTED PARTRIDGE *Rollulus rouloul*

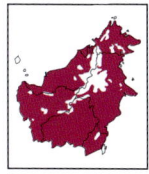

Identification 26 cm. Monotypic. **Adult male** Spectacular reddish-maroon upright bushy crest, forehead black with thin white line dividing it from crest, long filamentous plumes from above eyes, back and rump rich dark green, wings blue-brown, neck and underparts glossy blue; iris reddish-brown with extensive red skin around and extending behind eye, bill black with bright red base, legs and feet pinkish-red. **Adult female** Head grey with inconspicuous long feathers on forehead, wings chestnut-brown, rest of plumage grassy-green, darker on tail; iris reddish-brown with narrow duller red eye-ring, bill greyish-black. **Juvenile** Like female but with chestnut crown, greyer, more mottled upperparts and underparts, pale spots on wing-coverts. **Habitat** Primary and secondary lowland dipterocarp, peatswamp and kerangas forest, to 1,200 m. **Behaviour** Feeds on fallen fruits, seeds, insects, snails. Usually first detected by sound of raking leaf-litter. Usually in small parties. Secretive and shy. Has been known to associate with Bearded Pigs *Sus barbatus*. **Voice** Mournful *seeeool* repeated, rising then falling slightly in pitch (one note 1.5 s, 2–3 kHz). **Range & status** Thai-Malay Peninsula, Sumatra. **Borneo** Common resident Sabah and Brunei, uncommon Sarawak and Kalimantan. **Breeding** November–June; lays dull yellowish-white eggs in dome-shaped nest of leaves.

CRESTLESS FIREBACK *Lophura erythrophthalma*

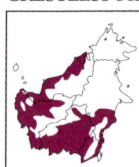

Identification Male 47–50 cm, female 42–44 cm. **Adult male *pyronota*** (endemic subspecies) Extensive scarlet facial wattles, neck, mantle, wings and breast dark blue with wide silvery-white feather-shafts and silvery-white vermiculations, lower back and rump dark maroon grading to blue uppertail-coverts, laterally compressed conspicuous yellow tail, rest of underparts glossy bluish-black; iris brown, bill greenish-grey, legs and feet bluish-grey with rear spur. **Adult female** Head brownish, throat greyish, rest of plumage glossy dark blue. **Juvenile** Like female but plumage with rusty feather-fringes. **Habitat** Primary lowland dipterocarp and alluvial forests, extreme lowland specialist to 200 m. **Behaviour** Feeds on insects, small berries, fallen fruit; very shy and secretive, often in small parties. **Voice** A low-pitched *tak-takrau*; alarm calls are a vibrating purr and short loud sharp *kek* (2 kHz); relatively quiet. **Range & status** Thai-Malay Peninsula, Sumatra. **Borneo** Very rare with recent records from Sarawak and E, C and W Kalimantan as well as Brunei and possibly E Sabah; largely absent from north and east. **Breeding** March–June; lays 3–5 plain buff eggs in depression in leaf-litter between buttresses of forest trees, or on top of soil termitaria; all incubation and chick-tending is by female.

CRESTED FIREBACK *Lophura ignita*

Identification Male 65–67 cm, female 56–57 cm. **Adult male *ignita*** (endemic subspecies) Distinctive plumed dark blue crest, extensive bright cobalt-blue facial skin-wattles, head and upperparts dark blue, wing-coverts dark blue with iridescent blue feather-fringes, flight feathers bluish-black, upper breast dark blue, lower breast and belly chestnut, central tail feathers cinnamon-buff, remaining tail feathers dark blue, lower back bright iridescent coppery-red (often not visible), rump blue with metallic margins; iris red, bill greyish-yellow, legs greyish-pink with long spur. **Adult male *nobilis*** Like *ignita* but larger. **Adult female** Head and short floppy crest chestnut, dull blue facial skin, chin and throat buffish-white, tail blackish-brown, upper breast chestnut with whitish streaks, lower breast and upper belly chestnut with thick white feather-fringes, lower belly buffish-white; no leg spurs. **Immature** Like female but upperwing-coverts with large black spots. **Habitat** Primary and secondary lowland dipterocarp forest especially near waterways; lowland specialist to 600 m. **Behaviour** Usually in groups with an adult male and 4–5 females and immatures; scratches in leaf-litter for insects, young leaves, berries, seeds, fallen fruit. **Voice** Groups are relatively noisy; gives soft clucking contact calls *chek-chek-chek* (0.9 kHz) and higher-pitched *kook* (2.2 kHz). Also a very quiet, repeated *keep keep*. **Range & status** Thai-Malay Peninsula, Sumatra. **Borneo** Race *ignita* uncommon resident in S Borneo, *nobilis* uncommon to locally common resident in N Borneo, appears to be more common in north. **Breeding** July–December; 4–8 creamy-buff eggs with faint brown spots laid in nest of dead leaves, grasses and feathers located between buttress roots or under thick low bushes.

BULWER'S PHEASANT *Lophura bulweri*

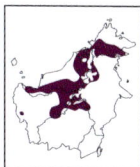

Identification Male 77–80 cm, female 55 cm. Monotypic. **Adult male** Extensive bright cobalt-blue wattles, throat and upper breast glossy purplish, overall plumage dark blackish-blue, upperparts finely tipped with blue feather-fringes, voluminous curved tail pure white and laterally compressed; iris ruby-red, fine eye-ring crimson, bill grey, legs and feet bright red. **Adult female** Blue facial skin, no crest, overall plumage plain rufous-brown. **Immature** Like female but upperwing-coverts with black marks and buff tips. **Habitat** Slope specialist, lower montane primary forest often near rivers, from 500 to 1,200 m, occasionally to 1,500 m. **Behaviour** Feeds on insects, fruit, worms; said to follow course of forest streams in search of crustaceans; nomadic, in search of fruiting trees; documented associating with migrating Bearded Pigs *Sus barbatus*. The male performs display in which tail is fluffed out sideways to frame wattles which are engorged and extended into an amazing elongated black-tipped mask. The red eye-ring is similarly engorged, creating very striking visage. **Voice** Described as a loud, harsh crow-like *bek kia* and penetrating metallic *kook kook*, also a soft, monotonous *gak*. **Range & status** Endemic, formerly described as common but now probably rare submontane resident, patchily distributed in foothills and adjacent lowlands from S Sabah to C Sarawak and W, C and E Kalimantan, apparently absent from southern and south-eastern edges of Kalimantan (no records within 200 km of east and south coast). **Breeding** Poorly known; one nest found with one oval, pinkish-cream egg located between buttress roots of large tree on forested ridge.

BORNEAN PEACOCK-PHEASANT
Polyplectron schleiermacheri

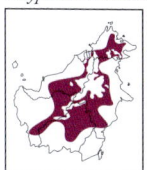

Identification Male 50 cm, female 35.5 cm. Monotypic. **Adult male** Bushy crest finely vermiculated black and white extending from above bill to nape, throat and sides of neck white, underparts metallic purple-green with white central stripe, upperparts rufous-brown with buff vermiculations and striking metallic blue-green ocelli; dorsally compressed, fan-shaped, black-tipped tail with rows of large blue-green ocelli; iris pale blue, facial skin orangey-red, bill dark grey, legs and feet grey with two spurs. **Adult female** Smaller and duller brown than male, no crest, plumage rufous-brown, ocelli dark metallic blue with buff fringes, no ocelli on uppertail-coverts; iris brown, no spurs. **Habitat** Primary lowland and alluvial riverine forest, to 1,000 m. **Behaviour** Very poorly known; probably gleans leaf-litter for insects and fallen fruits. The male spreads tail in fan-like fashion in display. **Voice** Call is a harsh double *cack cack*; song is a drawn out, melancholy *hoo-horrr...* (1.2-1.35 kHz,1.7 s), the second note much louder and longer, rising in pitch slightly; the phrases are given at rather long intervals of c 50 s. **Range & status** Endemic, very rare resident C Sarawak (one recent record) and C Borneo, from far east W Kalimantan to far southern E Kalimantan, with recent but provisional record from C Sabah (1996). Endangered. **Breeding** Undescribed.

21

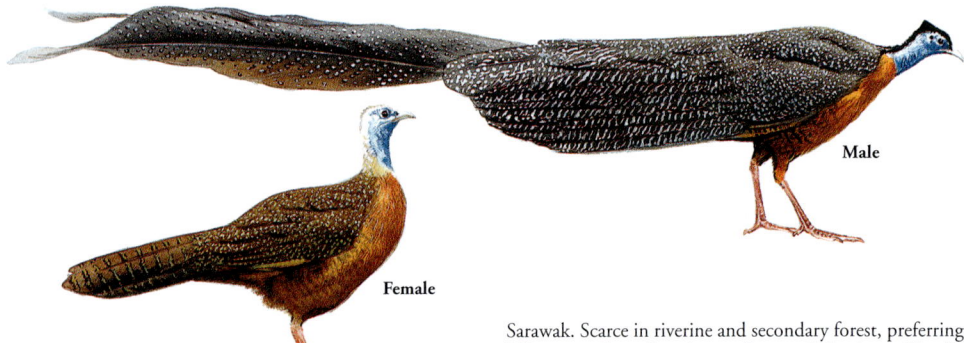

Male

Female

GREAT ARGUS *Argusianus argus*

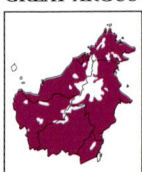

Identification Male 165 cm, female 60 cm. **Adult male** *grayi* Crown black with short crest of hair-like feathers, sparsely feathered skin of head and neck blue, overall plumage dark brown with complex pattern of black and white vermiculations and spots; huge, broad and greatly elongated secondaries with large ocelli (folded secondaries often hidden), upper breast orange-brown, lower back orange-brown, laterally compressed tail spotted white and silvery along top edge, incredibly long central tail feathers with corkscrew tips; iris dark brown, bill pale ivory, legs and feet bright pinkish-red, no spurs. **Adult female** Similar to male but smaller, darker with less distinct markings, no elongated secondaries, short tail, no ocelli. **Juvenile** like female but with more reddish tinge. **Habitat** Slope specialist, inhabits forest floor of primary and secondary lowland dipterocarp forest, to 1,200 m. One record from 2,170 m on G. Murud, Sarawak. Scarce in riverine and secondary forest, preferring hilly areas in tall primary forest. **Behaviour** Usually solitary, territorial with home ranges of 1–3 ha. Feeds on insects, small molluscs, fallen fruit, seeds, young leaves. The male clears small open area in forest, usually on ridge, by clearing fallen leaves and vegetation which functions as display ground. He announces himself with loud calls to attract females, then performs courtship dance with wings raised and spread fan-like, revealing ocelli, and tail held erect. Roosts in trees near display ground. **Voice** Very vocal; song is a resonant, repeated *kwow kwow kwow*... (1 note = 0.2 s uttered at 1 note/1.5 s; 0.7–1.3 kHz), gradually slowing to *kawow kawow* (1 note = 0.4 s uttered at 1 note/1.7 s) delivered over 1–1.5 minutes; call is a loud explosive *ka-wow* delivered on roughly level pitch (0.7–1.4 kHz), repeated at intervals of 15–30 s, often delivered from cleared display ground. **Range & status** Thai-Malay Peninsula, Sumatra. **Borneo** Widespread, locally common but declining resident throughout, and exterminated from many former areas. Many populations now isolated in small forest fragments. **Breeding** 2–3 creamy-white eggs with brown speckles laid in nest of dead grass located between buttress roots; male vocalisations decrease dramatically after February.

ANATIDAE: Ducks, geese & swans

Worldwide 167 species, 12 in Borneo. Small to large waterbirds with webbed feet and specialised broad, flattened bill. Largely affiliated with aquatic habitats. Gregarious. Ducks are generally sexually dimorphic, the males showing marked seasonal plumage variation. The eclipse or non-breeding plumage is similar to that of the female. Many species are long-distance migrants.

WANDERING WHISTLING-DUCK
Dendrocygna arcuata

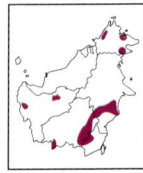

Identification 40–45 cm. **Adult** *arcuata* Crown and hindneck dark brown, sides of head and neck pale brown, upperparts dark brown with rufous edging on back and scapulars, upper breast buffish with black spotting, rest of underparts chestnut, distinctive creamy-white lanceolate plumes on flanks, tail black; iris red-brown, bill black, legs and feet black; in flight underwings dark brown, upperwing-coverts chestnut contrasting with dark grey flight feathers, distinctive buff-white U on rump, long neck extended and head carried lower than body. **Juvenile** Like adult but duller with pale centre of abdomen. **Similar species** See Lesser Whistling-duck. **Habitat** Rivers, oxbow lakes, lakes, swamps, paddyfields. **Behaviour** Usually in flocks. **Voice** Shrill twittering multi-syllabic whistle, descending in frequency (from 5.5 to 2.5 kHz), usually uttered in flight. **Range & status** Philippines, Indonesia, New Guinea, N Australia. **Borneo**

Adult

Adult

Common resident in suitable habitat in Kalimantan (up to 20,000 recorded Lake Jempang, E Kalimantan in 2004); status uncertain in Sabah where recorded regularly at Kota Belud, Sandakan and Tawau in recent years. **Breeding** Undescribed in Borneo.

LESSER WHISTLING-DUCK *Dendrocygna javanica*

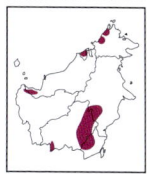

Identification 38–40 cm. **Adult *javanica*** Crown and nape dusky-brown, face, neck and breast unpatterned light bay-brown, upperparts purplish-brown with rufous fringes, underparts rufous-brown, lesser wing-coverts and uppertail-coverts bright rufous; iris dark brown, narrow eye-ring orange-yellow, bill dark grey, legs and feet dark grey; in flight upperwing-coverts rufous, flight feathers black, underwings black contrasting with rufous-brown underparts. **Juvenile** Duller with pale fringing dorsally. **Similar species** Smaller than Wandering Whistling-duck, lacks flank-plumes, no spots on sides of breast and neck. **Habitat** Freshwater wetlands, lakes, marshes, rivers, paddyfields; usually in pairs or small groups. **Voice** Disyllabic whistle: *see-sik*. **Range & status** Indian Subcontinent, SE Asia, Indonesia. **Borneo** Uncommon resident Sarawak, Brunei,

C and E Kalimantan, possibly in S Kalimantan; uncommon non-breeding visitor but possibly increasing in Sabah, August–March. **Breeding** Nest not yet recorded from Borneo.

COTTON PYGMY-GOOSE *Nettapus coromandelianus*

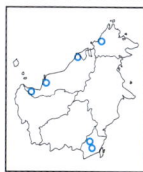

Identification 31–38 cm. Small white and green waterbird. **Adult male breeding *coromandelianus*** Forehead and crown metallic dark green-brown, face and neck white, iridescent green band at base of neck broadening on upper breast, upperparts metallic green and purple, prominent pale grey flanks, underparts white, uppertail-coverts pale mottled with dark brown contrasting with dark brown tail; iris dark red, bill small and black, legs and feet olive-green to black; in flight greenish-black on back and upperwing-coverts, broad white band across flight feathers above and below, black tips to primaries. **Adult male non-breeding** Narrow dark brown eyestripe, upperparts brown, wing-coverts glossy green. **Adult female** Crown and forehead brown, face white, prominent brown eyestripe, neck and upper breast white barred brown, lacks white collar, back brown-green with less iridescence than male; iris brown; in flight upperwing brown with narrow white trailing edge. **Juvenile** Like female but lacks iridescence, foreneck and breast mottled rather than barred brown. **Habitat** Deep freshwater lakes

and marshes with abundant aquatic vegetation. **Voice** Male gives repeated loud cackling *ka-ka-karwak*, female utters soft quacking. **Range & status** Indian Subcontinent, SE Asia, China, Philippines, Indonesia, New Guinea, NE Australia. **Borneo** Rare passage migrant and vagrant Sabah, Sarawak and S Kalimantan.

EURASIAN WIGEON *Anas penelope*

Identification 45–51 cm. Monotypic. **Adult male breeding** Centre of forehead and crown buffish-yellow, head and neck chestnut, back and flanks vermiculated grey and pale grey, broad white bar on rear flanks, breast pinkish-brown, belly white, undertail-coverts black, tail pointed; iris brown, short bill blue-grey with black tip, legs and feet grey; in flight upper forewing white, speculum green bordered with black, primaries dark, underwing pale grey, underparts white. **Adult male eclipse** Russet all over, greyer back. **Adult female** Head, neck, breast stippled brown; upperparts dark brown, flanks rufous-brown. **Similar species** differs from similar female Spot-billed Duck, Mallard and Northern Pintail by grey patch in leading edge of wing and sharply contrasting white belly in flight. **Habitat** Estuaries, lagoons, lakes, marshes. **Voice** Male gives a high, clear whistled *pwee-pwee* or *pyu-i* (1–3 kHz), female gives a gruff *hur* or *ga*. **Range & status** Europe, non-breeding visitor to Africa, Indian Subcontinent, East and SE Asia, Philippines. **Borneo** Uncommon non-breeding visitor Sabah, from November to February; rare vagrant Sarawak and Brunei.

23

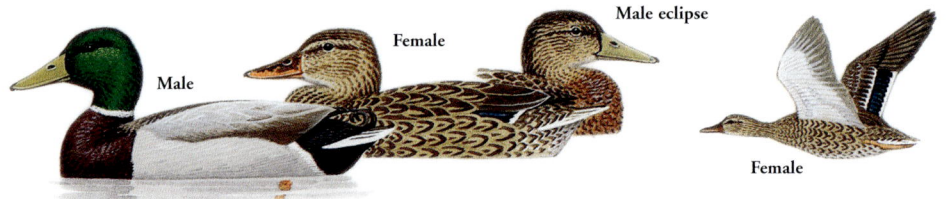

MALLARD *Anas platyrhynchos*

Identification 50–65 cm. **Adult male breeding** Head and neck bright glossy emerald-green, narrow neck-ring white, breast maroon-brown, back and mantle pale vermiculated grey, wings pale grey-brown, flanks and belly grey, underparts and flanks pale grey, rump and tail glossy black with curled central tail feathers; iris dark brown, bill yellow with grey-black tip, legs and feet orange; in flight broad glossy purple-blue speculum bordered front and rear by black and white bars, cream underwing-coverts contrasting with brown flight feathers. **Adult female** Head and neck streaked pale brown, prominent dark eye-stripe, body buffish-brown heavily streaked; bill dark brown mottled irregularly with orange, legs and feet dull orange. **Adult male eclipse** Like female but upperparts darker, less streaked; bill all yellow. **Juvenile** Like female but duller, breast with longitudinal streaks. **Habitat** Estuaries, lakes, reservoirs, ponds, rivers, grasslands, pastures; very adaptable and tolerant of humans. **Voice** Male soft wheezy calls *raaae-hb* (1–2 kHz), female louder raucous *kwak* repeated, slow-paced. **Range & status** N America, Palearctic, Indian Subcontinent, SE Asia; introduced Australia, New Zealand. **Borneo** Rare non-breeding visitor or vagrant to Sabah, Brunei and Sarawak, from September to November.

PACIFIC BLACK DUCK *Anas superciliosa*

Identification 47–60 cm. **Adult male** Crown black, prominent black eye-stripe contrasting with creamy-white supercilium and cheeks and throat, body dark grey-brown with pale edges to feathers; iris brown, bill dark grey, legs and feet grey; in flight speculum glossy dark green to purple with black edges, underwings white contrasting with darker body. **Adult female** Crown brown. **Juvenile** Like adult but streaky underparts. **Habitat** Estuaries, mudflats, lakes, rivers, grasslands, paddyfields, pastures; in Borneo recorded from rivers. **Voice** Female utters loud, raucous rapid quacking; less commonly heard male gives a softer *raab*. **Range & status** Australia, New Zealand, New Guinea, Pacific islands, Indonesia. **Borneo** Vagrant; one report (November) from E Kalimantan.

NORTHERN SHOVELER *Anas clypeata*

Identification 45–55 cm. Monotypic. Medium-sized, heavy-bodied duck with distinctive spatulate bill. **Adult male breeding** Head glossy green, breast white, belly and flanks chestnut, white rear flank-mark, undertail-coverts black; iris yellow to orange, bill grey-black, legs and feet orange-red; in flight upperwing-coverts pale blue, white central wing-bar, speculum green, underwing white, flight feathers grey. **Adult female** Plain brown, dark eyestripe, iris brown, bill grey with orange cutting edge. **Adult male eclipse** Like adult female but darker, speculum duller. **Habitat** Lakes, ponds, oxbow lakes, swamps, pastures. **Voice** Generally silent. **Range & status** Breeds Nearctic, Palearctic, migrates to Africa, Indian Subcontinent, East and SE Asia. **Borneo** Rare vagrant to Sarawak and Brunei, November–March; uncommon non-breeding visitor to Sabah, from December to March.

NORTHERN PINTAIL *Anas acuta*

Identification 50–55 cm (male's tail up to 10 cm more). Monotypic. **Adult male breeding** Head and neck dark chocolate-brown with darker crown and hindneck, narrow white stripe down rear sides of neck broadening to foreneck and breast, back and flanks vermiculated grey with long black scapulars edged pale grey, undertail-coverts black and vent creamy-yellow, tail grey with long black pointed streamers; iris brown, bill blue-grey with black culmen and tip, legs and feet dark grey; in flight bronzy-green speculum bordered by narrow rufous bar in front and white bar behind, underwing dull, centre of underparts white, pointed tail. **Adult female** Head warm brown unmarked, body mottled brown, darker on upperparts; bill darker with indistinct black culmen; in flight brown speculum bordered with white bars in front and behind. **Adult male eclipse** Like female but greyer. **Habitat** Estuaries, lakes, marshes, reservoirs. **Voice** Male high short whistled *pri pri* (1.5–2 kHz), female harsh *kwak kwak*. **Range & status** Breeds Nearctic, Palearctic, migrates to Central America, Africa, Indian Subcontinent and SE Asia. **Borneo** Uncommon non-breeding visitor to Sabah from October to January; rare non-breeding visitor to Sarawak and Brunei, October–March.

GARGANEY *Anas querquedula*

Identification 37–41 cm. Monotypic. **Adult male breeding** Head dark brown with broad white supercilium extending to hindneck, cheeks and foreneck with fine white streaks, upperparts brown with feathers edged paler, elongated scapulars black and grey with white shafts and edges, flanks silvery with fine black vermiculations, belly white; iris reddish-brown, bill dark grey, legs and feet grey; in flight pale blue-grey wing-coverts contrasting with brown back, speculum iridescent green bordered with white, underwing pale with darker leading edge. **Adult female** Crown and hindneck dark brown, blackish eyestripe bordered by buffish-white supercilium and cheek-stripe, upperparts mottled grey-brown, no elongated scapulars, belly white; bill paler grey. **Adult male eclipse** Like female but throat whiter, coarser streaking on head and neck. **Juvenile** Like female but belly streaked. **Habitat** Lakes, swamps, marshes, paddyfields, to 1,100 m. **Voice** Usually silent in Borneo; extralimitally, male gives mechanical rattling call *giririri…* (2–5 kHz), female a short *kwip*. **Range & status** Breeds Palearctic, migrates to Africa, Indian Subcontinent, E and SE Asia. **Borneo** Uncommon non-breeding visitor throughout, October–April.

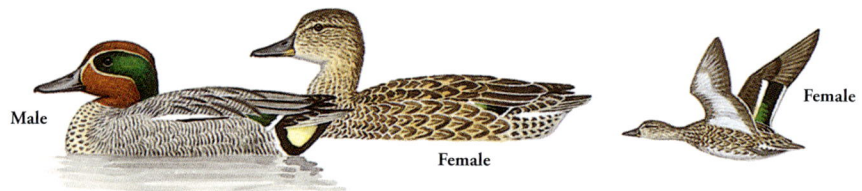

EURASIAN TEAL *Anas crecca*

Identification 34–43 cm. **Adult male breeding** *crecca* Head chestnut with long glossy green eye-patch bordered creamy-white to nape, upperparts and flanks grey with black vermiculations, breast buffish with black speckles, black-and-white stripe on folded wing, sides of vent creamy-yellow bordered black; iris reddish-brown, bill greyish-black, legs and feet olive-grey; in flight green speculum edged white front and behind, underwing pale with dark leading edge and white belly. **Adult female** Dark mottled brown with whitish abdomen, indistinct blackish eyestripe. **Adult male eclipse** Like female but eyestripe less distinct, darker overall. **Habitat** Lakes, ponds, marshes. Feeds close to water's edge in vegetation. **Voice** Male high, clear whistled *pwee pwee* (2 kHz) repeated, uttered at rest or in flight; female *gegege...* given relatively infrequently. **Range & status** Breeds N Palearctic, migrates to Africa, Middle East, Indian Subcontinent, SE Asia. **Borneo** Vagrant Sabah and Brunei.

SUNDA TEAL *Anas gibberifrons*

Identification 37–47 cm. **Adult male breeding** *gibberifrons* Distinctive bulbous forehead, head and neck speckled dark grey-brown, paler throat and cheeks contrasting with dark crown, body dark grey-brown with pale-edged feathers; iris red, bill grey, legs and feet grey; in flight upperwing with prominent white central bar in front of speculum, speculum black with green gloss and narrow white trailing edge, underwing dark grey-brown with white axillaries. **Adult female** Like male but lacks bulbous forehead. **Habitat** Estuaries, mangroves, swamps, lakes, paddyfields; in Borneo recorded in estuaries and rivers. **Voice** Loud and noisy, male loud whistled *pip*, female descending chuckle. **Range & status** Sumatra, Java, Sulawesi, Lesser Sundas, Timor. **Borneo** Status uncertain, recorded infrequently in E, S and C Kalimantan.

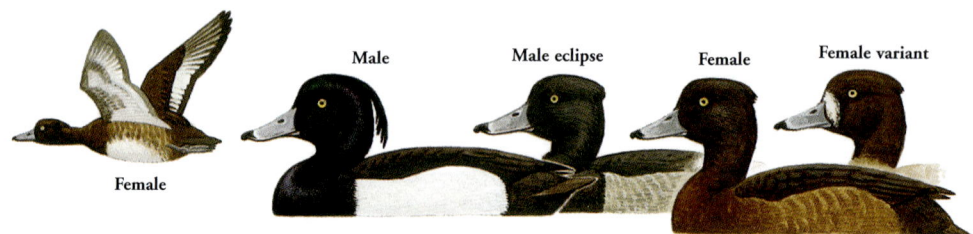

TUFTED DUCK *Aythya fuligula*

Identification 40–47 cm. Monotypic. Medium-sized diving duck with high forehead and distinctive long pendant tuft of feathers on rear of head. **Adult male breeding** Head and neck purple-brown, upperparts, breast and vent black, belly and flanks white, long tuft on back of head; iris bright yellow, bill blue-grey with black tip, legs and feet grey; in flight upperwing with broad central white bar, no speculum, underwing off-white. **Adult male eclipse** upperparts duller, crest short, belly and flanks greyish. **Adult female** Head and upperparts dark brown, underparts paler, crest shorter, sometimes with white around base of bill. **Habitat** Estuaries, deeper lakes and marshes. **Voice** Generally silent on wintering grounds. **Range & status** Breeds Palearctic, migrates to Indian Subcontinent, SE Asia, Philippines. **Borneo** Uncommon non-breeding visitor to Sabah, Brunei and Sarawak, October–January.

26

PROCELLARIIDAE: Petrels & shearwaters

Worldwide c.80 species, 3 in Borneo. Pelagic seabirds with long, tube-like nostrils and webbed feet. Flight is strong, with much gliding on stiff wings close to the water surface.

STREAKED SHEARWATER *Calonectris leucomelas*

Identification 48m. Monotypic. Large shearwater with pale face and streaked head. **Adult** Face whitish, upperparts greyish-brown with streaked crown, nape and hindneck, underparts white, underwings white with dark trailing edge and dark patches on primary coverts; long slender bill horn-coloured, legs pinkish. **Similar species** Only shearwater with pale head. **Voice** Rarely vocalises in flight; on breeding grounds loud raucous *kyuuiii*, *gwaaa*. **Habitat** Oceans. **Range & status** NW Pacific. **Borneo** Uncommon non-breeding visitor to N Borneo (Sabah, Brunei, Sarawak), with records August–May; nearest breeding colony Taiwan.

WEDGE-TAILED SHEARWATER *Puffinus pacificus*

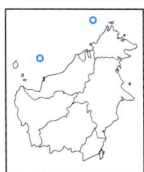

Identification 43 cm. Monotypic. Long wedge-shaped tail, long slender greyish bill with dark tip and flesh-white legs diagnostic. **Adult dark morph** All blackish-brown with blacker primaries and uppertail, paler on chin, throat and face. **Adult light morph** Upperparts paler greyish-brown, dark brown crown and nape giving hooded appearance, underparts white, undertail blackish, underwing whitish with dark trailing edge and tip. **Habitat** Oceans. **Range & status** Pacific and Indian Oceans. **Borneo** Rare non-breeding visitor; sight records from W Sarawak and Sabah.

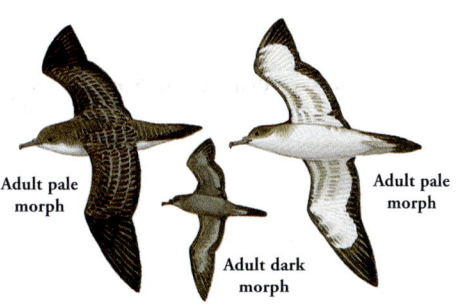

BULWER'S PETREL *Bulweria bulwerii*

Identification 26 cm. Monotypic. **Adult** Sooty-brown all over with slightly paler lores, chin and upper throat, pale greyish-brown band on upperwing; iris brown, bill black, pinkish legs with dark webs. **Habitat** Oceans. **Range & status** Atlantic, Indian and Pacific oceans. **Borneo** Rare coastal non-breeding visitor, nearest breeding colonies coastal islands of SE China; all records are sight records from Sarawak in September and December; none recent.

HYDROBATIDAE: Storm-petrels

Worldwide c.21 species, 1 in Borneo. Small pelagic seabirds with large head, fine hooked bill and long wings. Short bill with tube-like nostrils. Hover close to the water surface gleaning small fish and plankton.

SWINHOE'S STORM-PETREL *Oceanodroma monorhis*

Identification 20 cm. Small dark tubenose. **Adult** *monorhis* Blackish-brown with contrasting pale bar on upperwing, tail forked, legs do not project beyond tail in flight; bill and legs black. **Habitat** Open oceans. **Behaviour** Fast, swooping flight with erratic bounding close to sea surface. **Range & status** Nearest breeding colony Taiwan. **Borneo** Rare non-breeding visitor recorded from Sabah and E Sarawak in December and January.

27

PODICIPEDIDAE: Grebes

Worldwide c.21 species, 1 in Borneo. Small to medium-sized strong-swimming birds with short body and lobed feet. Generally frequent inland ponds and lakes. Sexes are similar with marked seasonal plumage variation. Feed by diving for small fish and aquatic invertebrates.

LITTLE GREBE *Tachybaptus ruficollis*

Identification 26 cm. **Adult breeding *philippensis*** Small waterbird, brown overall with blackish crown and hindneck, cheeks and throat rufous-chestnut; iris yellow, conspicuous yellow gape. **Adult non-breeding** Upperparts paler greyish-brown with pale buffish-brown cheeks, throat and underparts, gape inconspicuous. **Juvenile** Dusky grey upperparts with striped head and orange bill. **Voice** Territorial song is a shrill *kyuririri* (2–4 kHz). **Habitat** Wetlands, shallow freshwater small ponds and lakes. **Range & status** Europe; Africa south of Sahara; SE and NE Asia to New Guinea. **Borneo** Rare vagrant with only handful of records: collected once at Labuan, sight records from Brunei, W Kalimantan, and E Sabah.

CICONIIDAE: Storks

Worldwide 20 species, 2 in Borneo. Large, long-legged wetland birds with powerful bill, long neck and broad wings. Typically feeds by stalking in grasslands and shallow wetlands for large invertebrates and small vertebrates usually speared with long bill. Soars on thermals with neck and legs extended in flight. Sexes similar.

STORM'S STORK *Ciconia stormi*

SUKAU RIVER LODGE 9/6/10

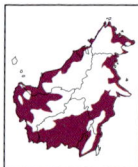

Identification 85 cm. Monotypic. **Adult breeding** Crown black, hindneck white contiguous with white throat, lower foreneck to breast black, body and wings glossy black, lower belly and undertail-coverts white; in flight underwings black; iris red surrounded by broad bright yellow orbital ring, dull orange facial skin, long straight bill bright orange-red, legs and feet pale orange. **Adult non-breeding** Bare parts duller. **Juvenile** Throat and bare parts duller than adult, bill tipped dusky. **Habitat** Lowland dipterocarp forest, floodplains of larger rivers, riverine swamp forest, mangroves, secondary forest, usually at sea-level but recorded at 1,600 m on G. Kinabalu. **Behaviour** Secretive; feeds at small pools within forest on small invertebrates; will also feed in recently disturbed areas. Sometimes seen on prominent perches in high trees; often soars in small groups on thermals. **Voice** A cow-like *krauu* has been recorded when taking flight. **Range & status** Thai-Malay Peninsula, Sumatra. **Borneo** Rare local lowland resident throughout, possibly absent from S Kalimantan. Borneo, in particular Sabah, is stronghold for this Endangered species. **Breeding** Details unknown in Borneo.

LESSER ADJUTANT *Leptoptilos javanicus*

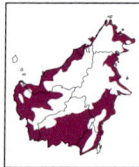

Identification 110–120 cm. Monotypic. Large, deep-billed stork with bare head and neck. **Adult non-breeding** Bare facial skin pale pink, forehead paler, frilly nuchal feathers on bare yellow to orange-yellow neck, upperparts glossy black, underparts white, neck-collar white sometimes spotted black; iris greyish-white, bill dirty yellow, legs and feet grey; in flight black underwing with white axillary spur, widely splayed primaries, flies with neck retracted. **Adult breeding** Face bright red, neck bright orange, white scalloping on tertials. **Juvenile** Woolly neck, upperparts dull brownish, bare parts duller. **Habitat** Mangroves, swamps, riverine forest, paddyfields. **Behaviour** Often in small groups; soars on thermals; forages on ground for small to medium invertebrates. **Voice** Silent away from nest; at nest clatters bill and gives soft guttural growls. **Range & status** Indian Subcontinent, SE Asia, Indonesia. **Borneo** Uncommon and local lowland resident throughout. **Breeding** November; recorded at Tanjung Puting, south C Kalimantan, and Mahakam Lakes, south-eastern E Kalimantan. No records of breeding in Sabah, Brunei or Sarawak since 1980s.

THRESKIORNITHIDAE: Ibises & spoonbills

Worldwide 32 species, 4 in Borneo. Gregarious medium to large long-legged wetland birds with highly specialised bill, short tail and long neck and legs. In ibises the bill is long and decurved, the spoonbills have a spatulate bill. Most have some bare skin on head. Strong fliers, usually with neck and legs extended. Sexes similar.

BLACK-HEADED IBIS *Threskiornis melanocephalus*

Identification 65–76 cm. Monotypic. Only white ibis in Borneo. **Adult breeding** Long decurved black bill, bare black head and neck, white plumage with grey tertial plumes, ruff of lanceolate feathers at base of neck, breast-plumes; iris dark red, bill black, legs black; broad-winged in flight with neck outstretched, bright red patch of skin near leading edge of underwing. **Adult non-breeding** No plumes. **Juvenile** Brown feathers on head and neck, black tips to outer primaries. **Habitat** Marshes, paddyfields, pasture. **Voice** Usually silent; noisy at breeding colonies, various harsh guttural honks (1–1.5 kHz). **Range & status** Indian Subcontinent, East and SE Asia, Indonesia. **Borneo** Rare, status uncertain Sabah and Sarawak.

WHITE-SHOULDERED IBIS *Pseudibis davisoni*

Identification 60–80 cm. Monotypic. **Adult** Plumage brownish-black with glossy bluish-black wings, bare head black with conspicuous bluish-white band of bare skin from chin to nape at base of skull, white patch on lesser wing-coverts (often not visible when wings folded); iris orange-red, large, decurved bill yellowish-grey, grey, legs and feet red; in flight distinctive white patch on inner forewings. **Juvenile** Tuft of brown feathers on nape; iris grey-brown, legs and feet dirty white. **Habitat** Extreme lowland specialist; open wetlands, woodlands, riparian forest, wide rivers with sandbanks, paddyfields, grasslands. **Behaviour** Usually in small groups; roosts communally in large trees. **Voice** Loud mournful calls described as 'weird and unearthly screams'; territorial call is a long, raspy, rather ethereal *pi-errrrrrh* (c.1.2 kHz, 2.5 s) and shorter, moaning *errrh* (c.1 s), sometimes repeated; also honking *errrrh owk owk owk owk* notes and more subdued *ohhaaa ohhaaa*. **Range & status** Formerly found throughout SE Asia to Thai-Malay Peninsula, now restricted to Indochina and Borneo. **Borneo** Rare, localised and declining resident in E and C Kalimantan where recent records are concentrated along upper and middle reaches of Mahakam River and tributaries (previously rather more widespread in C, E and S Kalimantan). **Breeding** Juvenile birds have been recorded in November; other details in Borneo are unknown.

GLOSSY IBIS *Plegadis falcinellus*

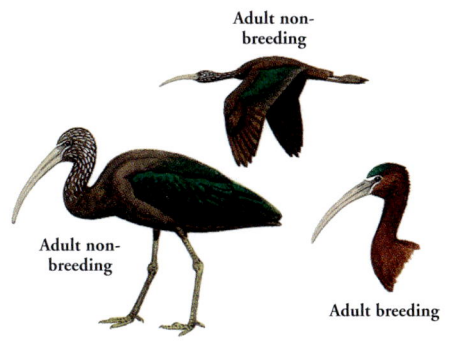

Identification 49–66 cm. Monotypic. **Adult breeding** Dark chestnut body with blackish wings with purple and green gloss; iris brown, facial skin cobalt-blue, bill dark brown, legs and feet yellow-green to dark brown; in flight appears all dark. **Adult non-breeding** As breeding adult but with fine white streaks on face and neck, facial skin brown with inconspicuous bordering white line. **Juvenile** Duller than non-breeding adult with shorter bill. **Habitat** Lakes, swamps, wetlands, grasslands. **Voice** Mostly silent; grunting sounds and soft chattering calls at breeding colonies, loud honking croak when flushed (1–3 kHz). **Range & status** S Europe, Africa, C Asia, Indian Subcontinent, Philippines, Indonesia, New Guinea, Australia. **Borneo** Vagrant to W Sabah, Brunei, E Kalimantan.

BLACK-FACED SPOONBILL *Platalea minor*

Identification 60–78 cm. Monotypic. **Adult breeding** All-white plumage with pale yellow nuchal crest and pale yellow spot on breast; iris black, bare facial skin black, distinctive spatulate bill greyish-black, legs and feet black; in flight neck outstretched and low-slung. **Adult non-breeding** Like breeding adult without crest and breast-spot. **Juvenile** Black on tips of wings, bill brown. **Similar species** Eurasian Spoonbill, which is larger with yellow tip to bill and white face, has yet to be recorded in Borneo. **Habitat** Estuaries, mudflats, marshes, paddyfields, mangroves. **Voice** Usually silent. **Range & status** Japan, Korea, China, Taiwan, N Vietnam. **Borneo** Vagrant; one definite sight record from Brunei; historic records from Sarawak, unidentified spoonbills recorded from W Sabah.

ARDEIDAE: Herons, egrets & bitterns

Worldwide c.60 species, 21 in Borneo. Small to large wetland birds with long neck and legs, and long, straight bill. Stalks in shallow water where it feeds on large invertebrates and small vertebrates by spearing prey in shallow water. Sexes similar, many develop elaborate plumes and coloured soft parts in the breeding season. Flies with deep, slow wing-beats.

GREAT BITTERN *Botaurus stellaris*

Identification 64–80 cm. **Adult *stellaris*** Largest bittern, heavily built; upperparts brown barred and mottled with dark brown, buff and rufous giving sandy appearance, crown and moustachial streak blackish-brown, sides of face unmarked sandy-buff, throat buff with brown gular stripe; iris yellow to brown, facial skin dull yellow to brown, bill dull yellow, legs and feet yellowish-green. **Juvenile** Crown and moustachial streak browner. **Habitat** Reedbeds, swamps, marshes. **Voice** Unlikely to be heard in Borneo; territorial call is a loud, foghorn-like, very low-pitched *boom* (167 Hz). **Range & status** Europe, Africa, Indian Subcontinent, C and E Asia, Philippines. **Borneo** Vagrant; one record each from Brunei and Sabah.

YELLOW BITTERN *Ixobrychus sinensis*

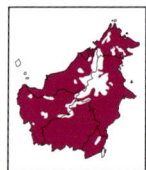

Identification 30–40 cm. Monotypic. Small buffish-yellow bittern with blackish crown and olive-brown upperparts. **Adult male** Crown black, throat cream to white with buff gular line, sides of neck and breast pinkish-brown, rest of underparts pale yellowish-brown fading to whiter lower belly, back olive-brown, wings yellowish-brown, rump pale grey-brown, tail black; iris golden-yellow, facial skin greenish-yellow, bill yellow with black culmen, legs and feet greenish-yellow; in flight black flight feathers and tail contrast strongly with yellow-brown wing-coverts and dark brown back, underwing-coverts white. **Adult female** Like male but crown browner and sometimes streaked, neck more strongly streaked, back streaked dark reddish-brown and buff, throat white with buff gular stripe. **Juvenile** Like female but darker, more heavily streaked. **Habitat** Reedbeds, paddyfields, edges of freshwater wetlands; shy and most often seen flying short distances, low over suitable habitat, to 1,100 m. **Voice** Territorial call is a slow, repeated *wo... wo... wo...* (0.5–1 kHz); may give staccato *kik kik kik* in flight. **Range & status** Indian Subcontinent, E and SE Asia, Indonesia, Philippines, New Guinea. **Borneo** Uncommon resident and non-breeding visitor throughout. **Breeding** Probably March–July.

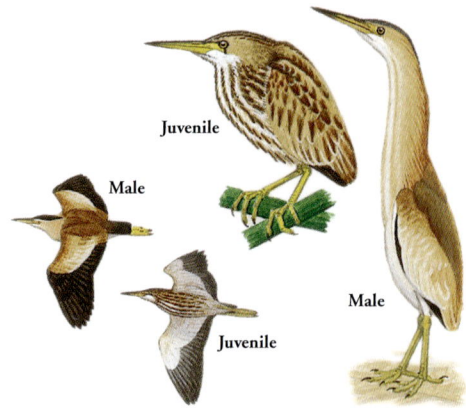

VON SCHRENCK'S BITTERN *Ixobrychus eurhythmus*

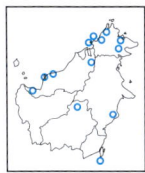
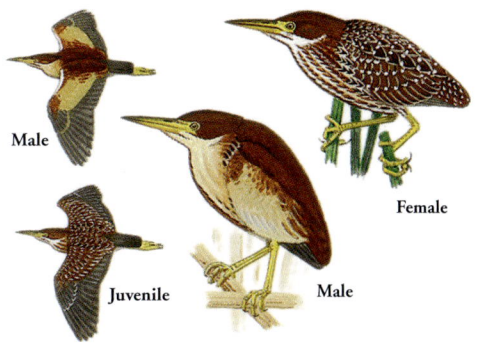

Identification 33–39 cm. Monotypic. **Adult male** Crown and nape blackish-grey, sides of face and hindneck rich purple-brown, throat buff with rufous gular line to upper belly, upperparts rich purple-brown, wing-coverts buff, tail dark brown; in flight rich purple-brown back and pale yellow-buff upperwing-coverts contrast with brownish-grey flight feathers, underwing grey; iris yellow, facial skin yellow, bill greenish-yellow with black culmen, legs light greenish-yellow. **Adult female** As male but upperparts dark reddish-brown with white spots on back and wing-coverts, broad white streaks on side of chestnut neck, throat buff with brown gular stripe, underparts buff streaked dark brown; in flight lacks contrasting upperparts and flight feathers. **Juvenile** Like female but browner and more heavily streaked. **Similar species** Like Cinnamon Bittern but dark upperparts contrast with lighter underparts and wing-coverts; in flight like Yellow Bittern but with paler grey primaries. **Habitat** Swampy areas in forest, wooded streamsides, secondary growth, paddyfields. **Voice** Territorial call is similar to Yellow Bittern with repeated *wo... wo... wo...* (0.5–1 kHz), but tempo faster. **Range & status** E and SE Asia, Indonesia, Philippines. **Borneo** Rare non-breeding visitor to Sarawak, Sabah, Brunei and C, S and E Kalimantan.

CINNAMON BITTERN *Ixobrychus cinnamomeus*

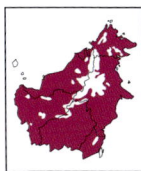

Identification 40 cm. Monotypic. **Adult male** Upperparts unmarked uniform rich cinnamon, underparts paler, prominent white malar stripe, throat buffish-white with dark brown gular stripe to upper breast; iris golden-yellow, facial skin greenish-yellow (turning red during courtship), bill yellow with black culmen, legs and feet greenish-yellow; in flight uniform cinnamon back and wings. **Adult female** Duller with some white streaks on less rich cinnamon upperparts, throat white with brown gular stripe, underparts buff streaked dull cinnamon. **Juvenile** Browner, barred and spotted with buff, streaked below. **Habitat** Freshwater swamps and ponds, reedbeds, paddyfields, to 1100 m. **Voice** Fast-paced frog-like *ka ka ka...* (1–2 kHz) when flushed. **Range & status** Indian Subcontinent, E and SE Asia, Indonesia, Philippines. **Borneo** Locally common resident throughout. **Breeding** June–August; platform nest is constructed in tall grass; elliptical eggs are dull white.

BLACK BITTERN *Dupetor flavicollis*

Identification 54–66 cm. **Adult male flavicollis** Upperparts dark grey-black (pale fringes in fresh plumage), distinctive cream to orange-buff stripe on sides of neck, throat white, neck and breast streaked broadly with black, rufous and buff, rest of underparts black; iris yellow to red, facial skin yellowish-brown, bill dark brown with lower mandible paler, legs and feet pinkish-grey to black; in flight can be confused with Little Heron but less compact, contrasting buff-yellow neck-stripe, longer trailing dark legs. **Adult female** Upperparts dark brown, underparts paler. **Juvenile** Upperparts brown with buff fringes, mottled buff and chestnut below. **Habitat** Estuaries, mangroves, swamps, reedbeds, forested streamsides, paddyfields. **Voice** Territorial call is low, loud boom uttered at 15 s intervals. **Range & status** Indian Subcontinent, south-east China, SE Asia, Indonesia, Philippines, New Guinea, northern Australia. **Borneo** Uncommon non-breeding visitor to Sabah from December to March; possible breeding resident in Sarawak, Brunei and Kalimantan. **Breeding** Juveniles have been reported in E Kalimantan but nests have not been described.

JAPANESE NIGHT-HERON *Gorsachius goisagi*

Identification 49 cm. Monotypic. **Adult non-breeding** Head, neck and upper back dark rufous, throat white with blackish gular stripe, back, rump and wings dark reddish-brown with fine buff vermiculations, underparts buff mottled and streaked brown and black, tail dark brown; iris yellow, facial skin greyish, bill dark grey, legs dark greenish-grey; in flight wing-coverts brown and flight feathers grey-black. **Adult breeding** Facial skin greenish-blue. **Juvenile** Crown greyish-black, head and neck blackish-brown finely barred with black, upperparts brown with fine buff bars, throat white with buff spots, underparts brown mottled with dark brown. **Similar species** Like Malaysian Night-heron but differs with shorter rufous crest, duller brown face and neck. **Habitat** Very secretive in dense primary and secondary forest, favouring forested streams; observed in Borneo on swampy ground in garden (near sea level). **Voice** Very like Malaysian Night-heron, slightly shorter and higher-pitched (0.5–1 kHz). **Range & status** Southern Japan, S China, Philippines, Sulawesi. **Borneo** Vagrant; one record from Brunei.

MALAYSIAN NIGHT-HERON *Gorsachius melanolophus*

Identification 49 cm. Monotypic. Medium-sized, stout heron with short legs and bill. **Adult** Head and upperparts cinnamon-rufous, wing-coverts with fine black vermiculations, crown and short pendant crest black, throat and chest buff streaked with black and brown, belly buff mottled with brown and rufous, tail blackish; iris greenish-yellow, facial skin greenish-blue, bill heavy with upper mandible black and lower grey, legs and feet dark green; in flight compact with short leg projection, brown wing-coverts and grey-black flight feathers, conspicuous rufous trailing edge, tips of primaries and coverts white. **Juvenile** Crown and nape black with large white spots, upperparts dark brown with fine buff bars, throat white with buff spots, underparts brown mottled with dark brown. **Habitat** Primary and secondary lowland dipterocarp forest. **Behaviour** Very secretive in dense, damp forest, favouring forested streams but sometimes found in gardens and plantations on migration. **Voice** Series of 5–6 deep, falling *bo* or *pwo* notes, given at night repeatedly during breeding season (1–2 kHz). **Range & status** S India and Sri Lanka, SE Asia, Taiwan, Philippines, Sumatra and Java. **Borneo** Uncommon to rare non-breeding visitor Sabah, Brunei and Sarawak.

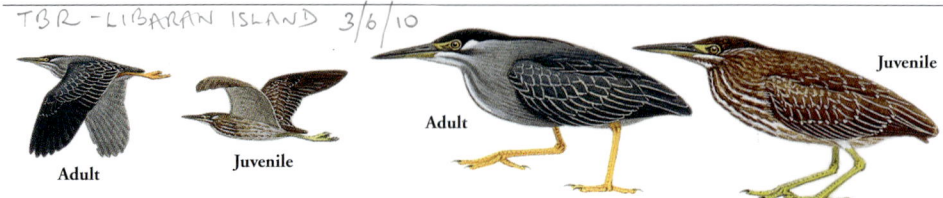

LITTLE HERON *Butorides striata*

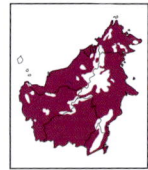

Identification 35–48 cm. Small, hunched appearance at rest. **Adult male non-breeding** *javanicus* Slaty-grey with blackish crown, long black nape-plumes, white bands on side of face, black streak below eye, white throat and central breast-stripe, prominent white fringes on upperwing-coverts; iris lemon-yellow to grey, facial skin greenish-yellow, bill black with yellowish or green base on lower mandible, legs and feet dull yellowish; in flight greyish upperwing contrasts with blackish flight feathers. Race *amurensis* larger. **Female** Like male but with brownish wash on sides of neck and flanks, more distinct spotting on throat. **Adult breeding** Legs bright yellow to orange-pink. **Juvenile** Brownish scaling and spots on upperparts and wing-coverts, streaked underparts; legs and feet greenish. **Habitat** Mudflats, estuaries, tidal rivers, mangroves, swamps, rocky shores, rivers, to 1,100 m. **Behaviour** Solitary. Often flushed from vegetation at water's edge or seen perched motionless. Usually flies low. **Voice** Alarm squawk when flushed; calls more at night; strong, strident *kyu* or *kyo* in flight (2 kHz). Rapid *kakaka* or *gagaga* on breeding grounds. **Range & status** Sub-Saharan Africa, C and S America, Indian Subcontinent, E and SE Asia, Indonesia, Philippines, Australia. **Borneo** Race *javanicus* common resident and *amurensis* common non-breeding visitor (although relative abundance unclear) throughout. **Breeding** March–August, Sabah and Sarawak; nests are described as soccerball-sized masses of sticks built high in isolated mangrove trees containing pale blue eggs.

RUFOUS NIGHT-HERON *Nycticorax caledonicus*

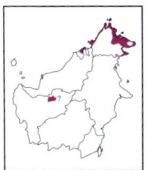

Identification 55–65 cm. **Adult *manillensis*** Crown and nape greyish-black, face pale cinnamon, 2–3 long whitish plumes from nape, upperparts deep cinnamon-rufous, underparts pale cinnamon from neck to upper breast, lower breast and belly white; iris yellow to orange, facial skin greenish to blue during courtship, bill black, legs and feet yellowish-green to bright pink during courtship; in flight underwing white with flight feathers pale cinnamon-rufous. **Juvenile** Head black-brown streaked buff, upperparts dark brown heavily spotted buff, upperwing barred dark brown and rufous, underparts streaked cream and brown; iris greenish-yellow, facial skin yellowish-olive, bill dull yellow with blackish culmen, legs and feet dull yellow; more rufous, less milky-brown tone than Black-crowned Night-heron. **Habitat** Estuaries, marshes, swamps, mangroves, offshore islands. **Behaviour** Similar to Black-crowned Night-Heron. **Voice** Usually silent but hoarse croaking *qu-ock* (1–5 kHz) calls when flushed or alarmed. **Range & status** Java, Philippines, Australia, New Zealand, western Pacific islands. **Borneo** Scarce resident Brunei and Sabah; unconfirmed from Danau Sentarum, W Kalimantan. **Breeding** Recorded in May in W Sabah.

BLACK-CROWNED NIGHT-HERON
Nycticorax nycticorax

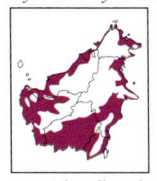

Identification 56–65 cm. **Adult non-breeding *nycticorax*** Crown and back black, one to three long white nape-plumes, forehead and line over eye white, throat, breast and belly white, wings and tail uniform grey, back black; iris red to reddish-orange, bill black with base of lower mandible pale greenish-yellow, legs and feet yellow; in flight compact and chunky, wings broad and rounded. **Adult male breeding** Bill all black, facial skin and legs pink in courtship, bluish gloss on black back, paler wings. **Adult female breeding** Greenish gloss to back. **Juvenile** Brown with bold buff spots and streaks on upperparts, streaking on breast. **Habitat** Estuaries, mangroves, rivers, swamps, pastures; roosts in trees near water. **Behaviour** Roosts in loose colonies in trees during the day often near water, flying out at dusk to feed in shallow wetlands. Slow, steady flight. **Voice** At night gives repeated squawking *kwa kwa kwa* in flight (1–5 kHz). **Range & status** Europe, Africa, N, C and S America, Indian Subcontinent, E and SE Asia, Philippines. **Borneo** Locally fairly common resident throughout, rarer in Kalimantan; population may be augmented by some non-breeding visitors. **Breeding** May–June, W Sabah and E Sarawak.

33

CHINESE POND-HERON *Ardeola bacchus*

Identification 45 cm. Monotypic. Short-necked, compact heron, white wings and tail (not visible at rest) contrasting with dark mantle in flight, possibly inseparable from Javan in non-breeding and immature plumage but may have more obvious dusky tips to outer primaries. **Adult non-breeding** Head, neck and breast whitish streaked with brown, back, scapulars and wings buff-brown, rest of plumage white; iris golden-yellow, lower mandible yellow with dark tip, upper mandible dusky, facial skin dull yellow, legs greenish-yellow. **Adult breeding** Dark maroon-chestnut head, neck and breast, long maroon breast-plumes, blackish-brown back, long blackish back-plumes extending beyond end of tail, wings, throat, belly and tail white; iris golden-yellow, facial skin yellow-green, bill yellow with bluish base and black tip, legs yellow to intense red during courtship. **Juvenile** Like non-breeding adult but brown on outer primaries, spotted below, paler streaks on buff on neck and breast with dusky bill. **Habitat** Estuaries, mudflats, mangroves, rivers, ponds, swamps, paddyfields; roosts in trees. **Behaviour** Stands motionless waiting for prey in shallow wetlands. **Voice** Harsh *kwa* on taking flight. **Range & status** China, SE Asia, Thai-Malay Peninsula. **Borneo** Regular, uncommon to rare non-breeding visitor Sabah, Brunei, Sarawak, C Kalimantan and Natunas.

JAVAN POND-HERON *Ardeola speciosa*

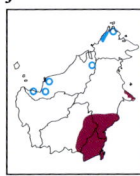

Identification 45 cm. **Adult non-breeding** *speciosa* As Chinese Pond-heron but may have less obvious dusky tips to outer primaries **Adult breeding** Head and neck pale orange-buff with two whitish long head-plumes, cinnamon breast with deep cinnamon plumes sharply demarcated from white belly, back black with long black plumes extending to end of tail, chin and throat white, wings, belly and tail white; iris yellow, bill yellow with bluish base and black tip, facial skin grey-blue, legs deep to pinkish-red. **Juvenile** As Chinese Pond-heron. **Habitat** Estuaries, rivers, mudflats, mangroves, ponds, swamps, paddyfields; roosts in trees. **Behaviour** As Chinese Pond-Heron. **Voice** Harsh *kwa* on taking flight. **Range & status** SE Asia, Indonesia. **Borneo** Common resident C, S and E Kalimantan, rare non-breeding visitor Sarawak, recently found to be uncommon but regular non-breeding visitor in W Sabah, not recorded Brunei. **Breeding** August–September, E Kalimantan; nests in low vegetation over water, lays 2–3 light blue eggs.

EASTERN CATTLE EGRET *Bubulcus coromandus*

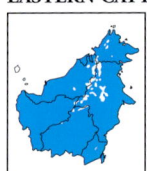

Identification 46–56 cm. **Adult non-breeding** *coromandus* All white sometimes with inconspicuous buff on crown, no plumes, short thick neck with bulging throat, rounded head; iris yellow, bill yellow with distinctive blunt shape, facial skin greenish-yellow, legs and feet dark green-grey to black; in flight compact appearance with feet extending slightly beyond tail, relatively short, rounded wings. **Adult breeding** Head, neck, breast, back pinkish-buff, rest of plumage white, variably pinkish-orange head-, neck- and back-plumes; during courtship iris red, bill bright orange with yellow tip, legs and feet yellowish, turning red during courtship. **Juvenile** Like non-breeding adult but bill and facial skin dull grey changing to grey-yellow. **Similar species** smaller with shorter, thicker neck than Pacific Reef-Egret and Little Egret. **Habitat** Swamps, shallow ponds, grasslands, paddyfields, pastures; associates with grazing livestock. **Behaviour** Often associates with large domestic animals. Usually seen in flocks in fields and pastures. Roosts communally. **Voice** Raucous, hoarse *ka* sometimes uttered in flight, softer than other egrets. **Range & status** SE Asia, Indonesia, Philippines. Formerly considered subspecies of Cattle Egret *Bubulcus ibis* of Indian Subcontinent, Africa, Europe and the Americas. **Borneo** Common non-breeding visitor and passage migrant throughout.

GREY HERON *Ardea cinerea*

Identification 90–98 cm. **Adult non-breeding** *jouyi* Large, mainly grey heron, white head and neck with prominent black line from eye to long pendant crest, black streaks on foreneck, underparts white with black pectoral tufts and flanks; in flight contrasting grey wing-coverts and black flight feathers; iris bright yellow, greenish-yellow facial skin, bill yellowish, legs and feet yellowish-grey. **Adult breeding** As non-breeding but bill bright orange, legs pink-orange. **Juvenile** Greyer head and neck, no crest. **Habitat** Mostly coastal in Borneo: estuaries, rivers, freshwater swamps and ponds, paddyfields; to 1,100 m. **Behaviour** Usually solitary. Flight is slow and laboured. Waits motionless for or slowly stalks fish in shallow wetlands. **Voice** Hoarse, raucous *gwaaa* yelp. **Range & status** Africa, Europe, Indian Subcontinent, E and SE Asia. **Borneo** Regular uncommon non-breeding visitor to Sabah and Sarawak, from November to mid-April; rare in Brunei and E Kalimantan.

GREAT-BILLED HERON *Ardea sumatrana*

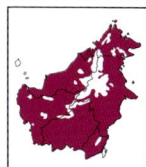

Identification 100–115 cm. **Adult non-breeding** *sumatrana* Large uniformly brown-grey heron with white chin and throat, large bill, elongated back-plumes, long nuchal crest, upper and underwings uniform dark grey; iris yellow, facial skin yellow-green, upper mandible black, lower mandible paler with yellow tip, legs and feet grey to yellow. **Adult breeding** Long, white-tipped plumes on foreneck, breast and scapulars. **Juvenile** Dull rufous, rufous markings on dark grey upperparts, pale-streaked grey underparts, lacks whitish plumes; facial skin bluish-green. **Habitat** Rivers often in interior forests, mangroves, estuaries, coastal mudflats. **Behaviour** Large territories, usually solitary or pairs. Often waits motionless for prey for long periods of time. **Voice** Loud, harsh croak on taking flight. **Range & status** SE Asia, Indonesia, Philippines, New Guinea, northern Australia. **Borneo** Locally uncommon resident throughout Borneo, widespread in Sabah, very uncommon in Brunei and Sarawak. **Breeding** Nests singly in mangroves.

PURPLE HERON *Ardea purpurea*

SUKAU RIVER LODGE 9/6/10

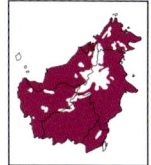

Identification 78–90 cm. **Adult** *manilensis* Crown black, long black crown-plumes, upperparts purple-grey with contrasting deep purple shoulder-patch, front of neck rufous with long black stripes, underparts deep maroon; in flight retracted neck large and bulging, upperwing-coverts dark grey with darker flight feathers and rufous leading edge, underwing-coverts rufous with black flight feathers; iris pale yellow, facial skin bright yellow, bill yellowish, legs and feet yellowish-grey. **Juvenile** Rufous-brown, brownish upperwing-coverts, dark grey flight feathers, reduced neck-stripes. **Similar species** Smaller but longer- and more slender-necked than Grey Heron. **Habitat** Freshwater ponds and lakes, swamps, rivers, paddyfields, occasionally to 1,100 m. **Behaviour** Similar to Grey Heron. **Voice** When alighting and taking off, utters a harsh *giii* or *gwawawaa*; also a long, hoarse, raucous growl *gwaaa* in flight. **Range & status** W Palearctic, Africa, Indian Subcontinent, E and SE Asia, Indonesia, Philippines.

Borneo Locally common resident and non-breeding visitor throughout. **Breeding** Probably February–December; breeding has been recorded coastal W Sabah, Sarawak, C and E Kalimantan; nests on or close to ground.

35

LIBARAN ISLAND   5/6/10

GREAT EGRET *Ardea alba*

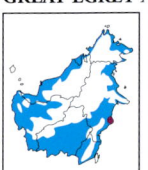

Identification 80–104 cm. Large all-white egret with heavy bill, long gape-line extending behind rear of eye, and long kinked neck. **Adult non-breeding** *modesta* Iris yellow, facial skin orange-yellow sometimes tinged blue, bill bright yellow, gape extends below and behind eye, legs black. **Adult breeding** Long back-plumes; bill black, facial skin deep greenish-blue, legs pinkish-red. **Juvenile** As non-breeding adult. **Similar species** See Intermediate Egret. **Habitat** Estuaries, mudflats, mangroves, lakes, swamps, rivers. **Behaviour** Flies with slow wingbeats. Often in association with other egrets. **Voice** Usually only calls in flight giving a hoarse, guttural *gwaaa, gaaw gaaw*. **Range & status** Europe, Africa, S, E and SE Asia, Australia, N, C and S America. **Borneo** Common non-breeding visitor and possibly rare resident throughout, less common on east coast. **Breeding** April–September; breeding in Borneo only confirmed from E Kalimantan; possibly breeds Sabah, Brunei, S Kalimantan.

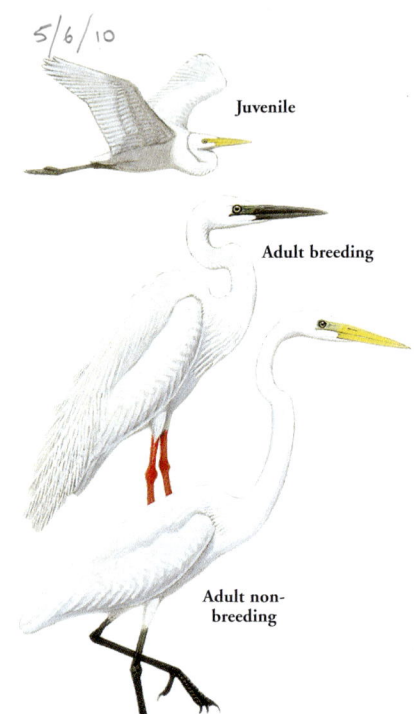

Juvenile

Adult breeding

Adult non-breeding

INTERMEDIATE EGRET *Mesophoyx intermedia*   BRUNEI   2/6/10 + 3/6/10

Identification 56–72 cm. Medium-sized all-white heron with relatively straight slim neck. **Adult non-breeding** *intermedia* Iris pale yellow, facial skin yellow, bill yellow with black tip, legs black. **Adult breeding** Long filamentous back and breast-plumes, iris red and bill black during courtship. **Juvenile** As adult non-breeding. **Similar species** Smaller than Great Egret, gape does not extend behind eye, bill shorter, small head with rounded crown, and thick neck less kinked. **Habitat** Estuaries, mudflats, mangroves, freshwater, lakes. **Behaviour** Tends to favour freshwater habitats. **Voice** Rarely calls except at breeding colonies, where it utters a harsh short repeated *ga, ga*. **Range & status** Sub-Saharan Africa, S and SE Asia, Japan, Indonesia, New Guinea, Australia. **Borneo** Locally common non-breeding visitor and possible rare breeding resident throughout. **Breeding** July–January; only confirmed in E Kalimantan.

Adult breeding

Juvenile

Adult non-breeding

LITTLE EGRET *Egretta garzetta*

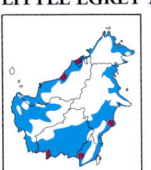

Identification 55–65 cm. Small, delicate all-white heron with long slender grey-black bill. **Adult breeding *nigripes*** Two long white nape-plumes, recurved filamentous dorsal plumes extending to end of tail, long straight breast-plumes; iris red during courtship fading to yellow, facial skin orange-yellow to reddish, bill black, legs and feet all black. **Adult non-breeding** Lacks crest and plumes, iris yellow, facial skin greenish-yellow. **Juvenile** As non-breeding adult but legs and feet duller, bill greyer. **Adult *garzetta*** Legs black with yellow feet. **Similar species** From similar Intermediate by smaller size, dark bill, less rounded head, black legs contrasting with yellow toes. **Habitat** Mangroves, lakes, rivers, swamps, paddyfields. **Behaviour** Active feeder in shallow wetlands. **Voice** Generally silent except at breeding colonies where it utters a harsh repeated *gwa gwa* with gargling quality; croaking call when alarmed or flushed. **Range & status** Europe, Africa, S, E and SE Asia, Indonesia, Australia, New Guinea, New Zealand. **Borneo** Uncommon resident and common non-breeding visitor throughout; both subspecies probably occur in roughly equal numbers. **Breeding** March–July in Brunei, C and E Kalimantan.

PACIFIC REEF-EGRET *Egretta sacra*

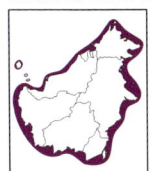

Identification 56–66 cm. Monotypic. Dimorphic. **Adult breeding** Short plumes on nape and lower foreneck, back-plumes to base of tail; iris orange-yellow, bill blackish-brown with yellowish base and lower mandible, facial skin dark grey to yellow, legs pale yellowish-green to greenish-black; **white morph** pure white, **dark morph** dark slaty bluish-grey to brownish-grey, some with white chin and throat-stripe. **Adult non-breeding** Lacks plumes, iris pale yellow, bill, lores, legs and feet as breeding adult. **Juvenile white morph** white, sometimes with dark brown streaks, **dark morph** browner, duller than adult, no plumes, bill brown, lores grey, legs and feet yellow. **Similar species** Little Egret has black bill and yellow feet, Eastern Cattle Egret is smaller with shorter bill. **Habitat** Estuaries, islands, atolls, rocky shorelines, coral cays, mudflats, mangroves, sandy beaches. **Behaviour** Seen singly or in pairs. Almost exclusively coastal. Stealthily stalks prey at water's edge. **Voice** Rarely vocalise, similar to other egrets with a grunting *ork*. **Range & status** SE Asia, Japan, Philippines, Indonesia, Australia, Pacific. **Borneo** Common resident in suitable habitat throughout, white phase rare in west. **Breeding** Recorded in June in W Sabah; nest is small pad of twigs usually located under small bush.

CHINESE EGRET *Egretta eulophotes*

Identification 65–68 cm. Monotypic. **Adult non-breeding** All white, lacks crest and back-plumes; bill dull grey-black with dull yellow base to lower mandible, iris brown-yellow, facial skin greenish-yellow, legs and feet dull greenish. **Adult breeding** Short, shaggy tuft of long nape-plumes distinctive, long straight dorsal plumes extending to end of tail; iris pale yellow, facial skin bright blue, bill bright orange-yellow sometimes with black tip, legs black with greenish-yellow feet. **Juvenile** As non-breeding adult. **Similar species** In non-breeding plumage differs from white-morph Pacific Reef-egret with longer legs and more slender bill; from Little Egret by leg colour, and more extensive pale area on lower mandible. **Habitat** Shallow estuaries, tidal mudflats, wetlands, bays. **Behaviour** Usually seen in tidal areas. More active feeder than Little Egret and Pacific Reef-Egret, actively pursues prey often with outstretched wings. **Voice** Rarely vocalises; hoarse short *gaa* or *ga*. **Range & status** Breeds China, Korea, Siberia; migrates from Japan to Sumatra and Philippines. Vulnerable. **Borneo** Formerly common, now declining non-breeding visitor September–April especially to coastal NW Borneo (Sabah, Sarawak, Brunei), scarce NE coastal Sabah, rare E Kalimantan.

PHAETHONTIDAE: Tropicbirds

Worldwide 3 species, 1 in Borneo. Delicate and graceful pantropical seabirds with mainly white plumage, webbed feet, short tail and long central tail feathers. Feeds by hovering before plunging into the water surface. Strong, direct flight, frequently soars. Sexes similar.

WHITE-TAILED TROPICBIRD *Phaethon lepturus*

Identification 38 cm (tail streamers up to 40 cm more). Race uncertain. **Adult** Head white with short black eyestripe, upperparts white with scapulars tipped black and black bar on innerwing, outer primaries on upperwing black, underparts white often with yellowish wash, long white tail-streamers; bill yellow or orange, legs and feet black. **Juvenile** Reduced black eyestripe; nape, mantle, upperwing-coverts, back and rump barred greyish-black, white tail tipped black with no streamers; bill dullish yellow with black tip. **Habitat** Oceans. **Range & status** Tropical and subtropical Pacific, Indian and Atlantic Oceans. **Borneo** Rare vagrant with one sight record from E Kalimantan; present on Spratly Islands (300 km NW of Sabah).

FREGATIDAE: Frigatebirds

Worldwide 5 species, 3 in Borneo. Large, aerial, pantropical seabirds with long hooked bill and very wide wingspan. Sexually dimorphic, females are larger and males have a prominent red gular pouch, which is often inflated during the breeding season. Plucks food from the water surface and kleptoparasitises other seabirds. Often soars almost motionless for long periods.

CHRISTMAS ISLAND FRIGATEBIRD
Fregata andrewsi

Identification 89–100 cm. Monotypic. **Adult male** Upperparts black with green and purple gloss, underparts black with white patch on lower belly and vent, underwing all black (no axillary spurs), large bright red gular pouch during breeding season, tail long and deeply forked; iris dark brown, eye-ring black, bill dark grey, legs and feet dull pink. **Adult female** Upperparts black with green and purple gloss, narrow white nuchal collar giving hooded appearance, head and throat black, underparts black with extensive white from upper breast to vent, extending onto underwings as conspicuous axillary spur; eye-ring pink, bill pink, brighter during courtship, legs and feet pink. **Juvenile** Similar to adult female but tawny head and throat, black breast-band, white patch from lower breast to vent, white axillary spurs (possibly broader than Lesser); eye-ring brown, bill grey, legs and feet brownish-grey. **Immature** like juvenile, gradually loses black breast-band and acquires adult plumage. **Habitat** Oceans, islets, inshore waters, often attracted to refuse from offshore oilrigs and coastal marketplaces. **Behaviour** Often in large flocks. Powerful flight on rigid wings. Pursues other birds, forcing them to drop prey. **Range & status** Indian Ocean; breeds Christmas Island. **Borneo** Common to uncommon non-breeding visitor to Sabah, rare in Kuching area (Sarawak), Brunei and Mahakam Delta (E Kalimantan). Critically Endangered.

GREAT FRIGATEBIRD *Fregata minor*

Identification 85–105 cm. **Adult male *minor*** All-black plumage with green and purple gloss diagnostic, brownish band across inner upperwing, large bright red gular pouch during breeding season, tail long and deeply forked; iris dark brown, eye-ring blackish-brown, bill dark-grey to black, legs and feet dull pink. **Adult female** Black with heart-shaped white patch on underparts from chin to upper belly (not extending onto underwing), lower belly black, scaly buff bar on inner upperwing; eye-ring pink, bill light grey to pinkish, iris, legs and feet as adult male. **Juvenile** Upperparts black, head and neck rusty-brown, wing-bar pale, centre of breast to legs white; eye-ring brown, bill pale grey, legs and feet brownish-grey. **Immature** Like juvenile, gradually loses black breast-band and acquires adult plumage. **Habitat** Oceans, islets, inshore waters. **Behaviour** As other frigatebirds. **Voice** Usually silent away from breeding colonies. **Range & status** Tropical and subtropical Indian and Pacific oceans. **Borneo** Uncommon non-breeding visitor to coastal areas of Sabah, Brunei, Sarawak and E Kalimantan.

LESSER FRIGATEBIRD *Fregata ariel*

Identification 71–81 cm. **Adult male *ariel*** Mostly black with green and purple gloss, conspicuous white patch on each side of underwing forming axillary spur, bright red gular pouch during breeding season, tail long and deeply forked; iris dark brown, eye-ring blackish-brown, bill dark grey with darker tip, legs and feet black to reddish-brown. **Adult female** Mostly black with white nuchal collar giving hooded appearance, hood forms V on throat, upper breast white contiguous with collar and white axillary spurs, scaly buff wing-bar on upperwing; iris dark brown, eye-ring red to blue, bill pink, legs and feet pink to red. **Juvenile** Head and throat tawny- or brownish-white, upperparts black, collar white, underparts white with black breast-band, white axillary spurs on black underwings, sometimes with black mottling on belly. **Immature** Like juvenile, gradually loses black breast-band and acquires adult plumage. **Habitat** Oceans, islets, inshore waters, often attracted to refuse from offshore oilrigs and coastal marketplaces. **Behaviour** As other frigatebirds. **Voice** Usually silent away from breeding colonies. **Range & status** Tropical and subtropical Indian and Pacific Oceans. **Borneo** Abundant non-breeding offshore visitor to Sabah (largely absent from April to mid-July) and Sarawak, regular uncommon visitor to Brunei and Kalimantan.

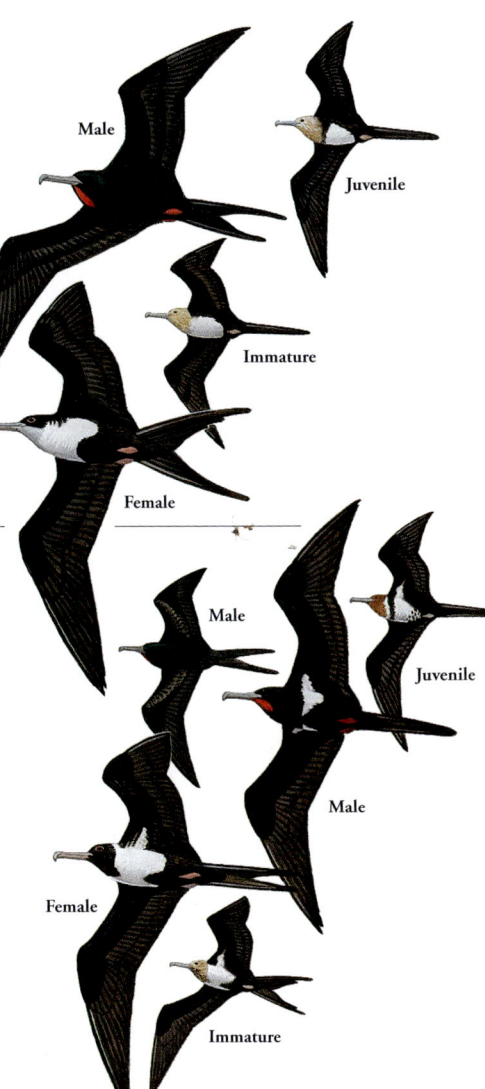

	Adult male	Adult female	Juvenile
Great Frigatebird	all black plumage	mostly black white from chin to upper belly belly black no axillary spurs	mostly black head and neck rusty-brown white from centre of breast to legs no axillary spurs black breast-band
Lesser Frigatebird	mostly black white axillary spurs	mostly black white nuchal collar hood white from upper breast to upper belly white axillary spurs	mostly black head and neck tawny or white black breast-band white from lower breast to vent sometimes with black mottling on belly white axillary spur

Christmas Island Frigatebird	mostly black
	white patch on lower
	  belly and vent
	no axillary spurs
		mostly black
		narrow white nuchal collar
		hood
		white from upper breast
		  to vent
		white axillary spurs
			mostly black
			head and throat tawny
			black breast-band
			white from lower breast to vent
			white axillary spurs
			  (possibly broader than Lesser)

SULIDAE: Boobies

Worldwide 9 species, 3 in Borneo. Large marine birds with heavy pointed bill, large rounded head with bare facial skin, and heavy body with short legs. Gregarious, forms large, noisy nesting colonies. Feeds on small fish by plunging into the water from high above the surface in a steep, long dive.

MASKED BOOBY *Sula dactylatra*

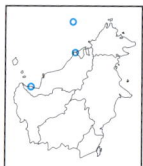

Identification 86 cm. **Adult** *personata* Conspicuous black face-mask, plumage white with black primaries and tail; in flight underwing and upperwing white with black trailing edge; iris yellow, bill yellowish, legs and feet yellowish-green. **Juvenile** Head and neck greyish-brown sometimes flecked white with white collar, back greyish-brown, upperwing-coverts greyish-brown with whitish edges; in flight shows dark brown central band across white underwing-coverts; iris dark, bill yellowish-green, bare facial skin blue-grey, feet grey. **Similar species** Juvenile Brown Booby has darker upperparts, no white collar, has brownish underwing-coverts and underparts; see Red-footed Booby. **Habitat** Oceans. **Range & status** Pantropical oceans. **Borneo** Rare vagrant; recorded from Sarawak.

RED-FOOTED BOOBY *Sula sula*

Identification 71 cm. **Adult** *rubripes* Variable, **white morph** head and body white with black primaries; iris dark with blue eye-ring and bare pink facial skin; bill pale blue, feet red; **dark morph** head and back brown, upperwing brown with darker primaries, underparts brown with white lower belly; bare parts as white morph. **Juvenile** Dark brown streaked darker on upperparts, and contrasting darker flight feathers and tail; iris grey, bare facial skin grey or pinkish, bill brown, legs and feet greyish-pink. **Similar species** Smaller than Masked Booby with all-white tail, note different colours of bare parts. **Habitat** Oceans. **Range & status** Pantropical oceans. **Borneo** Rare vagrant with records from Sabah and W Sarawak.

BROWN BOOBY *Sula leucogaster*

Identification 75–80 cm. **Male** *plotus* Upperparts dark brown, brown head and upper breast sharply demarcated from white lower breast to undertail-coverts; in flight underwing coverts white with brown fringes; iris silver, eye-ring blue, bare facial skin deep blue, bill and legs yellowish, legs and feet yellowish. **Female** As male but orbital ring and bare facial skin yellow. **Juvenile** As adults but duller brown with pale brownish belly and underwing-coverts contrasting with dark throat and flight feathers; bill and bare facial skin grey-blue, legs and feet pinkish. **Immature** indistinct streaky breast-band. **Similar species** Juvenile Red-footed Booby is more uniformly dark brown on underparts; see Masked Booby. **Habitat** Oceans, inshore seas, small islets. **Behaviour** Alternating flapping and gliding flight. Preys on fish by folding wings and diving steeply into water. **Range & status** Pantropical oceans. **Borneo** Uncommon resident and non-breeding visitor, regularly recorded in coastal areas and islands of N and W Borneo in small numbers (Sabah, Brunei and Sarawak). **Breeding** Breeds on Bankoran Island (Philippines), c.160 km north-east of Banggi Islands in Sulu Sea, and Layang Layang Island in Spratly group about 300 km west of Sabah.

PHALACROCORACIDAE: Cormorants

Worldwide c.38 species, 3 in Borneo. Large, dark waterbirds with long, hooked bill, long neck and body, and bare facial skin and throat pouch. Dives from the surface for fish. Soars in flight, swims partially submerged. Often stands with wings outspread to dry after fishing.

LITTLE BLACK CORMORANT
Phalacrocorax sulcirostris

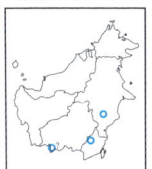

Identification 55–65 cm. Monotypic. **Adult breeding** Black with glossy sheen, upper back, wing-coverts and scapular feathers tinged silvery-grey, small tufts of white nuptial plumes over eye and behind ear; iris bright green, bill long and slender, dark grey-brown, legs and feet black. **Adult non-breeding** As breeding but nuptial plumes absent, plumage dull. **Juvenile** Dark brown; iris brown. **Habitat** Lakes and rivers. **Range & status** Australia, New Zealand, Indonesia, New Guinea. **Borneo** Vagrant or rare resident S Kalimantan, recent sight records from Mahakam Lakes area, E Kalimantan, in 2003 (2 birds) and 2004 (1 bird). Not recorded prior to this since 1851 when 4 specimens collected from S Borneo.

LITTLE CORMORANT *Phalacrocorax niger*

Identification 51–56 cm. Monotypic. **Adult breeding** Small; all bronze-black except for scattered white plumes on head above and behind eye, silvery margins to wing-coverts; iris black, slender bill dark grey, legs and feet black. **Adult non-breeding** Plumage duller with white patch on chin; bill flesh-coloured. **Juvenile** Duller and browner, throat whitish, underparts paler. **Habitat** Estuaries, freshwater ponds, rivers, lakes, paddyfields. **Range & status** Indian Subcontinent, SE Asia, Sumatra, Java. **Borneo** Rare vagrant and possible very rare resident with records from S Kalimantan and Sarawak, and possibly C Kalimantan. **Breeding** Nesting was recorded at Loagan Bunut, E Sarawak in 1987.

GREAT CORMORANT *Phalacrocorax carbo*

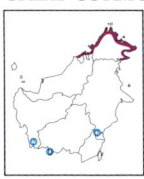

Identification 80–85 cm. **Adult breeding** *sinensis* Black with greenish sheen, white throat-patch extending to sides of face below eye, black nape-crest with whitish streaks, white oval thigh-patches; iris emerald-green, bare facial skin bright yellow, bill greyish, yellow at base, legs and feet black. **Adult non-breeding** As breeding but lacks crest, white streaking and thigh-patches, plumage fades and upperwing-coverts gain sandy edges. **Juvenile** Browner than adult; iris grey-brown, bare facial skin dull yellow. **Habitat** Rocky coasts and islands, mudflats, mangroves, estuaries, freshwater ponds. **Range & status** Australasia, Eurasia, Africa, north-east N America. **Borneo** Vagrant and uncommon resident in Sabah, Brunei, status uncertain in W, C and E Kalimantan. **Breeding** No confirmed breeding records.

ANHINGIDAE: Darters

Worldwide 4 species, 1 in Borneo. Pantropical diving birds with long, snake-like neck and spear-like bill. Uses sharp bill to spear fish. Swims partially submerged, often stands with wings outspread to dry.

SUKAU RIVER LODGE 9/6/10

ORIENTAL DARTER *Anhinga melanogaster*

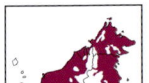

Adult non-breeding

Adult non-breeding

Identification 85–97 cm. Monotypic. Cormorant-like with long snake-like neck and spear-like bill, elongated body and long tail, distinct kink in neck. **Adult male breeding** Head, neck and tail blackish, upperparts glossy black with prominent whitish or greyish streaks on wing-coverts and scapulars, underparts brownish-black, rufous foreneck, black spots on white throat, strongly demarcated white or buff stripe from gape along sides of head and neck; iris yellow, facial skin yellow, bill yellow, legs and feet greyish-black. **Adult female breeding** As male but lacks black spots on throat. **Adult non-breeding** Head, neck and tail brownish, lacks rufous foreneck, pale throat. **Juvenile** Upperparts pale brownish, underparts brownish, whitish head and neck; bill, legs and feet dull yellow. **Habitat** Oxbow and freshwater lakes, wetlands, rivers, mangroves. **Behaviour** Favours undisturbed wetlands. Usually only head and neck visible when in the water. Swims underwater and spears fish with sharp bill. Perches on conspicuous branches with wings outstretched to dry. **Range & status** South and SE Asia, Philippines, Indonesia, Australia, New Guinea. **Borneo** Locally common to rare (W Sabah) but declining resident throughout, especially in coastal areas. **Breeding** Colonies have been noted in E Sabah, E and C Kalimantan; bred historically in W Sabah with eggs in mid-November.

FALCONIDAE: Falcons

Worldwide c.61 species, 7 in Borneo. Small to medium-sized diurnal birds of prey with notched beaks. Falconets are very small with short wings and tail, falcons are medium-sized with long, narrow and pointed wings, and long tail. The sexes are often similar but females are larger than males. Most are highly agile aerial hunters and catch prey on the wing, many also take prey from the ground.

Male — Male — Female — Female

Male — Female — Male

COMMON KESTREL *Falco tinnunculus*

Identification 32–39 cm. **Adult male interstinctus** Crown and nape grey, distinctive black moustachial stripe, throat pale buff, upperparts rich chestnut spotted black, primaries greyish-black, underparts buff streaked black, uppertail grey with black subterminal band and white tips, undertail pale grey with black subterminal band; iris brown with yellow eye-ring, cere yellow, bill blue-grey with black tip, legs and feet yellow; in flight wings long and pointed, tail relatively long, underwing-coverts buff densely spotted black, flight feathers pale grey faintly barred darker, upperwing-coverts rich chestnut spotted black, flight feathers black, rump grey. **Adult female** Larger than male, head pale brown finely streaked blackish-brown, dark brown moustachial stripe, upperparts chestnut-brown barred dark brown, primaries greyish-black, uppertail coverts and uppertail usually washed greyish and always barred darker with broader subterminal band, undertail paler, underparts buff streaked dark brown. **Juvenile** As female but more strongly and densely marked. **Habitat** Favours open country such as fields, paddyfields, marshes, plantations; has been recorded on G. Kinabalu at 1,200 m. **Behaviour** Feeds on small mammals, lizards, large insects. Hunts by flying slowly over open areas or hovers with tail fanned. **Voice** Very rarely vocalises outside breeding season. **Range & status** Africa, Palearctic, Indian Subcontinent, E and SE Asia, Philippines. **Borneo** Uncommon vagrant Sabah and Brunei, rare vagrant to Sarawak. No confirmed records from Kalimantan.

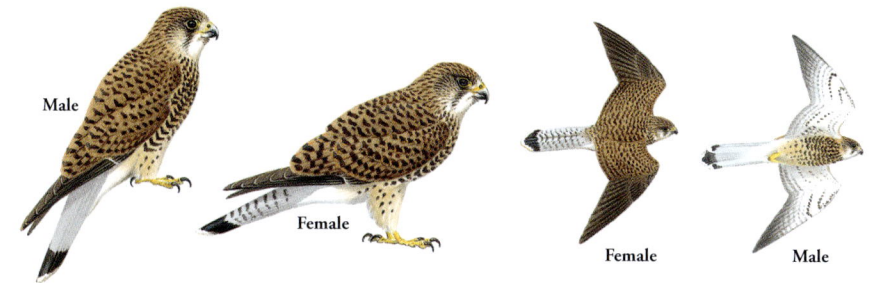

SPOTTED KESTREL *Falco moluccensis*

Identification 28–33 cm. **Adult male** *microbalia* Rather similar to Common Kestrel but head chestnut-brown streaked black, overall plumage darker, upperparts entirely barred black, underparts spotted and streaked black, rump and tail grey with broad subterminal band and white tips. **Adult female** As adult male but larger, uppertail grey with 7–8 narrow black bars and broader subterminal band and white tips. **Juvenile** Paler, tail brown with dark bands. **Habitat** Favours open country. **Behaviour** Very similar to Common Kestrel. **Voice** A sharp, rapid *kee-kee-kee-kee-kee-*... **Range & status** Java, Lesser Sundas, Moluccas. **Borneo** Rare vagrant with one record from mid-1800s probably from C or S Kalimantan.

BLACK-THIGHED FALCONET
Microhierax fringillarius

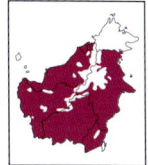

Identification 14–17 cm. Monotypic. Tiny falcon with prominent black and white head markings. **Adult** Crown black, small white forehead-patch, black band through eye, broad white downcurved supercilium wider towards back of head, upperparts black, upper breast white, lower breast and belly often with rufous suffusion, thighs black, undertail black with three or four central white bars; iris blackish-brown, cere and bill black, legs and feet black; in flight underwing-coverts white, flight feathers white narrowly barred black with black trailing edge. **Juvenile** As adult but rufous wash on white parts of head. **Habitat** Primary and secondary lowland dipterocarp and peatswamp forest, plantations, favours forest edges and clearings, to 1,000 m. **Behaviour** Feeds on large insects, small birds and lizards. Known to hunt over cultivated and burnt areas. Hunts from high, exposed perches sallying out to take prey in air, often returning to same perch for prolonged periods. Frequently bobs head when perched. Often in pairs or small groups. Flies with rapid wing-beats. **Voice** A loud, monotone and high-pitched *chee-chee-chee*... given in flight. **Range & status** Thai-Malay Peninsula, Indonesia. **Borneo** Common resident Sarawak, Brunei and Kalimantan, absent from Sabah (replaced by next species). **Breeding** December–June; builds nest in deserted nest-holes of woodpeckers or barbets.

WHITE-FRONTED FALCONET *Microhierax latifrons*

Identification 15–17 cm. Monotypic. Tiny with prominent white forehead and buffish wash on underparts. **Adult male** Entire front of head bright white, cheeks and throat white, broad black lores and eyestripe join black crown and nape merging into black upperparts, upper breast white, lower breast and belly washed pale buff, thighs black, undertail all black; iris blackish-brown, cere and bill black, legs and feet black. **Adult female** As male but front of head chestnut. **Juvenile** As male but underparts washed buffish-chestnut. **Habitat** Primary and secondary lowland dipterocarp forest, plantations, favours forest edges and clearings, to 1,200 m. **Behaviour** As previous species. **Voice** A trilling *kree-kree-kree*... **Range & status** Endemic, uncommon resident restricted to N Borneo where found throughout Sabah and in extreme E Sarawak bordering Sabah; status in Brunei uncertain; not recorded from Kalimantan. **Breeding** November–June; builds nest in deserted nest-holes of woodpeckers or barbets.

43

ORIENTAL HOBBY *Falco severus*

Identification 24–30 cm. Monotypic. **Adult** Crown to sides of head black giving hooded appearance, upperparts black fading to slaty-black on lower back and uppertail-coverts, throat and sides of neck buffish-rufous, underparts unmarked rich rufous, at rest wing-tips longer than tail-tip; iris brown, cere and eye-ring bright yellow, bill black, legs and feet yellow; in flight long pointed wings, relatively short tail, underwing-coverts unmarked rufous, flight feathers and undertail rufous narrowly barred. **Juvenile** As adult but underparts heavily streaked black, underwing-coverts streaked and barred. **Habitat** Forest clearings, paddyfields, limestone outcrops. **Behaviour** Feeds on large insects, small birds, bats; hunts from high exposed perch with direct rapid flights, mostly at dawn and dusk. **Voice** A monotone, repeated *ki-ki-ki-ki-*

ki... **Range & status** Indian Subcontinent, S China, SE Asia, Philippines, Java, Sulawesi, New Guinea, Solomon Islands. **Borneo** Rare vagrant recorded in Sabah and C Kalimantan; unconfirmed from Brunei and S Kalimantan.

EURASIAN HOBBY *Falco subbuteo*

Identification 28–36 cm. **Adult male *streichi*** Crown and nape black, throat and cheeks buffish-white, short black moustachial stripes, upperparts dark grey, underparts buff or white heavily and densely streaked blackish, thighs and vent rufous, at rest wing-tips longer than tail-tip; iris brown, cere and eye-ring yellow, bill grey, legs and feet yellow; in flight underwing barred dark on white, undertail finely barred. **Juvenile** Upperparts brown with buffish feather-fringes, underparts darker buff and more heavily marked, no rufous on thighs and vent. **Habitat** Open woodlands, plantations, paddyfields. **Behaviour** Feeds mainly on insects and small birds. Hunts with fast, acrobatic flight catching prey on wing. Most active at dawn and dusk. Has been recorded hunting migrant passerines on Layang Layang Island. **Voice** A

squeaky *ki-ki-ki-ki-* with slightly rising intonation, tempo increasing (14–15 phrases over 2.4 s, 3–4 kHz). **Range & status** Africa, Palearctic, Indian Subcontinent, East and SE Asia. **Borneo** Very rare vagrant with two sight records, one from Brunei, one from the Layang Layang Island (South China Sea 300 km north-west of Kota Kinabalu).

PEREGRINE FALCON *Falco peregrinus*

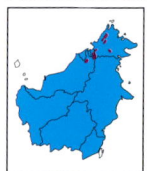

Identification 34–48 cm. Compact, robust falcon with long pointed wings. **Adult *ernesti*** Head black, solid black sides of head giving a hooded appearance, throat and sides of neck white, upperparts slaty-black, upper breast white with narrow black streaks, lower breast and belly barred grey and black, tail indistinctly barred black and grey with subterminal black band and grey tip; iris brown, cere and eye-ring yellow, bill grey with black tip, legs and feet yellow; in flight dense barring on underparts, relatively short tail. Female larger than male. **Juvenile *ernesti*** Hooded as adult, buffish underparts broadly streaked blackish-brown, cere and eye-ring paler. **Adult *calidus*** Larger, head black with black moustachial stripes (not hooded), white cheeks, upperparts brown with buffish feather-fringes, underparts pale buff with sparser dark bars. **Juvenile *calidus*** Brown moustachial stripes, underparts buff streaked dark brown; cere and eye-ring blue-grey, legs pale yellow. **Habitat** Lowland forest, hill forest, montane forest, cities, near cliffs, to 2,440 m. **Behaviour** Feeds mainly on small birds and bats; characteristic very agile yet strong direct flight. **Voice** Normally quiet away from its nest area, *ge-ge-ge-ge...* (c.12 notes to 2.4 s, 2-3 kHz). **Range & status** Worldwide; *ernesti* occurs in Thai-Malay Peninsula, Indonesia, Philippines, New Guinea. **Borneo** *ernesti* rare, mostly montane resident in N Borneo (Sabah and E Sarawak), *calidus* non-breeding visitor throughout (but favouring coastal areas) October-April. **Breeding** All reported nests have been located on cliffs.

PANDIONIDAE: Osprey

Worldwide 1 species, 1 in Borneo. Highly specialised large piscivorous raptor with spiky scales on underside of strong feet for grasping large fish in flight, the outer toe is reversible. The plumage is thick and oily. Sexes similar. Migratory and closely associated with water.

OSPREY *Pandion haliaetus*

Identification 50–58 cm. **Adult female** *haliaetus* Head and neck white with broad dark band through eye, short shaggy crest, upperparts dark brown, underparts white with dusky streaking on breast sometimes forming complete breast-band; iris yellow, cere blue-grey, bill grey, legs and feet pale grey; in flight underwing-coverts white with black carpal patches and rear edge of coverts, flight feathers grey with narrow darker barring contrasting with black wing-tips. **Adult male** Smaller than female, breast-band sparser or absent. **Juvenile** Crown and nape heavily streaked, upperparts with pale scaling; in flight upperwings show white lines down centre of wing and thin white trailing edge. **Habitat** Estuaries, lakes, mangroves, beaches, offshore islands; predominantly coastal but also on inland rivers in Borneo, to 700 m. **Behaviour** Glides and soars with bowed wings; flight is loose and shallow interrupted with long glides. **Voice** Call is a slow-paced whistled *pyo pyo pyo…* (1.5–2.5 kHz) uttered about 6 notes a second. **Range & status** N and S America, Africa, Palearctic, Indian Subcontinent, E and SE Asia, Philippines, Australia, New Guinea. **Borneo** Uncommon non-breeding visitor throughout, August–April. Records from May–July suggest it may be rare resident in E Kalimantan.

ACCIPITRIDAE: Hawks, eagles & allies

Worldwide c.239 species, 27 in Borneo. A diverse group of mostly diurnal birds of prey with specialised hooked bills, broad wings and strong talons. Mostly sexes are similar, females generally larger than males and many show a confusing array of age-related or colour morph plumages. Occupy a variety of habitats and take a wide variety of prey. Most are territorial and solitary.

JERDON'S BAZA *Aviceda jerdoni*

Identification 41–48 cm. Medium-sized raptor with distinctive erect crest. **Adult male** *borneensis* (endemic subspecies) Head and sides of neck pale rufous with variable dark shaft streaking, especially on the crown; sides of the head variably suffused with gray, throat pale rufous with dark gular stripe, long black crest tipped white usually held vertically, breast off-white with indistinct pale rufous streaks and blotches with variable grey suffusion, belly and thighs marked with broad rich rufous bars, tarsi feathered halfway to toes, back and rump dark brown, wings dark brown with a greyish cast, at rest wing-tips reach more than halfway down tail, uppertail dark brown with a grey cast, three dark bands visible with the subterminal band broader and white tips, black dark barring on under tail, undertail coverts softly barred and spotted rufous; iris yellow, cere pale grey, bill black, legs and feet yellow; in flight broad rounded wings, pale rufous and white underwing coverts, primaries greyish with blackish barring on primaries and broad, crisp black subterminal band in the secondaries, tail square with dark subterminal tail-band. **Adult female** Head paler with less rufous, paler rufous barring on belly with paler edging, subterminal band on secondaries not quite as black or broad, paler barring on primaries, narrower black subterminal band on secondaries, paler rufous barring on underwing coverts. **Juvenile** Head heavily streaked, paler below with prominent dark brown streaks on breast, tail brown with three tail bands, tail may be proportionally longer than either adult male or female; in flight subterminal band on secondaries grey and low contrast. **Similar species** Separated from Wallace's Hawk-eagle by amount of feathering on tarsi and length of wings relative to tail, light airy flight on flexible wings; from subadult Blyth's Hawk-eagle by longer wing projection at rest and broader white tip to crest. **Habitat** Riparian forests, lowland forests, logged forest, plantations; usually in lowlands. Voice A high-pitched, short pit-wee, second note descending (3–1.5 kHz). **Range & status** Indian Subcontinent, S China, SE Asia, Philippines, Indonesia. **Borneo** Uncommon resident throughout, possibly more common in E Borneo. **Breeding** Undescribed in Borneo.

ORIENTAL HONEY-BUZZARD *Pernis ptilorhynchus*

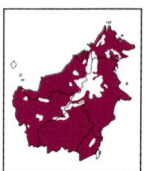

Identification 52–61 cm. Polymorphic; plumage highly variable but tail and wing-tip patterns consistent in adult male, adult female and juvenile; longish tail and distinctive pigeon-like head on long neck. **Adult male pale morph** *torquatus* Short crest on hindcrown, grey sides of face with dark-streaked malar stripes and gorget framing off-white throat with dark gular stripe, upperparts mostly uniform dark, lower breast to undertail-coverts dark brown to white with rufous bars, tail dark with wide paler band; iris yellow, cere grey, bill grey, legs and feet yellow, claws black; in flight from below primaries separated and upturned, wings broad, underwing-coverts barred rufous, flight feathers barred black and white and prominent black wing-tips, tail long with rounded corners. **Adult pale female** As male but sides of head brown, narrower barring on flight feathers and tail. **Adult dark morph** As pale morph but head, body and wings dark brown, underparts with whitish barring. **Juvenile** Variable, usually paler head, neck and underparts, iris typically darker, cere yellow, indistinct barring on flight feathers. **Adult** *orientalis* Pale to dark morphs, like *torquatus* but shorter crest; iris brown in male, yellow in female. **Habitat** Riparian forests, lowland forests, logged forest, plantations, to 1,000 m. **Behaviour** Feeds on wasps and bees, large insects, reptiles, small mammals and birds. Soars on flat wings or with shallow dihedral, often twisting head from side to side; may twist tail in kite-like manner. **Voice** High-pitched, loud slurred *pee-oo* (1.8–3 kHz). **Range & status** Palearctic, Indian Subcontinent, E and SE Asia, Philippines, Indonesia. **Borneo** Race *torquatus* common resident throughout; *orientalis* non-breeding visitor (abundance uncertain), October–March. **Breeding** Courtship behaviour has been recorded in Brunei and possibly in Sabah in early August.

BAT HAWK *Macheiramphus alcinus*

SUKAU RIVER LODGE 8/6/10

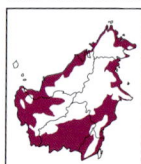

Identification 45 cm. Falcon-like, mainly crepuscular raptor (but also hunts at night, especially on moonlit nights). **Adult** *alcinus* Blackish-brown plumage, short crest, throat and breast white with thick black gular stripe; iris golden-yellow with broken white eye-ring, small bill black, legs and feet light grey; in flight long wings broad-based, note protruding carpal joint and short head, long tail. **Juvenile** Browner, more extensive white on throat and upper breast. **Similar species** In flight similar to Peregrine Falcon but always with noticeable sharp bend at wrists. **Habitat** Lowland forest, riparian forest, secondary forest, often associated with limestone outcrops and caves, to 200 m. **Behaviour** Requires tall, bare-boled trees for nesting in high canopy, and an abundant source of bats or swiftlets, but not necessarily continuous forest cover. Catches and devours prey in flight, flying level with or dropping through flocks. Known to feed around buildings but more commonly near caves and limestone outcrops. **Voice** High-pitched *kee*. **Range &**

status Africa, SE Asia, Indonesia, New Guinea. **Borneo** Uncommon resident throughout. **Breeding** Adults attending nests located in tall emergent trees have been observed in January–May and August in Sabah and E Sarawak; large nest is bulky accumulation of sticks on horizontal branch or fork in lower crown.

BLACK-SHOULDERED KITE *Elanus caeruleus*

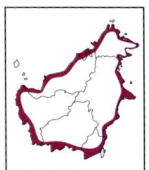

Identification 28–30 cm. Small, graceful kite with immaculate plumage. **Adult** *hypoleucos* Crown pale grey, back and wings pale grey, underparts pure white, black upperwing-coverts form distinctive shoulder-patch; dark eye-patch around large red iris, cere yellow, bill black, legs and feet yellow; in flight underparts and underwing white, wing-tips black. **Juvenile** Crown whitish with brown streaks, upperparts and wings brown with feathers edged white, underparts faintly streaked brownish; iris yellow. **Habitat** Open country, paddyfields, pastures, at sea level. **Behaviour** Active throughout the day, but mostly crepuscular; perches during day, often seen hovering at 45° to ground over fields and open areas, feeding on rodents, orthopterans, skinks, quail; flight is graceful, wings raised when gliding. **Voice** Thin, piping *kee-er*. **Range & status** Africa, Indian Subcontinent, SE Asia, Indonesia, Philippines, New Guinea. **Borneo** Locally uncommon, possibly increasing, resident throughout. **Breeding** January–March.

BLACK-EARED KITE *Milvus lineatus*

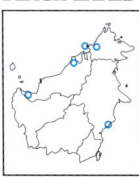

Identification 60–66 cm. Monotypic. **Adult** Plumage dark brown, ear-coverts dark, paler face and throat, slightly forked tail diagnostic; iris brown, cere blue-grey, bill dark brown, legs and feet yellow, in flight from below whitish patch at base of primaries. **Juvenile** More prominent black ear-coverts, head and underparts more grey-brown and streaked buff. **Habitat** Towns, villages, rubbish tips, rural areas. **Behaviour** Gregarious scavenger. **Voice** Call is a high-pitched tremulous whistle *pi-hyorororo* (2–3 kHz), also a shorter whistled *pi*. **Range & status** Breeds E Palearctic to N Indian Subcontinent; migrates to China, India, SE Asia. Formerly considered subspecies of Black Kite *M. migrans* of W Palearctic, Africa and Indian Subcontinent. **Borneo** Rare vagrant Sabah, Brunei, Sarawak and E Kalimantan.

BRAHMINY KITE *Haliastur indus*

Identification 45–51 cm. **Adult** *intermedius* Head, neck and breast white sometimes with narrow blackish-brown streaks, upperparts and belly rich chestnut; iris reddish-brown, cere yellow, bill yellowish-blue, legs and feet yellow; in flight underwing-coverts chestnut, flight feathers paler, wing-tips black. **Juvenile** Back and wings dark brown with feathers edged paler, head and underparts pale brown streaked buff; bill dark grey; in flight pale patch at base of primaries. **Similar species** Smaller than Black Kite with rounded tail. **Habitat** Open areas and forest edges near estuaries, lakes, rivers, along coast, to 1,100 m in Borneo. **Behaviour** Feeds on fish, snakes, lizards, large insects, carrion, refuse. **Voice** Quavering, shrill wail *cheee-ee-e* given in flight or when perched. **Range & status** Indian Subcontinent, S China, SE Asia, New Guinea, Australia. **Borneo** Common resident throughout; occurs inland but most abundant on coast. **Breeding** December–March; generally nests inland near water in tall trees, lays 1–2 dull white eggs in bulky nest of twigs.

47

Adult Adult Third year Juvenile Juvenile

WHITE-BELLIED SEA-EAGLE *Haliaeetus leucogaster*

Identification 75–85 cm. Monotypic. Large grey-and-white eagle with wedge-shaped tail. **Adult** Head and neck white, underparts white, back and wings grey; primaries black, iris dark brown, cere blue-grey, bill grey with darker tip, legs and feet dull yellow, tarsi unfeathered, claws black; in flight white underparts and underwing-coverts contrast with greyish-black flight feathers, wedge-shaped tail white with greyish-black base. **Juvenile** Head and neck buff with dark eye-stripe, upperparts dark brown streaked buff, underparts mottled brown to orange-buff; in flight wing-coverts buff with brown markings, secondaries and tips of primaries darker, large whitish patch on base of primaries, tail whitish with brown subterminal band; iris pale brown, bill dark grey. **Habitat** Offshore islands, harbours, estuaries, mangroves, beaches, lakes, swamps, to 200 m. **Behaviour** Glides and soars with strong dihedral. An opportunistic carnivore, feeding on carrion, fish, birds, snakes, etc. Snatches fish from water surface. Known to steal prey from other raptors. Performs spectacular display-flights. **Voice** Main call is a series of repeated, nasal honks *gank-gank-gank-gank…* (1.8–2.3 kHz). **Range & status** Indian Subcontinent, S China, SE Asia, Indonesia, New Guinea, Australia. **Borneo** Common resident along entire coast and offshore islands, less commonly on inland waterways. **Breeding** December–April; nest is very large, bulky collection of sticks located in tall tree.

GREY-HEADED FISH-EAGLE *Ichthyophaga ichthyaetus*

Identification 61–75 cm. Monotypic. Large, greyish-brown eagle with diagnostic white tail and sharply demarcated broad black terminal band. **Adult** Head to upper breast pale grey, upperparts and lower breast brownish-grey, belly white, tarsi unfeathered, uppertail white with broad black terminal band; iris pale yellow, cere grey, bill grey, legs and feet pale grey with black claws; in flight from below broad wings with bulging secondaries, wings dark, white belly and undertail contrasts with black terminal band. **Juvenile** Head and underparts pale brown with whitish streaks, faint whitish eyebrow, upperparts brown with pale fringes on feathers, tail lightly banded with dark brown terminal band; iris brown; in flight pale below, underwings white with lightly barred flight feathers. **Similar species** Lesser Fish-eagle is smaller, head, breast and mantle concolorous, some have pale fringing on scapulars and wing coverts, tail is all greyish-brown; at rest primaries longer, almost reaching tail tip; vocalisations differ. **Habitat** Favours rivers, lakes, lowland wetlands, occasional on coastlines and offshore islands, to 600 m. **Behaviour** Spends much time perched over water, swooping down to take fish or carrion from surface. Predation of snakes has been recorded. **Voice** Call is a loud, rasping *err-wuk* (0.5–1.4 kHz); first note dips, second note rises. **Range & status** Indian Subcontinent, SE Asia, Philippines, Indonesia. **Borneo** Uncommon lowland resident throughout. **Breeding** Poorly known in Borneo; nest with pure white egg recorded from coastal Sarawak.

Adult Juvenile Second/third year Adult Adult Juvenile

LESSER FISH-EAGLE *Ichthyophaga humilis*

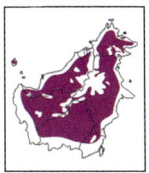

Identification 51–64 cm. **Adult *humilis*** Very similar to Grey-headed Fish-eagle but smaller, brownish tail with darker terminal band fading to paler base on undertail is diagnostic, plumage greyish-brown with white belly and thighs; iris pale yellow, cere and bill grey, legs and feet grey with black claws; in flight paler bases to primaries, V-shaped white vent contrasts with all brownish-grey tail. **Juvenile** Less heavily streaked than juvenile Grey-headed Fish-eagle, paler, tail darker, lacks pale eyebrow. **Similar species** See Grey-headed Fish-eagle. **Habitat** Narrow undisturbed forested waterways, mangroves, plantations, to 1,000 m. **Behaviour** Perches in large trees overhanging narrow rivers, often flushing ahead of canoe when travelling along interior rivers; glides and soars on flat wings, feeds on fish. **Voice** Call is a loud *nyooo-wer* (1–2 kHz), second note higher, also a slurred, whistled *foo-foo-foo-foooo* (1.9–2.6 kHz, 2.5 s). **Range & status** Himalayas, SE Asia, Indonesia. **Borneo** Uncommon resident of interior throughout, including N Natunas. **Breeding** Undescribed in Borneo.

CRESTED SERPENT-EAGLE *Spilornis cheela*

SUKAU RIVER LODGE 9/6/10

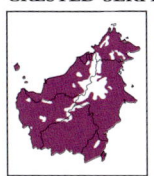

Identification 45–74 cm. Three endemic subspecies. **Adult *pallidus*** Crown black, fan-shaped short rounded nuchal crest with white marks, cheeks grey, upperparts dark brown with small white spots on wing-coverts, underparts rufous-chestnut with small white spots with black edgings on lower breast and belly, tarsi unfeathered, tail dark brown with broad pale subterminal band; male iris lemon-yellow, female iris darker yellow, bare facial skin deep yellow, cere yellow, bill grey, legs and feet rich yellow with black claws; in flight broad rounded wings are held slightly forward, gentle V-shaped dihedral, underwing-coverts rufous speckled white, trailing edge black with characteristic broad white band bordered black on inner wing. **Juvenile** Paler than adult with black face-patches, broad pale (white gradually changing to rufous) edging to feathers of head and back, underparts buff streaked brown, tail with two pale bands. **Adult *richmondi*** Smaller and paler. **Adult *natunensis*** Smaller, cheeks pale grey, short tail, upperparts grey-brown with little spotting. **Similar species** See Mountain Serpent-eagle. **Habitat** Lowland dipterocarp and swamp forest, mangroves, plantations, to 1,200 m (some

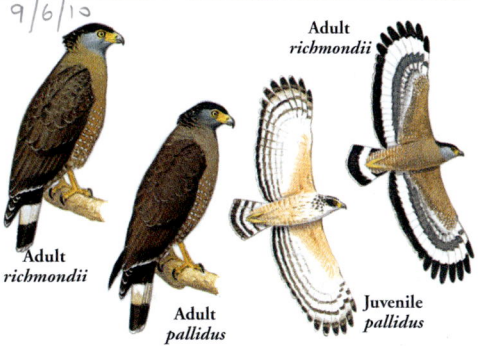

altitudinal overlap with Mountain Serpent-eagle). **Behaviour** Usually singly or in pairs; often soars circling over forest canopy; raises crest when alarmed. Feeds on snakes, small vertebrates. **Voice** Plaintive *kek kek kweee kweee kweee* with emphasis on last notes; also a longer *keee-er* usually uttered on wing. **Range & status** Indian Subcontinent, China, SE Asia, Indonesia. **Borneo** Common resident throughout, *pallidus* N Borneo, *richmondi* S Borneo, *natunensis* Natunas and Belitung Island. **Breeding** October–June.

MOUNTAIN SERPENT-EAGLE *Spilornis kinabaluensis*

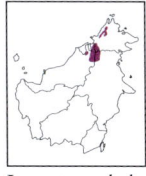

Identification 51–55 cm. Monotypic. **Adult** Similar to sympatric Crested Serpent-eagle race *pallidus* but larger, plumage darker, throat black, wings longer, clear white spots on breast and belly lack black edging, bolder and broader white bands on tail; in flight darker underwing-coverts, larger. **Immature** dark streaking on head and throat, dark vermiculations on breast, pale feather edging on upperparts. **Habitat** Strictly montane forests, 750–2,900 m. **Behaviour** As Crested Serpent-eagle; often soars circling over forest canopy but hugs ridges. Feeds on snakes and lizards. **Voice** Diagnostic (1.7–2.1 kHz, 3 s) *huit huit huit huiit hwoooo*, first notes brief leading into long slurred last note; less sharp and more drawn-out than Crested Serpent-eagle. **Range & status** Endemic, rare resident N Borneo in north-central

mountain ranges from G. Kinabalu to G. Murud and G. Mulu; few records from E Kalimantan (Sabah, Brunei, E Sarawak, E Kalimantan). **Breeding** Very poorly known; one record of an adult flying with two young at 900 m in November (Sabah).

49

EASTERN MARSH-HARRIER *Circus spilonotus*

Identification 47–55 cm. **Adult male** *spilonotus* Head blackish with varying amount of white streaking (sometimes entirely black), back black with white edgings, throat and breast white streaked blackish-brown, belly white; iris bright yellow, cere yellow, bill black, legs and feet yellow with black claws; in flight from above wing-coverts and back black mottled white, flight feathers whitish with black wing-tips, uppertail silvery-grey; in flight from below underwings whitish with thin black bands, primaries black. **Adult female** Head streaked dull brown, breast and upperparts brown streaked coarsely rufous and pale brown, belly and thighs rufous-brown; iris brown; in flight from above flight feathers banded off-white and grey, from below dark secondaries contrast with paler bases to primaries. **Juvenile** Head and throat buff, rest of plumage chocolate-brown with streaky buff breast-band and rufous-brown belly; in flight large pale patch on underwing contrasts with dark-tipped primaries. **Habitat** Marshes, swamps, lake edges, paddyfields, grasslands, pasture, to 1,100 m. **Behaviour** Flies low over grasslands and paddyfields; feeds on small vertebrates, fish, large insects. **Voice** Usually silent during migration; during breeding season call is a loud, short *kiiioo*. **Range & status** N, E and SE Asia, Philippines, Indonesia, New Guinea. **Borneo** Locally common non-breeding visitor and passage migrant to Sabah, Brunei and Sarawak, August–April; rare E Kalimantan.

HEN HARRIER *Circus cyaneus*

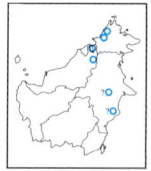

Identification 43–52 cm. **Adult male** *cyaneus* Upperparts pale grey with white patch on uppertail-coverts, primaries black, underparts white, at rest wing-tips falling well short of tail-tip; iris and cere yellow, bill dark grey, legs and feet yellow; in flight primaries tipped black, underwings grey with darker trailing edge, broad white band on rump. **Adult female** Pale face pattern with narrow pale rim to facial disk and whitish areas around eyes, dark mottled brown above, tawny-buff below heavily streaked brown; in flight prominent white uppertail-coverts, flight feathers boldly barred, tail with four broad bands. **Juvenile** Like female but bolder face pattern, slightly darker above, more rufous below streaked brown, uppertail-coverts white with narrow brown streaks. **Habitat** Open country, grasslands, wetlands, paddyfields. **Behaviour** Hunts flying low over open areas, feeding on small mammals and birds. **Voice** Generally silent in Borneo. **Range & status** Breeds Holarctic, NW and NE China; migrates to N Africa, Middle East, N Indian Subcontinent, S China, Korea, Japan and C America. **Borneo** Rare non-breeding visitor to Sabah and Sarawak; unconfirmed records from E Kalimantan.

PIED HARRIER *Circus melanoleucos*

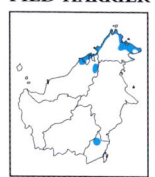

Identification 41–49 cm. Monotypic. **Adult male** Distinctive pied appearance, base colour is pale grey with head, back and upper breast black, forewing, rump and rest of underparts white, at rest wing-tips nearly reaching tail-tip; iris and cere yellow, bill black, legs and feet orange-yellow; in flight broad black wing-bar and primaries. **Adult female** Head streaked brown and white, indistinct face pattern, upperparts greyish, uppertail-coverts white, tail brown with five broad grey bars, underparts white heavily streaked brown; iris brown; in flight whitish leading edge on forewing, pale with bold streaks underneath, barred flight feathers. **Juvenile** More prominent face pattern, upperparts brown edged buff, underparts rich cinnamon, conspicuous white rump. **Habitat** Open ground, grasslands, swamps, marshes, paddyfields, to 1,200 m in Kelabit Highlands. **Behaviour** Prefers drier grasslands and fields, flying low in search of prey. **Voice** Generally silent in Borneo. **Range & status** Siberia, Indian Subcontinent, SE Asia, Philippines. **Borneo** Uncommon non-breeding visitor to Sabah, Brunei and Sarawak; one record from S Kalimantan.

WHITE-RUMPED VULTURE *Gyps bengalensis*

Identification 76–93 cm. Monotypic. **Adult** Overall plumage brownish-black, bare head and neck dark grey with sparse white fuzzy feathering, distinctive white neck-ruff, rump and lower back whitish; iris brownish-black, cere black, short heavy bill silvery-grey, legs and feet dark grey; in flight very deep wings and 2 m wingspan, whitish underwing-coverts contrasting with blackish flight feathers and underparts, black leading edge. **Juvenile** Grey-brown, head and neck with downy white plumage, underparts streaked whitish, lower back and rump brown, bill and cere blue-black. **Habitat** Open areas, human habitation. **Behaviour** Scavenging carnivore; soars high on rising thermals with wings held in shallow V; roosts in tall trees. **Voice** Harsh grunts and hisses. **Range & status** Indian Subcontinent, S China, SE Asia. Critically Endangered. **Borneo** Vagrant; recorded once (two birds) in Brunei. It is possible that this record pertains to Himalayan Griffon *G. himalayensis*, which has a paler buff-brown body and wing coverts (except in juvenile) and is larger (115–125 cm) and more heavily built.

51

CRESTED GOSHAWK *Accipiter trivirgatus*

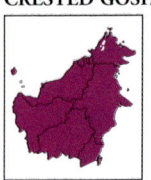
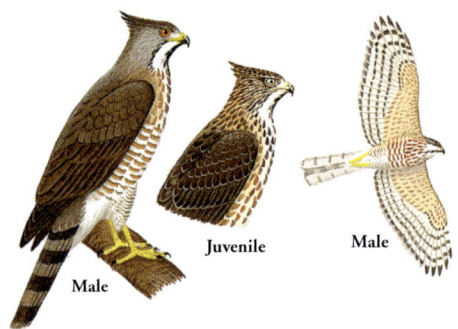

Identification 37–46 cm. **Adult male** *microstictus* (endemic subspecies) Crown and forehead blackish, short nuchal crest sometimes not visible, sides of head grey, chin and throat white with broad gular stripe and thin lateral throat-stripes, upperparts greyish-brown, upper breast white with rufous streaks, lower breast to belly barred rufous, long white undertail-coverts often giving impression of white rump in flight, tail barred evenly pale and dark; iris yellow, cere pale yellow, bill dark grey, legs and feet yellow with black claws; in flight wings and tail banded, undertail-coverts often fluffed up so that rump appears white. **Adult female** Larger and browner than male. **Juvenile** Crown streaked buff, dark streaks on cheek, sparse brown streaks on underparts. **Habitat** Primary and secondary lowland dipterocarp to upper montane forest, to 2,015 m. **Behaviour** Usually hunts from concealed perch; feeds on small mammals, small birds and nestlings, lizards, frogs, large insects. Display-flight of exaggerated stiff wing-flapping with wings depressed below the horizontal, alternating with normal flight. Known to breed in casuarina forest in Brunei. **Voice** Loud, high-pitched scream *keeee* 0.78 s (1–4.8 kHz). **Range & status** Indian Subcontinent, E Asia, Indonesia, Philippines. **Borneo** Common resident throughout including N Natunas. **Breeding** February–April; constructs nest in dense foliage in tall trees, laying 1–2 white eggs.

BESRA *Accipiter virgatus*

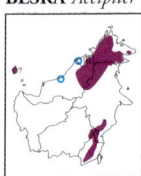

Identification 23–36 cm. **Adult male** *rufotibialis* (endemic subspecies) Upperparts dark grey, broad dark gular stripe on white throat, upper breast rufous streaked or unstreaked, lower breast and belly barred rufous, tail with dark and light bands of equal width; iris yellow, cere greenish-yellow, bill dark grey, legs and feet yellow. **Adult female** Larger than male, heavy dark streaks on breast, heavy dark barring on belly. **Juvenile** Upperparts brown, underparts pale with breast coarsely streaked blackish, belly and flanks mottled and barred. **Similar species** See Japanese Sparrowhawk. **Habitat** Hill to lower montane and kerangas forests, 300–1,900 m. **Behaviour** Mostly feeds on birds usually taken on wing after quick agile chase from concealed perch. **Voice** A high-pitched, rather squeaky rapid series of up to 10 short notes, *kyi-kyi-kyi*...with last notes speeding up (1.5 s, 1.5–2.2 kHz). **Range & status** Indian Subcontinent, C and S China, Taiwan, SE Asia, Indonesia, Philippines. **Borneo** An uncommon lower montane resident Sabah and E Sarawak; few records from E Kalimantan; one record of dead bird from Brunei; status uncertain in parts of Kalimantan and N Natunas. **Breeding** March–June.

CHINESE SPARROWHAWK *Accipiter soloensis*

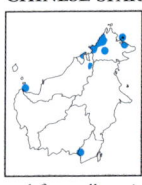

Identification 27–35 cm. Monotypic. **Adult male** Head and upperparts slaty-grey, throat white with faint grey streaking, underparts white with orange-rufous wash on breast and flanks with no barring, belly and undertail-coverts white; iris dark reddish-brown, bill dark grey, distinctive swollen orange cere, legs and feet yellow; in flight pale unmarked wings and underparts contrast with black wing-tips, four to five dark bands on undertail, uppertail unbanded. **Adult female** Larger, upperparts darker, underparts faintly barred pale rufous; iris yellow. **Juvenile** Head dark grey, throat streaked with broad dark gular stripe, dark brown above with feather-edges rufous to buff, breast broadly streaked rufous-brown, belly and flanks barred rufous-brown. **Habitat** Primary and secondary lowland dipterocarp forest, forest edges, to 500 m although recorded once at 1,100 m in Kelabit Highlands. **Behaviour** Solitary; mainly hunts from an open perch catching prey on ground; frogs are main prey but also small birds, lizards, large insects; migrates in small groups sometimes with other accipiters. **Voice** A flat but harsh, shrill *ki ki ki ki*... (*ki* repeated up to 11 times over 2.4 s, 1–10 kHz), but generally silent on migration. **Range & status** Breeds in Korea, China, Taiwan; migrates to SE Asia, Indonesia, Philippines. **Borneo** Very uncommon non-breeding visitor Sabah and Brunei, rare non-breeding visitor to Sarawak and S Kalimantan, recorded from October.

SUKAU RIVER LODGE   9/6/10

JAPANESE SPARROWHAWK *Accipiter gularis*

Identification Male 25–27 cm, female 28–30 cm. **Adult male** *gularis* Throat buffish-white with faint gular stripe, upperparts dark grey, underparts white with narrow rufous barring, narrow dark bands on uppertail, undertail-coverts white; iris dark red, cere yellow, bill black, legs and feet yellow; in flight from below uniform barring on flight feathers, tail shorter than other accipiters with narrower dark bands. **Adult female** Larger and darker than male with more prominent gular stripe, upperparts brownish-grey, underparts white barred greyish-brown; iris orange-yellow. **Juvenile** Throat white with narrow gular stripe (sometimes absent), upperparts dark brown with feathers edged rufous, upper breast streaked greyish-brown, lower breast and belly indistinctly mottled and barred. **Similar species** Distinguished from Besra in all plumages by very narrow (or no) gular stripe, narrower dark bands on uppertail; female Besra has coarse streaking on breast and bars on belly; juvenile Besra has blackish streaking on breast. **Habitat** Coastal forests, lowland swamp forest, primary and secondary lowland dipterocarp to lower montane forest, to 1,200 m in Kelabit Highlands. **Behaviour** Usually solitary, but seen in large flocks on migration; feeds mostly on small birds, has been recorded lingering on oilrigs off Sabah feeding on passerines. **Voice** Usually silent in Borneo; may utter a high-pitched, descending *kiii-ki-ki-ki-ki-ki* (1.5 s, 4 kHz). **Range & status** E and SE Asia, Indonesia, Philippines. **Borneo** Common non-breeding visitor and passage migrant throughout, from September to early April.

EURASIAN SPARROWHAWK *Accipiter nisus*

Identification Male 31–32 cm, female 39.5–40.5 cm. **Adult male** *nisosimilis* Distinctive rufous cheek-patch diagnostic, no gular stripe, upperparts dark grey, underparts white narrowly barred rufous, faint dark bands on uppertail, undertail barred; iris and cere yellow, bill black, legs and feet bright yellow; in flight rufous wash on underwing-coverts, flight feathers densely barred. **Adult female** Much larger than male, conspicuous broad white supercilium narrow behind eye, upperparts brownish-grey, dark bands on uppertail. **Juvenile** upperparts brown with rusty feather-fringes, broad rufous-brown barring on white or buffish breast and belly. **Similar species** larger than Besra and Japanese Sparrowhawk, upperparts paler, female has prominent supercilium. **Habitat** Primary and secondary forests, favouring more open woodlands. **Behaviour** Feeds almost exclusively on small birds; hunts by stealth in short flights from concealed perch. **Voice** Usually silent on migration, utters a *ki ki ki…* (*ki* repeated up to 16 times in 2.4 s, 2–5 kHz). **Range & status** Palearctic, E and SE Asia, Indian Subcontinent. **Borneo** Very rare vagrant with one confirmed record from Sarawak in 1895.

53

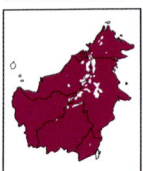

BLACK EAGLE *Ictinaetus malayensis*
Identification 67–81 cm. **Adult male** *malayensis* Plumage all black; iris brown, cere yellow, bill black, legs and feet yellow; in flight broad wings slightly narrow inwards, long narrow tail with inconspicuous darker banding, conspicuous yellow feet, pale patch at base of primaries on underwing. **Juvenile** Upperparts mottled brown, underparts brown with neck and breast buff streaked dark brown, tail with dark and light brown bars; in flight pale buffish underwing-coverts contrast with darker, faintly barred flight feathers. **Habitat** Primary lowland and hill forest, to 1,500 m. **Behaviour** Very often in pairs, often seen soaring over forested hillsides; possibly specialises in preying on canopy-dwelling birds, small mammals and reptiles. **Voice** A single high-pitched, whistle loud plaintive *klee-kee*. **Range & status** Indian Subcontinent, SE Asia, Indonesia. **Borneo** Uncommon resident throughout. **Breeding** Undescribed in Borneo; an adult with juvenile has been observed in October (Sarawak).

SUKAU RIVER LODGE

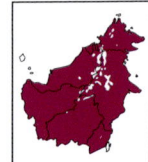

CHANGEABLE HAWK-EAGLE *Nisaetus limnaeetus*
Identification 57–66 cm. Polymorphic with two main morphs. **Adult pale morph male** *limnaeetus* Head buff with brown streaks, short nuchal crest, throat whitish with gular stripe, upperparts dark brown with buff feather-fringes, underparts white boldly streaked dark brown, undertail-coverts and feathered tarsi barred rufous, four dark bands on tail; iris bright yellow to brown, cere and bill black, legs and feet yellow or greenish-yellow with black claws; in flight paler barred flight feathers contrast with darker wing-coverts, wing-tips black, undertail barred with broader terminal band. **Adult female** Larger, more heavily marked below with more pronounced gular stripe than male. **Adult dark morph male** As pale morph but plumage all dark blackish-brown, tail with darker terminal band; iris usually brown in dark morph; in flight dark underwing-coverts contrast with slightly paler, faintly barred flight feathers, wing-tips darker. Dark morph can be confused with larger Black Eagle, which has all-dark underwings. **Juvenile** Head and underparts whitish, upperparts mottled brown and white, rump and uppertail white; in flight pale underneath with dark wing-tips and barred tail. **Habitat** Primary and secondary lowland and hill forest, plantations, preferring forest edges, to 1,400 m. **Behaviour** Feeds mostly on small to medium-sized birds but also reptiles, small mammals; hunts from concealed perch in short rapid flights. **Voice** Very vocal; piping, strident *whi-whi-whi-whi-whiii*, last note longest (3 s, 1.6–2.6 kHz). **Range & status** Indian Subcontinent, SE Asia, Indonesia, Philippines. **Borneo** Uncommon resident throughout; dark morph birds may predominate in Borneo. **Breeding** December–March; nest is large structure of sticks in tall tree; eggs are white with ochre stains.

54

BLYTH'S HAWK-EAGLE *Nisaetus alboniger*

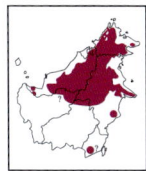

Identification 52–58 cm. Monotypic. **Adult** Striking black and white plumage, long black erect crest tipped white, head black, throat white with black gular stripe, upperparts black, breast streaked boldly black and white, belly barred black and white, tail black with broad greyish-white central band and narrow tip; iris yellowish-orange, cere and bill black, legs and feet yellow with black claws; in flight underwing-coverts white dotted black, flight feathers white with narrow black barring, wing-tips black, undertail black with broad white band. Female larger than male. **Juvenile** Long dark crest with white tips on pinkish-buff head, upperparts dark brown with buffish feather-fringes, underparts plain pinkish-buff becoming streaked later; in flight pale underneath with narrow, widely spaced dark barring on flight feathers and tail. Almost identical to juvenile Wallace's Hawk-eagle. **Habitat** Hill to upper montane forest, with records from plantations, 200–2,000 m. **Behaviour** Feeds on arboreal birds, mammals, reptiles, occasionally bats. **Voice** In flight a high-pitched, rapid *kek-keek kek-keek* or *speeoo-oo* descending at end; when perched utters short, high-pitched squeaks. **Range & status** Thai-Malay Peninsula, Sumatra. **Borneo** Uncommon resident N Borneo, recorded from Sabah, Brunei, Sarawak and E and C Kalimantan. **Breeding** Poorly known, possibly September–June.

WALLACE'S HAWK-EAGLE *Nisaetus nanus*

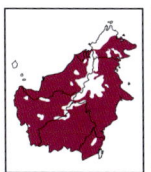

Identification 43–58 cm. **Adult *nanus*** Long erect black crest tipped white, head brown, upperparts brown, underparts buffish-white with brown streaks on breast and bars on belly, two pale and three dark bands in tail; iris yellow, cere and bill black, legs and feet lemon-yellow with black claws; in flight underwing-coverts buffish-rufous with dark mottling, flight feathers pale buffish-white with narrow dark bars and dark trailing edge. Female larger than male. **Juvenile** Almost indistinguishable from juvenile Blyth's Hawk-eagle but smaller with broader white tip on crest. **Similar species** Adult is very like subadult Blyth's Hawk-eagle but distinguished by tail pattern and smaller size; similar to Jerdon's Baza but wing-tips only extend halfway down tail, prominent brow, tarsi feathered to toes. **Habitat** Primary and secondary lowland dipterocarp, riverine, and swamp forest, plantations, to 1,000 m. **Behaviour** Canopy dweller; feeds on small birds, bats, reptiles. **Voice** A flat, piping *pit weeee* (1.4 s, 3.8 kHz). **Range & status** Thai-Malay Peninsula, Sumatra. **Borneo** Uncommon resident C and E Sabah, Brunei, E Sarawak, few records from W Sarawak and Kalimantan. Appears to be absent from N and W Sabah. **Breeding** Poorly known in Borneo.

RUFOUS-BELLIED EAGLE *Lophotriorchis kienerii*

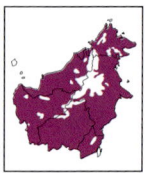

Identification 42–61 cm. **Adult** *formosus* Medium-sized eagle with shaggy black crest, prominent black hood contrasting with white throat, upperparts black, upper breast white with coarse black streaks on sides, lower breast, belly and underwing-coverts deep rufous with black streaks, wing-tips almost reaching to tail-tip, uppertail black with faint darker bands, undertail white with faint black bands and broad terminal bar, tarsi feathered; iris dark brown, cere bright yellow, bill dark grey, legs and feet greenish-yellow; in flight rufous underwing-coverts and abdomen contrast with pale, faintly barred flight feathers and undertail, pale primary panels, black sides of face give hooded appearance reminiscent of Peregrine Falcon, soars on level wings. **Juvenile** Distinctive black mask, upperparts brown with buffish fringes, underparts all white with blackish patch on flanks; in flight clean white underparts and underwing-coverts contrast with narrowly barred flight feathers. **Habitat** Primary and secondary forests, plantations, to 1,000 m. **Behaviour** Feeds on small birds and mammals; seems to favour forest edges and clearings, aerial hunter that makes spectacular stoops into the forest. **Voice** Loud, plaintive low-pitched *klee klee klee klee yii*, the last note rather weak and breathless. **Range & status** Isolated population in S India and Sri Lanka, eastern Himalayas, SE Asia, Indonesia, Philippines. **Borneo** Uncommon resident Sabah, Sarawak and Brunei, probably common in E Kalimantan, less so elsewhere in Kalimantan. **Breeding** Undescribed in Borneo.

GREY-FACED BUZZARD *Butastur indicus*

Identification 46 cm. Monotypic. **Adult male** Head grey, grey sides of face sharply demarcated from white throat with prominent dark submoustachial and gular stripes, indistinct whitish supercilium, upperparts and breast greyish-brown, rest of underparts white barred greyish-brown, uppertail-coverts white, at rest wing-tips almost reaching tail-tip, tail grey with three black bars; iris and cere yellow, bill black, legs and feet yellow; in flight dihedral almost flat, wing-tips dark, tail often broadly fanned, upperwings show rufous in primaries, underwings pale and flight feathers faintly and narrowly banded, wings relatively long and tail long and square. **Adult female** Head is not as grey as male, usually with clear white supercilium, more white markings on breast. **Juvenile** Whitish head streaked brown and broad brown mask, upperparts brown, underparts buffish-white with coarse rufous or brown streaks. **Habitat** Clearings in lowland to hill forest, to 1,500 m. **Behaviour** Usually solitary, but travels in groups on migration. Often perches in high, conspicuous trees. Feeds on lizards, large insects, small mammals. **Voice** Vocalises less frequently on migration; loud two-note *ki-WEE*, second note rising then descending (4.8–2.6 kHz, 1 s). **Range & status** E Asia, Indonesia, Philippines. **Borneo** Common non-breeding visitor and passage migrant to Sabah and Brunei, uncommon Sarawak, from September to early April. Not recorded from Kalimantan.

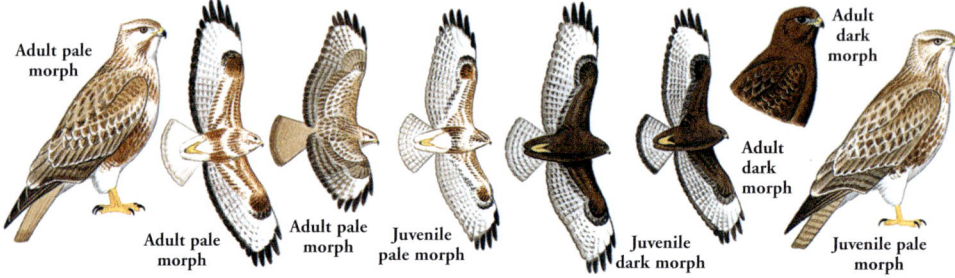

HIMALAYAN BUZZARD *Buteo burmanicus*

Identification 50–57 cm. Monotypic. **Adult** Upperparts dark brown with paler feather-bases and -fringes, breast white streaked brown, upper belly reddish-brown and lower belly white, tail either unmarked or faintly banded with dark subterminal band; iris brown, cere yellow, bill dark grey, legs and feet dull yellow; in flight broad rounded wings held in shallow V, black carpal patch and wing-tips contrasting with pale underwing. **Juvenile** Upperparts brown mottled with much white, underparts whitish streaked brown, tail with many narrow bars. **Habitat** Possible in any forested area. **Voice** Usually silent on migration. **Range & status** Breeds N Indian Subcontinent, China, Siberia, migrates to S Indian Subcontinent, SE Asia, Philippines. **Borneo** Vagrant; one confirmed record from Brunei.

RALLIDAE: Crakes, rails, gallinules & coots

Worldwide c.145 species, 14 in Borneo. Typically secretive (but some quite confiding and conspicuous), marsh-dwelling birds with laterally compressed body allowing movement through dense vegetation, short rounded wings, short tail and long legs. Most rarely fly, many species especially on small islands are flightless. Often very vocal. Diet is varied including invertebrates, small vertebrates and vegetable material.

RED-LEGGED CRAKE *Rallina fasciata*

Identification 23–25 cm. Monotypic. **Adult** Head to upper breast orange-red, lower breast and belly boldly barred black and white, back and tail brown, wings brown with extensive black and white bars and spots; iris bright red with red eye-ring, bill black, legs and feet red. **Juvenile** Head, neck and breast brown, throat paler, rest of underparts whitish with less defined barring, poorly defined bars on upperwing-coverts, legs and feet brown. **Habitat** Reedy swamps and marshes, forested streams, paddyfields, drainage ditches, to 900 m, one record from 1,550 m probably on migration. **Behaviour** Little known in Borneo; feeds on insects, especially beetles; secretive; migrates at night. **Voice** Territorial call is a loud, rapid, clucking *gogogogo…* (10–16 notes delivered in 1.5 s, 0.8 kHz), single note *gek* repeated every 3–7 s (0.8 kHz). Often both vocalisations delivered in conjunction by pairs. **Range & status** NE India, Myanmar to Thai-Malay Peninsula, Indonesia, Philippines. **Borneo** Uncommon resident and passage migrant (probably August–April), Sabah, Brunei, Sarawak and E and W Kalimantan, including S Natunas; status uncertain elsewhere in Kalimantan. **Breeding** Undescribed in Borneo.

BUFF-BANDED RAIL *Gallirallus philippensis*

Identification 25–33 cm. **Adult** *philippensis* Diagnostic head pattern with dark brown crown and eyestripe, conspicuous grey supercilium, chestnut nape, grey cheeks and throat; upperparts dark brown spotted and barred black and white, flight feathers barred rufous and black with white bars on outer edges, upper breast grey, buff breast-band, belly grey barred black, undertail-coverts buff barred black; iris brown, bill reddish-pink, legs and feet blackish-grey. **Juvenile** Like adult but duller, head pattern and breast-band indistinct, underparts barred grey; bill grey-black. **Habitat** Swamps, lake edges, rivers and streams, estuaries, mangroves, paddyfields. **Behaviour** Feeds on aquatic invertebrates, frogs, small fish, fruits and seeds; forages in shallow water and mud; generally sedentary but may be partially migratory. **Voice** A high-pitched, short squeak *kik* (4.5 kHz). **Range & status** Philippines, E Indonesia, New Guinea, Australia, New Zealand, SW Pacific. **Borneo** Rare vagrant with one record from W Sabah and two sight records in E Kalimantan (September 2004 and November 2006).

SLATY-BREASTED RAIL *Gallirallus striatus*

TAURAN BEACH RESORT 12/6/10

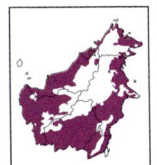
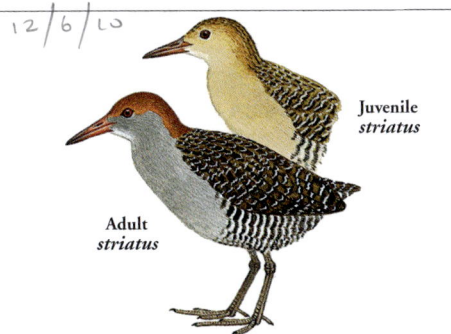

Identification 25–30 cm. **Adult** *striatus* Crown and nape chestnut; face to upper belly slaty-grey, chin pale grey; flanks to lower belly and undertail-coverts brown with broad white barring; upperparts greyish-brown with fine white bars and spots; iris reddish-brown, long bill pinkish-red with grey tip, legs and feet grey. **Adult** *gularis* Paler with whitish throat. **Juvenile** Overall plumage brownish, chin pale, underparts greyish-brown with indistinct pale barring, upperparts streaked; iris brown, bill grey with lower mandible tinged pink. **Habitat** Swamps and marshes, mangroves, nypa swamps, paddyfields, gardens, drainage ditches, to 1,200 m in Kelabit Highlands. **Behaviour** Feeds on insects, worms, small molluscs, seeds, grasses; generally solitary. **Voice** A sharp *terrik* and rapid *ketch-ketch-ketch…* increasing in volume. **Range & status** Indian Subcontinent, S China, SE Asia, Indonesia, Philippines. **Borneo** Common resident throughout. *G. s. striatus* in N Borneo; *G. s. gularis* in S Borneo. **Breeding** October–February; nest is small pad of dead grass situated in thick grass up to 30 cm from ground; eggs are pinkish-white with dark reddish-brown speckles and spots and lilac blotches.

EASTERN WATER RAIL *Rallus indicus*

Adult

Identification 25–28 cm. Monotypic. **Adult** Brown eyestripe on slaty-grey face, crown and nape brown with blackish streaks, chin whitish, underparts slaty-grey with brownish tinge, flanks and undertail-coverts barred black and white, upperparts olive-brown with dark brown streaks; iris reddish, distinctive long bill pink with grey culmen, legs and feet pinkish-grey. **Juvenile** Face and underparts mottled brown, dark eyestripe, supercilium buff, duller upperparts; iris brown. **Habitat** Reedbeds, swamps, marshes, paddyfields. **Behaviour** Feeds on aquatic invertebrates. **Voice** Territorial song is a loud, piping *kwee kwee kwee...* (2.5 kHz) repeated every 0.5 s in strophes of 8–10 notes; a grunting *kwa kwa kwa* is uttered alone or in concert with former. **Range & status** N India and E Siberia eastwards into E Asia and northern SE Asia. Formerly considered subspecies of Water Rail *R. aquaticus* of W Palearctic. **Borneo** Rare vagrant Brunei and Sarawak.

Juvenile

Adult
pusilla

BAILLON'S CRAKE *Porzana pusilla*

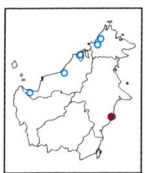

Identification 17–19 cm. **Adult *mira*** (endemic subspecies) tiny, face grey with brown ear-coverts, crown and upperparts warm rufous-brown with black and white streaks, throat and breast white, underparts grey with flanks and undertail-coverts barred brown, black and white; iris red, bill greenish-yellow, legs and feet greenish-grey. **Juvenile** Underparts mottled buff-brown, bare parts brown. **Adult *pusilla*** is larger, throat and breast grey, upperparts browner, underparts darker. **Habitat** Marshes, swamps, paddyfields, ponds. **Behaviour** Secretive; feeds on aquatic insects, small molluscs and crustaceans, worms; habits of *P. p. mira* unknown. **Voice** A creaky, staccato calls *kr-r-r-r-r-r...* and harsh, raspy *krrr-krrr-krrr...*; contact call is a soft *kik...kik...kik...* **Range & status** Africa, Europe, C and E Asia, Indian Subcontinent, SE Asia, Indonesia, Philippines, New Guinea, Australia, New Zealand. **Borneo** Race *mira* very rare resident SE Borneo (known from one specimen from E Kalimantan); *pusilla* rare non-breeding visitor to Sabah, Brunei and Sarawak, probably from January to October. **Breeding** Undescribed in Borneo.

RUDDY-BREASTED CRAKE *Porzana fusca*

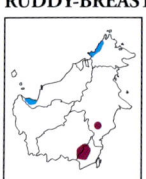

Identification 21–23 cm. **Adult *fusca*** Face and underparts rich rufous, throat buffish-white, lower belly and undertail banded black and white, upperparts uniform olive-brown; iris red, bill dark grey, legs and feet bright red. **Juvenile** Overall dull brown with faint white barring on underparts; iris brown. **Similar species** From other similar crakes by unmarked olive-brown wings. **Habitat** Swamps and marshes, paddyfields, drainage ditches. **Behaviour** Feeds on snails, aquatic insects, seeds. **Voice** A soft, short *kon, kon, kon* (0.95–1.6 kHz). **Range & status** Indian Subcontinent, E and SE Asia, Indonesia, Philippines. **Borneo** Status uncertain in Borneo; rare lowland resident or non-breeding visitor Sabah, Sarawak, E Kalimantan, S Borneo.

Adult

Juvenile

BAND-BELLIED CRAKE *Porzana paykullii*

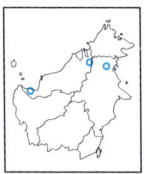

Identification 20–22 cm. Monotypic. **Adult** Crown and hindneck ashy-brown, face and foreneck orange-rufous, throat whitish, upperparts ashy-brown, breast orange-rufous, flanks and undertail-coverts barred black and white; iris bright red, bill greyish-green, legs and feet bright red. **Similar species** Red-legged Crake has all rufous-brown head, white barring on wings and barring on underparts is more extensive. **Habitat** Swampy areas of lowland rainforests, swamps, grasslands, paddyfields, to 1,200 m. **Behaviour** Favours thick cover, solitary. **Voice** Usually silent but territorial call is a loud metallic clangour running into brief trills. **Range & status** Russian Far East, NE China, Korea, SE Asia, Sumatra, Java. **Borneo** Rare non-breeding visitor Sarawak and E Kalimantan.

WHITE-BROWED CRAKE *Porzana cinerea*

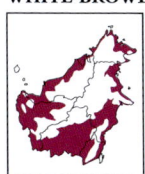

Identification 15–20 cm. Monotypic. **Adult** Distinctive facial pattern with black eye-line bordered above by short white supercilium and below by broad white stripe from chin to ear, head and breast ashy-grey, upperparts brown mottled buff, lower belly and undertail-coverts buff; iris red, bill olive-yellow with red base, legs and feet yellowish-green. **Juvenile** Face pattern less distinct, underparts brownish, lacks red base to bill. **Habitat** Marshes, swamps, rivers, creeks, lake edges, mangroves, paddyfields. **Behaviour** Forages at margins of watercourses, often on floating vegetation; not as shy as many rails. **Voice** High-pitched, strident *kek kek kek...* (1.4–3.4 kHz). **Range & status** Malaysia, Indonesia, Philippines, New Guinea, Melanesia, Micronesia, N

Australia. **Borneo** Locally common resident throughout. **Breeding** April–June; 3–4 buffish eggs with fine rufous-brown spots and blotches laid in bowl-shaped nest of dead grass located in grass over water.

WATERCOCK *Gallicrex cinerea*

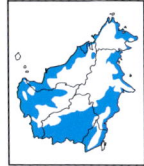

Identification 42–43 cm. Monotypic. **Adult male breeding** Black with variable buff fringes on mantle and wings, undertail-coverts finely fringed buff; iris reddish-brown, bill yellow with red base and striking red frontal shield, legs and feet red. **Adult female** Face and throat golden-buff, upperparts brown with broad buff fringes, underparts rufous-buff with fine dark barring; iris brown, bill dull yellow, legs and feet greenish-olive. **Adult male non-breeding** Like female but more distinct barring on underparts, legs and feet yellowish. **Juvenile** Like adult female but less barring on underparts. All plumages show white leading edge on wings in flight. **Habitat** Paddyfields, open swamps, to 200 m; has been recorded at 1,200 m in Kelabit Highlands. **Behaviour** Generally shy and skulking, largely crepuscular, preferring overcast weather; feeds on seeds, shoots, worms, snails, aquatic insects. **Voice** A clucking, throaty, accelerating *gyok gyok gyok...* (1.1 kHz). **Range & status** Indian Subcontinent, E Asia, SE Asia, Philippines, Indonesia. **Borneo** Has been regarded as an uncommon non-breeding visitor but breeding records and sightings throughout year indicate it may be resident.

BLACK-BACKED SWAMPHEN *Porphyrio indicus*

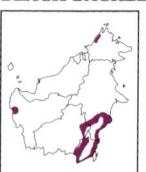

Identification 28–30 cm. **Adult** *indicus* Large gallinule with heavy triangular red bill and prominent red frontal shield, head and hindneck blackish, throat and upper breast greenish-turquoise, upperparts blackish-blue with green tinge, wings blackish with bright turquoise patch on coverts, underparts turquoise-blue, undertail-coverts white; iris red, legs and feet dull red. **Juvenile** Grey with duller bare parts. **Habitat** Strictly freshwater wetlands such as ponds, lakes, marshes, swamps, paddyfields, parks. **Behaviour** Feeds in open primarily on aquatic vegetation but also snails, leeches, insects, birds and nestlings, small mammals; often gregarious, not shy. **Voice** Very vocal; loud raucous *grek* almost like scream (1.6–5 kHz); also a more drawn-out duck-like *kraark*. **Range & status** Thailand, Indochina, Thai-Malay Peninsula, Indonesia, Sulawesi. **Borneo** Locally common resident Kalimantan, possibly spreading to other areas of Borneo; scarce vagrant or resident in Sabah, status in Sarawak and Brunei unclear. **Note** Formerly considered race of Purple Swamphen *Porphyrio porphyrio* (Sangster *et al.* 1998).

COMMON COOT *Fulica atra*

Identification 36–39 cm. **Adult** *atra* Overall plumage black, upperparts with slaty-blue gloss; iris brownish-red, bill and frontal shield white, legs and feet greenish-grey, toes lobed. **Juvenile** Face and underparts whitish, upperparts greyish without gloss; iris brown, bill and reduced frontal shield greyish-white. **Habitat** Lakes, ponds, swamps, rivers, paddyfields. **Behaviour** Aquatic, usually seen swimming on medium to large bodies of water, with characteristic 'duck dive'; runs along water grebe-like when taking flight; feeds on leaves and shoots of aquatic vegetation and insects; often seen in large congregations. **Voice** Call is a shrill, loud *kek… kek kek…* (1 kHz); also utters a slow *kachi kachi…* **Range & status** Europe, N Africa, C and E Asia, SE Asia, Indian Subcontinent, Philippines, Java, New Guinea, Australia, New Zealand. **Borneo** A rare vagrant recorded from Sabah and Brunei.

COMMON MOORHEN *Gallinula chloropus*

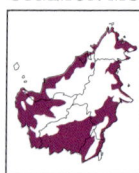

Identification 32–38 cm. **Adult** *chloropus* Head and neck black, underparts dark blue-black, back and wings dark brown, flanks streaked white in thin line, undertail-coverts black broadly bordered white; iris red, bill and frontal shield red, tip of bill yellow, legs and feet greenish-yellow, red at top of legs. **Juvenile** Overall plumage brown, face and sides of neck whitish, bill flesh-coloured, no frontal shield. **Adult** *orientalis* Like *chloropus* but smaller, with larger frontal shield, slaty-blue upperwing-coverts without brown wash. **Habitat** Freshwater wetlands including swamps, lakes, estuaries, rivers, paddyfields, parks; recorded to 1,200 m in Kelabit Highlands. **Behaviour** Constantly flicks tail, feeds on variety of vegetable matter and small animals including snails, insects and crustaceans. Often gregarious, not particularly shy. **Voice** A variety of clucking calls, including a rapid *kikek kikek kikek* (0.8–7.2 kHz) and warning *keek* or *kikuwerk*. **Range & status** N to S America, Europe, Africa, Indian Subcontinent, C to E Asia, SE Asia, Indonesia, Philippines, **Borneo** Uncommon resident and non-breeding visitor throughout; migrants probably belong to *chloropus* but status of this taxon is unclear. **Breeding** January–September; five elliptical buff eggs with sparse reddish-brown splotches laid in domed nest constructed in grass over water.

DUSKY MOORHEN *Gallinula tenebrosa*

Identification 35–40 cm. **Adult *frontata*** Similar to Common Moorhen but lacks prominent white streaking on flanks and shows red legs and feet with dark joints. **Juvenile** Browner, bill duller, lacks frontal shield. **Habitat** As for Common Moorhen. **Range & status** Sulawesi, Moluccas, Lesser Sundas, New Guinea, Australia. **Borneo** One historic record from S Kalimantan. Possibly a former resident in SE Borneo that may have declined since introduction of water hyacinth (*Eichhornia*), to which it is thought to be intolerant.

WHITE-BREASTED WATERHEN
Amaurornis phoenicurus

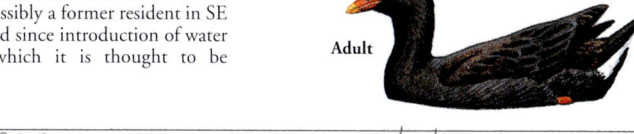

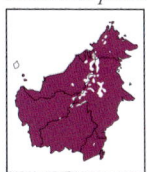

Identification 28–33 cm. **Adult male *phoenicurus*** Face and underparts white with black flanks, crown and rest of upperparts dark greyish-black, lower belly to undertail-coverts rufous; iris dark reddish-brown, bill greenish-yellow with red patch on base of upper mandible, legs and feet dull yellow. **Juvenile** Upperparts dark brownish-grey, underparts mottled greyish-white, undertail dull rufous; iris brown, bill grey, legs and feet brownish-grey. **Habitat** Edges of rivers, ponds and lakes; reedbeds, swamps, mangroves, paddyfields, drainage ditches, to 1,500 m. **Behaviour** Feeds on worms, insects, snails, seeds; often comes out from cover, especially after rain, bobbing tail up and down, frequently seen on roadsides. **Voice** An extraordinary range of loud grunts, croaks, bubbling gurgles. Main territorial call is a repeated *kuwaa kuwaa…* or *kraar kraar…* (0.7–1.4 kHz) uttered at 1 note/0.6 s. Also a softer, bubbling *ko ko ko….* Song is a clicking, punctuated *kok kok kok…* reminiscent of sound of small wooden gong. **Range & status** Indian Subcontinent, E and SE Asia, Indonesia, Philippines. **Borneo** Very common resident throughout, including S Natunas. **Breeding** all year, 2–4 whitish or buffish eggs with reddish-brown speckles and blotches.

BURHINIDAE: Thick-knees

Worldwide 10 species, 1 in Borneo. Medium-sized to large pantropical waders with big head, very big eyes, strong black or yellow bill, long pointed wings and long legs with prominent joints. Most are crepuscular or nocturnal and favour semi-arid habitats. Generally sedentary and feed on large invertebrates and small vertebrates. The sexes are similar.

BEACH THICK-KNEE *Esacus neglectus*

Identification 53–57 cm. Monotypic. Large wader with heavy bill and striking plumage. **Adult** Head boldly marked black, grey and white: crown blackish-grey, supercilium white, thick black band through eye to neck, short black malar stripes; throat and sides of neck white, neck and breast pale sandy, belly white, neck to uppertail brownish-grey, wings pale grey with blackish-brown band across top edge bordered white above and below; iris yellow, short, heavy bill black with yellow base, legs and feet yellow; in flight upperwing-coverts grey with contrasting black outer primaries and white inner primaries, underwing white with grey trailing edge. **Juvenile** Plumage edged greyish-buff, bare parts duller. **Habitat** Coastal: sandy and muddy beaches, coral reefs, estuaries, rocky foreshores, mangroves, at sea-level. **Behaviour** Sedentary; feeds on crabs and other crustaceans, stalks and chases prey. **Voice** Alarm call is a sharp, high-pitched *sweep* (3.5 kHz, 0.1–0.2 s) rapidly repeated; territorial call is a wailing *wee-LOO*. **Range & status** Andaman Islands, Thai-Malay Peninsula, Indonesia, Philippines, New Guinea, SW Pacific, N Australia. **Borneo** Rare resident on coast and offshore islands, no records from Kalimantan coast. **Breeding** Undescribed in Borneo.

RECURVIROSTRIDAE: Stilts & avocets

Worldwide c.11 species, 3 in Borneo. A small group of wading birds with extraordinarily long legs and bill. Most are gregarious and noisy. They feed by delicately plucking or sweeping water's surface in shallow areas.

BLACK-WINGED STILT *Himantopus himantopus*

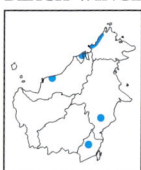

Identification 35–40 cm. Graceful wader with distinctive long, pink legs and needle-shaped bill. **Adult male breeding** *himantopus* Crown to hindneck white (sometimes with variable amount of black on head and hindneck), back and wings black, underparts white; iris red; distinctive long, thin, straight black bill; legs pink and very long; in flight feet extend well beyond tail, underwings black. **Adult female breeding** Like male but back and wings dull brownish. **Adult non-breeding** Crown to hindneck greyish. **Juvenile** Crown to hindneck dusky grey, upperparts greyish with buff edging. **Habitat** Marshes, swamps, lake edges, paddyfields at sea-level. **Behaviour** Usually in flocks near water; feeds on small aquatic invertebrates, tadpoles, small fish in shallow water; has been observed in flocks with White-headed Stilt. **Voice** Commonest call is a short, sharp, yelping *kek* (2.2 kHz). **Range & status** Europe, Africa, migrates to Indian Subcontinent, SE Asia. **Borneo** Locally common to uncommon non-breeding visitor to north-west coast (W Sabah, Brunei, E Sarawak) from September to March; during northern winter, rare in Kalimantan.

WHITE-HEADED STILT *Himantopus leucocephalus*

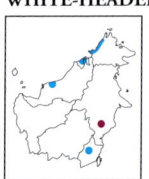

Identification 35–40 cm. Monotypic. Graceful wader with distinctive long, pink legs and needle-shaped bill. **Adult male breeding** Crown white, nape to hindneck with ridge of raised black feathers sometimes forming half-collar at base of neck, upper mantle white, back and wings black, underparts white; iris red; long, thin, straight black bill; legs pink and very long; in flight feet extend well beyond tail, underwings black. **Adult female breeding** Back and wings browner. **Adult non-breeding** Crown to hindneck greyish. **Juvenile** Crown to hindneck dusky grey, upperparts greyish with buff edging. **Habitat** Marshes, swamps, lake edges, paddyfields at sea-level. **Behaviour** As previous species. **Voice** A mellow, yapping *kak kak* (2.7 kHz), slightly higher-pitched than previous species. **Range & status** Australia, New Zealand; migrates to New Guinea, Indonesia, Philippines. **Borneo** Locally common to uncommon non-breeding visitor to north-west coast, rare in Brunei and Sarawak, from May to June; rare in Kalimantan with recent breeding record from E Kalimantan during southern winter.

PIED AVOCET *Recurvirostra avosetta*

Identification 42–45 cm. Monotypic. Distinctive black and white wader with long legs and slender, upcurved bill. **Adult male** Base plumage white with black head to nape, and black scapulars, lesser and median coverts and primaries; iris and bill black, legs bluish-grey. **Adult female** As male but bill shorter and more strongly upcurved. **Immature** Dark parts of plumage duller and greyish, greyish streaking on mantle and scapulars. **Habitat** Coastal wetlands, mudflats, estuaries, lakes. **Behaviour** Feeds on small invertebrates in shallow water. **Voice** A clear *kluit*. **Range & status** Breeds Africa, W, C Palearctic, E Asia; migrates to Middle East, Indian Subcontinent, S China, C Myanmar. **Borneo** Vagrant. One record from Kuching, W Sarawak.

VANELLIDAE: Lapwings & allies

Worldwide 24 species, 2 in Borneo. Small to medium-sized with short bill and long legs. They forage for invertebrates by running and stooping to pluck prey from the ground.

NORTHERN LAPWING *Vanellus vanellus*

Identification 28–31 cm. Monotypic. **Adult non-breeding** Forehead and long crest black, face buff with black eyestripe and cheek, chin and throat white, underparts white with broad black breast-band, undertail buffish-orange, upperparts glossy greenish-black, scapulars purplish-bronze, wings with buff fringes; iris brown, bill black, legs and feet pinkish-red, in flight tail white with black broad black terminal patch, underwing white with black flight feathers. **Adult male breeding** Face white, chin to breast all black. **Adult female breeding** Indistinct head markings with white flecks on throat, crest shorter. **Juvenile** Like non-breeding adult but crest short, buff fringes on upperparts, narrower brown breast-band. **Habitat** Wetlands, grasslands, paddyfields, pasture; recorded at sea-level in Borneo. **Behaviour** Gregarious; feeds on invertebrates; flight is agile and strong on broad wings. **Voice** Contact call is a whining, plaintive *myu ki ki* (delivered on more or less same pitch 3 kHz); probably silent on non-breeding grounds. **Range & status** Europe, N Africa, Palearctic, E Asia. **Borneo** Rare vagrant with two records from Brunei in December and January.

GREY-HEADED LAPWING *Vanellus cinereus*

Identification 34–37 cm. Monotypic. **Adult breeding** Head, neck and breast grey; blackish-grey breast-band separates white belly, back and wings sandy-brown, uppertail white with broad black subterminal band; iris red with narrow yellow eye-ring, bill yellow with black tip, long legs and feet yellow; in flight underwing white with black primaries, upperwing tricoloured with brown coverts contrasting with white secondaries and black primaries, toes project beyond tail. **Adult non-breeding** Head and neck brown, chin and throat white, indistinct breast-band. **Juvenile** Like non-breeding adult but upperparts with buff fringes, breast-band absent. **Habitat** Marshes, grasslands, paddyfields; recorded at sea-level in Borneo. **Behaviour** Gregarious; feeds on invertebrates. **Voice** A strong, rapid *ke ke ke...* (3 kHz) repeated; probably silent on non-breeding grounds. **Range & status** NE China, Japan, migrates to NE Indian Subcontinent, N Indochina. **Borneo** Rare vagrant with very few records from Sabah, Brunei and Sarawak.

PLUVIALIDAE: *Pluvialis* plovers

Worldwide 4 species, 2 in Borneo. Medium-sized shorebirds with large rounded head, short bill and stout body. Typically feed on invertebrates on the ground by running rapidly and pausing periodically to stoop and pluck prey.

PACIFIC GOLDEN PLOVER *Pluvialis fulva*

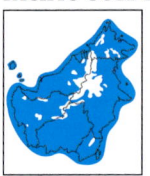

Identification 23–26 cm. Monotypic. Smaller than Grey Plover with general gold appearance and short, slender bill. **Adult non-breeding** Forehead and face pale buff with buffish-white supercilium, breast buffish-white with varying amounts of gold speckling, belly to undertail pale buffish-white, upperparts brown with gold speckling; in flight underwings pale grey, indistinct pale wing-bar at base of primaries, toes extend beyond tail-tip. **Adult breeding** Face and underparts black bordered by white line extending from forehead over eyes down flanks, upperparts speckled black and gold. **Similar species** Grey Plover is larger, greyer, with distinct white wing-bar, pale rump and distinctive black 'armpit'. **Habitat** Estuaries, mudflats, mangroves, paddyfields, lawns, airfields, to 1,200 m in Kelabit Highlands. **Behaviour** Usually gathers in small flocks but very large groups of several thousand have been recorded in Sabah. **Voice** A short, piercing *kaweet* (c.3 kHz), also a longer *kee-kuWEET* the last note dipping and drawn out. **Range & status** Siberia, W Alaska, E Africa, Indian Subcontinent, China, SE Asia, Indonesia, Philippines, New Guinea, Australia, SW Pacific, New Zealand. **Borneo** Common non-breeding visitor and passage migrant throughout from early September to April, with some records from June suggesting small numbers may remain in summer.

GREY PLOVER *Pluvialis squatarola*

Identification 28–31 cm. Large plover with large dark head, greyish plumage and relatively heavy bulbous bill. **Adult non-breeding** Pale buff forehead and supercilium, upperparts pale grey mottled with dark grey, rump whitish-grey, tail barred black and white, breast buffish-white with pale brownish-grey streaking, rest of underparts whitish; in flight (in breeding and non-breeding plumage) distinctive black 'armpits' contrast with white underwing, distinct white wing-bar. **Adult male breeding** Face and underparts black bordered by broad white line from forehead over eyes to sides of breast, vent to undertail white, upperparts speckled dark grey and white. **Adult female breeding** Underparts browner. **Juvenile** As non-breeding adult but upperparts darker with more distinct buffish speckling, breast washed buffish. **Habitat** Estuaries, mudflats, tidal reefs, mangroves, sandy beaches. **Behaviour** Usually in small flocks. **Voice** A fluty, melancholy, slurred trisyllabic whistle *tee-a-WEE* or *pee-uu-EE* the middle syllable lower-pitched (2.7–2 kHz, c.0.8 s). **Range & status** Arctic Circle, migrates to N and S America, W Europe, Africa, Indian Subcontinent, SE Asia, Indonesia, Australia. **Borneo** Common non-breeding visitor and passage migrant to coastal Sabah, Brunei, Sarawak, W and E Kalimantan, September–April.

CHARADRIIDAE: *Charadrius* plovers & allies

Worldwide c.38 species, 9 in Borneo. A large family of compact shorebirds with large eye, short bill and strong short legs. Most run rapidly and stop over short distances when foraging in grasslands, seashores or shallow wetlands for small invertebrates and plant material. Some species are sedentary, many are strongly migratory.

COMMON RINGED PLOVER *Charadrius hiaticula*

Identification 18–20 cm. Medium-sized *Charadrius* plover with single breast-band and bright orange and black bill. **Adult non-breeding *tundrae*** Forehead and supercilium buffish, crown olive-brown, throat and hind-collar white, broad dark breast-band joins narrow band around upper mantle, rest of upperparts olive-brown, underparts white; iris black, bill black, legs and feet orange; in flight shows long white upperwing-bar. **Adult male breeding** Forehead and supercilium white, black band over forecrown joining black mask from lores around eye to sides of neck, broad breast-band black; bill orange with black tip. **Adult female breeding** Narrower breast-band and ear-coverts with brownish tinge. **Juvenile** Similar to non-breeding adult but upperparts fringed buff, breast-band narrower, bill blackish, legs duller orange. **Similar species** See Little Ringed Plover. **Habitat** In Borneo recorded from mudflats and paddyfields at sea-level. **Voice** A short, upwardly inflected disyllabic whistle *tu-weet* (2.2–2.6 kHz). **Range & status** Arctic Circle, W Europe, Africa, Middle East, Indian Subcontinent. **Borneo** Vagrant to Brunei and W Sabah.

LONG-BILLED PLOVER *Charadrius placidus*

Identification 19–21 cm. Medium-sized *Charadrius* plover with brownish eyestripe and relatively long slender bill. **Adult non-breeding** Forehead white, dark band over forecrown, buffish supercilium, crown and cheeks brown, throat and narrow hind-collar white, narrow dark breast-band, rest of upperparts brown, underparts white; iris black, narrow yellow eye-ring, long bill black, legs and feet pinkish. **Adult breeding** Black band over forecrown, breast-band black. **Juvenile** Similar to non-breeding adult but band on forehead and breast-band browner, upperparts fringed buff. **Similar species** Larger with longer bill, narrower breast-band and browner eyestripe than Common and Little Ringed Plovers. **Habitat** Stony and gravelly freshwater riverbanks and islets and lake edges, paddyfields, mudflats, to 1,000 m (extralimital). **Behaviour** Usually solitary or in pairs. **Voice** A repeated, short, sharp *pee…pee…pee…* delivered on flat pitch (c.4 kHz). **Range & status** N and E Asia, Japan, NE Indian Subcontinent, Indochina. **Borneo** Vagrant; very few records from Sabah and Brunei.

LITTLE RINGED PLOVER *Charadrius dubius*

Identification 14–17 cm. Small plover with single breast-band and prominent yellow eye-ring. **Adult male non-breeding *dubius*** Forehead and supercilium buffish, crown and hindneck brown, throat and narrow hind-collar white, narrow brown breast-band, rest of upperparts brown, underparts white; iris black, bill black, legs and feet pinkish. **Adult male breeding** White forehead and black band over forecrown joining black mask from lores around eye to sides of neck with narrow white upper margin, thin black band from upper mantle to uneven broad breast-band; iris black with prominent yellow eye-ring. **Adult female breeding** Eye-ring narrower, breast-band with brownish tinge. **Juvenile** Similar to non-breeding adult but markings on head indistinct, upperparts fringed buff. **Similar species** Common Ringed Plover is larger, with orange legs, brighter bill, prominent white wing-bar in flight, no yellow eye-ring or narrow white margin above black head markings. **Habitat** Wetlands, rivers, estuaries, paddyfields, airfields, to 650 m. **Behaviour** Usually solitary but large gatherings of more than 100 have been recorded. **Voice** A far-carrying, sweet, downslurred *pee-oo* (3.4–2.7 kHz). **Range & status** Palearctic, Africa, Indian Subcontinent, Japan, China, SE Asia, Indonesia, Philippines, New Guinea. **Borneo** Common non-breeding visitor and passage migrant from coastal areas to interior throughout, August–April.

KENTISH PLOVER *Charadrius alexandrinus*

Identification 15–17.5 cm. Small elegant plover with white collar on hindneck and rufous cap. **Adult non-breeding *alexandrinus*** Forehead and broad supercilium white, collar and underparts white, brown patch on sides of breast, rest of upperparts olive-brown, may show rufous on head; bare parts black; in flight underwing white, white bar on upperwing, sides of uppertail-coverts and tail white. **Adult male breeding** Black bar on forecrown, hindcrown and nape rufous, eye-stripe black, patch on sides of breast black. **Juvenile** Paler with buff fringing on upperparts. **Similar species** Malaysian Plover avoids mixed flocks, has black hind-collar in male, and rufous breast-patches in female, legs and feet paler. **Habitat** Estuaries, coastal wetlands, sandy and muddy beaches, grasslands, at sea-level. **Behaviour** Usually single or in small numbers; often in mixed flocks with other plovers. **Voice** A sharp soft *pwit*; also a short trill *piruru* (2.5 kHz, c.0.2–0.3 s). **Range & status** N and S America, W Europe, Africa, Middle East, C and E Asia, Indian Subcontinent, SE Asia, Indonesia, Philippines. **Borneo** Uncommon non-breeding visitor to coastal Borneo (not yet recorded from C Kalimantan), September–April.

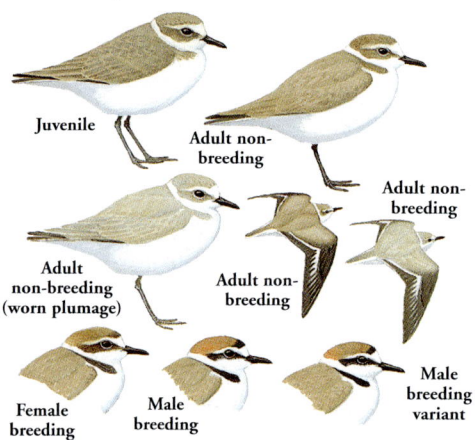

MALAYSIAN PLOVER *Charadrius peronii*

Identification 14–16 cm. Monotypic. Small plover with black collar on hindneck (male) or rufous breast-patches (female). **Adult male** Forehead and short supercilium white, black bar on forecrown, hindcrown and nape rufous, eye-stripe black, narrow collar and underparts white, patch on sides of breast black joining black hind-collar below white collar, rest of upperparts olive-brown; iris and bill black, legs and feet grey; in flight underwing, bar on upperwing and sides of uppertail-coverts and tail white. **Adult female** Like male but black on head and breast is replaced with rufous, sometimes with black flecks; lacks black hind-collar. **Juvenile** As female but never with black flecks. **Similar species** See Malaysian Plover. **Habitat** Favours undisturbed sandy beaches, but also recorded on muddy beaches and grasslands; sea-level. **Behaviour** Usually solitary or in pairs. **Voice** A soft *pwit*, similar to Kentish Plover. **Range & status** South SE Asia including Thai-Malay Peninsula, Sumatra, Philippines, Sulawesi, Lesser Sundas. **Borneo** Locally common (Sabah) to uncommon (Brunei, Sarawak) resident, rare in E Kalimantan. **Breeding** January–September; lays 2–3 creamy-buff eggs with dark brown and black scribbles and blotches in nest on sandy beaches.

LESSER SAND-PLOVER *Charadrius mongolus*

Identification 19–21 cm. Medium-sized *Charadrius* plover, rather plain brown in non-breeding plumage with slender bill and dark grey legs. **Adult non-breeding *atrifrons*** Crown, mask and upperparts greyish-brown, forehead and indistinct super-cilium whitish, underparts white with sides of breast greyish-brown; iris and bill black, legs and feet dark grey; in flight narrow white bar on upperwing, white sides to rump. **Adult breeding** Black forehead and mask, orange hindneck and breast encircles sharply delineated white throat. Female plumage duller. **Juvenile** Similar to non-breeding adult but upperparts fringed buff; forehead, supercilium and breast washed buffish-chestnut. **Similar species** Greater Sand-plover has proportionately longer, heavier bill and usually less rounded, more angular head with sloping forehead; longer and paler legs; when seen side by side Greater is usually notably bigger. **Habitat** Muddy or sandy beaches, lowland wetlands, estuaries, mangroves, at sea-level. **Behaviour** Feeds on polychaete worms, molluscs and other invertebrates in soft mud and sand; often in flocks with other waders. **Voice** A rapid four-note trilling *pir-r-r-ip* (3.5 kHz, c.0.2 s). **Range & status** Africa, Middle East, Indian Subcontinent, C and N Asia, SE Asia, Indonesia, Philippines, New Guinea, Australia. **Borneo** Common non-breeding visitor to coastal N Borneo (Sabah, Brunei, Sarawak, E Kalimantan), September–April.

WHITE-FACED PLOVER *Charadrius dealbatus*

Identification c.16–18 cm. Monotypic. **Adult male breeding** Forehead, lores, broad supercilium and lower ear coverts white, broad band over forehead black, crown chestnut, collar white, narrow lateral breast patches dark brown, scapulars and mantle sandy-brown with narrow paler fringes, upperwing coverts sandy-brown; bill black with ochre base on lower mandible, legs and feet flesh-grey; in flight pale mid-wing panel contrasts with darker marginal coverts and outer wing. **Adult non-breeding** Crown and lateral breast patches pale sandy-brown, scapulars and mantle browner. **Adult female breeding** Forehead and supercilium white, crown, upper ear coverts and lores sandy-brown, lateral breast patches pale sandy-brown. **Similar species** Kentish Plover has dark lores, upperparts of both sexes darker and browner, bill thinner and all black, legs usually dark, white collar bifurcated on nape by brown line, less extensive white on head, narrower band over forehead. Malaysian Plover has a thinner, shorter bill; head pattern similar but with less white on supercilium; lateral breast patches longer; note habitat and behaviour. **Habitat** Open, coastal sites. **Behaviour** Similar to Kentish but more active. **Range & Status** Breeds S China; winters to S Vietnam, Thai-Malay Peninsula, Singapore, Sumatra. **Borneo** Status uncertain; one record from Kuching.

GREATER SAND-PLOVER *Charadrius leschenaultii*

Identification 22–25 cm. Large *Charadrius* plover, rather plain brown in non-breeding plumage with robust bill and pale legs. **Adult non-breeding *leschenaultii*** Forehead and indistinct supercilium white; crown, mask and upperparts greyish-brown; underparts white with sides of breast greyish-brown; iris and bill black, legs and feet greenish-grey; in flight white bar on upperwing, white sides to rump. **Adult breeding** Forehead and narrow supercilium white, black band over forehead joining black mask from lores around eye to sides of neck, orange hindneck and breast-band encircles sharply delineated white throat. **Juvenile** Similar to non-breeding adult but upperparts fringed buff; forehead, supercilium and breast washed buffish-chestnut. **Similar species** See Lesser Sand-plover. **Habitat** Muddy and sandy beaches, estuaries, grasslands, at sea-level. **Behaviour** Feeds on polychaete worms, molluscs and other invertebrates in soft mud and sand, but favours harder substrates; often in flocks with other waders. **Voice** A rapid, five-note trilling *pir-r-r-r-ip* (c.3 kHz, c.0.25 s); similar to Lesser Sand-plover but slightly lower-pitched. **Range & status** Africa, Middle East, C Asia, Indian Subcontinent, SE Asia, Indonesia, Philippines, New Guinea, Australia.

Borneo Very common non-breeding visitor to coastal areas throughout, September–April; a few may remain in summer.

ORIENTAL PLOVER *Charadrius veredus*

Identification 22–25 cm. Monotypic. Somewhat long-necked plover with relatively long legs and wings, latter projecting beyond tail at rest. **Adult male non-breeding** Crown and ear-coverts brown; forehead, supercilium and throat buffish; buffish fringes on upperparts, breast pale brown grading into whitish underparts; iris and bill black, legs and feet yellow to dirty orange; in flight brown underwing contrasts with white belly, long-winged. **Adult male breeding** Head and neck creamy-white with olive-brown crown, breast orangey-rufous bordered black below, contrasting strongly with white belly to undertail-coverts. **Adult female breeding** Crown and ear-coverts darker, breast greyish-brown, lacks black border. **Juvenile** More contrasting paler buff fringing on upperparts, breast mottled buff and brown. **Habitat** Dry open fields and grasslands, mudflats, sandbanks, lawns, to 1,200 m in Kelabit Highlands. **Behaviour** Often in large flocks in other parts of its range, but usually seen singly in Borneo; fast, powerful flight; often far from water. **Voice** A very short, soft, metallic *chit* (3.4 kHz, 0.1 s) repeated every 1–1.5 s. **Range & status** N Asia, migrates to Indonesia, N Australia. **Borneo** Rare passage migrant along entire north-west coast (Sabah, Brunei, Sarawak) and in Kelabit Highlands, Sarawak. One record from E Kalimantan.

JACANIDAE: Jacanas

Worldwide 8 species, 2 in Borneo. A small pantropical family of very long-legged waterbirds with remarkably elongated toes adapted for walking on floating vegetation. Marked seasonal plumage variation. Polyandrous, females are larger but otherwise the sexes are similar. The female usually has a larger territory encompassing the territories of a number of males.

COMB-CRESTED JACANA *Irediparra gallinacea*

Identification Male 20–21 cm, female 24–27 cm. **Adult male** *gallinacea* Crown to hindneck black, narrow black line from base of bill to eye, face and throat white grading to pale orange on neck, broad black breast-band, rest of upperparts brownish-black, underparts white with buff tinge on undertail-coverts; iris golden-brown; very distinctive comb-like, fleshy wattle from forecrown and vertical comb varies from yellow to brilliant red dependent on mood, bill reddish tipped black, exceptionally long legs and feet dark olive; in flight underwing glossy black, long legs and feet trail conspicuously. **Adult female** Similar to male but much larger. **Juvenile** Upperparts brown, underparts white without black breast-band, frontal wattle and comb undeveloped. **Habitat** Floating aquatic vegetation in freshwater swamps, marshes, oxbow lakes, ponds. **Behaviour** Feeds on aquatic invertebrates and seeds which are gleaned from water surface and floating vegetation. **Voice** Variety of vocalisations consisting of shrill twitters and trills; main call is a rapidly repeated *ti ti ti ti...* (3.5 kHz). **Range & status** Indonesia, Philippines, New Guinea, Australia. **Borneo** Locally common resident confined to SE Borneo (S Kalimantan and probably southern E Kalimantan).

PHEASANT-TAILED JACANA *Hydrophasianus chirurgus*

Identification 39 cm (breeding adult's tail up to 20 cm more). Monotypic. **Adult breeding** Head and foreneck white, thin black line running down sides of neck from black patch on nape to upper breast separating white foreneck from golden-yellow hindneck; mantle and upper back dark brown with greenish gloss, lower back to uppertail blackish-brown, conspicuous white wings contrasting with blackish-brown underparts, elongated decurved central tail feathers; iris brown, bill slaty-blue, legs exceptionally long and feet pale bluish-grey; in flight underwing white with black trailing edge, long legs and feet trail conspicuously. **Adult non-breeding** Forehead to nape brownish, supercilium contiguous with dull golden-yellow hindneck, brownish line from lores through eye down sides of neck to thin dark breast-band dividing white foreneck from rest of underparts, upperparts pale brown, tail brown and short; bill brownish with yellow base, legs and feet duller. **Juvenile** Similar to non-breeding adult, cap rufous, paler, sides of neck buff, breast-band indistinct. **Habitat** Floating aquatic vegetation in freshwater swamps, marshes, oxbow lakes, ponds. **Behaviour** Feeds on aquatic invertebrates and seeds which are gleaned from water surface and floating vegetation. **Voice** Territorial call is a distinctive cat-like mewing (0.3–1.3 kHz, 4–5 notes/4 s); song is a mellow, liquid low-pitched *puwool puwool* (1.8–0.3 kHz). **Range & status** Indian Subcontinent, SE China, Taiwan, SE Asia, Indonesia, Philippines. **Borneo** Rare vagrant with one recent record from Sabah and historic records from S Kalimantan.

ROSTRATULIDAE: Painted-snipe

Worldwide 2 species, 1 in Borneo. A small family of cryptic wetland birds, resembling snipe, with large eye, long bill, and broad rounded wings. Sexually dimorphic with roles reversed, the female is brightly coloured and calls and defends a territory, the male incubates and raises young; polyandrous.

GREATER PAINTED-SNIPE *Rostratula benghalensis*

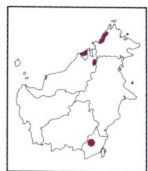

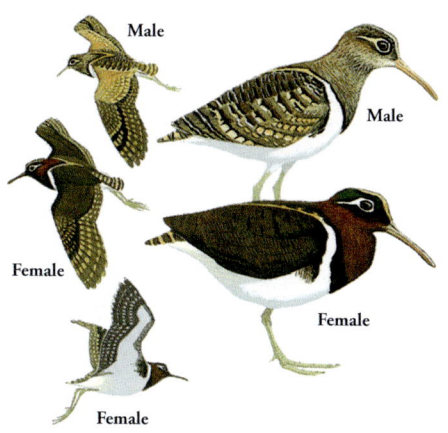

Identification 23–28 cm. **Adult female** *benghalensis* Crown dark grey with buff median stripe, distinctive white comma-shaped eye-patch, sides of head and throat rich chestnut-rufous, upperparts grey-brown with fine black barring, buffish-white stripe from sides of breast over shoulders creating V on mantle, underparts white; iris dark brown, long slightly drooping bill pale pink-grey, legs and feet yellowish-olive; in flight underwing-coverts white contrasting with darker flight feathers; takes flight with legs dangling. **Adult male** Comma-shaped eye-patch pale buff, crown dark brown with buff median stripe, sides of head to upper breast grey-brown with pale vermiculations, chin whitish, throat greyish streaked with white, white stripe with blackish borders running from sides of breast with mantle, upper-parts grey barred and vermiculated black, rump to uppertail mottled golden-buff, wing-coverts with large golden-buff bars and spots, underparts white. **Juvenile** Like adult male but wing-coverts grey with small buff spots, bill brownish. **Habitat** Shallow freshwater wetlands: lakes, ponds, swamps, marshes, paddyfields; possibly to 1,200 m. **Behaviour** Usually solitary or in pairs, shy, terrestrial, crepuscular and possibly nocturnal; feeds on vegetation, seeds, small invertebrates by probing soft ground and scything in shallow water. **Voice** Rarely vocalises outside breeding season; alarm call is a loud *kek* when flushed. During breeding season female utters a slow-tempo owl-like *ko ko ko…* (10–50 notes @ 1 note/s, 1 kHz). **Range & status** Africa, Madagascar, Indian Subcontinent, E and SE Asia, Indonesia, Philippines, Australia. **Borneo** Uncommon resident west coast Sabah and Brunei, rare resident S Kalimantan; one sight record from Kelabit Highlands, E Sarawak. **Breeding** May–June; four buffish-brown eggs with black streaks and blotches are laid in cup-shaped nest of rotting grass.

SCOLOPACIDAE: Snipe, sandpipers & allies

Worldwide c.91 species, 37 in Borneo. A large, very diverse family of small to large shorebirds most utilizing coastal habitats, but also woodlands, grasslands and fields. Bill size and shape varies depending largely on feeding method. Diet consists mainly of small invertebrates and prey is obtained by picking or probing with specialised bill. Most are strongly migratory, breeding in the far north and overwintering in tropical zones and further south. A range of seasonal, age-related, individual and geographic plumage variations often pose identification challenges. Typically sexes are similar.

EURASIAN WOODCOCK *Scolopax rusticola*

Identification 33–35 cm. Monotypic. A large, snipe-like wader with steep forehead and complex camouflage plumage. **Adult** Crown with thick transverse blackish-brown bars, eye-stripe from base of bill to behind eye and stripe below eye blackish, whitish around eye, back blackish-brown and wings rufous-brown with black, white and buff mottling; underparts pale brownish with brownish band from throat to upper breast and brownish barring on belly, short tail brown with dark subterminal band; iris black, long straight bill pinkish with black tip, short legs pinkish; in flight wings broad. **Juvenile** Like adult but forehead more spotted. **Habitat** Wet forests, swamps, marshes; recorded in weedy riverbank (Danum Valley) and short grass (Panaga, Brunei) in Borneo. **Behaviour** Crepuscular, migratory to SE Asia in non-breeding season; feeds on invertebrates, seeds, fruits by probing with long bill in damp soil. **Voice** Usually silent away from breeding grounds. A slow tempoed croaking *bu-bu-buchi* interspersed with a raspy, twittering *seewit* (rising and falling from 2–12 kHz, 0.1 s) given in flight at dusk. **Range & status** Europe, N Africa, C and E Asia, Himalayas, SE Asia. **Borneo** Rare vagrant to Sabah and Brunei.

PINTAIL SNIPE *Gallinago stenura*

Identification 25–27 cm. Monotypic. **Adult** Buff central crown-stripe, buff supercilium broader than brown eye-stripe and crown-stripe at base of bill, upperparts with parallel pale buffish lines, richly patterned plumage with buff, black and white camouflage mottling; whitish underparts finely barred, whitish centre of belly; primaries only just longer than tertials, tail projects only slightly beyond primaries, outertail feathers pin-shaped (rarely visible in field); iris brown; long, straight bill yellowish-grey with dark tip, legs greenish-yellow; in flight toes may project beyond tail-tip more than Swinhoe's, no white trailing edge. **Juvenile** Upperparts with finer marking than adult. **Similar species** Very similar to Swinhoe's Snipe: plumage differences have probably been overstated in past and both species share almost identical plumage patterns with no consistent differences; in most cases separation on size and structure, even when both species are side by side in field, is not possible unless outertail feathers are visible; flight calls may be species-specific but further research is required to establish this. Common Snipe has white trailing edge on wings in flight and narrower supercilium in front of eye.

Habitat In Borneo swamps, marshes, grasslands, paddyfields, streambanks; from sea-level to 1,100 m. **Behaviour** Feeds in moist soil on insects, worms and aquatic invertebrates as well as some plant material; shy, exploding from cover when approached. **Voice** May give a short, hoarse, squeaky *chek* when flushed (4 kHz), resembles a duck's *quack*. **Range & status** Russia to Siberia, migrating to Indian Subcontinent, S China, SE Asia, Indonesia, Philippines. **Borneo** Common non-breeding visitor throughout, August–April. Commonest snipe in W Sabah, Brunei and Sarawak. Status elsewhere is unclear owing to confusion with following species.

SWINHOE'S SNIPE *Gallinago megala*

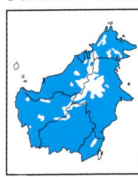

Identification 27–29 cm. Monotypic. **Adult** Buff central crown-stripe, buff supercilium broader than brown eye-stripe and crown-stripe at base of bill, upperparts with parallel pale buffish lines, richly patterned plumage with buff, black and white camouflage mottling; belly whitish; primaries longer than tertials, tail may project beyond primaries slightly more than Pintail Snipe, tail with white outer corners (rarely visible in field); iris brown; long straight bill yellowish-grey with dark tip, legs greenish-yellow; in flight toes may project beyond tail-tip less than Pintail, no white trailing edge. **Juvenile** Upperparts with finer marking than adult. **Similar species** See comments under Pintail Snipe. **Habitat** On breeding grounds: wetlands, meadows, tundra; on non-breeding grounds: swamps, marshes, grasslands, paddyfields, streambanks, from sea-level to 1,100 m in Borneo. **Behaviour** Feeds in moist soil on insects, worms and aquatic invertebrates as well as some plant material; shy, exploding from cover when approached. **Voice** Similar to Pintail Snipe

but possibly lower-pitched, usually below 3 kHz. **Range & status** Central Asia, migrating to Indian Subcontinent, South China, SE Asia, Indonesia, Philippines, New Guinea, northern Australia. **Borneo** Common to uncommon non-breeding visitor, possibly commoner in west than previous species but status is unclear owing to difficulty in differentiating Pintail and Swinhoe's Snipe in field.

COMMON SNIPE *Gallinago gallinago*

Identification 25–27 cm. **Adult** *gallinago* Buff central crown-stripe, buff supercilium narrower than brown eyestripe and crown-stripe at base of bill, upperparts with parallel pale buffish lines, richly patterned plumage with buff, black and white camouflage mottling; belly whitish; iris brown; long straight bill yellowish-grey with dark tip, legs greenish-yellow; in flight prominent white trailing edge to wing. **Juvenile** Very similar but with scaly pattern on wing-coverts. **Similar species** Pintail and Swinhoe's Snipe both lack white on trailing edge of wing and have broad supercilium in front of eye. **Habitat** Wetland edges, grasslands, paddyfields, mostly at sea-level in Borneo. **Behaviour** Feeds in moist soil on insects, worms and aquatic invertebrates as well as some plant material; shy, exploding from cover when approached. **Voice** A scratchy

squek (3 kHz) when flushed. **Range & status** Palearctic, Africa, Indian Subcontinent, E and SE Asia, W Indonesia, Philippines. **Borneo** Uncommon non-breeding visitor to N Borneo (Sabah and Brunei) November–March.

LONG-BILLED DOWITCHER
Limnodromus scolopaceus

Identification 26–30 cm. Monotypic. Long-billed wader with long greenish legs. **Adult non-breeding** Crown dark grey, prominent broad white supercilium, upperparts dark grey with pale edging on wings, upper breast washed grey, rest of underparts white with black bars on flanks and undertail; iris black, long bill dark grey slightly downturned at tip, legs and feet greenish-yellow; in flight underwing grey, toes extend slightly beyond tail. **Adult breeding** Crown chestnut with fine black streaks, head reddish-brown with prominent whitish supercilium, upperparts black with chestnut and buff edging, underparts dull rufous with fine black bars on breast and broad black bars on flanks and undertail. **Similar species** Asian Dowitcher is larger, has longer bill with distinctive bulbous tip, and dark legs. **Habitat** In Borneo recorded from coastal mudflats. **Voice** A very short, high-pitched *kip* (4.3 kHz). **Range & status** Breeds Siberia, Alaska, NW Canada; winters N and C America. **Borneo** Rare vagrant; Sabah and possibly Brunei.

ASIAN DOWITCHER *Limnodromus semipalmatus*

Identification 33–36 cm. Monotypic. Long-legged wader with long straight bill with swollen tip. **Adult non-breeding** Crown dark grey, prominent broad white supercilium, grey eyestripe, upperparts grey mottled black, underparts white with grey mottling on breast and grey barring on flanks; iris black, very long bill and long legs black; in flight pale grey wedge on lower back, rump and tail white barred black, underwing white, feet extend beyond tail. **Adult male breeding** Upperparts rufous with black and buff mottling on back and wings, neck and breast, belly to undertail white with flanks barred black. **Adult female breeding** Duller with more white in plumage. **Juvenile** Buff neck and breast streaked darker, upperparts blackish with buff fringes. **Similar species** See Long-billed Dowitcher; Bar-tailed Godwit has more slender, bicoloured bill without swollen tip. **Habitat** In Borneo recorded from coastal mudflats. **Behaviour** Characteristic 'sewing machine' feeding method as bill is repeatedly plunged deeply into soft mud in search of molluscs and polychaete worms. **Voice** A short, plaintive, yelping *chwep*. **Range & status** Breeds Siberia, Mongolia, NE China; winters from S Indian Subcontinent to Indonesia and Australia. **Borneo** Uncommon non-breeding visitor N Borneo (Sabah, Brunei, Sarawak), August–March; only one historic record from Kalimantan (West).

BLACK-TAILED GODWIT *Limosa limosa*

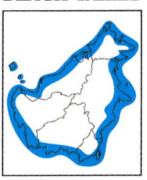

Identification 36–44 cm. Elegant wader with long straight pink bill and plain black uppertail. **Adult non-breeding *melanuroides*** Upperparts plain dark grey, prominent whitish supercilium, underparts pale grey grading into white belly, mottled grey on flanks; iris black, distinctive long, straight bill pink with black tip, legs and feet black; in flight long white bar in central upperwing, white uppertail-coverts contrast with black uppertail. **Adult male breeding** Head and neck rufous-brown with fine dark brown streaks, white supercilium, upperparts darker with complex pattern of rufous and dark brown mottling, underparts chestnut barred dark brown on flanks and belly. **Adult female non-breeding** Larger, plumage duller. **Juvenile** Like non-breeding but with buffish wash on head and breast, upperparts darker greyish-brown with buffish-chestnut feather-fringes. **Similar species** Bar-tailed Godwit has shorter, slightly upcurved bill; in flight shows greyish uppertail coverts and barred uppertail, lacks white on upperwing. **Habitat** Marshes, lakes, mudflats, mangroves, paddyfields, at sea-level. **Behaviour** Probes in sand and mud for molluscs and worms, also takes insects; often in small groups. **Voice** Outside breeding grounds a soft *ke* (3 kHz) uttered periodically. **Range & status** Europe, Africa, Indian Subcontinent, SE Asia, Indonesia, Australia. **Borneo** Uncommon non-breeding visitor and passage migrant throughout, August-April.

BAR-TAILED GODWIT *Limosa lapponica*

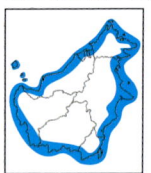

Identification 37–41 cm. Elegant wader with long, slightly upcurved bill and black-and-white-barred uppertail. **Adult non-breeding *baueri*** Supercilium brownish-white, upperparts greyish-brown with pale edging, neck and breast grey with fine dark streaks grading into white underparts; iris dark brown; slightly upcurved, long bill black with pink or yellowish base; legs and feet dark grey; in flight lacks white bar on wing, underwing-coverts barred dark brown and white, uppertail coverts greyish, uppertail barred. **Adult male breeding** Crown rufous-chestnut with fine darker streaks, dark brownish eyestripe, neck and underparts plain rufous-chestnut, upperparts chestnut with rich pattern of black and buff, tail barred brown and white. **Adult female breeding** Rufous-chestnut replaced by pale chestnut. **Juvenile** As non-breeding but upperparts dark brown with buff edging, neck and breast buffish-brown. **Similar species** See Black-tailed Godwit and Asian Dowitcher. **Habitat** Mudflats, estuaries, marshes, at sea-level. **Behaviour** Probes in sand and mud for molluscs and worms, also takes insects; often in small groups. **Voice** A short, nasal *ke...ke...* (2 kHz). **Range & status** Breeds Arctic Circle, migrates to coastal Europe, Africa, Middle East, Indian Subcontinent, E China, SE Asia, Indonesia, Philippines, New Guinea, Australia, New Zealand. **Borneo** Common to uncommon non-breeding visitor and passage migrant throughout, September-May.

WHIMBREL *Numenius phaeopus*

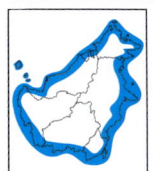

Identification 40–46 cm. Medium-sized curlew with long decurved bill and distinctive call. **Adult *variegatus*** Crown blackish-brown with pale brown central stripe, buff supercilium, dark brown eye-stripe, upperparts brown with whitish and buff spotting and fringing, underparts pale brown with brown streaking on neck and breast; iris dark brown, medium-sized bill dark grey with pink lower base and decurved more sharply at tip, legs and feet bluish-grey; in flight underwing-coverts brown with narrow whitish barring. **Juvenile** Breast more buffish, clearer buff spots on upperparts. **Habitat** Mudflats, estuaries, mangroves, sandy beaches, mostly at sea-level but records to 600 m. **Behaviour** Gleans and probes for crabs and other invertebrates on variety of substrates; often roosts in mangroves. **Voice** A highly distinctive tittering, musical *ti-ti-ti-ti-ti…* (2.6 kHz) uttered at rate of c.8 notes/s, usually given in flight; also a quavering two-note *kroo-ee*. **Range & status** Breeds Arctic Circle, migrates to Africa, Middle East, Indian Subcontinent, SE Asia, Indonesia, Philippines, New Guinea, Australia, S America. **Borneo** Common non-breeding visitor throughout, including offshore islands; dates are uncertain as some remain over northern summer.

EURASIAN CURLEW *Numenius arquata*

LIBARAN ISLAND 5/6/10

Identification 50–60 cm. Large, greyish-brown curlew with very long, decurved bill. **Adult non-breeding *orientalis*** Head and neck buffish with blackish-brown streaks, breast buffish with coarse blackish-brown streaks grading into white underparts, flanks prominently spotted blackish-brown, upperparts blackish-brown with broad buffish fringes; iris dark brown, long bill dark grey with pink lower base, legs and feet bluish-grey; in flight underwing-coverts white, lower back and rump white. **Adult breeding** Upperparts with brighter buffish fringing, head and breast more buffish. **Juvenile** Like adult breeding but more buffish with reduced streaking on underparts, more contrasting buffish edging on upperparts. **Habitat** Beaches, mudflats, estuaries, mangroves, at sea-level. **Behaviour** Probes long bill in soft mud for polychaete worms, molluscs and crabs. **Voice** A powerful, fluty *ker-REE*, the first note harsh and lower-pitched (1.6 kHz), the second sharply higher and louder (2.6 kHz), each phrase c.0.8 s.

Range & status Breeds W Europe to C Asia, migrating to S Europe, Africa, Middle East, Indian Subcontinent, E Asia, SE Asia, Indonesia, Philippines. **Borneo** Common to uncommon non-breeding visitor and passage migrant to coastal N Borneo (Sarawak, Brunei, Sabah, E Kalimantan) September–April.

FAR EASTERN CURLEW *Numenius madagascariensis*

Identification 60–66 cm. Monotypic. Largest curlew with an exceptionally long bill. **Adult non-breeding** Like Eurasian Curlew but larger with longer bill, rufous tinge on upperparts, underparts washed buffish-brown, bill longer in female; in flight underwing pale brown with close dark brown barring, rump and lower back brown. **Adult breeding** Brighter rufous tinge on upperparts, warmer buffish underparts. **Juvenile** More contrasting buffish edging on upperparts. **Habitat** Beaches, mudflats, estuaries, mangroves, at sea-level. **Behaviour** Probes long bill in soft mud for polychaete worms, molluscs and crabs. **Voice** A powerful, hoarse *ku-REE*, the first note lower-pitched (1.4 kHz), the second sharply higher (1.9 kHz) and louder, the two notes roughly equal in length, each phrase c.0.9 s; similar to Eurasian Curlew but somewhat flatter, less fluty and delivered at a more rapid rate; also a more rapid *krer-krer-krer-krer...* **Range & status** Breeds E Siberia to Kamchatka, migrating to Taiwan, Indonesia, New Guinea, Australia. **Borneo** Uncommon to locally common non-breeding visitor

and passage migrant to coastal N Borneo (Sarawak, Brunei, Sabah, E Kalimantan), August–March.

LITTLE CURLEW *Numenius minutus*

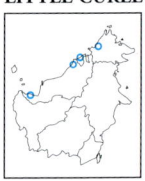

Identification 30–36 cm. Monotypic. Small curlew with short, only slightly downcurved bill. **Adult** Crown dark brown with pale brown central stripe, broad buff supercilium widening behind eye, indistinct dark brown eye-stripe, cheeks buff, back and wings brown with buff edging, underparts pale brown with brown streaking on foreneck and breast; iris black, short and slightly downcurved bill dark grey with pink base, legs and feet grey; in flight underwing-coverts buffish-brown. **Juvenile** Less streaking on breast. **Habitat** In Borneo recorded from mudflats, grasslands, airfields, at sea-level. **Voice** A soft, rapidly repeated whistle *weep…weep…weep…* (c.2.5 kHz); not recorded in Borneo. **Range & status** Breeds Siberia, migrates to New Guinea, Australia. **Borneo** Vagrant; coastal NW Borneo with few records from Sabah, Brunei and Sarawak.

TEREK SANDPIPER *Xenus cinereus*

Identification 22–25 cm. Monotypic. Small sandpiper with distinctive longish upturned bill and rather short orange legs. **Adult non-breeding** Upperparts pale brown with black on scapulars, prominent white supercilium extends just behind eye, dark grey line across lores, underparts white with finely streaked grey patches on sides of breast; iris dark brown, upturned bill grey with orange base, legs and feet orange. **Adult breeding** Crown and upperparts grey with prominent black lines on scapulars; bill all dark. **Juvenile** Like breeding adult but upperparts brownish with buff fringing, black lines on scapulars less distinctive. **Habitat** Beaches, estuaries, mudflats, at sea-level. **Behaviour** Favours mudflats in Borneo; often joins mixed flocks of waders; huge congregations of more than 2,700 have been recorded in Sarawak; frantic foraging behaviour is distinctive. **Voice** A fluty, piercing, slightly upslurred whistle *weet…weet…* (2–2.4 kHz) and more rapid *wit-wit-wit…* (2.4 kHz). **Range & status** Breeds Palearctic; migrates to Africa, Middle East, S Indian Subcontinent, SE Asia, Indonesia, Australia. **Borneo** Common non-breeding visitor and passage migrant throughout, including offshore islands, September–April.

GREY-TAILED TATTLER *Tringa brevipes*

Identification 24–27 cm. Monotypic. Medium-sized wader with short legs, long wings and tail, and distinctive vocalisations. **Adult non-breeding** Upperparts grey with narrow pale grey edging on wings, long pale grey supercilium, dark grey line across lores, throat and breast plain grey, primaries blackish-grey, underparts whitish; iris dark grey, bill dark brown, bill dark grey with yellow lower base, legs and feet pale yellow; in flight upperwing and underwing all grey, latter contrasting with white belly and undertail. **Adult breeding** Grey streaks on throat and breast and grey chevrons on flanks. **Juvenile** Like non-breeding adult but with small buffish-white spots on upperparts, tail feathers notched white. **Habitat** Sandy beaches, rocky foreshores, estuaries, mudflats, mangroves, at sea-level. **Behaviour** Usually seen singly; avoids freshwater habitats; walks with bobbing and teetering movements. **Voice** A pleasant, slurred disyllabic *tsu-wit* whistle, dipping then rising in pitch (2.7–3.5 kHz). **Range & status** Breeds Siberia; migrates to Taiwan, Thai-Malay Peninsula, Philippines, Indonesia, New Guinea, SW Pacific, Australia. **Borneo** Common non-breeding visitor and passage migrant to coastal N Borneo (Sabah, Brunei, Sarawak, E Kalimantan) September–May; some birds remain throughout year.

COMMON SANDPIPER *Actitis hypoleucos*

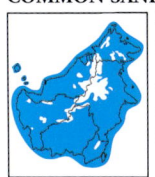

Identification 19–21 cm. Monotypic. Small, short-legged wader that constantly bobs its tail. **Adult non-breeding** Head and upperparts olive-brown, indistinct long white supercilium, indistinct dark grey eyestripe, neck and breast olive-brown, rest of underparts white with brownish patches on sides of breast; iris dark brown, short straight bill dark grey, legs and feet grey; in flight narrow white wing-bar contrasts with dark upperparts. **Adult breeding** Upperparts with darker streaks and bars, throat and breast streaked brown. **Juvenile** Upperparts with buff fringing and barring. **Habitat** Beaches, mangroves, waterways, plantations, paddyfields, from sea-level to 1,300 m in Kelabit Highlands. **Behaviour** Often seen singly or in small loose groups running along muddy riverbanks in interior; tail-bobbing action is distinctive. **Voice** Flight call is a short, squeaky, high-pitched repetitive *pi-pi-pi-pi...* (c.6 kHz). **Range & status** Breeds Palearctic; migrates to Africa, Middle East, Indian Subcontinent, E Asia, SE Asia, Philippines, Indonesia, New Guinea, Australia. **Borneo** Common non-breeding visitor and passage migrant throughout coastal and interior Borneo including offshore islands, August–May; small numbers remain year-round.

GREEN SANDPIPER *Tringa ochropus*

Identification 21–24 cm. Monotypic. **Adult non-breeding** Head to upper breast brownish with pale streaking, white supercilium in front of eye, black line over lores, upperparts dark olive-brown spotted white, rump and upper-tail-coverts white, tail barred black and white, rest of underparts white; iris dark brown, narrow white eye-ring, bill dark grey with yellowish lower base, legs and feet dirty yellow; in flight underwings dark brown finely barred white, feet project slightly beyond tail. **Adult breeding** Head and breast darker, larger white spots on upperparts. **Juvenile** Browner with buffish spots on upperparts. **Similar species** Wood Sandpiper is paler, white supercilium extends behind eye, has longer legs, in flight underwing is whitish, feet extend well beyond tail. **Habitat** Mudflats, freshwater wetlands, mangroves, small ponds, swamps, fields, paddyfields, generally recorded at sea-level in Borneo but possible in small waterbodies at higher elevations. **Behaviour** Usually singly or in small flocks; often observed feeding at very small bodies of water; favours freshwater wetlands. **Voice** When flushed, gives a high-pitched *tlueet-wit-wit*. **Range & status** Breeds N Palearctic; migrates to S Europe, Africa, Middle East, Indian Subcontinent, E Asia, SE Asia, Philippines. **Borneo** Uncommon non-breeding visitor to coastal N Borneo (Sabah, Brunei, Sarawak, E Kalimantan), August–April.

WOOD SANDPIPER *Tringa glareola*

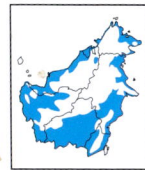

Identification 19–21 cm. Monotypic. **Adult non-breeding** Head to upper breast brownish with pale streaking, darker on crown; long white supercilium extends to ear-coverts, black line over lores, upperparts greyish-brown barred and spotted grey and white, rump and uppertail-coverts white, tail brown with narrow white barring, rest of underparts white; iris dark brown, narrow white eye-ring, bill dark grey with yellowish lower base, legs and feet dirty yellow; in flight underwing whitish, feet project well beyond tail. **Adult breeding** Upperparts more blackish-brown with bolder white spots and bars, more extensive, bolder streaking on breast. **Juvenile** Browner with buffish spots on upperparts. **Similar species** See Green Sandpiper. **Habitat** Mudflats, freshwater wetlands, paddyfields, to 1,200 m in Kelabit Highlands. **Behaviour** Seen singly or in small loose groups; favours inland freshwater wetlands; probes, gleans and sweeps for small aquatic invertebrates and fish in shallow water. **Voice** A loud piercing whistled three- or four-note *pee-pee-pit* (4 kHz). **Range & status** Breeds N Palearctic; migrates to Africa, Middle East, Indian Subcontinent, S China, SE Asia, Indonesia, Philippines, Australia. **Borneo** Very common non-breeding visitor and passage migrant to coastal and interior areas throughout, August–April; has been recorded throughout year in Brunei.

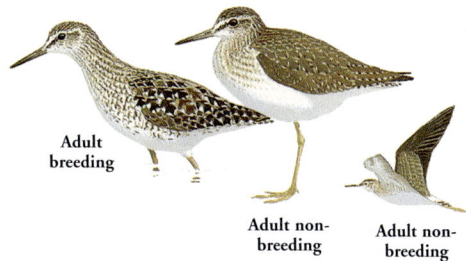

COMMON REDSHANK *Tringa totanus*

Identification 27–29 cm. **Adult non-breeding** *eurhinus* Lores blackish, upperparts brownish-grey with some narrow white fringes; underparts white with brownish-grey wash on breast, and narrow brownish streaking on breast, flanks and undertail; iris black, narrow white eye-ring, bill orange-red with black tip, legs and feet orange-red; in flight broad white inner trailing edge on upperwing, primaries blackish, lower back and rump white, underwing all white. **Adult breeding** Head and upperparts brownish mottled black and dark brown, underparts white with coarse blackish streaks and spots and brownish wash on breast. **Juvenile** Like non-breeding adult; upperparts browner with buff fringes, breast washed buffish-brown, darker streaking on underparts. **Similar species** Non-breeding Spotted Redshank is paler, has prominent whitish supercilium, has all-grey upperwing in flight. **Habitat** wetlands, mangroves, mudflats, paddyfields, to 100 m. **Behaviour** Roosts in large flocks; forages on muddy substrates for molluscs, crabs and polychaete worms. **Voice** A piercing, rather mournful three-note *cho-yo-yo*, the first note markedly downslurred, the second and very short third note delivered on flat pitch (3–2.3 kHz, 0.4 s); also a rapidly repeated, loud *pyo-pyo-pyo-pyo-pyo....* **Range & status** Palearctic, Indian Subcontinent, East and SE Asia, Philippines, Indonesia. **Borneo** Common non-breeding visitor throughout including offshore islands; dates are uncertain as some remain over northern summer.

SPOTTED REDSHANK *Tringa erythropus*

Identification 29–32 cm. Monotypic. **Adult non-breeding** Short white supercilium, black eyestripe, upperparts grey with white edges on flight feathers, lower back and rump white, uppertail barred black and white, underparts greyish-white; straight bill black with red base, legs and feet red; in flight wing-tips blackish, white rump and 'cigar-shaped' patch on back conspicuous and feet extend well beyond tail. **Adult breeding** All sooty-black with fine white edging on wings and back, lower back and rump white; slender bill black with scarlet base, slightly drooping at tip; legs and feet dark red. **Juvenile** Like adult non-breeding but darker and more densely barred underneath. **Similar species** Common Redshank has shorter bill, shorter legs, in flight broad white trailing edge of wings. **Habitat** Mudflats, coastal wetlands. **Behaviour** Recorded in flocks with Common Redshanks. **Voice** A sharp, rapid *chu-it* falling then rising in pitch. **Range & status** Breeds N Europe to NW Russia, migrating to Europe, Africa, Indian Subcontinent, SE China, Taiwan, SE Asia. **Borneo** Rare non-breeding visitor to coastal N Borneo (Sabah, Brunei and Sarawak).

MARSH SANDPIPER *Tringa stagnatilis*

Identification 22–25 cm. Monotypic. Delicate sandpiper with long, slender legs and needle-like straight bill. **Adult non-breeding** Face and supercilium white, upperparts greyish-brown with narrow pale fringes, underparts white with faint greyish streaking on breast; iris black, bill black with yellowish-green base, legs and feet greenish-grey; in flight shows long white area from back to uppertail, all-grey upperwing, toes project well beyond tail. **Adult breeding** Head and neck whitish with fine dark brown streaking, indistinct pale supercilium, upperparts dark brown with buffish-grey and white edging and bars, back and rump white, underparts white with dark brown streaks and bars on breast and flanks; legs and feet greenish-yellow. **Juvenile** Upperparts browner with buffish fringes. **Similar species** Common Greenshank is larger, has relatively shorter legs and thicker, upturned bill, in flight toes project slightly beyond tail. **Habitat** Coastal wetlands, mudflats, paddyfields, at sea-level. **Behaviour** Forages for small aquatic invertebrates including insects usually in shallow water, often in mixed flocks of waders. **Voice** A short, one note sharply downslurred *pyu...* repeated at varying intervals (3–2 kHz). **Range & status** Breeds W Russia to E Siberia, migrates to Africa, Middle East, Indian Subcontinent, SE Asia, Indonesia, Australia. **Borneo** Common non-breeding visitor throughout, September–May.

COMMON GREENSHANK *Tringa nebularia*

Identification 30–34 cm. Monotypic. Large wader with distinctive thick, slightly upturned bill and greenish legs. **Adult non-breeding** Head and neck greyish-white with fine dark grey streaking, indistinct pale supercilium, upperparts greyish-brown with narrow pale fringes, underparts all white; iris black, bill black with yellowish-green base, legs and feet greenish-yellow; in flight shows long white area from back to uppertail, upperwing all grey, underwing white finely barred brown, toes project slightly beyond tail. **Adult breeding** Head and neck whitish with fine dark brown streaking, lores blackish, upperparts dark brown with buffish-grey and white edging and bars, back and rump white, underparts white with dark brown streaks and bars on breast and flanks. **Juvenile** Upperparts browner with buffish fringes. **Similar species** See Marsh Sandpiper and Nordmann's Greenshank. **Habitat** Coastal wetlands, beaches, grasslands, paddyfields, at sea-level. **Behaviour** Generally solitary; forages for small aquatic invertebrates and small fish, often in shallow water. **Voice** A pleasant ringing, plaintive three- to five-note *tyu-tyu-tyu* each note sharply downslurred (3.2–2.4 kHz). **Range & status** Breeds Palearctic area, migrates to W Europe, Africa, Middle East, Indian Subcontinent, China, SE Asia, Indonesia, Philippines, New Guinea, Australia. **Borneo** Common (Sabah, Brunei) to uncommon (Sarawak, Kalimantan) non-breeding visitor throughout, from September to early June.

NORDMANN'S GREENSHANK *Tringa guttifer*

Identification 29–32 cm. Monotypic. Large wader with thick straight two-tone bill and short yellowish legs. **Adult non-breeding** Like Common Greenshank but upperparts paler, forehead and supercilium white, underparts white, smaller, straight bill black with basal half yellow, shorter legs yellow; in flight shows long white area from back to uppertail, upperwing all grey, underwing all white, toes do not project beyond tail. **Adult breeding** Upperparts dark brown with white fringes, underparts white with large brownish-black spots on breast and flanks. **Juvenile** Upperparts browner with buffish fringes, breast flecked brownish. **Habitat** In Borneo recorded from mudflats and grasslands at sea-level. **Range & status** Breeds Sakhalin Island; migrates to coastal NE India, E Asia and SE Asia. **Borneo** Rare vagrant, with very few records from Sabah and Sarawak. Endangered.

77

GREAT KNOT *Calidris tenuirostris*

Identification 26–28 cm. Monotypic. Large, bulky wader with oval-shaped body and short legs. **Adult non-breeding** Head and neck streaked brownish-grey, upperparts grey streaked brownish-grey and edged pale grey, underparts white with grey-streaked breast-band and flanks; in flight narrow white wing-bar, blackish primary coverts, white rump and uppertail-coverts contrasting with black uppertail, underwing white with brownish wash; iris dark brown, longish bill black with greenish deep base, legs and feet greenish-grey. **Adult breeding** Head streaked white and dark brown, upperparts dark brown with greyish-white fringes and chestnut band on scapulars, underparts white heavily mottled brown on breast, brown chevrons on flanks, white belly and undertail-coverts. **Juvenile** Upperparts browner with contrasting buffish-white fringes, breast and flanks spotted dark brown with buffish wash on breast. **Similar species** See Red Knot. **Habitat** Mudflats, mangroves, at sea-level. **Behaviour** Probes in soft mud mainly for molluscs; associates with other waders in mixed flocks. **Voice** A short, soft, single *nyut* uttered in flight. **Range & status** Breeds NE Siberia; migrates to Indian Subcontinent, SE Asia, Indonesia, Philippines, New Guinea, Australia. **Borneo** Uncommon non-breeding visitor and passage migrant to coastal N Borneo (Sabah, Brunei, Sarawak, E Kalimantan), September–May.

RED KNOT *Calidris canutus*

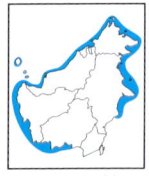

Identification 23–25 cm. Medium-sized, heavy wader with general oval shape and shortish bill relative to body size. **Adult non-breeding** *rogersi* Head and neck streaked brownish-grey, indistinct whitish supercilium, upperparts grey streaked brownish-grey and edged pale grey, underparts white with grey-streaked breast and flanks; iris dark brown, deep-based bill black, legs and feet greenish-grey; in flight distinct narrow white wing-bar, blackish primary coverts, uppertail-coverts barred grey, uppertail plain grey, underwing greyish-white. **Adult breeding** Crown and eyestripe streaked buff and dark brown, supercilium and face rufous, upperparts dark brown with broad chestnut fringing and pale grey tips, wing-coverts grey with white fringes, underparts rufous, paler on belly. **Juvenile** Upperparts brownish-buff with buff fringes, breast and flanks streaked dark brown with buffish wash on breast. **Similar species** Great Knot is larger with longer bill, stronger contrast between breast and belly, rump whiter contrasting with darker back and tail. **Habitat** Sandy beaches, mudflats, coastal wetlands, at sea-level. **Behaviour** Usually singly or in small flocks in Borneo; probes in soft mud mainly for molluscs and other small invertebrates. **Voice** In flight utters a short quiet low-pitched *krep… krep… krep…* (0.9 khz). **Range & status** Breeds Arctic Circle; migrates to NE and S America, Africa, W Europe, W Indonesia, Australia, New Zealand. **Borneo** Rare non-breeding visitor and passage migrant throughout except S Kalimantan, with very few records from April to June.

SANDERLING *Calidris alba*

Identification 20–21 cm. Monotypic. Stocky wader with short, heavy, slightly drooped bill and pale plumage. **Adult non-breeding** Forehead and lores white, crown and upperparts pale grey, underparts white; bare parts black; in flight bold white wing-bar, sides of rump and tail whitish. **Adult breeding** Head and breast chestnut streaked brown, breast sharply delineated from white underparts, upperparts blackish-brown with bold chestnut fringes and white notches. **Juvenile** Crown buffish streaked dark brown, pale buffish supercilium, upperparts dark brown with buffish-white spots and fringes, underparts white with buff wash on sides of breast. **Habitat** Sandy beaches, mudflats, strictly coastal at sea-level. **Behaviour** Favours sandy ocean beaches and sandflats; forages in very active manner, probing and pecking small invertebrates on shoreline. **Voice** Flight call is a quiet *twik*. **Range & status** Breeds Arctic Circle; migrates to N and S America, Europe, Africa, Middle East, Indian Subcontinent, E and SE Asia, Indonesia, New Guinea, Australia, New Zealand. **Borneo** Common non-breeding visitor and passage migrant to coastal N Borneo (Sabah, Brunei, Sarawak, E Kalimantan), September–May.

LITTLE STINT *Calidris minuta*

Identification 12–14 cm. Monotypic. Very similar to Red-necked Stint; differs as follows: **Adult non-breeding** Slightly longer legs and bill; upperparts browner. **Adult breeding** Head, neck and breast paler orange-rufous streaked brown; whitish supercilium, white throat, prominent creamy-white lines on mantle and upper scapulars. **Juvenile** More contrasting head pattern with darker centre of crown bordered white on each side, prominent white supercilium, upperparts darker and more rufous, prominent creamy-white lines on mantle and upper scapulars. **Habitat** Recorded at mudflats in Borneo. **Voice** A short *tsit*, similar to Red-necked Stint but higher and sharper. **Range & status** Breeds N Palearctic; migrates to S Europe, Africa, Middle East, Indian Subcontinent. **Borneo** Very rare vagrant with one substantiated record of three birds from NE Borneo (Sabah) and possibly Brunei.

RED-NECKED STINT *Calidris ruficollis*

Identification 13–16 cm. Monotypic. **Adult non-breeding** Upperparts grey with broad darker streaking, white supercilium, underparts white with greyish patches on sides of breast; bare parts black; in flight greyish-black flight feathers and primary coverts contrast with white wing-bar, sides of rump and tail white. **Adult breeding** Head to upper breast rufous with brown-streaked crown, rest of underparts white with brown spots on sides of breast, upperparts dark brown with narrow pale and broad chestnut fringes, wing-coverts greyish, white sides on dark brown tail and rump. **Juvenile** Crown and neck grey finely streaked brown, supercilium white, narrow dark grey eyestripe, upperparts brown with rufous and whitish fringes, underparts white with greyish and buffish wash across breast. **Similar species** See Little Stint. **Habitat** Mudflats, estuaries, sandy beaches, strictly coastal at sea-level. **Behaviour** Often observed in large flocks; pecks and sometimes probes very actively for very small invertebrates on muddy and sandy substrates. **Voice** Short, high-pitched *chit* calls (c.4.5 kHz), often repeated. **Range & status** Breeds NE Palearctic; migrates to E Indian Subcontinent, S China, Taiwan, SE Asia, Indonesia, Philippines, New Guinea, Australia. **Borneo** Common non-breeding visitor and passage migrant to coastal N Borneo (Sabah, Brunei, Sarawak, E Kalimantan) including offshore islands, August–May.

TEMMINCK'S STINT *Calidris temminckii*

Identification 13–15 cm. Monotypic. Tiny stint with pale legs. **Adult non-breeding** Head and upperparts plain grey, throat whitish, breast plain greyish-brown, rest of underparts white, tail projects noticeably beyond wing-tips at rest; iris dark brown; thin, slightly drooping bill black; legs and feet greenish-grey to yellowish-brown; in flight narrow white wing-bar, broad white outer tail feathers contrast with grey tail and rump. **Adult breeding** Head greyish-brown streaked brown, throat whitish, breast greyish-brown mottled buff, rest of underparts white, upperparts olive-brown with mottled pattern of dark brown, rufous and grey. **Juvenile** Like non-breeding but upperparts grey with dark brown and buff fringing, buffish-brown breast-band. **Similar species** See Long-toed Stint; also recalls miniature Common Sandpiper. **Habitat** Mudflats, estuaries, coastal wetlands, at sea-level. **Behaviour** Favours freshwater habitats; usually singly or in small groups; forages often in low vegetation in slow, methodical manner. **Voice** Flight call is a soft, rapid trilled *chiririri*. **Range & status** Breeds N Palearctic; migrates to Africa, Middle East, Indian Subcontinent, E and SE Asia, Philippines. **Borneo** Rare non-breeding visitor to N Borneo, recorded once from S Kalimantan, September–April.

LONG-TOED STINT *Calidris subminuta*

Identification 13–15 cm. Monotypic. Tiny long-necked wader with slender build, longish legs and shortish bill. **Adult non-breeding** Head grey with dark brown streaking, upperparts brownish-grey with broad dark feather-centres, breast washed greyish-brown with fine streaking; iris dark brown, shortish, slightly drooped bill black, legs and feet yellowish-brown to greenish-yellow; in flight faint white wing-bar, white sides to uppertail and rump. **Adult breeding** Crown and ear-coverts rufous streaked brown contrasting with prominent whitish supercilium, nape and neck pale brown streaked dark brown, upperparts dark brown with buff and rufous fringing, underparts white with flanks and rufous-washed breast streaked dark brown. **Juvenile** Like breeding adult but finer streaking on breast, whitish lines on mantle. **Similar species** Temminck's Stint is plainer with unstreaked breast; all other stints have dark legs. **Habitat** Coastal wetlands, marshes, grasslands, paddyfields, occasionally mudflats, to 1,200 m in Kelabit Highlands. **Behaviour** Favours inland freshwater habitats; singly or in small flocks; pecks small invertebrates at water's edge. **Voice** A soft *prrt*, dropping in pitch (3.6–3 kHz). **Range & status** Breeds C and E Palearctic; migrates to E Indian Subcontinent, Taiwan, SE Asia, Philippines, Indonesia, W and SE Australia. **Borneo** Very common non-breeding visitor and passage migrant to coastal and interior N Borneo (Sabah, Brunei, Sarawak, E Kalimantan), August–March.

SHARP-TAILED SANDPIPER *Calidris acuminata*

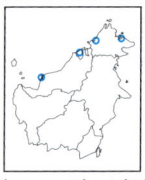

Identification 17–21 cm. Monotypic. Medium-sized wader with pale legs and short, slightly decurved bill. **Adult non-breeding** Crown rufous with brown streaks, distinct whitish supercilium, upperparts brown with dark feather-centres, breast greyish with faint brown streaking; iris dark brown, bill blackish-brown with pinkish-grey base on lower mandible, legs and feet greenish-grey; in flight narrow white wing-bar, rump and uppertail-coverts dark brown with broad white sides, under-wing-coverts white. **Adult breeding** Neck and upper breast buffish heavily streaked brown, rest of underparts white with bold black chevrons on lower breast and flanks, upperparts dark brown with chestnut and buff fringes. **Juvenile** Bright rufous crown, distinct white supercilium, upperparts dark brown with bright buff, chestnut and whitish fringes; breast washed bright buff with gorget of fine brown streaks, rest of underparts white. **Similar species** Pectoral Sandpiper (not yet recorded in Borneo) has breast pattern sharply delineated from rest of underparts and less distinct supercilium. **Habitat** Mudflats, coastal wetlands, at sea-level. **Behaviour** Recorded singly in mixed wader flocks in Borneo. **Voice** Flight call is a short, soft *weet weet…* repeated (3.5 kHz). **Range & status** Breeds N Siberia; migrates to New Guinea, SW Pacific, Australia, New Zealand. **Borneo** Rare non-breeding visitor and passage migrant with few records from coastal Sabah, Brunei and Sarawak, October–April.

DUNLIN *Calidris alpina*

Identification 16–22 cm. Medium-sized wader with longish bill decurved at tip and somewhat hunched posture. **Adult non-breeding** *sakhalina* Upperparts plain grey-brown with pale grey fringing on wing-coverts, throat and breast streaked greyish-brown, rest of underparts white; iris dark brown, bill and legs black; in flight narrow white wing-bar, centre of rump and uppertail-coverts blackish-brown bordered white. **Adult breeding** Head and neck streaked whitish and brown, supercilium whitish, upperparts dark brown boldly fringed bright chestnut and buffish-white, wing-coverts greyish-brown with paler fringes, underparts whitish streaked brownish on breast and large black patch on belly, undertail-coverts whitish. **Juvenile** Upperparts dark brown with buff and dark grey fringes, breast washed buff with brown streaks, lines of black spots on flanks and sides of belly. **Similar species** See Curlew Sandpiper; Broad-billed Sandpiper has 'split supercilium', is greyer in non-breeding plumage. **Habitat** Recorded at estuaries in Borneo. **Voice** Flight call is a rather soft, raspy and unclear *pree* (3.5 kHz). **Range & status** Breeds Arctic Circle; migrates to N America, Europe, Africa, Middle East, E Asia. **Borneo** Rare vagrant; very few records from Brunei.

CURLEW SANDPIPER *Calidris ferruginea*

Identification 18–23 cm. Monotypic. Medium-sized wader with long, markedly decurved bill and longish legs and neck. **Adult non-breeding** Upperparts plain greyish, long white supercilium, darker lores and ear-coverts, underparts white with grey wash on sides of breast; iris dark brown, bill and legs black; in flight narrow white wing-bar, rump and uppertail-coverts white with or without fine brown barring. **Adult male breeding** Head and underparts bright rufous with dark brown streaks on crown, undertail-coverts whitish, upperparts dark brown boldly fringed bright chestnut and buffish-white, wing-coverts greyish-brown with paler fringes. **Adult female breeding** Underparts paler rufous with whitish fringes and brown barring on belly. **Juvenile** Upperparts dark brown with buff and dark grey fringes, breast washed buff. **Similar species** Dunlin has shorter, less decurved bill, less distinct supercilium, lacks white rump-patch. **Habitat** Mudflats, paddyfields, at sea-level. **Behaviour** Pecks and probes in soft mud for small invertebrates, especially polychaete worms; often in large mixed wader flocks. **Voice** Flight call is a short trilled *prrrit* rising in pitch (3–3.5 kHz). **Range & status** Breeds N Palearctic; migrates to Africa, Middle East, Indian Subcontinent, SE Asia, Indonesia, Philippines, New Guinea, Australia. **Borneo** Uncommon non-breeding visitor and passage migrant to coastal N Borneo (Sabah, Brunei, Sarawak, E Kalimantan) and N Natunas, September–April.

BROAD-BILLED SANDPIPER *Limicola falcinellus*

Identification 14–16 cm. Small wader with distinctive double supercilium and broad-based bill with downward-kinked tip. **Adult non-breeding** *sibirica* White split supercilium contrasts with dark eyestripe, upperparts greyish-brown with dark feather-centres and pale fringes, underparts white with breast streaked greyish-brown; iris dark brown, bill black, legs and feet dark greenish-grey; in flight narrow white wing-bar, blackish rump and uppertail-coverts bordered white. **Adult breeding** Crown blackish-brown with narrow line over sides of crown and broad long white supercilium ('split supercilium'), dark lores and ear-coverts, cheeks brownish-white finely streaked brown, neck and breast washed brown and streaked darker, sharply delineated from white belly, upperparts blackish-brown with broad whitish and rufous fringes, wing-coverts blackish fringed buffish-white. **Juvenile** As breeding adult but upperparts with paler fringing, breast washed buffish-brown with faint streaking. **Similar species** See Dunlin. **Habitat** Mudflats, coastal wetlands, at sea-level. **Behaviour** Often in mixed wader flocks especially with stints; probes in soft mud for small invertebrates, especially polychaete worms. **Voice** Flight call is a soft, buzzing *chrreet*. **Range & status** Breeds N Palearctic; migrates to S and E Africa, Middle East, Indian Subcontinent, SE Asia, Indonesia, Philippines, New Guinea, Australia. **Borneo** Uncommon non-breeding visitor and passage migrant to coastal N Borneo (Sabah, Brunei, Sarawak, E Kalimantan), August–March.

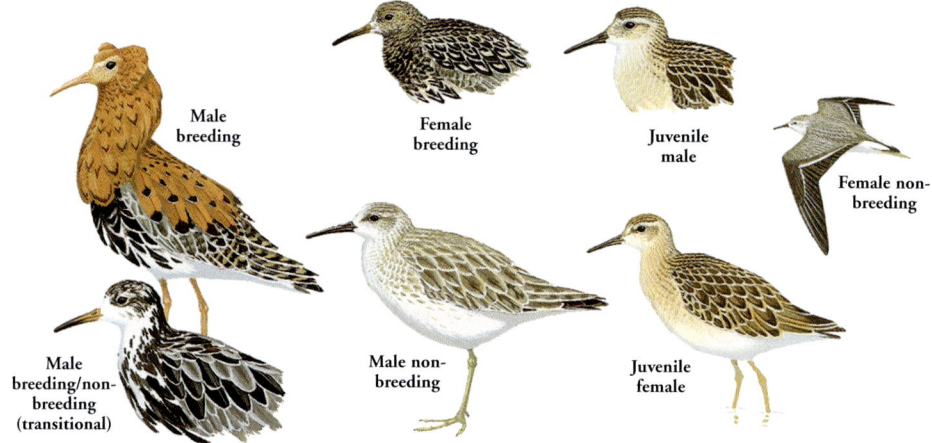

RUFF *Philomachus pugnax*

Identification Male 26–32 cm, female 20–25 cm. Monotypic. Medium-sized, markedly dimorphic wader with upright stance, relatively short, slightly decurved bill and longish neck and legs. **Adult non-breeding** Upperparts greyish-brown with buffish-white fringes, face whitish, underparts whitish with greyish mottling on breast; iris dark brown, bill grey, legs and feet yellowish; in flight narrow white wing-bar, broad white sides on dark grey rump. **Adult male breeding** Very striking and ornate head-tufts and neck-plumes variably barred or flecked buff, chestnut, black or white; upperparts black, brown, chestnut or white; bare facial skin dull yellow to brown, underparts dark contrasting with white lower belly and undertail-coverts, yellowish to pinkish-red with or without black tip, legs and feet reddish. **Adult female breeding** Smaller, lacks tufts and neck-plumes, upperparts dark brown with buff fringes, underparts whitish with black blotches on breast and flanks. **Juvenile** Face buff with pale throat, upperparts dark brown fringed buff, underparts buff grading into whitish belly. **Habitat** Mudflats, coastal wetlands, paddyfields, at sea-level. **Behaviour** Usually singly or in small groups in Borneo. **Voice** Usually quiet but may give a low *kuk* in flight. **Range & status** Breeds N Palearctic; migrates to S Europe, sub-Saharan Africa, Middle East, Indian Subcontinent, S China, SE Asia, Indonesia, Philippines, Australia. **Borneo** Rare non-breeding visitor and passage migrant to coastal N Borneo (Sabah, Brunei, Sarawak), August–April.

RUDDY TURNSTONE *Arenaria interpres*

Identification 21–26 cm. Stocky, short-legged wader with wedge-shaped bill and distinctive head pattern. **Adult male non-breeding** *interpres* Head brown streaked buffish, indistinct head pattern, upperparts dark brown with buffish fringing, breast-band blackish-brown; iris and bill black, legs and feet pink; in flight distinctive back pattern with white wing-bar, back and rump. **Adult male breeding** Top of crown streaky black and white, rest of head white with black line across forehead through eye continuing down side of neck, narrow black malar stripe, broad black breast-band extending to line up side of head, broad white collar, throat and rest of underparts white, upperparts rich chestnut boldly spotted and streaked black, tail black with white outer tips. **Adult female breeding** Duller head markings, more streaking on crown. **Juvenile** Like non-breeding adult but upperparts browner with buffish fringing. **Habitat** Sandy beaches, rocky foreshores, mudflats, estuaries, strictly coastal at sea-level. **Behaviour** Usually seen in small flocks; uses strong bill to turn over stones for small invertebrates. **Voice** A short, raspy *chit-kit*, also a staccato *tik-tik-tik-tik* (c.2.5–3 kHz). **Range & status** Breeds Arctic Circle; migrates to N and S America, W Europe, Africa, Middle East, Indian Subcontinent, E Asia, SE Asia, Indonesia, Philippines, New Guinea, SW Pacific,

Australia. **Borneo** Uncommon non-breeding visitor and passage migrant throughout including offshore islands, September–May; some birds remain throughout year.

RED-NECKED PHALAROPE *Phalaropus lobatus*

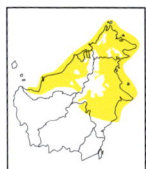

Identification 18–19 cm. Monotypic. Small graceful phalarope with needle-like bill and dark rump. **Adult non-breeding** Crown grey, face and neck white with conspicuous dark grey crescent-shaped eye-patch, underparts white with grey smudging on sides of breast and flanks, upperparts grey with white fringes; iris brown, bill black, legs and feet greyish-black; in flight dark upperwing with prominent narrow white wing-bar, dark grey rump and tail contrasts with white sides of rump. **Adult female breeding** Head and neck dark grey with white spot above eye, throat white with thin grey border, chestnut line from behind eye down sides of neck join chestnut upper breast, grey lower breast-band, rest of underparts white with broad dark grey smudges below breast-band, upperparts dark grey with prominent chestnut fringes on scapulars. **Adult male breeding** Like female but duller with less distinct markings, indistinct short whitish supercilium, upperparts more greyish-brown with more buff edging on mantle. **Juvenile** Crown and upperparts dark brown with rich buff fringes, underparts white with neck and breast washed pinkish-buff. **Similar species** Non-breeding Red Phalarope is larger, paler and plainer above; has shorter, deeper, broader bill with pale base. **Habitat** Open sea, estuaries, bays, rivers, paddyfields, to 1,200 m in Kelabit Highlands. **Behaviour** Gregarious on migration, often in large flocks; typically swims in tight circles pecking at small invertebrates. **Voice** Flight call is a rapidly repeated, squeaky *kik* (4.6 kHz), also a lower-pitched *kwik* (3 kHz). **Range & status** Breeds Arctic Circle; migrates to oceanic regions off S America, Middle East, C Indonesia. **Borneo** Locally common passage migrant to coastal and interior N Borneo (Sabah, Brunei, Sarawak, C and E Kalimantan), August–November, with occasional records March–early May.

RED PHALAROPE *Phalaropus fulicarius*

Identification 20–22 cm. Medium-sized phalarope with shortish, broad bill and chunky appearance. **Adult non-breeding** Head white with dark grey eye-patch and crown, underparts white with grey smudging on sides of breast and flanks, upperparts grey with narrow white fringes; iris dark brown, bill grey, legs and feet bluish-grey; in flight dark upperwing with prominent narrow white wing-bar, grey rump and tail contrasts with white sides of rump. **Adult female breeding** Brownish-black extends from chin through front of face over crown to hindneck, big white patch around eye to sides of face, sides of neck to underparts rich maroon-chestnut, upperparts blackish-brown with buffish-brown and whitish fringes. **Adult male breeding** Duller and paler, crown streaked chestnut. **Juvenile** Like non-breeding but upperparts blackish-brown with buffish-brown fringes, underparts white with neck and breast washed pinkish-buff. **Similar species** See Red-necked Phalarope. **Habitat** Open seas. **Behaviour** As Red-necked Phalarope. **Range & status** Breeds Arctic Circle; migrates to to oceanic regions off S America, Africa. **Borneo** Rare vagrant; one record from Sarawak.

GLAREOLIDAE: Pratincoles & coursers

Worldwide 17 species, 2 in Borneo. Small to medium-sized waders with long pointed wings and short decurved and pointed bills. The sexes are similar. The pratincoles are very agile aerial insectivores that hunt in flight. Most are gregarious and crepuscular.

ORIENTAL PRATINCOLE *Glareola maldivarum*

Identification 23–24 cm. Monotypic. **Adult breeding** Crown and upperparts greyish-brown, lores black, a thin black line from behind eye encircles buffish-yellow throat and cheeks, upper breast greyish-brown, lower breast washed rufous, belly and undertail white, long black primaries extend well beyond tail at rest; iris brown with narrow buffish-white eye-ring, bill black with bright red gape, legs and feet blackish-grey; in flight underwing chestnut with dark grey leading edge and greyish flight feathers; long, sickle-shaped wings, rump white, uppertail black and deeply forked. **Adult non-breeding** Lores paler, throat-band indistinct, red at base of bill duller. **Juvenile** Throat-band poorly defined or absent, upperparts mottled black and buff, tail less forked. **Habitat** In Borneo open grassland, heathland, paddyfields, pasture, airfields, to 1,200 m. **Behaviour** Crepuscular; gregarious; catches insects on wing, flight buoyant and direct; adopts an upright stance on ground. **Voice** A sharp, twittering *peet peet* (3 kHz), each note 0.1 s, usually given in flight. **Range & status** N and E Asia, Indian Subcontinent, migrating to SE Asia, Indonesia, Philippines, New Guinea, N Australia. **Borneo** Rare resident and locally common non-breeding visitor to Sabah, uncommon non-breeding visitor to Brunei (may be declining), Sarawak and Kalimantan, probably September–April. **Breeding** April–May; may not breed annually in Borneo, 1–2 brown-blotched eggs are laid in nest hidden in grass tussocks.

AUSTRALIAN PRATINCOLE *Stiltia isabella*

Identification 21–24 cm. Monotypic. **Adult breeding** Lores black, head and upperparts sandy-brown, throat whitish grading to pinkish-buff breast and chestnut belly, vent and undertail white, black primaries project much further than tail at rest; iris brown, bill red with black tip, legs and feet dark grey; in flight wings very long, upperwings sandy-brown contrasting with black primaries, underwing black with grey flight feathers, rump and short, square tail white with central black subterminal patch, legs project beyond tail. **Adult non-breeding** Duller, with duller black lores. **Juvenile** Lacks black lores, upperparts buff edged, bill all dark. **Habitat** Harvested paddyfields, bare pasture. **Behaviour** Migratory, movements influenced by rainfall in Australia; gregarious; crepuscular; feeds on insects, spiders and seeds, mostly taken from ground. **Voice** A pleasant, fluty *weeet-weet-wit* or *weeet-weet-wit-wit*, each note upslurred (2–3 kHz), the last note soft and short, given in flight. Alarm calls are short, sharp twitters (3.5 kHz). **Range & status** Australia, migrating to New Guinea, E Indonesia. **Borneo** Rare non-breeding vagrant to west coast of Sabah and W Sarawak; an old record from S Kalimantan.

STERCORARIIDAE: Skuas & jaegers

Worldwide 7 species, 2 in Borneo. Medium-sized to large, dark gull-like predatory and piratic seabirds with heavy hooked bill, long wings, and short tail with elongated central feathers. Powerful flyers and aggressive hunters and kleptoparasites. Most are long-distance migrants. Sexes are similar but the female is usually larger.

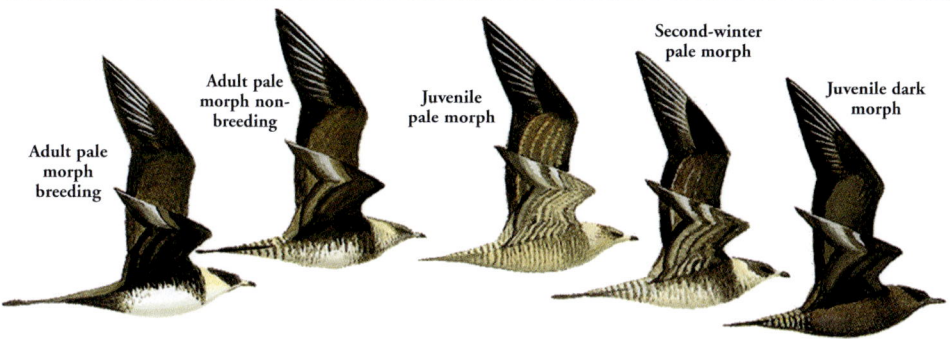

POMARINE JAEGER *Stercorarius pomarinus*

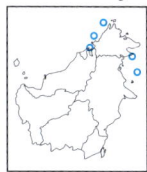

Identification 48–61 cm. Monotypic. Large, heavily built seabird with blackish-brown plumage, whitish belly, broad yellowish collar and distinctive elongated twisted tail feathers. **Adult breeding pale morph** Sooty-black cap from chin to nape, broad whitish collar with yellowish wash on sides of neck, upperparts blackish-brown, underparts buffish-white with mottled brown breast-band, undertail-coverts blackish-brown, tail blackish-brown with two elongated broad central tail feathers twisted at tip; in flight wings blackish-brown with base of primaries white; iris brown, bill grey with dark tip, legs and feet greyish-black. **Adult non-breeding pale morph** As breeding but head browner, throat and collar mottled brownish, tail-coverts barred brown and whitish, central tail feathers shorter. **Juvenile pale morph** Head brownish with dark face, upperparts brownish with buff edging, underwing and uppertail-coverts barred, double pale patch on underside of primaries, tail feathers only slightly elongated. **Adult dark morph** Blackish-brown overall with pale whitish base of primaries. **Similar species** Parasitic Jaeger is smaller, slenderer, has less defined cap, paler yellowish collar, and pointed tail-streamers. **Habitat** Open seas, occasionally inshore. **Behaviour** Usually solitary; slow, steady gull-like flight; pursues gulls and terns to force them to drop food which it retrieves in mid-air or from water. **Range & status** Breeds Arctic Circle, migrating south to Pacific, Atlantic and Indian Oceans. **Borneo** Rare passage migrant to N Borneo with few records from Sabah, Brunei, E Kalimantan.

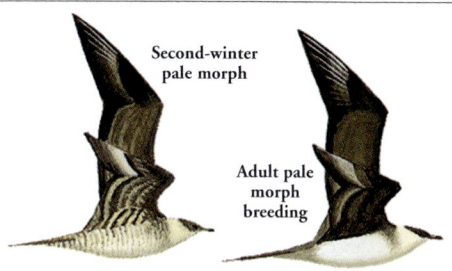

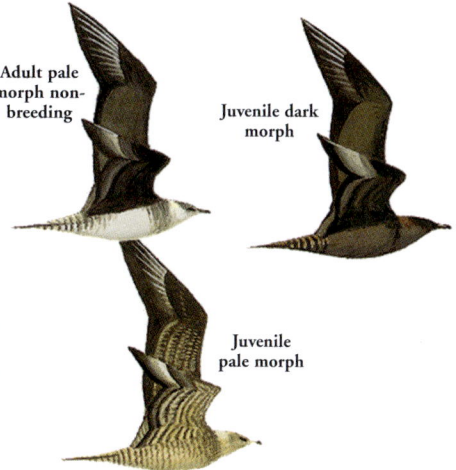

PARASITIC JAEGER *Stercorarius parasiticus*

Identification 42–54 cm. Monotypic. Medium-sized, gull-like seabird with pointed elongated central tail-streamers. **Adult breeding pale morph** Brownish cap from chin to nape, broad white collar with pale yellowish wash, upperparts brown, underparts white with grey undertail-coverts and variable breast-band, tail brown with pointed central tail feathers; in flight wings brown with whitish base to primaries; iris brown, bill greyish-black, legs and feet greyish-black. **Adult non-breeding pale morph** As breeding adult but less defined cap, dusky face and neck, upperparts edged buff, tail-coverts barred brown and white. **Juvenile pale morph** Variable but head and underparts usually brownish. **Adult dark morph** White in plumage replaced by dark brown. **Similar species** See Pomarine Jaeger. **Habitat** Open ocean, occasionally inshore. **Behaviour** Usually solitary; flight faster and more falcon-like than Pomarine Jaeger; robs gulls and terns in similar fashion. **Range & status** Breeds Arctic Circle, migrating south to Pacific, Atlantic and Indian Oceans. **Borneo** Vagrant; one record each from Sabah and Sarawak.

STERNIDAE: Terns

Worldwide 45 species, 16 in Borneo. Delicate seabirds with narrow, pointed wings and slender, pointed bill. Typically the plumage is mostly white with grey and black on the back and wings, often with brightly coloured red or yellow bill. Many have black on the crown during the breeding season. Flight is graceful and buoyant, they actively fish by plunge-diving or picking from the water surface. Many are migratory. Sexes are similar. Highly gregarious.

BROWN NODDY *Anous stolidus*

LIBARAN ISLAND 5/6/10

Identification 38–45 cm. Dark brown tern with whitish cap and long, wedge-shaped tail. **Adult** *pileatus* All dark brown with frosty white forehead and crown sharply demarcated from lores and merging into greyer nape; in flight paler brown band across upperwing-coverts, paler underwings; iris dark brown with broken white eye-ring, bill black, legs and feet dark brown. **Juvenile** Upperparts edged buff, browner on forecrown. **Similar species** See Black Noddy. **Habitat** Open seas, remote islets, at sea-level. **Voice** A harsh *karrk*. **Range & status** Tropical Pacific, Indian and Atlantic Oceans. **Borneo** Uncommon vagrant, with records from N Borneo (Sabah, Brunei, Sarawak and E Kalimantan) and offshore islands.

BLACK NODDY *Anous minutus*

Identification 35–39 cm. Blackish tern with whitish cap and long, slender bill. **Adult** *worcesteri* All blackish-brown with frosty white forehead and crown sharply demarcated from dark lores and merging into greyer nape; in flight wings uniform darker blackish-brown; iris dark brown with broken white eye-ring, bill and legs black. **Juvenile** Like adult but white restricted to forehead, wings edged buff. **Similar species** Brown Noddy is larger, with shorter bill, browner plumage, and longer tail; in flight wings paler. **Habitat** Open seas, offshore islands, at sea-level. **Behaviour** Flies with rapid wing-beats; nests in trees. **Voice** A nasal, rattling *chrrr…* **Range & status** Tropical Pacific and Atlantic Oceans. **Borneo** Rare vagrant, with two records from Sabah and Sarawak.

CASPIAN TERN *Hydroprogne caspia*

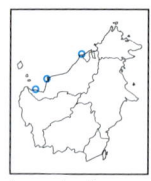

Identification 48–55 cm. Monotypic. Largest tern with huge black-tipped red bill. **Adult breeding** Black cap and mask with shaggy crest on nape, face and sides of neck white, back and wings pale grey with white rump and blackish primaries, short forked tail pale grey, underparts white, primaries extend well beyond tail at rest; in flight underwings white with blackish outer primaries; iris black, bill red with black tip, legs and feet black. **Adult non-breeding** Forehead and crown finely streaked white. **First winter** Like non-breeding adult but upperparts mottled brownish, bill duller red. **Habitat** Coastal mudflats and sandbars, estuaries, at sea-level. **Behaviour** Buoyant, strong flight with shallow wing-beats; plunges into water for small fish from 3–15 m above surface. **Voice** A deep, hoarse *kaaa*. **Range & status** N America, Europe, Africa, continental Asia, Indian Subcontinent, SE Asia, Australia, New Zealand. **Borneo** Rare vagrant with few records from Brunei and Sarawak.

LESSER CRESTED TERN *Thalasseus bengalensis*

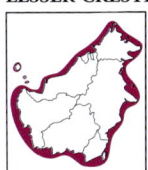

Identification 35–40 cm. **Adult breeding *bengalensis*** Black cap with shaggy crest on nape, face and neck white, rest of upperparts pale grey, underparts white; in flight underwing white with tips of primaries greyer; bill bright orange. **Adult non-breeding** Like non-breeding adult but forehead and crown white, black hindcrown streaked whitish, bill duller. **First winter** Outer primaries brown, wing-coverts with brown edging, bill duller. **Juvenile** Mantle and upperwing-coverts edged brown; bill greyish-yellow. **Similar species** Smaller than Great Crested Tern with more slender orange bill, paler grey upperparts and less streaking on hindcrown in non-breeding plumage. **Habitat** Open seas, sandy beaches, mudflats, estuaries. **Behaviour** More active than Great Crested Tern; graceful, buoyant flight. **Voice** A raspy, burring *kek'krrrk'krrrk'krrk...* **Range & status** NW Africa, Mediterranean Sea, Indian and SW Pacific oceans, Australia. **Borneo** Uncommon non-breeding visitor throughout, recorded at all times of year.

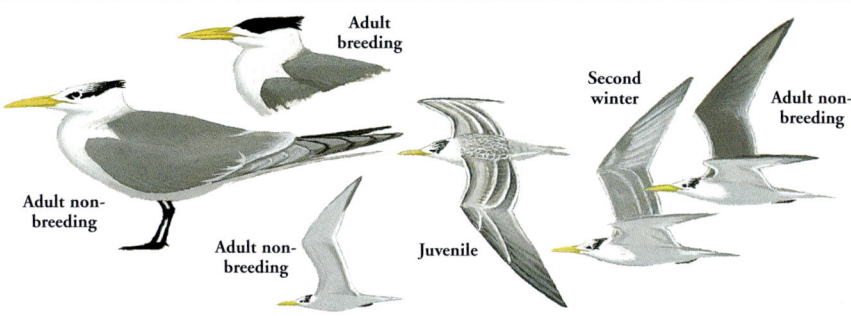

GREAT CRESTED TERN *Thalasseus bergii*

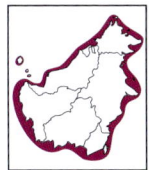

Identification 43–53 cm. Large, stocky tern with robust yellowish bill and dark grey upperparts. **Adult breeding *cristata*** Forehead white, cap black with shaggy crest on nape, face and sides of neck white, upperparts grey with paler rump, underparts white; in flight underwing white with dark grey tips on outer primaries; bill yellowish to greenish-yellow. **Adult non-breeding** Forehead to crown white, hindcrown to nape black with whitish streaks; bill duller. **Juvenile** Bill duller than non-breeding adult, upperparts brownish with whitish fringes, darker centres on wings, tail darker. **First winter** Like juvenile but mantle and scapulars uniform grey. **Similar species** See Lesser Crested Tern. **Habitat** Open seas, coastal beaches, mudflats, estuaries, offshore islands, at sea-level. **Behaviour** Flies rapidly with deep, slow wing-beats; plunge-dives, often seen sitting on driftwood and posts in shallow estuaries. **Voice** A raspy *krrraak*. **Range & status** S and E Africa, Madagascar, Indian Ocean, Middle East, Indian Subcontinent, E and SE Asia, Indonesia, Philippines, New Guinea, SW Pacific, Australia. **Borneo** Common non-breeding visitor throughout, with records from all times of year.

CHINESE CRESTED TERN *Thalasseus bernsteini*

Identification 38–43 cm. Monotypic. **Adult breeding** Black cap with shaggy crest on nape, upperparts pale grey with black primaries; in flight upperwing pale grey with contrasting blackish outer primaries; bill yellow with black tip. **Adult non-breeding** Forehead to forecrown white, hindcrown to nape streaked whitish. **Juvenile** Undescribed. **Similar species** Intermediate in size between Lesser and Great Crested Terns; slender yellow bill with black tip is diagnostic. **Habitat** Open seas, coastal areas, at sea-level. **Range & status** Breeds Taiwan and E China; migrates to Philippines. Critically Endangered. **Borneo** Very rare non-breeding visitor with three records from Sarawak; has not been reliably recorded from Borneo since 1913.

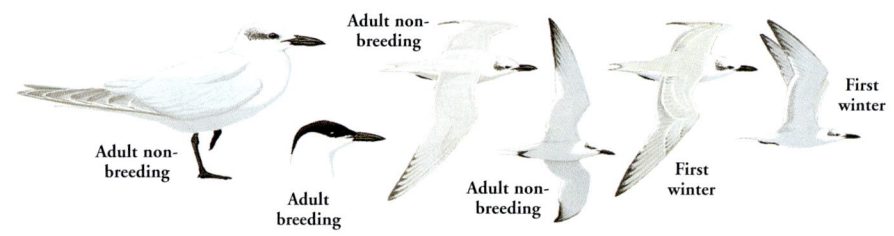

GULL-BILLED TERN *Gelochelidon nilotica*

Identification 35–43 cm. Large tern with distinctive heavy, black gull-like bill and shallow-forked tail. **Adult non-breeding** *addenda* Head white with dusky black mask extending to sides of face, upperparts pale grey, rump and shallow-forked tail silvery-grey, underparts white; iris dark brown, bill and legs black. **Adult breeding** As non-breeding adult but full black cap contrasts with white throat and sides of face. **Juvenile** As non-breeding adult but face-mask brownish, upperparts fringed with brown. **Habitat** Coasts, estuaries, marshes, lakes, mudflats, paddyfields at sea-level. **Behaviour** Usually hawks low over water, plucks prey from surface, seldom plunges. **Voice** Utters nasal *kek-kek* in flight. **Range & status** Palearctic, Africa, Indian Subcontinent, N & E Asia, SE Asia, Indonesia, Philippines, New Guinea, Australia, N & S America. **Borneo** Common non-breeding visitor and passage migrant throughout, including Natunas, September–June.

ROSEATE TERN *Sterna dougallii*

Identification 33–43 cm. **Adult breeding** *bangsi* Glossy black cap, rest of head white, upperparts pale grey, primaries darker, underparts often with pinkish wash, tail extends well beyond wings when perched; in flight dark leading edge to outer wing, very long tail-streamers; iris black, long slender bill black with red basal half, legs and feet dark red. **Adult non-breeding** As breeding adult but forehead white, tail-streamers shorter; bill all blackish, legs and feet brownish-orange. **Juvenile** Cap duller, upperparts grey with brownish scaling, tail lacks streamers. **First winter** Like non-breeding adult but in flight shows darker leading edge on outer wing, carpal bar on upperwing. **Similar species** In non-breeding plumage, paler upperparts and whiter underwing separate this species from Common Tern. **Habitat** Open seas, beaches, rocky islets, mudflats, at sea-level. **Behaviour** Flies gracefully with shallow, buoyant wing-beats. **Voice** A grating *karrk* and soft *chi-wip*. **Range & status** Coastal eastern N America, W Europe, Middle East, S and E Africa, Madagascar, Indian Ocean, Indian Subcontinent, E and SE Asia, Indonesia, Philippines, New Guinea, Australia, SW Pacific. **Borneo** Uncommon non-breeding visitor to N Borneo (Sabah, Brunei, Sarawak and E Kalimantan), recorded from S Kalimantan.

BLACK-NAPED TERN *Sterna sumatrana*

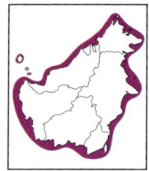

Identification 30–32 cm. Small, dainty tern with conspicuous black nape-band and long, pointed, deeply forked tail. **Adult breeding** *sumatrana* Head white with black band from eye joining on nape, upperparts pale grey, long deeply forked tail white, underparts white; in flight black outer edge on outer primaries; bare parts black. **Adult non-breeding** Dark streaks on hindcrown. **Juvenile** Like non-breeding adult but crown streaked brownish, upperparts with brownish centres; bill dusky yellow. **Similar species** Adult non-breeding Roseate Tern has different cap pattern, darker upperparts and darker grey primaries. **Habitat** Rocky islets, beaches, rarely seen in remote seas. **Behaviour** Often perches on lone offshore rocks, posts or buoys. **Voice** A repeated, hoarse *gee gee…* **Range & status** Indian Ocean, E and SE Asia, Indonesia, Philippines, New Guinea, SW Pacific, N Australia. **Borneo** Locally common coastal resident throughout, including offshore islands. **Breeding** April–July; two pale olive-buff eggs with heavy brown spots are laid on bare rock or small tuft of grass.

COMMON TERN *Sterna hirundo*

Identification 32–38 cm. Medium-sized tern with long wings and long, deeply forked tail. **Adult breeding *longipennis*** Black cap, mantle and wings pale grey, rump and tail white with black outer webs, underparts white with greyish wash; at rest wing-tips and tail about equal length; in flight underwing white with black tips; iris black, bill black, legs and feet blackish. **Adult non-breeding** Forehead white, crown to nape black with whitish streaks. **Juvenile** Upperparts with brownish fringes; bill with dark orange base, tail shorter. **Habitat** Open seas, beaches, estuaries, at sea-level. **Behaviour** Buoyant flight; hovers and plunge-dives. **Voice** A harsh, rapidly repeated *kee kee…* or *kik-kik-kik…* **Range & status** Breeds Palearctic, NW Africa, N India, Tibet, N America, Carribean; migrates to Southern Hemisphere. **Borneo** Uncommon to rare non-breeding visitor and passage migrant throughout, September–May.

SOOTY TERN *Onychoprion fuscatus*

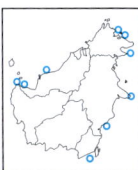

Identification 42–45 cm. Large tern with black upperparts and white forehead. **Adult breeding *nubilosa*** Forehead white extending over eye, black cap with thin black line from lores through eye, sides of face and neck white, upperparts dark blackish-grey with white outer tail feathers, underparts white; in flight underwing white with dark trailing edge, undertail white; bare parts black. **Adult non-breeding** More extensive white on forehead. **Juvenile** Head blackish-brown, upperparts blackish-brown with buff fringes, underparts blackish with whitish-grey undertail-coverts. **Similar species** See Bridled Tern. **Habitat** Opens seas, rocky islets, at sea-level. **Behaviour** Gregarious; more pelagic than Bridled Tern; rarely perches on floating debris; flies with stiff wing-beats. **Voice** A repeated, hoarse *kaa kaa…* and nasal *ker-wacky-wack.* **Range & status** Widespread throughout tropical and subtropical oceans. **Borneo** Uncommon vagrant to Sarawak, Sabah and SE coastal Kalimantan (East and South).

BRIDLED TERN *Onychoprion anaethetus*

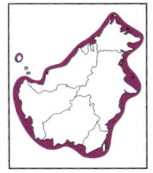

Identification 35–38 cm. Medium-sized tern with dark upperparts and white forehead and eyebrow. **Adult breeding *anaethetus*** Forehead and supercilium white, black cap with black line from lores through eye, sides of face and neck white extending to thin nuchal band, upperparts dark brownish-grey with white outer tail feathers, underparts white; in flight underwing white with dark trailing edge, undertail white; bare parts black. **Adult non-breeding** More extensive white on forehead. **Juvenile** Upperparts brown with buffish fringes. **Similar species** Sooty Tern is larger, has less extensive white over eye, upperparts blacker, lacks nuchal band. **Habitat** Open seas, rocky islets. **Behaviour** Favours offshore waters; swift, graceful flight low over water, skimming prey from surface; often perches on floating debris. **Voice** Yapping *wep wep…* **Range & status** W and E Africa, Indian Ocean, Indian Subcontinent, E and SE Asia, Indonesia, Philippines, Australia, SW Pacific, Carribean, C and northern S America. **Borneo** Uncommon resident throughout, including offshore islands. **Breeding** April–August; lays single pale buff egg with scattered dark spots in vegetation near shoreline.

ALEUTIAN TERN *Onychoprion aleuticus*

Identification 32–34 cm. Monotypic. **Adult breeding** Forehead white, crown and nape black, lores black, rump and tail white contrasting with dark grey upperparts and upper wing, underparts grey, tail deeply forked; in flight dark band on trailing edge of secondaries on underwing; bare parts black. **Adult non-breeding** More extensive white forehead and crown, black nape with whitish streaking, lores white, underparts white. **Juvenile/first winter** Forehead and cap duller and greyish-brown, upperparts greyish-brown with buff scaling, tail less deeply forked. **Second winter** As adult non-breeding but with dark bars on lesser coverts and darks tips to upper surface of secondaries. **Similar species** In non-breeding plumage, Common and Roseate Terns lack whitish crown and dark trailing edge to secondaries on underwing. **Habitat** Open seas. **Behaviour** Flies high over water with light, agile wing-beats. **Voice** A sharp *chit*. **Range & status** Breeds Bering Sea and NW coast of N America, migrates to Japan, coastal E Asia and SE Asia, Philippines, Indonesia. **Borneo** Rare non-breeding visitor to Sarawak (recorded in April from Pulau Bruit).

LITTLE TERN *Sternula albifrons*

Identification 22–28 cm. Small, delicate long-billed tern with short tail. **Adult breeding** *sinensis* Forehead white extending over eye, black cap with broad black line through eye to bill, sides of face and neck white, upperparts pale grey with white rump and tail, underparts white; in flight wings pale grey with blackish outer primaries; iris black, bill yellow with black tip, legs and feet yellow. **Adult non-breeding** Crown and lores white, hindcrown with whitish streaking, line from eye to nape black; bill and legs black. **Juvenile** Like non-breeding adult but upperparts edged brown; in flight dark leading edge to upperwing. **Habitat** Sandy beaches, mudflats, estuaries, bays. **Behaviour** Flies with rapid wing-beats; hovers and plunge-dives. **Voice** A high-pitched, repeated *kip kip...* uttered in flight. **Range & status** Africa, Europe, Middle East, Indian Ocean, Indian Subcontinent, E Asia, SE Asia, Indonesia, Philippines, SW Pacific, Australia, N & S America, Carribean. **Borneo** Uncommon non-breeding visitor throughout, including N Natunas, June–September, and rare resident Brunei and E Kalimantan. **Breeding** May–October; nest consists of a few loose sticks in thorny vegetation.

WHISKERED TERN *Chlidonias hybrida*

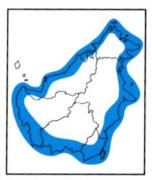

Identification 25–26 cm. **Adult non-breeding** *javanicus* Forehead white, crown streaked blackish, black streak through eye extends to black nape, upperparts pale grey, underparts white; iris black, bill black, legs and feet dark reddish. **Adult breeding** Black cap contrasts with white throat and sides of head, throat and rest of underparts dark grey, upperparts grey; bill and legs red. **Juvenile** Like non-breeding adult but back brown with blackish fringes. **Similar species** See White-winged Tern. **Habitat** Coastal and inland freshwater swamps, marshes and wetlands, at sea-level. **Behaviour** Usually seen in flocks foraging low over water. **Voice** A short, harsh *krek* usually uttered in flight. **Range & status** Europe, Africa, Middle East, Indian Subcontinent, N and E Asia, SE Asia, Australia. **Borneo** Uncommon non-breeding visitor throughout, September–May, with occasional records all year.

WHITE-WINGED TERN *Chlidonias leucopterus*

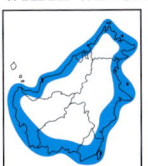

Identification 22–24 cm. Monotypic. Small tern with very shallowly forked, short tail and distinctive breeding plumage. **Adult non-breeding** Forehead and lores white, indistinct black crown extends to ear-coverts forming roundish ear-patch (sometimes isolated), sides of neck white, upperparts grey with white rump to tail, underparts white; bill black, legs and feet pinkish-black. **Adult breeding** Head and upperparts black with white rump and uppertail, wings grey with whitish shoulder, underparts black with contrasting white tail; in flight upperwing pale grey with darker trailing edge, black underwing-coverts with contrasting white flight feathers; iris black, bill and legs red. **Juvenile** Like non-breeding adult but upperparts dark brown with darker fringes, tail pale grey. **Similar species** Non-breeding Whiskered Tern lacks white rump, has different head pattern and longer, more forked tail. **Habitat** Beaches, estuaries, rivers, swamps, paddyfields, to 1,100 m in Kelabit Highlands. **Behaviour** Fluttering flight; often observed with Whiskered Tern; dips and skims, picking food off surface. **Voice** A buzzing, high-pitched *krip krip…* **Range & status** Breeds W and C Palearctic, E Asia; migrates to Africa, Indian Subcontinent, SE Asia, Australia. **Borneo** Common non-breeding visitor and passage migrant throughout, late August–May.

LARIDAE: Gulls

Worldwide c.53 species, 1 in Borneo. A widespread group of long-winged waterbirds with heavy bill, short neck, heavy body and short legs. Most are mainly white with grey and black in the wings. Sexes are similar but there is much variation due to season and age. Opportunistic, generalist feeders, gregarious and noisy.

BLACK-HEADED GULL *Chroicocephalus ridibundus*

Identification 35–39 cm. Monotypic. **Adult non-breeding** Head and underparts white with black spot behind eye and dark smudges on head, upperparts pale grey with black wing-tips; in flight white leading edge on outer upperwing, black tips on primaries; iris brown, bill red with black tip, legs and feet dark red. **Adult breeding** As non-breeding adult but shows blackish-brown hood, brighter bare parts. **First winter** Like non-breeding adult but bill paler, legs and feet duller red, wing-coverts mottled greyish-brown, blackish band on flight feathers, black subterminal tail-band. **Habitat** Coastal areas, farmland, urban areas, at sea-level. **Voice** Call is a high-pitched *kraah*. **Range & status** Breeds Palearctic, migrates to N Africa, Middle East, Indian Subcontinent, E Asia, Philippines, N America. **Borneo** Uncommon non-breeding visitor to Sabah, Brunei and Sarawak, November–February.

COLUMBIDAE: Pigeons & doves

Worldwide c.308 species, 21 in Borneo. A large, diverse family of mostly forest-dwelling birds with delicate bill, small head and robust body. Strong, fast fliers, often noisy in flight. All feed on grain or fruit. Usually highly vocal with distinctive coo-ing calls. Mostly the sexes are similar. The nest is usually a flimsy collection of twigs.

LIBARAN ISLAND   4/6/10

ROCK PIGEON *Columba livia*

Identification 31–34 cm. **Adult** Highly variable but generally grey with purple and green metallic gloss on neck, two black wing-bars and rump white or grey, tail-tip black; iris brown, bill black, legs and feet red. **Juvenile** Duller and browner, lacks metallic gloss on neck, wings greyish-brown. **Habitat** Cities, towns, parks, cultivated areas. **Behaviour** Gregarious, often forages on ground. **Voice** Soft cooing. **Range & status** Introduced; common resident around human habitation throughout.

Typical adult

Typical juvenile

Typical adult

Adult feral variants

SILVERY WOODPIGEON *Columba argentina*

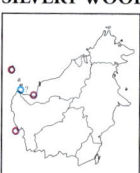

Identification 35–38 cm. Monotypic. Large pale grey pigeon with white uppertail contrasting with broad black terminal band. **Adult male** Overall pale silvery-grey, pale green wash on nape, uppertail-coverts white, tail white at base with terminal two-thirds black, flight feathers black; in flight underwing-coverts creamy-white with black flight feathers; iris red to yellow, eye-ring red, bill pale grey with reddish-brown base and cere, legs and feet grey. **Adult female** Similar to male but darker silvery-grey. **Similar species** Pied Imperial-pigeon is whiter, although juveniles often greyish; has more narrow black terminal band on tail, wedge-shaped on undertail; lacks any red on face; great care should be taken to distinguish these two species. **Habitat** Mangroves and woodlands of small islands. **Behaviour** Almost unknown; presumably wanders widely; may associate with Pied Imperial-pigeon. **Voice** Unknown. **Range & status** Offshore islands of Thai-Malay Peninsula, Sumatra.

Male

Critically Endangered. **Borneo** Very rare resident in W Sarawak and W Kalimantan, also N Natunas and Karimata Island. A recent sighting from Talang Talang island (W Sarawak) is unconfirmed; no reliable records since 1931. **Breeding** Said to be similar to Pied Imperial-pigeon but with larger, chalkier eggs.

METALLIC PIGEON *Columba vitiensis*

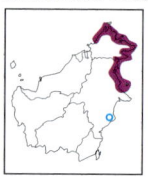

Identification 37–41 cm. Large, glossy metallic dark pigeon. **Adult** *griseogularis* Crown metallic purple with green gloss, cheeks and throat bluish-grey not strongly contrasting with head and breast, upperparts iridescent greyish-black with green and purple gloss, tail black, underparts greyish-black with weak purple and green gloss, underwings iridescent greyish-black with green gloss; iris orange to red, eye-ring dark red, bill red with yellow tip, legs and feet pink. **Juvenile** Duller with much reduced iridescence. **Adult** *anthracina* Smaller, underparts lack purple tinge, cheeks and throat dark grey not contrasting with head and underparts. **Habitat** In Borneo woodlands, gardens and plantations of small offshore islands. Some records from mangroves and riverine primary forest. **Behaviour** Not well known in Borneo; shy; solitary or in pairs, sometimes recorded in small groups; feeds on fruits and buds; forages in trees and bushes; nomadic. **Voice** Possibly not recorded from Borneo; from Philippines a deep *wuuuu woooo*, the first note upwardly inflected, the second level and lower pitched. **Range & status** Philippines (*griseogularis* and

Adult *griseogularis*

anthracina), E Indonesia, New Guinea, SW Pacific islands. **Borneo** Race *griseogularis* uncommon to rare resident on small islands of NE Borneo (Bohey Dulang, Sipadan, Maratuas) and one record from Mahakam River, E Kalimantan, *anthracina* uncommon resident on small islands off W Sabah (Mantanani, Tiga). **Breeding** Undescribed in Borneo; courtship behaviour observed in September.

RUDDY CUCKOO-DOVE *Macropygia emiliana*

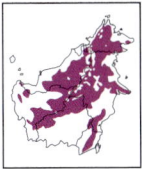

Identification 33–39 cm. Large, long-tailed, reddish-brown dove. **Adult male *borneensis*** (endemic subspecies) Crown dark chestnut contrasting with paler cheeks and throat, hindneck and mantle brown with green iridescence, wings dark brown speckled black, underparts reddish-brown with narrow black barring and purple iridescence, tail brown with black outer feathers; iris red, eye-ring pale blue, bill fleshy-brown, legs and feet red. **Adult female** Darker, lacks iridescence, hindneck chestnut barred black, throat pale buff with scaly black patch on lower throat. **Juvenile** Like female but more strongly barred. **Similar species** Little Cuckoo-dove smaller, head and underparts brighter cinnamon, breast mottled and spotted buff and black. **Habitat** Primary hill to lower montane forest, 300–1,550 m. **Behaviour** Slope specialist, usually found singly or in pairs; arboreal and frugivorous, foraging in canopy; resembles cuckoo or sparrowhawk in flight with powerful, direct wing-beats. **Voice** A loud, mournful *tok wao* or *wa-oo* repeated. **Range & status** Sumatra, Java, Lesser Sundas. **Borneo** Locally uncommon resident throughout. **Breeding** A nest consisting of sparse platform of twigs with one white egg was found low to ground in ferns in January.

LITTLE CUCKOO-DOVE *Macropygia ruficeps*

Identification 27–30 cm. Small, all-rufous dove with prominent black spotting on breast. **Adult male *nana*** (endemic subspecies) Head cinnamon, hindneck cinnamon with green and purple gloss, upperparts dark-brown with rufous fringes on wing-coverts, breast reddish-brown with variable amount of black and buff spotting, belly golden-brown; iris bluish-white, bill dark brown with black tip, legs and feet pinkish-red. **Adult female** Paler, lacks iridescence, breast heavily mottled black; bill black, legs and feet dull red. **Juvenile** Like female but redder, heavily barred and spotted overall. **Similar species** See Ruddy Cuckoo-dove. **Habitat** Primary and secondary forest, favouring lower montane forest edges, but recorded in Borneo from sea-level to 3,000 m. Has also been recorded on some offshore islands. **Behaviour** Eats small fruits and seeds; feeds on ground or forages in mid-storey and below canopy; breeds and roosts in montane areas but travels widely to lower elevations to feed; resembles cuckoo or sparrowhawk in flight with powerful, direct wing-beats. **Voice** A distinctive, buoyant *wook wook wook…*, each note brief and upslurred (0.1 s, 0.6–1 kHz), rapidly repeated every c.0.3 s. **Range & status** SE Asia, Thai-Malay Peninsula, Indonesia. **Borneo** Locally common to abundant resident throughout. **Breeding** January–October; lays 1–2 oval white eggs on flimsy platform of twigs and grass in thick low vegetation.

SPOTTED DOVE *Streptopelia chinensis*

Identification 31–33 cm. Medium-sized, slender dove with conspicuous white-spotted black collar and broad white outer tail-tips, notable in flight. **Adult *tigrina*** Head pale grey with narrow black line from gape to eye, nuchal collar black with white spots, throat and breast pinkish-brown fading into buffish-grey belly, undertail white, upperparts scalloped brown and buff, outer wing-coverts grey, graduated tail brown with black outer feathers broadly tipped white; in flight conspicuous white outer tips on long graduated tail, broad pale bar on wing-coverts contrasts with blackish flight feathers; iris orange, bill black, legs and feet pinkish-red. **Juvenile** Browner, nuchal collar unspotted dark grey, upperparts grey-brown, iris yellowish-brown. **Similar species** See Island Collared-dove. **Habitat** Secondary forest, open woodlands, cultivated areas, parks, gardens, to 1,000 m. **Behaviour** Mostly feeds on seeds, foraging on ground; usually in pairs or small groups. **Voice** A mellow *ku koo-koor* delivered on level pitch (c.7 kHz), each phrase c.1 s, repeated every 2 s or so. **Range & status** Indian Subcontinent, China, SE Asia, Philippines, Indonesia. **Borneo** Common resident throughout. **Breeding** Year-round; lays two white eggs on flimsy platform of twigs balanced on fork of tree.

ISLAND COLLARED-DOVE *Streptopelia bitorquata*

Identification 30–33 cm. Slender, medium-sized dove with distinct plain grey collar and plain brown upperparts. **Adult** *dussumieri* Head pale grey, dark grey nuchal collar with slight green gloss, below collar orange-brown, upperparts plain brown with grey outer wing-coverts, tail dark brown with outer feathers black and white, breast pinkish-brown, belly and undertail-coverts creamy-white; iris brown, bill dark grey, legs and feet dark red. **Juvenile** Like adult but paler with indistinct collar. **Similar species** Spotted Dove has broad white tips on outer tail feathers, distinct white spots on nuchal collar and dark streaks on upperparts. **Habitat** Mangroves, open woodland, cultivated areas generally in

lowlands to 800 m. **Behaviour** Mostly feeds on seeds, typically forages on ground; solitary or in pairs. **Voice** A mournful *tuk mm mm* and repeated, coarse *kook-koo-koo* (extralimital). **Range & status** Java and Bali, Lesser Sundas, Philippines. **Borneo** Rare vagrant; records from Sabah (Sandakan and off Semporna) and E Kalimantan (Kutai).

EMERALD DOVE *Chalcophaps indica*

Identification 23–27 cm. Medium-sized purplish-brown terrestrial dove with distinctive metallic green wings and pale cap. **Adult male** *indica* Forehead white blending into greyish-white crown, face and neck to breast purplish-brown, belly purplish-grey, mantle and wing-coverts iridescent bronze-green with small white patch on shoulder, lower back and rump greyish-black with two pale grey bars, flight feathers and tail grey-black; in flight underwing chestnut; iris brown, bill crimson, legs and feet pink. **Adult female** Like adult male but duller and browner, lacks white shoulder-patch, crown purplish-brown. **Juvenile** Head and underparts barred brown and buffish-rufous, wings barred dark brown and rufous with small amount of green on coverts. **Habitat** Primary and secondary lowland dipterocarp and peatswamp forest, mangroves, plantations, gardens, to 1,450 m. **Behaviour** Usually in pairs; forages on ground feeding on seeds, fallen fruit and small invertebrates; flies low, very fast and direct. **Voice** A slow, low-pitched, mournful *wup woooo*, the first note very short (0.02 s), the second long (0.9 s) delivered on same pitch (0.4 kHz); each phrase repeated every c.2 s. **Range & status** Indian Subcontinent, SE Asia,

Philippines, Indonesia. **Borneo** Locally common resident throughout, including offshore islands. **Breeding** December–March; lays two creamy-white eggs. **Note** Australasian form from Timor, New Guinea, Australia, SW Pacific now treated as distinct species, Green-winged Dove *C. chrysochlora*.

NICOBAR PIGEON *Caloenas nicobarica*

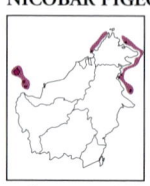

Identification 32–35 cm. Unusual, squat pigeon with spectacular glossy green and blue plumage and cape of long lanceolate feathers. **Adult male** *nicobarica* Head dark grey, nape and neck feathers highly elongated with green-and-blue iridescence, upperparts metallic bronzy-green and -blue, underparts dark grey with green-and-blue gloss, very short white tail conspicuous in flight; iris grey, bill black with enlarged knob-like greyish-black cere, legs and feet dark purplish-red to pink. **Adult female** Like male but shorter neck feathers, reduced cere, underparts browner. **Juvenile** Lacks hackles and iridescence, tail grey. **Habitat** Restricted to small forested offshore islands where it occurs in mangroves, coastal woodland, and lowland primary and secondary forest. **Behaviour** Usually solitary or in pairs; sparsely distributed outside breeding season, when large groups are sometimes reported; shy and easily flushed; forages on ground for fruit and seed; roosts in trees; highly nomadic, travelling long distances between islands following fruiting of trees. **Voice** Usually silent, but soft grunts and cooing have been reported. **Range & status** Andaman and Nicobar Islands, Philippines, Indonesia, offshore islands of New Guinea, Solomon Islands. **Borneo**

Uncommon resident on offshore islands of Sabah, Brunei and E Kalimantan (Maratuas); also Anambas, Natunas, and Tambelan Islands. **Breeding** Not described in Borneo; elsewhere lays one white egg on platform of sticks in tree 3–8 m above ground.

ZEBRA DOVE *Geopelia striata*

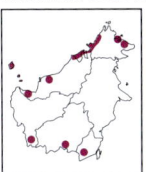

Identification 21 cm. Monotypic. Small, long-tailed, conspicuously barred dove. **Adult male** Face and throat bluish-grey, crown and nape greyish-brown, hindneck to sides of breast and flanks finely barred grey and black, centre of breast pinkish-brown fading to buffish-white belly, upperparts pale brown boldly barred black, graduated tail pale brown with black outer feathers tipped white; in flight underwing-coverts chestnut barred black, undertail white with black tip; iris white, eye-ring pale blue, bill grey with blue base, legs and feet pink. **Adult female** Like male but pinkish-brown centre of breast reduced. **Juvenile** Barred on crown and nape, underparts indistinctly barred. **Habitat** Open woodlands, plantations, cultivated areas, gardens, parks. **Behaviour** Feeds predominantly on seeds on ground; flushes when approached with clattering of wings. **Voice** A rapid, bubbly *kororo-ro-ro koor* (1.4 kHz), each phrase c.0.6 s. **Range & status** SE Asia, Thai-Malay Peninsula, Philippines (introduced), Indonesia. **Borneo** Locally common introduced resident around Kota Kinabalu and Sandakan, Sabah; throughout Brunei; around Kuching and Miri, Sarawak; C and S Kalimantan; and the Natunas.

JAMBU FRUIT-DOVE *Ptilinopus jambu*

Identification 22–27 cm. Monotypic. Small colourful fruit-dove, male with bright pink face and white underparts, female mostly green with purplish face. **Adult male** Forecrown and face to sides of throat plum-pink creating hood, hindcrown and upperparts emerald-green, primaries blackish-green, tip of uppertail yellow, centre of throat black, sides of neck white, underparts white with pink wash on breast, undertail-coverts chestnut, undertail dark grey with pale grey terminal band; iris orange, eye-ring bluish-white, bill orange, legs and feet red. **Adult female** Forehead dark purple, chin dull brown, underparts green with whitish belly, undertail-coverts pale brown. **Juvenile** Like female but lacks purple on face and dark chin. **Similar species** Female and juvenile Black-naped Fruit-doves have entirely green underparts. **Habitat** Primary and secondary lowland dipterocarp to lower montane forest, mangroves, to 1,600 m. **Behaviour** Shy; usually solitary or in pairs; strictly frugivorous; migratory and nomadic probably in response to fruiting. **Voice** Generally quiet; utters a repetitive, soft *hoo* delivered on flat pitch (0.55 kHz). **Range & status** Thai-Malay Peninsula, Sumatra, W Java. **Borneo** Locally uncommon resident throughout, with much local movement. **Breeding** November–July; nest with one egg has been recorded, but no other details.

BLACK-NAPED FRUIT-DOVE *Ptilinopus melanospila*

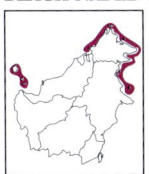

Identification 21–27 cm. Mostly green, plump fruit-dove with distinctive head pattern in male, female almost entirely green. **Adult male** *bangueyensis* Head pale grey with black patch on nape and pale yellow throat-patch, underparts olive-green, vent burnt orange blending into crimson undertail-coverts, undertail dark grey with light grey terminal band, upperparts olive-green; in flight underwing-coverts olive-green, flight feathers dark grey; iris yellow, bill yellowish-green, legs and feet red. **Adult female** Entirely olive-green except narrow yellow fringing on underparts and reddish wash on undertail-coverts. **Juvenile** Like female but with more yellow fringing to feathers. **Similar species** See Jambu Fruit-dove. **Habitat** Secondary forest, mangroves, parks, gardens on small to medium islands. **Behaviour** Solitary or in pairs, sometimes congregating at fruiting trees; strictly frugivorous, generally foraging below canopy; probably nomadic in response to fruiting. **Voice** A mellow two-note *woo…woo…* initially rising in pitch, before dropping (0.35–0.45 kHz), each note c.0.3 s, the phrase 1.5 s, repeated about every 3–5 s. **Range & status** Java and Bali, Lesser Sundas, south Philippines, Sulawesi. **Borneo** Uncommon resident of islands off Sabah and NE Kalimantan, and Natunas; old report from Matasiri Island, 86 km south of S Kalimantan. **Breeding** October–March; lays one plain buff egg on sparse platform of twigs located in lower storey 3–5 m from ground.

CINNAMON-HEADED GREEN-PIGEON
Treron fulvicollis

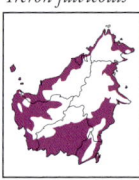

Identification 22–30 cm. A medium-sized *Treron*, male with distinctive chestnut head and breast, female all green with prominent red base of bill and cere. **Adult male** *baramensis* (endemic subspecies) Head, mantle and breast purplish-chestnut, belly greenish-grey, thighs yellowish, under-wing dark grey, undertail-coverts chestnut with pale tips, undertail black with grey terminal band, wing-coverts maroon, flight feathers black with yellow edges, back and rump grey, uppertail olive-green (outer feathers with black subterminal band and grey tip); iris yellow, eye-ring bluish-green, bill greenish with red base and cere, legs and feet pinkish-red. **Adult female** Forehead and crown greyish-green, upperparts olive-green with yellow-edged black flight feathers, breast green fading to greenish-grey belly, thighs yellowish, undertail-coverts buffish-white with green edging. **Juvenile** Like female but upperparts greyish, wing-coverts with yellow edging, tail with rufous tips. **Adult male** *fulvicollis* Like *baramensis* but throat and breast orangey-chestnut, belly yellowish-green, rump olive-green. **Adult female** *fulvicollis* Like *baramensis* but belly olive-green. **Adult male** *oberholseri* Underparts bright green, iris red. **Similar species** Female Thick-billed Green-pigeon has larger bill, broad eye-ring, and white-tipped green thighs; all other green-pigeons lack red cere and base of bill. **Habitat** Primary and secondary coastal and riverine forest, peatswamp forest, kerangas, mangroves; an extreme lowland specialist to 150 m. **Behaviour** Little known; frugivorous; numbers may fluctuate with seasonal fruiting. **Voice** Random, reeling *wii-ooo-wii* notes, typical of *Treron* pigeons. **Range & status** Thai-Malay Peninsula, Sumatra. **Borneo** Locally common (Sabah) to rare resident (Sarawak) throughout, in lowland areas; *baramensis* E

Sarawak, Sabah and islands north of Sabah, *oberholseri* the Natunas, *fulvicollis* Kalimantan and W Sarawak. **Breeding** Recorded in February; lays two white eggs on nest of twigs located in dense vegetation in tree at c.5 m.

LITTLE GREEN-PIGEON *Treron olax*

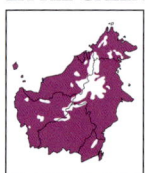

Identification 20–22 cm. Monotypic. Small, short-tailed green-pigeon, male with conspicuous orange breast and maroon mantle. **Adult male** Head to upper mantle bluish-grey, breast burnt orange blending to yellowish-green belly, flanks bluish-grey, lower mantle and wing-coverts deep maroon, flight feathers black with pale yellow edging, back to uppertail greyish-black with grey terminal band, thighs and undertail-coverts deep cinnamon, undertail black with grey terminal band; iris yellowish-white, narrow eye-ring pale blue, bill pale yellow with blue base, cere green, legs and feet pinkish-red. **Adult female** Like male but forehead and crown pale grey, back and wing-coverts dull green, throat to vent pale green, undertail-coverts buffish with broad green streaks. **Juvenile** As adult female but chestnut fringes on wing-coverts. **Similar species** Pink-necked Green-pigeon is larger, male having all-green upperparts and pinkish neck, female lacking grey on head; Thick-billed Green-pigeon is larger, both sexes with red cere and conspicuous greenish-blue eye-ring; Large Green-pigeon is much larger, male with all-green upperparts, female with faint orange breast-patch. **Habitat** Primary and secondary lowland dipterocarp to hill forest, peatswamp forest, parks, gardens, plantations, to 1,000 m. **Behaviour** Usually in small flocks; frugivorous, favouring figs. **Voice** A peculiar, undulating, strangulated sound typical of *Treron* pigeons: random, relatively high-pitched *wii…ooo…wii…* (2.5

kHz) with whining quality, uttered continuously. **Range & status** Thai-Malay Peninsula, Sumatra, Java. **Borneo** Locally common resident throughout, including the Natunas. **Breeding** February–July; lays two white eggs on flimsy platform of twigs.

PINK-NECKED GREEN-PIGEON *Treron vernans*

LIBARAN ISLAND 5/6/10

Identification 23–28 cm. Monotypic. Medium-sized colourful *Treron* with distinctive tail pattern and male with distinctive pink collar. **Adult male** Head grey, nape to upper breast purplish-pink, centre of breast burnt orange, lower breast to belly pale green, flanks and thighs olive-green broadly edged yellow, undertail-coverts chestnut, undertail black with grey terminal band, back and wing-coverts green with yellow edges on tertials, primaries black, uppertail grey with black subterminal band; iris reddish, bill pale grey, cere greenish-yellow, legs and feet pinkish-red. **Adult female** As male but head and neck olive-green, underparts all yellowish-green, undertail-coverts pale chestnut. **Juvenile** As adult female but buff fringes on wing-coverts. **Similar species** See Little Green-pigeon. **Habitat** Edges of primary and secondary lowland dipterocarp forest, peatswamp forest, kerangas, mangroves, plantations, parks, gardens, to 750 m. **Behaviour** Frugivorous, favouring figs and *Melastoma* fruits; usually seen in small flocks; favours more open areas. **Voice** Relatively quiet; utters a soft *coo*, nasal *waaa wi wi-wi-wi wi-wi-wi*, and said also to utter a sound like a siren winding up that then breaks off suddenly into chortles. **Range & status** Southern SE Asia, Thai-Malay Peninsula, Philippines, Indonesia. **Borneo** Common resident throughout, including offshore islands. **Breeding** February–October; lays two white eggs on flimsy platform of sticks.

THICK-BILLED GREEN-PIGEON *Treron curvirostra*

LIBARAN ISLAND 4/6/10

Identification 25–31 cm. Monotypic. Medium-sized *Treron* with distinctive red cere and broad greenish-blue eye-ring in both sexes. **Adult male** Forehead and crown pale grey, face and neck green, underparts yellowish-green, thighs and vent dark green broadly tipped white, undertail-coverts chestnut, undertail black with grey terminal band, mantle and wing-coverts maroon, flight feathers black with conspicuous yellow edging, back and rump yellowish-green, uppertail dark grey with black central band and pale grey tip to outer feathers; in flight underwing grey, iris dark, broad eye-ring bluish-green, bill yellowish with red base and cere, legs and feet pinkish-red. **Adult female** As male but mantle and wing-coverts olive-green, undertail-coverts green and white. **Juvenile** Like female but duller overall. **Similar species** See Little and Cinnamon-headed Green-pigeon. **Habitat** Primary and secondary lowland dipterocarp, peatswamp, coastal and riverine forests, mangroves, plantations, mainly to 750 m but also recorded from Kelabit Highlands and G. Kinabalu. **Behaviour** Usually in medium to large flocks; often noisy and conspicuous; frugivorous, with some nomadic movement in response to fruiting. **Voice** A typical meandering *Treron* song, a reeling *wiii-oo-wii… wuwii-wi-woo-wi* (1.6–2 kHz); also a soft cooing. **Range & status** NE Indian Subcontinent, SE Asia, Sumatra, Philippines (Mindoro and Palawan). **Borneo** Common resident throughout, including Natunas. **Breeding** August–May.

LARGE GREEN-PIGEON *Treron capellei*

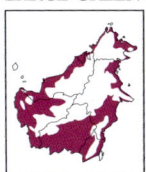

Identification 35–36 cm. Monotypic. Large, mostly green *Treron* with yellow legs and orange (male) or pale yellow (female) breast-patch. **Adult male** Face greyish-green, head and throat to rump pale green, breast orange, belly pale green, thighs pale green with buff tips, undertail-coverts dark chestnut, undertail black with grey terminal band, wing-coverts olive-green, flight feathers dark green with yellow edging, uppertail olive-green with outer feathers dark grey tipped pale grey; iris dark brown, narrow yellow eye-ring, robust greenish-white bill with dark green base and cere, legs and feet bright yellow. **Adult female** As male but breast pale yellow wash, undertail-coverts green and buff. **Similar species** Much larger than any other *Treron* in Borneo with distinctive plumage and yellow legs. **Habitat** Extreme lowland specialist of primary lowland dipterocarp, peatswamp and riverine forest; rarely in secondary and hill forest. **Behaviour** Usually solitary or in pairs in Borneo; frugivorous favouring large *Ficus* fruits (due to large size cannot feed on smaller figs growing on narrower branches); possibly quite sedentary. **Voice** Distinctive; a peculiar growling song with an interrogative quality *koh-kowoh-ko-kooh-ko-koh-ko-koh-koh*, main pitch c.0.75–0.9 kHz. **Range & status** Thai-Malay Peninsula, Sumatra, Java. **Borneo** Local and uncommon resident in lowland areas throughout, possibly declining. **Breeding** August–March.

SUKAU RIVER LODGE   8/6/10

GREEN IMPERIAL-PIGEON *Ducula aenea*

Adult *polia*

Adult *polia*

Identification 40–48 cm. Large pigeon with contrasting grey-and-green plumage. **Adult *polia*** Head and neck pinkish-grey, chin to belly pinkish-grey, undertail-coverts chestnut, undertail dark brown, upperparts metallic bronze-green, flight feathers black; iris red, bill grey with red base, legs and feet pinkish-red. **Juvenile** Similar to adult but duller. **Adult *palawanensis*** Tail darker and bluer, chin and throat dark and pinker. **Similar species** Mountain Imperial-pigeon is larger, lacks green gloss on upperparts and chestnut undertail-coverts, has pale iris and terminal band on tail. Grey Imperial-pigeon is smaller with reduced green gloss on upperparts and grey undertail. **Habitat** Primary and secondary lowland dipterocarp and hill forest, riverine forest, mangroves, to 1,050 m. **Behaviour** Seen singly and in small groups; may congregate at fruiting trees; frugivorous, feeding in canopy; powerful, direct flight often high above canopy; spectacular 'roller coaster' display-flight in which it flies up steeply before stalling, then suddenly dropping in very steep dive; partially nomadic in response to fruiting. **Voice** Song is a loud, growly, two-note *ka khoo*, the first note short and higher-pitched (0.3 s, 0.55 kHz), the second longer and lower (0.7 s, 0.35 kHz). **Range & status** Indian Subcontinent, South China, SE Asia, Philippines, Indonesia. **Borneo** Race *polia* locally very common lowland resident throughout, probably more common closer to coast, also the Natunas; *palawanensis* status unclear on Banggi Island. **Breeding** August–January; lays one smooth white egg.

GREY IMPERIAL-PIGEON *Ducula pickeringii*

Adult

Identification 37–40 cm. Medium-sized imperial-pigeon with pinkish-grey underparts and glossy brownish-grey upperparts. **Adult *pickeringii*** Head dull pinkish-grey, neck grey, whiter around eye and base of bill, underparts pinkish-grey, undertail-coverts buffish-grey, undertail grey, underwing pale grey, upperparts brownish-grey with slight green gloss, uppertail blackish-green; iris red, bill dark grey, legs and feet dull red. **Juvenile** Duller, iris brown, bill pale grey. **Similar species** See Green Imperial-pigeon. **Habitat** Primary and secondary forest on small, low islands; favours primary forest. **Behaviour** Small island specialist; may travel to mainland to feed, returning to small islands to roost; nomadic in response to fruiting; frugivorous; usually singly or in pairs but sometimes in small flocks. **Voice** A regular *woo woo woo woo woo woo woo...*, usually consisting of seven notes but sometimes fewer. Described as sounding like 'an object being swung, in an irregular manner, at the end of a piece of string' (Melville 1996). Also a loud, very deep *wa-roo* (0.7-0.4 kHz). **Range & status** South Philippines, NW Sulawesi. **Borneo** Locally uncommon resident on very small islands of Sabah (Banggi, Mantanani, Tiga, Sipadan and Semporna islands, and Tungku Abdul Rahman National Park); recent record from Derawan Islands, E Kalimantan; a few recent mainland records from Sabah and Sarawak (Similajau National Park). Historically abundant on some islands, but now declining throughout its range. **Breeding** Undescribed in Borneo.

MOUNTAIN IMPERIAL-PIGEON *Ducula badia*

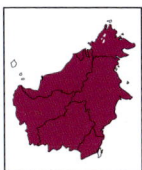

Identification 40–51 cm. Very large, robust pigeon with deep purplish upperparts and pale grey underparts. **Adult** *badia* Head and neck pale grey, throat white, hindneck pinkish-grey, underparts pale grey, undertail-coverts buff, undertail grey with pale grey terminal band, mantle to rump and wing-coverts maroon-brown, flight feathers blackish-brown, uppertail black with broad grey terminal band; iris greyish-white, eye-ring dark red, bill dark red with pale tip, legs and feet dull red. **Juvenile** Duller, upperparts browner. **Similar species** See Green Imperial-pigeon. **Habitat** Primary and secondary lowland dipterocarp to upper montane forest, mangroves, plantations, to 2,500 m. **Behaviour** Generally solitary but sometimes in small flocks; arboreal frugivore; sedentary but disperses daily into lowlands in search of food, essentially a bird of lower and upper montane forests. **Voice** A deep, three-note *ga-woo-woo*, delivered on same pitch (0.3 kHz), the first note very short and difficult to hear, the following two notes longer (0.3 s), each phrase c.1.2 s and repeated every 3–8 s. **Range & status** S India, E Himalayas, SE Asia, Sumatra, W Java. **Borneo** Locally common resident throughout. **Breeding** February–March; lays 1–2 smooth white eggs on simple stick platform (c.30 cm across) located c.5 m from ground.

PIED IMPERIAL-PIGEON *Ducula bicolor*

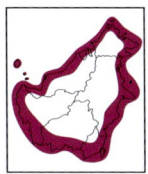

Identification 35–37 cm. Distinctive black-and-white, medium-sized imperial-pigeon. **Adult** *bicolor* Pure white overall, flight feathers and uppertail black, undertail white with black outer edges and triangular black terminal band; iris dark brown, bill bluish-grey, legs and feet bluish-grey. **Juvenile** Similar to adult but white parts greyish-white. **Similar species** See Silvery Woodpigeon. **Habitat** Forests and mangroves of coastal areas and offshore islands, at sea-level. **Behaviour** Feeds on fruits and buds; usually seen in flocks; daily and seasonal movements in search of food; nests on offshore islands. **Voice** A soft, mellow *wuk-wooo* (0.4 kHz, 0.5 s). **Range & status** Andaman and Nicobar Islands, SE Asia, Philippines, Indonesia. **Borneo** Common resident on offshore islands and in coastal areas throughout, less common in coastal areas. **Breeding** Recorded in June; eggs pure white, nests high in trees or coconut palms.

PSITTACIDAE: Parrots & parakeets

Worldwide c.332 species, 5 in Borneo. A very large family characterised by large head and powerful, hooked bill as well as harsh, raucous vocalisations. Many with very colourful plumage. Feed on seeds, nectar, flowers, buds and fruit. Able to use the dextrous bill and tongue as a third foot, and the feet are zygodactylic (the fourth toe is reversible), both these features allowing great agility. Highly gregarious and intelligent. All are cavity nesters.

BLUE-CROWNED HANGING-PARROT
Loriculus galgulus

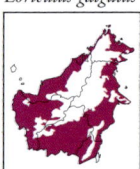

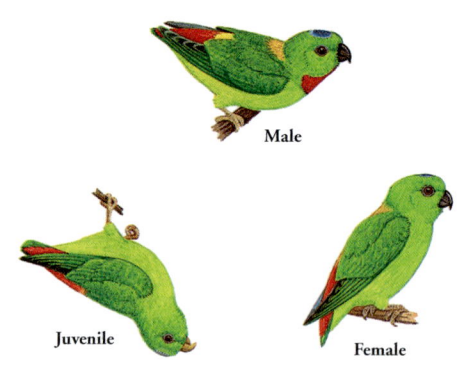

Identification 12 cm. Tiny green parrot with blue crown-patch and crimson bib. **Adult male** *galgulus* Head bright green with dark blue spot on crown, upperparts green with triangular patch golden on mantle, lower back yellow above crimson rump and undertail-coverts, bright crimson patch on upper breast; iris brown, bill black, legs and feet grey. **Adult female** Like male but lacks red throat-patch and yellow on lower back, duller reduced blue crown. **Immature** Duller; all green with yellow wash on mantle, bill yellow. **Habitat** Primary and secondary lowland dipterocarp forest, riverine and peatswamp forest, kerangas, mangroves, plantations; lowland specialist to 500 m. **Behaviour** Usually solitary or in pairs; most often seen flying fast and direct high overhead on whirring wings uttering flight calls; nectarivorous, feeding on flowers as well as small fruits and oil palm fruit; nests in small tree-hollows; roosts upside-down. **Voice** A distinctive, high-pitched buzzy *tseeet* (3.5 kHz) often uttered in flight. **Range & status** Thai-Malay Peninsula, Sumatra, W Java (introduced). **Borneo** Locally common resident throughout, including Banggi Island and Anambas. **Breeding** January–September; lays two dull white eggs stained brown in nest-holes.

BLUE-RUMPED PARROT *Psittinus cyanurus*

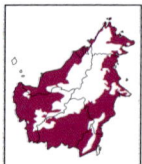

Identification 18 cm. A squat parrot with conspicuous red underwing-coverts and blue head and rump. **Adult male** *cyanurus* Head greyish-blue, underparts greyish-green, yellowish on vent, undertail yellow, mantle and back purplish-black mottled grey, wings green finely edged yellow with dark red shoulder-patch, lower back and rump blue, uppertail blue with yellow and green outer feathers; in flight scarlet underwing-coverts contrast with blackish flight feathers; iris yellowish-white, upper mandible red, lower mandible brown, legs and feet grey. **Adult female** As male but head brownish-grey, mantle green, bill all brown. **Juvenile** All green with yellow fringes on wing-coverts. **Similar species** Blue-naped Parrot is much larger, lacks blue on rump, all-red bill and different pattern on wing-coverts. **Habitat** Primary and secondary lowland dipterocarp forest, kerangas, plantations, mangroves; lowland specialist to 500 m. **Behaviour** Gregarious, often in large groups; feeds on oil palm nuts, fruits, seeds, buds; disperses over long distances, may be nomadic; nests in small tree-hollows. **Voice** A sharp, downslurred, high-pitched *tse-tsee-tsee...* uttered in flight (5–3 kHz). **Range & status** Thai-Malay Peninsula, Sumatra. **Borneo** Common (Sabah and Brunei) to uncommon (Sarawak and Kalimantan) lowland resident throughout. **Breeding** May–September.

BLUE-NAPED PARROT *Tanygnathus lucionensis*

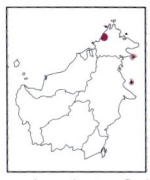

Identification 31 cm. Large, mostly green parrot with bright orange-red bill, blue nape and rounded tail. **Adult *salvadorii*** Head to rump bright green with bright blue crown and nape, wings blue and green with blackish shoulder and yellow margins on wing-coverts, underparts green with pale yellow undertail; in flight underwing-coverts green and flight feathers blackish; iris yellow, bill red with paler or yellowish tip, cere black, legs and feet grey. **Immature** Reduced blue on crown, duller markings on wing. **Similar species** See Blue-rumped Parrot. **Habitat** Secondary lowland dipterocarp forest, mangroves, plantations, gardens, at sea-level. **Behaviour** Usually in small flocks; feeds on fruits, seeds and some cultivated crops such as bananas and papayas; nest in large tree-hollows; probably sedentary. **Voice** Noisy; utters a loud, creaky, *krek-krek-krek…* (1.5–3 kHz). **Range & status** Philippines. **Borneo** Locally common resident, naturally

Male · Immature

occurring on Mantanani and Si Amil islands, Sabah and Maratuas, E Kalimantan; feral population Tanjung Aru, Kota Kinabalu. **Breeding** January–September; one observation of nest-hole in tree-stump.

RED-BREASTED PARAKEET *Psittacula alexandri*

Identification 33–38 cm. Bright green parakeet with blue-grey head and rosy breast. **Adult male *alexandri*** Head pale bluish-grey with thin black line from eye to cere, broad black band from chin tapering to sides of neck, breast pinkish-red, rest of underparts green, upperparts green with yellowish wash on wing-coverts, long tail blue with green outer feathers and tips; iris yellowish-white, bill all red, legs and feet greenish-grey. **Adult female** Head slightly paler grey, underparts duller pink, tail shorter. **Juvenile** All green. **Similar species** See Long-tailed Parakeet. **Habitat** Lowland forests including riverine forest, kerangas, mangroves and peatswamp forest, also plantations and gardens. **Behaviour** Gregarious; feeds on fruit, seeds, flowers; nest in tree-hollows. **Voice** A loud, raucous *kak…kak…kak…* uttered rapidly (1.6 kHz). **Range & status** Eastern Himalayas, SE Asia, Andaman Islands, offshore islands of Sumatra, Java and Bali. **Borneo**

Female · Male · Juvenile

Locally uncommon resident from far east corner of W Kalimantan to coastal south-east corner of S Kalimantan. **Breeding** Undescribed in Borneo.

LONG-TAILED PARAKEET *Psittacula longicauda*

SUKAU RIVER LODGE   8/6/10

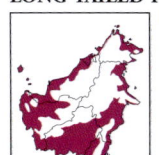

Identification 40–48 cm. Long-tailed, green parakeet with prominent red cheeks. **Adult male *longicauda*** Crown dark green, cheeks to nape rose-pink, chin to sides of neck black, underparts yellowish-green, mantle and upper back yellowish-green shading to blue on lower back and green on uppertail-coverts, wings green with blue tinge on primaries, elongated central tail blue with green outer feathers; iris yellow, upper mandible red, lower mandible black, legs and feet grey. **Adult female** Like male but cheeks dull pink and nape grey; iris white, bill all brown. **Adult male *defontainei*** Cheeks and nape redder, crown yellowish. **Similar species** Red-breasted Parakeet has grey cheeks, pinkish-red breast, primaries green and shorter tail. **Habitat** Lowland forests including riverine forest, kerangas, mangroves and peatswamp forest, also plantations and gardens, avoids primary forest; an extreme lowland specialist to 200 m. **Behaviour** Gregarious, usually in small flocks but sometimes in large congregations in response to fruiting or masting; feeds on fruit, seeds, flowers; nests in tree-hollows in colonies; seasonal movements are poorly understood. **Voice** A loud, raucous *rark…rark…rark…* (2 kHz). **Range & status** Andaman and Nicobar islands, Thai-Malay Peninsula,

Female *longicauda* · Male *longicauda* · Juvenile *longicauda*

Sumatra. **Borneo** Locally common resident throughout, including the Natunas (*defontainei*), more so in coastal areas; abundance fluctuates from year to year. **Breeding** June–July; nests in old woodpecker and barbet holes.

101

CUCULIDAE: Old World cuckoos

Worldwide c.139 species, 28 in Borneo. A diverse family of long-tailed and short-legged, mostly insectivorous birds with a short slender bill. Many but not all species are brood parasites; the malkohas, coucals and ground-cuckoos being notable exceptions. Parasitic cuckoos are particularly vocal during the breeding season. Arboreal or terrestrial. Sexes are similar with some exceptions, although some parasitic cuckoos exhibit a hepatic female phase.

CHESTNUT-WINGED CUCKOO
Clamator coromandus

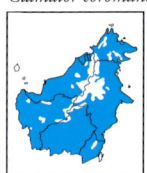

Identification 46 cm. Monotypic. **Adult** Distinctive black crest, upperparts glossy black, white on nape forms half-collar, wings chestnut, underparts white with chestnut throat and blackish vent, tail black with white tips (often not visible); iris pale brown to dark brown, bill black, feet dark dark grey; recalls small coucal in flight. **Juvenile** Duller; crest short, upperparts brown mottled and barred with buff feather-edges, underparts grey. **Habitat** Scrubby vegetation in primary and secondary lowland dipterocarp forest, woodlands, mangroves, plantations, villages, cultivated areas, to 1,200 m. **Behaviour** Brood parasite mainly of laughingthrushes; feeds on large invertebrates; sits quietly or clambers about in thick, low vegetation. **Voice** Territorial call is a clean, flat, bell-like double whistle *keep..keep*, repeated (2 kHz). Also a harsh *chek chek chek* (3 kHz). **Range & status** Himalayas, SE China, SE Asia, migrates to Indian Subcontinent, Thai-Malay Peninsula, Indonesia, Philippines. **Borneo** Uncommon non-breeding visitor and passage migrant throughout October–March.

LARGE HAWK-CUCKOO *Hierococcyx sparverioides*

Identification 38–40 cm. Monotypic. A large cuckoo with a hawk-like appearance. **Adult** Crown, face and neck slaty-grey, face paler in front of eye, chin black, dark streaks on throat, breast rufous streaked dark brown, belly white with brownish-black bars, undertail-coverts white, upperparts brown with white on bend of wing, long tail barred brownish-grey and black with broad black terminal bar tipped white; iris orange to buff, eye-ring lemon-yellow, bill black, feet yellow. **Juvenile** Forehead grey, upperparts barred rufous and brown, tail barred rufous and black, underparts buffish-white with black streaking on breast and barring on belly and undertail. **Similar species** Paler and larger than Dark Hawk-cuckoo; black bands in tail are broader than Malaysian Hawk-cuckoo. **Habitat** Lowland forest edges, secondary forest, mangroves, gardens, below 800 m. **Behaviour** Generally solitary in canopy; brood parasite mainly on laughingthrushes, whistling-thrushes, spiderhunters (extralimital data); feeds on insects including caterpillars and cockroaches, spiders, bird eggs, berries. **Voice** A loud strident two-note *pi peewer* (sometimes referred to as 'brain fe-ver'), the first note short (2.3 kHz), the second longer, rising then dropping (1.3–2.2 kHz), uttered in run of 4–8 phrases increasing in pitch and volume sounding increasingly frantic. Probably silent in non-breeding areas. **Range & status** Himalayas, E Asia, Indochina, migrates to Indian Subcontinent, Myanmar, Thailand, Thai-Malay Peninsula, Indonesia, Philippines. **Borneo** Uncommon to rare non-breeding visitor to lowlands throughout.

DARK HAWK-CUCKOO *Hierococcyx bocki*

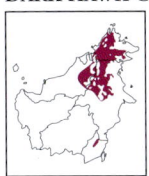

Identification 30–32 cm. Monotypic. **Adult** Crown, face and neck slaty-grey, chin and throat unstreaked grey, breast rufous unstreaked or with faint darker streaking, belly white with black bars, undertail-coverts white, back and rump slaty-grey, wings brown, white on bend of wing, long tail with broad grey and black bars with broad black terminal bar tipped white; iris orange to buff, eye-ring lemon-yellow, bill black above, greenish below, feet yellow. **Immature** Upperparts brownish-black with white feathers on nape, chin to breast slaty-brown, lower breast to undertail-coverts white with dark bars. **Similar species** Smaller and darker than Large Hawk-cuckoo, with unstreaked throat and breast. **Habitat** Primary and secondary hill to upper montane forest, from 800 to 1,550 m. **Behaviour** Arboreal and solitary; feeds on insects, spiders, bird eggs, berries. **Voice** Two-note *pui pee-ha*, the first note short, the second longer (1.6–2 kHz); mellower than Large Hawk-cuckoo. Sings from September to late May. **Range & status** Malay Peninsula. **Borneo**

Adult

Immature

Uncommon resident in north-central mountain ranges from G. Kinabalu to Usun Apau Plateau and G. Menyapa (Sabah, E Sarawak and E Kalimantan) and Meratus Mountains (S Kalimantan). **Breeding** Brood parasite; record of parasitism of Mountain Leaf-warbler from G. Kinabalu, otherwise undescribed in Borneo.

MOUSTACHED HAWK-CUCKOO *Hierococcyx vagans*

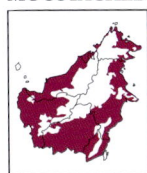

Identification 26 cm. Monotypic. Small hawk-like cuckoo with face pattern reminiscent of Eurasian Hobby. **Adult** Crown blackish-grey, face with broad black moustache from eye down sides of throat and narrower line extending behind eye, cheek and throat whitish, collar rufous-brown, upperparts dark greyish-brown with wings barred lighter brown, white on bend of wing, tail barred grey and black with white tips, underparts white with fine clean dark streaks, undertail-coverts white; iris brown, eye-ring bright yellow, bill black, yellowish-green below, legs and feet yellow; in flight underwings white, primaries with grey barring. **Juvenile** Crown blackish-brown, face blackish-brown with indistinct moustache, throat and chin blackish-brown, underparts with broad dark streaking, undertail-coverts whitish, upperparts blackish-brown with rufous edges, tail as adult. **Habitat** Primary and secondary lowland dipterocarp and riparian forest, forest edges; lowland specialist to 550 m. **Behaviour** Shy, solitary; feeds on large insects. **Voice** Main song is a

Adult

monotonous, melancholy two-note *kang-koh*, the first (1.8 kHz) slightly lower-pitched than the second (2 kHz). Singing probably peaks from January to March in Borneo. **Range & status** SE Asia, Thai-Malay Peninsula, Sumatra. **Borneo** Uncommon to rare resident throughout. **Breeding** brood parasite; has been recorded parasitising Rufous-winged Philentoma, otherwise undescribed in Borneo.

MALAYSIAN HAWK-CUCKOO *Hierococcyx fugax*

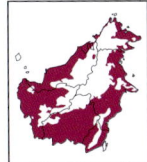

Identification 28–30 cm. Monotypic. **Adult** Upperparts slaty-grey, face grey with variable amount of white on sides of neck forming half-collar, chin grey, throat white, white on bend of wing, underparts whitish streaked brown and rufous with rufous wash on sides of neck and breast, undertail-coverts white, tail greyish-brown with blackish bars, broad greyish-black subterminal band with rufous tips; iris brown, eye-ring yellow, bill black with pale greenish tip and lower base, feet yellow. **Juvenile** Upperparts blackish-brown with buffish feather-edging, breast whitish heavily spotted with black, tail as adult; iris grey, bill black with yellow base. **Habitat** Primary and secondary lowland dipterocarp forests, woodland, plantations, to 1,600 m in Kelabit Highlands. **Behaviour** Feeds on insects and small fruits. **Voice** A quick, strident, high-pitched two-note *pi wit* (each note rising from c.3 to 4 kHz); also a shrill, rapid machine-gun-like *pipipipi…* delivered in a long, scrambled

Adult

Juvenile

sequence. **Range & status** Thai-Malay Peninsula, Sumatra, Java. **Borneo** Uncommon resident throughout. **Breeding** Brood parasite, recorded hosts including Grey-headed Canary-flycatcher and Black-throated Babbler, otherwise undescribed in Borneo.

NORTHERN HAWK-CUCKOO *Hierococcyx hyperythrus*

Identification 30 cm. Monotypic. **Adult** Face grey with white nape-patch, chin grey, throat white, breast and belly pale rufous, undertail-coverts white, tail light grey with narrow black and rufous barring, broad grey subterminal band with rufous tips, upperparts slaty-grey, white on bend of wing; iris brown, eye-ring yellow, bill black with pale greenish tip and lower base, feet yellow. **Juvenile** Crown blackish-brown, nape blotched white, upperparts blackish-brown with buffish feather-edging, breast whitish heavily spotted with black, tail as adult but barring more rufous. **Similar species** Larger than Malaysian Hawk-cuckoo with more extensive rufous wash on breast and belly. **Habitat** Primary and secondary lowland dipterocarp forest, plantations. **Behaviour** In Borneo unclear due to previous treatment as conspecific with *H. fugax*. **Voice** Song is a high-pitched, loud, strident, urgent *ju ichi* (3–4 kHz); also a 3–4 s series of chattering, short notes *pipipijujujupipipi* reaching a crescendo (2.5–5 kHz). Probably does not vocalise away from breeding area. **Range & status** NE Asia, migrating south to Philippines, E Indonesia. **Borneo** Uncommon to rare non-breeding visitor but status and distribution obscured by previous treatment as conspecific with *H. fugax*.

HODGSON'S HAWK-CUCKOO *Hierococcyx nisicolor*

Identification 28–30 cm. Monotypic. **Adult** Face grey, chin grey, throat white, breast and belly whitish streaked broadly rufous, undertail-coverts white, tail light grey with narrow black and rufous barring, broad grey subterminal band with rufous tips, upperparts slaty-grey, white on bend of wing; iris brown, eye-ring yellow, bill black with pale greenish tip and lower base, feet yellow. **Similar species** Less rufous below than Northern Hawk-cuckoo; Malaysian Hawk-cuckoo has less rufous on underparts. **Habitat** Primary and secondary lowland dipterocarp forests, plantations. **Behaviour** In Borneo unclear due to previous treatment as conspecific with *H. fugax*. **Voice** A loud, high-pitched, penetrating *ki wi* (the first note higher, 4.5 kHz, than the second, 4 kHz). Probably does not vocalise away from breeding area. **Range & status** China, E Himalayas, migrates south to Thailand, Thai-Malay Peninsula, Indonesia. **Borneo** Uncommon non-breeding visitor to NW Borneo, recorded once from SE Borneo. Status and distribution obscured by previous treatment as conspecific with *H. fugax*.

Adult

Juvenile

INDIAN CUCKOO *Cuculus micropterus*

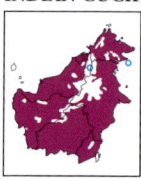

Identification 32 cm. **Adult male** *concretus* Head and wings grey, throat and upper breast pale grey, rest of underparts white with widely spaced black barring, upperparts brownish-grey, white in bend of wing, tail grey narrowly tipped white with broad black subterminal band and white notches on sides; iris reddish-brown, eye-ring yellow, bill black with yellow base, feet yellow. **Adult female** Like adult male but throat pale grey, breast brownish, barring on belly more narrow, tail with brownish-grey barring. **Juvenile** Crown and neck brownish with buffish fringes, upperparts brown with pale barring, underparts buff with brown barring. **Adult** *micropterus* Larger, paler. **Habitat** Primary and secondary lowland dipterocarp and hill forest, peatswamp forest, to 1,200 m. **Behaviour** Arboreal; feeds on insects, small fruits. **Voice** A loud, fluty, far-carrying *po po pa pyo* or *ka ka ko kyo*, the last note slightly lower-pitched (1.5–1.3 kHz), each phrase is about 0.9 s, repeated persistently; often transcribed as 'one more bottle'; vocalises October–April. **Range & status** Himalayas, Indian Subcontinent, E and SE Asia, Indonesia, Philippines. **Borneo** Race *concretus* locally common resident throughout; *micropterus* vagrant with records from Sipadan Island and Kelabit Highlands. **Breeding** Brood parasite; recorded hosts include drongos, shrikes, broadbills, otherwise undescribed in Borneo.

Female *concretus*

Male *concretus*

Juvenile *concretus*

ORIENTAL CUCKOO *Cuculus horsfieldi*

Male

Identification 32–33 cm. Monotypic. **Adult male** Upperparts dark grey, white on bend of wing, chin to upper breast grey, lower breast and belly white barred black, undertail-coverts buff unbarred or with fine black bars, tail black narrowly tipped white with white notches on sides and spots on shafts; iris brown, eye-ring yellow, bill black with yellow base, feet yellow. **Adult female** Like male but upper breast with rufous wash, narrower barring; **hepatic morph** has upperparts barred rufous and dark brown, underparts barred pale rufous and dark brown, lower breast tinged rufous. **Juvenile** Upperparts dark grey with white feather-edges, white patch on nape, chin to breast whitish with fine black barring, belly barred black and white, undertail-coverts buffish with incomplete black barring. **Similar species** Differs from very similar Himalayan Cuckoo in being larger and longer-winged, less conspicuous white edging on plumage of upperparts in juvenile, song lower-pitched; differs from Sunda Cuckoo by paler buff belly and undertail-coverts, larger, song lower-pitched with high soft introductory note. **Habitat** Mainly in primary and secondary lowland forest in Borneo, but occasionally in hill and montane forest. **Behaviour** Feeds on insects and small fruits; brood parasite, does not breed in Borneo. **Voice** On breeding grounds utters a repeated, slow-tempo, low-pitched *po po…po po…po po…* (0.5 kHz). **Range & status** Palearctic, E Asia, passage migrant SE Asia, non-breeding visitor to Thai-Malay Peninsula, Philippines, Indonesia, New Guinea, Australia. **Borneo** Rare non-breeding visitor throughout. Ratio of migratory Oriental to Himalayan Cuckoos in Borneo is thought to be 50:50.

Female hepatic morph

HIMALAYAN CUCKOO *Cuculus saturatus*

Male

Female hepatic morph

Juvenile

Juvenile female hepatic morph

Identification 32–33 cm. Monotypic. **Adult male** Head grey, upperparts dark grey, white on bend of wing, chin to upper breast grey, lower breast and belly white with buffish tinge and barred black, undertail-coverts buff unbarred or with fine black bars, tail black narrowly tipped white with white notches on sides and spots on shafts; iris brown, eye-ring yellow, bill black with yellow base, feet yellow. **Adult female** Like male but upper breast with rufous wash, barring more narrow; **hepatic morph** has upperparts barred rufous and dark brown, underparts barred pale buff and dark brown, lower breast tinged rufous. **Juvenile** Upperparts dark grey with white feather-edges, white patch on nape, chin to breast whitish with fine black barring, belly barred black and white, undertail-coverts buffish with incomplete black barring. **Similar species** Differs from very similar Oriental Cuckoo in being smaller and by more conspicuous white edging on plumage of upperparts in juvenile, song higher-pitched; from Sunda Cuckoo by paler buff belly and undertail-coverts, larger, song lower-pitched with high soft introductory note. **Habitat** Mainly in primary and secondary lowland dipterocarp forest in Borneo, but also hill and montane forest. **Behaviour** Feeds on insects and small fruits. **Voice** On breeding grounds song is a mellow four-note *po po-po-po*, the first note higher-pitched (0.5 kHz) than the next three (0.4 kHz). **Range & status** Himalayas, E Asia, non-breeding passage migrant and migrant to SE Asia, Thai-Malay Peninsula, Indonesia, Philippines. **Borneo** Rare non-breeding visitor throughout. Ratio of migratory Oriental to Himalayan Cuckoos in Borneo is thought to be 50:50.

SUNDA CUCKOO *Cuculus lepidus*

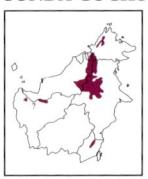

Identification 29–30 cm. **Adult male *insulindae*** Head and back dark grey, wings brownish-grey, white on bend of wing, chin to upper breast grey, lower breast and belly dark buff to light rufous barred black, undertail-coverts dark buff to light rufous unbarred or with fine black bars, tail black narrowly tipped white with white notches on sides and spots on shafts; iris brown, eye-ring yellow, bill black with yellow base, feet yellow. **Adult female** Like male but upper breast with rufous wash; **hepatic morph** has upperparts barred rufous and dark brown, underparts barred pale rufous and dark brown. **Juvenile** Upperparts dark grey with white feather-edges, white patch on nape, chin and throat whitish with fine black barring, breast to undertail-coverts barred black and white with rufous wash. **Habitat** Lower to upper montane forest from 750 to 2,750 m. **Behaviour** Feeds on insects and small fruits. **Voice** A three-note low- and even-pitched, mellow *poop poop-poop* (0.5 kHz), the first note quieter and shorter, delivered repeatedly; probably

Male

Female hepatic morph

mainly vocalises from February to April. **Range & status** Thai-Malay Peninsula, Sumatra, Java, Lesser Sundas. **Borneo** Locally common resident in north-central and western mountain ranges from G. Kinabalu to the Pueh Range (Sabah, Sarawak, E Kalimantan) as well as in the Meratus Mountains (S Kalimantan). Not recorded from Brunei. **Breeding** Brood parasite, recorded hosts include Mountain Leaf-warbler and Yellow-breasted Warbler, otherwise undescribed in Borneo.

BANDED BAY CUCKOO *Cacomantis sonneratii*

Identification 22 cm. **Adult *schlegeli*** Upperparts finely barred rufous and brown, barred whitish supercilium and rufous and brown eyestripe, plain white line under eye, tail barred rufous and brown with subterminal black band and white tip, underparts whitish with fine wavy brown barring, white on bend of wing; iris yellow to dark red, bill black and broad, feet grey. **Juvenile** Like adult but crown and mantle with white tips, face paler with less distinct pattern, barring on underparts narrower. **Similar species** Distinguished from hepatic morphs by pale supercilium and darkish eye stripe. **Habitat** Primary and secondary lowland dipterocarp forest, gardens, plantations, to 500 m. **Behaviour** Feeds on insects, especially caterpillars. **Voice** A sharp, repeated, four-note *weep weep-weep-weep*, each note descending in pitch and series of notes also descending (2.7–2 kHz), often transcribed as 'smoke yer pepper'; recalls Indian Cuckoo but faster and higher-pitched

Adult

Juvenile

(series is 0.8–1 s); heard October to February in Borneo. Another call is a loud series of rising notes, starting slow, increasing in pace to a crescendo and sudden stop (1.8–2.5 kHz). **Range & status** Indian Subcontinent, SE Asia, Sumatra, Java, Palawan. **Borneo** Common (Sabah) to uncommon resident throughout. **Breeding** Brood parasite; recorded hosts include Common Iora, Scarlet Minivet, bulbuls, possibly breeds around March.

PLAINTIVE CUCKOO *Cacomantis merulinus*

Identification 18–23 cm. **Adult male *threnodes*** Head grey, upperparts greyish-brown, tail blackish with white tips barred white below, white on bend of wing, chin to breast grey, belly to undertail-coverts pinkish-rufous; iris red, eye-ring blackish, bill black with yellow lower base, feet bright yellow. **Adult female** Like male but **hepatic morph** with upperparts barred rufous and brown, underparts whitish barred dark brown. **Juvenile** Like hepatic female but head pale rufous with brown streaking, throat whitish streaked brown; iris brown, gape orange, feet greenish-yellow. **Similar species** Rusty-breasted Cuckoo has rufous throat and breast, hepatic morph similar to Banded Bay Cuckoo which has white supercilium, broad bill and narrow white tips on tail feathers. **Habitat** Primary and secondary lowland dipterocarp, peatswamp and kerangas forest, gardens, plantations, to 1,000 m, commoner in lowlands. **Behaviour** Active, forage in tree canopy; feeds on insects especially caterpillars, small fruits. **Voice** Song is a plaintive but sharp descending series of notes *fi fi fi fi fi fi-fifi-fifififififi* accelerating and tapering off at end (3.2–2.2 kHz, each phrase 3.5 s). This is often followed by a piercing, insistent

Male

Juvenile

Female hepatic morph

Female hepatic morph variant

witit… weee wit weee, the first note softer, lower-pitched and rising (1.6–2.1 kHz), the next three with middle note slightly lower (2.5 kHz and 2 kHz). **Range & status** Indian Subcontinent, S China, SE Asia, Indonesia, Philippines. **Borneo** Common to abundant resident throughout. **Breeding** Brood parasite; recorded hosts include prinias, tailorbirds and spiderhunters, possibly breeds around March.

RUSTY-BREASTED CUCKOO *Cacomantis sepulcralis*

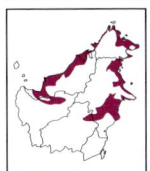

Female hepatic morph

Male

Juvenile

Identification 21–28 cm. **Adult male *sepulcralis*** Like Plaintive Cuckoo but darker, head grey, back and wings brown, white on bend of wing, tail barred black and rufous with white tips and white notches on outer edges, throat and underparts pinkish-rufous, undertail broadly barred brown with thin whitish notching on inner webs; iris brown, eye-ring yellow, bill black with orange base, feet yellow. **Adult female hepatic morph** Upperparts barred rufous and brown, underparts whitish barred dark brown. **Juvenile** Upperparts barred buff and dark brown, tail dark brown with rufous and whitish barring, white on bend of wing, underparts white with black barring, iris brown, eye-ring grey, bill black, feet greyish-yellow. **Similar species** Plaintive Cuckoo has grey throat and breast, somewhat paler grey upperparts and blackish eye-ring. **Habitat** Primary and secondary lowland dipterocarp, low hill, riverine and peatswamp forest, mangroves, plantations; lowland specialist to 300 m. **Behaviour** Feeds on insects, especially caterpillars, and other small invertebrates, small fruits. **Voice** A repeated, shrill *tea for two* or *fee fer fee*, the first and third notes (2.5 kHz) louder and higher-pitched than the second (1.9 kHz); another song is a repeated series of 5–6 clear mournful whistles, *weet weet weet…*, each note delivered with slight upward inflection (2.3–2.8 kHz), the series delivered on same pitch or slightly descending. **Range & status** S Thailand, Thai-Malay Peninsula, Indonesia, Philippines. **Borneo** Uncommon resident in lowland forests in Sabah and Sarawak, and hill forests of C and E Kalimantan. **Breeding** Brood parasite; elsewhere recorded hosts include shrikes, tailorbirds, forktails, flycatchers and sunbirds; possibly breeds around April.

VIOLET CUCKOO *Chrysococcyx xanthorhynchus*

Juvenile

Female

Male

Identification 16 cm. **Adult male *xanthorhynchus*** Head, upper breast and upperparts glossy violet-purple, lower breast and belly white barred blackish-purple, undertail blackish-violet with white tips; iris and eye-ring red, bill yellow with red base, feet greyish-olive. **Adult female** Crown coppery, face bronze-green with white speckling, upperparts bronze-green, underparts whitish finely barred bronze-green; bill yellowish with rufous base. **Juvenile** Upperparts rufous finely barred brown, underparts white barred irregularly blackish-brown; iris dark brown, bill dark brown with rufous base. **Similar species** Female Little Bronze Cuckoo has coarser barring on throat, lacks coppery crown, and never has red eye-ring. **Habitat** Forest edges, secondary forest, gardens, mangroves, plantations, to 1,300 m. **Behaviour** Feeds on insects, fruits; perches motionless, may sally out to catch insects or glean from foliage in lower and middle storeys. **Voice** Typical song is a repeated two-note *ki-wiT*, usually uttered in flight, the first note descending (4.5–4 kHz), the second upslurred (3.5–5.5 kHz, 1–2 phrases/s); also a high-pitched, descending trill given when perched and a courtship call consisting of a repeated *seer-se-seer*, ending in a woodpecker-like descending trill. **Range & status** SE Asia, Indonesia, Philippines. **Borneo** Common (Sabah, Brunei, E Kalimantan) to uncommon resident throughout, including N Natunas. **Breeding** Brood parasite; recorded hosts include sunbirds and spiderhunters; possibly breeds around April. Eggs are purplish-white with small black and white splotches.

LITTLE BRONZE CUCKOO *Chrysococcyx minutillus*

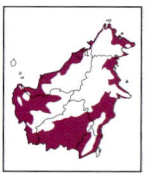

Male / Juvenile

Identification 15–16 cm. **Adult male** *aheneus* Crown bright green, forehead and supercilium whitish, upperparts glossy bronze-green, tail bronze-rufous with white tip and black-and-white barring on sides, underparts whitish with green-brown barring, undertail broadly banded black and white; iris red, eye-ring red, bill black, feet grey. **Adult female** Like male but upperparts not as glossy; iris brown, eye-ring may vary from white to brown. **Juvenile** Upperparts greyish-brown, underparts plain whitish with indistinct barring on flanks; iris brown, eye-ring pale. **Habitat** Primary and secondary lowland dipterocarp forest, mangroves, plantations to 250 m. **Behaviour** Feeds on insects, especially caterpillars. **Voice** Song given in breeding season is a 4–5 note *tiu tiu tiu tiu tiu* delivered at constant pitch (3 kHz, 1 phrase/0.8–1.2 s). Also a rapidly modulated, tinkling trill *ti ti ti ti ti...*, slightly descending, with rich layer of harmonics (3.4–2.7 kHz). The series can consist of 45 or more notes in 3 s. **Range & status** Thai-Malay Peninsula, Indonesia, Philippines, New Guinea, N Australia. **Borneo** Uncommon to rare resident Sabah, Brunei, Sarawak and W Kalimantan; common in E and S Kalimantan. **Breeding** Brood parasite; recorded hosts include sunbirds; possibly breeds July–November. **Note** Two taxa were previously treated as separate species: Little Bronze Cuckoo *C. m. cleis* and Gould's Bronze Cuckoo *C. russatus aheneus*. There has been much confusion regarding the taxonomy of the complex, and *C. russatus* has now been subsumed in *C. minutillus*, with *cleis* now generally regarded as synonym of *aheneus*.

HORSFIELD'S BRONZE CUCKOO
Chrysococcyx basalis

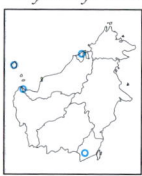

Adult

Identification 16–17 cm. Monotypic. **Adult** Head brown, prominent whitish supercilium bordered below by brown eyestripe curving down sides of neck, throat whitish lightly streaked, upperparts dull bronze-green with buff feather-edges, tail bronze-green with rufous edges, underparts whitish with incomplete brown barring, undertail dark grey with broad black and white bars and rufous on outer feathers; iris red, eye-ring grey, bill black, feet grey. **Juvenile** Like adult but duller with faint or no barring on underparts. **Habitat** Secondary forest, coastal scrub, mangroves; outside Borneo favours arid and semiarid zones, heathlands. **Behaviour** Feeds on insects, especially caterpillars; brood parasite. **Voice** A repeated, doleful *tsiuu*, downslurred (4.2–2.5 kHz, 1 note/s). **Range & status** Java, E Indonesia, New Guinea, Australia. **Borneo** Rare non-breeding vagrant with few records from Brunei, Sarawak, S Kalimantan and N Natunas, most June–August.

DRONGO CUCKOO *Surniculus lugubris*

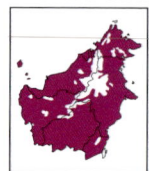

Adult / Juvenile

Identification 24 cm. Resembles small drongo but with distinctive slender, decurved bill. **Adult** *brachyurus* Upperparts glossy black, nape with inconspicuous white patch sometimes not visible, underparts black, undertail-coverts and undertail with narrow white barring, tail square or very slightly forked, broad at tip; iris reddish-brown, eye-ring black, bill black, feet dark grey. **Juvenile** Dull black spotted white. **Habitat** Forest edges and clearings of primary and secondary lowland dipterocarp forest, and peatswamp forest, kerangas, gardens, mangroves, to 1,300 m. **Behaviour** Feeds on insects, especially caterpillars, spiders, small fruits; forages in canopy; flight typical of cuckoo, smooth and direct, with no dip and loop as in drongos. **Voice** Song is a series of 6–7 loud, clear notes increasing in pitch (2.3–3.3 kHz, each phrase 2.5 s) ascending the scale, sometimes transcribed as *one two three four five six seven*. Often sings at night. Call is an unusual buzzy, hoarse *fee fee fee fee fi fifififififi* increasing in pitch, pace and volume (1.4–4.1 kHz), the last notes dropping off in both pitch and volume. Most vocal from December to April. **Range & status** S India, Himalayas, S China, SE Asia, Indonesia. **Borneo** Common resident throughout. **Breeding** Brood parasite; main hosts are babblers but others include bulbuls, ioras and shrikes; possibly breeds around April; egg is white with purple splotches.

ASIAN KOEL *Eudynamys scolopacea*

Identification 42–44 cm. **Adult male *malayana*** Glossy bluish-black all over, tail long and rounded; iris crimson, bill pale green, feet grey. **Adult female** Brown crown with buff streaks showing rufous wash, upperparts brown with rufous-buff spots and bars, throat and upper breast buff with coarse brown streaks and spots, rest of underparts buff washed rufous with brown barring; iris red. **Juvenile** Male is dull black with buff spots, female like adult female but darker with blackish head and breast; iris brown, bill black. **Adult *chinensis*** (recorded on offshore islands) Larger, female spotted and barred whitish, lacks rufous wash on crown. **Habitat** Secondary forest, coastal forests, plantations, orchards, gardens, mangroves, mainly at lower elevations in coastal areas but has been recorded to 1,200 m. **Behaviour** Arboreal, feeds on fruits, especially figs, and some insects. Brood parasite; known hosts include crows and mynas. Flight strong, swift and direct. **Voice** Territorial call is a strident, piercing *ko-el* in a series of 5–10 notes increasing in pitch, volume and pace to reach a crescendo (1.2–1.9 kHz); also a distinctive, rapid *wook kawook kawook kawook kawook kawook kawook kawook*, each note rising then falling (0.8–1.4 kHz). **Range & status** Indian Subcontinent, S China, SE Asia, Indonesia, Philippines, New Guinea. **Borneo** Uncommon non-breeding visitor throughout; most records September–April but some as late as June suggest possible resident status.

BORNEAN GROUND-CUCKOO *Carpococcyx radiatus*

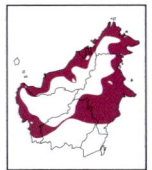

Identification 60 cm. Monotypic. Very large-bodied, ground-dwelling cuckoo with conspicuous barred underparts and long tail. **Adult** Head and throat glossy purple-black, mantle and back green with purple gloss, lower back and rump rufous with fine dark barring, wings and tail purple-black with coppery tinge, upper breast grey, rest of underparts white barred black; iris brown, bare facial skin around eye green, bill green, legs and feet green. **Juvenile** Like adult but crown greenish-brown, back brown, wings brown barred buff, underparts unbarred pale rufous. **Habitat** Primary lowland dipterocarp and riverine forest, an extreme lowland specialist to 50 m; probably requires extensive areas of primary forest, possibly favouring flat areas on limestone soils. **Behaviour** Terrestrial, inconspicuous and extremely wary; feeds on insects and fruit, known to follow feeding Bearded Pigs *Sus barbatus* and Sun Bears *Helarctos malayanus* gleaning soil invertebrates; nest is undescribed. **Voice** A low-pitched, single termulous *koo* (0.4 kHz, 0.3 s) or double *wu-koo* (0.4 kHz), the first note shorter than the second, each phrase delivered in 1 s, repeated every 4–5 s. Call is a nasal, pig-like grunt *arrk* (0.5 kHz). **Range & status** Endemic, uncommon to rare resident in suitable habitat throughout, except S Borneo. **Breeding** Very poorly known; observations of immatures August–December indicate hatching mid-year and breeding possibly February–July.

109

BLACK-BELLIED MALKOHA *Rhopodytes diardi*

Identification 38 cm. Large, long tailed, non-parasitic cuckoo. **Adult *borneensis*** (endemic subspecies) Upperparts dark grey, wings glossy dark blue-green, tail black with green gloss tipped white, throat and breast greenish-grey, belly and undertail-coverts blackish-grey, tail tipped white; iris pale blue, extensive crimson velvety bare facial skin around eye, edges of eyelids black, bill green with bluish-grey base, feet dark blue-grey. **Juvenile** Like adult but iris dark brown. **Similar species** Similar Chestnut-bellied Malkoha has rufous-chestnut belly and undertail-coverts and more orange-red facial skin. **Habitat** Primary and secondary lowland dipterocarp and peatswamp forest, mangroves, plantations, to 1,000 m, with occasional records to 1,700 m. **Behaviour** Feeds on insects; secretive, creeps around thick vegetation in middle storey and canopy, making short gliding flights from tree to tree; both sexes participate in nesting and rearing of chicks. **Voice** A brief, almost frog-like *kwauk* (1.2 kHz, 0.1 s). **Range & status** Thai-Malay Peninsula, Sumatra. **Borneo** Uncommon to rare resident throughout. **Breeding** Possibly breeds around March; eggs white.

CHESTNUT-BELLIED MALKOHA
Rhopodytes sumatranus

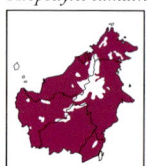

Identification 40 cm. Monotypic. **Adult** Head grey, back glossy dark green, wings glossy dark blue-green, tail black with green gloss and tipped white, throat and breast grey, belly and undertail-coverts rufous-chestnut; iris pale blue to red, extensive orange-red velvety bare facial skin around eye bordered black, bill green with bluish-grey base, feet dark blue-grey. **Juvenile** Like adult but iris dark brown. **Habitat** Forest edges, secondary lowland dipterocarp, peatswamp and riverine forests, kerangas, mangroves, plantations; favours coastal areas but occurs to 1,200 m. **Behaviour** Feeds on large insects, lizards, frogs; secretive, creeping around thick vegetation in middle storey and canopy; makes short gliding flights from tree to tree. **Voice** A knocking *kokokoko* and soft *chok chok*. **Range & status** Thai-Malay Peninsula, Sumatra. **Borneo** Uncommon resident throughout. **Breeding** June–October; both sexes participate in nesting and rearing of chicks, otherwise undescribed in Borneo.

RED-BILLED MALKOHA *Zanclostomus javanicus*

Identification 42 cm. **Adult *pallidus*** Forehead and lores rufous, head grey, back and wings glossy blue, rump grey, tail glossy dark blue tipped white, underparts rufous with broad pale grey breast-band; iris brown with broad blue bare facial skin around eye, bill red, feet slaty-grey. **Juvenile** Wing-coverts with rufous wash, bill red with black tip. **Habitat** Edges of primary lowland dipterocarp forest, secondary forest, lower montane forest, plantations; usually to 500 m, with occasional records to 1,300 m. **Behaviour** Usually in pairs; feeds on insects, spiders and crutaceans; creeps around thick vegetation in middle storey like squirrel, making short gliding flights from tree to tree. **Voice** A quiet, low-pitched croak (1.1 kHz), chattering bleat reminiscent of young goat, and a soft *cluck* (1.1 kHz). **Range & status** Thai-Malay Peninsula, Sumatra, Java. **Borneo** Uncommon resident throughout including the Natunas. **Breeding** February–April; egg all white; both sexes participate in nesting and rearing of chicks.

RAFFLES'S MALKOHA *Rhinortha chlorophaeus*

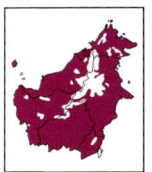

Identification 32 cm. Monotypic. Smallest malkoha. **Adult male** Upperparts rufous, tail black with fine grey barring and broad white tip, throat and breast paler rufous grading to dark grey belly, undertail-coverts grey; iris brown, bare facial skin around eye pale bluish-green, bill pale green, feet slaty-grey. **Adult female** Head, throat and mantle grey, rest of upperparts rufous with black subterminal band and white tips on tail, belly buffish with rufous vent. **Juvenile** Like adult, male with tail indistinctly barred, female with rufous to buffish throat. **Habitat** Primary and secondary lowland dipterocarp to lower montane forest, peatswamp forest, riverine forest, gardens, to 1,100 m. **Behaviour** Usually solitary or in pairs, secretive; feeds on insects creeping around thick vegetation in middle storey like squirrel, making short gliding flights from tree to tree. **Voice** A cat-like, mournful *kyar kyar-kyar-kyar-kyar*, the first note higher-pitched (2.5 kHz) than the following four which are delivered on an even pitch (1.9 kHz). Also a harsh, whiny *kyow kyow ki kyow*, the last note extended but on same pitch (2.3 kHz). **Range & status** Thai-Malay Peninsula, Sumatra. **Borneo** Common resident throughout, including N Natunas and Banggi Island. **Breeding** January–June; eggs are glossy white, the nest large and bulky built in dense vegetation 3–8 m from ground; both sexes participate in nesting and rearing of chicks.

Male

Female

CHESTNUT-BREASTED MALKOHA
Zanclostomus curvirostris

Identification 42–49 cm. **Adult *microrhinus*** (endemic subspecies) Head dark grey, upperparts glossy dark green, tail glossy dark green with broad chestnut terminal band (no white tips), underparts rich reddish-chestnut, undertail rufous; iris pale blue, bare facial skin around eye crimson, bill green with red lower mandible, feet grey. **Adult female** Like male but iris bright yellow. **Juvenile** Less extensive bare skin on face, bill slaty-grey. **Habitat** Primary and secondary lowland dipterocarp and peatswamp forest, plantations, gardens, to 1,200 m, but mostly below 800 m. **Behaviour** Usually solitary; feeds on insects, nestlings, small lizards and frogs; creeps around thick vegetation in middle storey like squirrel, making short gliding flights from tree to tree. **Voice** A brief, descending, soft *kauk* (1.4–0.9 kHz, 0.2 s); also a loud *wee-oo*. **Range & status** Thai-Malay Peninsula, Sumatra, Java, SW Philippines. **Borneo** Common resident throughout, including N Natunas and Banggi Islands. **Breeding** February–September; two white eggs are laid in nest consisting of loose construction of twigs lined with leaves placed high up in thick vegetation; both sexes participate in nesting and rearing of chicks.

Adult

SHORT-TOED COUCAL *Centropus rectunguis*

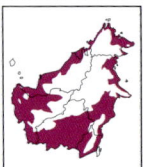

Identification 38–43 cm. Monotypic. **Adult** Head glossy black, underparts black, wings and back chestnut, relatively short tail black; iris crimson, bill black, feet black. Female slightly larger. **Juvenile** Head rufous with brown shaft-streaks, back and wings rufous with blackish barring, underparts and tail blackish-brown with whitish bars and spots; iris grey to brown. **Similar species** As Greater Coucal but smaller with shorter tail, different vocalisations and habitat, Short-toed being restricted to forest. **Habitat** Primary lowland dipterocarp, peatswamp and riverine forest; an extreme lowland specialist to 300 m. **Behaviour** As Greater Coucal; solitary and very inconspicuous. **Voice** Similar to Greater Coucal but a lower-pitched, slower *boo boo* (0.3 kHz, 2 notes/s). **Range & status** Thai-

Malay Peninsula, Sumatra. **Borneo** Locally uncommon to rare resident throughout; most recent records are from Brunei and E Sarawak. **Breeding** Undescribed in Borneo.

GREATER COUCAL *Centropus sinensis*

SUKAU RIVER LODGE 9/6/10

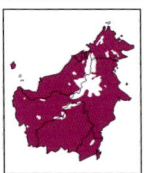

Identification 47–52 cm. **Adult** *bubutus* Head glossy black, underparts black, wings and back chestnut, long, broad black tail; iris crimson, bill black, feet black. Female larger. **Juvenile** Head, underparts and tail blackish-brown with whitish bars and spots, back and wings rufous barred black; iris grey to brown. **Habitat** Forest edges, secondary forest, peatswamp forest, grassland, scrubby vegetation, paddyfields, mangroves, overgrown plantations, gardens, to 1,200 m in Kelabit Highlands. **Behaviour** Often in pairs; feeds on small mammals, nestlings and eggs, lizards, frogs, large insects and invertebrates; creeps and clambers around low vegetation; flight is laboured and slow with alternate flapping and gliding. **Voice** A slow-paced, low-pitched constant *boo boo boo...* (0.35 kHz, 3–4 notes/s), often in duet with other bird giving a faster *bupup* (5 notes/s). **Range & status** Indian Subcontinent, S China, SE Asia, Indonesia, SW Philippines. **Borneo** Common resident throughout, including N Natunas. **Breeding** March–

December; lays 1–3 smooth, glossy white eggs; nest is large ball of grass and twigs with narrow entrance lined with dry leaves situated close to ground to 6 m.

LESSER COUCAL *Centropus bengalensis*

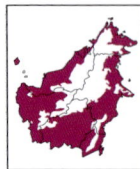

Identification 31–34 cm. **Adult breeding** *javanensis* Head and upper back glossy black, lower back and rump brown, wings chestnut, tail glossy black tipped white, underparts black; iris red, bill black, feet black; female larger. **Adult non-breeding** Head and upper back brown with prominent buffish-white shaft-streaks, wing-coverts dark brown with buffish shaft-streaks and feather-edging, flight feathers rufous, long uppertail-coverts brown barred buffish-rufous, tail black tipped white, underparts buff spotted white; bill pinkish with grey culmen. **Juvenile** Like non-breeding adult but more rufous with blackish barring on wings and tail and broader barring on underparts. **Habitat** Grasslands, swamps, peatswamp forest, scrubby vegetation, cultivation, recently cleared areas, to 700 m, with occasional records to 1,500 m. **Behaviour** Terrestrial, rarely known to climb trees; often in pairs; feeds on insects, spiders, lizards, fruit. **Voice** A bubbling, short, low-pitched *poop* (0.4 kHz, 0.05 s) interspersed with a higher-pitched fluty two-note *tukup* (1 kHz, 0.14 s) and repeated 1 phrase/s. **Range & status** Indian Subcontinent, S China, SE Asia, Indonesia, Philippines. **Borneo** Common resident throughout. **Breeding** February–December; egg dull white; nest is large ball of grass situated in low tangled vegetation.

TYTONIDAE: Barn-owls, grass-owls & bay owls

Worldwide c.18 species, 3 in Borneo. Large-headed, nocturnal or crepuscular birds of prey with soft plumage, allowing silent flight, and distinctive facial disk. Most are cavity nesters. Vocalisations are varied with a wide range of screeching, wailing, clicking and mechanical sounds. Feed mostly on small mammals located by sound. Female typically larger and darker than male.

COMMON BARN-OWL *Tyto alba*

Identification 34–36 cm. **Adult *javanica*** Heart-shaped facial disc white fringed with black, upperparts golden-buff with greyish wash and black and buff spots, wings and tail with fine blackish-brown barring, underparts white with black spots on breast, long legs densely feathered to toes; iris dark brown, bill pinkish-white, feet brown. **Juvenile** Plumage downy, more heavily spotted. **Similar species** See Eastern Grass-owl **Habitat** Introduced in oil palm plantations in N Borneo. **Behaviour** Strictly nocturnal; feeds on mice and rats as well as other small animals; buoyant flight with legs dangling. **Voice** A short, hoarse, unpleasant scream (3.6 kHz, 0.4 s). **Range & status** N America, S America, Europe, Africa, Indian Subcontinent, SE Asia, Indonesia, New Guinea, Australia. **Borneo** Introduced to Sabah and Sarawak, status uncertain.

EASTERN GRASS-OWL *Tyto longimembris*

Identification 35–36 cm. **Adult *amauronota*** As Common Barn-owl but upperparts dark brown with whitish spots and golden-buff markings, underparts with rufous wash, squarish facial disc white, edged dark brown on top and buffish on sides and bottom, small brown mark in front of small eyes; in flight contrasting dark upperwing and paler underwing, both with dark tips to primaries, golden-buff patch at base of primaries on upperwing, wings and legs long; iris dark brown, bill light brown, feet greyish. **Juvenile** Buffish downy plumage. **Similar species** Common Barn-owl is paler overall, lacks rufous wash on underparts; note habitat. **Habitat** Grasslands. **Behaviour** Strictly nocturnal; feeds on mice and rats as well as other small animals; hunts low over grass. **Voice** Similar to Common Barn-owl. **Range & status** Indian Subcontinent, S China, SE Asia, Philippines, W Indonesia, New Guinea, Australia, New Caledonia, Fiji. **Borneo** Rare breeding resident in N Borneo (Sabah). May be spreading in Borneo due to forest clearance. **Breeding** One nest on ground in July contained two chicks, another in January contained one chick and three eggs, both being situated in thick stands of leguminous ground cover; possibly nests at various times of year in Borneo.

ORIENTAL BAY OWL *Phodilus badius*

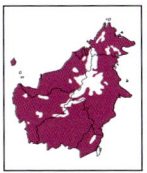

Identification 23–33 cm. **Adult *badius*** Pale pinkish-buff squarish facial disc with ear-like projections above eyes, chestnut feathering around eyes, outer edge of disc fringed chestnut-brown, crown and nape buffish speckled black and buff, back and wing-coverts chestnut with black and buff spots, flight feathers and tail chestnut barred black, underparts pinkish-buff spotted dark brown and buff; iris dark brown, bill pinkish-ivory, powerful legs and feet feathered to toes, toes pinkish-buff. **Adult *arixuthus*** Generally paler, larger pale spots on upperparts. **Juvenile** Downy plumage. **Habitat** Primary and secondary lowland dipterocarp forest, recorded to 1,200 m in Kelabit Highlands but generally restricted to lowlands. **Behaviour** Strictly nocturnal; feeds on small vertebrates and insects, hunting from perch in dense vegetation, rocking head from side to side as it watches potential prey. **Voice** An ethereal, piercing *hwee hwee...* of 3–6 notes, each note slightly upslurred (1–1.6 kHz); also a piercing screech. **Range & status** NE India, SW and S China, SE Asia, Java, Sumatra. **Borneo** Locally uncommon lowland resident throughout, *arixuthus* from N Natunas. **Breeding** October–December; nests in hollow trees and stumps.

113

STRIGIDAE: Typical owls

Worldwide c.187 species, 12 in Borneo. Large-headed, nocturnal and crepuscular birds of prey. Characterised by cryptic plumage, and large head and facial disk with forward-facing eyes. Flight is silent, and hearing and eyesight are particularly acute. Often highly vocal with diagnostic stereotypical hooting or whistling songs. Roost and nest in tree cavities. The taxonomy of smaller owls, *Otus* and *Ninox* in particular, is complex and still in a state of flux. Generally sexes are alike but the female slightly larger.

REDDISH SCOPS-OWL *Otus rufescens*

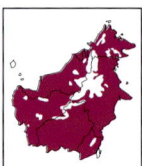

Identification 15–18 cm. **Adult *rufescens*** Prominent ear-tufts brownish flecked buff, indistinct facial disc buffish-rufous fringed dark brown, upperparts rufous-brown with small buff spots bordered black and larger on mantle and wing-coverts, flight feathers brown with dark brown barring, underparts pale rufous with distinct black spots, legs feathered buff almost to toes; iris brown, bill ivory, feet pale yellow. **Juvenile** Less spotted. **Similar species** More spotted than Mountain Scops-owl; lacks collar and is more rufous and spotted than Sunda Scops-owl. **Habitat** Primary and secondary lowland dipterocarp to lower montane forest, logged forest, to 1,500 m. **Behaviour** Nocturnal, very inconspicuous and shy; probably feeds mostly on insects in lower and middle storey of dense forest. **Voice** Song is a single note, soft *hyoo* (0.9 kHz, 0.4 s) repeated every 5–10 s. **Range & status** Thai-Malay Peninsula, Sumatra, Java. **Borneo** Uncommon resident throughout; probably under-recorded. **Breeding** Nests in tree-hollows, but undescribed in Borneo.

Adult

MOUNTAIN SCOPS-OWL *Otus spilocephalus*

Identification 18–20 cm. Small, grizzled black and buff inconspicuous owl. **Adult *luciae*** (endemic subspecies) Facial disc rufous-brown with whitish eyebrows, small ear-tufts and crown spotted black, upperparts rufous-brown with blackish bars, scapulars brown with row of black-tipped silvery spots, flight feathers and tail rufous-brown barred blackish, underparts rufous with black and buff vermiculations, legs feathered to toes; iris yellow, bill ivory, feet whitish to pale flesh-coloured. Much individual variation. **Juvenile** Markings duller; fluffier than adult. **Habitat** Confined to montane forest from 750 to 2,750 m. **Behaviour** Strictly nocturnal, very elusive, sedentary; feeds on insects, small birds and rodents in lower and middle storeys of dense forest; roosts in thick vegetation. **Voice** A pure, even-pitched *plew-plew* whistle (1.3 kHz, 1.2 s) uttered every 4–5 s with small interval between each note (0.5 s). **Range & status** Himalayas, S China, SE Asia, Sumatra. **Borneo** Locally common in north-central mountain ranges from G. Kinabalu to Dulit Range and G. Menyapa (Sabah, E Sarawak, E Kalimantan). **Breeding** Nests in tree-hollows, but undescribed in Borneo.

Adult
luciae

RAJAH SCOPS-OWL *Otus brookii*

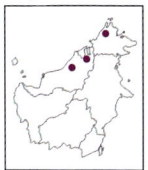

Identification 23 cm. **Adult *brookii*** (endemic) Ear-tufts white on inner side, white band on nape and white collar on hindneck, upperparts rich rufous-brown with black streaks and vermiculations and buff spots, scapulars with row of buff spots tipped black, underparts pale rufous-brown with buff and brown blotches and large spots, legs feathered almost to toes; iris orange, bill grey, feet pale yellow. **Juvenile** Race *brookii* undescribed; *solokensis* from Sumatra has dark rufous-brown upperparts with dark brown barring, underparts whitish-rufous with rufous freckles and streaks. **Habitat** Lower to upper montane forest from 900 to 2,000 m. **Behaviour** Very little known; feeds on insects and frogs; probably frequents middle storey. **Voice** Very poorly known in Borneo, where described by Hose (1929) as follows: 'Its note is clear, and at first almost startling, but is repeated monotonously with no change of inflection.' Call of *O. b. solokensis* of Sumatra is an explosive, harsh crow-like two-note *kra kra* (1-2-1 kHz, c.1 s) each note slightly downslurred. **Range & status** Sumatra.

Adult

Borneo Rare resident, with specimens from G. Dulit and G. Mulu, E Sarawak (1893), and one dead bird collected from G. Kinabalu in 1986; perhaps extinct in Borneo although a possible 1999 specimen from G. Kinabalu requires further investigation. **Breeding** Undescribed.

SUNDA SCOPS-OWL *Otus lempiji*

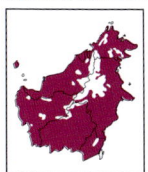

Identification 20–23 cm. Variable with two main morphs—greyish-brown and buffish-brown. **Adult *lempiji*** Facial disc rufous-brown with dark fringe, ear-tufts edged black, indistinct buff collar on hindneck, upperparts sandy-brown mottled black and buff, wings brown with buff barring, underparts buffish-brown to greyish-brown with blackish streaks and brown vermiculations, legs feathered to toes; iris brown, bill ivory to pale yellow, feet pale yellow. Race *lemurum* is here considered synonymous. **Juvenile** Paler than adult with more barring. **Habitat** Secondary forest, peatswamp forest, plantations, gardens, parks, to 1,100 m. **Behaviour** Strictly nocturnal; secretive; feeds on insects, nestlings, mice; nests in tree-hollows; roosts in thick vegetation, generally active in middle and lower storeys. **Voice** Call is a brief, interrogative, mellow *wooik* (1 kHz) with upward inflection, uttered at long intervals (10–15 s). **Range & status** Thai-Malay Peninsula, Sumatra, Java. **Borneo** Common resident throughout including N Natunas,

Adult

although current status uncertain and may be declining. **Breeding** January–June; lays two smooth white oval eggs; a nest has been observed in hollow base of tree.

MANTANANI SCOPS-OWL *Otus mantananensis*

Identification 18–20 cm. Two morphs occur—dark brown and rufous-brown. **Adult *mantananensis*** Facial disc buff with narrow dark border, eyebrows whitish, crown and ear-tufts brown spotted blackish-brown, upperparts dark brown to reddish-brown with blackish streaks and spots, scapulars with white spots, flight feathers and tail brown barred buff, breast rufous-brown grizzled blackish-brown grading into paler belly, legs feathered to above feet; iris yellow, bill grey, feet grey. **Juvenile** Not described for Bornean region; race *sibutuensis* of Sulu Archipelago is paler with heavy barring on wings and plain brown crown and breast. **Habitat** Restricted to small islands where it occurs in primary and secondary forest, plantations, coconut groves, casuarina forest, at sea-level. **Behaviour** Poorly known; nocturnal; mostly feeds on insects; nests in tree-hollows. **Voice** Call is a deep, goose-like *grrk* (0.9 kHz) which may be followed by a series of slightly longer, deep, grunting *waak-waak-*

Adult

waak... notes at rate of c.2 notes/s. **Range & status** Philippines. **Borneo** Common resident restricted to Mantanani Island, NW Borneo (Sabah). **Breeding** Possibly breeds in March; otherwise undescribed in Borneo.

115

BARRED EAGLE-OWL *Bubo sumatranus*

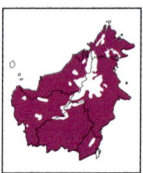

Identification 40–46 cm. **Adult *tenuifasciatus*** (endemic subspecies) Striking long, horizontal brown ear-tufts finely barred white, upperparts dark brown strongly barred rufous, scapulars with whitish spots, breast washed rufous with very dense, fine dark brown barring; rest of underparts greyish-white with dense brown barring, legs feathered to toes; iris dark brown, bill pale yellow, toes pale yellow. **Juvenile** Fluffy buffish-white with fine, wavy dark brown bars. **Habitat** Lowland primary and secondary dipterocarp forest, plantations, gardens, to 1,000 m. **Behaviour** Nocturnal, sometimes crepuscular; occupies large territories; roosts in tall trees with dense foliage usually close to trunk; feeds on small mammals and birds, snakes, large insects; nests in tree-hollows, very site-faithful, returning to same nest year after year. **Voice** Call is an eerie *whaa* (1.1 kHz, 0.6 s) uttered every 4–6 s; song is a two-note, lower-pitched *woo… hoo* (0.3–0.4 kHz) with 1.5 s between each note, the phrase uttered every 5–10 s. **Range & status** Thai-Malay Peninsula, Sumatra, Java and Bali. **Borneo** Sparsely distributed uncommon resident throughout. **Breeding** November–February; lays two eggs in tree-hole 1.5–15 m above ground.

Adult

BUFFY FISH-OWL *Ketupa ketupu*

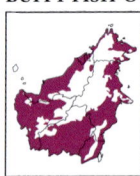

Identification 38–44 cm. **Adult *ketupu*** Face pale buff, eyebrows and lores white, long ear-tufts held horizontal, head and neck blackish-brown with rufous streaks, upperparts dark brown streaked rufous and spotted buffish-white and pale rufous, flight feathers dark brown broadly barred buff or fulvous, tail dark brown with 3–4 whitish-buff bands, underparts buff with broad brown streaks, streaks thinner and sparser on belly, legs unfeathered; iris yellow, bill dark grey, legs and feet pale greyish-yellow. **Adult *pageli*** Strongly tinged reddish above and below. **Juvenile** Like adult but upperparts more rufous with little or no buffish-white, tail with narrower, irregular whitish bars; underparts with narrower streaking. **Habitat** Frequents forested areas near water including forest-lined rivers and lakes, estuaries, paddyfields, parks and mangroves, essentially a lowland specialist to 400 m, with records from Kelabit Highlands to 1,100 m. **Behaviour** Nocturnal, sometimes crepuscular; hunts from perch near water; feeds on crustaceans, aquatic insects, small fish, frogs, small birds and mammals; nests in tree-hollows and large epiphytes; roosts in dense foliage in trees and palms. **Voice** A variety of calls including a harsh, upslurred scream (1.5–2.2 kHz), a long wailing *aaiee* (2.3 kHz), and fluty (like somebody blowing over bottle), melancholy *pop pop…* (0.5 kHz) repeated about every 0.5 s. **Range & status** SE Asia, Sumatra, Java and Bali. **Borneo** Race *ketupu* locally common resident in lowlands throughout (except NW); *pageli* locally common resident in lowlands of NW Borneo. **Breeding** November–August; lays two eggs in nest-hole.

Adult
ketupu

BROWN WOOD-OWL *Strix leptogrammica*

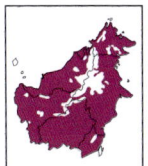

Identification 40–55 cm. **Adult *leptogrammica*** Facial disc rufous to buff with broad, dark-brown-edged rings around eyes; eyebrows paler, crown dark brown, mantle and back chestnut with dark brown barring, flight feathers and tail chestnut barred dark brown and buffish-cinnamon, throat and upper breast rufous-brown with fine dark brown barring, rest of underparts buffish-white with fine brown barring, legs feathered to toes; iris brown, bill black, feet dark grey. **Adult *vaga*** Larger, generally greyer, upper breast rich chestnut barred black, whitish throat-patch. **Juvenile** Facial disc buffish-brown with narrow brown rim, rest of plumage whitish-buff barred rufous with darker wings. **Habitat** Dense primary lowland dipterocarp and hill forest, to 1,000 m. **Behaviour** Strictly nocturnal; feeds on small mammals, birds and reptiles, and large insects; nests in tree-hollows; roosts in densest parts of tall trees. **Voice** A deep, mellow *boo-booo* (0.4 kHz) with both notes on same pitch, each phrase 1 s, uttered every 10–15 s; also a long, screeching *ii-ooow* (2 kHz, 1.2 s). **Range & status** Himalayas, S China, SE Asia, Sumatra, Java. **Borneo** Uncommon resident throughout; *vaga* in N Borneo, *leptogrammica* C and S Borneo. **Breeding** Undescribed in Borneo.

Juvenile *leptogrammica*

Adult *leptogrammica*

COLLARED OWLET *Glaucidium brodiei*

Identification 15–17 cm. Tiny owl with large, rounded head, plumage quite variable with two morphs—rufous and grey. **Adult *borneense*** (endemic subspecies) Head grey with buffish-white spots, eyebrows and lores whitish, white throat-patch, yellow and black eye-shaped pattern on nape, upperparts rufous-brown to greyish-brown barred buff and dark brown, upper breast and flanks brown barred greyish-white, lower breast and belly white with broad brown streaks, tail brown with rufous bars; iris yellow, bill yellow, legs and feet greenish-yellow. **Juvenile** Like adult but head streaked and tear-drop marks on breast. **Similar species** Lack of ear-tufts differentiate from scops-owls. **Habitat** Lower to upper montane forest, from 500 to 2,100 m, with records down to 240 m at Tawau, SE Sabah. **Behaviour** Little known in Borneo; often active during day when frequently mobbed by small birds; feeds on small birds and mammals, nestlings, lizards, large invertebrates; nests in tree-hollows. **Voice** A soft, mellow *poo* (pause) *pu-poo pu-poo* delivered on same pitch, delivered intermittently (differs from calls of this species in mainland Asia). **Range & status** Himalayas, S, C and E China, SE Asia, Sumatra. **Borneo** Uncommon resident of central mountain ranges from G. Kinabalu to Muller Range (Sabah, Brunei, E Sarawak, E and W Kalimantan). **Breeding** Undescribed in Borneo.

Adult

Adult

117

BROWN BOOBOOK *Ninox scutulata*

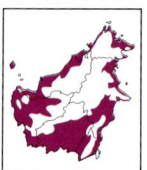

Identification 27–33 cm. Hawk-like owl with rounded head, long tail, and unstreaked dark brown upperparts. **Adult *borneensis*** (endemic subspecies) Head dark brown, lores white, upperparts uniform dark brown, long tail dark brown broadly barred pale brown and tipped white, underparts buffish-white with dense dark-brown streaks, legs feathered to toes; iris yellow, bill dark grey, feet yellow; female larger than male. **Juvenile** Like adult but plumage fluffy, underparts less streaked. **Habitat** Lowland specialist: primary lowland dipterocarp forest and mangroves. **Behaviour** Nocturnal and occasionally crepuscular; feeds on large insects and small vertebrates, often catching prey on wing; roosts under thick canopy or among creepers; nests in tree-hollows. **Voice** A distinctive, pleasant, mellow *hoo-wup* starting at 0.6 kHz, dipping slightly then rising to 0.8 kHz (0.5 s), uttered at rate of one per 1–1.5 s. **Range & status** Indian

Adult

Subcontinent, SE Asia, Indonesia. **Borneo** Common to uncommon resident throughout, including N Natunas. **Breeding** One record from February; almost spherical egg is white with slight gloss.

NORTHERN BOOBOOK *Ninox japonica*

Identification 27–33 cm. Hawk-like owl with rounded head, long wings and tail, and unstreaked dark brown upperparts. **Adult *japonica*** Head and upperparts brown, lores greyish-white, long tail dark brown broadly barred pale brown and tipped white, underparts white with distinct, broad dark-brown streaking, legs feathered to toes; iris yellow, bill dark grey, feet yellow. Female larger than male. **Juvenile** Like adult but plumage fluffy, underparts less streaked. **Similar species** Differs from Brown Boobook in being paler overall, longer-winged, different in voice. **Habitat** In Borneo, forests and woodlands especially on offshore islands, probably to 1,500 m; elsewhere, broadleaved deciduous and evergreen forest, plantations, parks, gardens. **Behaviour** Nocturnal and occasionally crepuscular; feeds on large insects and small vertebrates, often catching prey on wing; roosts under thick canopy or among creepers; nests in tree-hollows. **Voice** Rarely vocalises on non-breeding grounds. A short deep two-note *ho-ho* (1 kHz, < 1 s) repeated, often from prominent high

Adult

perch. **Range & status** Japan, China, Korea, migrating to Philippines, Indonesia. **Borneo** Uncommon non-breeding visitor N Borneo, especially offshore islands (Sabah, Brunei, Sarawak, and E Kalimantan).

SHORT-EARED OWL *Asio flammeus*

Identification 37–38 cm. Medium-sized owl with large, rounded head and inconspicuous short ear-tufts. **Adult *flammeus*** Facial disc greyish-white with black around eyes, small ear-tufts set close together at top of head, upperparts vary from greyish-white to buff with brown streaks and spots, underparts vary from greyish-white to buffish with heavy brown streaks; iris yellow, bill black, legs and feet feathered buff. **Habitat** Tundra, meadows, grasslands, heathlands (extralimital). **Behaviour** Diurnal and crepuscular; roosts on or close to ground; feeds on small mammals; buoyant flight with slow wing-beats and glides. **Voice** Unlikely to vocalise in Borneo; call is a harsh, squeaky *cheet* (2–3 kHz); during breeding season utters a low *bu bu bu…* in series of 10–20 notes. **Range & status** N and S America, Palearctic, N Africa, Indian Subcontinent, E Asia. **Borneo** Rare vagrant with two records (from Kuching, Sarawak, in 1910, and Brunei in 1976).

Adult

Adult

PODARGIDAE: Frogmouths

Worldwide 12 species, 6 in Borneo. Small to medium-sized, highly cryptic nocturnal birds with extraordinarily wide, heavy bills, forward-facing eyes and ornate head-plumes. Many species exhibit different colour morphs. They usually roost on well vegetated branches and are very difficult to detect during the day. Feed by gleaning and sallying for insects and small vertebrates.

LARGE FROGMOUTH *Batrachostomus auritus*

Adult

Identification 39–43 cm. Monotypic. Very large frogmouth with bold white spots on wing-coverts. **Adult** Upperparts chestnut to light brown, crown spotted or vermiculated buff, nuchal collar buffish-white with brown barring, buff stripe from lores to sides of head, buff moustachial stripe, pale buff bars and black spots on scapulars, wing-coverts with variable amount of bold buff or white spots, flight feathers and tail barred pale brown; underparts rufous-brown speckled brown with small buffish-white spots on breast, paler on belly; iris brown, bill brown with yellow at base and gape, legs and feet yellow. **Juvenile** Upperparts greyish-brown with pale buff vermiculations, lacks spots, underparts light greyish-brown with rufous tinge. **Similar species** Dulit Frogmouth is marginally smaller and darker with barred crown and less spotting on wing-coverts. **Habitat** Primary and secondary lowland dipterocarp forest and kerangas; extreme lowland specialist. **Behaviour** Poorly known, very elusive; nocturnal; feeds on cicadas and grasshoppers, hunting from perch taking prey from ground or nearby vegetation. **Voice** A slightly tremulous, mellow *kaaawoooo* delivered on an even (0.6–0.7 kHz) or slightly rising pitch (0.6–0.8 kHz). **Range & status** Thai-Malay Peninsula, Sumatra. **Borneo** Locally rare resident throughout, including N Natunas. **Breeding** Poorly known; the nest is a small circular pad of matted down attached to slender branch of small tree, containing a single egg.

DULIT FROGMOUTH *Batrachostomus harterti*

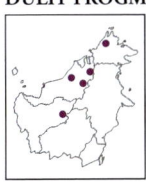

Adult

Identification 34–37 cm. Monotypic. Large, dark frogmouth found in hill and lower montane forest. **Adult** Crown dark brown barred buff, buff stripe from lores to sides of head, narrow pale buff nuchal collar, upperparts dark brown, wing-coverts spotted white, scapulars yellowish-brown barred brown and spotted black, flight feathers and tail barred paler brown, underparts brown barred buff, paler on belly and flanks; iris dark brown, bill pale greyish-brown, legs and feet pinkish-grey. **Juvenile** Unknown. **Similar species** See Large Frogmouth. **Habitat** Primary and secondary hill to lower montane forest, from 300 to 1,500 m. **Behaviour** Almost unknown; nocturnal. **Voice** Undescribed. **Range & status** Endemic, very rare resident known only from E Sarawak (G. Dulit, Usun Apau, Kelabit Highlands) and W Kalimantan (G. Liang Kubung). **Breeding** Undescribed.

GOULD'S FROGMOUTH *Batrachostomus stellatus*

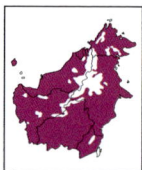

Identification 21–25 cm. Monotypic. Small to medium-sized frogmouth that occurs in two colour morphs. **Adult male** Upperparts rufous or dark brown, buff supercilium, narrow white collar, bold white spots on wing-coverts, scapulars with white or greyish spots, tail with paler brown barring, underparts buffish-white with rufous or brown edging; iris yellow, bill brown, legs and feet pinkish. **Adult female** Iris dark brown (this difference not yet proven), legs and feet pale yellow. **Juvenile** Plainer with less spotting, upperparts barred. **Similar species** Blyth's Frogmouth is smaller, darker and lacks white spots on wing-coverts, bold black spotting on upperparts (male) and bold white spots on underparts (female). Sunda Frogmouth lacks white spots on wing-coverts and has white throat. Bornean Frogmouth has shorter tail, more ornate whiskers and ear-tufts, less boldly spotted on underparts. **Habitat** Primary and secondary lowland dipterocarp and hill forest, to 920 m. **Behaviour** Nocturnal; feeds on crickets, cicadas, moths, beetles; perches low and pounces on prey in vegetation and on ground. **Voice** Male utters a throaty two-note *wuuuu-wau*, second note (1.6 kHz) much shorter and higher-pitched than first (1.2 kHz), each call about 1 s, uttered every 5–7 s. **Range & status** Thai-Malay Peninsula, Sumatra. **Borneo** Rare resident throughout, including N Natunas. **Breeding** Possibly breeds around April; nest is small circular pad of matted down attached to slender branch.

BORNEAN FROGMOUTH *Batrachostomus mixtus*

Identification 20–22 cm. Monotypic. Small brownish frogmouth with a relatively short tail. **Adult male** Upperparts reddish-brown with fine black vermiculations, narrow buffish-white collar, bold black-edged white spots on scapulars and wing-coverts, throat buffish-white speckled pale brown, rest of underparts light brown with bold white scalloping; iris yellow, bill greyish, legs and feet brown. **Adult female** Brighter reddish-brown with reduced white spotting and narrower collar. **Similar species** See Gould's Frogmouth. Blyth's Frogmouth has shorter whiskers and ear-tufts, male has black spots on upperparts, both sexes are more boldly spotted on underparts. Sunda Frogmouth is larger, male has black spots on upperparts, female has bolder white spots on underparts. **Habitat** Primary hill to upper montane forest, from 610 to 2,540 m. **Behaviour** Poorly known; nocturnal; probably feeds on beetles, crickets, and other insects. **Voice** A pure, whistled *pwau-* (1.6 kHz, c.1 s) repeated every 2–3 s. **Range & status** Endemic, rare resident in hills and mountains of north-west and isolated mountains of south-east (Sabah, Sarawak, S and E Kalimantan). **Breeding** February–April; nest is 7 cm wide saucer-shaped small pad made of cobwebs and soft material on horizontal branch c.1 m from ground; one contained single chick.

BLYTH'S FROGMOUTH *Batrachostomus affinis*

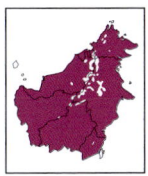

Identification 21–23 cm. **Adult male *affinis*** Upperparts brown with white speckles and black spots, head with whitish vermiculations, buffish supercilium, white collar with black markings, scapulars with bold white spots, flight feathers and tail barred paler brown, throat brownish-white with brown barring, breast brown speckled cinnamon, buff and white; belly and flanks buffish-white with brown edging and blackish spots; iris yellow, bill brown, legs and feet brown. **Adult female** Brighter, upperparts reddish-brown, scapulars with fewer white spots, underparts reddish-brown with bold white spots. **Juvenile** Paler and plainer. **Similar species** See Gould's and Bornean Frogmouths. Sunda Frogmouth is larger with less brown and black spotting. **Habitat** Primary and secondary lowland dipterocarp and hill forest, to 1,600 m. **Behaviour** Poorly known; nocturnal; feeds on variety of insects. **Voice** Female gives a four-note maniacal laugh *gyaa-gya-gya-gya* on downward pitch (1.4–0.8 kHz), each phrase about 1 s, repeated at irregular intervals (c.2–6 s); male gives a series of short yelps (1.6 kHz). **Range & status** SE Asia, Sumatra. **Borneo** Rare resident throughout, including Banggi Island. **Breeding** January–April; nest is soft whitish pad of mosses, lichens and downy feathers on slender branch.

SUNDA FROGMOUTH *Batrachostomus cornutus*

Identification 23–28 cm. Medium-sized frogmouth with marked polymorphism: tawny-brown or brown morphs also occur. **Adult male *cornutus*** Upperparts dark brown with buff, white and black speckling and spots; broad whitish supercilium and white collar, bold white spots on scapulars, flight feathers and tail barred paler brown, throat whitish barred brown, breast brown with buff, white and cinnamon speckles and spots; belly and flanks whitish with dark brown streaks and spots; iris yellow, bill pinkish-brown, legs and feet pale brown. Rufous or tawny-brown morphs also occur with more contrasting white spots on breast and scapulars. **Adult female** Upperparts reddish-brown with brown speckles, smaller white spots on scapulars, fewer bold white spots on underparts. **Juvenile** Paler and plainer. **Habitat** Secondary lowland dipterocarp forest, at sea-level (recorded to 1,000 m on Sumatra). **Behaviour** Very poorly known; nocturnal. **Voice** A clear, short, high-pitched whistled *phyu*, pitch rising then falling (1.4–2 kHz); also some growling *graa* notes. **Range & status** Sumatra, Kangean Island (Java). **Borneo** Rare resident throughout. **Breeding** February–May; lays single white egg in small circular nest made of down, moss and bark.

CAPRIMULGIDAE: Nightjars

Worldwide c.88 species, 5 in Borneo. Large-headed nocturnal or crepuscular insectivorous hunters with very wide mouth to catch insects on the wing. All have highly cryptic plumage and roost on the ground or along a branch during the day. Very vocal, most with diagnostic vocalisations. Fly silently on long wings with buoyant, erratic movements. Typically sexually dimorphic, the males usually with white patches on the wings and tail. Lays eggs directly on the ground.

Adult

Adult

MALAYSIAN EARED-NIGHTJAR
Eurostopodus temminckii

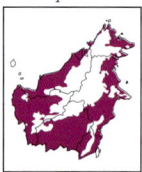

Identification 25–28 cm. Monotypic. Large nightjar with distinctive ear-tufts at rear of crown. **Adult** Crown and ear-tufts at rear of crown pale brown spotted blackish-brown, pale collar buffish on hindneck, upperparts brown speckled buff and cinnamon, scapulars black bordered broadly with buff, wing-coverts brown speckled and mottled buff and cinnamon, underparts pale brown barred dark brown, tail brown speckled and barred buffish-brown; in flight no white in wings or tail. **Similar species** Bonaparte's Nightjar is much smaller, lacks nuchal collar. **Habitat** Primary and secondary lowland dipterocarp and hill, kerangas and riverine forest, paddyfields, plantations, to 500 m. **Behaviour** Crepuscular and nocturnal; feeds on arboreal insects, foraging in flight over open water and clearings; roosts on ground and horizontal branches; usually sings in flight at dusk and dawn. **Voice** A distinctive far-carrying three-note *tok-tee-dow* (2–1.3 kHz, 1 s) with longer gap between first and second note, last note longer and downslurred. **Range & status** Thai-Malay Peninsula, Sumatra. **Borneo** Common resident throughout. **Breeding** One record of an adult incubating single egg on the ground, but otherwise undescribed in Borneo.

Male

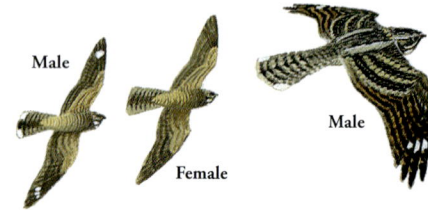

Male

Female

Male

GREY NIGHTJAR *Caprimulgus jotaka*

Identification 28–32 cm. **Adult male jotaka** Head greyish-black broadly streaked blackish-brown; upperparts intricately mottled black, grey, brown and buff; indistinct nuchal collar buffish-brown, buff malar stripe, white patch on sides of lower throat, wing-coverts greyish-brown with bold vermiculated greyish-white or buff spots, underparts narrowly barred grey, black and buff; in flight large white spot in wings and small white spots on outer tips of tail. **Adult female** As male but in flight shows small tawny-brown spot on wings and small buffish-brown outer tips to tail. **Similar species** Large-tailed Nightjar lacks bold spotting on wing-coverts, larger white (male) or buff (female) spots on outer tail-tips; Savanna Nightjar is smaller, lacks bold spots on wing-coverts, outer tail feathers all white (male) or plain (female). **Habitat** Primary and secondary lowland dipterocarp to upper montane forest, recorded to 2,000 m, commoner above 750 m. **Behaviour** Nocturnal; hawks arboreal insects with buoyant, acrobatic flight; roosts on ground or horizontal branch. **Voice** A loud, resonating *tok-tok-tok-tok-tok…* (1.5 kHz), sets of 8–14 rapidly uttered notes (4–5 note/s) repeated; more likely to be heard at dusk or dawn. **Range & status** N and E Asia, Indian Subcontinent, winters to SE Asia, Sumatra, Java, Philippines. **Borneo** Uncommon non-breeding visitor throughout, from September to March.

LIBARAN ISLAND 4/6/10

LARGE-TAILED NIGHTJAR *Caprimulgus macrurus*

Identification 25–29 cm. **Adult male** *salvadorii* (endemic subspecies) Head greyish-black broadly streaked blackish-brown with white malar stripe and large white throat-patch, upperparts dark greyish-black vermiculated blackish-brown, indistinct nuchal collar buffish-brown, wing-coverts greyish-brown with buff spots, scapulars black with bold buffish-white edging, underparts brown narrowly barred and speckled buff; in flight large white spot in wings and broad white spots on outer tips of tail. **Adult female** As male but in flight shows large tawny-brown spot on wings and buffish-brown outer tips to tail. **Similar species** See Grey Nightjar; Savanna Nightjar is smaller, greyer, with outer tail feathers entirely white (male) or tail plain (female). **Habitat** Secondary forest, kerangas, mangroves, scrub, cultivated areas, commonest below 400 m, with occasional records to 1,200 m. **Behaviour** Nocturnal; hawks and sallies for arboreal insects with buoyant, acrobatic flight; roosts on ground; often seen at night sitting on roads or tracks. **Voice** A loud, hollow-sounding *chonk…chonk…chonk…*, each note c.1.5 s, 1.6 kHz, repeated every 0.5 s or greater; also a low, grunting *grr grr grr…*. **Range & status** N and E Indian Subcontinent, S China, SE Asia, Indonesia, SW Philippines, New Guinea, N and NE Australia. **Borneo** Common resident W and N Borneo (Sabah, Sarawak, Brunei and far western areas of W and C Kalimantan bordering Sarawak including offshore islands) and patchily distributed elsewhere although not confirmed from E Kalimantan. **Breeding** April–November; lays 1–2 creamy-buff eggs with variable faint darker markings on bare ground.

SAVANNA NIGHTJAR *Caprimulgus affinis*

Identification 20 cm. **Adult male** *affinis* Upperparts brownish-grey vermiculated and speckled buff-white and tawny-brown, very indistinct buffish-white nuchal collar, scapulars black with indistinct buff edging, wing-coverts brown with bold tawny spots, small white patches on sides of lower throat, underparts tawny-brown finely barred and speckled greyish-brown, tail greyish-brown finely barred brownish-grey with white outer feathers; in flight large white spot on wing and white outer tail feathers. **Adult female** As male but more rufous, in flight shows buffish-brown wing spots and no white in tail. **Similar species** See Jungle and Large-tailed Nightjars. **Habitat** Swamps, cultivated areas, towns, in lowlands. **Behaviour** Nocturnal; hawks and sallies for arboreal insects with buoyant, acrobatic flight; roosts on ground. **Voice** A short high squeaky *kweek* (4.2 kHz, 0.2 s). **Range**

& status Indian Subcontinent, S China, SE Asia, Indonesia, Philippines. **Borneo** Common resident SE Borneo (C, S and E Kalimantan). **Breeding** Lays eggs on bare ground.

BONAPARTE'S NIGHTJAR *Caprimulgus concretus*

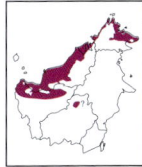

Identification 21–22 cm. Monotypic. **Adult male** Upperparts dark brown speckled chestnut, scapulars blackish-brown broadly edged buffish-chestnut, buffish-white malar stripe, large white throat-patch, breast blackish-brown barred chestnut, rest of underparts buffish-brown barred blackish-brown; in flight shows white throat and white tips on outer tail. **Adult female** Smaller white throat-patch; in flight darker, usually lacks white in tail. **Similar species** Darkest nightjar, the only small nightjar with no white in wings; see Malaysian Eared-nightjar. **Habitat** Primary and secondary lowland dipterocarp, riverine and kerangas forest; lowland specialist to 500 m. **Behaviour** Almost unknown; forages in clearings and forest edges of primary habitat; possibly usually found near water. **Voice** An unusual, disyllabic groaning *wuu-huuu* with mournful quality, the first part on higher, level pitch, the second part downslurred and lower-pitched (0.6–0.4 kHz),

each note c.1.2 s, repeated infrequently; also gives a short, low-pitched grunt (from Sumatra). **Range & status** Sumatra. **Borneo** Rare resident, very few recent records from Sabah, Brunei, Sarawak and W Kalimantan, no recent records from E, C and S Kalimantan. **Breeding** Undescribed.

APODIDAE: Swifts

Worldwide c.100 species, 14 in Borneo. Fast-flying aerial insectivores with long curved wings and very short legs and feet. The short bill with wide gape is adapted for catching insects on the wing. Treeswifts often perch upright on a branch. Typical swifts are unable to walk or perch on a horizontal surface, so they eat, sleep and mate entirely in flight and only land at the nest site during the breeding season; they are normally seen only in flight and many similar species are very difficult to identify. Vocalisations are high-pitched chatters and trills.

WATERFALL SWIFT *Hydrochrous gigas*

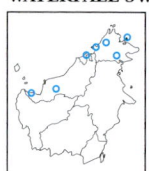

Identification 16 cm. Monotypic. Large, dark swiftlet with distinctive smooth, direct flight and deeply forked tail (usually held closed). **Adult** Upperparts uniform dark glossy blackish-brown, underparts brown with white margins on undertail-coverts, underwing paler greyish. **Juvenile** Less prominent white margins on undertail-coverts. **Habitat** Associated with waterfalls in primary lower and upper montane forest. **Behaviour** Poorly known; gregarious aerial insectivore; probably crepuscular as it is known not to use echolocation. **Voice** Utters a loud twittering call. **Range & status** W Java, Sumatra, Malay Peninsula. **Borneo** Rare local resident with few sight records from Sabah, Brunei and Sarawak.

GLOSSY SWIFTLET *Collocalia esculenta*   BRUNEI   2/6/10

Identification 9–10 cm. Tiny swiftlet with distinctive glossy blue-black upperparts contrasting with white belly. **Adult** *cyanoptila* Upperparts bluish-black with blue gloss, throat and upper breast greyish-brown, lower breast blotched whitish with grey blotching fading into white belly, undertail-coverts greyish-brown, square tail bluish-black, undertail paler; in flight underwing-coverts greyish-black, flight feathers paler. **Juvenile** Pale fringing on underparts. **Similar species** See Cave Swiftlet. **Habitat** A variety of habitats from forested areas and wetlands to human habitation. **Behaviour** Does not echolocate; gregarious aerial insectivore. **Voice** Usually silent. **Range & status** Thai-Malay Peninsula, Sumatra, Philippines, Sulawesi, Lesser Sundas, New Guinea, SW Pacific. **Borneo** Common resident throughout, including Natunas. **Breeding** Year-round, but main egg-laying periods are late March and early June; lays two white eggs in small half-cup of vegetable matter and saliva cement; nests in shallow caves and overhangs, in culverts, tunnels and buildings.

BORNEAN SWIFTLET *Collocalia dodgei*

Identification 10 cm. Monotypic. Tiny swiftlet with greenish-glossed blackish-brown upperparts contrasting with white belly. **Adult** Upperparts uniform blackish-brown with greenish gloss, throat and upper breast greyish-brown, lower breast blotched whitish with grey blotching fading into whitish belly, undertail-coverts greyish-brown, square tail bluish-black, undertail paler; in flight underwing-coverts greyish-black, flight feathers paler. **Juvenile** Pale fringing on underparts. **Similar species** Glossy Swiftlet has bluish gloss on upperparts. **Habitat** Primary upper montane forest, from 1,800 m. **Behaviour** Similar to Glossy Swiftlet; does not echolocate; gregarious aerial insectivore. **Voice** Call is a soft, high-pitched repeated *cheer-cheer...* **Range & status** Endemic, rare resident N Borneo where restricted to W and SW slopes of G. Kinabalu, recently found in the Maligan Range on the Sabah-Sarawak border, may occur in other nearby mountain ranges. **Breeding** As Glossy Swiftlet.

GOMANTONG CAVES 10/6/10

MOSSY-NEST SWIFTLET *Aerodramus salangana*

Identification 12 cm. Small, brownish swiftlet which constructs nest of vegetable material with little nest cement, giving an untidy appearance. **Adult** *natunae* Upperparts uniform dull brown, underparts greyish-brown, paler on throat, underwing pale greyish contrasting with dark underwing-coverts, tail shallowly forked. **Juvenile** Pale fringes on tips of tail feathers. **Similar species** Slightly darker with shallower tail-fork than Edible-nest and Mossy-nest Swiftlets; best distinguished on nest. **Habitat** A wide variety of habitats; breeds in caves. **Behaviour** Gregarious; forms large breeding colonies in cave systems; aerial insectivore found in large numbers near caves; feeds with other swiftlet species; uses echolocation. **Voice** Similar to Edible-nest Swiftlet. **Range & status** W Sumatra, Java. **Borneo** Abundant resident throughout including the Natunas. **Breeding** March–June; lays two white eggs in small half-saucer nest of mosses and other vegetable matter held together with saliva cement, usually attached to ledges of cave walls.

GOMANTONG CAVES 10/6/10

BLACK-NEST SWIFTLET *Aerodramus maximus*

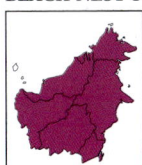

Identification 14 cm. Medium-sized, blackish-brown swiftlet which constructs whitish nest using nest cement containing many impurities. **Adult** *lowi* Upperparts glossy blackish-brown, underparts greyish, paler on throat, underwing pale grey contrasting with dark brown underwing-coverts, tail moderately forked. **Adult** *tichelmani* Smaller with paler greyish rump. **Similar species** Edible-nest Swiftlet is smaller with more deeply forked tail; Mossy-nest Swiftlet is smaller with squarish tail and darker underparts. **Habitat** A wide variety of habitats; breeds in caves. **Behaviour** Gregarious; forms large breeding colonies in cave systems; aerial insectivore found in large numbers near caves; feeds with other swiftlet species; uses echolocation to navigate cave systems. **Voice** Soft rattling twitter. **Range & status** SE Vietnam, Thai-Malay Peninsula, W Sumatra, W Java, Palawan. **Borneo** Abundant resident N and W Borneo (*lowi*) and SE Borneo (*tichelmani*). **Breeding** March–June; 1–2 white eggs are laid in shallow half-saucer nest composed of bird's own feathers and copious saliva cement, usually attached to cave wall.

GOMANTONG CAVES 10/6/10

EDIBLE-NEST SWIFTLET *Aerodramus fuciphaga*

Identification 12 cm. Small, blackish-brown swiftlet which constructs an all-white nest of nest cement. **Adult** *vestita* Upperparts glossy blackish-brown, rump is sometimes slightly paler, underparts brownish-grey, paler on throat, underwing pale grey with dark brown underwing-coverts, tail more deeply forked than Mossy-nest and Black-nest Swiftlets. **Similar species** See Mossy-nest and Black-nest Swiftlet. **Habitat** A wide variety of habitats; breeds in caves. **Behaviour** Gregarious; forms large breeding colonies in cave systems; aerial insectivore found in large numbers near caves; feeds with other swiftlet species; uses echolocation to navigate cave systems. **Voice** Repeated *chip* notes. **Range & status** Andaman and Nicobar Islands, Thai-Malay Peninsula, Sumatra, Java, Lesser Sundas. **Borneo** Abundant resident throughout including offshore islands. **Breeding** February–May; constructs shallow nest of copious nest cement attached to cave wall; this is the commercially valuable 'white' nest collected for trade.

SEPILOK 8/6/10

ASIAN PALM-SWIFT *Cypsiurus balasiensis*

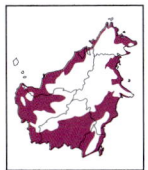

Identification 13 cm. Small all brownish-grey swift with long wings and long, thin forked tail (usually held closed). **Adult** *infumatus* Upperparts dark brownish-grey, underparts pale grey with paler throat and darker underwing-coverts. **Juvenile** Tail shorter and less deeply forked. **Habitat** Usually found in vicinity of fan palms in lowlands. **Behaviour** Gregarious, often in large flocks; nests and roosts in palm trees; aerial insectivore. **Voice** High-pitched trill. **Range & status** Indian Subcontinent, SE Asia, Indonesia, Philippines. **Borneo** Locally common throughout. **Breeding** Recorded in January–February; lays 1–3 white eggs in small nest of downy vegetable material attached to underside of palm-frond.

125

SILVER-RUMPED NEEDLETAIL
Rhaphidura leucopygialis

Identification 11 cm. Monotypic. Small, all-black needletail with contrasting white uppertail and distinctive shape in flight. **Adult** Head and mantle glossy black, rump and uppertail-coverts white, underparts all glossy black. **Juvenile** Less gloss, less extensive white on tail. **Habitat** Primary and secondary forest, plantations, often near water. **Behaviour** Usually in small flocks; aerial insectivore; recorded nesting in hollow trees; flight rapid with rocking from side to side. **Voice** A high-pitched chattering call uttered in flight. **Range & status** Thai-Malay Peninsula, Sumatra, Java. **Borneo** Locally common resident throughout. **Breeding** March–June; otherwise undescribed in Borneo.

WHITE-THROATED NEEDLETAIL
Hirundapus caudacutus

Identification 19–20 cm. Large, dark needletail with prominent contrasting white throat-patch and forehead, pale silvery saddle on back and white undertail. **Adult** *caudacutus* Upperparts dark olive-brown with white lores and forehead and silvery-white saddle on back, throat white, breast and upper flanks dark olive-brown, lower flanks and undertail-coverts white. **Juvenile** Lores and forehead pale greyish-brown, black streaking on white lower flanks, pale saddle less prominent. **Habitat** Can be seen feeding high over wide variety of habitats. **Behaviour** High-flying aerial insectivore; seen in large flocks on migration. **Voice** Rapid soft chattering. **Range & status** Breeds C Siberia, Japan, Himalayas; E China, SE Asia, Indonesia, S New Guinea, E Australia. **Borneo** Rarely recorded passage migrant N Borneo (Sabah, Brunei, Sarawak, E Kalimantan).

BROWN-BACKED NEEDLETAIL *Hirundapus giganteus*

SUKAU RIVER LODGE   10/6/10

Identification 25 cm. Very large dark brown needletail with white undertail-coverts, slightly paler on saddle and chin. **Adult** *giganteus* Upperparts brown with paler saddle, underparts brown, slightly paler on chin and throat, lower flanks and undertail-coverts white. **Juvenile** Dark fringing on white lower flanks and undertail-coverts. **Habitat** Can be seen feeding high over wide variety of habitats. **Behaviour** Gregarious, usually observed in small groups; high-flying aerial insectivore. **Voice** An insect-like trill. **Range & status** SW India, Sri Lanka, Andaman Islands, NE India, SE Asia, Sumatra, Java, Bali, Palawan. **Borneo** Uncommon resident throughout. **Breeding** Undescribed in Borneo.

HOUSE SWIFT *Apus affinis*

BRUNEI   2/6/10

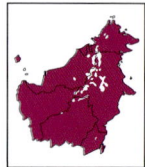

Identification 15 cm. Small, dark swift with whitish throat-patch, white rump and shallowly forked tail. **Adult** *subfurcatus* Upperparts black with brown forehead and lores and contrasting white rump, throat whitish, rest of underparts black. **Juvenile** Some pale fringing on flight feathers. **Similar species** Fork-tailed Swift is larger, longer-winged and with longer, more deeply forked tail. **Habitat** Towns and cities, to 1,450 m. **Behaviour** Highly gregarious, forms large colonies in urban areas; high-flying aerial insectivore. **Voice** A harsh twittering. **Range & status** E Himalayas, NE India, SE China, S Japan, SE Asia, Indonesia, Philippines. **Borneo** Common resident throughout, including Anambas and N Natunas. **Breeding** Year-round, laying 1–3 white eggs; nest is an untidy structure attached under rafters of houses, caves walls, cliffs and under bridges.

FORK-TAILED SWIFT *Apus pacificus*

Identification 17–18 cm. Blackish swift with prominent white rump and broad, deeply forked tail that is often held closed. **Adult *cooki*** Upperparts blackish with contrasting narrow white rump-band, underparts greyish-black with whitish fringing, paler on throat. **Adult *pacificus*** Upperparts browner, rump band broader. **Similar species** See House Swift. **Habitat** A wide variety of habitats in lowlands to montane areas. **Behaviour** Gregarious; high-flying aerial insectivore. **Voice** Wheezy, soft *sree*. **Range & status** E Palearctic, S India, Himalayas, China, SE Asia, Indonesia, New Guinea, Australia. **Borneo** Uncommon non-breeding visitor and passage migrant throughout, from late September to April.

GREY-RUMPED TREESWIFT *Hemiprocne longipennis*

Identification 18–21 cm. **Adult male *harterti*** Greenish-grey head with short upright forehead-crest and dark red ear-coverts, lores blackish, upperparts grey with pale rump, pale grey tertials contrasting with darker wings, throat greyish, rest of underparts greyish-white, at rest primaries extending beyond tail-tip; in flight pale grey rump contrasts with darker upperparts, underwing-coverts blackish. **Adult female** Like male but ear-coverts blackish. **Juvenile** Upperparts fringed brown, flight feathers and tail tipped white, underparts whitish with brown and white barring. **Similar species** Larger with longer tail than Whiskered Treeswift, plumage is greyer, tends to perch higher. **Habitat** A lowland specialist found over primary and secondary lowland dipterocarp, kerangas and peatswamp forest, mangroves, and plantations, to 1,050 m. **Behaviour** Holds wings below horizontal in gliding, wheeling flight; perches on prominent branch from where it sallies out to catch insects in flight; often seen in small flocks foraging over water or in clearings. **Voice** A short squeak reminiscent of child's squeeze-toy (4.3 kHz), uttered rapidly. **Range & status** Thai-Malay Peninsula, Indonesia, Philippines. **Borneo** Common lowland resident throughout, including Anambas and N Natunas. **Breeding** February–August; lays single greyish-white egg in tiny, shallow half-saucer nest made of bark and feathers held together with saliva cement and attached to side of branch.

WHISKERED TREESWIFT *Hemiprocne comata*

Identification 15–16.5 cm. **Adult male *comata*** Glossy dark blue crown with short crest, white lores and long narrow supercilium, distinctive long white line from chin to moustache forming 'whiskers', ear-coverts deep red, back to uppertail-coverts chocolate-brown, wings glossy dark blue with white tertials, throat glossy blue, rest of underparts chocolate-brown with white vent. **Adult female** As male but ear-coverts blackish. **Juvenile** Duller with reduced whiskers. **Similar species** See Grey-rumped Treeswift. **Habitat** Open areas in primary and secondary lowland dipterocarp and kerangas forest, mangroves, to 750 m. **Behaviour** Sallies out from perches in clearings usually at lower levels than Grey-rumped Treeswift, and flies for shorter periods of time; very acrobatic flight; often in pairs. **Voice** A rapid, squeaky, high-pitched *pit-pit-pit-pit-pit...* (5 kHz). **Range & status** Thai-Malay Peninsula, Sumatra, Philippines. **Borneo** Common resident throughout, including Anambas and N Natunas. **Breeding** Recorded in February; lays one white egg in tiny cup-shaped nest of down and feathers attached to side of branch.

TROGONIDAE: Trogons

Worldwide 40 species, 6 in Borneo. A pantropical family of typically colourful birds with short broad bill, large head and long, square tail. Generally insectivorous but takes some fruit. Inconspicuous when perched upright on a horizontal branch in a shady area in the mid-storey, from which it gleans insects in nearby foliage. Most give distinctive stereotypical monotone calls. Sexually dimorphic, the female is usually duller with different undertail pattern.

RED-NAPED TROGON *Harpactes kasumba*

Identification 31–34 cm. Large trogon with thin white breast-band and conspicuous red nape-stripe. **Adult male *impavidus*** (endemic subspecies) Forehead to hindcrown black, bright red nape-stripe extends from malar area, upperparts golden-brown with black and white vermiculated wing-coverts, primaries dark brown with white edging, tail broadly tipped black with black and white outer tail feathers, throat to upper breast black bordered below with narrow white breast-band, rest of underparts bright red, undertail white patterned with black on inner vanes; iris reddish-brown with broad blue orbital skin, bill cobalt-blue, legs and feet bluish-grey. **Adult female** Head, neck and breast greyish-brown, upperparts golden-brown with dark brown and yellow vermiculations on wing-coverts, underparts yellow-brown with no white breast-band, tail as male; iris brown with dull blue orbital skin, bill black, paler at base of lower mandible. **Juvenile** As adult female, older male intermediate between adult female and male. **Similar species** Male Diard's Trogon has dark purple hindcrown, pink nape-stripe, black-freckled undertail, pinkish breast-band, and violet orbital skin. **Habitat** Primary lowland dipterocarp, peatswamp and kerangas to lower montane forest, to 1,200 m. **Behaviour** Sallies out from perch in mid- to upper storey below canopy for large insects which it gleans or takes on wing; quiet and unobtrusive; usually solitary or in pairs. **Voice** Song is a slow,

Female   Male

sad sounding 5–8 note *pau pau pau pau pau…*, each short note slightly downslurred (1.5–1.2 kHz), delivered at rate of c.1 note/s; call is a soft, sharp *kwik*. **Range & status** Thai-Malay Peninsula, Sumatra. **Borneo** Common resident throughout. **Breeding** Poorly known in Borneo, may breed February–June; lays two white eggs in nest in rotten tree-stump; trogons generally excavate nest cavity using its bill.

DIARD'S TROGON *Harpactes diardii*

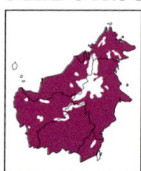

Identification 32–35 cm. Large trogon with contiguous pink nape-stripe and breast-band. **Adult male *diardii*** (endemic subspecies) Forehead to crown black, hindcrown with purplish wash, narrow nape-stripe pink, upperparts golden-brown with black and white vermiculated wing-coverts, primaries dark brown with white edging, tail broadly tipped black, outer tail feathers black and white, throat to upper breast black bordered below with indistinct pinkish line, rest of underparts pinkish-red, undertail white heavily flecked with black; iris reddish-brown with broad purplish-blue orbital skin, bill purplish-blue, legs and feet purplish-grey. **Adult female** As male but head, breast and upperparts olive-brown with dark brown and yellowish vermiculations on wing-coverts, rest of underparts pinkish. **Juvenile** Like female but underparts paler pink. **Similar species** See Red-naped Trogon. **Habitat** Primary and regenerated secondary lowland dipterocarp, riparian and kerangas to lower montane forest, to 1,200 m. **Behaviour** As for Red-naped Trogon; has been recorded eating figs. **Voice** Song is a mournful, quite rapid series of 15–20 *pau* notes, each note slightly downslurred and delivered at rate of 4–5 notes/s, entire series descending in pitch (1.2–9.4 kHz); lower-pitched and faster than Red-naped Trogon. **Range & status** Thai-Malay Peninsula, Sumatra. **Borneo** Common resident throughout. **Breeding** February–September; lays two white eggs in nest-hole in rotten stump c.1–2.5 m off ground.

Male   Female

WHITEHEAD'S TROGON *Harpactes whiteheadi*

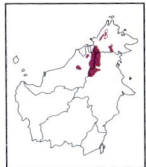

Identification 30–33 cm. Monotypic. Large trogon with bright red head (brown in female) and grey breast. **Adult male** Forehead to nape and ear-coverts crimson, rest of upperparts cinnamon-brown with fine black and white vermiculations on wing-coverts, primaries black with white edging, tail warm brown bordered black with white outer feathers, black throat grading into grey breast separating crimson underparts; iris reddish-brown with blue orbital skin, bill blue, legs and feet greyish. **Adult female** Similar to male but head and lower underparts cinnamon-brown, vermiculations on wing-coverts dark brown and yellowish. **Juvenile** Undescribed. **Habitat** Primary montane forest, from 900 to 2,000 m. **Behaviour** Very shy and unobtrusive, easily overlooked; rarely vocalises; sallies out from perch in upper storey below canopy in dense, damp forest for large insects which it gleans from foliage. **Voice** Song is a loud, slow-paced but urgent-sounding 4–5 note *kwau kwau kwau kwau…*, each note rising sharply in pitch (9.6–1.5 kHz, 2.5 s); a heavy churring or rolling *burr* call has also been described. **Range & status** Endemic, uncommon resident in north-central mountain ranges of N Borneo from G. Kinabalu to Dulit Range and Kayan Mentarang (Sabah, E Sarawak, E Kalimantan). **Breeding** Poorly known; one nest was cavity in rotten stump c.1.8 m from ground lined with dead bamboo leaves and plant fibres.

Male

Female

CINNAMON-RUMPED TROGON
Harpactes orrhophaeus

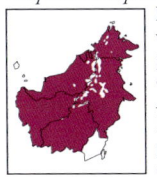

Identification 25–28 cm. Small trogon with entirely black head, scarlet underparts and cinnamon-brown rump contiguous with rest of upperparts. **Adult male** *vidua* (endemic subspecies) Head, neck and throat black, upperparts cinnamon-brown with fine black and white vermiculations on wing-coverts, primaries dark brown edged white, tail tipped black with black and white on outer feathers, underparts crimson becoming paler on undertail-coverts, undertail all white with black tip; iris brown with bright blue skin-patch above eye, bill bright blue with black culmen and tip, legs and feet grey. **Adult female** Head and back olive-brown with rusty-brown area around eye, wing-coverts vermiculated brown and yellowish, paler olive-buff on uppertail-coverts, throat olive-brown grading to yellowish-brown belly and pale yellow undertail-coverts. **Juvenile** Undescribed. **Similar species** Male Scarlet-rumped Trogon has bright scarlet rump, less fine vermiculations on wing-coverts, and brighter scarlet underparts; female Scarlet-rumped Trogon has pinkish rump, all-brownish head (lacks rusty-brown facial area of Cinnamon-rumped). **Habitat** Primary and secondary lowland dipterocarp to lower montane forest, to 1,550 m. **Behaviour** As for other trogons but relatively poorly known in Borneo. **Voice** A slow, mournful descending 3–4 note *taup-taup-taup-taup…* (1.4–1.1 kHz, c.1.6 s), each note monotone, last note shorter. **Range & status** Thai-Malay Peninsula, Sumatra. **Borneo** Uncommon resident throughout except S Kalimantan. **Breeding** Undescribed in Borneo, possibly breeds around March–July; elsewhere both sexes incubate and tend nestlings; lays two white eggs in cavity in rotten tree-stumps 1–1.5 m above ground.

Female

Male

SCARLET-RUMPED TROGON *Harpactes duvaucelii*

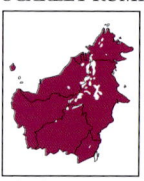

Identification 23–26 cm. Monotypic. Small trogon with entirely black head, scarlet underparts and rump contrasting with cinnamon-brown upperparts. **Adult male** Head, neck and throat black, mantle and back cinnamon-brown, vermiculated black and white on wing-coverts, primaries dark brown edged white, rump and uppertail-coverts scarlet, tail cinnamon-brown tipped black with black and white outer feathers, underparts scarlet, undertail all white with black tip; iris brown with bright blue skin-patch above eye, bill bright blue with black culmen and tip, legs and feet bluish-grey. **Adult female** Head and back plain olive-brown, wing-coverts vermiculated brown and yellowish, rump and undertail-coverts pinkish, throat olive-brown grading to paler yellowish-brown breast, rest of underparts pinkish. **Juvenile** Like adult female but undertail-coverts buffish, juvenile male gradually shows pinkish wash on underparts but otherwise underparts buffish-brown. **Similar species** See Cinnamon-rumped Trogon. **Habitat** Primary and secondary lowland dipterocarp, kerangas and peatswamp forest, to 1,000 m with one record at 1,500 m. **Behaviour** As for other trogons but more active at lower levels than other trogons; usually solitary. **Voice** Distinctive song is a rapid, 'bouncing ping-pong ball' song, a series of 18–20 short, rapid notes descending in pitch (2.1–1.7 kHz, c.8 notes/s), *teuk teuk teuk-teuk-euk-euk-euk-euk-euk-euk-euk-euk-euk-euk-euk-euk…*, the phrase starting slower then accelerating markedly. **Range & status** Thai-Malay Peninsula, Sumatra. **Borneo** Common resident throughout, including N Natunas. **Breeding** Undescribed in Borneo; elsewhere, nest is excavated in rotten tree-stump 1–1.5 m from ground, lays two plain white eggs.

ORANGE-BREASTED TROGON *Harpactes oreskios*

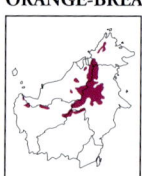

Identification 26–31 cm. Medium-sized trogon with uniform greenish head and orange lower breast; lacks any red in plumage. **Adult male** *dulitensis* (endemic subspecies) Head and neck olive-green, mantle to upper tail chestnut, tail tipped black with outer feathers black and white, wing-coverts vermiculated black and white, primaries black with white margins, upper breast bright olive-green, lower breast orange grading to bright yellow on flanks and belly, undertail mostly white; iris brown with blue orbital skin, bill cobalt-blue with black culmen and tip, legs and feet grey. **Adult female** Like male but duller, head and upperparts brownish-olive, duller and paler on uppertail-coverts, wing-coverts vermiculated brown and yellowish, upper breast greyish-olive, lower breast dull orange grading to yellow underparts. **Juvenile** Upperparts and breast brownish, underparts yellowish-white, wing-coverts buffish with blackish barring. **Habitat** Primary and secondary hill and lower montane forest, from 200 to 1,200 m, occasionally to 1,500 m. **Behaviour** As for other trogons; favours mid- to upper storey below canopy, roosts in understorey vegetation. **Voice** Usual song is a fairly rapid, monotone five-note *tu-tau-tau-tau-tau* (1.4 kHz, 0.7 s); call is a rapid, harsh *kek-kek-kek-kek-krrekkkk…*, the last note longer and trilled. **Range & status** SW China, SE Asia, Sumatra, Java. **Borneo** Uncommon resident along north-central to western mountain ranges of N Borneo, from G. Kinabalu (Sabah) to Pueh Range and Ulu Barito (Sarawak, E Kalimantan, northern parts of W and C Kalimantan). **Breeding** January–March; lays 1–2 smooth, glossy ivory-yellow eggs in cavity in rotten tree-stump probably 1–2 m from ground.

CORACIIDAE: Rollers

Worldwide 13 species, 1 in Borneo. Large-headed, short-billed colourful birds with robust bill, large head, long wings and tail. Usually seen singly or in pairs perched in dead trees or posts in open areas. Aerial insectivores, often acrobatic in flight. Cavity nester in trees, stumps or banks. Sexes similar.

DOLLARBIRD *Eurystomus orientalis*

LIBARAN ISLAND 5/6/10

Identification 25–28 cm. A stocky, large green-blue roller with broad, short red bill and conspicuous white circles in wings. **Adult *orientalis*** Head blackish-blue, throat purplish-blue, upperparts greenish-blue with purplish-blue flight feathers and tail, underparts greenish-blue; iris brown with narrow dark red eye-ring, bill and legs red; in flight striking large, round white patch on long broad wings; tail square. **Juvenile** As adult but upperparts duller, underparts slaty-blue, wing-patch smaller, upper mandible black, lower mandible yellow, legs and feet dull red. **Adult *calonyx*** Longer purple wings, shorter tail. **Habitat** Forested riverbanks, edges of primary and secondary lowland dipterocarp forest, mangroves, plantations, to 1,000 m. **Behaviour** Solitary or in pairs; favours high perches in dead trees; feeds mainly on large insects, caught on wing, also lizards; flight is slow and leisurely on long wings. **Voice** A short, raspy *chak* (2.8 kHz, 0.1 s) repeated slowly or a series of similar notes, *chak chak chak chak-chak-chak*…, repeated irregularly, more rapidly and accelerating. **Range & status** SW India, Sri Lanka, E and SE Asia, Indonesia, Philippines, New Guinea, Solomon Islands, Australia. **Borneo** Race *orientalis* common resident and common non-breeding visitor from SE Asia throughout; *calonyx* common non-breeding visitor throughout from NE Asia. **Breeding** November–May; lays 2–4 white eggs in nest-hole in dead tree; possibly uses woodpecker holes.

ALCEDINIDAE: Kingfishers

Worldwide 85 species, 11 in Borneo. Colourful, stocky and short-legged with large head and long straight bill. Flight is fast and direct and all excavate nest-holes with strong bill and feet. Most of the seven species of halcyoninae, or larger kingfishers, feed by diving steeply into water to catch fish, are often conspicuous and vocal, and in most species, but not all, the sexes are similar. The four species of alcedininae, or smaller kingfishers, usually forage for small invertebrates, fish and other small vertebrates near water, although *Ceyx* kingfishers may hunt some distance from water, and they are often shy and difficult to detect.

RUFOUS-COLLARED KINGFISHER
Actenoides concretus

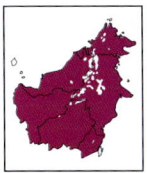

Identification 23–24 cm. An easily overlooked, forest-dwelling kingfisher with spectacular plumage, sexually dimorphic. **Adult male *borneanus*** (endemic subspecies) Cap green, black band through eye to nape, buffish supraloral line, collar and cheeks rufous, azure-blue moustache, back and wings azure-blue, rump light blue, underparts rufous paler on belly and throat; iris dark brown, bill yellow with black culmen, feet and legs yellowish-green. **Adult female** As male but back and wings dark green with prominent buff spots. **Juvenile** Duller than adults, bill grey-brown with yellowish tip, male with upperparts spotted. **Habitat** Dense primary lowland dipterocarp forest to lower montane forest, to 1,200 m, but recorded to 1,650 m. **Behaviour** Shy and unobtrusive in dense forest close to or far from waterways; feeds on large invertebrates and small fish, frogs and lizards; perches quietly in thick vegetation in lower to middle storey, taking prey mostly from ground. **Voice** Song is an upslurred, ringing *kweet…* (1.7–2.1 kHz, 0.5 s) repeated continuously at rate of about 1 note/s or sometimes at much longer intervals; call is a series of six sweet, trilling phrases, each phrase 0.5 s, the series lasting 5–6 s. **Range & status** Thai-Malay Peninsula, Sumatra. **Borneo** Uncommon to locally common resident throughout. **Breeding** December–April; lays two oval white eggs in nest-hole excavated in low earthen banks or rotten tree-trunks.

BANDED KINGFISHER *Lacedo pulchella*

Identification 20 cm. A highly sexually dimorphic, unobtrusive forest kingfisher with spectacular plumage in both male and female. **Adult male *melanops*** (endemic subspecies) Longish, shaggy crown feathers bright blue with narrow black and white bands; forehead, cheeks and collar black, throat white, centre of belly white, rest of underparts orange-rufous, upperparts strikingly banded silvery-blue and black; iris brown, bill red, legs and feet pinkish-brown. **Adult female** Head and upperparts banded rufous and black, underparts buffish-white with narrow black barring on breast and flanks, throat and centre of belly unbarred. **Juvenile** Duller, underparts heavily barred; upper mandible brown, lower mandible orange. **Adult male *pulchella*** Like male *melanops* but forehead, cheek and collar rufous. **Habitat** Primary and secondary lowland dipterocarp forest to lower montane forest, kerangas, peatswamp forest, to 1,500 m. **Behaviour** Solitary or in pairs in dense forest away from water; feeds on large invertebrates, small fish, lizards; hunts from perch in middle storey, sitting motionless for long periods of time, but often slowly raising and lowering crown feathers. **Voice** More often heard than seen. Song is a long, mournful series of *tu-wee* notes, the first longest and loudest (2 kHz, 0.5 s), speeding up and tapering off in volume towards end, the series of 14–16 notes delivered over 16–20 s. Each note upslurred rapidly, then downslurred. **Range & status** SE Asia, Sumatra, Java. **Borneo** Uncommon to rare resident throughout (*pulchella* on N Natunas). **Breeding** Recorded February–April; nest-hole is excavated with bill in rotten or fallen tree-stump or arboreal termitarium, one with two chicks seen 3 m above ground.

Male
melanops

Female
melanops

STORK-BILLED KINGFISHER *Pelargopsis capensis*

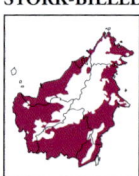

Identification 35 cm. Large kingfisher with huge red bill and conspicuous bright blue rump in flight. **Adult *cyanopteryx*** Head and neck buffish-orange, chin buffish-white, underparts buff-orange, back and wings greenish-blue, lower back and rump light azure-blue; iris brown, bill red with blackish tip, legs and feet red. **Juvenile** Like adult but with dusky breast-band. **Habitat** Forested rivers, streams, lakes, mangroves, wooded seashores, generally in lowlands to 400 m but also on Kelabit Highlands to 1,100 m. **Behaviour** Solitary; forms monogamous pairs during breeding season when very territorial; feeds on fish, crustaceans, small vertebrates, hunting from concealed perch over water. **Voice** Song is a piercing but plaintive, two-note whistle *fyu fyu* (2.2–1.9 kHz. 0.5 s), the second note softer and slightly lower than the first, each phrase repeated every 1–1.5 s for up to a minute. Call is rapid, raspy *kek kek kek...* (2.2 kHz), 10–15 notes run together. **Range & status** Indian Subcontinent, SE Asia, Indonesia, Philippines. **Borneo** Common resident throughout. **Breeding** Poorly known in Borneo; elsewhere known to excavate nest-hole in termite mounds or banks, laying 2–5 white eggs.

Adult

RUDDY KINGFISHER *Halcyon coromanda*

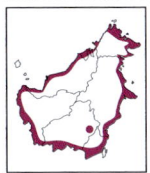

Identification 23 cm. Distinctive all-reddish, medium-sized kingfisher. **Adult *minor*** Upperparts rich rufous with purple wash, large rump-patch silvery-blue, chin pale rufous, underparts rich orange-rufous; iris dark brown, bill bright red, legs and feet bright red. **Juvenile** Upperparts darker without purple wash, rump purplish, dusky feather-edges on breast. **Adult *major*** Upperparts paler with little purple, small rump-patch blue, underparts pale rufous. **Habitat** Riverine forest, secondary lowland dipterocarp and peatswamp forest, mangroves, plantations, mainly in coastal areas at sea-level, with records from 200 km inland in C Kalimantan. **Behaviour** Shy; feeds on insects, small invertebrates, small fish, frogs which it hunts from perches in middle to lower storey. **Voice** Heard more often than seen; *H. c. minor* song is a pleasant, mournful, descending two-note *pee-wooo* phrase (1.9–1 kHz, 0.5 s), first note shorter than the second, repeated every 1–1.5 s. *H. c. major* song is a series of descending, tremulous notes with rich harmonics *kyorororo-ro...*, louder, then trailing off (2.3–1.7 kHz, series 1.5 s); probably silent outside breeding period. **Range & status** NE China, Korea, Japan, Taiwan, E Himalayas, SE Asia. Indonesia, Philippines. **Borneo** Race *minor* uncommon resident in coastal areas throughout, possibly commoner NW Borneo; *major* rare non-breeding visitor from NE Asia with few records from Sabah and Brunei. **Breeding** April–July; eggs are pure white; a nest excavated in an arboreal termitarium has been described, excavates nests in termite mounds and earthen banks.

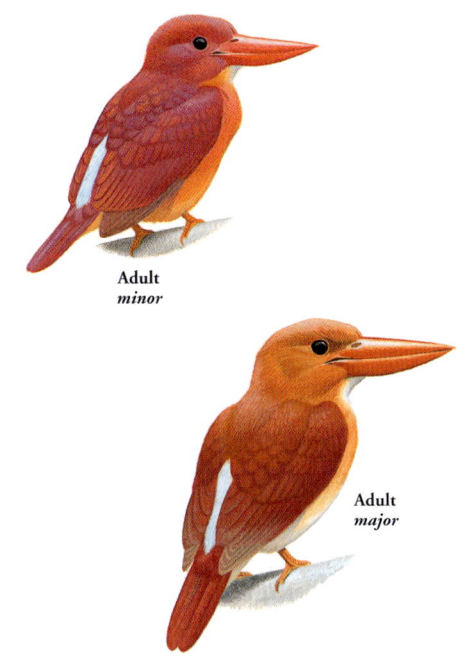

Adult *minor*

Adult *major*

BLACK-CAPPED KINGFISHER *Halcyon pileata*

Identification 28 cm. Monotypic. Strikingly plumaged medium-sized kingfisher with distinctive black cap and bright red bill contrasting with black back and white throat. **Adult** Head black, collar and throat to breast white, upperparts rich purple-black with black on shoulders, rest of underparts pale rufous; iris brown, bill bright red, legs and feet red; in flight shows large white wing-patch, underwing-coverts pale rufous. **Juvenile** Like adult with buffish loral spot and dusky scaling on breast feathers. **Habitat** Lagoons, swamps, estuaries, streams, mangroves, paddyfields, gardens, to 200 m. **Behaviour** Feeds mainly on insects, as well as frogs, small fish, crabs; hunts from conspicuous perches catching prey on wing, on ground, or from water surface; often faithful to same perch for prolonged periods. **Voice** Utters a cackling *kikikikiki* similar to Stork-billed Kingfisher but higher-pitched. **Range & status** Indian Subcontinent, E and SE Asia, Indonesia, S Philippines. **Borneo** Common to abundant non-breeding visitor in N Borneo, becoming less common further south, from late September to April.

Adult

Adult

SACRED KINGFISHER *Todiramphus sanctus*

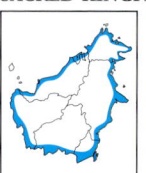

Identification 21 cm. Medium-sized, greenish-blue kingfisher with buff loral spot and buffish-white collar and underparts and large black bill. **Adult *sanctus*** Buff loral spot, crown greenish-blue, bluish-black mask extending to nape forming a band, buffish-white collar joining white throat, underparts white with buff wash on breast and flanks, upperparts blue, rump bright blue; iris brown, bill dark grey with pale pink lower base, legs and feet grey. **Juvenile** Duller; upperparts greener, underparts buffish with dusky feather-tips on breast and collar. **Similar species** Collared Kingfisher is larger and stockier, much cleaner-looking with white underparts and collar. **Habitat** Open woodlands, mangroves, riverine forest, at sea-level. **Behaviour** Very similar to Collared Kingfisher; migratory; feeds on insects, spiders and small vertebrates. **Voice** Call is a staccato *kek kek kek…* (3–4 kHz), similar to Collared Kingfisher but less strident and faster. **Range & status**

Adult

Australia, New Zealand, SW Pacific, migrating to Indonesia, New Guinea, Solomon Islands. **Borneo** Uncommon to rare non-breeding visitor throughout (not recorded from Brunei), commoner in S Borneo, from late April to September.

T.B.R. / LIBARAN ISLAND   3/6/10

COLLARED KINGFISHER *Todiramphus chloris*

Identification 23–25 cm. Medium-sized, greenish-blue kingfisher with white collar and underparts and large black bill. **Adult male *laubmannianus*** White supraloral spot, crown greenish-blue, dark blue mask extending to nape forming a band, white collar joining white throat and underparts, wings and rump bright blue, back blue; iris brown, bill dark grey with pale pink lower base, legs and feet grey. **Juvenile** Duller, upperparts greener, underparts buffish. **Similar species** Sacred Kingfisher is smaller, has buff loral spot, and underparts and collar washed buff. **Habitat** Coastal woodlands, mangroves, paddyfields, plantations, gardens, to 300 m, with records from Kelabit Highlands and G. Kinabalu to 1,500 m. **Behaviour** Noisy and conspicuous; defends territory year-round; feeds on crustaceans, insects, small fish, frogs, lizards. **Voice** Very vocal; main call is a coarse, grating *ke kek kek kek kek kek* (3.5 kHz), 3–6 notes of phrase uttered rapidly over 1.5–2 s. **Range & status** NE Africa, Middle East, Indian Subcontinent, SE Asia, Indonesia, Philippines, New Guinea,

Adult

Australia, SW Pacific. **Borneo** Common to abundant resident throughout, including offshore islands. **Breeding** April–October; lays three oval white eggs; nest-hole is excavated by pair in palm-stumps, termite mounds, dead tree-trunks and muddy banks, or uses natural tree-hollows.

RUFOUS-BACKED KINGFISHER *Ceyx rufidorsa*

Identification 14 cm. Tiny, brightly coloured, mostly reddish, fast-moving kingfisher. **Adult *motleyi*** Crown to mantle and uppertail lilac-rufous, bluish-black spot on forehead, cheek orange, neck-patch blue above and white below, wings black with blue edges on scapulars and wing-coverts, throat white, rest of underparts bright orange-yellow, there is much variation in the presence of dark coloration at the four plumage regions (forehead, neck patch, coverts and scapulars); iris brown, bill red, legs and feet red (with three toes). **Juvenile** Duller, underparts white, bill yellow-orange. **Similar species** Recent molecular studies suggest Black-backed Kingfisher *C. erithacus* probably does not occur in Borneo but it differs from Rufous-backed Kingfisher in having bluish-black back and mantle. **Habitat** Primary and secondary lowland dipterocarp forest to lower montane forest, peatswamp forest, kerangas, mangroves, often in lower to middle storey of dense forest far from water, to 1,500 m. **Behaviour** Solitary; predominantly feeds on insects, but also aquatic invertebrates,

Adult *motleyi*

spiders, small fish, frogs, taking prey from water, foliage or ground; nests in excavated burrows in steep banks, termite mounds or fallen trees, not always close to water. **Voice** Flight call is a short shrill high seet (6.5 kHz, 0.1 s), repeated but not conspicuous. **Range & status** Thai-Malay Peninsula, Indonesia, Philippines (Mindoro to Palawan). **Borneo** Common resident throughout. **Breeding** Nest-hole is excavated in muddy banks c.1 m from ground; two glossy white eggs.

BLUE-BANDED KINGFISHER *Alcedo euryzona*

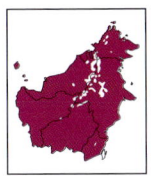

Male / Female

Identification 17 cm. Shy, sexually dimorphic kingfisher of forested waterways. Blackish upperparts contrast strongly with brilliant blue band from mantle to rump. **Adult male *peninsulae*** Head blackish-blue with ultramarine-blue feather-tips, rufous loral spot, white neck-stripe, back brilliant pale blue with silvery-azure rump, wings and tail bluish-black with small blue spots on wing-coverts, throat and underparts white with mottled blue breast-band; iris brown, bill black, legs and feet red. **Adult female** Like male but neck-stripe buffish, upperparts brownish, throat white and rest of underparts pale rufous with deeper rufous breast-band; lower mandible red. **Juvenile** Like adults but duller; male has pale rufous underparts. **Similar species** Common and Blue-eared Kingfishers both lack breast-band of male, brownish upperparts of female; pale blue back-band of Blue-banded much more contrasting. **Habitat** Edges of dense forested streams and rivers in primary lowland dipterocarp forest to lower montane forest, mangroves, to 1,400 m. **Behaviour** Poorly known; feeds on aquatic invertebrates, small fish and lizards; nests in burrows excavated in steep mud banks along forested waterways usually near running water. **Voice** Call uttered in flight similar to Common Kingfisher but louder and less squeaky. **Range & status** S Myanmar, Thai-Malay Peninsula, Sumatra, Java. **Borneo** Uncommon to locally common resident throughout although largely absent from south-central area. **Breeding** Possibly March–August; otherwise undescribed in Borneo.

SUKAU RIVER LODGE   8/6/10

BLUE-EARED KINGFISHER *Alcedo meninting*

Female / Juvenile

Identification 17 cm. Small, shy, forest-dwelling kingfisher with startling blue back-band contrasting with ultramarine upperparts. **Adult male *verreauxi*** Head, neck and ear-coverts ultramarine densely barred dark blue with rufous loral spot, white neck-stripe, throat white, underparts rich rufous, wings ultramarine with turquoise-blue spots, back and uppertail brilliant turquoise-blue; iris brown, bill black with reddish base, legs and feet scarlet. **Adult female** Like male but lower mandible or whole bill orange-red. **Juvenile** Duller, cheeks and ear-coverts rufous, breast-band greyish, bill initially all-red. **Similar species** Common Kingfisher has rufous ear-coverts, upperparts have slight greenish tinge, underparts paler rufous; *A. a. bengalensis* is bluer than other races and juvenile *A. meninting* has rufous ear-coverts, but differences listed above apply. **Habitat** Streams and creeks in primary lowland dipterocarp forest, peatswamp forest and mangroves, sometimes recorded in plantations; mainly in lowlands but locally to 1,100 m. **Behaviour** Solitary; dives steeply into water to catch aquatic invertebrates and small fish with sharp bill. **Voice** Call is a short, high-pitched *tseet* (7 kHz) uttered in flight. **Range & status** Indian Subcontinent, SE Asia, Indonesia, Palawan. **Borneo** Common to uncommon resident throughout. **Breeding** May–January; lays three white eggs in burrows excavated in steep mud banks along forested waterways and roads, usually near running water.

COMMON KINGFISHER *Alcedo atthis*

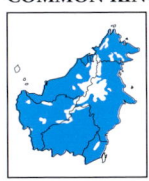

Male / Juvenile

Identification 16 cm. Small, greenish-tinged blue kingfisher found in open habitats. **Adult *bengalensis*** Crown and malar stripe turquoise-blue densely barred deep blue, loral spot and ear-coverts rufous, neck-stripe white, chin and throat white, bright turquoise-blue back and rump contrasting with darker blue wings, underparts rufous; iris dark brown, bill black with reddish gape, legs and feet bright red. **Adult female** Like male but lower mandible reddish-orange with black tip. **Juvenile** Like adult but duller overall with greyish breast-band, bill black with white tip. **Similar species** Blue-eared Kingfisher lacks rufous ear-coverts (except juvenile), has darker rufous underparts, deeper and richer blue overall. **Habitat** Lakes, ponds, streams, mangroves, ditches, to 1,100 m. **Behaviour** Hunts from perch over water; dives steeply into water to catch small fish and aquatic invertebrates with sharp bill; nests in burrows excavated in suitable sand and mud banks; pairs raise young. **Voice** A high-pitched, squeaky *chee* (4 kHz) repeated; usually uttered in flight. **Range & status** Europe, N Africa, Middle East, Indian Subcontinent, E and SE Asia, Philippines, Indonesia, New Guinea, Solomon Islands. **Borneo** Common non-breeding visitor throughout, September–May.

MEROPIDAE: Bee-eaters

Worldwide 26 species, 3 in Borneo. Graceful colourful and slender insectivores with slender curved bill, pointed wings, long tail and short legs. Flight is undulating with frequent glides. Typical bee-eaters are found in large groups in open country while the bearded bee-eater is inconspicuous in forest habitats, usually singly or in pairs.

RED-BEARDED BEE-EATER *Nyctyornis amictus*

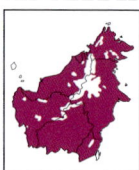

Identification 27–31 cm. Monotypic. An extraordinary, bright green forest-dwelling bee-eater with heavy decurved bill, brilliant crimson beard and square-ended tail. **Adult male** Forehead and crown pinkish-lilac, with narrow fringe of blue feathers at base of bill and around eye, long shaggy feathers of throat crimson, upperparts emerald-green, belly and undertail-coverts pale green, undertail bright orange-yellow with black terminal band; iris orange, bill black, paler at base, legs and feet dull green; in flight underwing buff. **Adult female** Like male but forehead red, smaller lilac crown-patch. **Juvenile** All green except for yellowish undertail and blue feathers at base of bill. **Habitat** Primary and secondary lowland dipterocarp to lower montane forest, peatswamp forest, to 1,200 m. **Behaviour** Sedentary; hawks arboreal insects from high leafy perches in middle storey near forest gaps; puffs beard out when vocalising. **Voice** Call is a very unusual, throaty and gruff *kwek-kwek-kwek-kwek-kwek-kwe-kwe-kwk*, starting louder and higher-pitched, then trailing off (3.5–1.7 kHz), each phrase c.1 s. **Range & status** S Myanmar, SW Thailand, Thai-Malay Peninsula, Sumatra. **Borneo** Locally common to uncommon resident throughout. **Breeding** January–June; lays 3–5 white eggs in burrow excavated in earthen banks or (elsewhere) termite mounds usually in dense forest.

BLUE-TAILED BEE-EATER *Merops philippinus*

Identification 24 cm (plus extended tail feathers of up to 6 cm). Monotypic. A large, greenish bee-eater with burnt-orange throat and bluish rump and tail. **Adult** Crown bronzy-green, black mask bordered blue above and below, chin yellow, throat orange-rufous, mantle and wings green, rump and tail blue, underparts pale green with pale blue undertail-coverts and grey undertail, tail-streamers broad and bluish-black; iris deep red, bill black, legs and feet brown. **Juvenile** Like adult but duller, bluer, throat buffish-rufous. **Similar species** Blue-throated Bee-eater has conspicuous chestnut cap and blue throat. **Habitat** Mangroves, estuaries, open woodlands, plantations, paddyfields, gardens, in lowlands. **Behaviour** Often in flocks; feeds on flying insects, especially bees, wasps and dragonflies; hawks prey from prominent perches; nests in colonies, excavating burrows in sandy soils. **Voice** A short, liquid *bip bip…* (2 kHz, 0.02 s) and more drawn-out, rolling *birip birip…* (3 kHz, 0.2 s). **Range & status** Indian Subcontinent, SE Asia, Indonesia, Philippines, New Guinea. **Borneo** Rare non-breeding visitor, Sabah, Sarawak and E Kalimantan; commoner SE Borneo (W, C and S Kalimantan) where breeding status is uncertain.

SUKAU RIVER LODGE   8/6/10

BLUE-THROATED BEE-EATER *Merops viridis*

Identification 22 cm (plus extended tail feathers of up to 9 cm). A medium-sized green bee-eater with prominent dark chestnut cap and long central tail-streamers. **Adult** *viridis* Crown and mantle dark chestnut, mask black, throat and cheeks blue, back and wings green, lower back to uppertail-coverts bright pale blue, tail blue with long central streamers; iris reddish-brown, bill black, legs and feet dark grey; in flight wings long and pointed; underwings pale rufous with blackish trailing edge. **Juvenile** Crown and mantle dark green, cheeks pale blue, pale buffish chin, throat and rest of underparts pale green. **Similar species** Blue-tailed Bee-eater has green crown and mantle, and rufous throat. **Habitat** Open woodlands, kerangas, marshes, mangroves, paddyfields, pastures, plantations, gardens, in lowlands to 500 m. **Behaviour** Often in flocks; feeds on flying insects, especially bees, wasps and dragonflies; hawks prey from prominent perches. **Voice** A pleasant, liquid *prrp prrp...* uttered at about 2–3 notes/s, medium-pitched (2.7 kHz). **Range & status** E and SE Asia, Sumatra, Java, Philippines. **Borneo** Common resident throughout with local movements to and from breeding grounds; status in S Kalimantan unclear. **Breeding** January–August; nests in colonies, excavating burrows in sandy soils; lays 1–4 almost round, pure white eggs.

UPUPIDAE: Hoopoes

Worldwide 2 species, 1 in Borneo. Unique, colourful bird with long slender decurved bill and extraordinary erectile crest. Broad wings and black, white and pink plumage distinctive. Typically seen foraging for insects on the ground. Generally migratory.

COMMON HOOPOE *Upupa epops*

Identification 26–32 cm. **Adult** *saturata* Remarkable long pinkish crown feathers tipped black; head, mantle and underparts pinkish, paler on undertail-coverts; wings, lower back and tail boldly striped black and white; iris black; very long, slender decurved bill grey; legs and feet grey. **Juvenile** Duller; crest and bill shorter. **Habitat** Open woodlands and fields, paddyfield stubble, parks. **Behaviour** Feeds on large insects and other invertebrates, foraging on ground using long bill to probe and dig in leaves, dirt and crevices; usually singly or in pairs. **Voice** Call is a pleasant, mellow *po-po-po* or *po-po* delivered on flat pitch (0.6 kHz), each phrase c.0.5 s. **Range & status** Africa, Europe, N, C and E Asia, Indian Subcontinent, SE Asia. **Borneo** Rare vagrant with handful of records from Sabah, Brunei and Sarawak.

BUCEROTIDAE: Hornbills

Worldwide 54 species, 8 in Borneo. Spectacular group of large birds with characteristic remarkably large bills. Most are black with white in plumage and colourful facial skin, casques and bills. Noisy and conspicuous with distinctive vocalisations, and noisy wing-beats in species which lack underwing-coverts. Mostly frugivorous but supplement the diet with large invertebrates and small vertebrates including nestlings. They exhibit a unique breeding strategy where the female is incarcerated in a tree cavity and fed by the male for the duration of incubation until the young are ready to fledge. Large size, frugivorous feeding behaviour and the need for large tree cavities make this group essentially reliant on large trees in old growth forest and thus their presence is an indicator of forest health.

BUSHY-CRESTED HORNBILL *Anorrhinus galeritus*

Identification 60–65 cm. Monotypic. Small hornbill with droopy crest, only hornbill with no white in plumage. **Adult male** Upperparts blackish-brown with greenish gloss and long, loose crown and nape feathers forming crest, underparts blackish-brown, tail dirty greyish-brown with broad blackish-brown terminal band; in flight all-dark underparts; iris red, bare orbital and gular skin pale blue, bill and low inconspicuous casque black, legs and feet greyish-black. **Adult female** Like male but smaller, iris reddish-brown, bill and casque yellow with black on base more extensive on lower mandible and variable amount on casque. **Juvenile** Like adult male but paler, iris brown, bare facial skin pale yellow, bill olive. **Habitat** Primary lowland dipterocarp forest, selectively logged forest, favouring foothills with high density of fig trees, to 1,300 m. **Behaviour** Territorial, usually in groups of up to 20; feeds on figs and wide variety of other fruits, as well as large insects, frogs and lizards, foraging mainly in dense forest below canopy. **Voice** Often very noisy; groups utter chorus of high-pitched, strident yelps *kee kee kee* (2.4 kHz). **Range & status** Thai-Malay Peninsula, Sumatra. **Borneo** Common resident throughout in suitable habitat, including the Natunas. **Breeding** Year-round, cooperative, breeding during fruiting peaks; lays 2–3 eggs; female is sealed in nest-hole at 10–25 m in trunk of live or dead tree, dominant pair of group breeding, the female attended by male and helpers (males and females) in groups of seven to ten birds; usually two, sometimes three young raised per nesting attempt and may breed again immediately after successful brood if food is available.

ORIENTAL PIED HORNBILL *Anthracoceros albirostris*

Identification 55–60 cm. Small pied hornbill. **Adult male *convexus*** Upperparts glossy black, wings black tipped white, upper breast glossy black, rest of underparts white, tail black with broad outer white tail-tips; iris dark red, bare facial skin around eye and throat-patch bluish-white, bill pale yellow with black base on lower mandible, casque shaped like cylinder from above bill-base tapering to protruding blade about half-way along, small patch of black at front and rear of casque, legs and feet dark grey; in flight underwing black with broad white trailing edge. **Adult female** Smaller than male, casque less pronounced with extensive black patch over front of casque and tip and edges of upper mandible, reddish-brown patches at sides and base of lower mandible; iris brown. **Juvenile** Less glossy black than adult, small bill all pale yellow, casque undeveloped; iris greyish-brown, bare facial skin pinkish-white. **Habitat** Extreme lowland specialist: secondary lowland dipterocarp, peatswamp, riverine and coastal forests, plantations, principally in coastal areas to 200 m. **Behaviour** Usually in pairs or family groups, may gather in large flocks outside breeding season; feeds mainly on fruit, also insects, spiders, small vertebrates. **Voice** A variable, harsh and loud, yelping *kek kek kuck kuck* (ca. 4 kHz), reminiscent of small, barking dog. **Range & status** NE Indian Subcontinent, S China, SE Asia, Indonesia. **Borneo** Locally common resident Sabah, Brunei and Kalimantan and uncommon resident Sarawak and N Natunas. **Breeding** January–June; lays 2–4 rough white eggs in natural tree cavity 5–15 m from ground; female is sealed into cavity with cement of droppings, vegetable matter, clay and saliva and attended by male until young fledge; male feeds female on nest.

BLACK HORNBILL *Anthracoceros malayanus*

Identification 60–65 cm. Small, all-black hornbill. Monotypic. **Adult male** Plumage black, sometimes with broad white to grey stripe over eye to nape (in Borneo most with pale grey), long tail with broad white tips on outer tail feathers; in flight all black with only small amount of white near tail-tip; iris red, bare facial skin black, sometimes with yellow patch below eye, bill pale yellow, casque shaped like cylinder from above bill-base tapering to protruding blade about half way along, and ridged along sides, black at bill-base and rear of casque, legs and feet black. **Adult female** Like male but smaller, bill and casque brown-grey, casque less pronounced; iris reddish-brown, bare orbital skin and submoustachial patch dull pink. **Juvenile** Iris brown, bare facial skin yellowish-orange, small bill pale green. **Habitat** Lowland specialist: primary lowland dipterocarp forest, secondary forest, coastal forest, kerangas, plantations; tolerates degraded forest, to 500 m. **Behaviour** Usually in pairs; mainly feeds on large fruit, but also insects and small vertebrates. **Voice** Call is an irregular, harsh, creaking *kyaa kyaa* (1.5 kHz). **Range & status** Thai-Malay Peninsula, Sumatra. **Borneo** Locally common resident throughout (less common on west coast of Sabah). **Breeding** Year-round possibly related to availability of fruit; 2–3 glossy white eggs are laid in sealed cavity nest; one nest was found at 4.5 m in live medium-sized tree; often only one chick is raised.

RHINOCEROS HORNBILL *Buceros rhinoceros*

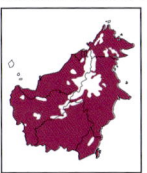

Identification 80–90 cm. Large, mostly black hornbill with distinctive casque and white tail with black central band. **Adult male *borneoensis*** (endemic subspecies) Upperparts black, throat to belly black, thighs and undertail-coverts white, tail white with broad black band across centre; iris red, eye-ring black, bill and casque yellow stained orange and red by preen oil, black at base of casque to base of bill, casque cylindrical with narrow black stripe on sides and strongly recurved at tip (with considerable individual variation), feet greenish-grey; in flight underwings all black, only hornbill in Borneo with white tail showing broad black central band. **Adult female** Plumage generally similar to male but smaller, iris white, eye-ring red, eyelids black, casque smaller with no black. **Juvenile** Iris pale blue, eye-ring brownish, bill small without casque. **Habitat** Primary lowland dipterocarp and hill forest, to 1,200 m, occasionally to 1,750 m. **Behaviour** Usually in pairs, sometimes in small flocks outside breeding season; feeds mainly on figs and other fruits, also large insects, spiders, lizards, eggs; nomadic in search of fruiting trees; flies in flaps and glides usually with male leading. **Voice** Often starts calling just before taking flight; male utters a loud, deep, far-carrying bark *grark* (0.9 kHz), bark of female is higher-pitched (2 kHz); in flight call develops into an antiphonal duet *ger-unk* or *eng-gang* (1.4–1.1 kHz) increasing in pace. **Range & status** Thai-Malay Peninsula, Sumatra, Java. **Borneo** Locally common resident in suitable habitat throughout; numbers may fluctuate depending on availability of fruiting trees. **Breeding** January–September; lays 1–2 white eggs mottled brown but usually only one chick is fledged; nests in natural holes in large forest trees; female is sealed into nest for c.50 days, attended by male and occasionally helpers; nesting coincides with fruiting peaks. Probably does not breed annually but may re-use nest-holes annually at times.

HELMETED HORNBILL *Rhinoplax vigil*

Identification 110–120 cm. Monotypic. Very unusual-looking, very large hornbill with extensive bare skin on head, elongated central tail feathers and uniquely shaped casque; only hornbill with solid ivory casque. **Adult male** Bristly upright crown feathers brown, bare and wrinkly skin on head and neck maroon-red, cheeks rufous-brown, upperparts and breast blackish-brown, belly and thighs white, tail white with black subterminal band, elongated central tail feathers grey with black subterminal band and white tip; iris reddish-brown; short, squat bill yellow with red sides and base from preen oil, casque heavy with blunt end halfway along bill stained red, legs and feet reddish-brown; in flight underwings black with broad white trailing edge, very elongated central tail feathers diagnostic. **Adult female** Basic plumage similar to male but smaller, bare head and neck pale blue, turquoise on throat. **Juvenile** Head and neck bare greenish-blue, short central tail feathers, bill small and yellow, casque reduced. **Habitat** Primary lowland dipterocarp and hill forest (avoids secondary forest), to 1,400 m, favouring foothills. **Behaviour** Usually in pairs; feeds mainly on fruit, especially figs; also hunts small animals including squirrels, birds, lizards, foraging in canopy of tall trees; has large home range size of c.770 ha. **Voice** Unique vocalisations immediately recognisable given from canopies of emergent trees and very far-carrying; song is a loud, low-pitched *poop… poop… poop…* repeated every 5–3 s (0.6 kHz, 0.1 s), gradually speeding up to a faster, double note *pupoop* (0.6 kHz, 0.6 s) every 3–0.3 s then descending into a rapid, higher-pitched, maniacal cackle *kakaka…*(1.6 kHz); each series may last from 1.5–4 mins. In flight a *kak* call (0.4 kHz) is uttered. **Range & status** Thai-Malay Peninsula, Sumatra. **Borneo** Uncommon resident throughout.

Breeding Year-round; breeds during fruiting peak, requires large dipterocarps for natural nest-holes in isolated forest trees; female is sealed in and lays 1–2 eggs but only one chick has ever been recorded with adults; male feeds female on sealed-in nest.

WHITE-CROWNED HORNBILL *Berenicornus comatus*

Identification 75–80 cm. Monotypic. Medium hornbill with unique full, spiky white crest and all-white tail contrasting with black upperparts. **Adult male** Shaggy, erect white crest; head, neck and underparts white, upperparts and thighs black; wings black tipped white, long tail white; in flight underwings black with white trailing edge, all-white undertail; iris pale yellow, bare skin around eye to sides of throat blue, bill and low casque dark grey with dull yellow base, legs and feet black. **Adult female** Like male but smaller with white crest and black face, neck and body. **Juvenile** All black with feathers tipped white on head and neck, tail black tipped white, bare facial skin grey, bill dull yellow. **Habitat** A slope specialist: primary lowland dipterocarp and hill forest, occasionally ranging over secondary forest and scrub, favouring areas with dense undergrowth, to 1,600 m, but usually above 500 m. **Behaviour** Inconspicuous, usually remaining well below canopy, regularly descending to ground; territorial, usually in groups of 4–8; feeds mostly on small animals such as large insects, lizards, birds, also fruits; unlike other hornbills flight is almost silent. **Voice** More often heard than seen due to habit of remaining below canopy; call is an owl- or pigeon-like mellow, low-pitched three-note *hu hoo-hoo*, the first note quieter and lower-pitched (0.6 kHz) than following two (0.7 kHz), the series delivered in 1 s and repeated at intervals of less than 0.5 s. **Range & status** Thai-Malay Peninsula, Sumatra. **Borneo** Uncommon to rare resident throughout at low densities.

Breeding Year-round, breeding during fruiting peaks; lays 1–2 eggs but usually only one chick is fledged; cooperative breeder, dominant pair assisted by other group members; female is sealed into nest in natural tree cavity 10–30 m above ground; same cavity may be used in successive years.

SUKAU RIVER LODGE   9/6/10

WRINKLED HORNBILL *Aceros corrugatus*

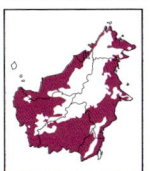

Identification 65–70 cm. Monotypic. Small hornbill with colourful face, bill and casque. **Adult male** Crown and upperparts black; sides of head, neck and upper breast white often stained ochre; lower breast to undertail-coverts black, tail white stained ochre with black base; in flight underwings all black with white undertail; iris reddish-brown, bare skin around eye blue; bare, inflatable throat-skin yellow, bill yellow with red base, ridged at base of lower mandible; high wrinkled casque red; legs and feet greyish-black. **Adult female** Like male but smaller with black head and neck, bare inflatable skin of throat blue, smaller bill and reduced casque yellow with brownish base. **Juvenile** Like adult male but bill small with no casque, pale yellow. **Similar species** Smaller than Wreathed Hornbill with more colourful face pattern; in flight base of tail is black. **Habitat** Extreme lowland specialist: lowland primary and selectively logged dipterocarp forest, favouring swamp forest, to 400 m but rarely above 30 m. **Behaviour** Highly mobile and nomadic, tracking fruiting trees, usually in pairs; feeds on fruits and small animals, forages in canopy of emergent trees. **Voice** Male utters a hoarse, coughing *kuk-kuk kuk-kuk-kuk* (0.4 kHz); female delivers similar call at slightly higher pitch (0.6 kHz). Loud, whooshing wing-beats. **Range & status** Thai-Malay Peninsula, Sumatra. **Borneo** Uncommon resident throughout, although status in S Kalimantan uncertain. Scarcer on west coast of Sabah. **Breeding** Breeding behaviour is little known with nest undescribed in Borneo.

WREATHED HORNBILL *Aceros undulatus*

Identification 75–85 cm. Monotypic. Large, mostly black hornbill with white tail and prominent gular pouch. **Adult male** Crown and nape chestnut, face to upper breast white, lower breast to undertail-coverts black, upperparts black, short tail white; in flight underwings all black with contrasting all-white tail; iris red with red orbital skin, bill pale yellow with ridges at base, low casque with reddish-brown corrugations, gular pouch yellow with black central stripe. **Adult female** Smaller, head and neck black, eye-ring pinkish-red, gular pouch blue with black band. **Juvenile** Like male, smaller bill with no casque. **Similar species** See Wrinkled Hornbill. **Habitat** Primary lowland dipterocarp forest and selectively logged areas, kerangas, to 3,000 m but favouring hill and lower montane forest. Requires large, unbroken tracts of forest. **Behaviour** Non-territorial, nomadic, in pairs or groups up to 20, may congregate in large numbers at fruiting trees, sometimes gathers in very large communal roosts; feeds mainly on fruits but also on small animals; flies high over canopy rarely gliding as other large hornbills do. **Voice** A raucous, loud, grunting *uk-guk*, the first note softer and lower-pitched (0.5 kHz) than the second (0.7 kHz), repeated every 1–2 s. Very loud, whooshing wing-beats distinctive. **Range & status** E Himalayas, SE Asia, Sumatra, Java and Bali. **Borneo** Locally common resident throughout in low densities, patchy distribution due to forest loss. **Breeding** January–May during fruiting peaks; 1–3 white eggs are laid in nest in natural tree cavities often in large emergent trees 18–26 m above ground; same cavities may be used in successive years; female is sealed in; usually only one, sometimes two, chicks are raised; non-cooperative breeders, pairs utilising tree-hollows.

RAMPHASTIDAE: Barbets

Worldwide 83 species, 9 in Borneo. The Asian barbets (Megalaiminae) are generally colourful birds with a thick, powerful bill surrounded by conspicuous rictal bristles. The very distinctive, repetitive vocalisations are uttered endlessly with bill closed. Most are green with diagnostic yellow, blue and red head patterns. Specialist frugivores, typically found in the forest canopy. All excavate nests in tree-trunks or branches. Typically the sexes are similar.

GOLD-WHISKERED BARBET *Megalaima chrysopogon*

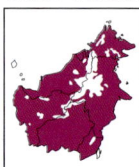

Identification 30 cm. **Adult *chrysopsis*** (endemic subspecies) Forehead yellow, crown and lores red, broad black face-mask bordered blue behind, broad malar area yellow, throat grey bordered blue below, underparts green, upperparts deep green; iris brown, eye-ring slaty-blue, large bill grey with black bristles at base, legs and feet olive-grey. **Juvenile** Duller, bill paler. **Similar species** Red-crowned and Red-throated Barbets are smaller and lack large yellow malar area. **Habitat** Primary and secondary lowland dipterocarp and hill forest, to 1,150 m. **Behaviour** Diet consists of large figs and berries, and some insects; forages in canopy. **Voice** Calls introduced by a rapid *tu-tu-tu-tu...* (c.14 notes/s) usually then followed by a resonant, mellow *tuu-tu-tu-toop* or *tu-tup* of varying length (0.6 kHz), often repeated endlessly. **Range & status** Thai-Malay Peninsula, Sumatra.

Borneo Common resident throughout. **Breeding** April–September; excavates nest cavity in arboreal termite nests and rotting tree-trunks.

RED-CROWNED BARBET *Megalaima rafflesii*

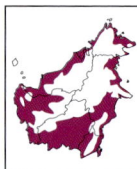

Identification 26 cm. Monotypic. **Adult male** Extensive red crown to nape, broad blue supercilium, red spot below eye and black ear-coverts, upperparts deep green, throat and upper breast blue, yellow patch on sides of neck and red spot on sides of breast, rest of underparts green, undertail pale blue; iris brown with black eye-ring, robust bill blackish-grey with black bristles at base, legs and feet olive-grey. **Juvenile** Duller, head markings indistinct. **Similar species** See Gold-whiskered Barbet; Red-throated Barbet has red throat and yellow forehead. **Habitat** Secondary coastal forest, peatswamp forest, kerangas; lowland specialist to 300 m. **Behaviour** Poorly known, diet consists mainly of fruits but also insects. **Voice** Two resonant low-pitched *poop poop* notes (0.5 kHz) introduce a long series of up to 40 notes *poop-poop-poop-poop...*, introductory notes separated by pause of c.0.3–0.5 s, the notes in the series

uttered at rate of c.4 notes/s. **Range & status** Thai-Malay Peninsula, Sumatra. **Borneo** Common (Sarawak, Brunei, Kalimantan) to uncommon (Sabah) resident throughout. **Breeding** March–July; excavates hole in dead tree or rotten stump; lays 2–3 eggs.

RED-THROATED BARBET *Megalaima mystacophanos*

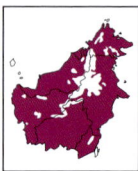

Identification 23 cm. **Adult male *mystacophanos*** Forehead yellow, crown and lores red, black eyestripe, cheek blue, throat red bordered blue below and by yellow malar area, red spot on sides of upper breast, underparts green, undertail pale blue, upperparts deep green; iris black, large bill black with black bristles at base, legs and feet grey. **Adult female** Paler, small yellow area in front of blue forehead, top of crown and lores red, face blue, throat pale yellow with small red spot of sides of breast; base of lower mandible yellowish-grey. **Juvenile** Dull green and grey; bill yellowish-grey. **Similar species** See Gold-whiskered and Red-throated Barbets. **Habitat** Primary and secondary lowland dipterocarp, kerangas and peatswamp forest, plantations, gardens, to 1,000 m. **Behaviour** Diet consists of fruit, especially figs, and insect larvae; forages in forest canopy. **Voice** An irregular, resonant *took...took took took*

took-took (0.8 kHz), higher-pitched than Gold-whiskered and Red-throated Barbets. **Range & status** Thai-Malay Peninsula, Sumatra. **Borneo** Common resident throughout. **Breeding** May–September; excavates nest cavity in arboreal termite nest or rotten tree-stump c.3 m from ground.

MOUNTAIN BARBET *Megalaima monticola*

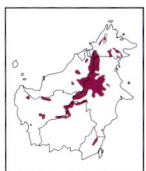

Identification 20–22 cm. Monotypic. **Adult male** Forehead streaky pale yellow, crown blue, hindcrown to nape red, ear-coverts streaky greenish-blue, upperparts dark green, throat and malar area scaly buffish-yellow and grey, small red spot on each side of upper breast, underparts yellowish-green; iris dark brown, bill black with black bristles at base, legs and feet olive-grey. **Juvenile** Duller, markings less distinct. **Similar species** Female Red-throated Barbet has red loral spot and larger bill. **Habitat** Primary and secondary hill to upper montane forest, montane kerangas, orchards, from 750 to 2,200 m. **Behaviour** Poorly known; arboreal frugivore, occasionally feeds on insects; forages from canopy to lower levels of forest. **Voice** A rapid, resonant, repetitive *tu-ruk tuk tuk tuk tuk tuk tuk tuk tuk...* (0.8 kHz, 4 notes/s) uttered incessantly, the two-note hiccup *tu-ruk* given every 19–21 notes. **Range & status** Endemic, locally common montane resident throughout. **Breeding** Poorly known, one nest seen in August in dead tree-trunk.

YELLOW-CROWNED BARBET *Megalaima henricii*

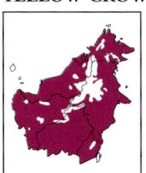

Identification 21.5–22.5 cm. **Adult *brachyrhyncha*** (endemic subspecies) Forehead to sides of crown yellow, central crown blue, black eyestripe, supercilium and cheeks to back of neck yellowish-green, narrow red collar, throat and sides of neck blue with small red spot on sides of upper breast, underparts green, upperparts deep green; iris dark brown, bill black with black bristles at base, legs and feet olive-grey. **Juvenile** Duller, head pattern indistinct. **Similar species** Golden-naped Barbet has blue forehead and no red in plumage. **Habitat** Primary and secondary lowland dipterocarp, peatswamp and kerangas forest, to 1,200 m but most common below 700 m, replaced at higher altitudes by Mountain Barbet. **Behaviour** Arboreal frugivore; feeds high in canopy and in emergent trees. **Voice** A relatively high-pitched, resonant *tuk tuk tuk tuk tkrrrrrk* (1.2 kHz), each phrase c.2 s. **Range & status** Thai-Malay Peninsula, Sumatra. **Borneo** Locally common to uncommon resident throughout. **Breeding** Undescribed in Borneo; elsewhere known to excavate nest-holes in tree c.9 m from ground.

GOLDEN-NAPED BARBET *Megalaima pulcherrima*

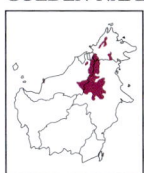

Identification 20–21.5 cm. Monotypic. **Adult male** Forehead to hindneck blue, lores black, sides of head yellowish-green, nape golden-yellow, upperparts deep green, throat blue, underparts green; iris black, relatively small stout bill black, legs and feet olive-grey. **Juvenile** Duller, lacks gold on nape. **Similar species** Only barbet on Borneo with plain blue crown and throat. **Habitat** Primary and secondary montane forest, from 1,100 to 2,500 m, with extreme records at 600 m and 3,200 m. **Behaviour** Poorly known; usually solitary; arboreal frugivore, also feeds on insects; forages in mid-storey and canopy. **Voice** A relatively high-pitched, mellow three-note *tuk tuk tukrrrk* (1.5 kHz, c.1.5 s); also a long trill *prrrrt* of 1–2 s, followed by gradually shortening similar phrases. **Range & status** Endemic, common resident in north-central mountain ranges from G. Kinabalu to G. Mulu and G. Murud and G. Menyapa (Sabah, E Sarawak, E Kalimantan). **Breeding** March–May; excavates nest-hole in dead or partly dead trees, one seen 8.5 m from ground.

BLUE-EARED BARBET *Megalaima australis*

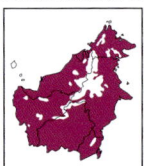

Identification 16–17 cm. **Adult *duvaucelii*** Forehead and forecrown black, hindcrown blue, ear-coverts black with red line above and red spot below, red spot below eye, black malar stripe connected to black ear-coverts, throat blue bordered by black breast-band, underparts green, undertail blue, upperparts deep green; iris dark brown, bill black, legs and feet olive-grey. **Juvenile** Duller with paler bill. **Similar species** Bornean Barbet has red crown, blue ears, black throat and yellow spot under eye. **Habitat** Primary and secondary lowland dipterocarp, peatswamp and kerangas to hill forest, mangroves, plantations, to 1,000 m. **Behaviour** Forages in canopy where it feeds mainly on fruit, especially figs, and some insects. **Voice** A rapid incessant two-note *tu-tuk tu-tuk tu-tuk tu-tuk…*, relatively high-pitched (2 kHz), the two notes identical, each phrase short (0.3 s), repeated at rate of c.2–3 phrases/s, with rather mechanical quality; also gives a short, repeated trilling *trrr trrr trrr…* (2.1 kHz). **Range & status** NE Indian Subcontinent, S China, SE Asia, Sumatra, Java and Bali. **Borneo** Common resident throughout. **Breeding** December–June; lays 2–3 white eggs in small nest-hole excavated in dead or rotting tree or branch or in an arboreal termite nest.

BORNEAN BARBET *Megalaima eximia*

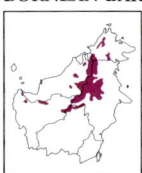

Identification 15–16 cm. **Adult *eximia*** Forehead and forecrown black, hindcrown deep red, supercilium and ear-coverts blue, orangey-yellow spot below eye, throat black with red spot on sides of neck and red breast-patch, underparts green, upperparts deep green; iris brown, bill black with long rictal bristles, legs and feet olive-grey. **Immature** Duller, red areas replaced with green, forehead and throat may be blue. **Adult *cyanea*** As nominate but forehead and throat blue (there is some dispute over status of this taxon). **Habitat** Primary lower montane forest; slope specialist from 900 to 2,100 m, with exceptional records as low as 425 m. **Behaviour** Very poorly known; frugivorous; forages from mid-storey to canopy. **Voice** A rapid, incessantly repeated single-note *tuk tuk tuk tuk tuk…* (1.8 kHz) uttered very rapidly at rate of c.5 notes/s. **Range & status** Endemic, uncommon resident in north-central and western mountain ranges from G. Kinabalu to Dulit Range and Pueh Range (Sabah, Sarawak, W, C and E Kalimantan); *cyanea* confined to G. Kinabalu. **Breeding** Documented in April; one seen excavating small nest cavity in dead branch, 19 m from ground.

BROWN BARBET *Calorhamphus fuliginosus*

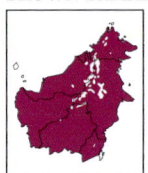

Identification 17–18 cm. **Adult male *fuliginosus*** (endemic subspecies) Upperparts dark brown, throat and breast pinkish-red fading into dirty buffish-brown underparts; iris brown; long, deep, slightly downcurved and hooked bill greyish-black; legs and feet bright orangey-red. **Adult female** As male but bill ivory or pale brown. **Juvenile** Duller. **Adult male *tertius*** (endemic subspecies) Like nominate but head paler brown, less extensive pinkish-red on throat and paler bill. **Habitat** Primary and secondary lowland dipterocarp, peatswamp and kerangas to hill forest, mangroves, to 1,500 m. **Behaviour** Gregarious, usually in vocal groups of 6–8; feeds on fruits and insects. **Voice** A thin, sibilant, rather soft but high-pitched *tseet tseet tseet…* (8 kHz), each short note (0.2–0.4 s) repeated somewhat irregularly at rate of 1–1.5/s. **Range & status** Thai-Malay Peninsula, Sumatra. **Borneo** Common resident throughout, *fuliginosus* in S Borneo (S Sarawak, Kalimantan) and *tertius* in N Borneo (Sabah, Brunei, E Sarawak). **Breeding** March–December; excavated nest-holes have been recorded in bees' nests, arboreal termite nests, rotten trees and at base of large fern.

INDICATORIDAE: Honeyguides

Worldwide 17 species, 1 in Borneo. Small, unobtrusive and nondescript arboreal birds with finch-like bill and short, strong legs. Feeds mostly on beeswax. Sexes similar. Breeding habits are poorly known in Borneo but are known to be parasitic elsewhere.

MALAYSIAN HONEYGUIDE *Indicator archipelagicus*

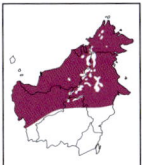

Male

Identification 16 cm. Monotypic. **Adult male** Nondescript; upperparts dark olive-brown with bright yellow patch on shoulder, chin whitish fading to grey throat, rest of underparts grey with faint brown streaks; iris red with narrow grey eye-ring, strong pointed bill pink with black tip, legs and feet olive-grey. **Adult female** As male but lacks yellow shoulder-patch, iris brown. **Juvenile** Upperparts greener, rump pale, underparts grey streaked olive, legs and feet pink. **Habitat** Primary lowland dipterocarp to lower montane forest, more rarely in secondary forest, plantations and gardens, to 1,300 m. **Behaviour** Very poorly known; inconspicuous; associates with bees; feeds on bees, bee larvae and beeswax, as well as other insects. **Voice** A crow-like *kiaw* (1.4 kHz) followed by very unusual, long, ascending, raspy almost frog-like trill, whole phrase c.4 s. **Range & status** Thai-Malay Peninsula, Sumatra. **Borneo** Rare resident with records from scattered localities in Sabah, Brunei, Sarawak and E, W and north C Kalimantan. **Breeding** Breeding habits in Borneo are unknown but may be parasitic (as many other members of family) on Brown Barbet, which it superficially resembles.

PICIDAE: Woodpeckers

Worldwide c.216 species, 18 in Borneo. A large family of birds characterised by strong claws, short legs and stiff tail for foraging on vertical surfaces. Sexes differ, the males usually have some red on the head. The strong, sharp bill is used for chiselling wood for invertebrate prey and nest-holes. The skull is reinforced and the tongue is highly elongated—both adaptions for the mode of feeding. The flight is rapid and deeply undulating. The simple vocalisations are accompanied by non-vocal territorial drumming.

RUFOUS PICULET *Sasia abnormis*

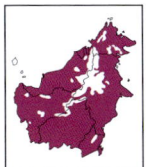

Female

Male

Juvenile

Identification 9 cm. Tiny woodpecker, olive-green upperparts, rufous underparts, appearing almost tailless. **Adult male *abnormis*** Forehead yellow, face and sides of neck rufous, crown and hindneck to upperparts olive-green, rump rufous, uppertail-coverts black, underparts rufous; iris and eye-ring red, upper mandible grey, lower mandible yellow, legs and feet orange. **Adult female** As male but forehead rufous. **Juvenile** Upperparts duller olive-green, underparts greenish-brown; iris brown, bill grey. **Habitat** Primary and secondary lowland dipterocarp and hill forest, peatswamp forest, plantations, to 1,200 m. Commoner in lowland forest. **Behaviour** Usually singly or in pairs; joins mixed feeding flocks; forages inconspicuously in dense undergrowth; feeds on insects especially ants, insect larvae, spiders; gleans prey from bark, bamboo, rattan and dead wood; often detected by sound of its loud and persistent tapping. **Voice** A squeaky (like child's toy), high-pitched one-note *peet* or two-note *pee-peet* (4–5 kHz) usually repeated; rapid drumming in bursts of 1–2 s. **Range & status** Thai-Malay Peninsula, Sumatra, Java. **Borneo** Common resident throughout. **Breeding** Poorly known, February–July; nests are excavated in small dead branches.

SPECKLED PICULET *Picumnus innominatus*

Identification 10 cm. Tiny, olive-green woodpecker with boldly spotted underparts and short, triangular bill. **Adult male *malayorum*** Forehead barred orange and black, crown and submoustachial stripe greyish-olive, blackish ear-coverts enclosed above by broad white supercilium and below by white moustachial stripe to sides of neck, chin and throat white, underparts buff-white boldly spotted black, upperparts olive-green, uppertail black with white central feathers; iris brown, bill dark grey, legs and feet bluish-grey. **Adult female** As male but forehead olive-green. **Juvenile** As female but duller with paler bill. **Habitat** Primary and secondary lowland dipterocarp and hill forest; occurs in wide altitudinal range in Borneo to 1,200 m. **Behaviour** Singly or in pairs; joins mixed feeding flocks; forages inconspicuously in dense undergrowth; diet consists of insects, insect larvae and small invertebrates; often detected by sound of its loud and persistent tapping. **Voice** Call is a high-pitched *sit-sit-sit*; drumming is surprisingly loud, rapid and persistent. **Range & status** S India, Himalayas, China, SE Asia, Sumatra. **Borneo** Rare resident Sabah and Brunei, status uncertain elsewhere with just one sight record from E Kalimantan. **Breeding** Undescribed in Borneo.

GREY-CAPPED PYGMY WOODPECKER
Dendrocopos canicapillus

Identification 14–15 cm. Very small blackish-brown and white woodpecker with orange-washed underparts. **Adult male *aurantiiventris*** (endemic subspecies) Forehead, crown and hindneck dark grey with red spot at sides of hindcrown, broad greyish-brown stripe from eye to sides of neck bordered above from eye to neck by broad white line, lores and cheeks to moustachial area buff-white, submoustachial stripe greyish-brown, chin and throat white, upperparts black barred white on back, uppertail black with white spots on outer feathers, underparts buffish-orange heavily streaked brown; iris brown, bill dark grey, legs and feet olive-grey. **Adult female** Lacks red on crown. **Juvenile** Darker. **Similar species** See Sunda Pygmy Woodpecker. **Habitat** Primary and secondary lowland dipterocarp forest, peatswamp forest, kerangas, mangroves, plantations, favours inland forest to 400 m, but with records to 1,700 m. **Behaviour** Solitary or in pairs; diet consists of variety of insects as well as fruits; forages in small branches and twigs of large trees and bushes, gleaning from bark, lichen and leaves and hammering dead branches. **Voice** A sharp, relatively soft, high-pitched *kik* (4.8 kHz), usually repeated 4–5 times over c.1.5 s. **Range & status** Himalayas, China, Siberia, Korea, SE Asia, Sumatra. **Borneo** Common resident throughout. **Breeding** April–May; excavates nest-hole in dead trees.

SUNDA PYGMY WOODPECKER
Dendrocopos moluccensis

LIBARAN ISLAND 6/6/10

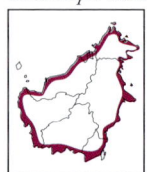

Identification 13 cm. Very small, brown and white woodpecker with heavy white barring above and brown streaking below. **Adult male *moluccensis*** Forehead, crown and hindneck dark brown with red spot at sides of hindcrown, broad dark brown stripe from eye to sides of neck bordered above from eye to neck by broad white line, lores and cheeks to moustachial area white, prominent submoustachial stripe dark brown, chin and throat white, upperparts dark brown barred and spotted with white, rump and uppertail-coverts white spotted with black, underparts whitish heavily streaked brown; iris brown, bill and legs dark grey. **Adult female** Lacks red on crown. **Juvenile** Duller and browner. **Similar species** Grey-capped Pygmy Woodpecker has blacker upperparts, underparts less streaked with an orange wash, less white on tail. **Habitat** Secondary forest, coastal woodlands, mangroves, parks, gardens, favours open habitats in coastal areas at sea-level. **Behaviour** Usually solitary or in pairs; forages on dead branches and trees for insects and small invertebrates. **Voice** A trilled, high-pitched, rapid series of *ki-ki-ki-ki...* notes (5 kHz), c.20 notes in a series lasting 1.5–2 s. **Range & status** Thai-Malay Peninsula, Indonesia. **Borneo** Common resident throughout chiefly in coastal areas, including near offshore islands. **Breeding** April–July; excavates nest-hole in tree-trunks c.10 m from ground.

WHITE-BELLIED WOODPECKER *Dryocopus javensis*

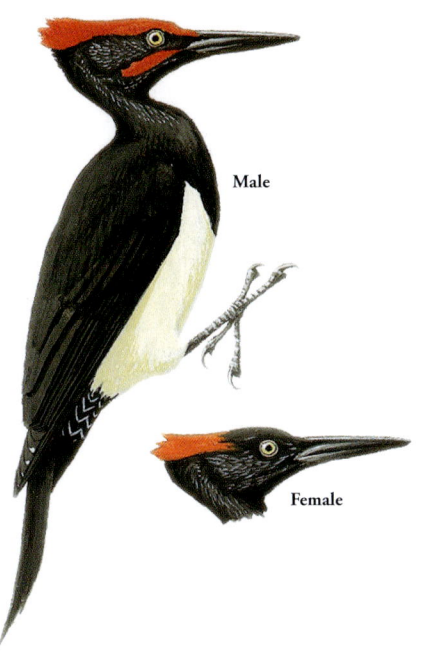

Identification 40–48 cm. Very large black and white woodpecker with crimson on head. **Adult male *javensis*** Forehead to nape and crest crimson, broad malar stripe crimson, rest of head and entire upperparts and breast black, ear-coverts and throat with fine white streaks, belly white, undertail-coverts and undertail black, underwing greyish-black with white coverts; iris yellow, bill dark grey, legs and feet dark grey. **Adult female** Crimson on head confined to crest. **Juvenile** Duller and browner with pale throat and grey iris. **Habitat** Primary and secondary lowland dipterocarp forest, peatswamp forest, kerangas, mangroves; much commoner in primary forest; lowland specialist found to 600 m. **Behaviour** Noisy and conspicuous; usually in pairs; diet consists of variety of insects; forages at all levels from upper limbs and trunks of tall trees to fallen timber on ground, nearly always on dead wood. **Voice** Range of vocalisations include a short loud far-carrying yelp *kiau* (2.5 kHz) and rapid *ke-ke-ke-ke…*; drumming is loud, accelerating and resonant. **Range & status** S India, SW China, Korea, SE Asia, Philippines, Sumatra, Java and Bali. **Borneo** Fairly common resident throughout, including N Natunas and Banggi Island. **Breeding** March–May; both sexes excavate nest in large dead or damaged trees 2–6 m from ground; 2–3 eggs.

RUFOUS WOODPECKER *Micropternus brachyurus*

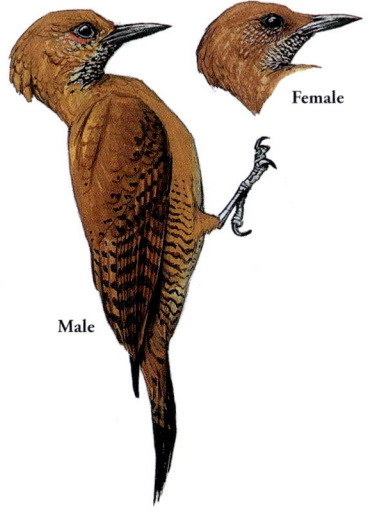

Identification 25 cm. All-rufous woodpecker with short crest and black bars on upperparts. **Adult male *badiosus*** (endemic subspecies) Forehead to nape and short crest dark brown, crimson patch below and behind eye, throat black scaled with chestnut and buff, upperparts rufous, wings and rump with narrow black bars, underparts rufous with fine black bars on flanks and undertail-coverts, tail black narrowly barred rufous; iris brown, bill dark grey, legs and feet dark grey. **Adult female** Lacks red on head. **Juvenile** Less heavily barred. **Habitat** Primary and secondary lowland dipterocarp forest, peatswamp forest, plantations; more common in primary forest below 200 m but recorded to 1,750 m. **Behaviour** Often in pairs; very active with bounding and dipping flight; feeds mainly on ants and termites, also figs and nectar; forages at all levels from ground to upper canopy. **Voice** Very vocal; utters a drawn-out series of 3–5 screaming notes *kee-kee-kee-kee-kee…* with plaintive quality, upslurred (2.7–3.5 kHz, 2.5 s); drumming is distinctive, starting off rapidly, gradually tapering off towards end, then stopping suddenly. **Range & status** S India, NE India, S China, SE Asia, Sumatra, Java. **Borneo** Common resident throughout including N Natunas. **Breeding** February–October; usually excavates nest in arboreal ant nests at heights of 3–15 m, the birds and ants occupying nest at same time; holes occasionally excavated in tree-trunks; lays 2–3 eggs; both adults incubate.

BANDED WOODPECKER *Chrysophlegma mineaceus*

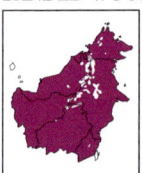

Identification 23–26 cm. Medium-sized woodpecker with predominantly reddish plumage, yellow nape, and narrow barring on underparts. **Adult male *malaccensis*** Crown brownish-red, paler on forehead and sides of head, nuchal crest brownish-red tipped yellow, throat to upper breast brownish-red, rest of underparts buff with dark brown barring, mantle and scapulars olive-brown with buff scaling, wing-coverts red, flight feathers brown edged red, rump yellow, uppertail black; iris dark reddish-brown, bill grey paler on lower mandible, legs and feet grey. **Adult female** Browner on head with buff spots on cheeks. **Juvenile** Duller, less barring on underparts. **Similar species** Crimson-winged Woodpecker has greener upperparts, all-green underparts with very little barring, lower mandible yellow; male has red moustache. **Habitat** Primary and secondary lowland dipterocarp to upper montane forest, peatswamp forest, mangroves, plantations, gardens, to 1,700 m, more common below 1,000 m; tolerant of disturbance with higher density in selectively logged forest and rural areas. **Behaviour** Unobtrusive, solitary or in pairs; feeds predominantly on ants and ant larvae; actively forages in dense vegetation pecking, gleaning and probing in vines, epiphytes, dead wood and amongst branches. **Voice** Call is a short, explosive *kau* (3.5 kHz, 0.3 s), sometimes repeated at 3–10 s intervals. **Range & status** Thai-Malay Peninsula, Sumatra, Java. **Borneo** Common resident throughout. **Breeding** January–October; lays 2–3 eggs in nest excavated in decayed stumps of live or dead trees or dead coconut palms at any height, both sexes making nests and caring for young.

Male

Female

CHECKER-THROATED WOODPECKER
Chrysophlegma mentalis

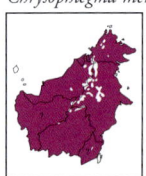

Identification 26–28 cm. Dark green, medium-sized woodpecker with distinctive chestnut neck and breast markings and black-and-white-spotted throat. **Adult male *humii*** Crown and face dark olive-green, nuchal crest bright yellow to hindneck, white-spotted brownish-green submoustachial stripe joins broad chestnut line from sides of neck to breast, throat checkered black and white, rest of underparts dark green, upperparts dark green with deep red wing-coverts barred darker on primaries, tail blackish; iris dark red, bill dark grey, paler below, legs and feet greenish-grey. **Adult female** Submoustachial stripe and band from sides of neck to breast duller chestnut. **Juvenile** Reduced red in wings, underparts all chestnut. **Similar species** Crimson-winged Woodpecker has red moustachial stripe, lacks chestnut around neck and breast. **Habitat** Primary lowland dipterocarp to upper montane forest with open understorey, to 1,700 m but occurs at higher densities in lowland forest; intolerant of habitat disturbance. **Behaviour** Usually solitary; often in mixed feeding flocks; eats variety of insects, also berries; forages in lower and middle storey. **Voice** Three- or four-note call, with somewhat sad, pleading tone, *ki kee kee kee*, delivered on level pitch (2.5 kHz) over c.1 s, also softer *kuwee*; relatively soft, rapid drumming. **Range & status** Thai-Malay Peninsula, Sumatra, W Java. **Borneo** Locally common resident in N Borneo (Sabah, Brunei, Sarawak, W, C and E Kalimantan), status uncertain in S Kalimantan. **Breeding** February–June; 2–3 eggs laid in nest excavated in dead stump.

Female

Male

CRIMSON-WINGED WOODPECKER *Picus puniceus*

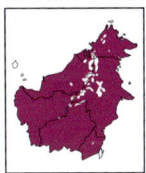

Male

Female

Identification 25 cm. Medium-sized, mostly green with contrasting crimson crest and wings, yellow nape and long, straight bicoloured bill. **Adult male** *observandus* Forehead and crown crimson with blackish lores, nuchal crest yellow to hindneck, rest of head olive-green with short crimson malar stripe, back and underparts olive-green with buff bars on flanks, wings crimson, rump yellow, uppertail brownish-black; in flight underwing brown with pale yellow barring; iris dark brown with pale blue eye-ring, upper mandible dark grey, lower yellow, legs and feet greenish-grey. **Adult female** Lacks crimson malar stripe. **Juvenile** Duller, less red on head and more barring on underparts. **Habitat** Primary and secondary lowland dipterocarp to upper montane forest, peatswamp forest, kerangas, plantations, to 1,700 m. **Behaviour** Mostly in pairs; joins mixed feeding flocks; eats mainly ants and termites including larvae obtained mostly by hammering and pecking, frequently on underside of branches in canopy. **Voice** Song is a laughing cackle, *kii kii kii kii ki*, descending in pitch (3.6–3 kHz, c.1 s) and volume; call is a strident, explosive *kau*, very like Banded Woodpecker but slightly longer (3.5 kHz, 0.4 s). **Range & status** Thai-Malay Peninsula, Sumatra, Java. **Borneo** Uncommon resident throughout. **Breeding** February–July; nests in small dead limbs 8–20 m up in large trees or in palms.

OLIVE-BACKED WOODPECKER *Dinopium rafflesii*

Female

Male

Identification 25–26 cm. Medium-sized woodpecker with olive-green plumage, white-spotted flanks and black and white head and neck pattern. **Adult male** *dulitense* (endemic subspecies) Crown and crest red narrowly edged black below, white supercilium from eye to nape, black eyestripe to hindneck, white cheek-stripe down side of neck to upper breast, thin black malar stripe broadening to upper breast, lores and throat buffish-yellow, malar area reddish to cinnamon, hindneck to upper mantle black, rest of upperparts olive-green with black primaries, uppertail black, underparts dark olive with white spots on flanks, undertail olive; iris brown, long bill greyish-black, legs and feet grey. **Adult female** Crown and crest black. **Juvenile** Duller. **Similar species** Common Flameback and Greater Flameback have conspicuous yellowish-green upperparts, red rump and black and white underparts. **Habitat** Primary and secondary lowland dipterocarp forest, peatswamp forest, kerangas, mangroves, to 400 m but has been recorded to 1,585 m; tends to avoid secondary forest. **Behaviour** Solitary or in pairs; feeds mainly on ants and ant larvae obtained mostly by gleaning; generally forages below 10 m; relatively slow-moving. **Voice** A rapid, machinegun-like series of strident *pi-pi-pi...* notes (1.6 kHz), 30–35 notes delivered in c.4 s; also a short, softer *chik* call; drumming regular and rapid (c.20/s). **Range & status** Thai-Malay Peninsula, Sumatra. **Borneo** Uncommon resident throughout. **Breeding** Poorly known in Borneo, possibly breeds February–October; one seen excavating nest-hole in tree 3 m from ground.

COMMON FLAMEBACK *Dinopium javanense*

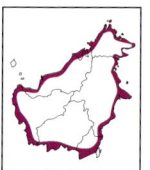

Identification 28–30 cm. Large woodpecker with distinctive black and white head pattern, yellow-green upperparts and bright red rump. **Adult male *javanense*** Forehead brownish-red, crown and crest crimson narrowly edged black below, white supercilium from eye to nape, broad white cheek-stripe to side of neck and upper breast, thin black malar stripe to upper breast, throat buff with small black spots, hindneck and upper mantle black, upperparts yellowish-green, lower back and rump crimson, uppertail black, underparts buffish-white with narrow black fringes; iris dark brown, bill dark grey with paler base, legs and feet grey. **Adult female** Crown and crest black with white flecks. **Juvenile** Like adults but more blackish-brown on breast. **Adult male *raveni*** (endemic subspecies) Underparts more buff with less black, throat broadly spotted. **Similar species** See Greater Flameback and Olive-backed Woodpecker. **Habitat** Primary and secondary open forest, peatswamp forest, coastal forest, mangroves, plantations, gardens, to 500 m. **Behaviour** Usually in pairs; favours more open woodlands; gleans and probes in search of ants and small invertebrates. **Voice** A 10-note staccato *ki-ki-ki-ki-ki-ki-ki-ki-ki-ki* (2.6 kHz, c.1 s). **Range & status** S India, SC China, SE Asia, Palawan, Sumatra, W Java. **Borneo** Locally common to uncommon resident in coastal areas throughout including NE offshore islands; *raveni* in Sabah and probably occurs along E Kalimantan coast. **Breeding** April–December; excavates nest-hole in dead coconut palm, lays 1–2 eggs.

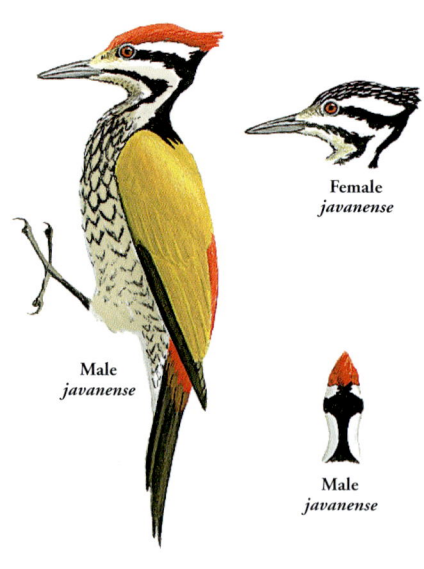

Female *javanense*

Male *javanense*

Male *javanense*

GREATER FLAMEBACK *Chrysocolaptes lucidus*

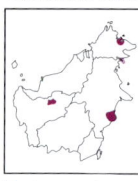

Identification 28–34 cm. Large woodpecker with distinctive black-and-white head pattern, yellow-green upperparts and bright red rump. **Adult male *andrewsi*** (endemic subspecies) Forehead, crown and crest crimson narrowly edged black below; broad white supercilium from eye to nape, black eyestripe to sides of neck enclosing white hindneck, white cheek-stripe to side of throat, split black malar stripe enclosing white patch, upperparts yellowish-green, lower back and rump crimson, uppertail black, throat white with thin central black line, underparts buffish-white with narrow black fringes; iris white, long bill dark grey, legs and feet grey. **Adult female** Crown and crest black with white spots. **Juvenile** Duller with more olive upperparts. **Similar species** Common Flameback has shorter bill, pointier crest, black hindneck, solid black malar stripe and dark iris. **Habitat** Possibly restricted to mangroves and swamp forest in Borneo. **Behaviour** Very poorly known in Borneo; usually in pairs; feeds on caterpillars, wood-borer larvae and ants obtained by hammering and pecking, rarely gleans; forages in large trees and snags. **Voice** Poorly known in Borneo; gives rapid staccato 5–10 note *kikikikiki...* (3 kHz, 0.5–1 s); loud rapid drumming fades out towards end. **Range & status** Indian Subcontinent, SW China, SE Asia, Sumatra, Java, Bali, Philippines. **Borneo** Rare resident NE Sabah, common in mangroves in Mahakam Delta, E Kalimantan; one record from Danau Sentarum, W Kalimantan. **Breeding** Undescribed in Borneo.

Male

Female

MAROON WOODPECKER *Blythipicus rubiginosus*

Identification 23 cm. Monotypic. Fairly small, all purplish-brown woodpecker with distinctive long yellow bill. **Adult male** Head olive-brown, sides of neck and nape red, malar area variably tipped red, upperparts purplish-brown, flight with indistinct reddish barring, tail dark brown with indistinct paler brown barring, underparts blackish-brown; iris brownish-red, long straight bill yellow, legs and feet bluish-black. **Adult female** Shorter bill, no red on head. **Juvenile** Upperparts tinged orange, more red on crown. **Habitat** Primary and secondary lowland dipterocarp to upper montane forest, peatswamp forest, mangroves, plantations, gardens, with dense undergrowth, recorded to 1,800 m, probably more common in primary lowland forests. **Behaviour** Found singly or in pairs; feeds mainly on beetle and wood-borer larvae and ants, foraging in lower and middle storey by hammering and pecking. **Voice** A short sharp squeaky *kik* (4.5 kHz) repeated rather slowly (c.2 notes/s), higher-pitched than other similar-sized woodpeckers. Sounds like child's toy, somewhat similar to Rufous Piculet but more regular and louder. **Range & status** Thai-Malay Peninsula, Sumatra. **Borneo** Common resident throughout. **Breeding** January–July; constructs nest in rather small dead limbs, 20 m or more from ground in large trees.

ORANGE-BACKED WOODPECKER
Reinwardtipicus validus

Identification 30 cm. Medium-large woodpecker with dark wings and tail contrasting with red and orange (male) or greyish-brown (female) head, back and underparts. **Adult male** *xanthopygius* Forehead to short crest dark red, sides of face orangey-brown, chin and malar area buffish-orange, nape and hindneck to back white with orange wash on lower back blending into orange rump, tail blackish-brown, wings blackish-brown with 3–5 broad reddish-brown bars on flight feathers, underparts dark red; iris brown, upper mandible grey, lower yellow, legs and feet olive-brown. **Adult female** Like male but forehead to short crest dark brown, rest of head greyish-brown, rump white, underparts greyish-brown. **Juvenile** Similar to adult female, juvenile male showing some red and orange in plumage. **Habitat** Primary and secondary lowland dipterocarp to upper montane forest, peatswamp forest, to 1,900 m. **Behaviour** Nearly always in pairs; dead-wood specialist foraging mostly in middle storey; feeds on beetle larvae, termites, ants, caterpillars and other insects. **Voice** A series of squeaky, clucking notes *chik-chik-chik-chik-kichik* (2.8 kHz), last note at higher pitch (4 kHz); drumming is soft in very short bursts. **Range & status** Thai-Malay Peninsula, Sumatra, W Java. **Borneo** Common (Sabah and Brunei) to uncommon (Sarawak and Kalimantan) resident throughout, including Bangka Island and N Natunas. **Breeding** February–October; lays glossy white eggs in nest-hole excavated in dead tree 10 m from ground.

BUFF-RUMPED WOODPECKER *Meiglyptes tristis*

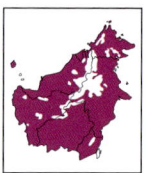

Identification 17–18 cm. Very small, short-tailed woodpecker with dense barring all over except for plain buff rump. **Adult male *grammithorax*** Head buffish-brown with narrow dark brown vermiculations, lores and eye-ring buffish, crimson malar stripe, mantle and back narrowly barred buffish-brown and black, wings black with broad buffish-brown bars, rump plain buffish-brown, underparts barred buffish-brown and dark brown, more narrowly on throat broadening to undertail; iris brown, bill black, legs and feet greenish-grey. **Adult female** Lacks red malar stripe. **Juvenile** Duller, more broadly barred, underparts darker and less barred. **Similar species** Buff-necked Woodpecker is larger, has prominent buffish neck-patch, lacks plain buffish-brown rump. **Habitat** Primary and secondary lowland dipterocarp to lower montane forest, peatswamp forest, plantations, to 1,100 m; commoner in primary or secondary lowland forest between 200–400 m. **Behaviour** Often in mixed feeding flocks; feeds mainly on ants and other insects (may specialise on ants associated with *Macaranga* trees) in small branches of upper canopy, obtaining food by gleaning, probing and hammering, favouring forest edges, clearings and gaps; often associates with Buff-necked Woodpecker (species feed in different strata). **Voice** A distinctive very rapid, high-pitched trill *kikikikiki…* (4.5 kHz), c.18 notes/s, each phrase c.1.5–2.5 s; also a quiet *seet seet*; drumming is quite soft and slow-paced (c.16/s), in short bursts of c.1.5–3 s. **Range & status** Thai-Malay Peninsula, Sumatra, W Java. **Borneo** Common resident throughout, including the Nias, Bangka and N Natuna Islands. **Breeding** April–August; probably lays two eggs in nest excavated in limb of dead or live trees at 6–8 m.

Female

Male

BUFF-NECKED WOODPECKER *Meiglyptes tukki*

Identification 21 cm. Small, brown and buff barred woodpecker with conspicuous large buffish patch on neck. **Adult male *tukki*** Crown and sides of head plain brown with red malar stripe, large buff patch on side of neck, chin and upper throat narrowly barred buff and brown, lower throat darker and sometimes unbarred, underparts finely barred buff and brown, upperparts blackish-brown narrowly barred buff; iris brown, bill black, legs and feet brown. **Adult female** Lacks red malar stripe. **Juvenile** Broader barring. **Adult *percnerpes*** (endemic subspecies) Browner with reddish brown, strongly barred. **Adult *pulonis*** (endemic subspecies) Longer-billed, browner with paler throat. **Habitat** Primary and secondary lowland dipterocarp and peatswamp forest, plantations, to 800 m. Tolerant of logged forest, occurring in equal densities in primary and secondary forest. **Behaviour** Usually in pairs or mixed feeding flocks in middle and lower strata; feeds on ants and termites by gleaning, probing and hammering on outer branches, epiphytes and nests of arboreal ants and termites. **Voice** A rapid, high-pitched, trilling *kikikikiki…* (3.7 kHz), c.14 notes/s; lower-pitched and slightly slower than similar call of Buff-rumped Woodpecker; drumming is soft, slightly faster-paced (c.19/s) than Buff-rumped. **Range & status** Thai-Malay Peninsula, Sumatra. **Borneo** Common resident throughout; *tukki* N Borneo and Bangka and N Natunas, *percnerpes* S Borneo, *pulonis* Banggi Island. **Breeding** March–September; probably lays two eggs in nest excavated in dead limbs of live trees or more often rotten dead trees 1–6.5 m above ground; both adults attend young.

Female *tukki*

Male *tukki*

GREY-AND-BUFF WOODPECKER
Hemicircus concretus

Identification 13–14 cm. Tiny grey and buff woodpecker with remarkable long triangular crest and very short tail. **Adult male** *sordidus* Forehead to point of crest scarlet; rear of crest, face and neck grey; upperparts boldly checkered black and buff, rump plain buff, underparts grey with buff barring on flanks; iris brown, bill and legs grey. **Adult female** Crest all grey. **Juvenile** Crown buff, upperparts checkered black and reddish-buff, underparts barred grey and reddish-buff. **Habitat** Primary and secondary lowland dipterocarp and hill forest, peatswamp forest, kerangas, plantations, gardens, mainly to 1,000 m but with records to 1,525 m. **Behaviour** usually solitary or in pairs; forages in canopy on small branches and twigs for insects and overripe fruit, gleaning and pecking leaves and fruits; feeding activity resembles nuthatch. **Voice** An explosive short high but downslurred *skreee* (6–3.5 kHz); also a rapid chattering *ke-ke-ke-ke-ke... ke-ke-ke-ke-ke...* (4 kHz). **Range & status** Thai-Malay Peninsula, Sumatra, Java. **Borneo** Locally uncommon resident throughout. **Breeding** Poorly known in Borneo, probably breeds February–July; excavates nest-hole in dead or partly dead tree c.3.5 m from ground.

GREAT SLATY WOODPECKER
Mulleripicus pulverulentus

Identification 50 cm. Huge all-grey woodpecker with long thin neck and very long, bicoloured bill and buffish throat. **Adult male** *pulverulentus* Overall slaty-grey, head and neck speckled whitish, wings and tail darker, chin and throat buffish-yellow, prominent red cheek-patch; iris dark brown, upper mandible grey with yellow base, lower yellow, legs and feet grey. **Adult female** Lacks red cheek-patch. **Juvenile** Brownish with whiter chin and throat. **Habitat** Primary lowland dipterocarp forest, riverine and peatswamp forest, to 500 m; a lowland specialist intolerant of logged forest. **Behaviour** Usually in pairs or family groups; diet consists mainly of ants and wood-borer larvae, obtained mainly by gleaning from bark in upper storey; forages in emergent trees, requiring large live trees for foraging on stingless bee, ant and termite nests that are located on large branches and tree-trunks. **Voice** Noisy; a loud, far-carrying, whinnying *wit-wit-wit-wee* (4 kHz). **Range & status** NE Himalayas, SE Asia, E Sumatra, W Java, Palawan. **Borneo** Locally uncommon resident throughout including N Natunas. **Breeding** March–August; excavates nest-hole in dead or partly dead tree or stump; 2–4 eggs.

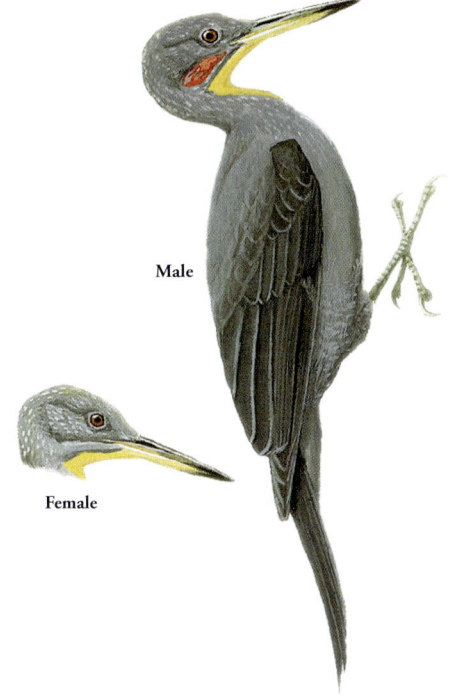

EURYLAIMIDAE: Broadbills

Worldwide 15 species, 8 in Borneo. A small family of diverse, colourful tropical birds with large head and very broad bill. Arboreal foliage-gleaning insectivores, generally unobtrusive in the mid-storey. Most are seen in pairs, some are usually in small groups. Build bulky, pendulous nests with a long tail often suspended in a conspicuous location.

GREEN BROADBILL *Calyptomena viridis*

Identification 14–17 cm. Stocky, vivid green broadbill with short tail, black markings on wings and almost obscured bill. **Adult male** *viridis* Iridescent bright green, tuft of feathers on forehead almost obscuring short bill, black spot on rear ear-coverts, three black bars on wings, flight feathers green edged black; iris dark brown, bill greyish-yellow, legs and feet olive-grey. **Adult female** Paler dull green, with no black markings on ear-coverts and wings. **Juvenile** Like female but paler with brownish flight feathers. **Similar species** Hose's Broadbill is larger with blue underparts and spots rather than bars on wings; Whitehead's Broadbill is much larger with black patch on upper breast. **Habitat** Primary and secondary lowland dipterocarp, peatswamp, kerangas and hill forest, overgrown plantations near forest, to 700 m (occasionally to 1,250 m). **Behaviour** Relatively slow-moving, foraging mostly in lower strata; eats fruits, particularly figs, and some insects; usually singly or in pairs but small groups congregate at fruiting trees. **Voice** Song is a quiet, unusual 'bouncing ball' trill, *boi, boi boi-boi-boi-boik*, starting slowly and increasing in tempo (1.5 kHz), each phrase c.1.2 s; a much quieter *kwoo kwoo*, often while feeding (1 kHz). **Range & status** Thai-Malay Peninsula, Sumatra. **Borneo** Common resident throughout, including N Natunas. **Breeding** January–June; gourd-shaped nest of woven plant material is suspended across horizontal branch often in understorey; lays two creamy-white eggs tinged pale brown.

Male

Female

HOSE'S BROADBILL *Calyptomena hosii*

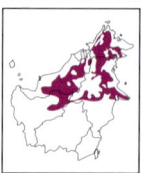

Identification 19–21 cm. Monotypic. Bright green broadbill with striking blue underparts. **Adult male** Iridescent bright green, tuft of feathers on forehead obscures most of bill, black spot on rear ear-coverts, small black spot in front of eye, black nape-patch and line across top of mantle, rows of black spots on wing-coverts, flight feathers black edged green, underparts azure-blue, tail black; iris dark brown, bill grey, legs and feet grey. **Adult female** Upperparts paler dull green, forehead tuft reduced, no black on head except for small pre-ocular spot, underparts yellowish-green with yellow flanks and blue centre of belly to undertail-coverts. **Juvenile** As female with darker nape. **Similar species** See Green Broadbill; Whitehead's Broadbill is larger with black upper breast-patch, lacks blue on underparts. **Habitat** Primary hill to lower montane forest; slope specialist from 300 to 1,200 m. **Behaviour** Very poorly known; mainly eats fruit, including figs and berries, and some insects; usually singly or in pairs but small groups recorded at fruiting tree. **Voice** A low-pitched, soft, dove-like *coo-wooo*, last, long note upslurred (0.76 kHz, 1.5 s). **Range & status** Endemic, patchily distributed (common to rare) submontane resident in north-central ranges from G. Kinabalu to Dulit Range and Kayan Mentarang, south-western ranges in Muller Mountains and eastern ranges in Sambaliung Mountains (NW Sabah, E Sarawak, W and E Kalimantan); said to be commoner in E Sarawak. **Breeding** April–October; nest (not been documented for over a century) is ball of dead leaves, mosses and lichens with long tail slung from low branch; lays 2–4 creamy-white eggs.

Female

Male

WHITEHEAD'S BROADBILL *Calyptomena whiteheadi*

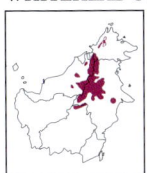

Identification 24–27 cm. Monotypic. Large bright green and black broadbill with prominent black breast-patch. **Adult male** Iridescent vivid green, tuft of feathers on forehead hides most of bill, obscure black spot on crown, large black spot on rear ear-coverts and nape, small black pre-ocular spot, black upper breast-patch, underparts bright green streaked black, mantle and back streaked green and black, wing-coverts iridescent bright green mottled black, flight feathers black with secondaries edged green, tail black; iris black, bill and legs grey. **Adult female** Upperparts duller green with reduced black markings, reduced forehead-tuft, throat black, underparts all green. **Habitat** Primary tall lower and upper montane forest, 600–1,850 m, usually above 900 m. **Behaviour** Sometimes loud and conspicuous but often sits quietly for long periods; usually solitary, sometimes in small groups at fruiting trees; diet mainly fruits and insects. **Voice** Song is a raspy *ki-chrrrr*, the *ki* very high and squeaky (3.3 kHz), the *chrrrr* drawn-out (1–2 s); call a staccato *kikikiki...* (3 kHz), recalling woodpecker (like Greater Flameback). **Range & status** Endemic, uncommon resident in north-central mountain ranges from G. Kinabalu to Usun Apau Plateau (NW Sabah, E Sarawak, C and E Kalimantan). **Breeding** March–May; slings nest of mosses, lichens and leaves with long 'tail' from thin horizontal branch in mid-storey, c.15 m up; lays 1–2 glossy creamy-white eggs.

Male

Female

LONG-TAILED BROADBILL *Psarisomus dalhousiae*

Identification 23–26 cm. Very striking bright green, blue, black and yellow broadbill with long tail. **Adult *borneensis*** (endemic subspecies) Black helmet-like head pattern with blue patch on top of crown and yellow spot on sides of nape, face and throat bright yellow, incomplete white collar bordering yellow throat across upper breast, small blue nuchal patch, underparts green, upperparts bright green with bright blue primaries, long tail ultramarine-blue; iris brown, bill pale green, legs and feet greenish-yellow; in flight underwing blue with white patch on flight feathers. **Juvenile** Crown green and black, throat greenish-yellow; bill yellowish-grey. **Habitat** Primary lower montane forest, from 900 to 1,700 m. **Behaviour** Sometimes in small, noisy flocks; forages in mid-storey mostly on insects. **Voice** A high piercing seven-note *puiii puii puii puii puii puii puipi* (6–4 kHz), each short note downslurred (0.5 s), the first usually loudest and highest, the last briefly rising markedly in pitch, the series c.4.5 s (G. Murud, Sarawak). **Range & status** Himalayas, S China, SE Asia, Sumatra. **Borneo** Locally uncommon to rare resident in north-central mountain ranges from G. Kinabalu to Dulit Range and Kayan Mentarang (W Sabah, E Sarawak and E Kalimantan). **Breeding** March–August; constructs large football-shaped nest of dead leaves and rootlets in lower branches of tree over steep slope.

Juvenile

Adult

155

DUSKY BROADBILL *Corydon sumatranus*

Identification 24–28 cm. Large, robust, dark broadbill with huge pink bill. **Adult *brunnescens*** (endemic subspecies) Head and body dark brown with olive tinge, bright red patch on mantle usually not visible, throat and upper breast rufous-brown, small white patch at base of primaries, undertail brown with variable white bars; iris dark brown, bare skin around eye and lores pink; huge wide bill pink with grey tip; legs and feet grey; in flight white patches on wings and tail. **Juvenile** Brown all over except for reduced white patch on wings, throat and upper breast only slightly paler than rest of underparts; bill all pale pink with reddish gape. **Habitat** Primary riverine forest and lowland dipterocarp to upper montane forest, to 1,800 m (G. Kinabalu) but commonest in lowlands. **Behaviour** Gregarious and noisy; forages for large insects and small vertebrates in groups of up to 10 in canopy. **Voice** A penetrating, harsh *kweer kweer kweer kweer...* with screaming quality, each note delivered on much the same pitch (2.5 kHz), each note c.0.3 s, 6–8 notes repeated rapidly; also a series of very rapid, squeaky *pwi pwi pwi pwi...* notes interspersed with similar notes uttered at slower pace, reminiscent of child's squeeze-toy. **Range & status** SE Asia, Sumatra. **Borneo** Uncommon resident throughout, including N Natunas. **Breeding** April–November; cooperative breeder; nest is large ball-shaped pendant structure of moss, leaves, twigs and other plant matter slung from hanging vegetation in middle storey often in open places; thought to be protection against predators.

Adult

Juvenile

BLACK-AND-RED BROADBILL
Cymbirhynchus macrorhynchos

Identification 20–24 cm. Striking black and deep-red broadbill with remarkable blue and yellow bill. **Adult *macrorhynchos*** Forehead and chin to hindneck black, extending into broad black breast-band dividing deep maroon throat and underparts, back and wings black with white bar on scapulars, bend of wing bright orange, lower back and rump deep maroon, tail black; iris dark blue, broad prominent bill with upper mandible bright aquablue, lower pale yellow, legs and feet greyish-blue. **Juvenile** Duller, brown with maroon on throat and rump, blackish breast-band, reduced white patch on scapulars. **Habitat** Primary and secondary lowland dipterocarp forest usually near moving water in riverine and peatswamp forest, mangroves, and overgrown plantations, to 750 m. **Behaviour** Usually in pairs; feeds on insects and other small invertebrates, small fruits. **Voice** A relatively low-key rasping, chucking *krrk krrk krrk*, the short notes repeated (2.5 kHz); less often an accelerating, raspy cicada-like trill. **Range & status** SE Asia, Sumatra. **Borneo** Common resident throughout. **Breeding** December–September; nest is large, untidy ball-shaped dangling mass of twigs, leaves and other vegetation suspended from branch over water, looking like flood debris; eggs two, pale pink with darker speckles.

Juvenile

Adult

BANDED BROADBILL *Eurylaimus javanicus*

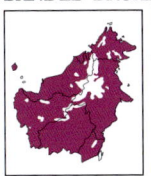

Identification 21–23 cm. Purplish-red broadbill with striking brown and yellow wings and broad blue bill. **Adult male** *brookei* (endemic subspecies) Forecrown and lores black, head and underparts purplish-red with pinkish throat, indistinct pinkish-black breast-band bordered greyish below, undertail black with white spots, mantle dark purplish-red, back to uppertail-coverts black with prominent yellow streaks, wings dark brown with striking yellow markings, bend of wing yellow, uppertail black; iris greyish-white to bluish, bill blue with black edges, legs and feet bluish-grey. **Adult female** As male but less black on forehead, upper breast greyish, lacks breast-band. **Juvenile** Head and upperparts pale brown with yellow markings, throat pale yellow, underparts pinky-yellow; bill yellowish-grey. **Similar species** Black-and-yellow Broadbill much smaller but vocalisations superficially similar; see Voice under that species. **Habitat** Primary and secondary lowland dipterocarp to lower montane forest, kerangas and peatswamp forest, to 1,200 m. **Behaviour** Usually in pairs; feeds predominantly on insects; perches quietly in mid-storey, flying out to glean prey from nearby foliage. **Voice** Song is remarkable, cicada-like frantic trill of c.7–9 s, introduced by single sudden loud *pwau* (1.5 kHz, 0.4 s), then starting off very rapidly (11 notes/s), building in pitch and volume (1.4–1.8 kHz) before reaching crescendo where pace slows (7 notes/s) and gradually dies off in volume; call is a short loud screaming *kwau-* (1.6 kHz, 0.6 s). **Range & status** SE Asia, Sumatra, Java. **Borneo** Common resident throughout, including N Natunas (somewhat less common than Black-and-yellow Broadbill). **Breeding** Probably March–August; otherwise undescribed in Borneo; elsewhere, pear-shaped pendulous ragged nest is made from dead leaves, green moss and thin twigs suspended by thin 'string' on branch

c.15 m above ground, the entrance close to top of nest and obscured by overhanging porch; nest has 'tail' of leaves and twigs hanging from main body; may be positioned near beehives as protection from predators.

BLACK-AND-YELLOW BROADBILL
Eurylaimus ochromalus

Identification 13–15 cm. Monotypic. Small, colourful broadbill with conspicuous white collar and pink underparts. **Adult male** Head black, white collar from back of neck to upper breast under black throat, narrow black breast-band, breast to belly pink fading into yellow undertail-coverts, back black with prominent yellow streaks, wings black with bright yellow markings, tail black with subterminal white spots; iris yellow, bill blue with black edges, legs and feet pink. **Adult female** As male but breast-band incomplete in middle. **Juvenile** Browner with less distinct yellow markings and supercilium, throat white, lacks breast-band, streaking on breast. **Habitat** Primary and secondary lowland dipterocarp to lower montane forest, peatswamp forest, overgrown plantations, to 1,200 m. **Behaviour** Similar to Banded Broadbill; takes smaller prey, sometimes in small groups. **Voice** Song is remarkable, cicada-like frantic trill of c.10–13 s, starting off relatively slowly (c.4.5 notes/s), building in pitch, volume and tempo (1.6–2.5 kHz) before reaching crescendo (c.12.5 notes/s) then finishing suddenly (similar to Banded Broadbill but lacks loud introductory note, accelerates more slowly and finishes abruptly); call is a short loud, squeaky *kwee-* (2.1 kHz, 0.4 s). **Range & status** Thai-Malay Peninsula, Sumatra. **Borneo** Common resident throughout, including N Natunas (slightly more common than Banded Broadbill). **Breeding** March–August; bulky

nest with side-entrance is made of grasses and twigs suspended from branch c.5–18 m from ground and usually located close to bee's nest; two eggs are usually laid.

157

PITTIDAE: Pittas

Worldwide c.32 species, 10 in Borneo. Small to medium-sized terrestrial birds with large head, plump body, rounded wings, long legs and short tail, most are highly coloured. Feed on invertebrates on the ground, turning over leaf-litter in the manner of thrushes. Hops on the ground with an upright posture. Shy and easily overlooked but can be highly vocal at times, calls from the ground or a perch below the canopy. Usually solitary or in pairs.

HOODED PITTA *Pitta sordida*

Identification 16–19 cm. Small green pitta with distinctive black hood. **Adult mulleri** Head and throat all black, back and mantle bright emerald-green, wings bright emerald-green with bright turquoise-blue patch, primaries black with thin white stripe (not always visible), uppertail-coverts turquoise-blue, tail black, underparts paler green with bright red centre of belly and undertail-coverts; iris and bill black, legs and feet pinkish-grey; in flight large white patch on wing variable in size. **Juvenile** duller with brownish underparts. **Habitat** Primary and secondary lowland dipterocarp, riverine and peatswamp forest, mangroves, plantations; lowland specialist to 400 m. **Behaviour** Not as shy as many pittas; usually found near water; consumes variety of insects, as well as snails and worms; roosts on lianas and low vegetation. **Voice** Call is a loud, short, sharp *kwee* (3.3 kHz, 0.2 s) repeated every 4–5 s; song is a loud sharp *kee-kee*, both notes on same pitch (1.8 kHz) and equally loud, each phrase c.0.7 s, repeated rapidly every 2–4 s. **Range & status** NE Indian Subcontinent, SE Asia, Philippines, Sumatra, W Java, N Sulawesi, New Guinea. **Borneo** Uncommon resident throughout. **Breeding** December–October; three creamy-white eggs with reddish-brown lines and spots and underlying light purple spots are laid in football-shaped nest of dead leaves, grass, bark and roots on or close to ground at base of understorey vegetation; said to look like flood debris.

FAIRY PITTA *Pitta nympha*

Identification 16–19 cm. Monotypic. **Adult** Crown to nape black, broad buffish-chestnut crown-sides and narrow buff supercilium, sides of head black, throat white, underparts pale buff with bright red centre of lower breast to undertail-coverts, upperparts green with glossy turquoise-blue wing-coverts and pale blue rump, primaries black with short white edge, tail black; iris and bill black, legs and feet pink; in flight small, round white wing-patches contrast with black flight feathers. **Similar species** See Blue-winged Pitta; Mangrove Pitta is larger, has larger bill, different head pattern and vocalisations. **Habitat** Primary lowland dipterocarp to lower montane forest, to 1,070 m in Borneo. **Behaviour** Poorly known in Borneo; diet known to consist of various insects and arthropods, snails and earthworms. **Voice** Two loud disyllabic notes *kawau kawau* (1–2 kHz, 1.3 s), very similar to Blue-winged Pitta but higher-pitched and each note slower with much shorter gap between two notes (extralimital). **Range & status** E China, Japan, Korea; winters to S China, Taiwan, Vietnam. **Borneo** Rare non-breeding visitor (October to March) to Sarawak, W Sabah and Brunei October–March; very rarely recorded from Kalimantan and E Sabah; declining throughout its range. Vulnerable.

BLUE-WINGED PITTA *Pitta moluccensis*

Identification 18–21 cm. Monotypic. Medium-sized, very colourful pitta with prominent buffish crown-stripe on black head and blue wings. **Adult** Crown to nape black, broad crown-stripe buffish-brown, sides of head black, throat white, underparts brownish-buff with bright red centre of belly to undertail-coverts, upperparts green with glossy blue wing-coverts and dark blue rump, primaries black with white edge, tail black; iris and bill black, legs and feet pink; in flight large round white wing-patches contrast conspicuously with black flight feathers. **Juvenile** Duller with grey bill tipped red and reddish gape. **Similar species** Fairy Pitta is smaller, has buffish supercilium and chestnut crown-stripe, paler buff underparts, paler green upperparts and smaller white wing-patches in flight; Mangrove Pitta has larger bill, less contrasting supercilium, different habitat; vocalisations all differ. **Habitat** Primary and secondary lowland forest, mangroves, to 200 m, reported on migration up to 1,800 m. **Behaviour** Eats insects, worms, snails. **Voice** A loud fluty crowing *kawau kawau*, each note 0.3 s and disyllabic (1–1.7 kHz), the phrase 1.1 s; often calls from perches; alarm call is a short loud screechy *skree-*. **Range & status** S China, SE Asia, Sumatra. **Borneo** Uncommon non-breeding visitor (late September to mid-May) and possible resident throughout.

Adult

Juvenile

Adult

MANGROVE PITTA *Pitta megarhyncha*

Identification 18–21 cm. Monotypic. **Adult** Narrow central crown-stripe to nape black, broad crown-sides brown, sides of head black, throat white, underparts brownish-buff with bright red centre of belly to undertail-coverts, upperparts green, wing-coverts glossy blue, primaries black edged white, rump dark blue, tail black; iris and very large bill black, legs and feet pink; in flight large round white wing-patch contrast conspicuously with black flight feathers. **Juvenile** Duller; crown brownish with darker scaling, little blue on wings and rump. **Habitat** Exclusively dependent on mangroves. **Behaviour** Diet consists of insects, molluscs and crabs taken from amongst roots and mud in mangroves. **Voice** A loud two-note *kawa-kwa*, first note longer than second (1–1.6 kHz, 0.9 s), each rising then falling in pitch, without disyllabic properties of notes of Blue-winged and Fairy Pittas (extralimital). **Range & status** Bangladesh, Myanmar, Thai-Malay Peninsula, Sumatra. **Borneo** Status uncertain as only one specimen from Sarawak exists, the provenance of which is questionable.

Adult

Juvenile

159

BLUE-HEADED PITTA *Pitta baudii*

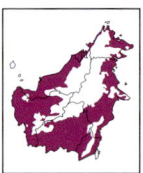

Identification 16–17 cm. Monotypic. Small pitta with brilliant blue (male) or reddish (female) head and reddish upperparts. **Adult male** Forehead to nape glossy bright blue, broad black mask to hindneck, throat to sides of neck white, centre of breast black, rest of underparts deep blue, upperparts reddish-brown with black wing-coverts and distinctive white line, rump and tail deep blue; iris and bill black, legs and feet pinkish-grey. **Adult female** Head and upperparts reddish-brown, wing-coverts black with white stripe, rump and tail blue, throat pale buff, underparts pale brown. **Juvenile** Like female but duller with mottled underparts, bill black tipped red. **Habitat** Primary and secondary lowland dipterocarp forest; lowland specialist to 500 m. **Behaviour** Feeds on ground in leaf-litter, taking caterpillars and other insects, earthworms, arthropods; sometimes seen hopping along forest trails. **Voice** Alarm call is a rather loud, high-pitched, explosive *kawow-*, upslurring quickly before tapering off slowly (3.1–1.8 kHz, c.1 s); song is a shorter, mellow, disyllabic *por-wii…-* with purring quality, rising then dipping in middle before tapering off quickly (1.2–1.6 kHz, c.0.8 s), usually repeated every 2–5 s. **Range & status** Endemic, uncommon to locally common lowland resident throughout, commonest in E Sabah and rarer in south. **Breeding** March–June; nest is ball of dead leaves at base of understorey vegetation; lays two glossy white eggs with purplish-brown speckles.

Male

Female

BLUE-BANDED PITTA *Pitta arquata*

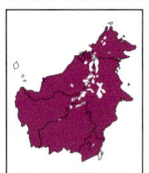

Identification 15–17 cm. Monotypic. Strikingly red, small pitta with bright blue markings on head and breast. **Adult** Crown to upper mantle bright orange, thin bright turquoise-blue line behind eye, face and throat buffish-orange, underparts bright red with bright turquoise-blue breast-band, upperparts dark green with turquoise-blue patch on wing-coverts, tail blue; iris pale grey, bill grey with red on base of lower mandible and tip, legs and feet bluish-grey. **Juvenile** Brown with paler brown belly, flanks reddish, bill grey with orange gape. **Habitat** Primary and secondary hill and lower montane forest, favouring bamboo stands; possibly a slope specialist recorded from 150 to 1,500 m but commonest at 600–1,200 m. **Behaviour** Very poorly known; unobtrusive; keeps to dense undergrowth; calls from perches up to 3 m from ground; feeds on variety of insects. **Voice** Very similar to Rail-babbler and Garnet and Black-and-crimson Pittas; low, pure whistle delivered on level pitch, steadily increasing in power (c.1.3 kHz, 2-2.2 s) with no modulation. **Range & status** Endemic, rare resident probably throughout, but not yet recorded from Brunei and S Kalimantan. **Breeding** March–September; poorly known but one nest was round, made of dead leaves and fibre; egg is white with grey and brown spots.

Adult

Juvenile

BLACK-AND-CRIMSON PITTA *Pitta ussheri*

Identification 13–16 cm. Monotypic. Small blue, black and red pitta. **Adult** All-black head with thin turquoise-blue line behind eye, throat black, breast blackish-blue, rest of underparts red, upperparts deep purplish-blue with glossy bright blue on wing-coverts; iris dark brown, bill black, legs and feet dark grey. **Juvenile** As Garnet Pitta but lacks red on nape. **Similar species** See Garnet Pitta. **Habitat** Primary and secondary lowland dipterocarp forest, plantations; lowland specialist to 300 m. **Behaviour** Shy; favours thickly vegetated gullies; diet consists of variety of insects, spiders, small snails; usually detected by call and more approachable than many other pittas. **Voice** A long clear whistle (1.2-1.3 kHz, 3-3.2 s) increasing in volume and ending abruptly; ventriloquial; longer and less modulated than similar call of Garnet Pitta. **Range & status** Endemic, locally common resident confined to lowlands of N Borneo, south to Sabah–Sarawak and Sabah–Kalimantan borders. **Breeding** February–August; nest is dome of dead leaves and decaying vegetation located on ground amongst understorey vegetation; eggs two, white with light grey or reddish spots.

Adult

Juvenile

GARNET PITTA *Pitta granatina*

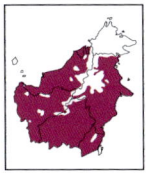

Identification 14–16 cm. Small blue, black and red pitta. **Adult** *granatina* (endemic subspecies) Forehead and forecrown black, hindcrown to upper mantle bright red, thin turquoise-blue line behind eye divides red crown and black sides of face and neck, throat black, breast blackish-blue, rest of underparts bright red, upperparts deep purplish-blue with glossy bright blue on wing-coverts; iris dark brown, bill black, legs and feet dark grey. **Juvenile** Brown with red on nape and belly, bill black with red tip and gape. **Similar species** Allopatric Black-and-crimson Pitta has all-black head, different vocalisations. **Habitat** Primary and secondary lowland dipterocarp forest, rarely in kerangas; lowland specialist below 300 m, handful of records up to 1,000 m. **Behaviour** Shy; consumes variety of invertebrates, small snails, small fruits; often calls from medium to high perches; usually detected by call and more approachable than many other pittas. **Voice** A long, clear, slightly modulated whistle (1.2-1.3 kHz, c.2 s), increasing in volume and very slightly upwardly inflected, downslurred abruptly the end; ventriloquial. **Range & status** Thai-Malay Peninsula, Sumatra. **Borneo** Locally common resident, widely distributed in lowland areas of Sarawak, Brunei and Kalimantan, absent from Sabah. **Breeding** Domed nest is made of dead leaves and strands of creepers located on ground near understorey vegetation; egg is off-white with sparse dark wine-coloured spots.

Adult

Juvenile

161

GIANT PITTA *Pitta caerulea*

Identification 25–29 cm. Very large pitta with conspicuous eyestripe and solid blue (male) or reddish-brown (female) upperparts. **Adult male** *hosei* (endemic subspecies) Head greyish-brown with black scaling, crown to nape black, black eyestripe to sides of head, thin black collar extending from black nape to narrow breast-band, underparts pale buffish-brown, upperparts blue; iris dark brown, bill dark grey, legs and feet pinkish-brown. **Adult female** Head brown with fine black scaling, black stripe behind eye to sides of head, thin black collar and breast-band, underparts brown, upperparts reddish-brown, rump and tail blue. **Juvenile** Head buffish-brown mottled dark brown, blackish stripe behind eye, throat white, breast and flanks dark brown, belly mottled brown and buff, upperparts dark brown, tail blue; bill black with red tip and base, legs and feet bluish-grey. **Habitat** Primary and secondary lowland dipterocarp and hill forest, to 900 m but commonest in lowlands. **Behaviour** Shy and elusive; feeds in leaf-litter on snails, earthworms, spiders and insects. **Voice** A mellow slow single whistle *phyew* delivered on a level pitch (1.4 kHz), each note c.1 s, repeated every 1–2 s; most likely to call October–March. **Range & status** Thai-Malay Peninsula, Sumatra. **Borneo** Rare resident N Borneo (E Sabah, Sarawak, E Kalimantan), one record from W Kalimantan. **Breeding** Undescribed in Borneo; elsewhere domed nest of leaves and twigs constructed close to ground.

BANDED PITTA *Pitta guajana*

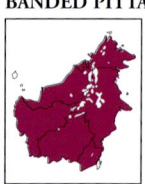

Identification 21–24 cm. Medium-sized pitta with distinctive yellow, black, blue and brown markings. **Adult male** *schwaneri* (endemic subspecies) Crown black, supercilium bright yellow, broad mask black, white throat to yellow sides of neck, underparts barred deep purplish-blue and yellow with deep purplish-blue patch in centre of belly, back chestnut-brown, wing-coverts black with broad white stripe, rump and tail deep blue; iris dark brown, bill black, legs and feet pinkish-grey. **Adult female** As male but forehead chestnut-brown, supercilium buffish, breast to belly barred black and buff, no blue patch on belly. **Juvenile** Browner speckled buff, supercilium and reduced wing-stripe buff, breast streaked or barred brown and buff. **Habitat** Primary and secondary lowland dipterocarp forest, possibly favouring drier ridgetops; recorded to 1,500 m but commonest between 600–1,200 m. **Behaviour** Very elusive especially when not vocalising, rarely comes into open; diet consists of insects, snails, earthworms. **Voice** One call is a short, tremulous *prurr...* (1 kHz, c.0.4 s) repeated every 2–4 s; another is a louder, strident, downslurred *pwow* (1.3–1 kHz, 0.2 s) repeated irregularly. **Range & status** Thai-Malay Peninsula, Sumatra, Java. **Borneo** Locally uncommon resident throughout. **Breeding** January–August; lays 3–4 creamy-white eggs with greyish mottling in nest made of dead leaves on or just off ground in understorey plants.

VIREONIDAE: Shrike-babblers, epornis & allies

Worldwide c.58 species, 2 in Borneo. Small, generally plain and stout-bodied songbirds usually with a heavy pointed bill with small hooked tip and short, strong legs. The shrike-babblers are sexually dimorphic. Generally quite vocal especially when foraging. The songs consist of simple, loud repeated phrases. Often join mixed feeding flocks.

WHITE-BROWED SHRIKE-BABBLER
Pteruthius flaviscapis

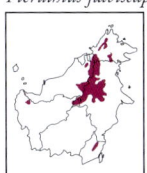

Identification 14–15 cm. Stocky, medium-sized arboreal passerine with distinctive black and white plumage in male, female grey and dull green. **Adult male *robinsoni*** (endemic subspecies) Crown and sides of head black with long broad white supercilium from above eye, back to uppertail-coverts grey, wings glossy black with chestnut and yellow tertials, white tips on primaries, tail glossy back, throat and underparts pale grey with pinkish wash on flanks; iris greyish, bill grey, legs and feet pinkish. **Adult female** Head and back grey with indistinct pale supercilium, wings and tail olive-brown with yellowish fringing and variable chestnut on tertials, underparts buffish with olive wash on lower flanks. **Juvenile** Like adult female but head and back grey with olive tinge. **Habitat** Primary and secondary hill to upper montane forest, from 750 to 3,100 m. **Behaviour** Foliage-gleaning insectivore, active in upper storey; also eats small fruits and seeds; usually encountered in pairs; sometimes joins mixed feeding flocks. **Voice** Song is a strident, loud and rather high-pitched phrase *jip-jip* (pause) *jip-ji-jip*, the first one or two notes rather weak, each note sharply downturned (3.6–2.7 kHz, c.1 s), the phrase repeated continually; also a similar *ji-jip* (pause) *jip-jip* (3.5–2.2 kHz), the first note softer. **Range & status** Himalayas, S China, SE Asia, Sumatra, Java. **Borneo** Uncommon resident in north-central and west mountain ranges from G. Kinabalu to Pueh Range and G. Menyapa (Sabah, Sarawak, W and E Kalimantan) and in Meratus Mountains, S Kalimantan. **Breeding** Possibly breeds March–May; nest is cup of fine roots slung between fork, usually three eggs. **Note** Formerly considered a babbler but molecular studies suggest that *Pteruthius* should be placed in family Vireonidae (vireos and allies).

Female

Male

WHITE-BELLIED ERPORNIS *Erpornis zantholeuca*

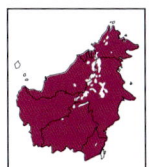

Identification 11–13 cm. Nondescript small greenish yuhina-like bird with short crest. **Adult *brunnescens*** (endemic subspecies) Crown and upperparts olive-green, lores and area around eye to cheek greyish, throat to centre of belly whitish, rest of underparts washed grey with pale yellow undertail-coverts; iris grey, upper mandible black, bill pink with grey culmen, legs and feet pinkish. **Juvenile** Duller with reduced crest. **Habitat** Primary and secondary lowland dipterocarp to lower montane forest, occasionally kerangas and peatswamp forest, to 1,750 m. **Behaviour** Usually solitary but sometimes joins mixed feeding flocks; not very vocal; feeds on insects and less often on fruit in mid-storey. **Voice** One song is a rapid series of sharp *si-si-si-si-si-si...* notes (c.3.4 kHz, 6 notes/s); also a wheezy, high-pitched *shee-shee-shi-shee* rising and falling (7–4.5 kHz); calls consist of various peevish, nasal buzzing notes. **Range & status** NE Indian Subcontinent, SE China, Taiwan, SE Asia, NW Sumatra. **Borneo** Common resident Sabah, uncommon Sarawak, Brunei and Kalimantan. **Breeding** Possibly breeds year-round, otherwise undescribed in Borneo. **Note** Formerly known as White-bellied Yuhina *Yuhina zantholeuca* in babbler family but molecular studies suggest it belongs in family Vireonidae.

Juvenile

Adult

ACANTHIZIDAE: Thornbills & allies

Worldwide c.60 species, 1 in Borneo. Small to medium-sized, mostly drab olive-green birds with slender bill. Active feeders on the ground or in the foliage of trees and bushes. Sexes alike. The vocalisations are melodious, loud and distinctive, some species incorporate mimicry.

GOLDEN-BELLIED GERYGONE *Gerygone sulphurea*

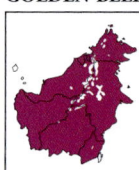

Identification 9.5–10.5 cm. **Adult *sulphurea*** Cheeks and ear-coverts dark grey, lores whitish, rest of upperparts greyish-brown with subterminal white tips on tail, throat yellow fading into yellowish-white belly and white undertail-coverts; iris black, bill and legs greyish-black. **Juvenile** Upperparts paler with greyish-brown ear-coverts, underparts paler, narrow whitish eye-ring, pinkish base to bill. **Habitat** Primary and secondary lowland dipterocarp, hill and kerangas forest, mangroves, coastal woodland, plantations (especially old rubber plantations), occasionally to 1,700 m. **Behaviour** An arboreal insectivore; gleans foliage in mid- to upper storey; often joins mixed feeding flocks. **Voice** A beautiful series of glissading whistles, with rising and falling cadence, *zwee-zii-zree-zwee-zree-zi-zeee...* (c.7–2.8 kHz, each phrase c.7.5 s); described as somewhat reminiscent of *Malacopteron* babbler but with buzzing quality. **Range & status** Thai-Malay Peninsula, Indonesia, Philippines. **Borneo** Common to uncommon resident throughout (possibly often overlooked). **Breeding** Undescribed in Borneo; elsewhere lays 2–3 whitish eggs with reddish-brown dots and speckles in purse-shaped nest with side entrance near top suspended from branch in tree.

EUPETIDAE: Jewel-babblers & allies

Worldwide 10 species, 1 in Borneo. A small, rather diverse family of shy and secretive birds with short bill, strong legs and long, wide tail. Most species with striking patterns in a combination of black, white, brown, orange, or blue. Occupy a variety of wooded habitats. Most are terrestrial insectivores, also consume small vertebrates and seeds. More often heard than seen.

RAIL-BABBLER *Eupetes macrocerus*

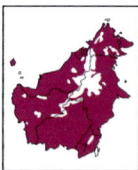

Identification 28–30 cm. Distinctive rail-like ground-dweller with notably long neck and tail, longish legs. **Adult *borneensis*** (endemic subspecies) Head rich brown with bold bright white supercilium from in front of eye to sides of neck, conspicuous broad black stripe through and below eye from lores to sides of neck, thin patch of bright blue skin running along neck-side below eye-stripe (sometimes inflated when calling), rest of upperparts reddish-brown with tail brighter red, underparts rufous with belly washed grey; iris black, bill black, legs and feet bluish-black. **Juvenile** Duller and greyer with whitish throat, underparts brownish-grey. **Habitat** Primary lowland dipterocarp and hill forest, kerangas, to 1,100 m. **Behaviour** Very shy, inconspicuous and easily overlooked; pursues invertebrate prey in thick vegetation on forest floor, often repeatedly following same path; rarely flies. **Voice** Song is a long, clear whistle delivered on flat pitch (1.7 kHz, c.1.7 s) and increasing in volume, very like Black-and-crimson (1.2–1.4 kHz, 2.9 s) and Blue-banded Pittas but monotone, higher and shorter, and delivered more frequently; call is a very soft clucking (extralimital). **Range & status** Thai-Malay Peninsula, Sumatra. **Borneo** Rare resident throughout (no confirmed records for S Kalimantan). **Breeding** Undescribed in Borneo; elsewhere breeds January–June; lays two white eggs in shallow, loose nest of plant fibres close to ground in thick vegetation.

PACHYCEPHALIDAE: Whistlers

Worldwide c.41 species, 3 in Borneo. A somewhat homogeneous family of small to medium-sized birds with short strong bill, large rounded head, sturdy body, strong legs and feet, and medium length tail. Often known as 'thickheads'. Most have plumage of browns, greys and olives, some with more striking yellow, white or red markings. Usually solitary. Methodically gleans insects in the treetops. Typically the sexes are alike. The name whistler refers to the distinctive whistling songs.

MANGROVE WHISTLER *Pachycephala cinerea*

Identification 17 cm. **Adult *cinerea*** Lores pale grey, upperparts brownish-grey with brownish wash on flight feathers and tail, underparts white with throat faintly mottled brownish, greyish-brown wash on breast; iris dark brown, thick bill and legs greyish-black. **Juvenile** Upperparts browner with rusty-brown edges on wing-coverts, underparts white; bill pinkish-brown. **Habitat** Coastal and peatswamp forest, kerangas, mangroves, plantations, to 200 m. **Behaviour** Sallies and gleans for insects in mid- to upper storey; often joins mixed feeding flocks. **Voice** Distinctive, beautiful liquid song, the first four or five notes delivered on an even pitch with last whipcrack note rising suddenly *weet-weet-weet-weet-weeit* (1.4–4.1 kHz, 1.5 s). **Range & status** Coastal NE India, SE Asia, Sumatra, Java, Palawan. **Borneo** Common resident in coastal areas throughout, including offshore islands. **Breeding** January–June; nest is deep cup of fibres and mosses located in thick vegetation c.1–4 m from ground.

WHITE-VENTED WHISTLER *Pachycephala homeyeri*

Identification 16–17 cm. **Adult *homeyeri*** Upperparts rufous-brown with wings and tail more reddish, underparts white with pale brown wash on breast; iris dark brown, bill black, legs and feet dark grey. **Juvenile** Like adult but with rufous edging on wing-coverts and tail. **Habitat** Island forest, at sea-level. **Behaviour** Forages for insects in lower to mid-storey; joins mixed feeding flocks. **Voice** Quite variable but generally a loud liquid series of four notes, *oo-oo-wi-chee*, the first upslurred, the high-pitched last note falling off in pitch rapidly (1.7–2.9 kHz, 1.5 s). **Range & status** C and S Philippines. **Borneo** Common resident NE Borneo islands (only recorded from Si-Amil, Sipidan and Pandanan islands, Sabah). **Breeding** Undescribed in Borneo.

BORNEAN WHISTLER *Pachycephala hypoxantha*

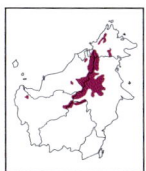

Identification 16 cm. **Adult *hypoxantha*** Lores greyish, upperparts olive-green, brighter on rump and greyer on wings, tail blackish with olive-green edging, underparts bright yellow with greenish wash on lower throat and flanks; iris dark brown, bill black, legs and feet pale grey. **Adult *sarawacensis*** Greenish wash on underparts reduced. **Juvenile** Rufous-brown plumage with some yellow on underparts; legs and feet pinkish. **Habitat** Primary and secondary lower to upper montane forest, 650–2,950 m. **Behaviour** Actively hawks and gleans insects in mid- to upper storey; often joins mixed feeding flocks. **Voice** A variety of clear, liquid songs are given but commonly a seesawing series of eight high and low notes *wee-sit-wee-sit-wee-sit-wee-sit*, the *wee* notes flat and high-pitched (4.5 kHz), the *sit* notes sharply upslurred (1.5–2.2 kHz), the entire phrase c.2.5 s; also a *dit-doo-dee-dee-dee-dee*, the last notes described as like whipcracks. **Range & status** Endemic, common resident in north-central and western mountain ranges from G. Kinabalu to Pueh Range and G. Menyapa (Sabah, Sarawak, W, C and E Kalimantan), *P. h. hypoxantha* from N and C Borneo and *P. h. sarawacensis* W Borneo. **Breeding** November–June; otherwise undescribed.

CAMPEPHAGIDAE: Cuckooshrikes, trillers and minivets

Worldwide c.82 species, 8 in Borneo. Small to medium-sized insectivores with short bill with pronounced rictal bristles, largish head, long body, longish tail and shortish wings and legs. Plumage mostly greyish and whitish in cuckooshrikes and yellow or red on black in minivets. Flight is strong and undulating. Cuckooshrikes are generally quiet and unobtrusive, while the gregarious minivets are noisy and active. Sexually dimorphic.

SUNDA CUCKOOSHRIKE *Coracina larvata*

Identification 22.5 cm. Small cuckooshrike with conspicuous black mask. **Adult male** *normani* (endemic subspecies) Forehead, face and throat black, plumage mostly slaty-grey, primaries black with grey fringing, tail black; iris dark brown, bill and legs black. **Adult female** Reduced dark mask, throat grey. **Juvenile** Upperparts grey, underparts strongly barred. **Habitat** Primary and secondary hill to upper montane forest, 750–2,550 m. **Behaviour** Feeds in upper storey on fruit and large invertebrates and small vertebrates such as geckos; noisy and conspicuous; usually solitary or in pairs. **Voice** A low-pitched whistled *pit-teeoh*, descending on last syllable; also loud shrieks and squeaks. **Range & status** Sumatra, Java. **Borneo** Uncommon resident in north-central mountain ranges from G. Kinabalu to Dulit Range, Barito Ulu and G. Menyapa (Sabah, E Sarawak, E and C Kalimantan). **Breeding** Undescribed in Borneo except for one record of fledged young in June.

Male

Female

BAR-BELLIED CUCKOOSHRIKE *Coracina striata*

Identification 27.5–30 cm. **Adult male** *sumatrensis* Mostly pale slaty-grey plumage, lores slightly darker grey, primaries blackish-grey with grey fringing, flanks faintly barred darker, rump and uppertail-coverts barred grey and blackish, tail black with grey tip; in flight underwing-coverts barred grey and blackish; iris pale yellow, bill and legs black. **Adult female** As male but lores paler, lower breast to undertail-coverts white barred black, stronger black barring on rump; in flight underwing-coverts boldly barred black and white. **Juvenile** Grey plumage fringed pale and dark grey, creating scaly appearance, flight feathers fringed whitish. **Habitat** Primary and secondary lowland dipterocarp, peatswamp, riparian and kerangas forest, plantations; essentially a lowland species to 600 m, with occasional records to 1,250 m. **Behaviour** Forages in upper storey; generally flies high; sometimes in noisy parties of 5–6 individuals. **Voice** Call is a squeaky, whinnying *priririt* or *kliu-kliu-kliu-kliu* (3.2–2 kHz, c.0.4 s), also a high-pitched, rather parrot-like *keeuk-keeuk*. **Range & status** Thai-Malay Peninsula, Sumatra, Philippines. **Borneo** Uncommon lowland resident throughout, including Anambas and Natunas. **Breeding** Undescribed in Borneo.

Juvenile

Male

Female

TAURAN BEACH RESORT *13/6/10*

LESSER CUCKOOSHRIKE *Coracina fimbriata*

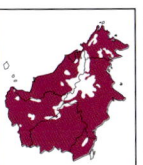

Identification 17.5 cm. **Adult male** *schierbrandii* Upperparts dark grey with darker blackish-grey wings and tail, throat grey grading over underparts to pale grey undertail-coverts; iris dark brown, bill and legs black. **Adult female** Paler with barring on underparts. **Juvenile** Paler with heavy buffish-white and brownish scaling. **Habitat** Primary and secondary lowland dipterocarp, peatswamp and hill forest, plantations, to 1,000 m. **Behaviour** Feeds on small invertebrates and fruit in upper storey; joins mixed feeding flocks. **Voice** A sweet, loud *whi-ti-whi-ti-wheet-ti-wheet-ti-wheee...* the last note descending (4-2.5 kHz, c.2 s). **Range & status** Thai-Malay Peninsula, Sumatra, Java, Bali. **Borneo** Common resident throughout. **Breeding** January–September; one nest was small compact structure of fibres and bark held together with cobwebs located on top of old tree with two young.

Male

Female

LIBARAN ISLAND *4/6/10*

PIED TRILLER *Lalage nigra*

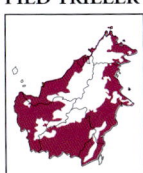

Identification 16 cm. **Adult male** *nigra* Forehead to nape black, broad white supercilium, lores and eyestripe black, black mantle sharply demarcated from grey back to uppertail-coverts, wings black with large white patch on coverts and white fringing on flight feathers, tail black with white tips, underparts white with grey wash on breast; iris brown, bill and legs black. **Adult female** Like male but upperparts tinged brown, rump and underparts finely barred blackish. **Juvenile** Upperparts with buffish-white fringing, underparts buffish-white with indistinct brownish streaking on throat and breast. **Habitat** Coastal kerangas and woodlands, mangroves, cultivated areas, gardens, to 450 m. **Behaviour** Generally forages in foliage of upper storey for insects but will come to ground; usually solitary or in pairs. **Voice** Song is a high-pitched two-note *wheek-chuk* or *per-whek* (5 kHz, 0.6 s), the second note dipping, and repeated at regular rate of about 1 phrase/s; call is a harsh grating *chat*. **Range & status** Nicobar Islands, Malay Peninsula, Sumatra, Java, Philippines. **Borneo** Common resident throughout, including NE offshore islands.

Female

Juvenile

Male

Breeding March–September; builds small compact cup-shaped nest of fine roots and fibres, bark or grass stems held together with cobwebs in fork of tree 2–8 m from ground; lays two yellowish eggs with grey spots and olive-brown flecks, both sexes attending nest.

ASHY MINIVET *Pericrocotus divaricatus*

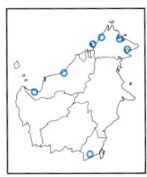

Identification 18.5–20 cm. **Adult male** *divaricatus* Forehead and forecrown white, lores through eye black joining with black hindcrown to nape, upperparts grey, darker on wings and tail, tail with white outer feathers, sides of neck and underparts white; in flight prominent white band at base of primaries; iris brown, bill and legs black. **Adult female** Like male but crown and nape grey as rest of upperparts with white band across forehead and black lores. **Habitat** Mangroves, coastal woodlands, gardens, lowland forest edge, at sea-level. **Behaviour** Elsewhere in region usually in small flocks in upper storey. **Voice** In flight utters a high-pitched jingling trill. **Range & status** Breeds NE Asia, migrating to SE Asia, Sumatra, Philippines. **Borneo** Rare non-breeding visitor to coastal areas with few records from Sabah, Sarawak and S Kalimantan.

Male

Female

FIERY MINIVET *Pericrocotus igneus*

Identification 15–15.5 cm. **Adult male *igneus*** Head, throat and upperparts glossy black with bright orange-red uppertail-coverts and wing-patch, tail black with bright orange-red outer feathers, rest of underparts bright orange-red; iris dark brown, bill and legs grey. **Adult female** Narrow yellow line across forehead to above eye, crown to back grey, orange patch on darker grey wings, uppertail-coverts orange-red, tail dark grey with bright red outer feathers, underparts yellow. **Juvenile** Like female but head and back brownish with buffish fringing, underparts whitish with pale brown barring. **Similar species** Scarlet Minivet is larger, lacks orange tinge to plumage, more red on tail and has second, smaller wing-patch. **Habitat** Primary and secondary lowland dipterocarp and kerangas forest, casuarina woodland, plantations; lowland specialist to 600 m. **Behaviour** Arboreal insectivore; usually seen in active flocks flitting from treetop to treetop; often joins mixed feeding flocks. **Voice** In flight utters a slightly upslurred *swee-eet*. **Range & status** Thai-Malay Peninsula, Sumatra, Palawan. **Borneo** Uncommon lowland resident throughout. **Breeding** Possibly March–September; otherwise undescribed in Borneo.

GREY-CHINNED MINIVET *Pericrocotus solaris*

KINABALU 11/6/10

Identification 16–17 cm. **Adult male *cinereigula*** (endemic subspecies) Head and upperparts glossy black with scarlet uppertail-coverts and wing-patches, tail black with scarlet outer feathers, throat dark grey, rest of underparts scarlet; iris brown, bill and legs black. **Adult female** Head and upperparts grey with olive-yellow rump and yellow wing-patch, tail darker grey with yellow outer feathers, throat yellowish-grey, rest of underparts yellow. **Juvenile** Like female but upperparts fringed yellowish. **Similar species** See Scarlet Minivet. **Habitat** Primary and secondary hill to upper montane forest, from 650 to 2,450 m. **Behaviour** Arboreal insectivore; often joins mixed feeding flocks. **Voice** A short, thin high-pitched repeated *tsee* uttered in flight (4.5–3.8 kHz). **Range & status** E Himalayas, S China, SE Asia, W Sumatra. **Borneo** Common montane resident in north-central mountain ranges from G. Kinabalu to Dulit Range and G. Menyapa (Sabah, E Sarawak and E Kalimantan). **Breeding** Undescribed in Borneo; fledglings have been seen in July.

SCARLET MINIVET *Pericrocotus speciosus*

KINABALU 11/6/10

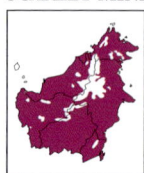

Identification 17–19 cm. **Adult male *insulanus*** (endemic subspecies) Head, throat and upperparts glossy black with scarlet uppertail-coverts, distinctive scarlet wing-patches, one large trapezoid-shaped patch on coverts and secondaries and smaller isolated one on tertials, tail mostly scarlet with black central feathers, rest of underparts scarlet; iris dark brown, bill and legs grey. **Adult female** Yellowish-grey line across forehead to above eye yellow, ear-coverts yellowish-grey, crown to back grey, yellow patches on darker grey wings, uppertail-coverts olive-yellow, tail dark grey with yellow outer feathers, underparts yellow. **Juvenile** Like female but head and back greyish with yellowish fringing, underparts yellow with indistinct pale olive-grey barring on throat, breast and flanks. **Similar species** See Fiery Minivet; male Grey-chinned Minivet has dark grey throat (often difficult to discern in field), female lacks yellow on forehead, ear-coverts and throat. Different wing pattern in both. **Habitat** Primary and secondary lowland dipterocarp to lower montane forest, to 1,200 m. **Behaviour** Arboreal insectivore, usually in active flocks in upper storey. **Voice** Song is a very rapid, high-pitched twittering *sweet-sweet-sweet-sweet…* (4–7 kHz); call is a softer, raspy *fee-fee-fee…* **Range & status** Indian Subcontinent, China, SE Asia, Sumatra, Java, Bali, Lombok, Philippines. **Borneo** Locally common resident throughout, possibly commoner in N Borneo (Sabah). **Breeding** January–November; one nest was made of green moss and lined with green fibres containined one white egg with rufous markings, located on side of rock.

ORIOLIDAE: Old World orioles

Worldwide c.29 species, 5 in Borneo. Medium-sized, robust arboreal forest-dwelling birds with strong mid-length slightly curved bill, long pointed wings, mid-length tail and strong legs. The males are typically brightly plumaged yellow or red with black, the females duller. Most forage quietly in the canopy for large invertebrates and fruit. Most are highly vocal with rich, varied songs.

BLACK ORIOLE *Oriolus hosii*

Identification 21 cm. Monotypic. **Adult male** Plumage entirely black except for chestnut undertail-coverts; iris dark red, bill dull pink, legs and feet grey. **Adult female** Like male but dark throat and breast contrast with paler grey rest of underparts. **Similar species** Black-and-crimson Oriole has red or chestnut on breast and grey bill. **Habitat** Primary lower and upper montane forest, 900–2,000 m. **Behaviour** Poorly known; forages quietly in mid- to upper storey in fruiting trees often in small parties. **Voice** Described as a clear whistle with downward inflection. **Range & status** Endemic, rare resident, known from G. Murud, Dulit Range and Usun Apau (E Sarawak) and Batu Tibang (E Kalimantan). Recently reported from far north Kayan Mentarang (E Kalimantan). **Breeding** Undescribed.

BLACK-AND-CRIMSON ORIOLE *Oriolus cruentus*

Identification 21 cm. **Adult *vulneratus*** (endemic subspecies) Upperparts and chin to upper breast glossy black, glossy crimson patch on wing and large, square-cut crimson patch on lower breast and upper belly, rest of underparts black without gloss; iris dark brown, bill slaty-grey, legs and feet grey (male and female similar in Borneo). **Juvenile** Lacks red in plumage, has dull chestnut streaks on lower breast and upper belly. **Similar species** See Black Oriole. **Habitat** Primary and secondary tall hill to upper montane forest, 600–2,300 m. **Behaviour** Feeds on insects, especially caterpillars, and fruit in mid- to upper storey; usually solitary or in pairs, often in mixed feeding flocks. **Voice** Call is a long, mewing downslurred *kweee* (5.3–4.6 kHz, 0.6 s). **Range & status** Malay Peninsula, Sumatra, Java. **Borneo** Common resident in central-north mountain ranges from G. Kinabalu to G. Latuk and G. Menyapa (Sabah, E Sarawak and C and E Kalimantan). **Breeding** Possibly February–July; otherwise undescribed in Borneo.

BLACK-NAPED ORIOLE *Oriolus chinensis*

Identification 24.5–27.5 cm. **Adult male *maculatus*** Head, back and underparts bright yellow with broad black band from lores through eye broadening across nape, wings black with yellow wing-coverts and fringes to flight feathers, tail black tipped yellow; iris dark red, bill pink, legs and feet bluish-grey. **Adult female** As male but back and wing-coverts washed greenish. **Juvenile** Upperparts olive-green with obscure band through eye and darker flight feathers and tail fringed olive, underparts whitish streaked blackish, undertail-coverts greenish-yellow; iris brown, bill grey. **Habitat** Mangroves, secondary scrub, plantations, gardens, to 600 m. **Voice** Song is a distinctive, loud, rich, liquid *kau kwa-oo* (1.7–0.9 kHz, c.0.5 s) with variations; call is a rasping, nasal *chraii*. **Range & status** Indian Subcontinent, SE Asia, Indonesia, Philippines. **Borneo** Rare resident with few records from Sarawak, W, E and S Kalimantan; introduced Sabah (two records of probable escapees).

DARK-THROATED ORIOLE *Oriolus xanthonotus*

Identification 18–20 cm. **Adult male** *consobrinus* (endemic subspecies) Head to nape and upper breast black creating hooded appearance, upperparts yellow with black wings and tail fringed yellow and whitish, lower breast to belly white with broad black streaks, undertail-coverts and undertail yellow; iris dark red, bill deep pink, legs and feet grey. **Adult female** *consobrinus* Like male but crown and nape grey with streaked throat and upper breast suffused dark grey, upperparts olive-green with grey wings and tail, uppertail-coverts brighter, undertail-coverts pale yellow. **Juvenile** Like female but bill duller, crown and nape olive-green. **Adult male** *xanthonotus* Less yellow on tail. **Adult female** *xanthonotus* Head and upperparts olive-green with brighter uppertail-coverts, throat and underparts white with olive-grey streaking, undertail-coverts pale yellow, narrow yellow eye-ring. **Similar species** See Black-hooded Oriole. **Habitat** Primary and secondary lowland dipterocarp, peatswamp and kerangas forest, to 750 m. **Behaviour** Active in upper storey; usually solitary or in pairs; sometimes joins mixed feeding flocks; generalist feeder, takes small invertebrates and figs. **Voice** Song is a distinctive loud fluty *phi-phu-phuwip* (1.5–1.2 kHz, 0.8 s) repeated every 1–2 seconds; call is a harsh, deep repeated *chuk*. **Range & status** Thai-Malay Peninsula, Sumatra, Java, Palawan. **Borneo** Common resident throughout, *consobrinus* N Borneo, *xanthonotus* SW Borneo. **Breeding** February–September; lays two pale pink eggs with sparse purplish-brown spots in nest made of twigs, strips of bark and plant fibres decorated with lichen and cocoons located in fork of outer branches of tree.

BLACK-HOODED ORIOLE *Oriolus xanthornus*

Identification 22–23 cm. **Adult male** *tanakae* (endemic subspecies) Head to nape and upper breast black creating hooded appearance, rest of plumage bright yellow, flight feathers black with yellow fringes, black tail broadly bordered yellow; iris dark red, bill deep pink, legs and feet grey. **Adult female** As male but with olive wash on upperparts, slightly duller yellow on underparts. **Juvenile** Duller, yellow streaks on forehead, crown streaked olive, whitish throat streaked black, streaks extending onto yellow underparts; iris brown with narrow yellow eye-ring, bill black. **Similar species** Dark-throated Oriole has black wing-coverts, broad black streaking on whitish underparts and all-black uppertail. **Habitat** Secondary and riparian forest, forest edges, gardens, at sea-level. **Behaviour** Poorly known in Borneo, probably similar habits to other orioles. **Voice** Song is a rich, fluty *phu phi-woo* (0.8–1.5 kHz, c.0.7 s), the first note quiet, the second slurred, higher-pitched and much louder. **Range & status** N and S India, Sri Lanka, Andaman Islands, SE Asia, Sumatra. **Borneo** Uncommon to rare resident coastal NE Borneo from Sandakan to Tawau (Sabah), and Maratuas. **Breeding** Undescribed in Borneo.

GENERA INCERTAE SEDIS: Woodshrikes, flycatcher-shrikes & philentomas

Worldwide 8 species, 5 in Borneo. Small to medium-sized shrike-like, typically noisy and sociable insectivores with stout body, short tail and robust bill. Rather slow moving, generally inhabit the mid-storey. Occupy a variety of wooded habitats. Most are foliage gleaning or sallying insectivores.

LARGE WOODSHRIKE *Tephrodornis gularis*

Male, Female, Juvenile

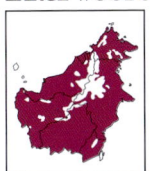

Identification 17–18 cm. Medium-sized bulky grey or brown woodshrike with large, hooked bill and prominent black face-mask. **Adult male** *frenatus* (endemic subspecies) Broad black face-mask from lores to ear-coverts, upperparts dark grey with white rump and black tail, underparts white with greyish wash on breast, iris yellowish-green, bill and legs black; in flight white rump noticeable. **Adult female** Like male but upperparts brown with fine brown streaking on back, smaller face-mask dark brown, underparts greyish. **Juvenile** Upperparts brown with buff spotting and barring, flight feathers and tail edged and tipped buff, underparts whitish. **Habitat** Primary and secondary lowland dipterocarp and lower montane forest, peatswamp forest, kerangas, plantations, to 1,200 m. **Behaviour** In noisy pairs or small groups; usually seen high in canopy; feeds on large insects hawking from exposed perch or gleaning foliage. **Voice** Noisy, with wide repertoire of whistles and harsh notes, more often heard than seen; in Borneo call is a harsh squeaky rattling, quite high-pitched: *chreee-chee-chi-chi-chi* (5.2 kHz); song is a series of clear staccato whistles *too-too-too-too-too...* delivered on level pitch (c.2.4 kHz), c.8 notes/s (extralimital). **Range & status** SW and NE India, S China, SE Asia, Sumatra, Java. **Borneo** Uncommon resident throughout. **Breeding** February–July; lays three creamy-buff eggs with large rufous-brown blotches and underlying purplish-grey spots; nest undescribed.

BAR-WINGED FLYCATCHER-SHRIKE
Hemipus picatus

Male, Female, Juvenile

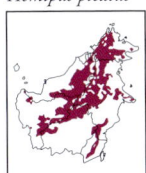

Identification 12.5–14.5 cm. **Adult male** *intermedius* Upperparts glossy black with white rump and prominent long white bar on wings, outertail feathers white, chin and margin of throat white, throat to breast and flanks smoky-grey, belly and undertail-coverts white; iris brown, bill and legs black. **Adult female** As male but upperparts blackish-brown. **Juvenile** Like female but upperparts fringed buffish, wing-patch buffish-white with narrow brown barring, underparts off-white. **Similar species** Black-winged Flycatcher-shrike lacks white on wings. **Habitat** Primary and secondary hill to lower montane and upland kerangas forest, generally from 500 to 1,500 m, with occasional extreme records 50–1,830 m. **Behaviour** Sallies after flying insects and foliage-gleans from mid-storey, often returning to same perch; usually solitary or in pairs, but joins mixed feeding flocks. **Voice** A high-pitched staccato *sittititiiti...* (c.6–7 kHz). **Range & status** Himalayas, Indian Subcontinent, SW China, SE Asia, Sumatra. **Borneo** Common resident throughout. **Breeding** Possibly February–July but otherwise undescribed in Borneo.

BLACK-WINGED FLYCATCHER-SHRIKE
Hemipus hirundinaceus

Male, Juvenile, Female

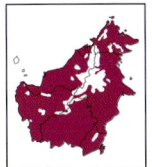

Identification 13.5–14.5 cm. Monotypic. **Adult male** Upperparts all glossy black except for white rump, underparts white with grey wash on breast; iris brown, bill and legs black. **Adult female** As male but upperparts dark brown. **Juvenile** Like female but upperparts fringed buffish, wing-patch buffish-white with narrow brown barring, underparts whitish with brownish wash on breast. **Similar species** See Bar-winged Flycatcher-shrike. **Habitat** Primary and secondary lowland dipterocarp, hill and kerangas forest, mangroves, plantations, cultivated areas, to 950 m, with occasional records to 1,200 m. **Behaviour** As for preceding; usually replaces latter at lower altitudes but they overlap at mid-levels. **Voice** A buzzing *dee-dit-doo*, descending in pitch; also an ascending *zee-zit-zit* and an undulating buzz. **Range & status** Malay Peninsula, Sumatra, Java, Bali. **Borneo** Common resident throughout. **Breeding** April–October; cup-shaped nest is made of mosses and lichens swathed in cobwebs located on horizontal branch to look like broken-off stump 8–11 m from ground.

RUFOUS-WINGED PHILENTOMA
Philentoma pyrhoptera

Male blue morph   Female   Male typical morph

Identification 15–17 cm. Flycatcher-like philentoma with blue plumage and usually with distinctive chestnut wings and tail. **Adult male *pyrhoptera*** Head and back to throat and breast cobalt-blue, wings and tail rich chestnut, rest of underparts buffish-white; iris red, bill black, legs and feet bluish-grey. **Adult male blue morph** Upperparts and underparts completely cobalt-blue, slightly paler on lower belly and undertail-coverts. **Adult female** Upperparts dull greyish-brown with rufous-brown wing-coverts and tail, underparts buffish-white with brownish wash on breast and flanks. **Juvenile** As female but head and mantle brownish, underparts buffish-white with orange-rufous wash on breast. **Habitat** Primary and secondary lowland dipterocarp forest, peatswamp forest, mangroves, to 1,500 m on Kelabit Highlands, but usually below 1,000 m. **Behaviour** Usually seen singly or in pairs; foliage-gleaning insectivore in lower storey; generally inconspicuous; joins mixed feeding flocks. **Voice** A pure whistled *pi-tuuuu*, the quieter first note slightly higher-pitched and short (3.4 kHz, 0.1 s), the second lower and longer (3.2 kHz, 1 s), getting louder towards end; alarm call is a raspy scolding short repeated *chek-chek-chek...* **Range & status** S Vietnam, S Thailand, Thai-Malay Peninsula, Sumatra. **Borneo** Common resident throughout, including N Natunas. **Breeding** Possibly February–August; otherwise undescribed in Borneo.

MAROON-BREASTED PHILENTOMA
Philentoma velatum

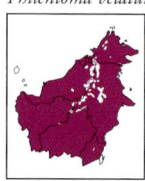

Male   Female

Identification 19–20 cm. Flycatcher-like philentoma with distinctive dark face and deep purple breast. **Adult male *caesium*** Crown and upperparts cobalt-blue, black face from forehead around eye to throat, lower throat and breast deep maroon, rest of underparts cobalt-blue; iris red, bill black, legs and feet bluish-black. **Adult female** Dull cobalt-blue all over except for darker face and throat. **Juvenile** Upperparts and underparts patchy blue and brown, wings and tail cobalt-blue with chestnut wing-coverts; iris brown. **Habitat** Primary and secondary lowland dipterocarp to lower montane forest, peatswamp forest, kerangas, plantations, to 1,650 m. **Behaviour** Solitary or in pairs; usually seen in lower and mid-storey of primary forest, often in swampy areas. **Voice** A series of loud, raspy harsh notes, *chazz chazz chazz...*, also a quick, chirpy *chup-chup-chup-CHUP-chup* (3 kHz, 0.7 s). **Range & status** Thai-Malay Peninsula, Sumatra, Java. **Borneo** Uncommon resident throughout. **Breeding** Possibly February–June; one nest located in fork of rotting tree but otherwise undescribed in Borneo.

ARTAMIDAE: Woodswallows

Worldwide 10 species, 1 in Borneo. Aerial insectivore, typically of tropical areas with broad-based pointed bill, large head, broad-based pointed wings and square tail. Flight is strong and graceful, insects are caught in flight in open areas. Gregarious, often perch huddled together in conspicuous places and have the habit of wagging tail from side to side. Sexes alike.

WHITE-BREASTED WOODSWALLOW
Artamus leucorynchus

LIBARAN ISLAND   3/6/10

Adult   Juvenile   Adult

Identification 16.5-18.5 cm. **Adult *leucorynchus*** Ashy-grey with bright white underparts from breast to undertail-coverts, rump and uppertail-coverts white; in flight broad-based triangular wings, white underparts and underwing-coverts contrast with ashy-grey undertail and throat; iris black, bill bluish-grey with black tip, legs and feet greyish-black. **Juvenile** Upperparts browner with whitish feather-tips, underparts whitish with darker barring, darker on sides of throat. **Habitat** Open areas near mangroves, plantations, paddyfields, to 1,900 m. **Behaviour** Catches insects in flight with feet and eats them on wing; huddles together in small groups on powerlines and bare branches; often wags fanned tail from side to side when perched. **Voice** Call is a sharp, irregularly repeated *chee chee...* (c.3 kHz). **Range & status** Andaman Islands, Thai-Malay Peninsula, Indonesia, Philippines, New Guinea, Australia, SW Pacific. **Borneo** Common resident throughout, including offshore islands. **Breeding** October–June; lays 2–4 creamy-white eggs with grey and light brown spots in nest of twigs and roots located in fork of tree.

AEGITHINIDAE: Ioras

Worldwide 4 species, 2 in Borneo. Small arboreal leaf-gleaning insectivores with slender, pointed bill, and slender body and short, thin legs. The sexes differ, males are brightly plumaged yellow and green. Joins mixed feeding flocks. Found in a variety of wooded habitats. Highly vocal with rich, varied song.

COMMON IORA *Aegithina tiphia*

Male *viridis* — Female *viridis*

Identification 12–14 cm. **Adult male *aequanimis*** Forehead and lores yellow, head to uppertail-coverts dull yellowish-green, wings black with two broad white wing-bars, underparts yellow grading to yellowish-green belly and undertail-coverts, tail black; iris dark brown with yellow eye-ring, bill and legs grey. **Adult male *viridis*** (endemic subspecies) Underparts paler. **Adult female** As adult male but duller with duller wing-bars. **Juvenile** Like female but paler with wing-bars less distinct. **Habitat** Primary forest edges, secondary forest, scrub, mangroves, plantations, gardens, to 1,000 m. **Behaviour** Usually solitary or in pairs; gleans foliage for small invertebrates in treetops. **Voice** Song is varied and musical, gives a strident series of glissading notes as well as a sweet whistled *di-dwi-dwi-dwi-dwi-dwee*, the first, short note sharply downslurred but otherwise monotone (1.9 kHz, 1.2 s); also *ee-chong*, the first note long and harsh, the second short, sweet and sharply downslurred, and a series of 7–8 staccato *doo* notes. **Range & status** Indian Subcontinent, SW China, SE Asia, Sumatra, Java, Bali, Palawan. **Borneo** Common resident throughout, including offshore islands: *aequanimis* in Sabah, *viridis* elsewhere. **Breeding** February–July; lays two creamy-white eggs with reddish-brown spots and greyish flecks in small, deep, tight cup of rootlets and grass held together with cobwebs located in fork of small tree 3–8 m from ground.

GREEN IORA *Aegithina viridissima*

Male — Female

Identification 12.5 cm. **Adult male *viridissima*** Head to uppertail-coverts dark green, lores blackish, wings black with broad two white bars across coverts, primaries fringed yellowish-white, tail black, throat and upper breast green grading to greenish-yellow belly and undertail-coverts; iris brown with broad broken bright yellow eye-ring, bill pale bluish-grey, legs and feet slaty-blue. **Adult female** As male but lores yellow, narrower yellow wing-bars, underparts all yellow, tail greenish. **Juvenile** Like female but paler. **Habitat** Disturbed areas of primary forest and secondary lowland dipterocarp, kerangas, peatswamp, forest edges, mangroves, overgrown plantations, to 600 m. **Behaviour** Gleans foliage for small invertebrates at all levels; often joins mixed feeding flocks; seen singly or in small parties. **Voice** Song is a squeaky, high-pitched *zee-zee-zee-zee…* (5.4 kHz); chattering and staccato phrases are also given. **Range & status** Thai-Malay Peninsula, Sumatra. **Borneo** Common resident throughout, including N Natunas, Anambas and Banggi islands. **Breeding** Possibly breeds January–July but otherwise undescribed in Borneo.

RHIPIDURIDAE: Fantails

Worldwide 42 species, 3 in Borneo. A rather homogeneous family of small birds with small bill and long rictal bristles, short legs and long, rounded tail. Noisy and active insectivores, forages in thick foliage with jerky movements; wags and fans tail to disturb insects. Sexes similar.

PIED FANTAIL *Rhipidura javanica*

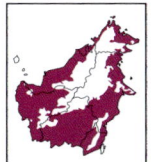

Adult

Identification 17.5–19.5 cm. Very active, black and white lowland fantail. **Adult *longicauda*** Head and upperparts dark grey with short white supercilium, tail with broad white tips, chin dark grey, throat and underparts white with dark grey breast-band and sides of upper breast, buffish wash on belly and undertail-coverts; iris brown, bill and legs black. **Juvenile** Duller and browner, breast-band less distinct. **Similar species** See White-throated Fantail. **Habitat** Peatswamp forest, secondary growth, plantations, cultivated land, gardens, to 750 m. **Behaviour** Very active insectivore; constantly fans tail when flycatching and sallying; feeds in lower to mid-storey. **Voice** A high-pitched, squeaky *wi-tit-weet-weet-weet-wit*, of 4–6 notes, the last falling (5.3–3 kHz, 2 s). **Range & status** SE Asia, Sumatra, Java, Bali, Philippines. **Borneo** Common lowland resident throughout. **Breeding** Year-round, lays 2–3 pale buff eggs with brown and grey spots in small, deep cup-shaped nest of fine woven fibres covered with cobwebs usually located in small fork or on horizontal branch.

KINABALU 12/6/10

WHITE-THROATED FANTAIL *Rhipidura albicollis*

Identification 17.5–20.5 cm. Bold, active, black and white montane fantail. **Adult *kinabalu*** (endemic subspecies) Upperparts brownish-black with bold white supercilium, tail with prominent white tips, chin and throat white, rest of underparts dark grey; iris brown, bill and legs black. **Juvenile** Darker with brownish edging, buffish underparts, reduced throat-patch. **Adult *sarawacensis*** (endemic subspecies) Upperparts browner, narrow throat-stripe, breast and centre of belly mottled white, bolder white tail-tips. **Similar species** Pied Fantail is found in lowland habitats and has white underparts. **Habitat** Primary and secondary hill and montane forest, gardens, 700–2,750 m. **Behaviour** Very active insectivore; catches insects on wing generally in lower to mid-storey, often fans tail; joins mixed feeding flocks. **Voice** A series of 4–6 thin, high-pitched notes, first three on descending scale, then a short rising note and final drawn-out descending note *dee-dee-dee-dit-dooo* (5.2–3 kHz, 2 s). **Range & status** Himalayas, S China, SE Asia, Sumatra. **Borneo** Common montane resident throughout, *kinabalu* in N Borneo and *sarawacensis* in W Borneo, race uncertain in S Kalimantan. **Breeding** November–June; lays two white eggs with reddish spots in nest of moss and fine grasses located in mossy bank.

Juvenile *kinabalu* Adult *kinabalu*

TURTLE ISLAND 7/6/10

SPOTTED FANTAIL *Rhipidura perlata*

Identification 17–18 cm. Monotypic. Dainty black and white fantail with distinctive spotting on breast. **Adult** Upperparts blackish-grey with narrow white eyebrow, string of small white spots on wing-coverts, tail black with broad white tips, throat and breast blackish-grey spotted white, flanks blackish-grey, rest of underparts whitish; iris brown, bill and legs black. **Juvenile** Upperparts brownish with buffish tips on wing-coverts. **Habitat** Primary and secondary lowland dipterocarp and kerangas to lower montane forest, to 1,650 m; favours old growth forest. **Behaviour** Active insectivore; usually seen singly or in pairs in mid- to upper storey; often joins mixed feeding flocks; tends to sit with upright posture. **Voice** Song is a rich, melodious series of 7–8 notes, *wee-chit-chit-wee-chit-wichit-cheee* (2–3 kHz, 1.5 s), sometimes described as 'whistle while you work'; call is a grating *chwik* or *cheewick*. **Range & status** Thai-Malay Peninsula, Sumatra, W Java. **Borneo** Common resident throughout. **Breeding** February–July; otherwise undescribed in Borneo.

Adult

MONARCHIDAE: Monarchs, paradise-flycatchers & allies

Worldwide c.85 species, 3 in Borneo. Small arboreal insectivores with long or very long tail and broad, flat bill with prominent rictal bristles. Glean flushed insects in dense vegetation in short sallies while flicking wings and fanning tail. Sometimes joins mixed feeding flocks. Typically sexually dimorphic.

SUKAU RIVER LODGE 8/6/10

BLACK-NAPED MONARCH *Hypothymis azurea*

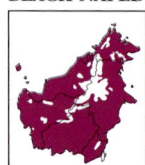

Identification 15–17 cm. Small, active and noisy insectivore with short crest giving square-headed appearance. **Adult male *prophata*** Plumage azure-blue with black spot on nape and narrow black band above bill, black stripe across upper breast, and whitish belly to undertail-coverts, undertail greyish-blue; iris blackish-brown with bright blue eye-wattle, bill blue, mouth yellow-green, legs black. **Adult female** Head and breast dull blue with narrow black line over bill, rest of upperparts brown with bluish tinge, rest of underparts whitish. **Juvenile** Like female. **Habitat** Primary and secondary lowland dipterocarp, kerangas and peatswamp to lower montane forest, plantations, to 1,200 m. **Behaviour** Usually seen singly or in pairs; active insectivore, foraging in lower to mid-storey; noisy but often difficult to observe. **Voice** Call is wheezy *shweet shweet...* (6 kHz); song is a ringing *weet-weet-weet...* (4 kHz, c.6 notes/s). **Range & status** Indian Subcontinent, S China, Taiwan, SE Asia, Indonesia, Philippines. **Borneo** Common resident throughout including offshore islands. **Breeding** March–October; lays two eggs in cup-shaped nest of moss, twigs and rootlets located 1.5–2 m from ground in understorey vegetation; eggs are creamy-white to pinkish-white with brown and grey splotches, spots or specks.

Male Female

ASIAN PARADISE-FLYCATCHER *Terpsiphone paradisi*

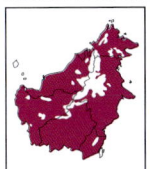

Male white morph

Male rufous morph

Female

Juvenile

Identification 20 cm (excluding male's elongated tail feathers). Striking monarch flycatcher with bright white plumage and very long tail in male. **Adult male *borneensis* white morph** (endemic subspecies) Head with short crest and throat glossy black, rest of plumage white with black edging on wing and tail feathers, tail with elongated central feathers up to 30 cm long; iris brown with blue eye-wattle, bill blue with black tip, mouth yellow, legs and feet greyish-blue; **rufous morph** (very rare in Borneo) like white morph but back and tail rufous-brown, underparts washed grey. **Adult female** Like rufous morph male but duller with short tail. **Juvenile** Like female but head brownish, scaling on breast. **Habitat** Primary and secondary lowland dipterocarp and peatswamp to lower montane forest, plantations, to 1,200 m. **Behaviour** Arboreal insectivore, hawking for insects from inconspicuous perch; usually singly or in pairs, but joins mixed feeding flocks. **Voice** Call is a wheezy, two- or three-note *shweet-shweet-shweet* (c.4 kHz, 0.7 s); song is a rich, ringing, continuously repeated *wit-wit-wit...* (2 kHz, c.5 notes/s), both call and song lower-pitched than song of Black-naped Monarch. **Range & status** C, E and N Asia, Indian Subcontinent, SE Asia, Indonesia. **Borneo** Common resident throughout. **Breeding** February–August; lays 1–2 glossy pale cream to pinkish eggs with reddish spots in deep cup-shaped nest of mosses, rootlets, bark and leaves, outside covered in lichens and cobwebs with long tail, usually located in fork of sapling c.3 m from ground.

JAPANESE PARADISE-FLYCATCHER
Terpsiphone atrocaudata

Male

Female

Identification 17.5–20 cm (excluding male's elongated tail feathers). Dark monarch with short crest and very long tail in male. **Adult male *atrocaudata*** Head and breast black, upperparts glossy black and purplish-brown, belly to undertail-coverts white. **Adult female** Smaller, duller, upperparts brownish. Duller than female Asian Paradise-flycatcher, crown lacks gloss and has a more clear-cut line between dark breast and white belly. **Habitat** Migrants in region have been recorded in forest and mangroves to 700 m. **Behaviour** As Asian Paradise-flycatcher. **Voice** The call is very similar to Asian Paradise-flycatcher but slightly less wheezy. **Range & status** Breeds Korea, Japan, Taiwan; migrates to SE Asia, Sumatra, Philippines. **Borneo** Vagrant with one record from G. Kinabalu, Sabah, in 1992.

DICRURIDAE: Drongos

Worldwide c.23 species, 6 in Borneo. Small to medium-sized insectivorous, mostly black birds with a robust hook-tipped bill with prominent rictal bristles, slender body and long forked tail. Some have short crest or modified tail feathers. Bold and noisy, perching upright in a prominent position and sallying out conspicuously to catch insects on the wing. Drongos often lead mixed feeding flocks. The vocalisations are varied, often harsh and raucous, with much mimicry.

BLACK DRONGO *Dicrurus macrocercus*

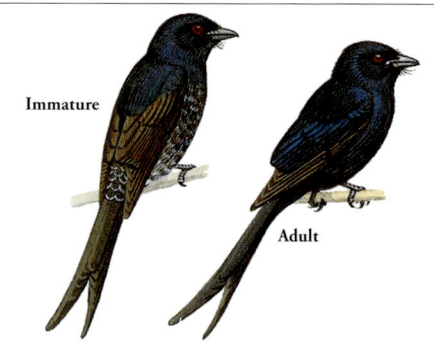

Identification 27–28.5 cm. Large all-black drongo (race uncertain) with long, deeply forked tail. **Adult** Plumage entirely black with moderate gloss, often with white spot in front of eye, distinctive long, deeply forked tail slightly curled upwards at tips; iris brown, bill and legs black. **Immature** Duller with brownish tinge, underparts and uppertail-coverts greyer and fringed whitish. **Habitat** On Borneo recorded from paddyfields, cultivated areas, at sea-level. **Behaviour** Perches on low posts and fences as well as on cattle in open areas, hawking disturbed insects close to ground; often flicks tail when perched and in flight. **Voice** A distinctive, rasping *jeez*, also *kerrr chu*, the last note short and high-pitched. **Range & status** Indian Subcontinent, S China, SE Asia, Sumatra, Java, Bali. **Borneo** Rare non-breeding visitor with few records from coastal N Borneo (Sabah).

ASHY DRONGO *Dicrurus leucophaeus*

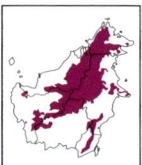

Identification 25–29 cm. Unmistakable light grey drongo with red eyes. **Adult** *stigmatops* (endemic subspecies) Plumage all pale grey with prominent white lores, long deeply forked tail; iris orange-red, bill and legs black. **Juvenile** No white lores, underparts brownish-grey; iris brown. **Habitat** Primary lower to upper montane forest, 550–2,400 m. **Behaviour** Hawks insects from prominent high perch; one of most visible birds at higher altitudes. **Voice** Song is a piercing, high-pitched *pit-ee-pit pit*, each note higher in pitch (3–5.3 kHz, 0.5 s); call is a harsher *prrt*. **Range & status** C and N Asia, Indian Subcontinent, S China, SE Asia, Sumatra, Java, Bali, Lombok, Palawan. **Borneo** Common resident in hill and mountain ranges throughout. **Breeding** January–July; lays 2–3 pale pink or ochraceous-buff eggs with pale spots in nest of plant fibres, roots and grasses suspended from branch of tree.

CROW-BILLED DRONGO *Dicrurus annectans*

Identification 27–32 cm. Monotypic. Large drongo with broad long bill and shallow forked tail upcurled on outer tips. **Adult** All-black plumage, glossy on head and mantle, tail shallowly forked and turned up strongly at tips; iris dark red, heavy bill and legs black. **Immature** Duller; underparts fringed whitish, tail less curled at tips; iris brown. **Similar species** Black Drongo has slimmer bill, tail is longer and more deeply forked and only slightly turned-up at ends. **Habitat** Primary lowland dipterocarp, kerangas and peatswamp forest, mangroves, coastal woodland, to 400 m. **Behaviour** Sallies out from shaded perches to catch insects on wing; relatively inconspicuous. **Voice** Churrs and loud musical whistles, *tjeep tjeep tjeep tchou tchou*. **Range & status** Breeds NE Indian Subcontinent, S China; migrates to SE Asia, Sumatra, Java. **Borneo** Uncommon non-breeding visitor N and W Borneo (Sabah, Brunei, Sarawak, E Kalimantan).

BRONZED DRONGO *Dicrurus aeneus*

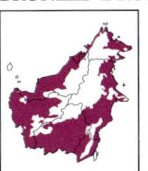

Identification 20–23 cm. Small, fine-billed drongo with strong gloss on black plumage. **Adult** *malayensis* All-black plumage strongly glossed on upperparts, throat and breast, forked tail lacks turn-ups at tips; iris dark red, bill and legs black. **Juvenile** All black with underparts matt-black. **Habitat** Primary lowland dipterocarp, riparian and peatswamp forest, to 500 m. **Behaviour** Sallies out in pursuit of insects from shaded perch in mid- to upper storey; favours open areas within forest. **Voice** Song is a sharp combination of two notes, one an upslurred *sweep* (3–4 kHz, 0.2 s), the other a more sharply downslurred *tsit* (5.2–3.2 kHz, 0.1 s), notes uttered in various combinations at rate of c.1 note/s. **Range & status** Indian Subcontinent, S China, Taiwan, SE Asia, Sumatra. **Borneo** Common resident throughout. **Breeding** March–June; constructs tiny cup-shaped nest woven from lichen, bark and hairlike threads on slender branch.

GREATER RACKET-TAILED DRONGO
Dicrurus paradiseus

Identification 30 cm (up to 60 cm with rackets). Unmistakable large drongo with short forehead-tuft and spectacular long tail-rackets. **Adult** *brachyphorus* (endemic subspecies) Plumage all black, glossed dark blue on upperparts, prominent short crest on forehead, shallowly forked tail with highly elongated outer feathers, up to 30 cm, with bare shafts and twisted terminal rackets (many birds may have outer tail feathers at various stages of development in which they are shorter and sometimes still feathered on shafts); iris dark red, bill and legs black. **Juvenile** Duller with brownish tinge, shorter crest, no elongated tail feathers. **Similar species** Confusion with Crow-billed Drongo may arise when rackets are not developed, in which case Crow-billed has more deeply forked tail with turned-up tips. **Habitat** Primary and secondary lowland dipterocarp, kerangas and peatswamp forest, mangroves, plantations; lowland specialist to 650 m. **Behaviour** Often in mixed feeding flocks; noisy and conspicuous; more often encountered within forest than other drongos. **Voice** Highly varied loud rasping, squeaking and churring notes, with some whistling notes and mimicry. **Range & status** Subcontinent, S China, SE Asia, Sumatra, Java, Bali. **Borneo** Common resident throughout, including N Natunas and Anambas. **Breeding** Possibly January–August; otherwise undescribed in Borneo.

HAIR-CRESTED DRONGO *Dicrurus hottentottus*

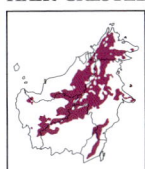

Identification 29–33 cm. Large drongo with very distinctive broad, forked tail with pronounced upcurled outer tips. **Adult** *borneensis* (endemic subspecies) All-black plumage with strong dark greenish gloss on wings and tail, glossy blue spangles on crown to throat and breast, broad, almost unforked tail prominently curved up and out at tips, crest of hair-like plumes on head often difficult to see in field; iris dark red, bill and legs black. **Juvenile** Duller brownish-black with shorter plumes on head and less curled tail. **Habitat** Primary and secondary hill to lower montane forest, 500–1,700 m, with occasional records down to 220 m. **Behaviour** Hawks insects from prominent perch in clearings; noisy and conspicuous. **Voice** Highly varied loud chirps, peeps, whistles and rasping notes; also a loud, fluty *wee-oo-wit* (1.3–1.9 kHz, 0.5 s), the second short note highest-pitched. **Range & status** India, S China, SE Asia, Bali, E Indonesia. **Borneo** Common resident throughout. **Breeding** February–July; lays two white to salmon-pink eggs with red spots and grey to reddish blotches in shallow nest made of roots located in outer branches of tree.

177

CORVIDAE: Crows, jays, magpies & treepies

Worldwide c.121 species, 9 in Borneo. Large, often gregarious, social and intelligent birds with noisy vocalisations, strong legs and feet, and powerful, straight all purpose bill. Occupy a very wide range of habitats. Most are arboreal and omnivorous. Social organisation is highly developed. Sexes alike.

SUKAU RIVER LODGE   8/6/10

SLENDER-BILLED CROW *Corvus enca*

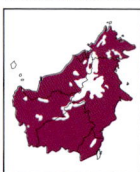

Identification 43–47 cm. **Adult** *compilator* Plumage entirely black, upperparts glossed; iris dark brown, bill and legs black. **Juvenile** Duller, less glossy. **Similar species** Difficult to separate from Large-billed Crow; in flight Slender-billed has squarer tail, shorter, more rounded wings, and faster-shivering wing-beats with wings held below horizontal; when perched has slenderer build, less steep-angled forehead, no throat-hackles, unglossed underparts and thinner bill with less arched culmen. **Habitat** Primary and secondary lowland dipterocarp, riparian and peatswamp forest, plantations, to 1,000 m. **Behaviour** Relatively shy, avoids human habitation; often in small flocks; feeds on invertebrates and small vertebrates, and may occasionally take carrion. **Voice** A hoarse, throaty *kaa-kaa-kaa-kaa...* or shorter *ka-ka-ka...* (at c.1.4 kHz higher-pitched than Large-billed Crow), sometimes given with series of chuckles and yelps. **Range & status** Thai-Malay Peninsula, Indonesia, Philippines. **Borneo** Common lowland resident throughout. **Breeding** Possibly year-round, constructs typical corvid nest of twigs and sticks.

SOUTHERN JUNGLE CROW *Corvus macrorhynchos*

Identification 48–59 cm. **Adult male** *macrorhynchos* Plumage entirely purplish-glossed black with erectile crown feathers and longish throat-hackles, large bill strongly arched; iris dark brown, bill and legs black. **Adult female** Less strongly arched bill. **Juvenile** Duller and browner. **Similar species** See Slender-billed Crow. **Habitat** Extralimitally in cultivated areas, plantations, human habitation. **Voice** Deep throaty *kaaa-kaaa-kaaa...* (1.9 kHz). **Range & status** Thai-Malay Peninsula, Lesser Sundas, Philippines. **Borneo** Status uncertain, with handful of unconfirmed sight records from Sabah, Sarawak and W, C and S Kalimantan, and specimens from Sabah, Labuan and S Kalimantan.

HOUSE CROW *Corvus splendens*

Identification 40-43 cm. **Adult** *protogatus* Plumage black with greyish nape and mantle to neck and breast; iris dark brown, bare parts black. **Juvenile** Duller, browner. **Similar species** Smaller than Large-billed Crow and Slender-billed Crow, which both lack grey in plumage. **Habitat** Urban and cultivated areas. **Behaviour** Feeds on invertebrates and small vertebrates, and carrion and refuse; roosts communally. **Voice** A hoarse, relatively weak *kaa kaaa* and a lower pitched *kowk*. **Range & status** Indian Subcontinent, SW China, Myanmar, Thai-Malay Peninsula. **Borneo** Recently established common resident in the Filipino Market in Kota Kinabalu, W Sabah.

178

COMMON GREEN MAGPIE *Cissa chinensis*

Adult

Identification 31–34.5 cm. **Adult *minor*** Crown and nape green with yellow wash on forecrown, black mask from lores through eye to nape, upperparts bright green with maroon-red wings and black and white barred tertials, graduated tail tipped black and white on outer feathers and white on central feathers, underparts bright green; iris bright red, bill and legs bright pinkish-red. **Juvenile** Like adult but mask narrower and duller, iris brown, bill and legs duller. **Similar species** Short-tailed Magpie has shorter, white-tipped tail, lacks black and white on tertials and has all-green crown; note habitat and voice. **Habitat** Secondary forest, scrub, overgrown cultivation, from 550 to 1,800 m. **Behaviour** Forages in dense foliage close to ground, gleaning for insects; usually in small parties; noisy but often quite elusive. **Voice** Song is a loud, long, whipping *sweeek* or *kleeep* (3–5 kHz, 0.3 s), repeated; call is a grating, urgent *krik-krik...* **Range & status** E Himalayas, SE Asia, Sumatra. **Borneo** Uncommon resident NW Borneo from G. Kinabalu to Kelabit Highlands (Sabah, E Sarawak, E Kalimantan). **Breeding** January–March; lays 1–3 white eggs with pale grey and bronze flecks; nest located in thick undergrowth.

SHORT-TAILED GREEN MAGPIE *Cissa thalassina*

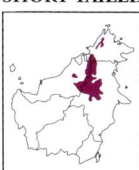

Adult

Identification 30–32 cm. **Adult *jeffreyi*** (endemic subspecies) Crown and upperparts bright green with maroon-red wings, black mask from lores through eye to nape, graduated tail tipped white on outer feathers, underparts bright green; iris whitish with red eyering, bill and legs bright pinkish-red. **Juvenile** Like adult but mask narrower and duller, iris brown, bill and legs yellow. **Similar species** See Common Green Magpie. **Habitat** Primary and secondary lower to upper montane forest, 900–2,450 m. **Behaviour** Often joins mixed feeding flocks in lower to mid-storey of tall forest; usually in small parties; noisy but often quite elusive. **Voice** Many varied notes and phrases including a sweet, piping *wit-wit-wit-tswit-tswit-wu-wooo*, the *wit* notes short and monotone, the whipped *tswit* notes very sharply downslurred, the last note long and downslurred (5.1–2 kHz); calls include sharp, discordant whistles, nasal growls and chatters. **Range & status** Java. **Borneo** Common resident in north-central mountain ranges from G. Kinabalu to Dulit Range and G. Menyapa (Sabah, E Sarawak, E Kalimantan). **Breeding** Poorly known, fledglings noted in April.

BORNEAN BLACK MAGPIE *Platysmurus aterrimus*

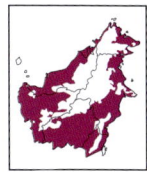

Adult
Juvenile

Identification 36–38 cm. **Adult** All black with short erect crest on forehead and long broad tail; iris red, bill and legs black. **Juvenile** Duller, lacks crest. **Habitat** Primary lowland dipterocarp, peatswamp and kerangas forest; lowland specialist to 550 m. **Behaviour** Often in pairs but sometimes in quite large parties; noisy and active foliage-gleaning insectivore in mid-storey; joins mixed feeding flocks. **Voice** Call is a harsh, rasping rattled *kek'ke'ke'ke'ke...*; song is a long, monotone, mellow, repeated whistle with quality of bamboo flute, *whooo...whooo...* (1.4 kHz, each note c.0.6 s) each note increasing in volume; may also include some mimicry. **Borneo** Endemic, local and uncommon lowland resident throughout. **Breeding** Poorly known, possibly breeds March–September; constructs nest of twigs.

RACKET-TAILED TREEPIE *Crypsirina temia*

Identification 31–32.5 cm. Monotypic. **Adult** All greenish-glossed black plumage with short erectile feathers on forehead and lores, very long distinctive spatulate tail; iris bright blue, bill and legs black. **Juvenile** Duller and browner, tail lacks spatulate tip; iris dark brown. **Habitat** Extralimitally in primary and secondary forest edges, bamboo, mangroves, coastal scrub, to 900 m. **Behaviour** Arboreal insectivore, often in pairs or small parties. **Voice** A short, ringing *chu*, deep rasping, throaty *churg-churg*, and harsh *chraak-chraak* (2-3.5 kHz). **Range & status** SW China, SE Asia, Java, Bali. **Borneo** Resident or former resident, known from two specimens probably collected in S Kalimantan in mid-nineteenth century.

BORNEAN TREEPIE *Dendrocitta cinerascens*

Identification 40 cm. Monotypic. **Adult** Forehead fawn-brown, black line above forehead and over eye, crown to nape silvery-grey, sides of face and underparts fawn-brown, upperparts grey with white patch on black wings, paler on rump, long graduated tail grey with black outer feathers and broad black band on end, underparts pale brown; iris reddish-brown, bill and legs black. **Juvenile** Darker and duller. **Habitat** Primary and secondary hill to upper montane forest, 550–2,900 m. **Behaviour** Generalist feeder, taking insects and fruits; noisy and conspicuous, usually singly or in pairs foraging or vocalising in treetops. **Voice** Call is a repeated harsh, grating *krek-krek...* (1.8 kHz); also a higher-pitched throaty, bell-like *chow* or *choing* (2.3 kHz). **Range & status** Endemic, locally common resident in north-central and south-western mountain ranges from G. Kinabalu to G. Menyapa and Muller Ranges (Sabah, E and C Sarawak, northern W and C Kalimantan, and E Kalimantan). **Breeding** November–May; lays two greenish-white eggs with brown dots in simple shallow cup-shaped nest of twigs lined with grass and roots.

CRESTED JAY *Platylophus galericulatus*

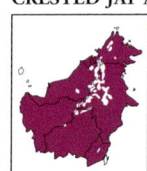

Identification 25–28 cm. **Adult *coronatus*** All tawny-brown plumage with large white patch on side of neck with edges bordered blackish, long erect crest blackish-brown; iris dark red with white spot above and below eye, bill black, legs and feet greenish-black. **Juvenile** Shorter crest, duller with buffish-white spots on wing-coverts and underparts streaked and barred buffish-white. **Habitat** Primary lowland dipterocarp and kerangas to lower montane forest, to 1,300 m. **Behaviour** Usually encountered in small parties; noisy but often quite elusive in thick vegetation in mid-storey where it gleans small to large invertebrates; known by Iban as 'rain bird' as its call is said to foretell a storm. **Voice** Song is a distinctive loud machinegun-rattle, *tit-tut-tut-tut-tut-tut...* (4.4 kHz), typically uttered in six-note phrases of c.0.5 s. **Range & status** Thai-Malay Peninsula, Sumatra, Java. **Borneo** Locally common resident throughout. **Breeding** Undescribed in Borneo.

PITYRIASEIDAE: Bristlehead

Worldwide 1 species, 1 in Borneo. An endemic monospecific family. The bristlehead is a highly nomadic, vociferous bird with a large heavy, hooked bill, and black plumage with red and yellow on head and thighs. The plumage on the head and neck is coarse and stiff, hence the English name. This species represents a relict lineage from the early diversification of shrike-like birds across the Old World tropics.

BORNEAN BRISTLEHEAD *Pityriasis gymnocephala*

Identification 25 cm. Monotypic genus and family. Very unusual black bird with striking yellow and crimson head, very large hooked bill and short tail. **Adult male** Name derives from stiff feathers on yellow-orange crown; face, throat and neck bright red with black patch on cheek, rest of upperparts and underparts black with bright red patch on thighs; iris and bill black, legs and feet pink; in flight white wing-patch. **Adult female** As male but with red spots on flanks. **Juvenile** As adult but reduced red on head and breast, no black patch on cheek, thighs black, eye-ring red. **Habitat** Primary and secondary lowland dipterocarp and hill forest, kerangas, peatswamp forest, occasionally plantations, to 600 m, with records to 1,200 m. **Behaviour** Highly nomadic arboreal insectivore; favours forest canopy where usually seen in small noisy flocks of 6–10, sometimes in mixed feeding flocks. **Voice** Very varied, unusual and distinctive, with nasal contact calls, series of high-pitched whining screams and whistles *pit-pit-PIOU* or *pit-prree-PO* (3 kHz), wails and a harsh, low-pitched *kaw* (1.8 kHz). **Range & status** Endemic, uncommon resident throughout. **Breeding** Poorly known, possibly May–October; egg is white with large brown and grey spots, nest undescribed; possibly communal breeder.

LANIIDAE: Shrikes

Worldwide c.31 species, 4 in Borneo. Active predators with large head, black face-mask, hooked bill, short rounded wings and long tail. Hunts by dropping from a perch and swooping down to catch prey (large insects or small invertebrates) on or near the ground. Flight is strong and undulating. Perches upright in open areas. Sexes may differ slightly.

TIGER SHRIKE *Lanius tigrinus*

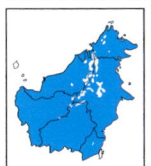

Identification 18 cm. Monotypic. Medium-sized shrike with characteristic black and rufous 'tiger' pattern on upperparts and heavy bill. **Adult male** Head to upper mantle light grey with broad black mask from forehead to ear-coverts, upperparts rufous-brown narrowly barred dark brown, wings and tail plain reddish-brown, underparts white; iris dark brown, heavy hooked bill bluish-black with black tip. **Adult female** Duller, less extensive black face-mask, underparts creamy-white barred brown on breast and flanks. **Juvenile** Upperparts rufous-brown with heavy dark brown barring, sides of face peppered black, white and rufous; underparts whitish with heavy blackish barring on sides of breast and flanks. **Similar species** Brown Shrike has longer tail and smaller bill, lacks barring on reddish-brown upperparts; juvenile has blackish face-mask, less barring on underparts. **Habitat** Primary lowland dipterocarp and lower montane forest edges, secondary forest, coastal woodlands, to 1,300 m. **Behaviour** Solitary and retiring; tends to sit quietly on perch in mid- to lower storey, pouncing on prey or gleaning from foliage; feeds on invertebrates and small vertebrates. **Voice** Call is a harsh, grating *tchek-* and rapid chattering *tchi-tchi-tchi-* (c.3 kHz). **Range & status** Breeds E Palearctic, E Asia; migrates to S China, SE Asia, Indonesia, Philippines. **Borneo** Common non-breeding visitor and passage migrant throughout, September–May.

BROWN SHRIKE *Lanius cristatus*

Identification 17–19 cm. Medium-sized shrike with plain brownish back and buffish underparts. **Adult male *lucionensis*** Head grey, forehead and narrow supercilium white above black face-mask, upperparts greyish-brown; flight feathers, rump and tail darker, tinged rufous; throat white with rest of underparts pale buffish-brown; iris brown, bill black, legs and feet dark grey. **Adult male *confusus*** Like *lucionensis* but head and upperparts warmer brown, underparts more buff. **Adult female** Duller, sometimes with buffy supercilium, faint barring on sides of breast and flanks. **Juvenile** Upperparts brown with fine dark brown barring, poorly defined darker face-mask, underparts buffish-white with fine dark brown barring on sides of breast and flanks; bill grey with black tip. **Similar species** See Tiger Shrike; juvenile Long-tailed Shrike is larger with longer tail and small white patch on wing. **Habitat** Primary lowland dipterocarp and lower montane forest edges, peatswamp and secondary forest, coastal woodlands, mangroves, cultivated areas, gardens, plantations, to 1,700 m. **Behaviour** Usually solitary; hunts invertebrates and small vertebrates from exposed perches, usually close to ground. **Voice** Call is a harsh, grating, repeated chattering *je-je-je-je-* (c.4.5 kHz), higher-pitched than Tiger Shrike. **Range & status** Breeds E Palearctic, E Asia; migrates to SE China, Indian Subcontinent, SE Asia, Indonesia, Philippines. **Borneo** Common non-breeding visitor and passage migrant throughout, including offshore islands, September–May.

LONG-TAILED SHRIKE *Lanius schach*

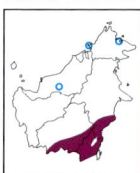

Identification 23–27 cm. Large shrike with long tail and striking rufous, grey, black and white plumage. **Adult *bentet*** Forehead and broad face-mask black, hindcrown and upper mantle grey fading into rufous back and rump, wings black with small white spot at base of primaries, and whitish fringes on tertials, tail black, underparts white with rufous on sides of breast and flanks; iris dark brown, bill and legs black. **Adult *nasutus*** As *bentet* but forehead to hindneck black, upper mantle and back grey. **Juvenile** Duller, face-mask dull blackish-grey, crown and mantle scaly buff and dark grey, underparts washed buffish with fine wavy barring on breast and flanks. **Habitat** Forest edges, plantations, paddyfields, grasslands, cultivated areas. **Behaviour** Usually solitary; perches on stumps and fences from where it pounces on large invertebrates and small vertebrates. **Voice** Call is a harsh, scratchy *shak-shak-shak...*, song is a jumble of scratchy squawks and chirps (1.5-4 kHz). **Range & status** Indian Subcontinent, C Asia, China, Taiwan, SE Asia, Indonesia, Philippines, New Guinea. **Borneo** Race *nasutus* rare non-breeding migrant to N Borneo (Sabah, Sarawak) recorded in February and March; *bentet* common resident SE Borneo (E, C, S Kalimantan).

SOUTHERN GREY SHRIKE *Lanius meridionalis*

Identification 24–25 cm. Large grey-and-white shrike with striking black-and-white wings and black face-mask. **Adult male *pallidirostris*** Thin white supercilium above black lores and face mask, crown to back plain pale grey, rump white, wings black edged white with white patch at base of primaries, tail black with white outer feathers, underparts white sometimes with a pinkish tinge; iris dark brown, bill grey, legs and feet black; in flight upperwing black with prominent white outer wing bar. **Adult female** Mask more weakly defined from behind eye. **First winter** Duller and paler, bill pinkish, lores pale, face mask brownish, wing coverts edged buff, underparts greyish with faint barring. **Habitat** Recorded in paddyfields in Borneo. **Voice** Calls are described as a nasal *chree-chree-* (extralimital). **Range & status** SW Europe, N Africa, Middle East, C Asia, Indian Subcontinent. **Borneo** Rare vagrant; one record from Brunei.

NECTARINIDAE: Sunbirds & spiderhunters

Worldwide c.129 species, 18 in Borneo. A large family of smallish, active birds that feed on nectar and invertebrates. Highly arboreal with long, decurved bills, short rounded wings and tails, strong legs and a fast, direct flight on whirring wings. Male sunbirds are often brightly coloured with an iridescent metallic sheen, the females are typically drab. Spiderhunters are typically sexually monomorphic with dull olive plumage.

PLAIN SUNBIRD *Anthreptes simplex*

Identification 12.5 cm. Monotypic. Medium-sized, dull olive-green sunbird with yellow on underparts and short, slightly curved bill. **Adult male** Upperparts olive-green with metallic purple on forehead, underparts greyish-olive with grey throat and yellowish centre of belly and undertail-coverts; iris deep red, bill black, legs and feet greyish-brown. **Adult female** As adult male but lacks metallic purple on forehead. **Juvenile** Like adult female but bill pinkish, legs and feet orange-yellow. **Similar species** Female Brown-throated, Red-throated and Olive-backed Sunbirds have brighter yellow on underparts; female Van Hasselt's Sunbird has pale markings on face; female Copper-throated Sunbird has greyish-brown forehead; female Crimson Sunbird has olive-yellow rump; female Temminck's Sunbird has olive-brown upperparts and reddish wash on wings and tail. **Habitat** Primary and secondary lowland dipterocarp and kerangas forest, plantations, to 400 m. **Behaviour** Generalist, feeding on invertebrates, nectar, fruits; leaf-gleans in warbler-like fashion. **Voice** A metallic, high-pitched repeated *seep*. **Range & status** Thai-Malay Peninsula, Sumatra. **Borneo** Common resident throughout including N Natunas. **Breeding** Possibly February–August but otherwise undescribed in Borneo.

BROWN-THROATED SUNBIRD *Anthreptes malacensis*

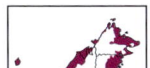

Identification 12.5 cm. Stocky sunbird with heavy, thick bill. **Adult male** *borneensis* (endemic subspecies) Upperparts metallic green with bright metallic purple on shoulders and back to uppertail-coverts, tail glossy blue, wings purplish-brown, cheeks and throat brownish-purple with metallic purple malar stripe, underparts yellow, bright yellow pectoral tufts; iris deep red, bill and legs dark grey. **Adult female** Upperparts olive-green with yellow around eye, wings yellowish, tail brownish, underparts bright greenish-yellow. **Juvenile** As adult female but bill paler. **Adult male** *malacensis* Cheeks olive-green. **Similar species** Red-throated Sunbird has more reddish throat and sides of head, maroon band across upper back, more reddish wings and greenish underparts; female Red-throated Sunbird has narrower yellow eye-ring, less yellow underparts. **Habitat** Secondary lowland dipterocarp, peatswamp, kerangas forest, mangroves, plantations, gardens, favouring open and disturbed habitats, to 500 m with occasional records up to 950 m. **Behaviour** Feeds primarily on invertebrates, also nectar and over-ripe fruits. **Voice** Call is a high-pitched *tsweet*; song is a sharp, see-sawing *swit-sweet-swit-sweet* (the first note c.4.5 kHz, the second c.5.2 kHz). **Range & status** W Burma, Thai-Malay Peninsula, Indochina, Sumatra, Java, Sulawesi, Lesser Sundas, Philippines. **Borneo** Common resident throughout, including offshore islands where often abundant. **Breeding** January–August; lays two pale pink eggs with purplish-black lines and blotches in nest of plant fibres and grasses held together with cobwebs and suspended from branch.

RED-THROATED SUNBIRD *Anthreptes rhodolaema*

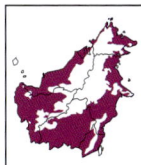

Identification 12.5 cm. Monotypic. **Adult male** Crown and mantle metallic green, back to uppertail-coverts violet with maroon band across lower back, small bright metallic blue patch on shoulders, wings reddish-brown, tail glossy purple, brownish-maroon sides of face and deep red throat divided by metallic purple malar stripe, underparts yellowish-olive; iris red, bill and legs dark grey. **Adult female** Upperparts greyish-olive with narrow yellowish eye-ring, underparts olive-yellow, brighter yellow on lower breast and belly. **Juvenile** Like adult female but underparts less yellow. **Similar species** See Brown-throated Sunbird. **Habitat** Forest edges, secondary lowland dipterocarp, peatswamp and kerangas forest, mangroves, plantations, gardens, to 500 m; possibly favours inland wooded habitats. **Behaviour** Leaf-gleans small invertebrates at all levels; also feeds on nectar and over-ripe fruits. **Voice** A high-pitched whistled *wee-oo* with emphasis on first note. **Range & status** Thai-Malay Peninsula, Sumatra. **Borneo** Very uncommon resident throughout. **Breeding** Poorly known, possibly June–September; nest is pendulous pouch of plant fibres and dead leaves.

RUBY-CHEEKED SUNBIRD *Chalcoparia singalensis*

Identification 11 cm. Small sunbird with glossy green upperparts, orangey throat and breast, and short straight bill. **Adult male** *borneana* (endemic subspecies) Ear-coverts and cheeks copper-red, upperparts bright metallic green with wings and tail blackish, chin to breast apricot-orange, rest of underparts yellow; iris deep red, bill and legs blackish-grey. **Adult female** Like adult male but upperparts olive-brown, yellowish-green on flight feathers. **Juvenile** Like female but lacks apricot-orange on throat. **Adult male** *pallida* (endemic subspecies) Less extensive apricot-orange on throat, underparts paler yellow. **Habitat** Primary and secondary lowland dipterocarp to hill forest, peatswamp and heath forest, mangroves, plantations, gardens, to 500 m with one record from 1,200 m. **Behaviour** Observed singly or in small groups; feeds on small invertebrates, fruits and nectar in mid- to upper storey; often feeds at spiders' webs. **Voice** Call is a shrill, squeaky *tswee*, repeated (6 kHz); song is described as a shrill, rising trill ending in two distinct notes. **Range & status** NE Indian Subcontinent, SE Asia, Sumatra, Java. **Borneo** Common resident throughout including N Natunas (*pallida*). **Breeding** January–September; nest is cradle of plant fibres, mosses and grasses held together with cobwebs built behind thick vegetation in bank; lays two pale lilac eggs with fine reddish-brown lines and speckles.

COPPER-THROATED SUNBIRD *Leptocoma calcostetha*

Identification 13 cm. Monotypic. Large, long-tailed sunbird with dark metallic plumage appearing all black in poor light. **Adult male** Upperparts metallic green with glossy black wings and tail, throat metallic coppery-red, breast metallic purplish-blue, rest of underparts black, yellowish-orange pectoral tufts; iris dark brown, bill and legs black. **Adult female** Crown grey, rest of upperparts olive-green, tail blackish-grey with bold white tips, underparts yellowish with pale grey throat and breast. **Juvenile** Like female but throat yellowish. **Similar species** See Plain Sunbird; female Brown-throated Sunbird has yellow on face and throat; female Red-throated Sunbird has yellow throat and yellower underparts; female Van Hasselt's Sunbird has greenish-yellow throat; female Crimson and Temminck's Sunbird lack white on tail and grey throat, latter also having reddish wash on wings and tail. **Habitat** Secondary lowland dipterocarp and kerangas forest, coastal vegetation, mangroves, plantations, gardens, at sea-level; commonest in mangroves. **Behaviour** Often feeds at mangrove flowers, also on small invertebrates; actively flits from flower to flower at all levels. **Voice** Described as a deep, melodious trill, recalling Yellow-bellied Prinia. **Range & status** SE Asia, Sumatra, Java, Palawan. **Borneo** Locally common resident in coastal areas throughout, including offshore islands. **Breeding** March–July; lays two eggs in pear-shaped nest made of plant fibres, grasses and mosses held together with cobwebs and suspended from narrow branches and twigs.

VAN HASSELT'S SUNBIRD *Leptocoma brasiliana*

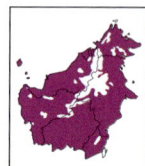
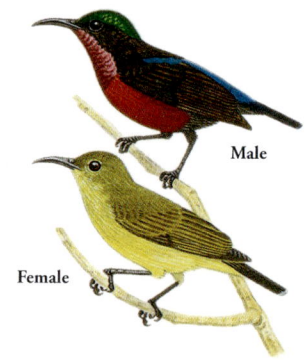

Identification 9 cm. Small dark sunbird with dark purple throat. **Adult male** *brasiliana* Crown and nape metallic green, face and upperparts blackish-purple with metallic purple-blue rump and shoulder-patch, tail black, throat metallic purple, breast and upper belly deep purplish-red, lower belly to undertail-coverts dark greyish-brown; iris dark brown, bill and legs black. **Adult female** Upperparts olive-brown with reddish-brown tinge to flight feathers, tail black, underparts buffish-yellow. **Juvenile** As female. **Similar species** See Plain and Copper-throated Sunbirds; Brown-throated and Red-throated Sunbirds have yellow underparts; female Olive-backed Sunbird has white tips on black tail; female Crimson Sunbird has more olive underparts and longer tail; female Temminck's Sunbird is browner with greyer head and red wash on wings and tail. **Habitat** Disturbed areas of lowland dipterocarp to hill forest, kerangas, peatswamp forest, mangroves, plantations, to 1,000 m. **Behaviour** Very active, usually in upper storey; gleans foliage for small invertebrates, also feeds on nectar and fruit. **Voice** A series of high-pitched, short notes *chit-chit-chit-chit* (7 kHz) and lower-pitched short trills (4.6 kHz, 0.2 s). **Range & status** NE Indian Subcontinent, SE Asia, Sumatra, Java. **Borneo** Uncommon resident patchily distributed throughout, including offshore islands. **Breeding** January–September; purse-shaped nest of plant fibres is suspended from narrow branch; eggs creamy-white with reddish-brown or purplish streaks.

OLIVE-BACKED SUNBIRD *Cinnyris jugularis*

Identification 10 cm. Small sunbird with long decurved bill and contrasting metallic blackish-purple and yellow underparts. **Adult male** *ornatus* Forehead metallic blackish-purple, rest of upperparts olive-green, tail black with broad white tips, throat and breast metallic blackish-purple, underparts bright yellow, pectoral tufts orange; iris dark brown, bill and legs black. **Adult male non-breeding** Metallic blackish-purple confined to centre of throat and breast. **Adult female** Like male but lacks metallic blackish-purple in plumage, pale yellow supercilium. **Juvenile** As female. **Habitat** Secondary lowland dipterocarp and kerangas to lower montane forest, coastal scrub, mangroves, plantations, gardens, to 1,500 m. **Behaviour** Primarily feeds on nectar as well as small invertebrates; usually singly or in pairs; aggressive and active; usually feeds at lower to mid-levels. **Voice** Call is a short, rising *sweet* (4.5–7 kHz, 0.2 s); song is a rapid, unmusical *sweet chiwit chiwit chit-chit-chit…* **Range & status** SE Asia, S China, Sumatra, Java, Philippines, Sulawesi, New Guinea, NE Australia. **Borneo** Common resident throughout, including offshore islands where often abundant. **Breeding** Year-round; lays two white eggs with fine olive-grey and light brown speckles in straggly-tailed pear-shaped nest made of plant fibres, grasses, hair, moss and cobwebs, decorated with bark, lichen, dead leaves and cocoons, and slung from narrow twig or exposed root near bank.

CRIMSON SUNBIRD *Aethopyga siparaja*

Identification 9–10 cm. Striking, bright crimson sunbird with graduated tail showing elongated central tail feathers. **Adult male** *siparaja* Forehead and forecrown glossy purple, malar stripe purple; hindcrown, neck, shoulders and back crimson; wings olive-grey, rump yellow, tail glossy purple, chin to upper breast crimson with fine yellow streaks, rest of underparts grey; iris dark brown, bill and legs grey. **Adult male non-breeding** No crimson on head and breast. **Adult female** Crown to upper mantle greyish-olive, back olive, rump and uppertail-coverts yellowish-olive, shorter tail black, throat and breast greyish, rest of underparts olive with yellowish streaking on upper belly, undertail-coverts yellow. **Juvenile** Like adult female but throat tinged reddish in male. **Adult male** *natunae* (endemic subspecies) Underparts paler grey. **Similar species** Male Temminck's Sunbird has scarlet tail and yellow rump, female has olive-green upperparts and reddish wash on wings and tail. **Habitat** Secondary lowland dipterocarp forest, kerangas, coastal scrub, mangroves, plantations, gardens, recorded to 1,150 m but generally below 600 m. **Behaviour** Feeds on insects and nectar; usually forages in lower storey, often in pairs. **Voice** A harsh, staccato *tsit-tsit-tsit-tsit-tsit-tsit* (4.5–6 kHz, 0.5 s) and squeaky *tsee-wit* (7 kHz, 0.3 s). **Range & status** NE Indian Subcontinent, S China, SE Asia, Sumatra, Java, Sulawesi, Philippines. **Borneo** Common resident throughout, including offshore islands. **Breeding** December–September; lays two pale pink eggs with darker blotches and dark red spots in long pocket nest of dead grass and plant fibres slung from exposed roots on overhanging embankment behind thick vegetation.

TEMMINCK'S SUNBIRD *Aethopyga temminckii*

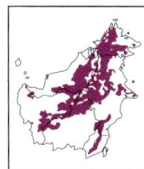

Identification 11 cm. Monotypic. Striking scarlet sunbird with yellow rump and elongated scarlet tail. **Adult male** Forehead and upperparts scarlet with metallic purple sides of crown and moustachial stripe, flight feathers dark brown, rump yellow and uppertail-coverts metallic purple; chin to breast scarlet contrasting with light grey belly to undertail-coverts; iris dark brown, bill and legs black. **Adult female** Head grey, upperparts olive-green with reddish wash on wings and tail, underparts yellowish-olive, tail shorter. **Juvenile** Like female but underparts greyer. **Similar species** See Crimson Sunbird. **Habitat** Primary and secondary lowland dipterocarp and peatswamp to lower montane forest; generally submontane but records from 150–1,680 m. **Behaviour** Feeds primarily on small invertebrates but also nectar and small fruits; very active; often feeds in lower storey. **Voice** Call is a rapid, continually repeated, almost barbet-like *chi-tit* (7 kHz, each phrase 0.15 s). **Range & status** Thai-Malay Peninsula, Sumatra. **Borneo** Common resident, patchily distributed throughout. **Breeding** Possibly December–June but otherwise undescribed in Borneo.

185

PURPLE-NAPED SUNBIRD
Hypogramma hypogrammicum

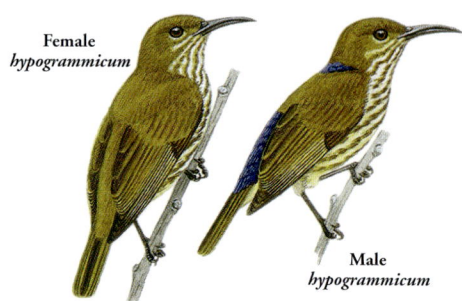
Female *hypogrammicum*
Male *hypogrammicum*

Identification 14 cm. Large olive-green sunbird with streaked underparts and purple nape and rump often not visible in the field. **Adult male** *hypogrammicum* Upperparts olive-green with inconspicuous metallic purple-blue nape, lower back to uppertail-coverts metallic purple-blue, tail olive-green, underparts yellow with broad olive streaks; iris red, bill black, legs and feet brownish. **Adult female** Smaller, lacks metallic purple-blue on nape and rump. **Adult male** *natunense* (endemic subspecies) More purple nape and rump, finer streaking on throat, larger bill. **Habitat** Primary and secondary lowland dipterocarp, riparian, peatswamp, and kerangas forest, plantations, gardens, to 1,000 m. **Behaviour** Reminiscent of small babbler; forages for small invertebrates, fruit and nectar in lower to mid-storey, especially favouring banana flowers; fans and flicks tail. **Voice** A loud, sharp, short, downslurred *tsip* uttered in phrases of 2–4 notes (6.5 kHz). **Range & status** SE Asia, Sumatra. **Borneo** Locally common resident throughout including N Natunas (*natunense*). **Breeding** January–August; nest is pendulous pear-shaped purse of grasses and plant fibres with hair and bark woven in.

GREY-BREASTED SPIDERHUNTER
Arachnothera modesta

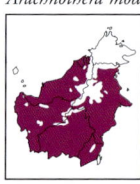

Adult

Identification 16 cm. Medium-sized spiderhunter with long stout bill and streaky underparts. **Adult** *modesta* Upperparts golden olive-green, underparts pale grey with narrow dark grey streaking from throat to breast, tail olive-green with dark blackish terminal band; iris brown, bill blackish-brown, legs and feet fleshy-pink. **Juvenile** Lacks streaking on underparts. **Adult** *pars* (endemic subspecies) Upperparts more greenish, underparts more heavily streaked. **Similar species** The very similar Streaky-breasted Spiderhunter is larger, has longer bill, belly is whiter, and streaking on underparts extends from chin to lower belly. **Habitat** Primary and secondary lowland dipterocarp and hill forest, peatswamp forest, gardens, to 1,200 m. **Behaviour** Feeds on invertebrates and nectar; very active; flies low and fast through under- and mid-storey. **Voice** Song is a continuous, harsh *tsee-chu*, rising then falling. **Range & status** Thai-Malay Peninsula, Sumatra. **Borneo** Uncommon resident, patchily distributed in Sarawak, Brunei and Kalimantan (*pars* in E Borneo); recent molecular studies confirm that only *A. affinis* occurs in Sabah and previous records recorded of *A. modesta* are attributable to *A. a. everetti*. **Breeding** Poorly known; possibly lays two glossy olive-brown and brown eggs.

STREAKY-BREASTED SPIDERHUNTER
Arachnothera affinis

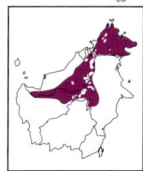

Adult

Identification 18 cm. Large, long-billed spiderhunter with extensive streaking on underparts. **Adult** *everetti* (endemic subspecies) Upperparts dark olive-green with darker scaling on crown, underparts grey with broad dark grey streaking from chin to lower belly, finer on throat; iris brown, bill blackish-grey, legs and feet fleshy-pink. **Juvenile** Lacks streaking on underparts. **Similar species** Grey-breasted Spiderhunter is smaller with stouter, shorter bill, less streaking below, greyer belly, more golden upperparts. **Habitat** Primary and secondary lowland dipterocarp to lower montane forest, plantations, gardens, to 1,500 m. **Behaviour** Feeds on nectar and small invertebrates; highly mobile, flying rapidly through lower storey in search of flowers. **Voice** Call is a squeaky harsh *chit-chit-chit* (c.6 kHz. 0.3 s). **Range & status** Java, Bali. **Borneo** Uncommon montane resident in Sarawak and W and E Kalimantan; uncommon lowland and montane resident Sabah. **Breeding** Possibly year-round; lays two glossy deep olive-brown eggs mottled and speckled with grey and black in cup-like nest of plant fibres suspended by cobwebs from underside of large leaf. **Note** Previously this distinctive subspecies was treated as an endemic, Bornean Spiderhunter *A. everetti*, but *A. affinis* on Java and Bali shows many similarities and thus both taxa are better treated as one species *A. affinis* (*A. a. everetti* from Borneo, *A. a. affinis* from Java and Bali).

KINABALU 12/6/10

LITTLE SPIDERHUNTER *Arachnothera longirostra*

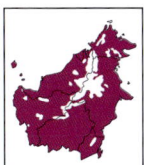

Adult *buettikoferi*

Identification 15–16.5 cm. Small, very long-billed sunbird with distinctive whitish-grey throat. **Adult male *buettikoferi*** (endemic subspecies) Area around eye whitish with dark grey stripe through eye, upperparts brownish-green, pale orange pectoral tufts, tail blackish with white tips, blackish-grey moustachial stripe, throat pale whitish-grey merging into bright yellow underparts; iris brown, bill and legs black. **Adult female** Smaller, lacks pectoral tufts. **Juvenile** Like female but browner. **Adult *atita*** (endemic subspecies) Underparts brighter yellow, bill longer. **Adult *rothschildi*** (endemic subspecies) Vent whitish, bill shorter. **Similar species** Only spiderhunter with whitish-grey throat. **Habitat** Primary and secondary lowland dipterocarp and hill forest, kerangas and peatswamp forest, mangroves, plantations, gardens, to 1,500 m but commonest below 1,000 m. **Behaviour** Very active; flies rapidly through lower storey where it feeds on nectar and small invertebrates; often frequents spiders' webs; pierces base of flowers to extract nectar, especially banana and ginger flowers. **Voice** Call is a sharp, harsh *chit-chit* (6 kHz, 0.2 s); song is an endlessly repeated, upslurred *swit-swit-swit*... (2.5–4.3 kHz). **Range & status** S India, NE Indian Subcontinent, SE Asia, W Yunnan, Sumatra, Java, Philippines. **Borneo** Abundant resident throughout including the N (*rothschildi*) and S (*atita*) Natunas. **Breeding** Possibly year-round; lays two white or pinkish-white eggs with bright reddish-brown speckles in nest of dead leaves, plant fibres and cobwebs attached to underside of large leaf or built in tunnel created by sewing together banana or ginger leaves.

THICK-BILLED SPIDERHUNTER
Arachnothera crassirostris

Adult

Identification 15 cm. Monotypic. Small spiderhunter with long, relatively thick decurved bill. **Adult male** Upperparts dark olive-green with greyish-yellow edging on wings and tips to tail, broken yellow eye-ring with dark olive line through eye, throat and breast greyish-green, orange pectoral tufts, rest of underparts yellow; iris brown, bill dark grey, paler at base, bill and legs black. **Adult female** Lacks pectoral tufts. **Juvenile** Browner with paler bill. **Similar species** Little Spiderhunter has whitish-grey throat, Streaky-breasted and Grey-breasted Spiderhunters have streaking on underparts, Spectacled and Yellow-eared Spiderhunters lack dark line through eye. **Habitat** Primary and secondary lowland dipterocarp, kerangas to lower montane forest, plantations, to 1,200 m. **Behaviour** Feeds on invertebrates and nectar usually in mid-storey; often in pairs. **Voice** A noisy, nasal *chit-chit*. **Range & status** Thai-Malay Peninsula, Sumatra. **Borneo** Uncommon resident throughout. **Breeding** Poorly known in Borneo; nest is like that of Long-billed Spiderhunter but smaller.

LONG-BILLED SPIDERHUNTER
Arachnothera robusta

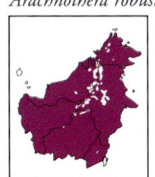

Adult

Identification 22 cm. Large, very long-billed sunbird with dark, white-tipped tail. **Adult male *robusta*** Upperparts olive-green, flight feathers edged yellowish, tail brownish-black with white outer tips, underparts yellow with greyish-green streaking on yellowish-green throat and breast, orange pectoral tufts; iris brown, bill and legs black. **Adult female** Smaller, lacks pectoral tufts. **Juvenile** Undescribed. **Similar species** Little, Thick-billed, Spectacled and Yellow-eared Spiderhunters all lack streaking on underparts; Streaky-breasted and Grey-breasted Sunbirds lack yellow on underparts. **Habitat** Primary and secondary lowland dipterocarp to lower montane forest, plantations, to 1,500 m. **Behaviour** Very aggressive; feeds predominantly on invertebrates and nectar in upper storey. **Voice** Call is a squeaky, relatively mellow, staccato *kwee-kwee-kwee-kwit* (3.3 kHz, 0.6 s) of 2–5 notes; song is described as a rising *choi, choi, choi, choi*... **Range & status** Thai-Malay Peninsula, Sumatra, Java. **Borneo** Uncommon resident, patchily distributed throughout. **Breeding** March–August; lays two white eggs with fine black lines in large, bulky, tube-shaped nest of plant fibres, mosses and leaves attached to underside of large leaf or two large leaves sewn together.

SPECTACLED SPIDERHUNTER
Arachnothera flavigaster

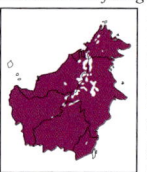

Adult

Identification 22 cm. Monotypic. Large spiderhunter with large triangular ear-patch and broad yellow eye-ring. **Adult** Upperparts dark olive-green, broad eye-ring yellow, triangular patch on ear-coverts yellow, throat and breast greenish-yellow, rest of underparts yellow; iris brown, bill dark grey, legs and feet pinkish-brown. **Juvenile** Undescribed. **Similar species** Very similar Yellow-eared Spiderhunter is smaller with longer, finer bill, larger tufted ear-patch, narrower eye-ring and indistinct streaking on throat and breast; see also Thick-billed Spiderhunter. **Habitat** Disturbed areas in primary and secondary lowland dipterocarp to upper montane forest, plantations, gardens, to 1,680 m. **Behaviour** Aggressive; feeds on invertebrates, fruit and nectar; forages in forest canopy. **Voice** A harsh rattling *chi-chi-chit* (4.5 kHz, 0.3 s). **Range & status** Thai-Malay Peninsula, Sumatra. **Borneo** Uncommon to rare resident patchily distributed throughout. **Breeding** April–August; nest is compact shallow cup of palm fibres slung from underside of leaves, typically of palm-fronds.

YELLOW-EARED SPIDERHUNTER
Arachnothera chrysogenys

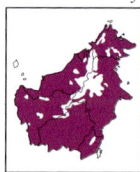

Adult *chrysogenys*

Identification 18 cm. Large spiderhunter with long fine bill and large yellow cheek-patch of elongated feathers. **Adult male** *chrysogenys* Upperparts olive-green, large yellow tuft of feathers on cheeks, narrow yellow eye-ring, underparts yellowish-green with indistinct greenish streaking on throat to breast, brighter yellow on belly and undertail-coverts, grey pectoral tufts; iris brown, bill black, legs and feet pinkish-brown. **Adult female** Lacks pectoral tufts. **Juvenile** Undescribed. **Adult** *harrissoni* (endemic subspecies) Paler and duller than *chrysogenys*. **Similar species** See Spectacled Spiderhunter; from all other spiderhunters by streaking on underparts and yellow eye-ring without black line. **Habitat** Primary and secondary lowland dipterocarp, peatswamp and kerangas to lower montane forest, mangroves, plantations, gardens, to 1,200 m. **Behaviour** Usually seen singly; consumes insects, fruit and nectar, foraging high in canopy where it hovers, flutters and hangs upside-down. **Voice** Call is a high-pitched *twit-twit-twit-tweeee*. **Range & status** Thai-Malay Peninsula, Sumatra, Java. **Borneo** Uncommon resident throughout, *chrysogenys* in W Borneo, *harrissoni* in E Borneo. **Breeding** May–September; lays two white eggs in elongated nest made of plant fibres and attached to underside of large leaf.

WHITEHEAD'S SPIDERHUNTER *Arachnothera juliae*

Adult

Identification 18 cm. Monotypic. Large, distinctive dark brown spiderhunter with heavily streaked head and underparts and conspicuous bright yellow vent and uppertail-coverts. **Adult** Upperparts chocolate-brown with narrow white streaking on head and back, underparts brown broadly streaked white, finer on throat, uppertail and undertail-coverts bright yellow; iris brown, bill and legs black. **Juvenile** Undescribed. **Habitat** Primary and secondary lower and upper montane forest, 930–2,100 m. **Behaviour** Usually seen singly or in pairs in canopy but sometimes in mid-canopy; has been observed in mixed flocks (pers. obs.); relatively sedate. **Voice** Very distinctive; call is a wheezy *wee-chit* (4 kHz); also a complex series of nasal but wheezy twitters and trills with rich harmonics *wit-wit-wit-wt'wt'wt'weehee...* (3–8 kHz). **Range & status** Endemic, locally common resident in north-central mountain ranges from G. Kinabalu to Dulit Range and Kayan Mentarang in N Borneo (Sabah, E Sarawak, E Kalimantan). **Breeding** Undescribed; one nest observed in March.

DICAEIDAE: Flowerpeckers

Worldwide c.45 species, 12 in Borneo. A family of tiny arboreal birds with short bill, round body, short wings and tail, and strong legs. They feed very actively on fruit and nectar in epiphytes and mistletoes, for which they are an important dispersing agent. In most species the sexes differ, the male typically with a patch of red on the head, upperparts or underparts, the female dull.

THICK-BILLED FLOWERPECKER *Dicaeum agile*

Identification 10 cm. Large plain flowerpecker with brownish upperparts and streaked underparts. **Adult *modestum*** Upperparts olive-brown, underparts whitish with indistinct brownish streaking, white pectoral tufts, very faint white spots on tail-tips; iris brown to dark red, thick bill and legs black. **Juvenile** Underparts less streaked with yellowish wash on lower belly and undertail-coverts; bill flesh-coloured. **Similar species** See Brown-backed Flowerpecker. **Habitat** Primary lowland dipterocarp forest, plantations, gardens, to 200 m. **Behaviour** Has distinctive habit of fanning and wagging tail from side to side; feeds on small fruits and invertebrates. **Voice** Call is a loud, sharp *chip-chip*; song is high-pitched *chit-chit* notes and rattling trills. **Range & status** Indian Subcontinent, SE Asia, Thai-Malay Peninsula, Sumatra, Java, Lesser Sundas, Philippines. **Borneo** Rare resident E Sabah, E Sarawak and E Kalimantan but recent records only from Sabah. **Breeding** Undescribed in Borneo.

BROWN-BACKED FLOWERPECKER
Dicaeum everetti

Identification 10 cm. Large plain flowerpecker with brown upperparts and faintly streaked dull underparts. **Adult *everetti*** Upperparts olive-brown, underparts greyish-brown with faint darker streaking, whitish on throat, central belly and undertail-coverts; iris pale yellow to orange, bill and legs greyish. **Adult *bungurense*** (endemic subspecies) Upperparts darker, underparts greyer with streaking on throat to belly. **Similar species** Thick-billed Flowerpecker is browner, with finer bill, more streaked underparts and faint white spots on tail; note habitat. **Habitat** Secondary lowland dipterocarp forest, kerangas, mangroves, plantations at sea-level. **Behaviour** Feeds on small fruits and invertebrates in forests on poor soils. **Voice** A sharp *chip chip*. **Range & status** Malay Peninsula. **Borneo** Rare resident Sabah, Brunei, Sarawak, W Kalimantan and N Natunas (*bungurense*). **Breeding** Poorly known; one nest described as felty pouch of kapok or grass heads suspended from outer branches of tree 5–6 m from ground.

YELLOW-BREASTED FLOWERPECKER
Prionochilus maculatus

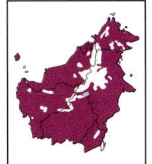

Identification 9–10 cm. Olive-green flowerpecker with distinctive red crown-patch and dark-streaked yellow underparts. **Adult *maculatus*** Upperparts dark olive-green with conspicuous orange-red patch on crown, tail with black tip, moustachial stripe and throat white, malar stripe olive-green, underparts yellow boldly streaked olive-green, centre of belly unstreaked brighter yellow; iris dark red, bill and legs blackish-grey. **Juvenile** Upperparts olive-green, lacks crown-patch, underparts paler olive-green with pale yellow centre of belly; bill yellowish. **Adult *natunensis*** (endemic subspecies) Underparts brighter yellow with darker streaking, throat washed yellow. **Habitat** Primary and secondary lowland dipterocarp and hill forest, plantations, gardens, to 1,250 m. **Behaviour** Forages for small berries and nectar at all levels; usually solitary or in pairs. **Voice** A high-pitched *tswik*. **Range & status** Thai-Malay Peninsula, Sumatra. **Borneo** Common resident throughout, including N Natunas (*natunensis*). **Breeding** Undescribed in Borneo.

CRIMSON-BREASTED FLOWERPECKER
Prionochilus percussus

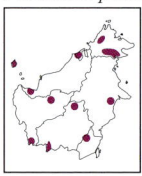

Male

Juvenile

Female

Identification 9.5–10 cm. Slaty-blue flowerpecker with contrasting bright yellow underparts and red patch on breast. **Adult male *ignicapilla*** Upperparts slaty-blue with small bright red crown-patch and prominent white submoustachial stripe, white pectoral tuft, underparts bright yellow fading into pale yellow undertail-coverts with red patch in centre of breast, flanks greyish; iris brown, bill and legs black. **Adult female** Upperparts olive-green with dull orange crown-patch, indistinct whitish submoustachial stripe, throat pale grey, underparts dull olive-green with yellow centre of breast and pale undertail-coverts. **Juvenile** Like female but duller, underparts all olive-grey; bill pinkish. **Similar species** Lacks yellow rump of Yellow-rumped Flowerpecker, which lacks white malar stripes and has smaller red breast-patch, female also with yellow rump, greyer upperparts and no indistinct malar stripes, not known to occur together; female Scarlet-breasted Flowerpecker has white throat, yellowish rump and undertail-coverts, black tail. **Habitat** Primary and secondary lowland dipterocarp and hill forest, peatswamp forest, to 1,050 m. **Behaviour** Forages for small fruits and nectar from lower to upper storey. **Voice** A thin, high-pitched repeated *tsi-tsi-tsee* on an ascending scale (4-6 kHz, 0.7 s) and a longer downslurred *tseee* (7.7-6.7 kHz, 1 s). **Range & status** Thai-Malay Peninsula, Sumatra, W Java. **Borneo** Rare resident, patchily distributed throughout, including N Natunas; rarer in north where once thought to be absent. **Breeding** Undescribed in Borneo.

YELLOW-RUMPED FLOWERPECKER
Prionochilus xanthopygius

Male

Female

Identification 9.5–10 cm. Monotypic. Very like previous species but with distinctive yellow rump. **Adult male** Upperparts slaty-blue with small bright red crown-patch, white pectoral tuft and underwing-coverts, rump bright yellow, underparts bright yellow with red patch in mid-breast fading to pale yellow undertail-coverts, flanks greyish; iris brown, bill and legs black. **Adult female** Crown greyish-blue with small dull orange crown-patch, upperparts greyish-green with yellow rump, sides of face bluish-grey, throat and flanks grey, rest of underparts dull olive-green with yellow centre of breast and pale undertail-coverts. **Juvenile** Wings and tail blackish-brown, rest of upperparts bluish-grey, underparts greenish-grey, rump dull yellow; bill pinkish. **Similar species** Crimson-breasted Flowerpecker has white malar stripe, lacks yellow rump; female Scarlet-breasted Flowerpecker is larger, brighter, has yellow undertail-coverts. **Habitat** Primary lowland dipterocarp to lower montane, peatswamp, heath and kerangas forest, plantations, to 1,760 m. **Behaviour** Forages for small fruits, nectar and small invertebrates at all levels. **Voice** A thin, high-pitched staccato phrase, the first long *seee* note on descending pitch followed by rapid *tsik-tsik-tsik* on rising pitch: *seee tsik-tsik-tsik... seee tsik-tsik-tsik...* (8.1–4.1 kHz), each phrase c.1s. **Range & status** Endemic, common resident in N Borneo (Sabah, Brunei, E Sarawak, E Kalimantan, northern areas of W and C Kalimantan, N Natunas). **Breeding** Possibly February–September; lays 1–2 white eggs.

SCARLET-BREASTED FLOWERPECKER
Dicaeum thoracicus

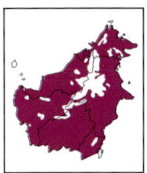

Identification 9 cm. Monotypic. Small black-and-yellow flowerpecker with conspicuous scarlet breast-patch. **Adult male** Black head with small red patch on crown, large scarlet patch on throat and breast bordered on sides and lower breast by broad black band, mantle and back yellowish-green, rump and uppertail-coverts yellow, wings and tail black, rest of underparts yellow; iris brown, bill and legs blackish. **Adult female** Head greyish sometimes with dull olive-yellow patch on crown, upperparts olive-green with yellowish uppertail-coverts, throat greyish, underparts greyish-olive with dull orange breast-patch and yellowish belly. **Juvenile** Like female but underparts greyer, bill pinkish at base. **Similar species** See Crimson-breasted and Yellow-rumped Flowerpecker; female Black-sided Flowerpecker lacks orange and yellow on underparts; female Orange-bellied Flowerpecker lacks black tail and has orange in rump and uppertail-coverts. **Habitat** Primary and secondary lowland dipterocarp, peatswamp and heath forest, coastal vegetation, plantations, to 1,000 m. **Behaviour** Forages for small fruits, especially mistletoes, nectar and small invertebrates at all levels. **Voice** Gives high-pitched insect-like series of *seek* notes and metallic twitter. **Range & status** S Vietnam, Malay Peninsula, Sumatra. **Borneo** Uncommon resident throughout. **Breeding** Undescribed in Borneo.

ORANGE-BELLIED FLOWERPECKER
Dicaeum trigonostigma

BRUNEI 2/6/10

Identification 8 cm. Tiny, distinctively blue-and-orange flowerpecker. **Adult male *dayakanum*** (endemic subspecies) Upperparts dark blue with orange back to uppertail-coverts, throat and upper breast bluish-grey, rest of underparts bright orange, white pectoral tuft; iris brown, bill black, legs and feet dark grey. **Adult female** Upperparts dark olive-brown, rump greenish-orange, throat yellowish-white, breast greyish-blue with rest of underparts washed yellowish. **Juvenile** Like female but underparts entirely greyish, legs and feet paler. **Adult male *megastoma*** (endemic subspecies) Upperparts darker, bill longer. **Similar species** See Scarlet-backed Flowerpecker. **Habitat** Primary and secondary lowland dipterocarp to lower montane forest, peatswamp forest, kerangas, plantations, gardens, to 1,650 m. **Behaviour** Feeds on small fruits, especially mistletoes, and small invertebrates, with nectar constituting important part of diet. **Voice** Call is a series of sharp metallic chips; song is a high-pitched *sip-sip-sip…* (7.5-8 kHz) **Range & status** Indian Subcontinent, SE Asia, Thai-Malay Peninsula, Sumatra, Java, Philippines. **Borneo** Common resident throughout, *dayakanum* on the mainland and adjacent offshore northern islands, *megastoma* on N Natunas. **Breeding** December–September; eggs are bluish-white with tiny brown speckles; nest is small pouch-shaped felty mass of plant fibres and down suspended from outer branches 2.5–9 m from ground.

YELLOW-VENTED FLOWERPECKER
Dicaeum chrysorrheum

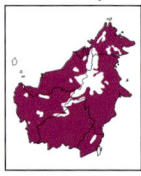

Adult

Identification 9.5 cm. Olive-green flowerpecker with conspicuous streaked underparts and bright yellow undertail-coverts. **Adult *chrysorrheum*** Upperparts olive-green with blackish wings and tail, underparts white boldly streaked blackish-olive with thick malar stripe bordering white throat, undertail-coverts bright yellow; iris whitish, bill and legs dark grey. **Juvenile** Upperparts duller, underparts greyish-white with greyish-brown streaking, undertail-coverts pale yellow. **Habitat** Primary and secondary lowland and lower montane forest, kerangas, plantations, to 1,100 m. **Behaviour** Feeds on small fruits, especially mistletoes, nectar and small invertebrates at all levels. **Voice** Contact call is a harsh *dzeep*; song is described as *chip-a-chip-treee*. **Range & status** NE Indian Subcontinent, SE Asia, Thai-Malay Peninsula, Sumatra, Java. **Borneo** Uncommon resident throughout. **Breeding** Undescribed in Borneo.

PLAIN FLOWERPECKER *Dicaeum minullum*

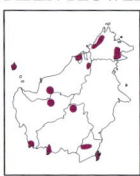

Adult

Identification 8 cm. Tiny, active and very plain flowerpecker with notably thin bill. **Adult *borneanum*** Upperparts brownish-olive, lores and area around eye pale brown, white pectoral tuft, underparts greyish with buffish-white throat and centre of belly, undertail-coverts tinged yellowish-green; iris brown, bill dark grey, legs and feet bluish-black. **Juvenile** Browner with less olive on upperparts. **Similar species** Both Thick-billed and Brown-backed Flowerpeckers have larger, thicker bills; female Black-sided Flowerpecker has olive-green upperparts, whiter on throat. **Habitat** Secondary lowland dipterocarp to lower montane forest, gardens, 200–1,100 m. **Behaviour** Feeds on small fruits and invertebrates in lower levels. **Voice** Call is a sharp *chip-chip* typical of flowerpeckers; song is a high-pitched trill. **Range & status** South India, NE Indian Subcontinent, S China, SE Asia, Sumatra, Java. **Borneo** Very uncommon resident with patchy distribution throughout, including N Natunas. **Breeding** January–July; lays two pale orange-pink eggs with reddish-brown flecks.

KINABALU 11/6/10

BLACK-SIDED FLOWERPECKER
Dicaeum monticolum

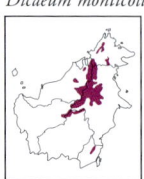

Male

Female

Identification 8 cm. Monotypic. Tiny flowerpecker with diagnostic crimson throat and upper breast in male. **Adult male** Upperparts dark glossy blackish-blue, chin white, throat and upper breast bright crimson bordered blackish, rest of underparts dark grey with buffish wash on lower belly and undertail-coverts, pectoral tufts white; iris dark brown, bill and legs black. **Adult female** Upperparts olive-green with yellowish wash on rump, underparts mostly greyish with whitish throat and buffy flanks, pectoral tufts white. **Juvenile** Like female but underparts darker greyish-olive, male with some crimson on breast. **Similar species** See Plain Flowerpecker. **Habitat** Primary and secondary hill to upper montane forest, kerangas, gardens, 460–2,540 m. **Behaviour** Feeds on small fruits, seeds, nectar and invertebrates, usually at lower levels. **Voice** A high-pitched, metallic *zit*; also a rapid *tsit-tsit* and slurred *tsweet tsweet*. **Range & status** Endemic, common resident in north-central mountain ranges from G. Kinabalu to G. Menyapa and Muller Range, and Meratus Mountains (Sabah, Sarawak and W, E and S Kalimantan). **Breeding** November–February; lays three eggs in nest made of moss and lined with tree-fern fibres decorated with lichen.

192

SCARLET-BACKED FLOWERPECKER
Dicaeum cruentatum

Identification 8 cm. An active, aggressive flowerpecker with distinctive red stripe from crown down back. **Adult male *nigrimentum*** (endemic subspecies) Crown, back and rump bright red, wings and tail black, throat and upper breast black with variable amounts of buffish-white through centre of throat and breast, rest of underparts buffish-white with black flanks; iris dark brown, bill and legs black. **Adult female** Upperparts dark olive-green, lower back and rump bright red, tail black, underparts buffish-olive with greyish-white throat and undertail-coverts. **Juvenile** Like female but lacks red on rump, underparts buffier. **Similar species** Female Orange-bellied Flowerpecker lacks red on back; female Scarlet-headed Flowerpecker has whitish underparts and reddish wash on crown and mantle. **Habitat** Secondary scrub, mangroves, kerangas, plantations, gardens, to 700 m. **Behaviour** Usually in pairs or small groups; feeds on small fruits, especially mistletoes, seeds, nectar and small invertebrates at all levels. **Voice** Call is a short high-pitched repeated *tsit* (8.4 kHz); song is buzzy see-saw *see-sit*. **Range & status** NE Indian Subcontinent, SE Asia, S China, Sumatra. **Borneo** Common resident throughout. **Breeding** December–June; lays single whitish egg with brownish flecks in pocket-shaped nest made of seed heads, kapok and down decorated with bark and leaves and suspended from outer branches 5–9 m from ground.

SCARLET-HEADED FLOWERPECKER
Dicaeum trochileum

Identification 8 cm. Tiny flowerpecker with contrasting scarlet and black upperparts in male. **Adult male *trochileum*** Head to upper breast bright red, upperparts bright red with glossy black wings and tail, rest of underparts greyish-white with darker grey lower breast and flanks, undertail-coverts and pectoral tufts white; iris dark brown, bill and legs black. **Adult female** Upperparts greyish-brown with reddish wash on head and mantle, rump scarlet, wings and tail blackish, underparts greyish with whitish centre of breast and belly. **Juvenile** Upperparts greenish-brown with reddish wash on rump, underparts greyish with paler throat and centre of belly. **Similar species** See Scarlet-backed Flowerpecker. **Habitat** Lowland secondary growth, mangroves, gardens, to 600 m. **Behaviour** Insectivore and frugivore, foraging in lower levels often in small groups of 2–4 birds. **Voice** Call is a staccato, high-pitched *zit-zit-zit*; song is a high-pitched see-sawing double note. **Range & status** S Sumatra, Java, Bali, Lombok. **Borneo** Uncommon resident south eastern Kalimantan. **Breeding** Undescribed in Borneo.

CHLOROPSEIDAE: Leafbirds

Worldwide 10 species, 4 in Borneo. Small family of smallish arboreal, green and yellow birds with blue and black on face and wings and small slender bill, slender body and short legs. Typically forage for insects in the canopy but also feed on fruit and nectar. Sociable, joins mixed feeding flocks. Sexes differ, the male is generally more strongly coloured and marked than female. The vocalisations are melodious incorporating some mimicry.

GREATER GREEN LEAFBIRD *Chloropsis sonnerati*

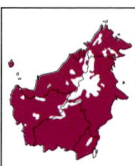

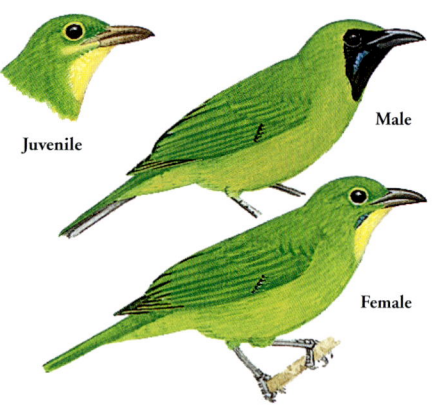

Identification 20.5–22.5 cm. **Adult male** *zosterops* Bright green, slightly darker on upperparts, face and throat black with glossy dark blue malar stripe, sometimes showing blue shoulder-patch; iris brown, bill black, legs and feet bluish-grey. **Adult female** Like male but with bright yellow eye-ring, throat yellow bordered above by faint blue malar stripe. **Juvenile** Like adult female but with yellow submoustachial streak, no blue malar stripe, broader yellow eye-ring. **Similar species** Male Lesser Green Leafbird (nominate *cyanopogon*) is very like Greater but is smaller, male has narrow, indistinct yellow border around black face and throat, female lacks yellow on throat, juvenile lacks yellow submoustachial streak. **Habitat** Primary and secondary lowland dipterocarp, kerangas and peatswamp forest, plantations, to 1,200 m. **Behaviour** Feeds on small invertebrates, fruits and nectar in upper storey; usually solitary or in pairs; joins mixed feeding flocks. **Voice** Song is a complex series of loud, rich, varied notes, *wee-chit-wu-wi-tsit-wu-wee-chit-wu-wu* (2.2–5.8 kHz), rising on *wee* and falling on *chit* notes, interspersed with loud chattering. **Range & status** Thai-Malay Peninsula, Sumatra, Java. **Borneo** Common resident throughout, including N Natunas. **Breeding** Possibly breeds January–October but otherwise undescribed in Borneo.

LESSER GREEN LEAFBIRD *Chloropsis cyanopogon*

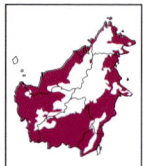

Identification 16–19 cm. **Adult male** *cyanopogon* As Greater Green Leafbird but black face and throat with narrow yellow border. **Adult female** All grass-green with blue malar stripe. **Juvenile** As adult female but lacks blue malar stripe. **Similar species** See Greater Green Leafbird. **Habitat** Primary and secondary lowland dipterocarp and peatswamp forest, plantations, to 600 m. **Behaviour** Often in mixed feeding flocks; generalist feeder, foraging in mid- to upper storey; often occurs with Greater Green Leafbird. **Voice** A quite high-pitched, varied series of notes, *pit-whee-whee-pit-pit* (2.6–3.2 kHz). **Range & status** Thai-Malay Peninsula, Sumatra. **Borneo** Common resident throughout. **Breeding** February–August; one nest found 10–12 m from ground in large tree.

BORNEAN LEAFBIRD *Chloropsis kinabaluensis*

Identification 16–18 cm. Monotypic. **Adult male** Similar to Blue-winged Leafbird but black mask bordered yellowish-green, malar stripe larger and bluer, blue of wings and tail brighter, and bill heavier and hooked. **Adult female** Like male but black mask bordered bluish-green and lacks blue malar stripe. **Juvenile** Lacks black mask. **Similar species** See Blue-winged Leafbird. **Habitat** Primary and secondary lower and upper montane forest, 900–2,200 m; where Blue-winged Leafbird is absent descends to 550 m. **Behaviour** As other leafbirds. **Voice** a high-pitched twittering *prrt...prrt...prrt...* (4.7-3.7 kHz), also a rapidly repeated *chit*. **Range & status** Endemic, common montane resident in north-central ranges from G. Kinabalu to Dulit Range, Usun Apau plateau, and G. Menyapa (Sabah, E Sarawak, E Kalimantan). **Breeding** One possible record from November; otherwise undescribed.

BLUE-WINGED LEAFBIRD *Chloropsis cochinchinensis*

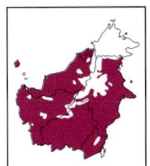

Identification 16–18 cm. **Adult male *viridinucha*** (endemic subspecies) Forehead bright yellow, face to upper breast black forming mask with deep blue malar stripe and bordered by yellow, rest of plumage grass-green with dark cobalt-blue shoulder-patch and outer fringes of secondaries and primaries, upper tail cobalt-blue; iris brown, bill black, legs and feet greenish-grey. **Adult female** As male but lacks mask, has pale blue malar patch. **Juvenile** Like adult female but duller, lacks malar patch. **Adult *moluccensis*** (N Natuna) golden-yellow on nape. **Similar species** Bornean Leafbird lives at higher altitudes and female has black throat; see species account. **Habitat** Primary and secondary lowland dipterocarp, kerangas and peatswamp forest, to 900 m. **Behaviour** Often in mixed feeding flocks; generalist feeder, foraging in mid- to upper storey; usually solitary or in pairs. **Voice** A high-pitched varied *pit-wee-pit-wee…* (3–4.4 kHz) interspersed with harsh *cheet* notes. **Range & status** Indian Subcontinent, SW China, SE Asia, Sumatra, Java. **Borneo** Common lowland resident in Brunei, Sarawak and Kalimantan (absent from Sabah), including the Natunas. **Breeding** One record from November.

IRENIDAE: Fairy-bluebirds

Worldwide 2 species, 1 in Borneo. A small family of medium-sized arboreal birds with red iris and oriole-like structure. The males are strikingly blue and black, the females duller. May be partially nomadic in search of fruiting trees, also consume nectar and insects. Usually in pairs.

ASIAN FAIRY-BLUEBIRD *Irena puella*

Identification 24–26 cm. An unmistakable, startlingly deep-blue and velvet-black bird with red eyes. **Adult male *crinigera*** Forehead to long upper tail-coverts brilliant glossy cobalt-blue (tail-coverts extend almost to end of tail), square tail black, flight feathers black, lores and face to belly black, undertail-coverts glossy cobalt-blue; iris red, bill and legs greyish-black. **Adult female** Plumage all duller turquoise-blue with blackish flight feathers and tail (black tail almost obscured by long blue tail-coverts). **Juvenile** Like female but duller with brownish-tinged wings. **Habitat** Primary and secondary lowland dipterocarp, kerangas and peatswamp to lower montane forest, to 1,600 m. **Behaviour** Often joins mixed feeding flocks; arboreal frugivore but occasionally takes insects; generally feeds in mid-storey. **Voice** A rapid, loud, rollicking 4–10 note *hwit-hwit-hwit-hwit-*, each whipping note rising in pitch (1.5–4 kHz, 5–6 notes/s); call is a similar loud liquid *hwiit* note, but much more drawn-out. **Range & status** Indian Subcontinent, SE Asia, Sumatra, Java, Palawan. **Borneo** Common resident throughout. **Breeding** December–August; one nest was large shallow cup of fibres, rootlets and twigs padded with moss located in fork of tree 7 m from ground, with one pale bluish-green egg with brown and purplish-grey blotches and spots.

SITTIDAE: Nuthatches

Worldwide c.26 species, 1 in Borneo. A small group of short-tailed, small arboreal insectivores with large head and chisel-shaped bill, specialised for gleaning small invertebrates from the bark of tree-trunks and larger branches. Typically with a dark face-mask and bluish upperparts. Undulating flight. Joins mixed feeding flocks.

VELVET-FRONTED NUTHATCH *Sitta frontalis*

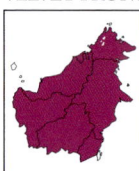

Identification 12.5 cm. **Adult male** *corallipes* (endemic subspecies) Black forehead and lores with narrow black postocular stripe, upperparts violet-blue with black flight feathers, underparts ashy-blue; iris bright yellow with red eye-ring, bill red with blackish tip, legs and feet bright pinkish-red. **Adult female** As male but lacks black postocular stripe. **Juvenile** Upperparts duller and greyer, underparts buffish with rufous barring on undertail-coverts; bill black. **Habitat** Primary and secondary lowland dipterocarp, hill and swamp forest, mangroves, plantations, to 2,200 m. **Behaviour** Usually seen creeping on trunks and large branches of trees in search of small invertebrates in bark; often in mixed feeding flocks. **Voice** Song is a rapid series of loud, high-pitched *sit* notes (6.7 kHz, 7 notes/s); call is a quiet *chweet-chweet*. **Range & status** Indian Subcontinent, S China, Sumatra, Java, Palawan. **Borneo** Common resident throughout, including Maratuas. **Breeding** February–August; lays three whitish eggs with rusty-brown speckles in nest made in small woodpecker or barbet hole.

ESTRILDIDAE: Avadavats, parrotfinches, munias & allies

Worldwide c.139 species, 8 in Borneo. Small finch-like, gregarious and often colourful seed-eaters with short conical bill, slim body, short wings and short pointed tail. Mostly found in tropical areas in open dry habitats. All build large, untidy domed nests. Sexes usually similar.

JAVA SPARROW *Padda oryzivora*

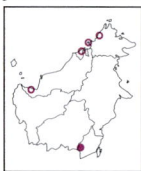

Identification 17 cm. Monotypic. Unmistakable large finch-like bird with conspicuous white cheek-patch and pink underparts. **Adult** Head black with large white cheek-patch, upperparts and breast bluish-grey, uppertail-coverts and tail black, rest of underparts pale pink with white lower flanks and undertail-coverts; iris red, large bill pinkish-red, legs and feet pink. **Juvenile** Crown greyish-brown, cheek and throat pale buffish-white, upperparts pale olive-brown with rufous-brown-tinged flight feathers, underparts buffish-brown with faint dark streaking on breast; bill grey with pinkish base. **Habitat** Grasslands, scrub, paddyfields, at sea-level. **Behaviour** Often in large flocks; relatively sedentary and slow-moving. **Voice** Call is a liquid *tup* and a sharp *tak*; song is a series of bell-like notes followed by a trill, finishing with a long metallic whistle. **Range & status** Java, Bali, Lombok, Sumbawa. Introduced in parts of SE Asia, Subcontinent, Hawaii, Fiji, Americas, S Africa. **Borneo** Introduced, uncommon resident Kota Kinabalu, Kuching, Labuan, Brunei, and S Kalimantan. **Breeding** Observed nesting in building eaves.

DUSKY MUNIA *Lonchura fuscans*

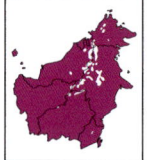

Identification 10 cm. Monotypic. Small, entirely dark munia with contrasting pale grey bill. **Adult** Entirely blackish-brown with darker fringes creating scalloped pattern; iris black, upper mandible black, lower pale bluish-grey, legs and feet bluish-grey. **Juvenile** Duller, lacks dark fringing, bill all black. **Habitat** Primary forest edge, secondary forest, paddyfields, grasslands, young plantations, gardens, to 1,600 m. **Behaviour** Relatively secretive; spends time on ground and low in vegetation; feeds on rice and grass seeds; small parties roost in old nests. **Voice** A shrill *pee pee* and thin *chirrup*. **Range & status** Essentially endemic, with small population on Cagayan Sulu in Philippines; common to abundant resident throughout, including the Natunas. **Breeding** Year-round; lays 1–7 white eggs, nest large ball of grass with side entrance located in crevice in bank or in dense foliage of small tree 1–2 m from ground.

TBR — LIBARAN ISLAND 3/6/10

SCALY-BREASTED MUNIA *Lonchura punctulata*

Identification 10 cm. Small brown munia with distinctive scaly breast. **Adult** *cabanisi* Face and chin dark ginger-brown, upperparts light brown with buffish streaks, uppertail brown with yellowish edging, lower throat and underparts buffish-white with brown scaling; iris dark brown, bill lead-grey, legs and feet bluish-grey. **Adult** *nisoria* Face and breast rufous-brown, upperparts brown with rump grey and finely spotted yellowish-olive uppertail-coverts, underparts white with dark brown fringing giving scaly appearance, vent and undertail-coverts plain whitish. **Juvenile** Buffish-brown, darker on upperparts, belly whitish; bill paler. **Habitat** Paddyfields, long grass, at sea-level. **Behaviour** Usually in small to large flocks in low grass. **Voice** Call is a repeated *kitty-kitty-kitty…*, song a very soft series of fluty, slurred whistles. **Range & status** Indian Subcontinent, S China, SE Asia, Indonesia, Philippines. **Borneo** Race *cabanisi* common recent colonist in W Sabah and Brunei from Philippines, *nisoria* introduced or colonist to southern W, C and S Kalimantan from Java.

Adult *cabanisi*

Juvenile *cabanisi*

TAURAN BEACH RESORT 12/6/10 ??

WHITE-BELLIED MUNIA *Lonchura leucogastra*

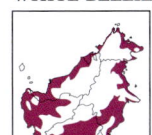

Identification 9.5–11.5 cm. Smallish brown munia with contrasting black and white underparts and yellowish tail. **Adult** *smythiesi* (endemic subspecies) Face to breast and flanks to undertail-coverts blackish-brown, upperparts greyish-brown with buffish streaks, tail dark brown with yellowish fringes, belly to vent white; iris dark brown, bill lead-grey, legs and feet grey. **Adult** *castanonota* (endemic subspecies) Crown and upperparts chestnut, face to breast and flanks to undertail-coverts black, belly to vent white with black spots on upper belly. **Adult** *palawana* Very similar to *smythiesi* but with less brown on flanks. **Juvenile** Duller with less yellow on tail, bill black. **Habitat** Long grass, scrub, overgrown plantations, an extreme lowland specialist to 200 m. **Behaviour** Shy, often solitary or in pairs, sometimes in larger flocks; skulking in long grass. **Voice** Call is a soft *chee-ee-ee* or a high-pitched piping *prrit prrit*. **Range & status** Thai-Malay Peninsula, Sumatra, Philippines. **Borneo** Rare resident throughout, *smythiesi* W Sarawak, *castanonota* S Borneo, *palawana* Sabah, Brunei, and northern E Kalimantan. **Breeding** February–October; nest is large ball of dry leaves located in palms or trees.

Adult *smythiesi*

TURAN BEACH RESORT — LIBARAN ISLAND 3/6/10

CHESTNUT MUNIA *Lonchura atricapilla*

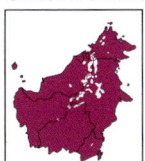

Identification 11–12.5 cm. Medium-sized chestnut munia with distinctive black hood. **Adult** *jagori* Forehead to nape and upper breast black, rest of upperparts chestnut-brown, orange-yellow fringes on uppertail-coverts and tail, underparts rich brown with black belly and undertail-coverts; iris dark brown, bill lead-grey, legs and feet bluish-grey. **Juvenile** Upperparts buffish-brown, underparts buffish. **Habitat** Long grass, scrub, paddyfields, overgrown plantations, to 1,700 m. **Behaviour** Highly sociable, usually seen in large to very large flocks. **Voice** Call is a tinkling, reedy *preep*. **Range & status** NE Indian Subcontinent, SW China, Taiwan, SE Asia, Sumatra, Philippines, Sulawesi. **Borneo** Abundant resident throughout, including the Natunas. **Breeding** Year-round; lays 3–6 white eggs; nest is ball of grasses situated in bushes, trees and palms 0–3 m from ground.

Adult

Juvenile

197

RED AVADAVAT *Amandava amandava*

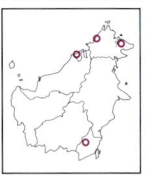

Identification 10 cm. Unmistakable white-spotted red finch-like bird. **Adult male breeding** *amandava* Upperparts brownish-red with white spots on wings and bright red rump, underparts bright red with white spots on breast and flanks, undertail-coverts brown; iris red, bill and legs pink. **Adult female** Upperparts greyish-brown with white spots on wing-coverts, bright red rump, underparts plain brownish. **Adult male non-breeding** Like adult female but white spots on uppertail-coverts and larger white spots on wing-coverts. **Juvenile** Upperparts browner with buffish fringes on wings, bill darker. **Voice** A thin *tsee* and high-pitched squeaks; song is a weak high-pitched warble. **Range & status** Indian Subcontinent, SE China, SE Asia, Java, Lesser Sundas. **Borneo** Rare, introduced W Sabah and Brunei; one record from S Kalimantan.

TAWNY-BREASTED PARROTFINCH
Erythrura hyperythra

Identification 10 cm. Small colourful parrotfinch with bright green upperparts and tawny underparts. **Adult male** *borneensis* (endemic subspecies) Thin black band on front of forehead, forehead to hindcrown bright blue, rest of upperparts bright green with orange rump, underparts orange-buff with greenish wash on sides of breast and flanks; iris dark brown, bill black, legs and feet pink. **Adult female** Upperparts duller green with less blue on head. **Juvenile** Paler, lacks blue on head, bill yellow with black tip. **Similar species** Pin-tailed Parrotfinch has longer, pointed, red tail and blue face. **Habitat** Bamboo stands in primary lower and upper montane forest, paddyfields, 1,200–3,300 m. **Behaviour** Feeds on bamboo seeds, grass seeds, figs, and possibly small insects in small parties. **Voice** Call is a weak thin *prrrt*, repeated; song is described as a very soft series of notes followed by four bell-like notes. **Range & status** Malay Peninsula, Philippines, Java, Sulawesi, Lesser Sundas. **Borneo** Rare resident in north-central mountain ranges from G. Kinabalu to G. Mulu and Kayan Mantarang (Sabah, E Sarawak and E Kalimantan). **Breeding** Undescribed in Borneo.

PIN-TAILED PARROTFINCH *Erythrura prasina*

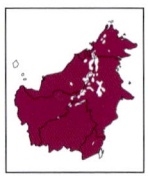

Identification male 15 cm, female 12.5–13 cm. Colourful blue, green, orange-brown and red parrotfinch with long pointed tail. **Adult male** *coelica* (endemic subspecies) Forehead and face to lower breast bright blue, upperparts bright green with long pointed red tail, rest of underparts orange-brown with red patch in centre of belly; iris and bill black, legs and feet pink. **Adult female** Upperparts paler green, shorter tail red, face to centre of breast washed blue, rest of underparts paler without red patch. **Juvenile** Like adult female but duller and paler, lower mandible yellowish. **Habitat** Scrub, paddyfields, to 1,500 m. **Behaviour** Poorly known; usually in small flocks, but recorded in flocks of up to 60 birds descending on rice; also feeds on bamboo seeds. **Voice** Rapid, sharp *tsit-tsit* calls. **Range & status** Thai-Malay Peninsula, Sumatra, Java. **Borneo** Rare resident throughout. **Breeding** Undescribed in Borneo.

PASSERIDAE: Old World sparrows

Worldwide c.40 species, 1 in Borneo. Small to medium-sized seed-eating birds with plump body, large rounded head, short stout deep-based bill, and strong legs. Plumage is generally a combination of black, brown and grey. Typically move with a hopping gait. Most are gregarious, highly vocal and nest in cavities in trees or buildings.

EURASIAN TREE-SPARROW *Passer montanus*

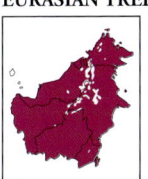

Identification 14 cm. **Adult** *malaccensis* Crown and nape chestnut-brown, cheek white with black spot, upperparts streaked black and rufous, small black bib on buffish-brown underparts; iris and bill black, legs and feet pinkish. **Juvenile** Duller with indistinct black markings on head; base of bill pinkish. **Habitat** Anywhere near human habitation, to 1,400 m. **Voice** Call is a sharp, churring *chip*. **Range & status** Europe, C, N and E Asia, Indian Subcontinent, SE Asia, Indonesia, Philippines. Introduced N America, Australia. **Borneo** Introduced; abundant around human habitation throughout.

EMBERIZIDAE: Buntings

Worldwide c.321 species, 3 in Borneo. A large family of rather finch-like seed eaters with pointed conical bill and long, notched tail usually with contrasting white outer feathers. The flight is strong and undulating. The males are often brightly coloured with seasonal plumage variation, while the females are duller.

BLACK-HEADED BUNTING *Emberiza melanocephala*

Identification 16–18 cm. Monotypic. **Adult male non-breeding** Crown and sides of head blackish with buffish scaling, upperparts chestnut with buffish fringing, darker on wings with pale fringing, underparts buffish-yellow, undertail-coverts pale yellow. **Adult male breeding** Crown and sides of head plain black, back and wing-coverts chestnut, underparts bright yellow. **Adult female** Like male but paler with upperparts buffish with fine darker streaking. **Habitat** In Borneo recorded in grass and paddyfields. **Voice** Calls are a sparrow-like *chleep* and metallic *tzik*. **Range & status** Breeds Eurasia, migrating to Indian Subcontinent. **Borneo** Vagrant, with two confirmed records from Pulau Tiga (Island), W Sabah.

LITTLE BUNTING *Emberiza pusilla*

Identification 12–14 cm. Monotypic. **Adult non-breeding** Lores and crown chestnut with black lateral crown-stripes and eyestripe, rufous ear-coverts bordered black, upperparts brown with grey streaking, throat buffish with narrow brown malar stripe, underparts greyish-white with fine black streaks; iris brown with narrow whitish eye-ring. **Adult breeding** Like non-breeding but chestnut on head brighter, crown- and eyestripes more defined. **Juvenile** Duller with less distinct head markings and streaking. **Habitat** Open cultivated areas, gardens. **Voice** Call is a short sharp *tzit*. **Range & status** Breeds N Eurasia, migrating to Indian Subcontinent, SE Asia, Philippines. **Borneo** Vagrant, with two records from Sarawak and W Sabah.

YELLOW-BREASTED BUNTING *Emberiza aureola*

Identification 15 cm. **Adult male non-breeding** *ornata* Crown chestnut with buffish fringes, supercilium buffish, ear-coverts streaky buffish with dark border, upperparts chestnut with darker streaking and two white bars on wing-coverts, underparts yellow with brown breast-band and streaks on flanks. **Adult male breeding** Face and throat black, breast-band and upperparts plain bright chestnut. **Adult female** Paler, lacks breast-band. **Juvenile** Like female but paler still with indistinct head markings. **Habitat** In Borneo recorded at golf course and paddyfields. **Behaviour** Seen feeding with wagtails in E Sabah. **Voice** Call is a short metallic *tik*. **Range & status** Breeds N Europe, N Asia; migrates to Indochina. **Borneo** Vagrant; four records from W Sarawak, Brunei and W Sabah.

MOTACILLIDAE: Pipits & wagtails

Worldwide c.66 species, 9 in Borneo. Slender, terrestrial insectivores with slender pointed bill, long tail and long legs. Sex and age-related plumage variation pronounced in wagtails, less so in pipits. Frequently bobs head when walking, often wagging tail. Strong and deeply undulating flight, utters distinctive calls in flight. Many are long distance migrants.

RED-THROATED PIPIT *Anthus cervinus*

Identification 14–15 cm. Monotypic. **Adult breeding** Dull reddish supercilium, face and throat to upper breast; ear-coverts often buffish, upperparts pale brown heavily streaked blackish, darker wings and tail edged buff, outer tail feathers tipped white, rest of underparts buffish-white with bold blackish-brown streaking on lower breast and flanks; iris dark brown, bill grey with pinkish lower base, legs and feet pink. **Adult winter** Red less extensive and paler on throat and head. Supercilium buffish-white, underparts all buffish-white with bold streaking, blackish-brown malar stripe. **First winter** Lacks red on head and throat, more boldly streaked on breast, flanks and mantle. Shows two pale mantle stripes (not as distinct as in Pechora Pipit). **Similar species** Crown and upperparts browner than Olive-backed Pipit, upperparts and flanks more heavily dark-streaked, underparts paler; note voice, habitat and behaviour. See also Pechora Pipit. **Habitat** Grasslands, airfields, plantations, to 1,200 m in Kelabit Highlands. **Behaviour** Forages on ground in open areas predominantly for insects; has been recorded in very large groups of 150 or more. **Voice** A short abrupt rich *keep* (7.5 kHz, 0.2 s) usually uttered in flight or when flushed. **Range & status** Breeds Arctic Circle; winters to Africa, N Indian Subcontinent, S China, SE Asia, Sumatra, Philippines. **Borneo** Uncommon non-breeding visitor and passage migrant to Sabah, Brunei, Sarawak and E Kalimantan, September–April; has been recorded throughout year in Brunei.

OLIVE-BACKED PIPIT *Anthus hodgsoni*

First winter

Adult

Identification 15–17 cm. **Adult *yunnanensis*** Crown and upperparts olive-green with bold, fine black streaks on crown and indistinct streaks on mantle; supercilium buff in front of eye and white behind, moustachial area buffish-white and malar stripe blackish, indistinct black spot below white spot on rear of olive-green ear-coverts; flight feathers and tail blackish edged green, underparts white washed buff and boldly streaked black on breast and flanks; iris dark brown, bill greyish with pink lower base, legs and feet pink. **First winter** Upperparts browner, with heavier but poorly defined streaking on underparts. **Similar species** See Red-throated and Pechora Pipits. **Habitat** Secondary forest, narrow roads and tracks, plantations, beaches, to 1,250 m. **Behaviour** Often in small groups; forages unobtrusively for small invertebrates in leaf-litter and grass on ground, flushes as group into nearby trees when disturbed. **Voice** Call is a short, harsh, shrill *tzeet*, note downslurred giving somewhat plaintive quality (7.7–6.2 kHz, 0.2 s). **Range & status** Breeds C, E Palearctic, Japan, China, Indian Subcontinent, winters SE Asia, S China, Philippines. **Borneo** Uncommon non-breeding visitor recorded from Sabah, Brunei, Sarawak and E Kalimantan, probably December–April.

PECHORA PIPIT *Anthus gustavi*

Adult

Identification 14–15 cm. **Adult *gustavi*** Narrow buffish-white supercilium, buffish ear-coverts mottled blackish, black malar stripe connecting to large black patch on sides of throat, throat clear buffish-white, upperparts pale brown heavily streaked blackish with broad whitish fringes on back forming two lines, darker wings and tail edged buff, underparts buffish-white streaked boldly blackish-brown; iris dark brown, bill pinkish with grey culmen, legs and feet pink. **First winter** Streaking on underparts less defined and extending to throat. **Similar species** From duller Red-throated Pipit by heavier, more defined streaking on underparts and distinctive whitish lines on back. **Habitat** In Borneo recorded from coastal forest, mudflats, at sea-level. **Behaviour** Forages on ground in open areas for small invertebrates; flushes into nearby trees when disturbed. **Voice** When flushed utters a thin, high-pitched *tsee*. **Range & status** Breeds N Russia to Kamchatka, NE China; migrates to Philippines, Wallacea. **Borneo** Rare non-breeding visitor to N Borneo (Sabah, Brunei and Sarawak), November–April.

RICHARD'S PIPIT *Anthus richardi*

Adult

Adult worn

First winter

Identification 17–18 cm. **Adult *richardi*** Very like Paddyfield Pipit but larger, supercilium buffish, upperparts more rufous-tinged, underparts paler with more elongate markings on breast. **First winter** More coarsely streaked on breast, narrow white fringes to wing coverts. **Similar species** See Paddyfield Pipit. **Habitat** Grasslands, fields, paddyfields, plantations, airfields, at sea-level. **Behaviour** Forages for small invertebrates on open ground, usually singly or in pairs. **Voice** A short, squeaky *skeep* (5 kHz). **Range & status** C, N and E Asia, Indian Subcontinent, SE Asia. **Borneo** Uncommon non-breeding visitor throughout; migration dates and distribution somewhat unclear owing to confusion with Paddyfield Pipit, which was previously considered conspecific.

LIBARAN ISLAND 4/6/10

PADDYFIELD PIPIT *Anthus rufulus*

Adult worn

Adult

Juvenile

Identification 15–16 cm. **Adult *malayensis*** Crown greyish-brown finely streaked dark brown, long whitish supercilium, darkish eyestripe, buffish-white moustachial stripe, narrow brown malar stripe, underparts whitish with buffish-white breast spotted brown and buffish wash on flanks, upperparts greyish-brown heavily streaked blackish-brown, wings dark brown fringed buffish-white, outer tail feathers white; iris brown, bill pinkish with grey culmen, legs and feet pink. **Juvenile** Buffish lores, upperparts appear scaly, underparts more spotted. **Similar species** Richard's Pipit is larger, has more upright stance, longer legs, markings on breast more elongate and heavier; note voice. **Habitat** Grasslands, fields, paddyfields, plantations, airfields, at sea-level. **Behaviour** Forages for small invertebrates on open ground, usually singly or in pairs. **Voice** A very short, high-pitched, raspy *chwit* (6.8 kHz). **Range & status** Indian Subcontinent, S China, SE Asia, Indonesia, Philippines. **Borneo** Common (Sabah) to uncommon (Brunei, Sarawak, E Kalimantan) resident in N Borneo. One record from C Kalimantan. **Breeding** January–June; nests on ground amongst grass tussocks; elsewhere lays 2–4 dirty white eggs with brownish speckles.

FOREST WAGTAIL *Dendronanthus indicus*

Adult

Identification 16–18 cm. Monotypic. Unusual wagtail with olive upperparts and distinctive black and white wing pattern. **Adult** Upperparts brownish-olive with long buffish-white supercilium, wing-coverts blackish with two bold buffish-white bars, underparts white with double breast-band, black upper band broader in centre, olive-brown lower band usually broken in middle; iris brown, upper mandible grey, lower mandible pink, legs and feet pink. **Juvenile** Browner overall; narrower breast-bands brownish. **Habitat** Primary and secondary lowland forest edges, rocky streams, mangroves, plantations, to 1,000 m. **Behaviour** Usually solitary or in pairs; forages on ground for small invertebrates; avoids open areas; when disturbed flies up into nearby trees. **Voice** Call is a short, metallic *pink* (4 kHz, 0.2 s); song (unlikely to be heard in Borneo) is a see-sawing, two-note *too-wit* repeated quickly 4–5 times, the first note much lower (2.5 kHz) than the second (4.4 kHz). **Range & status** S India, Sri Lanka, N and E Asia, S Japan, SE Asia, Sumatra, W Java. **Borneo** Uncommon to rare non-breeding visitor to N Borneo (Sabah, Brunei, Sarawak).

GREY WAGTAIL *Motacilla cinerea*

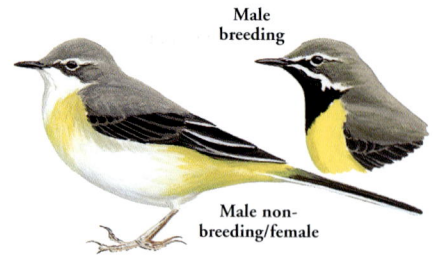

Male breeding

Male non-breeding/female

Identification 17–20 cm. Typical wagtail with all-grey upperparts and contrasting yellow rump, distinctive black throat in breeding plumage. **Adult male non-breeding *cinerea*** Narrow supercilium and throat whitish, upperparts slaty-grey, flight feathers black with white fringes, uppertail-coverts yellow, tail blackish-grey with white outer feathers, underparts yellow and white; iris and bill black, narrow white eye-ring, legs and feet pinkish-grey. **Adult non-breeding female** Underparts paler, throat more buffish. **Adult male breeding** White malar stripe divides black throat and grey sides of head, underparts all yellow. **Adult female breeding** Slightly duller, throat and upper breast whitish with black flecks. **Juvenile** Like non-breeding female but underparts and supercilium more buffish, upperparts tinged olive. **Similar species** See Eastern Yellow Wagtail. **Habitat** Streams in primary and secondary lowland and lower montane forest, fields, roadsides, to 1,600 m but much commoner in hill and montane areas. **Behaviour** Favours narrow wooded rocky streams and roads; actively forages on ground, darting and running for small invertebrates; pumps tail up and down when stationary. **Voice** Varied short sharp notes, *chi-chi…chi-chi…tsi-tsi-tsi…*, the first series of notes lower-pitched (6.8 kHz) than the second (7.8 kHz). **Range & status** Europe, N Africa, Middle East, C, N and E Asia, Indian Subcontinent, SE Asia, Indonesia, Philippines New Guinea. **Borneo** Common non-breeding visitor and passage migrant throughout, from August to early May.

WHITE WAGTAIL *Motacilla alba*

Identification 16–18 cm. Distinctive black, grey and white wagtail. **Adult male breeding *ocularis*** Forehead and forecrown white with narrow blackish eyestripe, hindcrown to hindneck black, upperparts grey with whitish panel on wing-coverts and flight feathers blackish edged white, malar area and sides of neck white, chin to upper breast black, rest of underparts white, tail blackish-grey with white outer feathers; bare parts blackish. **Adult female breeding** Head pattern more greyish. **Adult non-breeding** Brownish wash on crown and nape, underparts all white with black mottling restricted to lower throat and breast. **Juvenile** Duller with less distinct head pattern tinged buff, underparts greyish with brownish gorget. **Habitat** Roadsides, grasslands, fields, paddyfields, parks, to 600 m in Borneo. **Behaviour** Solitary or in pairs; actively forages on ground, darting and running for small invertebrates; pumps tail up and down when stationary. **Voice** A sharp, high-pitched *chi chi chi...* (5 kHz) and bolder, fluty *churi...churi...* **Range & status** Africa, Middle East, Palearctic, Indian Subcontinent, C and E Asia, SE Asia, Philippines. **Borneo** Uncommon non-breeding visitor to Sabah, Brunei and Sarawak, October–April.

Juvenile

Male non-breeding

Male breeding

EASTERN YELLOW WAGTAIL *Motacilla tschutschensis*

Identification 16–17 cm. Typical wagtail with grey or green head and green upperparts. **Adult male breeding *simillima*** Head grey with long narrow white supercilium, rest of upperparts greenish with wings and tail darker fringed yellowish, outer tail feathers white, throat and underparts yellow; iris dark brown, bill and legs blackish-grey. **Adult female breeding** Duller, head greyish-brown, supercilium buffish-white, upperparts brownish, underparts paler. **Adult non-breeding** Like female but browner. **Juvenile** Underparts paler. **Adult male breeding *taivana*** Crown and upperparts green, long broad bright yellow supercilium, broad eyestripe dark green, wings darker with yellow fringes, outer tail feathers yellow, underparts yellow with green wash on flanks. **Adult female breeding** Duller with greenish-brown ear-coverts and paler supercilium. **Similar species** Grey Wagtail in all plumages has all-grey upperparts, longer tail. **Habitat** Mangroves, paddyfields, fields, plantations, roadsides, to 600 m. **Behaviour** Observed in large flocks in Borneo; predominantly seen on passage in September/October and April/May; actively forages on ground, darting and running for small invertebrates; pumps tail up and down when stationary. **Voice** A low-key, monotonous, short *chee* (6 kHz). **Range & status** Eastern Palearctic, SE Asia, Indonesia, Philippines, New Guinea, N Australia. **Borneo** Common non-breeding visitor and passage migrant throughout, September–May; both *simillima* and *taivana* seen on migration but former is more common in Borneo.

Male breeding *simillima*

Male breeding *taivana*

Female *taivana*

STURNIDAE: Starlings & mynas

Worldwide c.114 species, 10 in Borneo. Gregarious and bold small to medium-sized birds with stout body, pointed bill and wings, and strong legs and feet. Plumage typically has some metallic sheen. Some have crests or wattles on the head. Highly vocal with a wide range of calls, often incorporating mimicry. Occupy a wide range of habitats and feed on insects and fruit, some are omnivorous. Most nest in holes in trees, banks or buildings. Sexes usually alike.

CRESTED MYNA *Acridotheres cristatellus*

SEPILOK (ON ROAD) 8/6/10

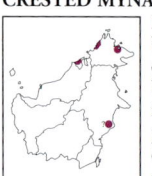

Identification 22–26 cm. Largely black myna with conspicuous short crest on forehead and ivory-coloured bill. **Adult** *cristatellus* All black except for white tips on tail and white wing-patch (conspicuous in flight), undertail-coverts edged white, elongated feathers on forehead forming short crest at base of bill; iris orange, bill ivory-white, legs and feet dull yellow. **Juvenile** As adult but brownish, crest shorter, white on tail-tips and undertail-coverts much reduced. **Habitat** Paddyfields, parks, gardens. **Behaviour** Usually in small flocks; frugivore and insectivore; forages on ground. **Voice** A harsh *churr churr churr*; known to mimic other bird species. **Range & status** C to SE China, N SE Asia, Taiwan. **Borneo** Uncommon but very localised introduced resident in coastal Sabah and Brunei. **Breeding** Undescribed in Borneo.

JAVAN MYNA *Acridotheres javanicus*

Identification 25–26 cm. Monotypic. **Adult** Small tufted crest on forehead, upperparts greyish-black, white wing-patch (conspicuous in flight), underparts paler greyish-black with white undertail-coverts, tail black with white tips; iris lemon-yellow, bill and legs orange-yellow. **Juvenile** Paler and browner overall with streaking on underparts, reduced crest; iris duller. **Habitat** Towns and cities (in Borneo). **Behaviour** Usually seen in pairs or groups; forages for invertebrates on ground. **Voice** Very similar to Common Myna. **Range & status** Java, Bali, S Sulawesi; introduced Malay Peninsula, Singapore, Sumatra. **Borneo** Common introduced resident Kuching, Sarawak, possibly present in S Kalimantan. **Breeding** Undescribed in Borneo.

COMMON MYNA *Acridotheres tristis*

SUKAU RIVER LODGE 9/6/10 ??

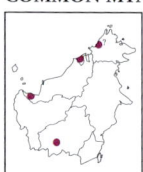

Identification 25–26 cm. **Adult** *tristis* Head, neck and upper breast greyish-black, rest of plumage brown with white wing-patch (conspicuous in flight) and whitish belly and undertail-coverts, tail brownish-black with white tips; in flight underwing-coverts white; iris brown with bright yellow eye-ring, bill and legs yellow. **Juvenile** Head and neck browner; paler and duller overall. **Habitat** Towns and cities (in Borneo). **Behaviour** Usually seen singly or in pairs; forages for invertebrates on ground. **Voice** Highly vocal with wide diversity of calls, including loud fluty whistles, harsh notes and snarling churrs uttered continuously and randomly. **Range & status** Middle East, Indian Subcontinent, SE Asia, Malay Peninsula; widely introduced. **Borneo** Uncommon introduced resident Brunei and Kuching, Sarawak; recent records from SW Sabah, one record from C Kalimantan. **Breeding** Undescribed in Borneo.

SUKAU RIVER LODGE   9/6/10

COMMON HILL-MYNA *Gracula religiosa*

Identification 28–30 cm. Stocky, glossy black myna with conspicuous yellow head-wattles. **Adult** *religiosa* All black with purple gloss except for white wing-patch (conspicuous in flight), and large bright yellow wattle extending from behind eye around nape and separate small wattle below eye; iris dark brown, bill orange-red with yellow tip, legs and feet yellow. **Juvenile** Lacks gloss in plumage, reduced yellow wattles. **Habitat** Primary and secondary lowland dipterocarp forest, peatswamp forest, mangroves, plantations, to 1,200 m on Kelabit Highlands. **Behaviour** Strictly arboreal frugivore and insectivore; usually in pairs or small flocks; nests in tree-hollows. **Voice** Very diverse range of songs and calls; commonest call is a loud, ringing, downslurred *tee-ong* (2.3–1.2 kHz, 0.3 s), first note high-pitched, second descending abruptly. **Range & status** India, SE Asia, Indonesia, Palawan. **Borneo** Common resident in lowlands throughout, including offshore islands. **Breeding** January–October; lays two pale greenish or bluish eggs with dark flecks in nest of grasses, twigs, feathers and bark built in tree-hollow.

ASIAN GLOSSY STARLING *Aplonis panayensis*

BRUNEI   2/6/10

Identification 17–20 cm. Gregarious, all glossy-black starling with conspicuous red eye. **Adult** *strigata* All black with greenish gloss; iris bright red, bill and legs black. **Juvenile** Upperparts brown, underparts buffish-white heavily streaked brown; iris yellow, orange or pink, increasing in intensity with age. **Habitat** Primary and secondary lowland forest, mangroves, gardens, villages, to 200 m. **Behaviour** Primarily frugivorous; breeds and roosts communally in large numbers, often perching in tall dead trees and on powerlines. **Voice** Call is a clear loud metallic note uttered in flight and when feeding. **Range & status** NE India, Myanmar, S Indochina, Thai-Malay Peninsula, Indonesia, Philippines. **Borneo** Abundant resident in coastal areas throughout, including offshore islands. **Breeding** Year-round; lays 2–3 pale blue eggs with brown splotches in nest of dry grass and bamboo leaves located in crown of palms, buildings, tree-hollows or cliffs.

BLACK-COLLARED STARLING *Gracupica nigricollis*

Identification 26–30 cm. Monotypic. Large pied starling with conspicuous yellow eye-wattle. **Adult** Head and underparts greyish-white with broad black collar, upperparts brownish-black with white wing markings and rump, tail dark brown with white tips; iris pale grey with conspicuous yellow eye-patch, bill black, legs and feet yellowish to greyish. **Juvenile** Head and underparts brownish-grey, no black collar, upperparts browner. **Habitat** Grassland, paddyfields, cultivated areas, towns. **Behaviour** Usually forages on ground for insects and other small invertebrates; often in small groups; single bird observed in October in Brunei may have been an escape. **Voice** Song is a complex series of loud coarse notes, *tee tchew tee tchew tchew* (1.8–4.4 kHz). **Range & status** S China, SE Asia. **Borneo** Vagrant; one record from Brunei.

205

WHITE-SHOULDERED STARLING *Sturnus sinensis*

Identification 17–18 cm. Monotypic. **Adult male** Head and back smoky-grey, rump buffish-white, upperwing-coverts and scapulars white, flight feathers black with dark green gloss, throat and breast smoky-grey fading to whitish belly, tail black tipped white (white in plumage often washed pinkish); iris pale blue, bill and legs bluish-grey. **Adult female** Greyer overall, wings brownish with smaller white shoulder-patch. **Habitat** Open areas, paddyfields, towns. **Behaviour** Mainly arboreal insectivore; often in small flocks. **Voice** Soft *preep* in flight; also a harsh *kaar* described when taking flight. **Range & status** Breeds S China; migrates to SE Asia, N Philippines, Taiwan. **Borneo** Vagrant; one specimen from Sarawak, sight records from Brunei and E Kalimantan.

PURPLE-BACKED STARLING *Sturnus sturninus*

Identification 16–17 cm. Monotypic. **Adult male** Head and underparts grey with glossy purple patch on nape and creamy-white centre of belly and undertail-coverts, mantle and back glossy purple, rump pale brownish-white, wings dark green with whitish wing-bars and buffish fringing on flight feathers, tail glossy green; iris dark brown, bill grey, legs and feet greenish-grey. **Adult female** Upperparts mousy-brown, underparts paler, belly white, tail brown with weak purplish gloss, wings brown with whitish wing-bars. **Habitat** Forest edges, rural areas. **Behaviour** Mainly insectivorous; usually in small flocks. **Voice** Call is a soft, harsh *kyu kyu* or *kaa kek*. **Range & status** Breeds in C and E Asia; migrates to SE Asia, Sumatra, Java. **Borneo** Vagrant; one specimen from Sarawak.

CHESTNUT-CHEEKED STARLING
Sturnus philippensis

Identification 16–18 cm. Monotypic. Small, sexually dimorphic starling with conspicuous chestnut cheek-patch. **Adult male** Head buffish-white with reddish-brown cheeks and sides of neck, mantle and back glossy purple, wings black with white wing-bars, rump pinkish-buff, tail black with greenish gloss, underparts pale grey with centre of breast and belly whitish; iris dark brown, bill grey, legs and feet greenish-grey. **Adult female** Head and back brownish-grey, wings dark brown with narrow whitish wing-bars, tail glossy black, underparts buffish-white. **Habitat** Secondary growth, rural areas, plantations. **Behaviour** Often congregates in large flocks; feeds on small fruits and invertebrates. **Voice** In flight utters a soft melodious *chrueruchu*; song has been described as simple babbling of call notes, *kyukyukyururu*; alarm call is a sharp *kya*. **Range & status** Breeds E Siberia, N Japan; migrates Taiwan, Philippines. **Borneo** Uncommon non-breeding visitor to N Borneo (Sabah, Brunei, E Sarawak, S and E Kalimantan), September–April.

206

ROSY STARLING *Sturnus roseus*

Identification 19–22 cm. Monotypic. **Adult non-breeding** Black hood; back, rump and underparts dull pink, wings and tail black, undertail-coverts black edged buffish; iris black, bill brownish-pink with greyish culmen, legs and feet pinkish-grey. **Juvenile** Greyish-brown overall with paler underparts; iris black with pale eye-ring, bill grey with yellow base, legs and feet pinkish-yellow. **Habitat** Woodlands, cultivated areas, towns. **Behaviour** Feeds on insects and small fruits, often on ground; usually in small to very large flocks; single bird in non-breeding plumage was observed in Kota Kinabalu feeding on insects in December 1999. **Voice** Wintering flocks utter continuous excited chatter. **Range & status** Breeds C Asia; migrates to Indian Subcontinent. **Borneo** Vagrant; one record from Kota Kinabalu, Sabah; status uncertain.

TURDIDAE: Thrushes & allies

Worldwide 147 species, 8 in Borneo. A diverse and very large family of medium-sized, mostly terrestrial birds with strong bill, plump body, and longish legs and tail. Feeds on small invertebrates and fruit, typically turning over leaf-litter for small invertebrates or arboreal for insects, fruit and seeds. Many with complex, beautiful songs often given from a high prominent perch. Many are long distance migrants. Most are sexually dimorphic. Flight is strong and undulating.

ISLAND THRUSH *Turdus poliocephalus*

Identification 24–25.5 cm. **Adult *seebohmi*** (endemic subspecies) Head, breast and upperparts blackish-brown; lower breast to belly chestnut, undertail-coverts blackish-brown streaked buff and white; iris brown, eye-ring yellow, bill yellow, legs and feet yellow. **Juvenile** Duller, mottled and streaked buff, ear-coverts mottled rufous, dark malar stripe. **Habitat** Upper montane scrub, 1,500–3,650 m. **Behaviour** Mainly eats small fruits but also insects; semi-nomadic in response to availability of fruit. **Voice** Call is a clucking *chk chk...* and rattling alarm; song is a complex, fluty series of varied musical phrases gradually increasing in tempo and volume (c.2–4.5 kHz). **Range & status** Taiwan, Philippines, Indonesia, New Guinea, SW Pacific. **Borneo** Locally common resident on upper slopes of G. Kinabalu, Trus Madi and Tambuyukon (W Sabah). **Breeding** February–March; lays one egg in compact woven nest of rootlets, leaves, grass, moss and lichen located in fork in thick bush.

EYEBROWED THRUSH *Turdus obscurus*

Identification 21–23 cm. Monotypic. **Adult male** Head and throat grey with white supercilium, small white patch below eye and white chin and malar area, upperparts brown, breast and flanks orangey-brown, central belly and undertail-coverts white; iris black, bill grey with yellow base of lower mandible, legs and feet orange. **Adult female** As male but head olive-brown, more white on throat. **Juvenile** Upperparts brown with bold buff streaks, underparts dull orangey-brown with bold dark brown spots. **Habitat** Primary and secondary lowland dipterocarp to upper montane forest, to 3,300 m. **Behaviour** Often in small flocks of up to 15 birds; eats small invertebrates and fruits, mainly latter in Borneo; forages on forest floor for fallen fruits and visits fruiting trees. **Voice** Commonest vocalisation in Borneo is a short, thin, high-pitched disyllabic *tsit-chee*, first part of note much louder, second part a soft trill (7.5 kHz, 0.9 s). **Range & status** Siberia, Mongolia, E Asia, SE Asia, Philippines, Indonesia. **Borneo** Uncommon non-breeding visitor and passage migrant to Sabah, Brunei and Sarawak, October–April; no records from Kalimantan.

WHITE'S THRUSH *Zoothera aurea*

Adult

Identification 24–30 cm. **Adult** Race uncertain: head and throat finely scaled black and gold, black mark on ear-coverts, upperparts golden-brown broadly scaled blackish, underparts buffish-white with broad crescent-shaped black edging on feathers giving scaly appearance; in flight bold black and white lines on underwing, white tips on outer tail feathers; iris black, bill greyish-black, legs and feet pale pink. **Juvenile** As adult but upperparts more yellowish, underparts spotted rather than scaly. **Habitat** In Borneo found in lowland gardens; elsewhere known from variety of forest habitats. **Behaviour** Shy; forages on ground or in understorey for earthworms, snails, insects, small fruits; most active at dawn and dusk. **Voice** Not described from Borneo; elsewhere a thin unobtrusive *pui* (2 kHz) or *fui* (3 kHz), each note c.1 s. **Range & status** Breeds from Urals east to Siberia, Korea, Japan; migrates to E Himalayas, S China, SE Asia, Indonesia, Philippines. **Borneo** Rare vagrant; three confirmed records from Kota Kinabalu, Manukan Island and Mantanani Island (Sabah).

SIBERIAN THRUSH *Zoothera sibirica*

First-winter male

Male

Female

Identification 20.5–23 cm. **Adult male** *sibirica* Dark slaty bluish-black with broad, long white supercilium, whitish centre of belly, and broad white tips on undertail-coverts; iris and bill black, legs and feet yellowy-orange. **Adult female** Upperparts brown with scaly brown and buff supercilium, streaky buff cheek, buffish throat and dark brown malar stripe, underparts scaly brown and buff grading into buff undertail-coverts. **Habitat** In Borneo records are from montane forest, human habitation and an oilrig; elsewhere variety of forest types with thick understorey. **Behaviour** Shy and secretive; usually solitary or in pairs; eats earthworms, insects, small fruits; forages on ground or in understorey, also visits fruiting trees. **Voice** Undescribed in Borneo; song is a loud, halting series of phrases, *choi chuririri* (1.6–4 kHz), the last note reverberating with strong harmonics. **Range & status** N Asia, Japan, S China, SE Asia, Sumatra, Java and Bali. **Borneo** Rare vagrant; three records from Sabah and Sarawak (two of these offshore).

ORANGE-HEADED THRUSH *Zoothera citrina*

Male

Female

Juvenile

Identification 20–23 cm. **Adult male** *aurata* (endemic subspecies) Head, neck and underparts deep chestnut-orange; throat pale orange, mantle and wings to tail dark grey with white bar on wing-coverts, vent and undertail-coverts white; iris black, bill grey, legs and feet pink. **Adult female** Similar but dark grey on upperparts replaced by olive-grey, wing-bar duller. **Juvenile** Dull dark brown mottled buff, indistinct stripes on face and throat, mottled blackish on breast. **Habitat** Primary and secondary lower montane forest, 750–1,800 m. **Behaviour** Shy and unobtrusive; forages on ground or in understorey for earthworms, snails, insects, small fruits. **Voice** Not well known in Borneo; call is a rattling harsh *chrrr* or *chrrr chrr* (c.5.5 kHz). **Range & status** Himalayas, S India and Sri Lanka, S China, SE Asia, Java and Bali. **Borneo** Rare resident N Borneo, confined to Crocker Range, Sabah and G. Palung, W Kalimantan (one sight record). **Breeding** Possibly breeds November–May but otherwise undescribed in Borneo.

EVERETT'S THRUSH *Zoothera everetti*

Adult

Identification 19–20 cm. Monotypic. **Adult** Head and upperparts greyish-brown, lores and throat buffish-white with grey malar stripe, rest of underparts orangey-brown with white centre of belly; in flight wide white stripe on underwing; iris dark brown, bill blackish-grey, legs and feet pink. **Juvenile** As adult but wing-coverts tipped buff, underparts scaly brown and buff. **Habitat** Primary mossy lower and upper montane forest, recorded 1,200–2,140 m. **Behaviour** Shy and secretive; forages on ground in damp forest for earthworms, snails and insects. **Voice** Poorly known; described as a quiet clicking or muttering in flight; also a sharp *tsak tsak* when alarmed. **Range & status** Endemic, rare resident G. Kinabalu to Dulit Range and Kelabit Highlands (W Sabah and E Sarawak). **Breeding** Undescribed.

CHESTNUT-CAPPED THRUSH *Zoothera interpres*

Adult / Juvenile

Identification 15–18 cm. Monotypic. **Adult** Forehead to hindneck chestnut, lores white, face and throat black with white patch on cheek, throat and breast black grading into white belly and flanks with bold black spots, lower belly and undertail-coverts white, upperparts dark grey with two broad white bars on wings; iris dark brown, incomplete white eye-ring, bill black, legs and feet pink. **Juvenile** Crown to rump streaky chestnut, wings greyish with buffish wing-bars, underparts buffish-chestnut with dark stripes on face and throat, black spots on breast and belly fading to buffish-white undertail-coverts. **Habitat** Primary and secondary lowland dipterocarp forest, more rarely in tree plantations, usually below 400 m but with records to 1,300 m. **Behaviour** Shy and easily overlooked; takes earthworms, snails, insects, small fruits; forages on ground or in understorey. **Voice** Call is a soft but harsh *tsit-tsit* as well as a thin, descending *tsi-i-i-i*; in breeding season a varied sweet song, *too wee too wii-tu* (1.8–6.5 kHz), each phrase quite short (c.1.5 s) and varied with repetition: *wee too trr wi-tu-tu*. **Range & status** Thai-Malay Peninsula, SW Philippines, Java, Lesser Sundas. **Borneo** Uncommon, possibly nomadic, resident in Sabah, rare resident in Brunei, Sarawak and E Kalimantan. **Breeding** April–September; cup-shaped nest 1.6 m from ground in fork of sapling held two pale grey eggs with reddish-brown splotches.

FRUIT-HUNTER *Chlamydochaera jefferyi*

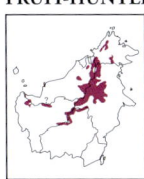

Male / Juvenile / Female

Identification 22.5 cm. Monotypic. **Adult male** Forehead, throat and cheeks pale buffish-brown; crown pale grey; long broad black stripe covering lores, eyestripe and supercilium continues to back of neck; upperparts grey with black primaries, tail grey with black outer feathers and black subterminal band and white tips, large black breast-shield, rest of underparts pale grey; iris dark red, bill black, legs and feet black. **Adult female** As male but grey on upperparts replaced by brown and underparts buffish-brown. Forecrown, ear coverts and throat rufous. **Juvenile** Brown speckled black on head and breast. **Habitat** Primary and secondary lower and upper montane forest, 700–3,200 m. **Behaviour** Arboreal frugivore but also recorded feeding on land snails; unobtrusive; forages in mid-storey and joins mixed feeding flocks; nomadic in reponse to fruiting; usually in pairs but may congregate in large numbers at fruiting trees. **Voice** Only known vocalisation is an easily overlooked soft, high-pitched drawn-out *see-eeep* (7-7.5 kHz, c.1 s) the first part of the note is upslurred before flattening out, repeated at 5–10 s intervals. **Range & status** Endemic, local and uncommon resident in north-central, western and south-western mountain ranges of G. Kinabalu to Pueh Range and Schwaner Range (Sabah, Sarawak, W and C Kalimantan). **Breeding** Probably March–September; otherwise undescribed.

MUSCICAPIDAE: Old World flycatchers including chats, forktails & allies

Worldwide c.300 species, 44 in Borneo. Diverse small to medium-sized short-legged, upright-perching insectivores with large head, broad bill with well developed rictal bristles, short wings and longish tail. Most catch prey by flycatching and sallying out from a perch at different levels in the forest. Some are long distance migrants. Vocalisations very varied. In most species the sexes differ.

BORNEAN WHISTLING-THRUSH
Myophonus borneensis

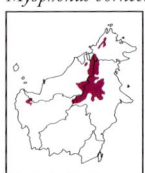

Identification 24–26 cm. Monotypic. **Adult male** Upperparts glossy bluish-black with bright blue spangles in plumage (appearing all black in poor light), bluish sheen on throat and wings, small bright blue patch on shoulder, primaries and lower back to uppertail tinged brown, underparts bluish-black with brown tinge; bare parts all black. **Adult female** All blackish-brown. **Habitat** Primary lower and upper montane forest usually near rocky streams, 650–2,750 m, probably commonest at 1,000–2,200 m, but there are also rare records of birds in limestone areas of extreme lowlands in W Sarawak. **Voice** A harsh, high-pitched *cheet* (5 kHz) can be heard clearly over sound of fast-running water. **Behaviour** Usually solitary; forages near streams around rocks and in leaf-litter for insects and larvae, small invertebrates, frogs and, less frequently, small fruits; frequently fans tail downwards (diagnostic); constructs nest of plant material in rock crevices near streams. **Range & status** Endemic, uncommon resident in north-central and western mountain ranges from G. Kinabalu to Tegora and G. Menyapa (Sabah, Sarawak, E and W Kalimantan). **Breeding** November–April; lays two creamy-white eggs with reddish speckles in nest built in crevice near streams and rivers, often between boulders.

BLUE ROCK-THRUSH *Monticola solitarius*

Identification 20–23 cm. **Adult male breeding** *philippensis* Head, upperparts, throat and upper breast slaty-blue, flanks and thighs blue, rest of underparts chestnut; iris and bill black, legs and feet greyish-black. **Adult male non-breeding** Duller overall with greyish-blue upperparts, breast and flanks fringed paler giving scaly appearance. **Adult non-breeding female** Upperparts ashy-grey barred black and buff, lower back and uppertail tinged blue, underparts buffish-brown with black scalloping; bill brownish-black. **Juvenile** Darker brown, more strongly spotted and scaled buff. **Habitat** Gardens, urban areas, rocky outcrops, coastal areas, to 2,100 m. **Behaviour** Usually solitary; perches with upright stance on buildings, rocks, tree-stumps; diet consists of insects, other small invertebrates, berries, small lizards. **Voice** Usually silent in Borneo but may give a scolding *chk chk chk* (2.7 kHz) and high-pitched *seep* (5.4 kHz); elsewhere, song is a fluid, complex musical *uit uit* whistle. **Range & status** Europe, N Africa, Middle East, Indian Subcontinent, E Asia, SE Asia, Indonesia, Philippines. **Borneo** Uncommon non-breeding visitor to Sabah, Brunei and Sarawak, also recorded from N Natunas and Pulau Laut, S Kalimantan; September–April.

WHITE-BROWED SHORTWING
Brachypteryx montana

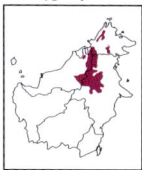

Juvenile

Female

Male

Identification 12–13 cm. A long-legged, short-tailed bird that hops on ground in densely vegetated gullies. **Adult male *erythrogyna*** (endemic subspecies) Upperparts dark blackish-blue, short inconspicuous white supercilium from forehead to above eye, underparts deep blue with paler blue mottling and greyish centre of belly; iris and bill black, legs and feet black. **Adult female** Head and underparts rufous-brown, upperparts blackish-blue with wings tinged brown. **Juvenile** Dark brown mottled buff on head and white streaks on underparts. **Habitat** Gullies and ravines in primary and secondary lower and upper montane forest, 900–3,600 m. **Behaviour** Skulking and elusive, much more often heard than seen; forages for small invertebrates on or near ground, in thick undergrowth, with rapid, darting movements; nest in Borneo is undescribed. **Voice** A beautiful, lilting, very powerful song, a complex jumble of notes, tempo initially slow but gradually increasing in speed and volume (2.6–5.6 kHz, each phrase c.13 s). **Range & status** Himalayas, S China, NW Thailand to N Indochina, Philippines, Sumatra, Java, Flores. **Borneo** Uncommon resident in north-central mountain ranges from G. Kinabalu to Kelabit Highlands and G. Menyapa (Sabah, E Sarawak, E Kalimantan). **Breeding** Possibly breeds around February; otherwise undescribed in Borneo.

RED-FLANKED BLUETAIL *Tarsiger cyanurus*

Male

Female

Identification 15 cm. Monotypic. **Adult male** Upperparts and sides of breast deep blue with paler blue supercilium and rump, underparts white with rufous-orange flanks. **Adult female** Like male but upperparts brown with blue rump to uppertail. **Juvenile** Brown with buffish-orange speckles and streaks, paler on belly, rump to uppertail tinged blue. **Habitat** Open forests on migration. **Behaviour** Arboreal insectivore; perches in lower storey with upright posture. **Range & status** Breeds W(north-east),C,E Palearctic, NE China, N Korea, Japan; migrates to NE India, S China, Taiwan, SE Asia. **Borneo** Rare vagrant with two sight records from Sabah

SIBERIAN BLUE ROBIN *Luscinia cyane*

Female

Male

First-winter female

Identification 14 cm. **Adult male *bochaiensis*** Broad black line from lores to sides of breast and flanks, rest of upperparts dark blue, darker on ear-coverts, rest of underparts white; iris dark brown, bill black, legs and feet pale pink. **Adult female** Lore buffish-brown, upperparts brown with dull blue rump and uppertail-coverts, chin and throat whitish, sides of throat and breast brownish-white with darker scaling, rest of underparts whitish. **First-winter female** As adult female but greater coverts tipped pale, breast more scaly and tail often lacks blue. **Habitat** Primary and secondary lowland dipterocarp, peatswamp and kerangas forest, overgrown plantations, gardens, to 500 m with occasional records to 1,680 m. **Behaviour** Terrestrial insectivore; vibrates tail up and down as it walks inconspicuously on forest floor. **Voice** On non-breeding grounds utters a low-pitched *tek-tek-tek...*. **Range & status** Breeds S Siberia, NE China, Korea, Japan; migrates to SE China, SE Asia, Sumatra. **Borneo** Common to uncommon non-breeding visitor and passage migrant throughout, from mid-September to mid-April.

SIBERIAN RUBYTHROAT *Luscinia calliope*

Identification 16 cm. Monotypic. **Adult non-breeding male** (darker in breeding adult) Lores and ear-coverts black, short supercilium and moustachial stripe white, black malar stripe borders bright red chin and throat, crown and upperparts brown, breast washed greyish, darker in breeding adult, rest of underparts brownish, paler on belly; irs dark brown, bill dark grey, legs and feet pinkish-brown. **Adult female** Like adult male but duller, throat whitish, supercilium and malar stripe indistinct. **Habitat** On migration favours scrub, thickets, overgrown gardens. **Range & status** Breeds Siberia, N Japan, NE China; migrates to NE India, S China, SE Asia, Philippines. **Borneo** Rare vagrant; recorded once from Brunei and once from G. Kinabalu, Sabah.

Male non-breeding

Female

NORTHERN WHEATEAR *Oenanthe oenanthe*

Identification 15 cm. **Adult male breeding** *oenanthe* Crown to back grey, broad black patch through eye from lores to ear-coverts, wings black, rump white, tail black with white base to outer feathers, underparts white with pale orange wash on throat and breast. **Adult male non-breeding** As breeding male but upperparts sandy-brown, cinnamon tinge on throat and sides of neck. **Adult female** Upperparts sandy-brown with paler supercilium and dark brown edging on flight feathers, tail dark brown with white base to outer tail feathers, breast pale cinnamon. **First winter** As female but with paler edges to flight feathers, more extensive cinnamon below and tail tipped white. **Habitat** In Borneo recorded at racecourse, an oilrig, and from Kelabit Highlands (1,100 m). **Behaviour** Forages on ground for small invertebrates; upright posture. **Range & status** Breeds Europe, NW Africa, C and N Asia, N America, Greenland; migrates to Africa, Middle East, NW India.

Male breeding

Female

Borneo Rare vagrant; four records from Sabah and Sarawak, October–March.

EASTERN STONECHAT *Saxicola maurus*

Identification 14 cm. **Adult male non-breeding** *stejnegeri* Crown and rest of upperparts blackish with buffish streaks, lores and ear-coverts flecked black, wings black edged buffish with indistinct whitish patch on wing-coverts, uppertail-coverts white with broad buffish-orange tips, tail black with buffish tips, throat and sides of neck white, rest of underparts pale rufous with paler undertail-coverts; iris black, bill and legs black. **Adult male breeding** Head and throat black, upperparts black with rufous-buffish fringing and whitish rump. **Adult female** Like non-breeding male but lores and ear-coverts speckled black and buffish, upperparts brown streaked blackish-brown, uppertail-coverts plain cinnamon. **Similar species** Female Pied Bushchat is much darker, has dark streaking and rufous uppertail-coverts, lacks white on wing. **Habitat** Marshes, grasslands, paddyfields. **Behaviour** Perches in open on prominent low bushes and grass stems from where it sallies out to catch flying insects; typically solitary; wags tail from side to side. **Range & status** Breeds E Palearctic, N Indian Subcontinent; migrates to Middle East, NE Africa, Indian Subcontinent, China, Taiwan, northern SE Asia, Sumatra, Philippines. **Borneo** Rare vagrant; recorded from W Sabah, Brunei, Sarawak, from December to early April.

Male non-breeding/immature

Male breeding

Female non-breeding

PIED BUSHCHAT *Saxicola caprata*

Identification 14 cm. **Adult male breeding** All black with contrasting white wing-patch, uppertail-coverts and belly. **Adult male non-breeding** Generally blackish with brownish fringing, broad white wing-stripe and undertail-coverts, rump and uppertail-coverts white with rufous tips; iris black, bill and legs black. **Adult female** Upperparts greyish-brown with rufous uppertail-coverts, underparts warm brown with paler throat (more streaked in breeding plumage), belly and undertail-coverts tinged rufous, lacks wing-stripe. **Juvenile** Mottled pale grey and grey with rufous edging on wings. **Similar species** See Eastern Stonechat. **Habitat** Paddyfields, grasslands, open areas, recorded at 1,550 m in Borneo. **Behaviour** Perches in open on prominent low bushes and grass stems from where it sallies out to catch flying insects. **Range & status** C Asia, Indian Subcontinent, SW China, SE Asia, Java, Bali, Sulawesi, Lesser Sundas, Philippines, New Guinea. **Borneo** Rare vagrant; recorded once from Sabah.

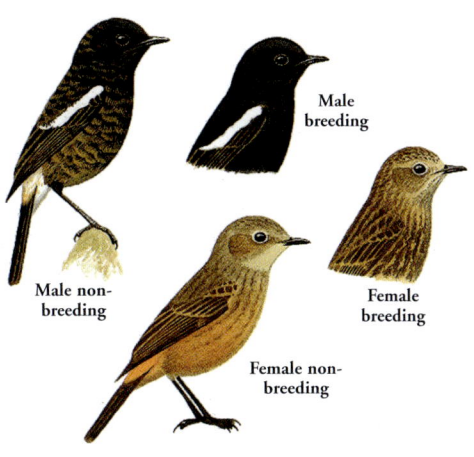

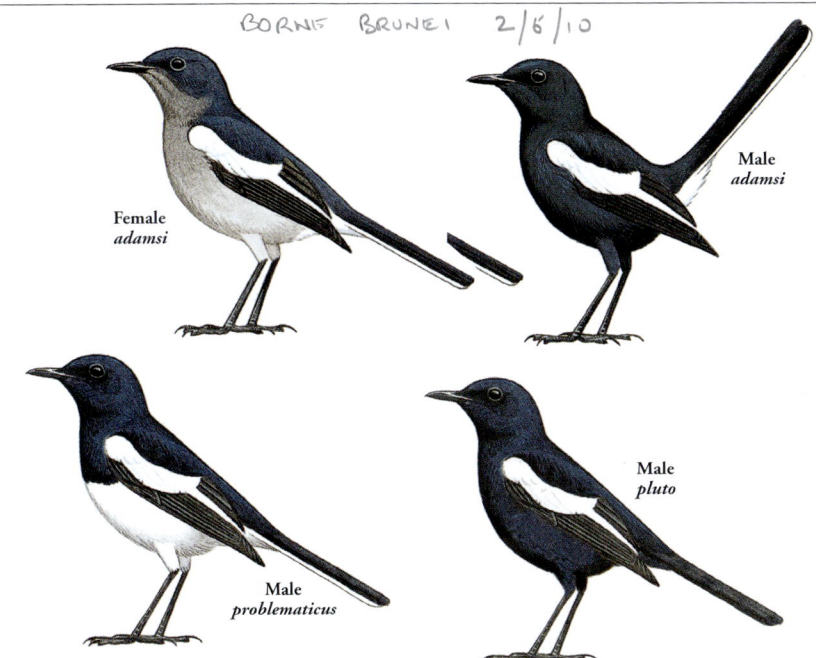

ORIENTAL MAGPIE-ROBIN *Copsychus saularis*

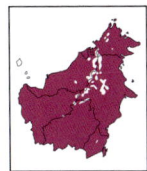

Identification 20 cm. **Adult male *adamsi*** (endemic subspecies) Upperparts glossy black with broad white stripe on centre of wing, tail black with white outer tail feathers, underparts black with white undertail-coverts; iris dark brown, bill and legs black. **Adult female** Upperparts greyish-black, underparts grey. **Adult male *problematicus*** (endemic subspecies) As *adamsi* but chin to breast glossy black with belly and undertail-coverts white. **Adult female** Upperparts black. **Adult male *pluto*** (endemic subspecies) As *adamsi* but underparts all black, tail all black. **Adult female** Upperparts black, underparts all grey. **Juvenile** Breast mottled buffish. **Habitat** Coastal woodlands, mangroves, cultivated areas, villages, gardens, plantations, to 1,450 m. **Behaviour** Feeds on invertebrates and occasionally small vertebrates such as geckos; pounces on prey on ground from prominent perch; usually seen in pairs; aggressive and very territorial. **Voice** Powerful and varied song with series of plaintive whistles on different pitches, inflected up and down (2-5.5 kHz); known to mimic other birds including Plaintive Cuckoo, Pied Fantail and Yellow-bellied Prinia. **Range & status** Indian Subcontinent, S China, SE Asia, Sumatra, Java, Bali, Philippines (except Palawan). **Borneo** Common resident throughout; *adamsi* from N Borneo (Sabah and Banggi Island), *problematicus* from SW and W Borneo (Sarawak and S and W Kalimantan), *pluto* from E Borneo (E and C Kalimantan and Maratuas). **Breeding** Year-round; lays 3–4 pale glossy greenish-blue eggs with reddish-brown blotches in large loose nest of fine roots hidden in thick branches or in tree cavity.

SUKAU RIVER LODGE   9/6/10

WHITE-CROWNED SHAMA *Copsychus stricklandii*

Identification 27 cm. **Adult male** *stricklandii* Upperparts glossy black with prominent white stripe over crown from upper forehead to nape and white lower back to uppertail-coverts, black tail long and graduated with white outer feathers, throat to upper breast glossy black sharply delineated from rufous underparts; iris black, bill black, legs and feet pinkish. **Adult female** Slightly duller, tail shorter. **Adult male** *barbouri* As *stricklandii* but no white in tail, longer wings and tarsi. **Juvenile** Upperparts sooty-brown with forehead and ear-coverts speckled buffish, wing-coverts with rufous spots and tips, chin and throat pale tawny, warm brown on breast with sooty edging giving scaly pattern, rest of underparts whitish. **Habitat** Primary and secondary lowland dipterocarp, peatswamp and riparian to lower montane forest, coastal vegetation, kerangas, mangroves, plantations, to 1,200 m. **Behaviour** Stays in thick cover; hops and runs with short flights in understorey where it gleans foliage for insects, occasionally taking berries; usually solitary; cocks and fans tail when giving alarm call. **Voice** Extraordinarily rich, melodious song with bubbly quality is highly varied and incorporates some mimicry, quite low-pitched (c.1–2.7 kHz), consisting of strings of two- or three-note phrases, bee-baw-bee, and long chuckles; tchak alarm call sounds like breaking stick. **Range & status** Endemic, *stricklandii* common resident Sabah and northern E Kalimantan; *barbouri* Maratua Islands. **Breeding** January–October; builds nest of fibres, rootlets and dead leaves in holes in trees 2.5–4 m from ground, laying 2–3 pale green eggs heavily flecked with light brown and sparse purplish spots.

Male *stricklandi*

WHITE-RUMPED SHAMA *Copsychus malabaricus*

Identification 27 cm. **Adult male** *suavis* (endemic subspecies) As White-crowned Shama but lacks white on crown. **Adult female** Slightly duller, tail shorter. **Juvenile** As White-crowned Shama. **Habitat** Primary and secondary lowland dipterocarp, peatswamp and riparian to lower montane forest, coastal vegetation, kerangas, mangroves, plantations, to 1,200 m. **Behaviour** as White-crowned Shama. **Voice** As White-crowned Shama. **Range & status** Indian Subcontinent, S China, SE Asia, Sumatra, Java. **Borneo** Common resident including offshore islands, *suavis* Brunei, Sarawak, Kalimantan; *tricolor* Natuna and Anamba Islands (Sumatra, W Java, Karimata Islands). Breeding as White-crowned Shama. **Note** Ranges of *C. stricklandii* and *C. malabaricus* overlap in south W Sabah and far E Sarawak.

Male   Female   Juvenile

RUFOUS-TAILED SHAMA *Trichixos pyrropyga*

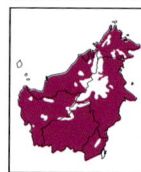

Identification 20 cm. Monotypic. **Adult male** Upperparts sooty-black with short white spot over eye, rump to tail rufous, apical third of tail black, chin to upper breast grey, rest of under-parts rufous with paler belly; iris brown, bill black, legs and feet pinkish. **Adult female** Upperparts brown with buffish mottling on ear-coverts, rump and tail as male, underparts whitish with cinnamon wash on throat to upper breast and flanks. **Juvenile** Like female but with buffish-orange streaks on head and back and spots on wing-coverts, throat and breast duller with dark streaks. **Habitat** Primary lowland dipterocarp, peatswamp and kerangas to hill forest, to 900 m. **Behaviour** Shy; usually solitary; gleans foliage in lower to upper storey for small invertebrates. **Voice** Two to four loud, rich notes, *weet-weet-weet-wee*, with mournful quality, alternating between series of upslurred then downslurred notes from c.1.4–2.2 kHz.

Male   Juvenile   Female

Range & status Thai-Malay Peninsula, Sumatra. **Borneo** Uncommon resident throughout. **Breeding** Possibly breeds February–June but otherwise undescribed in Borneo.

CHESTNUT-NAPED FORKTAIL *Enicurus ruficapillus*

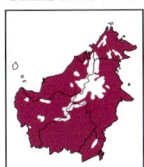

Identification 18 cm. Monotypic. **Adult male** Forehead white bordered by black lores and narrow frontal band, crown to upper neck bright chestnut, mantle and upper back black, lower back to uppertail-coverts white, wings black with bold white horizontal line, long, deeply forked tail barred black and white with broad white tips, chin and throat black, rest of underparts white with marbled black scaly pattern on breast; iris and bill black, legs and feet pinkish-white. **Adult female** Like male but chestnut extends from crown to lower back. **Juvenile** Like female but duller, throat and cheeks white with black line from lores below eye to sides of face and thin black malar stripe, breast pattern smudgy. **Habitat** Shady streams in primary lowland dipterocarp and hill forest, to 1,250 m. **Behaviour** Shy and easily disturbed; forages for small invertebrates on rocks in undisturbed, fast-flowing streams; intolerant of disturbed forest. **Voice** Call is a pentrating, high-pitched monotone whistle *kreeee*; also a loud, high-pitched two- to four-note *kee-sweet-keet-kee* (4.8–6.6 kHz), the second note sharply downslurred. **Range & status** Thai-Malay Peninsula, Sumatra. **Borneo** Common resident throughout. **Breeding** Possibly breeds February–May but otherwise undescribed in Borneo.

WHITE-CROWNED FORKTAIL *Enicurus leschenaulti*

Identification 20–23 cm. **Adult frontalis** Steep forehead to hindcrown bright white, face to upper back and chin to lower breast black sharply demarcated from white belly to undertail-coverts, lower back and uppertail-coverts white, wings black with bold white horizontal line and white tips on inner secondaries, long, deeply forked tail barred black and white; iris and bill black, legs and feet pinkish-white. **Juvenile** Duller, tinged brownish, no white on crown, pale shafts on breast, tail shorter. **Habitat** Fast-flowing rocky streams in primary lowland dipterocarp forest. **Behaviour** Shy, restless and easily disturbed; when disturbed flies rapidly out of view while uttering loud call; actively forages for small invertebrates on rocks and banks of well-vegetated streams; occasionally on narrow roads especially after rain; intolerant of disturbed forest. **Voice** Call is a loud high grating *screeee* (5 kHz, c.1 s). **Range & status** Thai-Malay

Peninsula, Sumatra, Java, Bali. **Borneo** Common resident throughout in lowlands. **Breeding** February–July; lays two white eggs with reddish-brown spots in cup-shaped nest of loosely woven fibres located near streambank, usually between boulders or tree-roots.

BORNEAN FORKTAIL *Enicurus borneensis*

Identification 23 cm. Monotypic. **Adult** As White-crowned Forktail but larger with longer tail, white on crown does not extend as far back. **Juvenile** As White-crowned Forktail, slightly more prominent pale shaft streaks on dark breast. **Habitat** Fast-flowing rocky streams in lower to upper montane forest, 900–1,950 m. **Behaviour** As White-crowned Forktail. **Voice** As White-crowned Forktail. **Range & status** Endemic, montane areas of Sabah to E Sarawak and W Kalimantan. **Breeding** Not well known.

PALE BLUE FLYCATCHER *Cyornis unicolor*

Identification 16.5–18 cm. **Adult male** *harterti* Upperparts bright pale blue with paler blue supercilium and blackish lores, chin to breast paler blue, rest of underparts greyish-blue; iris dark brown, bill black, legs and feet greyish-black. **Adult female** Upperparts brown with rufous-brown edges to wings and tail, underparts buffish-brown, paler on centre of belly to undertail-coverts; narrow pale eye-ring. **Juvenile** Upperparts olive-brown with buffish spots and speckles, chin to breast brownish with heavy dark bars and scales, paler on belly. **Similar species** See Verditer Flycatcher. **Habitat** Primary lowland dipterocarp forest, to 400 m with some records up to 1,400 m. **Behaviour** Canopy-dweller in primary forest, possibly therefore much overlooked; hawks insects from prominent perch. **Voice** Song is a rich, melodious series of notes ending with harsh long note, *di-ti-di-ti-ti-tee-too-too chiii* (3 kHz, c.2.2 s). **Range & status** E Himalayas, NE India, S China, N Indochina, Thai-Malay Peninsula, Sumatra, Java. **Borneo** Uncommon to rare resident in Sabah, Brunei, Sarawak and W and E Kalimantan. **Breeding** Possibly breeds February–May but otherwise undescribed in Borneo.

SUKAU RIVER LODGE 8/6/10

MALAYSIAN BLUE FLYCATCHER *Cyornis turcosus*

Identification 13–14 cm. **Adult male** *turcosus* (endemic subspecies) Lores blackish, upperparts blue with shining blue forehead and supercilium and rump to uppertail, chin and throat bright blue, breast and flanks rufous-orange fading to whitish belly and undertail-coverts; iris dark brown, bill black, legs and feet pinkish-grey. **Adult male** *rupatensis* Breast and flanks deeper rufous-orange. **Adult female** Like adult male but upperparts duller blue, throat buffish, rest of underparts paler. **Juvenile** Upperparts greyish-brown heavily spotted buffish-orange, flight feathers and tail edged bluish, buffish underparts scaled and barred dark brown. **Similar species** Large-billed Blue Flycatcher has less extensive pale blue on forehead, black chin, pale orange throat, and duller blue wing-coverts. **Habitat** Primary and secondary lowland dipterocarp and riparian forest, to 900 m. **Behaviour** In Borneo usually seen near rivers and waterways where it forages from exposed low perches for flying insects; solitary or in pairs. **Voice** Song is a rather thin, high-pitched *tsee-tsi-tsi-tseee*, the last note slightly higher (3.3–4 kHz, c.1.5 s), continually repeated; call is a harsh *tik-tk-tk*. **Range & status** Malay Peninsula, Sumatra. **Borneo** Common resident throughout, *turcosus* in E Borneo, *rupatensis* in W Borneo. **Breeding** January–September; lays two bluish-grey eggs with reddish-brown markings in shallow mossy cup-shaped nest 1 m or higher from ground.

BORNEAN BLUE FLYCATCHER *Cyornis superbus*

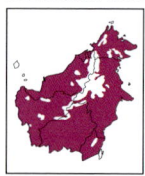

Identification 15 cm. Monotypic. **Adult male** Face and ear-coverts black, upperparts deep blue with bright shining blue forehead and supercilium to nape, lower back to rump bright shining blue, chin and throat pale orange, breast and flanks deeper orange fading to whitish belly and undertail-coverts; iris and bill black, legs and feet pinkish to dark grey. **Adult female** Forehead and short supercilium pale rufous, narrow pale eye-ring, upperparts brown with bright rufous rump to uppertail, flight feathers fringed rufous, chin and throat pale orange, breast orange-brown, rest of underparts whitish. **Juvenile** Undescribed. **Similar species** More extensive bright shining blue on head and back than any other blue flycatcher. **Habitat** Primary and secondary lowland dipterocarp and hill forest, to 1,000 m. **Behaviour** Favours interior forest, often near waterways; usually solitary or in pairs; sallies in pursuit of flying insects from perch in lower to mid-storey. **Voice** Song is a thin tinkling high-pitched phrase of five notes, *wee-ti-wee-ti-wi*, second note highest, fourth lowest (alternating between 4.8–3 kHz and 5.5–4 kHz, each phrase c.1 s), phrase interspersed with shorter, three-note *wee-tee-wi* phrases with emphasis on second note. **Range & status** Endemic, uncommon resident throughout. **Breeding** Possibly breeds February–June but otherwise undescribed.

LARGE-BILLED BLUE FLYCATCHER
Cyornis caerulatus

Identification 14 cm. **Adult male** *caerulatus* (endemic subspecies) Lores and cheeks blackish-blue, upperparts dark blue with brighter blue forehead, chin and sides of throat blackish-blue, centre of throat pale orange grading to deep orange breast, belly paler, undertail-coverts whitish; iris black, relatively large bill black, legs and feet greyish-black. **Adult female** *caerulatus* Upperparts brown, sometimes with blue wash on wing-coverts, lower back to tail dull blue, underparts buffish with pale orange breast-band. **Adult male** *rufifrons* (endemic subspecies) Rufous wash on forehead, underparts deeper orange. **Adult female** *rufifrons* Bluer wing-coverts. **Juvenile** Undescribed. **Similar species** See Mangrove and Malaysian Blue Flycatchers. **Habitat** Primary lowland dipterocarp forest; lowland specialist to 500 m. **Behaviour** Favours interior forest, avoiding riparian habitats; forages in lower storey from prominent perch, sallying to catch insects on wing; often in pairs. **Voice** Song is a varied series of pleasant, mellow phrases *whu-whi-whi-whi*, first note lower-pitched, the next three on an even pitch (2.4-3 kHz, 0.7 s); also a modulated three-note *phwu-phi-phee* the first note lowest-pitched, the second highest and the third falling (1.8-4.4 kHz, 1.3 s), these interspersed with various, unhurried rising and falling notes around 2-3.5 kHz. **Range & status** Sumatra. **Borneo** Common resident throughout (status in S and W Kalimantan uncertain), *rufifrons* from W Borneo. **Breeding** Possibly breeds February–July but otherwise undescribed in Borneo.

Male *rufifrons*
Female *rufifrons*
Male *caerulatus*
Female *caerulatus*

HILL BLUE FLYCATCHER *Cyornis banyumas*

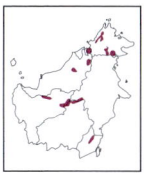

Identification 14–15.5 cm. **Adult male** *coeruleatus* (endemic subspecies) Lores to sides of face and chin black, upperparts dark blue with bright pale blue forehead and supercilium in front of eye and bright pale blue rump, throat to lower breast and flanks rufous-orange fading to greyish-white belly and undertail-coverts; iris dark brown, bill black, legs and feet grey to pinkish-grey. **Adult female** Upperparts warm brown with rufous-brown rump and tail, underparts pale rufous-orange fading to whitish belly and undertail-coverts; narrow buffish eye-ring. **Juvenile** Upperparts dark brown with buffish spots, throat and breast buffish with dark scaling, rest of underparts whitish with greyish mottling. **Similar species** see Mangrove Blue Flycatcher **Habitat** Primary hill and lower montane forest, usually 900–1,100 m but down to sea-level where Mangrove Blue Flycatcher is absent, usually replacing Bornean Blue Flycatcher at higher elevations. **Behaviour** Usually solitary; forages quietly from concealed perch in lower to mid-storey. **Voice** A melodious, lilting, loud song of 5–7 notes, *cheet-chee-chee-chew…* (5–3 kHz, c.1 s). **Range & status** E Himalayas, SC China, SE Asia, Java. **Borneo** Uncommon to rare resident in Sabah, Brunei, Sarawak and W Kalimantan; common resident in Meratus Mountains, S Kalimantan. **Breeding** Poorly known; two glossy pale olive-buff eggs covered with soft brown flecks collected in March.

Male
Female
Juvenile

MANGROVE BLUE FLYCATCHER *Cyornis rufigastra*

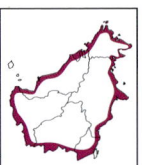

Female
Male

Identification 14–15 cm. **Adult male** *rufigastra* Lores and cheeks black, upperparts deep blue with paler blue forehead and supercilium, flight feathers edged black, chin black, throat and breast to upper flanks orange grading to paler lower flanks and whitish undertail-coverts; iris and bill black, legs and feet pinkish-grey. **Adult female** Like male but with distinctive pale whitish forehead and lores, pale whitish chin. **Juvenile** Upperparts dark brown with buffish spots and streaks, underparts paler with dark scaling, vent whitish. **Similar species** Large-billed Blue Flycatcher has brighter blue forehead and lower back and rump; Hill Blue Flycatcher has brighter, more extensive blue on forehead. **Habitat** Coastal kerangas and peatswamp forest, mangroves, coastal forest. **Behaviour** Feeds on insects, sallying from perch in lower storey; usually solitary or in pairs. **Voice** A melodious complex warbling song, *dee-doo-di-do-deee…* and other variations, last note rising (2.5–3.2 kHz); call is a sharp, rapid but quite soft *ch-ch-ch-ch…* **Range & status** Thai-Malay Peninsula, Sumatra, Java, Sulawesi, Philippines. **Borneo** Common resident in coastal areas throughout including offshore islands. **Breeding** February–August; nest is shallow cup composed of fibres, rootlets and dead leaves, often at base of palm-frond where it joins trunk.

WHITE-TAILED FLYCATCHER *Cyornis concretus*

Female
Male

Identification 18–19 cm. **Adult male** *everetti* (endemic subspecies) Forehead and area over eye bright blue, lores black, rest of upperparts dark ashy-blue with blackish flight feathers, tail dark blue with no white on outer feathers, chin to breast and flanks ashy-blue, belly and undertail-coverts white; iris and bill black, legs and feet pinkish. **Adult female** Lores buffish, upperparts brown, tail rufous-brown with some white at base of outer feathers, throat and breast pale brown with white triangle on lower throat, rest of underparts greyish-white. **Juvenile** Brownish with buffish and rufous spots and speckles on upperparts, darker barring and scaling on underparts. **Similar species** See Blue-and-white Flycatcher. **Habitat** Primary hill and lower montane forest, 150–1,700 m but usually above 600 m. **Behaviour** Gleans and hawks for insects in lower to mid-storey; usually solitary or in pairs. **Voice** Call is a soft, slightly upslurred, drawn-out *pwee…* (3–3.5 kHz, 0.5 s); extralimitally, song is a series of rich, penetrating notes with variable phrases, often with an introductory *tee-too*, first note rising, second falling (4.3–2.8 kHz). **Range & status** NE India, NW Myanmar, S China, N Indochina, Thai-Malay Peninsula, Sumatra. **Borneo** Uncommon sub-montane resident Sabah, E Sarawak and W, C and E Kalimantan. **Breeding** Possibly breeds February–June but otherwise undescribed in Borneo.

BLUE-AND-WHITE FLYCATCHER
Cyanoptila cyanomelana

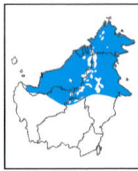

Immature male
Male
Female

Identification 16–17 cm. **Adult male** *cyanomelana* Sides of face to upper breast and flanks black, rest of upperparts rich deep cobalt-blue with primaries edged black, white base on outer tail feathers, rest of underparts white; iris and bill black, legs and feet brownish-black. **Adult female** Upperparts greyish-brown, cheeks lightly streaked buffish, warmer brown on rump, wings darker with rufous-brown edging, centre of lower throat pale buffish-white, breast pale brown clearly demarcated from white belly and undertail-coverts. **Immature** Male like adult female but with blue on scapulars, wings, back and uppertail-coverts. **Similar species** White-tailed Flycatcher is not as deep blue, has blue face, and lacks white in tail. **Habitat** Primary and secondary lowland dipterocarp to lower montane forest, favouring submontane forest to 1,550 m. **Behaviour** Feeds on insects and berries; typically sallies from perch in mid-storey to catch insects on wing; also gleans foliage. **Voice** Generally silent on non-breeding grounds. **Range & status** Breeds Siberia, NE China, Korea, Japan; migrates to Taiwan, Indochina, Sumatra, Java, Philippines. **Borneo** Uncommon non-breeding visitor and passage migrant N Borneo (Sabah, Sarawak, E and C Kalimantan), from late October to late April.

VERDITER FLYCATCHER *Eumyias thalassina*

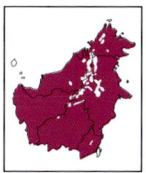

Identification 15–17 cm. **Adult male *thalassoides*** Upperparts turquoise-blue with prominent black lores and narrow frontal band, flight feathers edged black, chin black, underparts slightly paler turquoise-blue with whitish tips on undertail-coverts; iris black, bill and legs greyish-black. **Adult female** Paler with pale greyish-white lores, chin and throat finely barred whitish. **Juvenile** Dull greyish-blue with buffish centres to feathers, wings and tail dull blue. **Similar species** Pale Blue Flycatcher is bluer with shorter tail, longer bill, more contrast between blue breast and greyish-blue belly, no white tips on undertail-coverts. **Habitat** Primary and secondary lowland dipterocarp and riparian to lower montane forest, plantations, to 1,300 m. **Behaviour** Usually solitary or in pairs; sallies for flying insects from exposed perch in mid- to upper storey, often returning to same perch. **Voice** A jumble of thin, hurried, high-pitched notes, *pi-ti-pi-ti-pwee-tee-pwee-pwee* (3–8 kHz, c.1.5 s), repeated at intervals of 6–8 s; usually given from high perch. **Range & status**

Himalayas, Indian Subcontinent, C and S China, SE Asia, Sumatra. **Borneo** Uncommon resident throughout. **Breeding** Possibly breeds February–June but otherwise undescribed in Borneo.

INDIGO FLYCATCHER *Eumyias indigo*

KINABALU

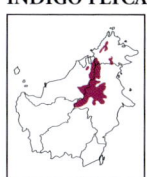

11/6/10

Identification 14 cm. **Adult *cerviniventris*** (endemic subspecies) Forehead bright azure-blue, lores and area around eye black, rest of upperparts deep indigo-blue, darker edging on flight feathers and tail, white base of outer tail feathers often not visible in field, throat and breast deep blue fading to bluish-grey belly and buffish-yellow undertail-coverts; iris, bill and legs black. **Juvenile** Upperparts greyish-blue with darker feather-edging giving barred effect, darker rump spotted and streaked buffish and black, underparts greyish with buffish centres to feathers. **Habitat** Primary and secondary lower and upper montane forest, 900–2,650 m. **Behaviour** Tame and approachable; feeds on insects and some berries; gleans and hawks insects generally in mid-storey; sometimes joins mixed feeding flocks. **Voice** Song is a thin see-sawing series of notes, *wit-wee-wit-wee-wit-wee...* (4–5 kHz, c.7 s), repeated at intervals. **Range & status** Sumatra, Java. **Borneo** Common resident in north-central mountain ranges from G. Kinabalu to G. Murud

and G. Menyapa (Sabah, E Sarawak, E Kalimantan). **Breeding** March–June; constructs small cup-shaped nest of woven rootlets, twigs and dead grass lined with down on rocky ledges or in trees up to 6 m from ground.

PYGMY BLUE FLYCATCHER *Muscicapella hodgsoni*

Identification 9–10 cm. **Adult male *sondaica*** Crown bright blue, lores and forehead to cheeks black, rest of upperparts deep blue, underparts deep orange fading into paler lower belly and whitish undertail-coverts; iris black, bill black, legs and feet pinkish-grey. **Adult female** Upperparts brown, rufous-tinged on wings and tail, underparts buffish with whitish throat and belly to undertail-coverts. **Juvenile** Undescribed. **Similar species** From Snowy-browed Flycatcher by bluer upperparts and no white eyebrow or blackish flight feathers and tail. **Habitat** Primary lower and upper montane forest, 1,200–2,200 m, with one record at 850 m. **Behaviour** Unobtrusive and easily overlooked, but with distinctive habit of cocking tail and down-flicking wings; usually solitary or in pairs, foraging in lower storey. **Voice** Song is a piping, high-pitched *tsit-tsit-tsit* (5.3 kHz, c.1.5 s) with staccato *churrr...* **Range & status** E Himalayas, NE India, S China, NW Myanmar, NW

Thailand, C Indochina, Malay Peninsula, Sumatra. **Borneo** Rare resident in north-central mountain ranges, known only from G. Kinabalu, G. Dulit and G. Mulu (Sabah and E Sarawak) with anomalous record from Barito Ulu at 850 m (C Kalimantan). **Breeding** Undescribed in Borneo.

YELLOW-RUMPED FLYCATCHER
Ficedula zanthopygia

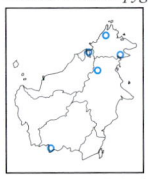

Identification 13–13.5 cm. Monotypic. **Adult male** Upperparts black with prominent broad white supercilium and white stripe on wing, lower back and rump bright yellow, underparts bright orange-yellow with whitish undertail-coverts (orange flush on throat and breast in northern spring); iris, bill and legs black. **Adult female** Upperparts greyish-olive with paler yellow rump and darker wings and tail, white patch on wings, underparts whitish with greyish speckling on throat and upper breast, pale buffish-yellow on breast; narrow whitish eye-ring. **Juvenile** Like adult female but with buffish mottling on upperparts. **Similar species** See Narcissus Flycatcher. **Habitat** Primary and secondary lowland dipterocarp forest, gardens, mangroves. **Voice** Generally silent on non-breeding grounds. **Range & status** Breeds SE Siberia, NE Asia, C and E China; migrates to SE Asia, Sumatra. **Borneo** Rare vagrant with six records from Sabah, Brunei and E and C Kalimantan.

Female

Male winter

Male spring

NARCISSUS FLYCATCHER *Ficedula narcissina*

Identification 13–13.5 cm. **Adult male *narcissina*** Upperparts black with long, broad yellowish-orange supercilium and white patch on wings, lower back and rump bright yellow, bright orange-yellow on throat fading through yellow belly to whitish undertail-coverts; iris black, bill and legs greyish-black. **Adult female** Upperparts olive-green with darker wings, tertials and coverts edged buffish, underparts greyish-white. **Juvenile** Upperparts browner with buffish spots and speckles. **Similar species** Yellow-rumped Flycatcher has white supercilium, no white on underparts and yellow lower back and rump. **Habitat** Primary lowland dipterocarp and lower montane forest, upland heath, to 1,350 m. **Behaviour** Usually seen singly or in pairs; sallies from perch in mid-storey to catch insects on wing. **Voice** Generally silent on non-breeding grounds. **Range & status** Breeds Japan, E China; migrates to Hainan, Thai-Malay Peninsula, Philippines. **Borneo** Uncommon non-breeding visitor and passage migrant to Sabah and Sarawak, with one record from C Kalimantan, from early September to mid-April.

Female

Male

RUFOUS-CHESTED FLYCATCHER
Ficedula dumetoria

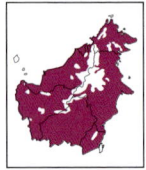

Identification 11–12 cm. **Adult male *muelleri*** Upperparts slaty-black with long white supercilium and prominent white stripe on wings, white base to outer tail, chin to breast burnt-orange, white belly and undertail-coverts; iris dark brown, bill black, legs and feet pinkish to black. **Adult female** upperparts olive-brown with pale lores and eye-ring, rump and tail washed rufous, wing-coverts fringed pale rufous. **Juvenile** Upperparts dark brown with buffish-rufous spots and streaks, chin and throat pale buffish-orange, breast buffish-orange spotted pale brown, rest of underparts buffish-white. **Similar species** See Mugimaki Flycatcher. **Habitat** Primary lowland dipterocarp to hill forest and kerangas, to 1,200 m. **Behaviour** Shy and inconspicuous; usually singly or in pairs, foraging for insects in dense lower to mid-storey by sallying from perch; also gleans from foliage in warbler-like fashion. **Voice** Song is a high-pitched, tinkling three- or four-note *tsi-tsi-tsee-tsee* (6–7 kHz, c.1 s); call is a soft *sst-sst*. **Range & status** Thai-Malay Peninsula, Sumatra, Java, Lesser Sundas. **Borneo** Locally common resident throughout. **Breeding** Possibly breeds November–June but otherwise undescribed in Borneo.

Female

Male

SNOWY-BROWED FLYCATCHER *Ficedula hyperythra*

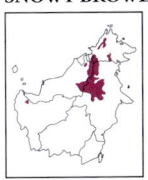

Identification 11–13 cm. **Adult male *sumatrana*** Upperparts slaty-blue with prominent bright white eyebrow from above eye to top of bill, wings and tail blackish-brown, inconspicuous white base to outer tail, chin slaty-blue, throat to belly deep rufous-orange with whitish centre of belly and undertail-coverts; iris dark brown, bill black, legs and feet pinkish-grey to grey. **Adult female** Pale orange forehead and eye-ring, upperparts greyish-brown, tail washed rufous, throat to belly buffish-orange, rest of underparts greyish-white. **Juvenile** Upperparts brown with buffish feather-centres giving speckled appearance. **Adult male *mjobergi*** (endemic subspecies) Face and sides of throat black, centre of throat pale orange, deeper orange on breast with greyish flanks. **Habitat** Primary and secondary lower to upper montane forest, 1,200–3,700 m. **Behaviour** Tame and often inquisitive; perches on sides of trunks and exposed roosts to forage on or near ground for insects; sometimes hops on ground; usually encountered singly or in pairs. **Voice** Song is a high-pitched, squeaky four-note *tsee-tsee-tsi-tsee* on descending scale (7.2–6 kHz, c.1 s); call is a thin upslurred *seep*. **Range & status** Himalayas, NE India, S China, Taiwan, SE Asia, Indonesia, Philippines. **Borneo** Common resident, *sumatrana* from G. Kinabalu to G. Mulu and G. Menyapa (Sabah, E Sarawak, E Kalimantan); *mjobergi* an isolated population in G. Niut and Pueh Range (S Sarawak and W Kalimantan). **Breeding** March–September; lays two white eggs in moss-lined cup hidden in loose moss on side of tree.

Male *sumatrana*

Female *sumatrana*

Juvenile *sumatrana*

MUGIMAKI FLYCATCHER *Ficedula mugimaki*

Identification 12.5–13.5 cm. Monotypic. **Adult male** Upperparts blackish with short white supercilium behind eye and white patch on upperwing, white base to outer tail, chin and breast rich rufous-orange grading to white lower belly and undertail-coverts; iris dark brown, bill black, legs and feet pinkish-grey to brownish-grey. **Adult female** Upperparts brownish with indistinct pale brownish supercilium, darker wings edged whitish, chin to lower breast paler rufous-orange. **Immature** male like adult female but richer rufous underparts, some white at base of outer tail feathers. **Similar species** Red-chested Flycatcher is smaller, white supercilium is longer, different shaped wing patch, orange on underparts less extensive. **Habitat** Primary and secondary lowland dipterocarp and lower montane forest, coastal woodland, mangroves, gardens, to 1,750 m. **Behaviour** Usually seen singly or in pairs; sallies out from perch in mid-storey to catch insects on wing; gleans from foliage of tall fruiting and flowering trees; also known to eat berries. **Voice** Generally silent on non-breeding grounds. **Range & status** Breeds SE Siberia, NE China, Korea; migrates to SE China, SE Asia, Sumatra, Java, Sulawesi, Philippines. **Borneo** Uncommon non-breeding visitor and passage migrant to Sabah, Brunei, Sarawak, E Kalimantan, from late October to mid-May.

Immature male

Male

Female

LITTLE PIED FLYCATCHER *Ficedula westermanni*

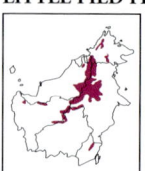

Identification 10–11 cm. **Adult male westermanni** Upperparts black with prominent broad white supercilium and broad white wing-stripe, white base to outer tail feathers, underparts white, undertail black; iris dark brown, bill and legs black. **Adult female** Upperparts grey with brownish rump and uppertail-coverts, underparts greyish-white. **Juvenile** Upperparts heavily spotted and speckled buff. **Habitat** Primary and secondary lower to upper montane forest, 850–3,100 m. **Behaviour** Sallies from perch in mid- to upper storey to catch insects on wing and glean from foliage; usually solitary but often in pairs in breeding season. **Voice** A thin, piping *tsi-tsi-tsi-tsi* followed by a soft, rattling *trrr* (5 kHz, c.3 s). **Range & status** C Himalayas, NE India, S China, SE Asia, Indonesia, Philippines. **Borneo** Common resident in north-central and western mountain ranges from G. Kinabalu to Pueh Range and G. Menyapa (Sabah, Sarawak, W, C and E Kalimantan) and in Meratus Mountains (S Kalimantan). **Breeding** March–August; one fawn-coloured egg was found in deep mossy nest lined with fine white roots located in creeper 12 m from ground.

TAIGA FLYCATCHER *Ficedula albicilla*

Identification 11.5 cm. Monotypic. **Adult male non-breeding/female** Upperparts brown, tail darker with white outer feathers on upper tail (especially conspicuous in flight), underparts whitish with buffish wash on breast and flanks; iris dark brown, narrow whitish eye-ring, bill and legs greyish-black. **Adult male breeding** Face greyish, small triangular area of orangey-red on chin and centre of throat bordered grey. **First winter** As female but wing-coverts tipped buff forming a narrow wing-bar. **Habitat** On non-breeding grounds recorded in lowland forest edge, woodland, secondary growth, plantations, gardens. **Behaviour** Sallies from perch in lower to mid-storey to catch insects on wing or from ground. **Voice** Call is a rapid, raspy *tssk...*, sometimes repeated (5.5–6.5 kHz, 0.3 s). **Range & status** Breeds C and E Asia, Siberia; migrates to E Indian Subcontinent, SE China, SE Asia. **Borneo** Rare vagrant to Sabah, Brunei and Sarawak, October–March.

GREY-STREAKED FLYCATCHER *Muscicapa griseisticta*

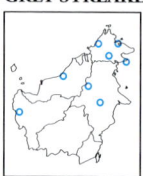

Identification 12.5–14 cm. Monotypic. Small, greyish flycatcher with prominent streaking on underparts. **Adult** Upperparts brownish-grey with pale lores and line over top of bill and buffish-white tips to wing-coverts, greyish-white sub-moustachial stripe, brownish-grey malar stripe, throat white, underparts white broadly streaked dark grey on breast and flanks, undertail-coverts whitish; iris brown with narrow whitish eye-ring, bill and legs black. **Juvenile** Like adult but duller with buffish streaks and spots on upperparts, streaking on underparts indistinct. **Similar species** Combination of pale lores, heavy streaks on underparts and long wings diagnostic. **Habitat** Primary lowland dipterocarp and peatswamp forest, coastal woodland, to 1,500 m. **Behaviour** Arboreal insectivore; sallies from high, prominent perch; usually solitary. **Voice** A metallic high-pitched rattling *tzit tzit* has been described in Borneo. **Range & status** Breeds NE Asia, Siberia; migrates to S China, Taiwan, Sulawesi, Moluccas, Philippines, New Guinea. **Borneo** Rare non-breeding visitor to Sabah, Sarawak, W and E Kalimantan, from September to mid-March.

BROWN-STREAKED FLYCATCHER *Muscicapa williamsoni*

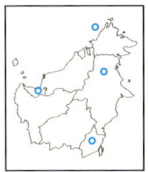

Identification 12–14 cm. Monotypic. **Adult** Like Asian Brown Flycatcher but upperparts browner, breast and flanks buffish-brown broadly streaked brownish; base of lower mandible pale yellowish. **Juvenile** As juvenile Asian Brown Flycatcher but uppertail-coverts tinged rufous, wing-coverts and tail tipped creamy-buff. **Similar species** See Asian Brown, Grey-streaked and Dark-sided Flycatchers. **Habitat** Primary and secondary lowland dipterocarp forest, plantations, gardens. **Behaviour** As Asian Brown Flycatcher. **Voice** As Asian Brown Flycatcher. **Range & status** Breeds SE Asia, migrates to Sumatra and Borneo. **Borneo** Uncommon non-breeding visitor and passage migrant to Sarawak, Sabah, E and S Kalimantan, from August to November. Status in Borneo is somewhat obscured by previous treatment as a subspecies of *M. dauurica*.

ASIAN BROWN FLYCATCHER *Muscicapa dauurica*

dauurica

umbrosa

Identification 12–14 cm. **Adult *dauurica*** Upperparts greyish-brown with whitish lores, short whitish sub-moustachial stripe and indistinct dark malar stripe, flight feathers dark grey with tertials and wing-coverts fringed greyish-white, underparts whitish with sides of throat and breast washed dirty greyish-brown; iris brown with narrow pale grey eye-ring, bill black with base of lower mandible yellowish, legs and feet black. **Juvenile** Upperparts spotted buffish, underparts whiter. **Adult *umbrosa*** (endemic subspecies) Darker than nominate, eye-ring less distinct. **Similar species** See Grey-streaked, Brown-streaked and Dark-sided Flycatchers. **Habitat** Resident race is confined to primary and secondary lowland dipterocarp forest to 230 m; migrants have been recorded in coastal woodlands, scrub, plantations, gardens, to 1,600 m. **Behaviour** Arboreal insectivore; usually solitary; forages mostly in mid-storey from prominent perch, sallying to catch insects on wing. **Voice** Call is a sharp *chi* or loud *seet seet*; song is a complex, sweet *chi jo chi-chi-chi cho-chu-chu-chu* (2.5–6.5 kHz). **Range & status** Resident in S India, Myanmar, NW Thailand, S Vietnam; breeds Siberia, N and E Asia, Himalayas; migrates to S China, Peninsular India, Sri Lanka, SE Asia, Sumatra, Java, Philippines. **Borneo** Race *umbrosa* uncommon resident in N Borneo (Sabah, E Kalimantan), *dauurica* uncommon non-breeding visitor and passage migrant throughout including offshore islands, from early August to late April. **Breeding** Possibly breeds January–July but otherwise undescribed in Borneo.

DARK-SIDED FLYCATCHER *Muscicapa sibirica*

Identification 13–14 cm. Small greyish-brown flycatcher with indistinct streaking on breast and flanks. **Adult *sibirica*** Upperparts brownish-grey with pale lores, greyish-white sub-moustachial stripe often mottled, grey malar stripe, centre of throat white often extending to sides of neck to form half-collar, upper breast and flanks brownish streaked brownish-grey, rest of underparts white, dark centres to undertail-coverts; iris brown with thin white eye-ring, bill and legs black. **Juvenile** Darker with buffish streaks and spots on upperparts, underparts buffish, bill black with paler base of lower mandible. **Similar species** See Grey-streaked Flycatcher; told from Asian Brown Flycatcher by more prominent whitish submoustachial stripe and half-collar, heavier grey on breast and flanks, dark centres to undertail-coverts and longer primary projection. **Habitat** Primary and secondary lowland dipterocarp to lower montane forest, to 1,600 m. **Behaviour** Arboreal insectivore; sits upright on prominent perch and sallies to catch insects on wing, often returning to same perch. **Voice** Call is a sharp *jii* or trilling *jiriri…*; song on breeding grounds is a tinkling high-pitched melodious *cho chii-chi-cho chii-chi-cho…* (2.5–8.5 kHz, c.3 s). **Range & status** Breeds Siberia, N and E Asia, Himalayas, C and SW China; migrates to S China, SE Asia, Sumatra. **Borneo** Uncommon non-breeding visitor and passage migrant to N Borneo (Sabah, Brunei, Sarawak, E, W and S Kalimantan), from August to mid-April.

FERRUGINOUS FLYCATCHER *Muscicapa ferruginea*

Identification 12–13 cm. Monotypic. **Adult** Head and face dark grey with buffish-orange lores, upperparts rufous with grey tinge, darker grey wings fringed rufous, uppertail-coverts bright rufous, indistinct pale submoustachial stripe and greyish malar stripe, underparts pale rufous with white throat and centre of belly; iris black with narrow white eye-ring, bill dark grey with pinkish or yellowish base of lower mandible, legs and feet pink. **Juvenile** Upperparts spotted buffish, mottled on throat and breast, rest of underparts paler rufous. **Habitat** Primary and secondary lowland dipterocarp to lower montane forest, to 1,550 m. **Behaviour** Shy; usually solitary; forages in lower to mid-storey, sallying out from an exposed perch. **Voice** Generally silent away from breeding grounds. **Range & status** Breeds C and E Himalayas, NE India, Taiwan, N Vietnam; migrates to Indochina, Thai-Malay Peninsula, Sumatra, Java, Philippines. **Borneo** Uncommon non-breeding visitor and passage migrant to N Borneo (Sabah, Sarawak, E Kalimantan) from late October to February.

BROWN-CHESTED JUNGLE-FLYCATCHER
Rhinomyias brunneatus

Identification 15 cm. Medium-sized brownish flycatcher with brownish breast-band and large pointed bill, hooked at tip. **Adult *brunneatus*** Upperparts olive-brown, lores paler, warm rufous-brown on uppertail-coverts, throat whitish with greyish scaling, indistinct broad brownish breast-band, underparts white with brownish flanks; iris brown, bill black with pinkish base to lower mandible, legs and feet pinkish. **Juvenile** Like adult but buffish centres of feathers on upperparts give scaly appearance. **Habitat** Secondary forest, plantations. **Range & status** Resident Nicobar Islands; nominate race breeds SE China, migrates to SE Asia. **Borneo** Vagrant; one record from Brunei.

FULVOUS-CHESTED JUNGLE-FLYCATCHER
Rhinomyias olivacea

Identification 14–15 cm. Medium-sized, brownish flycatcher with broad indistinct tawny-brown breast-band and large, pointed bill, hooked at tip. **Adult *olivacea*** Upperparts olive-brown with buffish flecks on cheeks and ear-coverts, rump to uppertail warmer brown, lores buffish-brown, chin and throat white, rest of underparts greyish-white with tawny-brown breast-band and flanks; iris brown with narrow greyish eye-ring, bill dark grey, legs and feet pink. **Juvenile** Upperparts browner with buffish feather-centres giving scaly appearance, underparts mottled brown and buff. **Similar species** Grey-chested Jungle-flycatcher has greyer breast-band and darker upperparts. **Habitat** Primary and secondary lowland dipterocarp and coastal to hill forest, mangroves, plantations, to 900 m but mostly in coastal and lowland areas. **Behaviour** Sallies and hawks for insects in lower to mid-storey; usually solitary. **Voice** Call is a harsh *churr*...; song is a lilting five-note phrase, *see-swee-see-see-swee*, first note highest, then falling, rising and the last two notes lower (5–3.5 kHz, 1 s). **Range & status** Thai-Malay Peninsula, Sumatra, Java. **Borneo** Locally uncommon resident in lowlands and offshore islands of N and C Borneo (Sabah, Brunei, C Kalimantan) and N Natunas. **Breeding** February–June; lays 2–3 brownish-white eggs with faint reddish-brown spots in cup-shaped nest of moss and small sticks.

GREY-CHESTED JUNGLE-FLYCATCHER
Rhinomyias umbratilis

Identification 15 cm. Monotypic. Medium-sized brownish flycatcher with indistinct grey breast-band and large pointed bill, hooked at tip. **Adult** Upperparts dark brown, warmer on uppertail, whitish lores and dark malar area, chin and throat bright white, underparts white with darker grey breast-band and flanks; iris brown, bill dark grey, legs and feet pinkish. **Juvenile** Upperparts darker with pale tips, breast-band mottled darker. **Similar species** See Fulvous-chested Jungle-flycatcher. **Habitat** Primary and secondary lowland dipterocarp, peatswamp and kerangas forest, plantations, to 500 m. **Behaviour** Sallies, hawks and gleans for insects in lower to mid-storey; usually solitary. **Voice** Call is a chattering *trrt-trrt-trrt...*; song is a repetitive, pretty *wee-tee-tee*, first note highest (3.8–3 kHz, c.2 s), and a five-note song on descending scale (7–3 kHz, 1.5 s). **Range & status** Thai-Malay Peninsula, Sumatra. **Borneo** Common resident in lowland and coastal areas throughout, including offshore islands where previous species is absent. **Breeding** March–August; eggs and nest like Fulvous-chested Flycatcher.

RUFOUS-TAILED JUNGLE-FLYCATCHER
Rhinomyias ruficauda

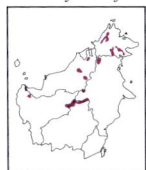

Identification 14.5–15 cm. Medium-sized brownish flycatcher with bright rufous tail and large pointed bill, hooked at tip. **Adult** *ruficrissa* (endemic subspecies) Upperparts olive-brown, lores paler, warmer brown on rump and uppertail-coverts, flight feathers dark brown, tail bright rufous, chin and throat white, indistinct breast-band and flanks brownish-grey, rest of underparts white; iris brown, bill black, legs and feet pinkish to pale bluish. **Juvenile** Like adult but buffish centres and dark edges of feathers give scaly appearance. **Adult** *isola* (endemic subspecies) Throat buffish-yellow, breast-band greyer, rufous wash on primaries. **Habitat** Primary lower montane forest, 950–1,250 m. **Behaviour** Poorly known; solitary; forages in mid-storey. **Voice** In the Philippines the song is a high-pitched raspy *chi-chi-chi-chi* (2.8-3.5 kHz, 0.5 s) and a soft, burry twitter. **Range & status** Philippines. **Borneo** Uncommon to rare resident in north-central and western mountain ranges from G. Kinabalu (*ruficrissa*) to Pueh Range (Sabah, Sarawak, E, C and W Kalimantan). **Breeding** Undescribed in Borneo.

EYEBROWED JUNGLE-FLYCATCHER
Rhinomyias gularis

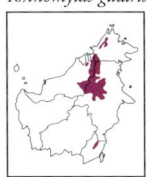

Identification 15 cm. Monotypic. Medium-sized, rich brown flycatcher with prominent eyebrow and large pointed bill, hooked at tip. **Adult** Upperparts rich reddish-brown with long white eyebrow, chin and throat white sharply demarcated from grey breast, flanks and upper belly grey, rest of underparts whitish; iris brown, bill black, legs and feet bluish-grey. **Juvenile** Like adult but with buffish centres of feathers giving scaled appearance. **Habitat** Primary and secondary lower and upper montane forest, 900–3,300 m but mostly 1,500–2,150 m. **Behaviour** Usually solitary, sometimes in small groups; stays close to ground. **Voice** Alarm call is a sharp *prrt*. **Range & status** Endemic, common resident in north-central mountain ranges from G. Kinabalu to G. Murud and G. Menyapa (Sabah, E Sarawak, E Kalimantan), also recorded from Meratus Mountains (S Kalimantan). **Breeding** January–September; lays pale olive-green eggs with reddish spots in large, untidy ball-shaped nest of moss, small sticks and dead leaves, lined with rootlets and fibres; one was suspended from tip of climbing bamboo.

STENOSTIRIDAE: Canary-flycatchers & allies

Worldwide 8 species, 1 in Borneo. Small, often-confiding African and Asian flycatcher-like insectivores. Feed by sallying out from a perch. Often join mixed feeding flocks.

GREY-HEADED CANARY-FLYCATCHER
Culicicapa ceylonensis

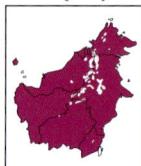

Identification 12–13 cm. **Adult *antioxantha*** Head with slight crest to nape and breast grey, upperparts olive-green, tail and flight feathers with yellowish edging, rest of underparts yellow; iris black with narrow whitish eye-ring, bill dark grey with pinkish base to lower mandible, legs and feet pinkish. **Juvenile** Like adult but head brownish with greyish lores, yellow tips to wing-coverts, underparts duller. **Habitat** Primary lowland dipterocarp to lower montane forest, to 1,700 m. **Behaviour** Not shy; usually solitary; actively forages for insects and other small invertebrates at all levels; often flicks tail when perched. **Voice** Song is a squeaky, loud, constantly repeated *sil-ly-bil-ly-me* (5 kHz, c. 1 s), first note slurred, following four on same pitch; call is a harsh *chap*. **Range & status** Indian Subcontinent, C and S China, SE Asia, Indonesia. **Borneo** Common resident throughout. **Breeding** April–October; eggs are glossy white with brown spots and grey mottling; one nest was simple pocket constructed in hanging moss.

Juvenile

Adult

PARIDAE: Tits

Worldwide 56 species, 1 in Borneo. Tiny to small insectivores with large head, short rounded wings and short stubby tail. Energetic and inquisitive. Most forage actively and acrobatically, gleaning insects in the treetops. Sexes similar.

GREY TIT *Parus cinereus*

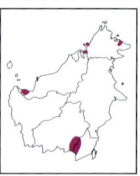

Identification 12.5–14 cm. **Adult male *sarawacensis*** (endemic subspecies) Head black with large white patch over cheek and ear-coverts, upperparts dark grey with whitish wing-bar, uppertail-coverts black, tail black with grey fringes and white outer feathers, throat and sides of neck black, breast and belly pale greyish-white with broad black ventral band; iris and bill black, legs and feet greyish-black. **Adult female** Duller with narrower ventral stripe. **Juvenile** Like female but browner. **Habitat** Mangroves, nipah and swamp forest, at sea-level. **Behaviour** Poorly known in Borneo; arboreal insectivore. **Voice** Extralimitally, a loud *kee-chee*, first note higher-pitched (6.6 kHz) than second (4.1 kHz). **Range & status** SW Turkmenistan, NE Iran, Afghanistan, Indian Subcontinent, C Asia to E Asia and Japan, SE Asia, Indonesia. **Borneo** Patchily distributed, uncommon resident Sabah, Sarawak, C and S Kalimantan. **Breeding** Undescribed in Borneo; elsewhere nest of plant fibres and wool is contructed in tree-hole; lays 5–12 eggs.

Male

Juvenile

ALAUDIDAE: Larks

Worldwide 91 species, 2 in Borneo. Generally rather plain mostly ground-dwelling birds with heavy, conical bill and many with a short crest. Typically occur in dry, open habitats. Diet consists of small invertebrates, seeds and small fruits. The rich and varied song is often given in a hovering and circling display-flight. Nest on the ground.

AUSTRALASIAN BUSHLARK *Mirafra javanica*

Identification 14–15 cm. **Adult *javanica*** Buffish supercilium, upperparts reddish-brown with heavy black mottling, primaries rufous, tail with white outer feathers, underparts pale buffish-brown with darker streaking on upper breast; iris dark brown, stout bill pinkish with grey culmen, legs and feet pinkish. **Juvenile** Paler and duller with less streaking. **Habitat** Grasslands, airports, at sea-level. **Behaviour** Sings as it flies up from ground in undulating flight, then flutters down. **Voice** Sweet, complex series of notes incorporating mimicry. **Range & status** S China, SE Asia, Java, Bali, Lesser Sundas, Philippines, New Guinea, Australia. **Borneo** Uncommon resident in coastal southern Borneo (W, C and S Kalimantan), first recorded in 1976; recorded recently on G. Menyapa, E Kalimantan.

ORIENTAL SKYLARK *Alauda gulgula*

Identification 16.5–18 cm. **Adult *gulgula*** Short crest, upperparts pale brown with dark streaking, rusty ear-coverts, underparts pale buffish-white with clear dark streaks on breast; iris dark brown, bill pinkish with grey culmen, legs and feet pinkish. **Juvenile** Crown and mantle paler with whitish fringing, wing-coverts tipped whitish, breast-streaking more diffuse. **Habitat** In Borneo recorded on golf course and in coastal grassland. **Voice** Liquid, bubbling song often uttered in flight. **Range & status** C Asia, Indian Subcontinent, China, Taiwan, SE Asia. **Borneo** Vagrant, with two records from W Sarawak and E Sabah.

PYCNONOTIDAE: Bulbuls

Worldwide 137 species, 24 in Borneo. A large family of mostly tropical and subtropical medium-sized arboreal birds. Generally long-tailed and short-winged with upright posture and subdued plumage. Found in a wide range of habitats. Vary from noisy and conspicuous to shy and unobstrusive. The diet spans a wide range of fruits, nectar, pollen, insects, and small invertebrates. Many are important dispersers of pollen and seeds. Sexes similar.

SCALY-BREASTED BULBUL *Pycnonotus squamatus*

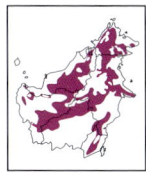 

Identification 14–15 cm. Small, highly coloured bulbul with striking black and white head pattern, and scaly breast. **Adult *borneensis*** (endemic subspecies) Head to hindneck and cheeks black contrasting with white throat, upperparts bronze-green, tail black with white outer tips, breast and flanks black with white fringing creating scaly pattern, belly white, undertail-coverts bright yellow; iris dark red, bill and legs black. **Juvenile** Poorly known, upper breast smudgy black, lower breast white (Malay Peninsula data). **Habitat** Primary and secondary lowland dipterocarp to lower montane forest; slope specialist at 300–1,200 m. **Behaviour** Usually in pairs or small groups; an arboreal foliage-gleaning frugivore, occasionally taking small insects, known to hover at edge of foliage; gathers at fruiting trees, foraging in forest canopy and edges. **Voice** Described as a metallic, descending *prrt prrt*. **Range & status** Thai-Malay Peninsula, Sumatra, Java. **Borneo** Uncommon resident in hills and mountain ranges throughout. **Breeding** Undescribed in Borneo.

227

BLACK-HEADED BULBUL *Pycnonotus atriceps*

Identification 16–18 cm. Medium-sized olive-green bulbul with black head and pale blue iris. **Adult male *atriceps*** Head to nape and throat black with greenish sheen, lower hindneck to back yellowish-green fading to bright yellow on lower back to uppertail, tail tipped yellow with broad black subterminal band, wings olive-green with black primaries, underparts bright yellow with darker olive-green wash on breast and flanks; iris pale blue, bill and legs black. **Juvenile** Duller, head and throat brownish; iris brownish. **Habitat** Primary and secondary lowland to lower montane forest, kerangas, plantations, to 1,600 m. **Behaviour** Nomadic in response to fruiting; feeds on figs and other fruits, and insects; usually in pairs or small groups; inconspicuous but active; gathers in congregations at fruiting trees. **Voice** Call is a very short, emphatic, high-pitched, downslurred *tswit* (4.6–2 kHz, 0.1 s); song is a similar note repeated rapidly; a staccato *doo-da-dit-dit-doo* song is also described, the *doo* notes on lower pitch than the faster *dit* notes. **Range & status** NE Indian Subcontinent, SW China, SE Asia, Sumatra, Java, Palawan. **Borneo** Large fluctuations in abundance but generally common resident throughout, including offshore islands. **Breeding** January–August; nest is small cup of dead, tightly woven grass and bark fibres attached to twigs in outer branches of bush c.1.2 m from ground; lays two buffish eggs.

Juvenile

Adult

Adult (greener variant)

BORNEAN BULBUL *Pycnonotus montis*

Identification 17–18 cm. Monotypic. Medium-sized olive-green bulbul with yellow throat and moderately long crest on black head. **Adult** Head and crest black, upperparts olive-green, throat yellow, underparts yellowish-green fading to yellowish undertail-coverts, undertail greyish; iris dark red, bill black, legs and feet greyish-black. **Juvenile** Probably duller and browner. **Habitat** Secondary forest and cultivated areas; slope specialist from 600 to 1,550 m, generally above 800 m. **Behaviour** An arboreal frugivore but also takes flying insects; usually solitary or in pairs but small groups congregate at fruiting trees. **Voice** Song is a loud, sweet, emphatic *wee-wit-it-weet*, the last notes louder and upwardly inflected at end (2.6–3.5 kHz, 0.5 s), sometimes introduced by two quiet *wit-wit...* notes. **Range & status** Endemic, uncommon in north-central mountain ranges from G. Kinabalu to Ulu Barito and G. Menyapa (Sabah, E Sarawak, E, C and north W Kalimantan). **Breeding** Poorly known; one nest found in January held two eggs with dark reddish speckles and heavy bluish-green splodges. **Note** Previously subsumed within Black-crested Bulbul *Pycnonotus melanicterus* of Indian Subcontinent, SE Asia and S China.

Adult

BLACK-AND-WHITE BULBUL
Pycnonotus melanoleucos

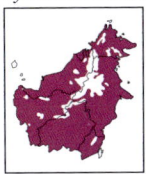

Identification 16–18 cm. Monotypic. Unmistakable medium-sized black and white bulbul. **Adult male** Plumage all black except for contrasting white wing-coverts; iris reddish-brown, bill and legs black. **Adult female** As male but brownish with reduced white on wing-coverts. **Juvenile** Upperparts dark brown with paler fringing, underparts whitish mottled pale brown; iris greyish-brown. **Habitat** Primary and secondary lowland dipterocarp, peatswamp, kerangas and lower montane forest, to 1,250 m, with one record from 3,050 m. **Behaviour** Feeds mainly on figs and other fruits, also caterpillars; nomadic over wide areas; attracted to fruiting trees. **Voice** Generally quiet; a clear, upwardly inflected repeated disyllabic *too-wit* call has been described. **Range & status** Thai-Malay Peninsula, Sumatra. **Borneo** Uncommon resident throughout. **Breeding** Recorded in January; cup-shaped nest is made of woven fibres or sticks bound together with vines located 6 m from ground in fork in outer branches of tree; eggs are pale fawn with darker freckles.

STRAW-HEADED BULBUL *Pycnonotus zeylanicus*

Identification 28–29 cm. Monotypic. Large bulbul with distinctive straw-coloured crown and beautiful, powerful song. **Adult** Crown and cheeks golden-yellow, narrow black eyestripe and broader black malar stripe, mantle and back greyish-olive with fine pale grey streaking; wings, rump and tail olive; throat white; underparts mottled olive-brown and streaked white, darker on breast; undertail-coverts buffish-yellow; iris red, bill and legs greyish-black. **Juvenile** Duller, crown and cheeks pale yellow; iris brown. **Habitat** Riverine vegetation in primary and secondary lowland dipterocarp and peatswamp forest, occasionally in nearby gardens, plantations, paddyfields, orchards, to 1,500 m but generally below 1,000 m. **Behaviour** Feeds on small fruits and berries, occasionally small invertebrates; forages low in bushes near water, usually in small groups, sometimes on ground. **Voice** A rich and melodious, powerful, far-carrying warbled series with repeated phrase, *wit-wooti'woo* (3–1.6 kHz). **Range & status** Thai-Malay Peninsula, NW and SW Sumatra. **Borneo** Uncommon resident throughout (except S Kalimantan, where status uncertain), formerly common but now rare owing to cagebird trade and, to lesser extent, habitat loss. **Breeding** December–August; lays two whitish eggs with greyish and reddish spots and speckles in nest of rough grass and weeds 1.5–5 m above ground in bush.

GREY-BELLIED BULBUL *Pycnonotus cyaniventris*

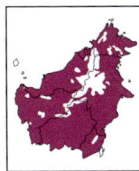

Identification 16–17 cm. Medium-sized grey bulbul with green back and wings, and striking yellow undertail-coverts. **Adult *paroticalis*** (endemic subspecies) Head dark smoky-grey with faint short pale supercilium in front of eye, upperparts olive-green, tail black with olive fringing, underparts smoky-grey with contrasting bright yellow undertail-coverts, centre of belly paler; iris dark brown, bill and legs blackish-grey. **Juvenile** Undescribed. **Habitat** Primary and secondary lowland dipterocarp to lower montane forest, plantations, to 1,100 m. **Behaviour** Inconspicuous; usually in mixed feeding flocks; mid-storey foliage-gleaning frugivore/insectivore. **Voice** Song is a series of notes rising in pitch *pi-pi-pi-pi-pi...*, reminiscent of Grey-headed Canary-flycatcher; call is described as *clewk*. **Range & status** Thai-Malay Peninsula, Sumatra. **Borneo** Uncommon resident throughout. **Breeding** December–September; nest is made of dead grass, rootlets and moss; lays two pinkish-white eggs with heavy purplish-brown speckles.

SOOTY-HEADED BULBUL *Pycnonotus aurigaster*

Identification 19–21 cm. Short-crested largish bulbul with black cap and distinctive golden-yellow undertail-coverts. **Adult *aurigaster*** Head and crest from nape around eye and lores dull black, ear-coverts pale brownish-white, underparts buffish-white sometimes with smudgy grey spots on breast, undertail-coverts bright yellow, hindneck and mantle buffish-brown, rest of upperparts greyish-brown with prominent white rump, tail brownish-black broadly tipped white; iris reddish-brown, bill and legs black. **Juvenile** Crown brownish, undertail-coverts paler. **Habitat** Secondary forest, scrub, plantations, cultivated areas, gardens. **Behaviour** An opportunistic feeder, favouring disturbed habitat near human habitation. **Voice** A bubbly, cheerful repetitive *witti-wi-i-wit*, first note sharply down- then upwardly inflected, middle notes highest (1.9–3 kHz). **Range & status** S China, SE Asia, Java, Bali; introduced Singapore, Sumatra, Sulawesi. **Borneo** Introduced (probably cagebird escapes); uncommon throughout Kalimantan, possibly spreading.

Adult

PUFF-BACKED BULBUL *Pycnonotus eutilotus*

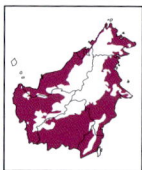 

Identification 20–22 cm. Monotypic. Large bulbul with short crest, contrasting brown upperparts and whitish underparts. **Adult** Head with short crest and upperparts brown, darker on crown; long feathers on rump ('puffback') usually not visible in field, tail with outer feathers tipped white, underparts buffish-white fading to pale yellow undertail-coverts with paler wash on breast; iris reddish-brown, bill and legs blackish-grey. **Juvenile** Like adult but with pale fringing on tail. **Habitat** Primary lowland dipterocarp, peatswamp and kerangas forest, to 600 m, with one record from 1,300 m. **Behaviour** Usually singly or in pairs, inconspicuous; joins mixed feeding flocks; foliage-gleaning frugivore/insectivore, generally foraging in lower to mid-storey. **Voice** Song is a loud, high-pitched *chee-oo-chee-tsoo*, notes rising and falling in pitch, last note downwardly inflected (4.4–2.3 kHz, c.1 s). **Range & status** Thai-Malay Peninsula, Sumatra. **Borneo** Uncommon resident throughout. **Breeding** February–July; otherwise undescribed in Borneo.

Adult

BLUE-WATTLED BULBUL *Pycnonotus nieuwenhuisii*

Identification 18 cm. Monotypic. Taxonomic status uncertain and perhaps a hybrid of *Pycnonotus* species, possibly *P. atriceps* and *P. cyaniventris*, or rare morph of commoner species; former explanation is most likely. **Adult** Head and throat dark grey giving hooded appearance, upperparts olive-green, darker on wings and paler on uppertail-coverts, tail greenish-black with whitish tips, underparts yellowish-olive; iris brown with fleshy blue eye-ring, bill and legs black. **Habitat** Primary lowland dipterocarp and hill forest, 60–650 m. **Behaviour** Poorly known; has been observed feeding in fruiting trees in Brunei. **Voice** Possibly utters two harsh but quiet notes. **Range & status** Sumatra. **Borneo** Rare resident in Brunei and E Kalimantan.

Adult

PALE-FACED BULBUL *Pycnonotus leucops*

Identification 17.5–19 cm. Medium-sized dull bulbul with white face-patch, giving wide-eyed appearance, and conspicuous bright yellow undertail-coverts. **Adult** Forehead to crown and hindneck greyish-brown, face from lores over and behind eye to throat whitish, upperparts dull olive, flight feathers and tail darker, underparts pale grey with indistinct grey streaking and bright yellow undertail-coverts; iris black, bill and legs greyish-black. **Juvenile** Undescribed. **Similar species** Yellow-vented Bulbul has black lores. **Habitat** Primary and secondary montane forest and heath; high-altitude specialist, 900–3,500 m. **Behaviour** Conspicuous, usually in pairs or small groups; mainly feeds on small fruits; known to forage for berries above treeline. **Voice** Song is a bubbly, emphatic *kw't-kw't tu-weeti-weeti*, the first two quick notes introducing the sweet phrase (2–3.2 kHz, c.1 s); calls consist of harsh, clucking notes. **Range & status** Endemic, locally common resident in north-central mountain ranges from G. Kinabalu to G. Murud and G. Menyapa (Sabah, E Sarawak, E Kalimantan). **Breeding** Undescribed. **Note** Previously subsumed within Flavescent Bulbul *Pycnonotus flavescens*.

Adult

YELLOW-VENTED BULBUL *Pycnonotus goiavier*

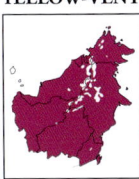

Identification 19–20 cm. Medium-sized, noisy and conspicuous bulbul with distinctive head pattern. **Adult *gourdini*** (endemic subspecies) Short narrow crest dark olive-brown, broad supercilium and face whitish with brownish ear-coverts, lores and eye-ring black, upperparts olive-brown, underparts whitish with brownish smudges on breast and yellow undertail-coverts; iris brown, bill and legs greyish-black. **Juvenile** Paler with less distinct head markings. **Similar species** See Flavescent Bulbul. **Habitat** Secondary lowland dipterocarp to lower montane forest, peatswamp forest, mangroves, plantations, cultivated areas, gardens, to 1,600 m. **Behaviour** In small flocks; feeds on small fruits and berries, small invertebrates; usually forages near ground. **Voice** A distinctive cheery, bubbly *pirit pirit pirit pirit prrt...* (1.6–2.7 kHz). **Range & status** SE Asia, Philippines, Sumatra, Java, Bali, Lombok, Sumbawa. **Borneo** Abundant resident throughout. **Breeding** Year-round, peaking in January–March and August; cup-shaped nest is made of woven fibres, leaves and grass located low in fork of bush; lays two pinkish-white eggs with purplish-brown spots and speckles and underlying greyish markings.

Juvenile

Adult

OLIVE-WINGED BULBUL *Pycnonotus plumosus*

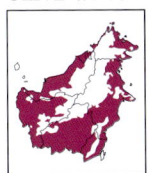

Identification 20–20.5 cm. Medium-sized, very nondescript bulbul with red iris and faint streaking on ear-coverts. **Adult *plumosus*** Dark brown lores and eye-ring, face greyish with faint whitish streaks on ear-coverts, upperparts brownish with olive-green fringes on wings and tail, underparts paler greyish-brown with buffish undertail-coverts, throat paler; iris red, bill greyish-black, legs and feet dark red. **Adult *hutzi*** (endemic subspecies) Upperparts slightly darker, underparts greyer with less yellow. **Adult *insularis*** Upperparts more olive, underparts tinged yellowish. **Juvenile** Browner, lacks whitish streaking on face, iris brown. **Habitat** Primary and secondary lowland dipterocarp, peatswamp and kerangas forest, scrub, mangroves, to 600 m, sometimes to 1,200 m. **Behaviour** Feeds on berries, small fruits and small invertebrates. **Voice** Song is a repeated bubbly *whip-whip-wit-witty-witit* (c. 2 kHz, 1.5 s). **Range & status** Thai-Malay Peninsula, Sumatra, Java, Bali, W Philippines. **Borneo** Common resident throughout including near-shore islands (*hutzi* in N and E Borneo, *insularis* N Borneo islands). **Breeding** January–September; cup-shaped nest of woven grass, rootlets and fibres located in thick bushes; lays two pale pink eggs heavily marked with purplish-red.

Adult *plumosus*

Juvenile *plumosus*

CREAM-VENTED BULBUL *Pycnonotus simplex*

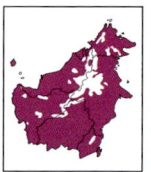

Identification 18 cm. Medium-sized, very nondescript bulbul best distinguished from other plain bulbuls by creamy-white vent. **Adult** *simplex* Upperparts olive-brown, tail dark olive-brown tinged rufous, throat creamy-white, rest of underparts pale brown, slightly darker on breast and flanks with creamy-white undertail-coverts; in Borneo iris usually red, less often whitish, bill black, legs and feet brown. **Juvenile** Upperparts browner, iris greyish-brown. **Similar species** See Red-eyed Bulbul. **Habitat** Primary and secondary lowland dipterocarp, peatswamp and kerangas forest to lower montane forest, plantations, to 1,300 m in Kelabit Highlands. **Behaviour** Feeds on fruits and small invertebrates; usually in pairs or small groups; often joins mixed feeding flocks. **Voice** Call is a quiet trilling *prrrr* (2.2 kHz); song is a squeaky, rapid *bee-quick-bee-kee-quick* (1.5–2.5 kHz). **Range & status** Thai-Malay Peninsula, Sumatra, Java. **Borneo** Common resident throughout, including the Anambas and N Natunas. **Breeding** February–September; egg is white with fine greyish and reddish flecks.

RED-EYED BULBUL *Pycnonotus brunneus*

Identification 19 cm. Medium-sized nondescript brownish bulbul with orange-red iris and buffish vent. **Adult** *brunneus* Upperparts olive-brown with paler olive fringing on wings, throat whitish-brown, underparts pale brown with buffish wash, undertail-coverts buffish; iris two-toned orange-red (red outer ring, orange inner ring), bill greyish, legs and feet pinkish-brown. **Juvenile** Upperparts paler and browner, iris pale grey. **Similar species** Cream-vented Bulbul is slightly smaller, iris usually red not orange, underparts paler. **Habitat** Secondary lowland dipterocarp, peatswamp and kerangas forest to lower montane forest, less commonly in primary forest, mangroves, plantations, to 1,200 m. **Behaviour** Foliage-gleaning frugivore and insectivore; usually in pairs or small groups. **Voice** Utters a repeated cheery, upwardly inflected series of breathless whistles, *whit-whit-whit-whit-wit-wit*, last two notes sharply louder and higher (2.5–3.5 kHz). **Range & status** Thai-Malay Peninsula, Sumatra. **Borneo** Common resident throughout

including the Anamba and Banggi Islands. **Breeding** June–October; one nest described as compact and tidy, located 2 m from ground on top of broken-off sapling.

SPECTACLED BULBUL *Pycnonotus erythropthalmos*

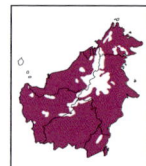

Identification 16–18 cm. Monotypic. Medium-small olive-brown bulbul with distinctive narrow yellow eye-ring. **Adult** Upperparts olive-brown, rump and uppertail-coverts tinged rufous, underparts greyish-brown with buffish tinge on flanks, throat somewhat paler; in flight underwing-coverts yellow; iris red with narrow yellow eye-ring, gape yellowish, bill black, legs and feet pinkish-brown. **Juvenile** Upperparts paler and browner, iris brown to reddish-brown. **Similar species** From Red-eyed and Cream-vented Bulbuls by narrow yellow eye-ring and yellow underwing-coverts. **Habitat** Primary and old secondary lowland dipterocarp and peatswamp forest to lower montane forest, mangroves, overgrown plantations, to 1,000 m. **Behaviour** Foliage-gleaning frugivore and insectivore in lower to mid-storey; usually singly in pairs. **Voice** Song is a sweet, complex series of relatively high-pitched notes (2.4–4.2 kHz), *pi-pi-pi-*

dee-dee-dee… **Range & status** Thai-Malay Peninsula, Sumatra. **Borneo** Common resident throughout. **Breeding** January–September; two off-white eggs with purplish-brown and greyish speckles are laid in deep cup of dead leaves, rootlets and fibres lined with fine grass located 1.5–9 m off ground in fork of bush or small tree.

HOOK-BILLED BULBUL *Setornis criniger*

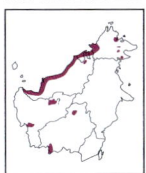

Identification 20 cm. Monotypic. A robust bulbul with chunky, hooked bill and prominent white supercilium. **Adult** Head dark brown with short whitish supercilium, black eyestripe and malar stripe, ear-coverts greyish, upperparts brown, tail broadly tipped white, underparts white with grey wash on flanks and buffish wash on lower belly; iris dark brown, bill and legs black. **Juvenile** Undescribed. **Habitat** Primary coastal peatswamp and kerangas forest; an extreme lowland specialist to 200 m. **Behaviour** Usually in pairs or small groups; forages for small fruits and invertebrates in lower to mid-storey. **Voice** Song is a nasal rattling series of notes (3.5 kHz, 11 notes/s); also a soft *crrrk*. **Range & status** Sumatra. **Borneo** Scarce to locally common resident with patchy distribution, rarer in north and absent from east, not recorded from E and S Kalimantan. **Breeding** Possibly breeds May–August but otherwise undescribed in Borneo.

Adult

BUFF-VENTED BULBUL *Iole olivacea*

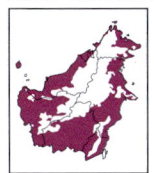

Identification 20–21 cm. Medium-sized bulbul with slight crest, long slender bill, pale iris and buffish vent. **Adult** *charlottae* Crown and upperparts warm brown, face buffish-grey, throat whitish, rest of underparts buffish-grey, undertail-coverts buffish; iris greyish-white, bill pinkish-grey with grey culmen, legs and feet pink. **Juvenile** Pale margins on wing feathers; iris light brown, bill paler. **Habitat** Primary and secondary lowland dipterocarp and peatswamp forest, to 400 m. **Behaviour** Forages at all levels for small fruits and invertebrates. **Voice** Call is a rapidly repeated nasal *chi-wit* (3.1 kHz); song is a musical *er-whit* or *wher-it*. **Range & status** Thai-Malay Peninsula, Sumatra. **Borneo** Uncommon resident throughout including Banggi, the N Natuna and Anamba Islands. **Breeding** Possibly breeds February–October but otherwise undescribed in Borneo.

Adult

HAIRY-BACKED BULBUL *Tricholestes criniger*

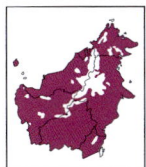

Identification 16–17 cm. Small olive and yellow bulbul with pale yellow face giving wide-eye appearance. **Adult** *viridis* Lores and area around eye pale yellow, upperparts olive with rufous tinge on wings and uppertail, underparts yellow mottled grey on breast, long hairlike plumes on back rarely visible in field; iris brown, bill bluish-grey, legs and feet pink. **Juvenile** Iris grey. **Habitat** Primary and secondary lowland dipterocarp and kerangas forest, overgrown plantations, to 850 m. **Behaviour** Forages for small fruits and invertebrates in lower to mid-storey; usually singly or in pairs; often encountered in mixed feeding flocks. **Voice** Call is a single clean whistle, *phweee* (3.3 kHz, 0.7 s); song is a series of rather quiet scratchy, jumbled notes. **Range & status** Thai-Malay Peninsula, Sumatra. **Borneo** Common resident throughout including N Natunas. **Breeding** Possibly breeds April–August but otherwise undescribed in Borneo.

Adult

233

FINSCH'S BULBUL *Alophoixus finschii*

Identification 16–17 cm. Monotypic. Medium-small bulbul with thick short bill and creamy-yellow throat. **Adult** Upperparts olive-brown, yellow throat often puffed out, breast and flanks olive-green fading into yellowish-green belly and undertail-coverts; iris reddish-brown, bill pinkish-grey, legs and feet reddish-brown. **Juvenile** Similar to adult. **Similar species** Hairy-backed Bulbul is smaller and lacks contrasting yellow throat. **Habitat** Primary and secondary lowland dipterocarp and kerangas forest, plantations, 130–400 m. **Behaviour** Forages at all levels for small fruits and invertebrates; usually singly or in pairs. **Voice** Poorly known and usually quiet; a whistled song, *choi-choi-chong-choi, choi-choi*, has been described; call is a nasal, upslurred *skweeet* (2.5-5.5 kHz). **Range & status** Malay Peninsula,

Sumatra. **Borneo** Rare resident throughout. **Breeding** Possibly breeds in March; otherwise undescribed in Borneo.

YELLOW-BELLIED BULBUL *Alophoixus phaeocephalus*

Identification 20–20.5 cm. Large, inconspicuous bulbul with grey head contrasting with white throat, olive upperparts and yellow underparts. **Adult** *connectens* (endemic subspecies) Head dark grey with whitish lores, sides of face paler, upperparts olive with brownish tinge on wings and tail, throat buffish-white, underparts bright yellow with olive wash on sides of breast; iris reddish-brown, bill bluish-grey, legs and feet pink. **Adult** *diardi* (endemic subspecies) As *connectens* but with broad yellow tips to tail. **Adult** *sulphuratus* (endemic subspecies) Intermediate between *connectens* and *diardi*. **Juvenile** As adult but iris and bill brownish. **Habitat** Primary and secondary lowland dipterocarp, peatswamp and kerangas forest, to 600 m. **Behaviour** Usually encountered singly or in pairs; forages in lower to mid-storey for fruits and small invertebrates; sometimes joins mixed feeding flocks. **Voice** Calls are a repeated high raspy *kwee kwee kwee* (4.3 kHz). **Range & status** Thai-Malay Peninsula, Sumatra. **Borneo** Common resident throughout including N Natunas (*connectens* NE Borneo, *diardi* W Borneo, *sulphuratus* C Borneo). **Breeding** February–July.

GREY-CHEEKED BULBUL *Alophoixus bres*

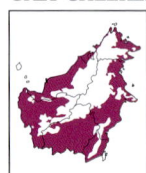

Identification 21–23 cm. A large chunky bulbul with prominent white throat usually puffed out and upright crest. **Adult** *gutturalis* (endemic subspecies) Crest and upperparts brown, lores and ear-coverts greyish-brown, throat white, underparts pale yellowish-olive, undertail-coverts buffish; iris dark red, bill grey, legs and feet pinkish-brown. **Juvenile** Upperparts more rufous; iris brown. **Similar species** See Ochraceous Bulbul. **Habitat** Primary and old secondary lowland dipterocarp forest, overgrown plantations, to 700 m with some records up to 1,500 m; probably replaced by Ochraceous Bulbul at higher altitudes. **Behaviour** Arboreal foliage-gleaning frugivore and insectivore; forages in lower and mid-storey; often joins mixed feeding flocks. **Voice** Song is a melodious ringing mournful series of irregular notes, first rising then descending in pitch, *phwee-wit, pwee-pee-pee-pee-peerrt* (2.4–4 kHz, c.3 s), but this is variable. **Range & status** Thai-Malay Peninsula, Sumatra, Java, W Philippines. **Borneo** Common resident throughout. **Breeding** Possibly breeds February–June but otherwise undescribed in Borneo.

OCHRACEOUS BULBUL *Alophoixus ochraceus*

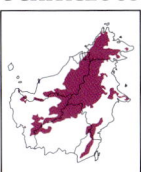

Identification 19–22 cm. A large chunky bulbul with prominent white puffy throat and upright crest. **Adult *ruficrissus*** (endemic subspecies) Crest and upperparts rufous-brown, lores and ear-coverts greyish-brown, throat white, underparts pale olive-brown, undertail-coverts rich rufous-brown; iris dark red, bill grey, legs and feet pinkish-brown. **Adult *fowleri*** (endemic subspecies) Crest greyish-brown, upperparts less rufous, ear-coverts and underparts greyer. **Juvenile** Upperparts more rufous; iris brown. **Similar species** Grey-cheeked Bulbul has less prominent crest, underparts yellower, undertail-coverts buffy. **Habitat** Primary and secondary lower and upper montane forest, 600–2,650 m. **Behaviour** Conspicuous and noisy; predominantly frugivorous but takes some insects; forages in mid-storey; usually in small loose groups. **Voice** Song is a rapid series of varied even-pitched notes, *kchit-kchit-phew-phew-phew-phew-phew*, first notes harsh and raspy, rest fluty (ca. 2.5 kHz). **Range & status** Vietnam, SW Thailand, Thai-Malay Peninsula, Sumatra. **Borneo** Common resident in mountain ranges throughout (*ruficrissus* G. Kinabalu, *fowleri* elsewhere). **Breeding** December–August; eggs are white, sparsely spotted greyish and reddish.

Adult *ruficrissus*

Adult *fowleri*

STREAKED BULBUL *Ixos malaccensis*

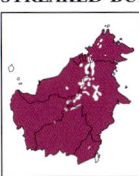

Identification 23 cm. Monotypic. Medium-large bulbul with long slender bill, streaky underparts and white vent, lacks crest. **Adult** Head and upperparts olive-green, throat and breast greyish with broad whitish streaking fading to white on undertail-coverts; iris red, bill grey with pink lower base, legs and feet pinkish-grey. **Juvenile** Upperparts brown, reduced streaking on underparts; iris brown. **Habitat** Primary and secondary lowland dipterocarp to lower montane, peatswamp and kerangas forest, to 1,300 m. **Behaviour** Sometimes joins mixed feeding flocks; arboreal frugivore and insectivore; usually singly or in pairs. **Voice** A distinctive squeaky upslurred *sweet-sweet-sweet…* (5–6 kHz), repeated. **Range & status** Thai-Malay Peninsula, Sumatra. **Borneo** Uncommon resident throughout. **Breeding** Possibly breeds February–August; eggs are pinkish-white with maroon and chestnut spots and blotches.

Juvenile

Adult

CINEREOUS BULBUL *Hemixos cinereus*

Identification 20–21 cm. Medium-large bulbul with shaggy crest and throat feathers often puffed out. **Adult *connectens*** (endemic subspecies) Face and moustachial area dark brownish-black contrasting with white throat, upperparts olive-brown with yellowish-green fringing on wings and tail, underparts greyish-white, vent and undertail-coverts bright yellow, undertail olive-brown; iris dark red, bill and legs black. **Juvenile** Face pattern less distinct. **Habitat** Primary and secondary lower and upper montane and kerangas forest; slope specialist at 700–2,750 m. **Behaviour** An arboreal insectivore and frugivore, often gathering at fruiting trees where noisy and conspicuous, otherwise usually silent. **Voice** Gives a short, nasal *di-deet-deet* (2–3.3 kHz). **Range & status** Thai-Malay Peninsula, Sumatra. **Borneo** Common resident in mountain ranges throughout. **Breeding** Possibly breeds December–July but otherwise undescribed in Borneo. **Note** Previously subsumed within Ashy Bulbul *Hemixos flavala* of SE Asia.

Adult

235

HIRUNDINIDAE: Swallows & martins

Worldwide c.88 species, 5 in Borneo. Agile, very active streamlined aerial insectivores with slender body, small bill, short legs and long, pointed wings. Frequently perch on horizontal exposed branches and telephone lines. Often in large flocks, breed in colonies. Many are long distance migrants.

ASIAN HOUSE-MARTIN *Delichon dasypus*

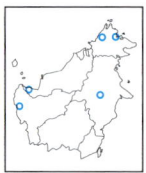

Identification 12–13 cm. **Adult *dasypus*** Crown and back glossy blackish-blue, broad white rump with inconspicuous grey streaks, wings and slightly forked tail brownish-black, underparts white, legs feathered white; in flight underwing grey. **Juvenile** Duller; upperparts brownish with whitish tips on tertials, squarer tail. **Habitat** In Borneo recorded from forested valleys, airfields and bare hills, to 975 m. **Behaviour** Forages for insects, often in flocks and often in higher airspace. **Voice** A soft twittering. **Range & status** Himalayas, S Russia, China, Japan, Korea, SE Asia, Indonesia, Philippines. **Borneo** Vagrant; records from Sabah, Sarawak and E and W Kalimantan, September–December.

COMMON SAND-MARTIN *Riparia riparia*

Identification 12 cm. **Adult male *ijimae*** Upperparts greyish-brown, flight feathers and tail darker, underparts from chin to undertail-coverts white with broad greyish-brown band across upper breast, tail shallowly forked, bare parts black. **Juvenile** Paler, back and wing-coverts with buffish fringes, tail somewhat shorter. **Habitat** Coastal wetlands, grasslands and paddyfields. **Behaviour** Forages for small insects in flight over open ground or freshwater; may join flocks of other hirundines. **Voice** Harsh twittering. **Range & status** Breeds N and C America, Palearctic, N Africa; migrates to S America, sub-Sahara Africa, S China, SE Asia, Philippines. **Borneo** Rare non-breeding visitor to N Borneo (Sabah, Brunei and Sarawak; only one record from C Kalimantan) from August to late May.

STRIATED SWALLOW *Cecropis striolata*

Identification 19 cm. **Adult *striolata*** Crown and upperparts glossy blackish-blue with broad dark-streaked orange-red rump, sides of face whitish finely streaked black with rufous wash on rear ear-coverts; underparts white with bold, heavy black streaking; undertail blackish-blue, tail deeply forked; bare parts black; in flight underwing-coverts buffish. **Juvenile** Duller, upperparts brownish with buff tips on wing-coverts. **Habitat** Open hillsides, cleared forest, to 600 m. **Behaviour** Usually seen singly in Borneo; joins mixed flocks with other hirundines to forage for insects over open areas. **Voice** A harsh wheezy *scree* (c.5 kHz, 0.4–0.5 s). **Range & status** NE India, S China, Taiwan, SE Asia, Philippines, Indonesia. **Borneo** Uncommon non-breeding visitor recorded in Sabah, Brunei, Sarawak, E and S Kalimantan, September–June.

BARN SWALLOW *Hirundo rustica*

Identification 14–17.5 cm. **Adult breeding *gutturalis*** Forehead rich brick-red, crown and upperparts glossy blackish-blue, throat and upper breast brick-red bordered below by blackish-blue breast-band, rest of underparts creamy-white, forked tail with row of small subterminal white spots and greatly elongated outer streamers; bare parts black; in flight underwing-coverts white. **Adult non-breeding** Lacks tail-streamers. **Juvenile** Duller and paler with short tail. **Similar species** House Swallow lacks breast-band and long tail-streamers, has grey underwing-coverts in flight; Striated Swallow is larger, has streaky underparts and reddish rump, lacks breast-band and tail-streamers. **Habitat** Open country including cities and towns, to 2,400 m. **Behaviour** Huge numbers roost communally; aerial insectivore, forages for small insects in flight over open ground or freshwater. **Voice** A harsh twittering, followed by a lower, mechanical trill *chi-chi-chi-piririri...* **Range & status** Breeds N America, Palearctic, Himalayas, Indochina; migrates to S America, Africa, Indian Subcontinent, SE Asia, Philippines, Indonesia, New Guinea, N Australia. **Borneo** Abundant non-breeding visitor and passage migrant throughout including offshore islands, July–May.

HOUSE SWALLOW *Hirundo tahitica*

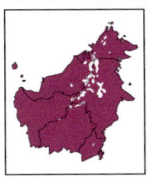

Identification 11–14 cm. **Adult male *javanica*** Forehead rich brick-red, crown and upperparts glossy blackish-blue, throat and upper breast brick-red, rest of underparts greyish-white with dark greyish mottling on vent, shallowly forked tail with large subterminal whitish spots; bare parts black; in flight underwing-coverts grey. **Juvenile** Duller and paler with short tail. **Similar species** See Barn Swallow. **Habitat** Open areas in primary and secondary forest, freshwater wetlands, estuaries, beaches, paddyfields, towns, to 1,600 m. **Behaviour** Often in mixed flocks with other hirundines; aerial insectivore, foraging for small insects over open ground or freshwater. **Voice** A short sharp high repeated *tseep* (6.4 kHz), sometimes slower-paced or run together in a harsh twittering. **Range & status** SE Asia, Philippines, Indonesia, New Guinea, SW Pacific. **Borneo** Common resident throughout, including offshore islands. **Breeding** Year-round; builds saucer-shaped mud nests under rafters, culverts and bridges, laying 2–4 white eggs with light grey spots.

CETTIIDAE: *Abroscopus* warblers, Mountain Tailorbird, *Cettia* bush-warblers, stubtails & allies

Worldwide c.34 species, 4 in Borneo. A varied family of small, active insectivores with stubby bodies and fine, pointed bills. Tesias and stubtails are almost tail-less. Most are secretive and forage in thick vegetation.

YELLOW-BELLIED WARBLER *Abroscopus superciliaris*

KINABALU 11/6/10

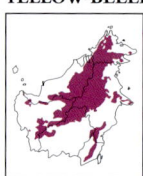

Identification 9 cm. Rather plain warbler with grey and white head pattern and pale yellow underparts. **Adult** *schwaneri* (endemic subspecies) Crown and nape grey, prominent greyish-white supercilium, lores and ear-coverts grey, throat and upper breast white, rest of underparts lemon-yellow, upperparts olive-green; iris dark brown, bill dark grey, legs and feet pinkish-brown. **Juvenile** Upperparts with brownish tinge, underparts paler. **Habitat** Thick undergrowth and bamboo stands in primary and secondary lowland dipterocarp to lower montane forest; slope specialist, usually 1,000–1,800 m, with records down to 200 m. **Behaviour** Foliage-gleaning insectivore, foraging in thick vegetation in lower to mid-storey. **Voice** A pleasant piercing tinkling series of 6–8 descending notes, *di-dee-dee-dee-dee-dee-dee-dit* (6.7–3.4 kHz, c.1.4 s). **Range & status** Himalayas, SE Asia, S China, Sumatra, Java. **Borneo** Common resident throughout, rare in Brunei. **Breeding** March–July; eggs are white with red flecks, but nest undescribed in Borneo.

MOUNTAIN TAILORBIRD *Phyllergates cucullatus*

KINABALU 12/16/10

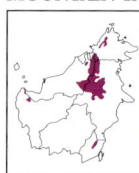

Identification 10–12 cm. Colourful tailorbird with distinctive orange crown and bright yellow underparts. **Adult** *cinereicollis* Forehead and crown bright orange-rufous, narrow supercilium pale grey, lores, ear-coverts, nape and mantle dark grey, rest of upperparts olive-green, throat and breast whitish, sides of breast pale grey, flanks and belly bright yellow; iris brown; long, slender bill grey; legs and feet pale pink. **Juvenile** Duller; lacks rufous on crown, throat and breast yellowish. **Similar species** See Dark-necked Tailorbird. **Habitat** Primary and secondary lower and upper montane forest, 1,150–2,650 m. **Behaviour** Skulking; gleans tiny invertebrates from foliage in thickets, bamboo stands and dense vegetation. **Voice** Has three different songs, often uttered in sequence, all sweet, musical whistles: *dee dee-dee-dee-di'di'di*, first note quiet and hesitant, rest louder and lilting (4.8–4.1 kHz); *didi-dwee-di-di-dee* on lower pitch than other phrases, last note loudest (3.8 kHz); and *tsi-tsi tsweee*, first two notes higher (5.2) than longer, louder third note (4.5 kHz); call is an inconspicuous *cht*. **Range & status** NE India, S China, SE Asia, Indonesia, Philippines. **Borneo** Common resident in north-central and western mountain ranges from G. Kinabalu to Pueh Range and G. Menyapa (Sabah, Sarawak and W and E Kalimantan) and Meratus Mountains (S Kalimantan). **Breeding** Possibly breeds November–July but otherwise undescribed in Borneo; elsewhere nest is pouch made of soft dead leaves and fibres at base of leaves or bamboos.

BORNEAN STUBTAIL *Urosphena whiteheadi*

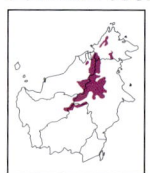

Identification 10 cm. Monotypic. Tiny, short-tailed terrestrial warbler with long buffish supercilium and exceptionally high-pitched voice. **Adult** Crown and upperparts brown, long supercilium and cheeks buffish-brown, eyestripe grey, underparts greyish-white with grey flanks; iris and bill black, legs and feet pale pink. **Habitat** Primary and secondary lower and upper montane forest, 750–3,150 m. **Behaviour** Poorly known; hops and creeps unobtrusively but often confidingly on ground or in low undergrowth. **Voice** Song is a short, very high-pitched single note (9.5 kHz, 0.3–0.5 s); call is a thin, high *tsit-tst tseee* (9.5 kHz); another trilled spot *piririt* is lower (8.2 kHz, 0.7 s). **Range & status** Endemic, uncommon resident N Borneo, confined to north-central mountain ranges from G. Kinabalu to Dulit Range and G. Menyapa (Sabah, E Sarawak, north W, C and E Kalimantan). **Breeding** Poorly known; a nest found in April was composed of reddish fibres and located close to ground in mossy bank, with two pink eggs with darker spots.

SUNDA BUSH-WARBLER *Cettia vulcania*

Identification 12–13 cm. Long-tailed, brownish warbler with paler underparts and long supercilium which skulks in thick vegetation. **Adult *oreophila*** (endemic subspecies) Crown and upperparts chestnut-brown, slightly darker on primaries and tail; long supercilium buffish-yellow, eyestripe dark brown, cheek and ear-coverts greyish; underparts greyish-white streaked darker, buffish-brown on undertail-coverts and flanks; iris brown, bill grey with yellowish lower mandible, legs and feet pinkish-grey. **Adult *banksi*** (endemic subspecies) As *oreophila* but darker. **Similar species** Friendly Bush-warbler is larger, darker, with more spotting on underparts. **Habitat** Dense undergrowth in primary and secondary lower and upper montane forest, 1,450–3,700 m. **Behaviour** Skulks in thickets, gleaning small invertebrates from vegetation, especially near road cuttings. **Voice** Alarm call is a harsh 'broken stick' *chrr*, repeated; song is a very distinctive slurred phrase of 4 short notes followed by a long note, that rises and falls noticeably *wit-wi-t-a-wit weeee-ik* (2.8–5.5 kHz,1.4 s). **Range & status** Sumatra, Java and Bali, Lesser Sundas, Palawan. **Borneo** Common resident in north-central mountain ranges from G. Kinabalu (*oreophila*) to G. Murud and G. Menyapa (Sabah, E Sarawak, E Kalimantan). **Breeding** February–July; nest consists of dead grasses woven into live ones.

Adult *oreophila*

PHYLLOSCOPIDAE: *Seicercus* & *Phylloscopus* warblers

Worldwide c.74 species, 4 in Borneo. Tiny to medium-sized, mostly arboreal insectivores with short slender bill, short wings and medium to long tail. Plumage is generally dull or subtle with prominent crown-stripe and supercilium. Many have complex, diagnostic vocalisations. Sexes are generally similar. Many species pose identification challenges.

YELLOW-BREASTED WARBLER *Seicercus montis*

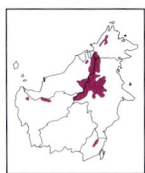

Identification 9–10 cm. Distinctive green-and-yellow warbler with striking chestnut and black head pattern. **Adult *montis*** (endemic subspecies) Crown and face chestnut with black lateral crown-stripes to nape, upperparts olive-green with two yellow wing-bars and grading to yellow rump, tail darker fringed olive-yellow, throat and underparts bright yellow; iris brown with white eye-ring, bill pinkish with grey culmen, legs and feet pinkish-brown. **Juvenile** Duller with less well-defined head pattern. **Habitat** Primary and secondary lower and upper montane forest, 1,050–2,450 m. **Behaviour** Commonly joins mixed feeding flocks; gleans small invertebrates from foliage in mid- to upper storey. **Voice** Song is a series of slurred, piercing, delicate notes, very high-pitched but not very loud, *t-tzi-tzi-tzi-tzwee* (8.4–6.5 kHz, c.1 s); this is often interspersed with a short sharp downslurred *prrit* call. **Range & status** Thai-Malay Peninsula, Sumatra, Palawan, Lesser Sundas. **Borneo** Common resident in north-central and western mountain ranges from G. Kinabalu to G. Menyapa and Pueh Range (Sabah, Sarawak and W and E Kalimantan); also recorded from S Kalimantan (Meratus Mountains) where probably uncommon. **Breeding** December–October; nest is made of moss and fibres and hidden in mossy banks.

Juvenile

Adult

239

KINABALU 12/6/10

MOUNTAIN LEAF-WARBLER *Phylloscopus trivirgatus*

Adult *kinabaluensis*

Adult *sarawacensis*

Juvenile *kinabaluensis*

Identification 10–11 cm. Small yellowish warbler with distinctive head pattern and plain upperparts. **Adult *kinabaluensis*** (endemic subspecies) Crown dark greyish-green with indistinct paler crown-stripe and broad yellowish supercilium, dark greyish-green eye-stripe and lores, ear-coverts pale yellow, upperparts greyish-green without wing-bars, underparts pale yellow; iris brown, bill orange with grey culmen, legs and feet pinkish. **Juvenile** Upperparts duller, underparts yellowish. **Adult *sarawacensis*** (endemic subspecies) More clearly defined head pattern, upperparts greener, underparts richer yellow. **Habitat** Primary and secondary lower and upper montane forest, 1,100–3,350 m. **Behaviour** Commonly in mixed feeding flocks; gleans insects in foliage in mid- to upper storey. **Voice** A pretty melodious whistle, *tsee-wi-chi-wi-chi-wi-chit...* (3.4–7.5 kHz, c.2.5 s); call is a short, inconspicuous *tst tst tst...* (5.7 kHz). **Range & status** Thai-Malay Peninsula, Sumatra, Java, Lesser Sundas, Philippines. **Borneo** Common montane resident in north-central, western and south ranges from G. Kinabalu to G. Menyapa and Pueh Range and Meratus Mountains (Sabah, Sarawak, W, E and S Kalimantan), *kinabaluensis* confined to G. Kinabalu, *sarawacensis* west to Pueh Range, elsewhere race uncertain. **Breeding** Possibly breeds June–November but otherwise undescribed in Borneo.

ARCTIC WARBLER *Phylloscopus borealis*

Adult *borealis* (worn)

Adult *borealis* (fresh)

Adult *xanthodryas*

Identification 11–13 cm. Largest, plainest *Phylloscopus* warbler in Borneo with conspicuous supercilium. **Adult *borealis*** Forehead and crown olive-green, long buffish-white supercilium, dark olive eyestripe, ear-coverts buffish mottled olive, upperparts olive-green with single buffish-white wing-bar (sometimes shows indistinct second wing-bar), underparts whitish with indistinct greyish streaking on sides of breast and flanks; iris brown, bill pink with grey culmen, legs and feet pink. **Juvenile** As adult but upperparts greyish, underparts greyish-white with brown wash on flanks. **Adult *xanthodryas*** Upperparts greener, supercilium and underparts yellower. **Habitat** Primary and secondary lowland forests, peatswamp forest, to 1,700 m. **Behaviour** Arboreal insectivore; usually seen foraging in mid- to upper storey; often joins mixed feeding flocks. **Voice** Call is a very brief, high-pitched *dzit* (5.8 kHz, 0.1 s); unlikely to sing away from breeding grounds. **Range & status** Breeds N Palearctic; migrates to S China, Taiwan, SE Asia, Indonesia, Philippines. **Borneo** Common non-breeding visitor and passage migrant throughout, including offshore islands, September–April.

YELLOW-BROWED WARBLER *Phylloscopus inornatus*

Adult (worn)

Adult (fresh)

Identification 10–11 cm. Monotypic. Small greenish warbler with two wing-bars and pale yellow supercilium. **Adult** Crown, lores and eyestripe olive-brown, long pale yellow supercilium, ear-coverts olive-brown mottled buff, upperparts olive-green with two prominent yellowish-white wing-bars, whitish tips on tertials, underparts whitish; iris brown, bill brownish-grey with pink base, legs and feet pinkish-brown. **Juvenile** Upperparts darker, underparts with yellow wash. **Habitat** In Borneo recorded in coastal woodland, elsewhere recorded in wide variety of wooded habitats. **Behaviour** On migration usually solitary; gleans insects from foliage in canopy. **Voice** A short, sweet *tsee-weet*, first note sharply downslurred, second equally sharply upwardly inflected (6.9–4.7 kHz, 0.3 s). **Range & status** Breeds E Palearctic; winters NE India, SE Asia. **Borneo** Vagrant; one record from Kuching, W Sarawak.

TIMALIIDAE: Babblers

Worldwide c.432 species, 40 in Borneo. A very large, very diverse mostly Asian group of sociable, noisy but skulking arboreal birds with soft plumage, strong legs and long tail. Many are weak fliers with short, rounded wings. Occupy a range of habitats, most are insectivorous. Most are highly sedentary and sexually monomorphic. Vocalisations are typically distinctive, loud and complex. The systematics of this family is in a state of flux and many species may belong to other groups.

BROWN FULVETTA *Alcippe brunneicauda*

Identification 14–15 cm. Monotypic. Small, very nondescript brown babbler. **Adult** Forehead to nape dull greyish-brown, face grey with fine paler streaking, upperparts brown, warmer on rump and uppertail-coverts, throat and belly whitish, grey wash across breast and flanks; iris brown, bill brownish-grey, paler on lower mandible, legs and feet pinkish- to brownish-grey. **Juvenile** Base of lower mandible yellowish. **Habitat** Primary and older secondary lowland dipterocarp to lower montane forest, to 1,200 m. **Behaviour** Gleans foliage for small insects and fruit in mid-storey; often joins mixed feeding flocks; nondescript and often overlooked, usually detected by distinctive song. **Voice** Song is a loud, sweet, up-and-down *di-ti-di-ti-du-dit* in 5–6 lilting notes, last note lowest (4.4–3.2 kHz, 1.2 s); call is a shrill, metallic *swit*. **Range & status** Thai-Malay Peninsula, Sumatra. **Borneo** Common resident throughout, including N Natunas. **Breeding** February–August; otherwise undescribed in Borneo.

CHESTNUT-CRESTED YUHINA *Staphida everetti*

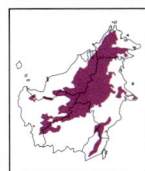

Identification 14–15 cm. Monotypic. Small, highly mobile tit-like babbler with short chestnut crest. **Adult** Forehead and crown to sides of face chestnut, lores and short narrow supercilium white, submoustachial area white with narrow chestnut malar stripe, upperparts grey, darker on wings and tail with white outer tail feathers, underparts white; iris reddish-brown, bill grey, legs and feet greyish-brown to pinkish-grey. **Juvenile** As adult. **Habitat** Primary and secondary hill to upper montane and kerangas forest, 550–2,600 m. **Behaviour** Typically in large single-species flocks of 10–30 birds seen sweeping rapidly through canopy, pausing to glean insects from foliage. **Voice** Calls consist of soft buzzing notes, and chattering notes uttered in flight. **Range & status** Endemic, common resident in mountain ranges throughout. **Breeding** November–August; cup-shaped nest of moss and fibres is made in small hole in mossy bank c.0.5 m from ground; lays 1–6 white to pinkish-white eggs with dark reddish and grey spots, possibly cooperative breeder.

ORIENTAL WHITE-EYE *Zosterops palpebrosus*

Identification 10.5–11 cm. **Adult** *auriventer* Lores black, front of forehead yellow grading into lime-green crown and upperparts, sides of face and throat to upper breast yellow, underparts whitish-grey with yellow stripe from throat to vent, undertail-coverts yellow; iris brown with broad bright white eye-ring, bill grey, legs and feet dark grey. **Juvenile** Lacks white eye-ring and ventral stripe. **Similar species** See Black-capped and Everett's White-eyes. **Habitat** Mangroves, coastal scrub, swamp forest, at sea-level. **Behaviour** Usually in active, noisy flocks; gleans foliage for insects in canopy. **Voice** Call is a constantly uttered, rather high-pitched, shrill *chee-chee-chee…* (4.8 kHz). **Range & status** Indian Subcontinent, SW China, SE Asia, Sumatra, Java, Bali, Lesser Sundas. **Borneo** Rare resident in W Sabah, Brunei, Sarawak, northern W Kalimantan and the S Natunas. **Breeding** Poorly known in Borneo, breeding behaviour observed March–April.

BLACK-CAPPED WHITE-EYE *Zosterops atricapilla*

Identification 9.5–11 cm. **Adult *atricapilla*** Forehead, lores and chin black, upperparts olive-green, darker on flight feathers and tail, throat paler olive-green, underparts grey with broad yellowish-green stripe on centre of belly and olive-green undertail-coverts; iris brown with broad bright white eye-ring, bill and legs grey. **Juvenile** Reduced black on face. **Similar species** Oriental White-eye lacks black on face, has darker upperparts and paler grey underparts with narrower, longer yellow ventral stripe. **Habitat** Primary and secondary lower and upper montane forest, 950–2,900 m. **Behaviour** Usually in flocks, often joining mixed feeding flocks; gleans small invertebrates from foliage and moss in mid- to upper storey; also eats fruit and nectar. **Voice** Call is a repeated squeaky *tseet* (5.5 kHz), also 2–3 softer liquid notes *prrrt... prrt...* (5–3.4 kHz). **Range & status** Sumatra. **Borneo** Common resident in north-central mountain ranges from G. Kinabalu to G. Menyapa (Sabah, E Sarawak and E Kalimantan) and Meratus Mountains (S Kalimantan). **Breeding** Possibly November–September; one nest was made of fine roots on underside of mossy branch.

Adult

EVERETT'S WHITE-EYE *Zosterops everetti*

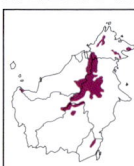

Identification 9.5–11.5 cm. **Adult *tahanensis*** Lores black, crown and upperparts olive-green, throat yellowish-green, underparts grey with broad yellow ventral stripe to yellow undertail-coverts; iris brown with broad bright white eye-ring, bill and legs grey. **Juvenile** Duller with paler, reduced ventral stripe and green fringes to flight feathers. **Similar species** Oriental White-eye has yellowish forehead, paler grey flanks and narrower ventral stripe; Black-capped White-eye is darker on head, with less yellow on underparts. **Habitat** Primary and secondary lower montane forest, 200–1,800 m. **Behaviour** Arboreal foliage-gleaning insectivore; usually in flocks. **Voice** Call is a high-pitched buzzing *dzee*. **Range & status** Thai-Malay Peninsula, Philippines, N Sulawesi. **Borneo** Uncommon resident in north-central and western mountain ranges from G. Kinabalu to Pueh Range (Sabah, Brunei, Sarawak, C and E Kalimantan) and Meratus Mountains (S Kalimantan). **Breeding** Undescribed in Borneo.

Adult

JAVAN WHITE-EYE *Zosterops flavus*

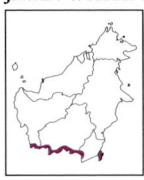

Identification 9.5–11 cm. Monotypic. **Adult** No black on lores, upperparts all yellowish-green, short tail with greenish edges, underparts yellow; iris brown with bright white eye-ring, bill and legs grey. **Similar species** Yellow-bellied White-eye is larger, with black lores and no green fringes on tail. **Habitat** Mangroves, coastal scrub, at sea-level. **Behaviour** Gleans small invertebrates from treetop foliage. **Voice** Call is a rapid, high-pitched squeaky *tsee-tsee-tsee...* uttered in phrases of 1–3 notes (4–5.6 kHz). **Range & status** NW Java. **Borneo** Common resident in SE Borneo (W, C and S Kalimantan). **Breeding** Undescribed in Borneo.

Adult

242

YELLOW-BELLIED WHITE-EYE *Zosterops chloris*

Adult

Identification 10–11 cm. **Adult** *maxi* Lores and thin line under eye black, upperparts olive-green, underparts pale yellow; iris brown with white eye-ring, bill and legs grey. **Similar species** See Javan White-eye. **Habitat** Mangroves, coastal woodlands, plantations, at sea-level. **Behaviour** Usually in small flocks; gleans foliage for small invertebrates at all strata of coastal vegetation. **Voice** Thin high-pitched *tsit* calls. **Range & status** Sulawesi, Lesser Sundas. **Borneo** Only recorded on Karimata Islands (W Kalimantan) and Matasirih and Marabatuan islands (S Kalimantan). **Breeding** Undescribed in Borneo.

PYGMY WHITE-EYE *Oculocincta squamifrons*

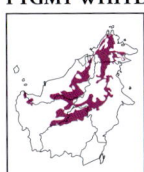

Adult

Identification 9 cm. Monotypic. **Adult** Upperparts and throat olive-grey, forehead speckled with white, underparts whitish-yellow with greyish flanks, brighter yellow on belly; iris buffish-white with thin white eye-ring, bill brownish-black, legs and feet pale greenish-grey. **Juvenile** Undescribed. **Habitat** Primary and secondary hill to lower montane and kerangas forest, 50–2,100 m but usually 550–1,000 m. **Behaviour** Nomadic frugivore with warbler-like movements; tiny and fast-moving in small flocks; often in mixed feeding flocks. **Voice** Call is an unobtrusive, high-pitched *tsee tsee tsee* (5.5-6.5 kHz). **Range & status** Endemic, uncommon in north-central and western mountain ranges from G. Kinabalu to G. Penrissen, Barito Ulu and G. Menyapa (Sabah, Sarawak, W, C and E Kalimantan). **Breeding** Undescribed.

MOUNTAIN BLACKEYE *Chlorocharis emiliae*

Adult *emiliae*

Identification 12–14 cm. **Adult** *emiliae* Lores and area around eye black, bordered bright yellowish-green on supercilium and throat, upperparts dark olive-green, underparts paler olive-green, undertail grey; iris yellowish-brown, long pointed bill pink, legs and feet yellow. **Juvenile** Iris brown, bill duller. **Adult** *trinitae* Underparts pale yellow to green. **Adult** *fusciceps* Crown brownish, underparts yellow. **Adult** *moultoni* Underparts dark green. **Habitat** Primary upper montane forest and scrub, 1,500–2,600 m. **Behaviour** Feeds on small invertebrates and nectar at all levels; often in small groups; commonest bird in summit scrub on G. Kinabalu and G. Trus Madi. **Voice** Song is a sweet melodious thrush-like *wit-weet-weet-weet-weetee-weetee-tee* (3.5–2.4 kHz, c.2 s); call is a sharper *pweet*. **Range & status** Endemic, common resident in north-central and west mountain ranges from G. Kinabalu to Pueh Range (Sabah, Sarawak and E and W Kalimantan), *emiliae* G. Kinabalu, *trinitae* G. Trus Madi, *fusciceps* E Sarawak, *moultoni* W Sarawak. **Breeding** February–September; nest is shallow cup made of brown rootlets and dead grasses lined with moss and decorated with lichen, located in fork of tree or in dense heath.

243

BLACK-THROATED BABBLER *Stachyris nigricollis*

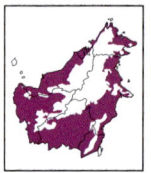

Identification 15–16 cm. Monotypic. Medium-sized babbler with rich brown upperparts and distinctive black face with white supercilium and malar patch. **Adult** Forecrown black with fine whitish streaking, lores black, short white supercilium behind eye, ear-coverts and sides of neck grey, hindcrown and upperparts rufous-brown, darker on wings and tail, chin to upper breast black bordered below with broken white line, prominent broad white malar spot, rest of underparts grey merging into dark chestnut lower flanks and undertail-coverts; iris reddish-brown, upper mandible black, lower mandible bluish-grey, legs and feet dark grey. **Juvenile** Duller; white on forehead absent, malar patch reduced, underparts uniform grey with no white necklace. **Habitat** Primary forest edges, secondary and disturbed lowland dipterocarp forest, riparian, peatswamp and kerangas forest; lowland specialist to 600 m. **Behaviour** Arboreal foliage-gleaning insectivore; active in lower to mid-storey usually in pairs or small parties; sometimes joins mixed feeding flocks. **Voice** Song is a long series of mellow fluty whistles, *pu pu-pu-pu-pu-pu-pu-pu-pu-pu-pu-pupu-pu...* delivered on an even pitch (1 kHz, c.5–6 notes/s) with slight pause after first note, often accompanied by nasal churring notes from mate. **Range & status** Thai-Malay Peninsula, Sumatra. **Borneo** Locally common lowland resident throughout. **Breeding** Possibly breeds April–September but otherwise undescribed in Borneo.

Juvenile

Adult

WHITE-NECKED BABBLER *Stachyris leucotis*

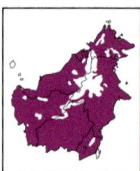

Identification 14–15 cm. Medium-sized chestnut, grey and black babbler with distinctive string of white spots around eye to neck. **Adult *obscurata*** (endemic subspecies) Crown dark grey, lores buffish-rufous, white (sometimes broken) supercilium running into string of white spots on black on necksides around rear of dark grey ear-coverts, upperparts warm brown with buffish-brown spots on wing-coverts, chin and throat black extending on neck to join black behind ear-coverts, rest of underparts bluish-grey with dull olive-brown lower belly to undertail-coverts; iris reddish-brown, bill grey, paler on lower mandible, legs and feet grey. **Juvenile** Duller with brownish ear-coverts, supercilium and spots on neck buffish, underparts dark brown. **Habitat** Slope specialist in primary lowland dipterocarp and hill forest, to 1,000 m but mostly above 600 m. **Behaviour** Shy and secretive, occurring at low densities in parties of 2–4; foliage-gleaning insectivore in thick vegetation in lower storey. **Voice** A clear loud four-note *woo-wee-wit-wit*, first note long, second shorter and higher, then two dipping notes (3–2.5 kHz, 1.2 s), or more monotone three-note *woo-wee-wit* with last note slightly downslurred (2.3–2 kHz, 1.2 s). **Range & status** Thai-Malay Peninsula, Sumatra. **Borneo** Rare resident Sabah, Brunei, Sarawak, W, C and E Kalimantan, status in S Kalimantan uncertain. **Breeding** December–June; one nest was compact cup of grass, roots and fibres containing three white eggs.

Adult

GOMANTONG CAVE 10/6/10

GREY-HEADED BABBLER *Stachyris poliocephala*

Adult

Juvenile

Identification 13–15 cm. Monotypic. Rufous-brown babbler with distinctive dark hood. **Adult** Dark blackish-grey hood with narrow white streaking on forehead and throat, upperparts dark brown with rufous tinge on wings and tail, rest of underparts chestnut-brown; iris golden-yellow, bill dark grey, legs and feet grey. **Juvenile** Duller, lacks streaking on head; iris brownish. **Habitat** Primary and secondary lowland dipterocarp to lower montane forest, plantations, to 1,200 m. **Behaviour** Shy and skulking; gleans foliage for small insects in lower to mid-storey. **Voice** Song is a clear, high-pitched, glissading *pee-chee-puwee* (3.1–2.3 kHz, 1.8 s). **Range & status** Thai-Malay Peninsula, Sumatra. **Borneo** Locally common resident N Borneo (Sabah, Brunei and Sarawak, E Kalimantan) and S Kalimantan, but possibly more widespread. **Breeding** April–September; makes compact cup-shaped nest of fine roots and fibres decorated with moss well concealed on ground, two white eggs.

GREY-THROATED BABBLER *Stachyris nigriceps*

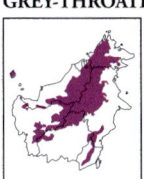

Adult *borneensis*

Identification 12–13 cm. Small active noisy babbler with distinctive head pattern, usually in thick undergrowth. **Adult** *borneensis* (endemic subspecies) Crown black with faint paler streaking, short pale grey supercilium behind eye, lores and moustachial area to throat blackish with prominent white sub-moustachial patch, upperparts brown, sides of neck and rest of underparts buffish-brown with grey flecks on upper breast below throat; iris yellowish-brown, bill grey, legs and feet pinkish-grey. **Adult** *hartleyi* (endemic subspecies) Greyer crown. **Juvenile** Poorly known but probably duller with buffish submoustachial patch. **Habitat** Primary and secondary hill to upper montane forest, 500–2,200 m, with records to 3,300 m on G. Kinabalu. **Behaviour** Usually in small, noisy and active groups of 5–8 individuals; gleans foliage for small insects in dense vegetation in lower to mid-storey. **Voice** Song is a rapid high-pitched monotone *tsi-tee-ti-ti-ti-ti-ti-ti-ti-* (4 kHz, 2.5 s); contact call is a soft churring *chi-chi-chi-chi…* **Range & status** NE Indian Subcontinent, S China, SE Asia, Sumatra. **Borneo** Common submontane resident in north-central, western and southern mountain ranges from G. Kinabalu to Pueh Range, G. Palung and Meratus Mountains; *borneensis* N Borneo (NE Sabah), *hartleyi* W Borneo (Sarawak and Kalimantan, race in S Kalimantan uncertain), including N Natunas. **Breeding** December–August; nest is large ball of grasses and leaves with side entrance located low down in dense vegetation; lays 2–5 glossy white eggs.

CHESTNUT-WINGED BABBLER *Stachyris erythroptera*

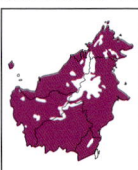

Identification 12.5–13.5 cm. Small grey and chesnut babbler with prominent blue eye-ring. **Adult *bicolor*** (endemic subspecies) Crown to nape and breast dark slaty-grey, upperparts chestnut-brown, rest of underparts buffish-brown; iris reddish-brown, bill dark grey, legs and feet pinkish-grey; when singing, inflated blue skin shows on neck-sides. **Adult *rufa*** (endemic subspecies) Upperparts richer rufous-chestnut. **Juvenile** More rufous upperparts with duller facial skin, underparts paler. **Habitat** Primary and secondary lowland dipterocarp and peatswamp forest, edges of mangroves, plantations, to 1,220 m. **Behaviour** Active and noisy foliage-gleaning insectivore; usually in small parties in thick vegetation in mid-storey; often joins mixed feeding flocks. **Voice** Song is a mellow, slow-paced 5–12-note *hu-hu-hu-hu-hu...* (0.9 kHz, 5–6 notes/s), often with accompanying churring notes (probably from female); also a faster series of *hu-u-u-u-u-* notes at rate of c.12 notes/s. **Range & status** Thai-Malay Peninsula, Sumatra. **Borneo** Common resident throughout, including N Natunas and Banggi Island, *bicolor* N Borneo, *rufa* S Borneo. **Breeding** March–October; nest is ball of dead leaves and moss with side entrance built in small tree 1–4 m from ground; more than two adults have been seen building nest, suggesting cooperative breeding.

Adult *bicolor*

CHESTNUT-RUMPED BABBLER *Stachyris maculata*

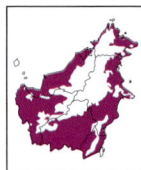

Identification 17–18.5 cm. Large heavy-billed babbler with pronounced black streaking on underparts and bright chestnut rump. **Adult *maculata*** Forehead and forecrown streaked black and whitish, lores blackish, cheek and ear-coverts grey, hindcrown and rest of upperparts olive-brown with bright chestnut lower back to uppertail-coverts, chin and throat black grading into broad black streaks on white breast to belly, lower flanks and undertail-coverts dull brown; iris yellow with broad blue orbital skin, bill dark grey, paler at base of lower mandible, legs and feet grey; when singing, inflated blue skin shows on neck-sides. **Juvenile** Upperparts brighter, chin to breast greyish with some black streaking, underparts plainer; iris grey, base of lower mandible yellow. **Habitat** Primary and secondary lowland dipterocarp, riverine swamp and peatswamp forest, old plantations, to 550 m. **Behaviour** Active and noisy foliage- and bark-gleaning insectivore; usually in small parties in thick vegetation in lower to mid-storey; often joins mixed feeding flocks. **Voice** Song is a cheery, low-pitched hooting *woop-oop-woop...* (1 kHz, 0.5 s), usually with an accompanying cacophony of nasal churrs (probably from female) and a rapid, piping *pupupupupu...* (1.4 kHz, 10 notes/s), as well as various other jumbled trills and hoots. **Range & status** Thai-Malay Peninsula, Sumatra. **Borneo** Common resident throughout. **Breeding** February–September; loose, ball-shaped nest of dry leaves is held together with grass and roots; lays three dull white eggs.

Adult

CHESTNUT-BACKED SCIMITAR-BABBLER
Pomatorhinus montanus

Adult

Identification 19–21 cm. Small scimitar-babbler with long white supercilium and black head contrasting with rich chestnut upperparts. **Adult *bornensis*** (endemic subspecies) Head black with prominent long white supercilium to nape, upperparts bright chestnut, wings fringed brownish, tail blackish-brown, throat and underparts white with chestnut flanks and vent; iris yellow, longish decurved bill grey with yellowish base of lower mandible, legs and feet bluish-grey. **Juvenile** Duller, more chestnut on head, less extensive chestnut on flanks. **Habitat** Primary and secondary lowland dipterocarp to lower montane forest, to 2,200 m. **Behaviour** Gleans bark and foliage in mid- to upper storey; often joins mixed feeding flocks; fairly unobtrusive but easily detected by distinctive vocalisations. **Voice** Song is a low-pitched four-note phrase, *grrt-put-put-pweet*, first note a short, quiet growl, middle notes louder hoots and last longest and sharply upslurred (1.2–2.4 kHz, 1 s), and a resonant *hwu-hu-hu*, first note higher (1.6–1.2 kHz); also a shorter, mellow, even-pitched *wup-wup-woo* (1.2 kHz, 0.7 s). **Range & status** Thai-Malay Peninsula, Sumatra, Java, Bali. **Borneo** Uncommon resident throughout. **Breeding** January–October; lays 2–3 glossy white eggs in large ball-shaped nest of grasses and leaves.

RUFOUS-FRONTED BABBLER *Stachyridopsis rufifrons*

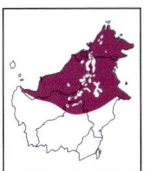

Adult *poliogaster*

Identification 11–12 cm. Very small, active, rather nondescript arboreal babbler with chestnut or rufous crown and orange-buff on underparts. **Adult *poliogaster*** Crown chestnut, face pale grey, rest of upperparts olive-brown, chin to upper breast buffish-white with fine dark streaks, faint breast-band buffish-orange, centre of belly whitish with rest of underparts greyish; iris reddish-brown, bill grey, legs and feet pinkish-grey. **Adult *sarawacensis*** (endemic subspecies) Crown more orange-rufous, face greyer; iris brownish-yellow, bill black. **Juvenile** Crown paler, wings and tail edged rufous. **Habitat** Dense undergrowth in primary and secondary lowland dipterocarp, kerangas and hill forest, to 1,500 m. **Behaviour** Usually seen in pairs or small groups; often joins mixed feeding flocks; forages in dense foliage for small invertebrates in lower to mid-storey. **Voice** Song is a simple but rapid series of 8–10 mellow monotone notes (1.8 kHz, 1.5 s), *pu pu-pu-pu-pu-pu-pu-pu-pu...* sometimes with pause after first note. **Range & status** NE Indian Subcontinent, S China, SE Asia, Sumatra. **Borneo** Uncommon resident Sabah, Sarawak, and W, C and E Kalimantan. **Breeding** February–July; nest is ball of large leaves bound by long grasses and with side entrance 4–6 m up in tree.

BOLD-STRIPED TIT-BABBLER *Macronous bornensis*

Identification 12 cm. Small noisy babbler with chestnut upperparts and boldly black and white streaked underparts. **Adult *bornensis*** (endemic) Lores and ear-coverts blackish-grey, crown and upperparts chestnut, underparts white with bold black streaking shading on belly to pale yellow with narrow indistinct streaking, flanks and undertail-coverts plain pale grey; iris pale yellow with blue orbital skin, bill grey, legs and feet pinkish-grey. **Adult *montanus*** (endemic subspecies) Like *bornensis* but crown to mantle greyish-brown, underparts buffier. **Juvenile** Underparts unstreaked buffish-white. **Habitat** Disturbed primary and secondary lowland dipterocarp, swamp and riparian forest, mangroves, scrub, cultivated areas, gardens, plantations, to 1,600 m. **Behaviour** Very noisy and active arboreal insectivore; gleans dense foliage in small parties at all levels; not shy but rather skulking and often difficult to see. **Voice** Song is a paced, mellow *chonk-chonk-chonk-chonk...* (1 kHz, 3–4 notes/s), usually accompanied by a constant *chk-chk-chk-chk-chk...* uttered by female. **Range & status** W and C Java, Bangka and Belitung islands (off E Sumatra). **Borneo** Abundant resident throughout, *montanus* confined to G. Kinabalu area, *bornensis* elsewhere, also on N Natunas and Banggi and Malawali islands (represented by various races). **Breeding** Year-round; nest is loose ball of dry leaves and grasses lined with fine rootlets and fibres with side entrance located in thick scrubby vegetation on or near ground; lays two white or pinkish-white eggs with reddish spots.

Adult *montanus*

Adult *bornensis*

FLUFFY-BACKED TIT-BABBLER *Macronous ptilosus*

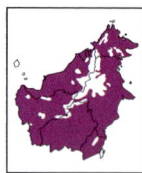

Identification 16–17 cm. Large, rich chestnut babbler with bright crown, black throat and conspicuous blue eye-ring. **Adult *reclusus*** Forehead to nape rich rufous, upperparts chestnut-brown, wings and tail darker blackish-brown, moustachial area to throat black, underparts chestnut-brown; iris reddish-brown, orbital skin bright blue, bill and legs black; when singing, inflated pale blue skin sometimes shows on neck-sides; eponymous long plumes on rump and flanks usually not visible in field. **Juvenile** Duller with paler orbital skin, lower mandible yellowish. **Habitat** Disturbed areas of primary and secondary lowland dipterocarp, hill and swamp forest, mangroves, to 1,000 m. **Behaviour** Foliage-gleaning insectivore, typically found in pairs or small parties foraging in thick vegetation in lower storey. **Voice** Song is a low-pitched, mellow *poop* (pause) *poop-poop-poop* (1 kHz, c.1 s), usually with a strange, very throaty churring, probably uttered by female; also gives a low *poo-poo* (pause) *poo-poo* (0.7 kHz). **Range & status** Thai-Malay Peninsula, Sumatra. **Borneo** Locally common resident throughout. **Breeding** November–July; nest is small loose ball of dead leaves lined with fine roots located close to ground; lays two glossy white to pinkish eggs with reddish and brownish blotches.

Adult

248

TEMMINCK'S BABBLER *Pellorneum pyrrogenys*

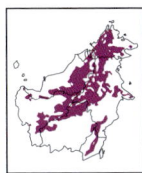

Identification 14–15 cm. Small, rather nondescript babbler with dark crown and rufous breast-band on white underparts. **Adult *canicapillus*** (endemic subspecies) Crown blackish-grey with pale streaks, lores and supercilium grey, ear-coverts rufous-brown streaked darker, rest of upperparts brown, warmer on flight feathers and tail, underparts white with rufous-brown breast-band extending onto flanks; iris reddish-brown, bill greyish-black, legs and feet pinkish-grey. **Adult *longstaffi*** (endemic subspecies) Crown blackish, broader breast-band with deeper rufous on flanks extending to vent. **Adult *erythrote*** (endemic subspecies) More rufous on sides of face, breast-band more defined. **Juvenile** Undescribed. **Habitat** Primary and secondary lower montane forest, 500–1,550 m. **Behaviour** Foliage-gleaning insectivore, foraging on or near ground in thick vegetation; sometimes joins other lower-storey species in mixed feeding flocks. **Voice** Song is a loud jolly whistled *pi-choo* (3.8–2 kHz, 0.5 s) uttered irregularly, first note upslurred, longer second note downslurred; also a longer, more complex song consisting of a rapid *pit-pit-pit-pit-pit-chooo...*, last note downslurred; call is a repeated quavering *prrt-prrt-prrt...* **Range & status** Java. **Borneo** Uncommon hill and montane resident throughout, *canicapillus* W Sabah, *longstaffi* E Sarawak and E Kalimantan, *erythrote* W Borneo. **Breeding** December–April; lays two blue or dull green eggs with brown and purplish-grey spots in compact nest hidden in base of shrub or tree-root.

Adult *longstaffi*

BLACK-CAPPED BABBLER *Pellorneum capistratum*

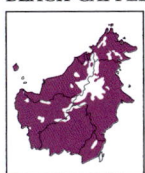

Identification 15–17 cm. Small terrestrial babbler with distinctive head pattern and black, rufous and white plumage. **Adult *morrelli*** (endemic subspecies) Forehead to nape black, long whitish supercilium to hindneck, lores and ear-coverts dark greyish-brown with darker streaks, faint narrow dark grey malar stripe, upperparts chestnut-brown, throat and submoustachial area white, rest of underparts rufous-brown; iris dark brown, bill grey with pinkish-grey lower mandible, legs and feet pinkish. **Adult *capistratoides*** (endemic subspecies) Like *morrelli* but head and ear-coverts blacker, darker overall. **Juvenile** Crown browner, rufous wash on throat. **Habitat** Primary and secondary lowland dipterocarp, peatswamp and kerangas forest, old plantations, usually below 1,000 m but up to 1,400 m in Kelabit Highlands. **Behaviour** Terrestrial insectivore; usually encountered singly or in pairs gleaning leaf-litter on or very near ground; walks and runs, sometimes taking short flights. **Voice** A disyllabic clear sweet whistle, *pii-yuu*, rising slightly then falling in pitch (3.6–4.5 kHz, 0.5 s); also a rather mournful three-note *too-ii-tyou* (4.3–3.1 kHz, c.1 s), short middle note highest. **Range & status** Thai-Malay Peninsula, Sumatra, Java. **Borneo** Common lowland resident throughout, including N Natunas and Banggi Island, *P. c. morrelli* Sabah, *P. c. capistratoides* Sarawak and Kalimantan. **Breeding** Possibly breeds March–August but otherwise undescribed in Borneo.

Adult *morrelli*

MOUSTACHED BABBLER *Malacopteron magnirostre*

Identification 16–18 cm. Medium-sized, rather plain babbler with dark crown and moustache and chestnut tail. **Adult** *cinereocapilla* (endemic subspecies) Forehead and crown dark grey, lores, supercilium and ear-coverts grey, narrow dark grey moustachial stripe, wings and back olive-brown, tail chestnut-brown, underparts greyish-white with pale grey wash on breast (sometimes streaked); iris reddish-brown, bill grey, legs and feet bluish-grey. **Juvenile** Crown duller, moustachial stripe indistinct, base of lower mandible yellowish. **Similar species** Sooty-capped Babbler has more defined browner crown, darker tail and no moustachial stripe. **Habitat** Primary lowland dipterocarp, kerangas and peatswamp forest, old plantations, usually to 600–900 m but with records to 1,200 m. **Behaviour** Gleans foliage in mid-storey for small invertebrates; usually in pairs or small groups; joins mixed feeding flocks often with other *Malacopteron* babblers. **Voice** Song is a loud, melancholy 3–6-note *di-doo-doo-doo-dooo*, descending scale (3.4–2.2 kHz, c.2.3 s), also a two-phrase *doo-da-doo* on one pitch followed by four descending notes; call is a quite soft but harsh, churring *prrrt*. **Range & status** Thai-Malay Peninsula, Sumatra. **Borneo** Common resident throughout. **Breeding** Possibly breeds February–September but otherwise undescribed in Borneo.

Adult

SOOTY-CAPPED BABBLER *Malacopteron affine*

Identification 15–17 cm. Medium-sized, rather plain babbler with prominent brownish cap and dark chestnut tail. **Adult** *phoeniceum* (endemic subspecies) Forehead to nape greyish-brown, lores, supercilium and ear-coverts grey, wings and back olive-brown, tail chestnut-brown, underparts whitish with grey streaky wash on breast; iris reddish-brown, bill grey, paler on lower mandible, legs and feet grey. **Juvenile** Cap duller, flight feathers edged rufous, tail brighter, breast unstreaked; lower mandible pale yellow. **Similar species** See Moustached Babbler. **Habitat** Primary and secondary lowland dipterocarp, riparian and kerangas forest, forest edges, plantations, to 550 m. **Behaviour** Favours secondary growth and areas of natural disturbance; forages for insects in lower to mid-storey; usually in small parties, often joining mixed feeding flocks. **Voice** Very distinctive rambling but pleasant song, a series of rather slow plaintive clear whistles, *phu-phi-phu-phoo-phi-phoo-phu-phi…*, seemingly randomly rising and falling in pitch (3–1.5 kHz, each phrase c.10–15 s), each note short and uttered at rate of 2–3 notes/s; also a jollier song in two three-note phrases, *wi-ti-woo wi-ti-woo*, the *wi* note rising then two notes descending, each phrase c.1 s. **Range & status** Thai-Malay Peninsula, Sumatra. **Borneo** Common lowland resident throughout. **Breeding** June–October; makes nest using bark fibres in dense foliage.

Adult

SCALY-CROWNED BABBLER *Malacopteron cinereum*

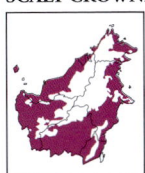

Identification 14–16 cm. Medium-sized babbler with black-speckled rufous cap and pinkish legs. **Adult** *cinereum* Forehead to crown bright rufous with black tips, nape black; lores, supercilium and sides of face grey with buffish streaks on ear-coverts, upperparts olive-brown, tail chestnut-brown, underparts whitish with grey wash on breast and flanks; iris reddish-brown, bill grey, paler on lower mandible, legs and feet pinkish. **Juvenile** Warmer edging on flight feathers. **Similar species** Rufous-crowned Babbler is larger, has grey streaking on throat and breast, lacks black tips on crown feathers and has bluish-grey legs. **Habitat** Primary lowland dipterocarp and kerangas forest, occasionally old plantations, to 550 m. **Behaviour** Arboreal insectivore, active, acrobatic and conspicuous in mid- to upper storey; usually encountered in small parties, occasionally joining mixed feeding flocks. **Voice** Usual song in Borneo is a melancholy clear whistled *dui-dii-doo...* on rising scale, first note slightly dipping (3–3.6 kHz, 1 s); call is a rapid chattering nasal *chit-chit-chit-chit-weet-weet-weet...* **Range & status** SE Asia, Sumatra, Java. **Borneo** Common lowland resident throughout, including N Natunas. **Breeding** May–August; lays two pale green eggs densely splotched pale brown.

RUFOUS-CROWNED BABBLER
Malacopteron magnum

Identification 17–19 cm. Medium-large babbler with rufous cap, black nape, grey streaks on throat and breast, and heavy hooked bill. **Adult** *saba* (endemic subspecies) Forehead to crown rufous, nape black; lores, supercilium and sides of face grey with paler flecks, wings and back olive-brown, rump and tail rufous-brown, underparts white with broad grey streaks on greyish-washed throat and breast; iris reddish, bill grey, paler on lower mandible, legs and feet bluish-grey. **Adult** *magnum* Less extensive rufous on head from forehead to forecrown, hindcrown to nape black. **Juvenile** Iris greyish-brown, lower mandible yellowish. **Similar species** See Scaly-crowned Babbler. **Habitat** Primary lowland dipterocarp, kerangas, peatswamp and riparian forest, old plantations, to 700 m, occasionally to 1,000 m. **Behaviour** Arboreal insectivore, gleaning foliage for small invertebrates in mid- to upper storey; usually in pairs or small parties, often joining mixed feeding flocks. **Voice** A slightly complaining whistled series of notes on descending scale, each note downslurred but evenly pitched overall, *pui-pui-pui-pii-pii-pui-pii-pui-pii-pui-pii-pui...*(3.4–2.3 kHz, 3 notes/s); also a wandering song similar to Sooty-crowned Babbler but slightly slower-paced with longer notes. **Range & status** Thai-Malay Peninsula, Sumatra. **Borneo** Common lowland resident throughout, *M. m. saba* from Sabah and Brunei, *M. m. magnum* from Sarawak, Kalimantan and N Natunas. **Breeding** Possibly breeds March–October but otherwise undescribed in Borneo.

GREY-BREASTED BABBLER *Ophrydornis albogularis*

Identification 14.5–16 cm. Small, almost flycatcher-like babbler with white eyebrow and throat contrasting with dark grey head and grey breast. **Adult** *moultoni* (endemic subspecies) Head dark grey with white or yellow (N Borneo) lores and short white supercilium with distinctive kink over eye, ear-coverts dark grey, upperparts olive-brown with rufous fringes on wings, rump and short tail chestnut-brown, throat and submoustachial area white contrasting with broad grey breast-band, rest of underparts white with buffish flanks; iris reddish, bill grey with paler lower mandible, legs and feet bluish-grey. **Juvenile** Undescribed. **Habitat** Occurs in nutrient-poor forests with thick understorey: primary peatswamp and kerangas forest, essentially a lowland specialist to 300 m with records to 915 m in Sarawak. **Behaviour** Arboreal insectivore, gleaning foliage in lower storey; usually in pairs and occasionally in small parties but does not join mixed feeding flocks. **Voice** Relatively quiet but often first located by characteristic scolding of observer, a repeated loud *prrt-prrt-prrt...* (2.7 kHz); song is described as a series of 4–10 clear whistled *whit-woo* phrases on an ascending scale. **Range & status** Malay Peninsula, Sumatra. **Borneo** Rare resident Sabah and E Kalimantan, locally common to uncommon resident C and W Kalimantan, and Sarawak. **Breeding** Undescribed in Borneo. **Note** Previously placed in *Malacopteron*, but now in *Ophrydornis* owing to marked differences in morphology, plumage and behaviour.

BORNEAN GROUND-BABBLER
Ptilocichla leucogrammica

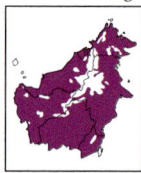

Adult

Identification 15–16 cm. Monotypic. Medium-sized ground-dwelling babbler with long hooked-tipped bill and distinctive white-streaked dark underparts. **Adult** Forehead and crown brown with indistinct blackish scaling, sides of head scaly whitish and grey, darker on ear-coverts, throat and submoustachial area whitish streaked grey with thin dark grey malar stripe, upperparts chestnut-brown, tail blackish-brown, rest of underparts black with broad white streaks fading to dull chestnut on lower flanks and undertail-coverts; iris dark brown, bill dark grey with paler lower mandible, legs and feet grey. **Juvenile** Faint streaking on crown, upperparts duller. **Habitat** Primary lowland dipterocarp, kerangas and peatswamp forest, to 900 m; probably highly sensitive to habitat disturbance. **Behaviour** Secretive and shy ground-dwelling insectivore; gleans leaf-litter in densely vegetated gullies; best detected by distinctive vocalisations; moves like small rail. **Voice** Song is a clear sweet mournful *doo-dee* or *doo-dee-doo*, each note even-pitched and slightly higher than last (1.8–2.2 kHz, 1.4–2 s); call is a harsh *prr, prr*. **Range & status** Endemic, locally uncommon lowland resident throughout, possibly commoner in north. **Breeding** Poorly known; possibly breeds July–October.

WHITE-CHESTED BABBLER *Trichastoma rostratum*

SUKAU RIVER LODGE   8/6/10 ??

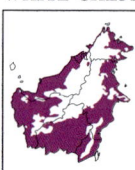

Adult

Identification 14–15 cm. Small, rather nondescript brown babbler with whitish underparts, long slender bill with hooked tip and short tail. **Adult macropterum** (endemic subspecies) Lores and face pale brown, crown olive-brown with greyish tinge, rest of upperparts warm olive-brown with darker greyish fringing on wings and tail, underparts white with pale grey sides of breast and flanks; iris dark brown, bill grey, legs and feet pinkish-grey. **Juvenile** As adult. **Similar species** Ferruginous Babbler is brighter rufous with longer tail and different behaviour and habitat. **Habitat** Primary and secondary lowland riverine forest, peatswamp, mangroves, overgrown plantations, usually to 500 m with records to 1,100 m on Kelabit Highlands. **Behaviour** A riverbank specialist, usually found near water; forages for insects on ground, rocks and roots at water's edge, also makes short sallying flights; often in pairs. **Voice** Male song is a cheerful, ringing *wee-ti-weeit* or *min-ta-duit*, last note rising then falling in pitch (2–3.5 kHz, c.0.9 s); female gives a loud sharp downslurred repeated *pwee* (4 kHz) in response to male song; call is a harsh rattle. **Range & status** Thai-Malay Peninsula, Sumatra. **Borneo** Locally common resident throughout. **Breeding** Possibly breeds around June but otherwise undescribed in Borneo.

FERRUGINOUS BABBLER *Trichastoma bicolor*

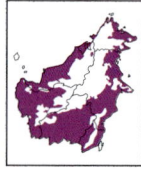

Adult

Identification 16–18 cm. Monotypic. Small babbler with long tail and distinctive rufous plumage contrasting with whitish underparts. **Adult** Lores and face pale buffish-brown, upperparts rufous-brown, brighter on wings and tail, underparts creamy-white, some with buffish wash on breast; iris brown, bill brown with paler lower mandible, legs and feet pinkish. **Juvenile** Upperparts brighter rufous. **Similar species** See White-chested Babbler. **Habitat** Primary and secondary lowland dipterocarp and swamp forest; lowland specialist to 600 m, with population on Kelabit Highlands above 900 m. **Behaviour** Forages for insects, especially ants, in lower storey; usually quite inconspicuous; often joins mixed feeding flocks. **Voice** A simple short high-pitched *hweet* (2.4–4 kHz, 0.3 s), sharply upslurred and repeated at intervals of 1–5 s; also a shorter, slightly lower-pitched downslurred *phew*. **Range & status** Thai-Malay Peninsula, Sumatra. **Borneo** Locally common resident throughout. **Breeding** March–September; lays two pale pink eggs with reddish-brown spots at larger end in small untidy nest of twigs and leaves located in bank or tree.

ABBOTT'S BABBLER *Malacocincla abbotti*

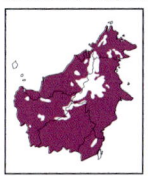

Adult

Identification 14–17 cm. Chunky, short-tailed small babbler with large, hook-tipped bill. **Adult *concreta*** Lores and supercilium greyish, upperparts olive-brown, underparts uniform greyish-white with lower flanks to undertail-coverts washed pale buffish-brown; iris reddish-brown, bill grey with paler lower mandible, legs and feet pinkish-grey. **Juvenile** Upperparts warmer brown. **Similar species** See Horsfield's Babbler. **Habitat** Lowland coastal plains, lower riverine forests often associated with nipa palms, mangroves, peatswamp forest, to 1,150 m. **Behaviour** Foliage-gleaning insectivore, foraging in lower storey; often quite inconspicuous. **Voice** Song a loud rich *fwee-feee-fwi* dipping in pitch on second note (2.2–1.5 kHz, c.1.5 s), also a four-note *wee-fwi-wii-fwee*, first two notes on level pitch, then rising and dipping. **Range & status** N and NE Indian Subcontinent, SE Asia, Sumatra. **Borneo** Rare lowland resident throughout with only 21 confirmed records; reportedly common in C Kalimantan in association with nipa; not confirmed from Brunei. **Breeding** Undescribed in Borneo.

HORSFIELD'S BABBLER *Malacocincla sepiaria*

Adult
rufiventris

Identification 14–16 cm. Chunky, short-tailed small babbler with contrasting dark crown and olive-brown upperparts. **Adult *harterti*** (endemic subspecies) Crown dark grey, lores and supercilium pale grey, ear-coverts buffish-brown with faint greyish streaking, rest of upperparts olive-brown, chin and throat white, grey wash across breast and indistinct darker streaking on lower throat and breast, centre of belly white with rufous flanks and undertail-coverts; iris reddish-brown, bill grey, legs and feet pinkish. **Adult *rufiventris*** (endemic subspecies) More pronounced contrast between head and back, more richly coloured underparts. **Juvenile** Upperparts more rufous. **Similar species** Nearly identical in plumage to Abbott's Babbler but crown darker grey, back darker and more olive, brighter, more extensive rufous coloration on flanks and undertail-coverts, indistinct streaking on upper breast, tail shorter. **Habitat** Primary lowland dipterocarp forest, to 500 m with an anomalous record from 1,700 m on G. Kinabalu. **Behaviour** Inconspicuous; usually in pairs or solitary; forages in thick vegetation for small invertebrates in lower storey. **Voice** Call is a short, grating *chrrr* repeated; song is a distinctive *tip-top-tiu...* with two short notes, first sharply high-pitched and downslurred, second lowest, last long and downslurred (3.8–1.5 kHz, 2 s). **Range & status** Thai-Malay Peninsula, Sumatra, Java, Bali. **Borneo** Locally common lowland resident throughout, *harterti* N Borneo, *rufiventris* S Borneo. **Breeding** February–November; one nest was cup of fine rootlets on base of dry leaves.

SHORT-TAILED BABBLER *Malacocincla malaccensis*

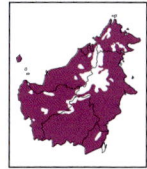

Adult

Identification 12.5–14.5 cm. Small terrestrial babbler with very short tail and conspicuous moustachial stripe. **Adult *poliogenys*** (endemic subspecies) Crown rufous-brown, lores and supercilium grey, ear-coverts grey with darker streaking bordered below with narrow blackish moustachial stripe, upperparts olive-brown, chin and throat white, pale tawny-rufous wash on breast and tawny-rufous flanks with centre of belly white; iris reddish-brown, bill grey with paler lower mandible, legs and feet pinkish. **Juvenile** Crown paler, upperparts more rufescent, throat washed buffish. **Similar species** Smaller with shorter tail than Abbott's and Horsfield's Babblers, which both lack blackish moustachial stripe. **Habitat** Primary and secondary lowland dipterocarp, peatswamp and kerangas to hill forest, old plantations, to 1,600 m. **Behaviour** Terrestrial insectivore; usually solitary or in pairs. **Voice** A mournful song consisting of a series of quite long, descending whistles, *phwee-phwee-phwee-phwee...* (3.2–2.1 kHz, each note c.0.5 s) uttered at rate of 2 notes/s; call is a harsh rapid chacking followed by a series of whining notes, *chk-chk-chk-chk-pii-pii-pii....* **Range & status** Thai-Malay Peninsula, Sumatra. **Borneo** Locally common lowland resident throughout including the Anambas, N Natunas and Bangka islands. **Breeding** Possibly January–November; otherwise undescribed in Borneo.

BLACK-BROWED BABBLER *Malacocincla perspicillata*

Adult

Identification 15 cm. Monotypic. Small babbler with broad black eyebrow and large, strong bill. **Adult** Crown brown, broad black supercilium extends to side of nape, lores pale grey with blackish spot in front of eye, ear-coverts pale grey with paler streaking, rest of upperparts dark brown, throat white merging with pale grey breast, flanks and belly to undertail-coverts brownish; iris colour unknown, bill grey, legs and feet dull brownish. **Juvenile** Undescribed. **Habitat** Unknown but probably lowland forest. **Behaviour** Undescribed. **Voice** Undescribed. **Range & status** Endemic, very rare resident S Borneo, known from one specimen probably collected in S Kalimantan, possibly extinct.

STRIPED WREN-BABBLER *Kenopia striata*

Juvenile

Adult

Identification 14–15 cm. Monotypic. Small, boldly patterned terrestrial babbler with white face giving wide-eyed look and prominent streaking on head and back. **Adult** Forehead to nape black with white streaks on centre of crown to nape, face white with yellow bristly lores and greyish ear-coverts, upperparts chestnut-brown with broad white streaks on mantle and wing-coverts, underparts white with grey mottling on sides of breast and chestnut-streaked flanks; iris dark brown, bill grey, legs and feet pink. **Juvenile** Crown browner with less streaking, lores whitish, streaking on upperparts buffish, breast and sides of breast streaked brownish. **Habitat** Primary and secondary lowland dipterocarp and kerangas forest, to 550 m, with anomalous records up to 1,220 m. **Behaviour** Terrestrial insectivore; gleans small insects from leaf-litter in thick vegetation; usually encountered singly or in pairs; moves by hopping. **Voice** Song is an even-pitched clear piercing pleasant *pit-ee-peeee...* (2.5 kHz, 0.7 s), first two notes very short; call is a harsh *chuk chuk chuk...* **Range & status** Thai-Malay Peninsula, Sumatra. **Borneo** Locally uncommon to rare resident throughout. **Breeding** Possibly breeds February–May but otherwise undescribed in Borneo.

BLACK-THROATED WREN-BABBLER
Turdinus atrigularis

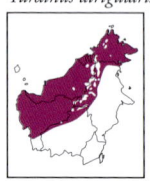

Adult

Identification 18 cm. Monotypic. Large terrestrial babbler with distinctive blue post-ocular patch and black face and throat. **Adult** Crown brown edged black, lores buffish, patch of blue skin behind eye, back and scapulars warm brown with broad black fringing, wings brown with rufous-brown fringing, tail dark brown, sides of face and throat to upper breast black with pale buffish moustachial stripe and thin malar stripe, lower breast to belly buffish with broad black scaling fading into plain lower belly and rufous flanks and undertail-coverts; iris reddish-brown, bill black, legs and feet pinkish-grey. **Juvenile** Upperparts tinged reddish, underparts buffish with blackish streaking on throat, breast and flanks. **Similar species** Bornean Wren-babbler is smaller and lacks black throat. **Habitat** Primary lowland dipterocarp forest, to 500 m, with records up to 1,500 m. **Behaviour** Ground-dwelling insectivore; gleans leaf-litter, flicking leaves, in densely vegetated gullies; encountered in pairs and small parties. **Voice** A loud, crowing monotone *dit-dee-dooo-doooo* (1.5 kHz, c.2 s); also a series of up to 50 plaintive, downslurred whistles (1.9–1.7 kHz) uttered at rate of 2 notes/s; calls are a deep gruff *we-ah, we-ah,we-ah...* **Range & status** Endemic, uncommon lowland resident in Sabah, E Sarawak, E, W and C Kalimantan. In Kalimantan, recorded from Kayan Mentarang, E Kalimantan, Barito Ulu, C Kalimantan and in far south W Kalimantan. **Breeding** January–April; egg is white with rufous splotches, nest is possibly big untidy cup of dead leaves with finer lining built close to ground in thick vegetation.

MOUNTAIN WREN-BABBLER *Napothera crassa*

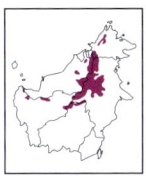

Identification 14 cm. Monotypic. Small, short-tailed, streaky terrestrial babbler with whitish supercilium and throat. **Adult** Forehead and crown to back dark greyish-brown with buffish streaks, lores and supercilium whitish-grey with dark spot in front of eye, ear-coverts brown with pale streaks, wings and tail olive-brown, throat and upper breast whitish shading through greyish lower breast to buffish-rufous belly with paler streaks to dark brown vent; iris reddish-brown, bill grey, paler on lower mandible, legs and feet greyish-brown. **Juvenile** Undescribed. **Similar species** Eyebrowed Wren-babbler is smaller, paler and buffier on throat and breast, with diagnostic buffish-white spots on wing-coverts. **Habitat** Primary lower and upper montane forest, 900–2,900 m. **Behaviour** Terrestrial insectivore; favours densely vegetated rocky gullies; usually in noisy, often inquisitive family groups of 4–6. **Voice** Typical song is a jolly *pee-tee-pee-ti-pee-ti* delivered on much the same pitch (3.7 kHz) with fourth and sixth short notes dipping (2.6

kHz), each phrase c.1 second repeated at intervals of 1–3 seconds; also a three-note *hee-hee-htee* on descending scale (3.3–2.4 kHz, 1 s), last note undulating; calls are a chirpy grating *chi-chi-chi-pipipi....* **Range & status** Endemic, locally uncommon to common resident in north-central and western mountain ranges from G. Kinabalu to Pueh Range (Sabah, Sarawak, E, C and W Kalimantan). **Breeding** March–July; lays two reddish-brown eggs with brown blotches in nest constructed in mossy bank.

EYEBROWED WREN-BABBLER *Napothera epilepidota*

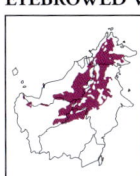

Identification 10–11 cm. Very small, almost tailless terrestrial babbler with long whitish supercilium and buffish-white spots on wing-coverts. **Adult** *exsul* (endemic subspecies) Forehead and crown to back dark brown with buffish streaks, long whitish supercilium, lores and eyestripe grey, ear-coverts and submoustachial area grey with pale streaks, wings and tail warm brown with prominent buffish-white spots on tips of wing-coverts, chin and throat buffish-white, underparts buffish-rufous with paler streaks; iris brown, bill grey, paler on lower mandible, legs and feet pinkish-brown to greyish-brown. **Juvenile** Upperparts duller with buffier wing-spots. **Habitat** Primary hill to lower montane forest, 700–1,675 m. **Behaviour** Hops on ground as it gleans leaf-litter for small invertebrates; usually in pairs or small family parties. **Voice** Song is a rather mournful pure clear whistle *pweee* (3.2 kHz, 0.8 s), repeated every 2–5 s; call is a chacking *pit pit pit*. **Range & status** NE Indian Subcontinent, S China,

SE Asia, Sumatra, Java. **Borneo** Rare submontane resident in north-central and western mountain ranges from G. Kinabalu to Barito Ulu and Pueh Range (Sabah, Sarawak and E, C and W Kalimantan). **Breeding** A nest from October was loose cup of roots, tendrils and moss placed in clump of grass, with two pale greenish-white eggs with reddish-brown markings.

SUNDA LAUGHINGTHRUSH *Garrulax palliatus*

Identification 24–25 cm. **Adult** *schistochlamys* (endemic subspecies) Lores blackish, head and mantle slaty-grey, back, wings and tail chestnut-brown, underparts slaty-grey with darker streaks on chin and throat, flanks to vent chestnut; iris black with broad aquablue eye-ring, bill and legs dark grey. **Juvenile** Duller with brown mixed with grey on upperparts. **Habitat** Primary and secondary lower and upper montane forest, 300–2,000 m but usually above 800 m. **Behaviour** Usually in loose groups, often in mixed feeding flocks; forages for small invertebrates and berries at all levels and will feed on ground. **Voice** Flock song is a low mellow ringing *koo-koo-koo-koo...* (1.7 kHz), reaching a rapid high-pitched chattering crescendo, *wit-wit-wit-witty-witty...* (3.6 kHz) and tapering off with a *wicka-wicka-wicka-wicka...* (2.2kHz); contact call is a descending mew. **Range & status** Sumatra. **Borneo** Common resident in north-central mountain ranges from G. Kinabalu to Dulit Range and G. Menyapa (Sabah, E Sarawak, E Kalimantan). **Breeding** December–March; cup-shaped nest of woven fibres.

CHESTNUT-HOODED LAUGHINGTHRUSH
Rhinocichla treacheri

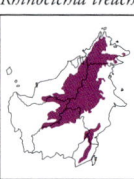

Identification 22–24 cm. **Adult *treacheri*** Lores and forehead to nape and chin chestnut, upperparts slaty-grey with white primaries forming prominent wing-patch, tail darker with black tips, throat to breast buffish-ochre with narrow buffish streaks, flanks grey, belly to undertail-coverts chestnut; iris brown with bright yellow half eye-ring below eye, bill orange, legs and feet dull orange. **Juvenile** Like adult but duller. **Adult *damnata*** Less streaking on duller breast. **Adult *griswoldi*** Richer chestnut on undertail-coverts. **Habitat** Primary and secondary hill and montane forest, forest edges and cultivation, 200–3,350 m but usually above 600 m. **Behaviour** Conspicuous; forages on ground to upper storey for small invertebrates and fruits; usually in small groups, often joining mixed feeding flocks. **Voice** Song is a repeated loud slurred whistle *wee-oo…*, rising then falling in pitch (1.5–2 kHz, 0.3 s); also a series of up to 12 shorter upslurred notes *wi-wi-wi-wi-wi…*; call is a raspy churr. **Range & status** Endemic, common montane resident in north-central ranges from G. Kinabalu to Barito Ulu, and in Meratus Mountains (Sabah, E Sarawak, E and S Kalimantan); *treacheri* Sabah, *griswoldi* C Borneo, *damnata* E Sarawak and E Kalimantan. **Breeding** February–October; lays 1–2 bright or pale greenish-blue egg in cup-shaped nest of dead leaves and roots located 3–10 m from ground in thick vegetation. **Note** Previously subsumed within Chestnut-capped Laughingthrush *Garrulax mitratus* of Peninsular Malaysia and Sumatra.

Adult *treacheri*

BARE-HEADED LAUGHINGTHRUSH
Melanocichla calva

Identification 25–26 cm. Monotypic. **Adult** Lores, area around eye and forehead to hindcrown bare yellowish skin, submoustachial blue skin-patch, rest of plumage dirty blackish-brown; iris dark brown, bill orange-red, legs and feet dirty yellow. **Juvenile** Like adult but forehead to crown feathered with bare skin behind eye. **Habitat** Primary and secondary lower montane forest, 750–1,600 m. **Behaviour** Usually in pairs or small flocks; forages for small invertebrates, often creeping about in columns of dense vegetation in mid-storey; less active than other laughingthrushes. **Voice** Call is a very low soft hollow series of 3–20 short notes, *hoo hoo hoo hoo…* (0.5 kHz); also a grating querulous *queer-queer-hoop-hoop-hoop*. **Range & status** Endemic, locally uncommon resident in north-central mountain ranges from G. Kinabalu to G. Dulit and some outlying peaks (Sabah and E Sarawak). **Breeding** Undescribed.

Juvenile

Adult

ACROCEPHALIDAE: *Acrocephalus* warblers & allies

Worldwide c.46 species, 2 in Borneo. Small to large brownish-plumaged warblers with powerful pointed bills and strong legs and often with paler supercilium. Feed on small invertebrates in tall grass and reeds. Vocalisations are often powerful and varied.

ORIENTAL REED-WARBLER *Acrocephalus orientalis*

Identification 16–18 cm. Monotypic. Generally plain olive-brown warbler, paler underneath, with distinct whitish supercilium. **Adult** Upperparts olive-brown with distinct buffish-white supercilium and darker greyish eye-stripe and lores, underparts whitish with tawny-buffish wash on flanks and vent, often with faint grey streaking on throat and breast, tail with whitish outer tips; iris brown, bill pinkish with grey culmen, gape bright pink, legs and feet grey. **Juvenile** Upperparts brighter, flight feathers edged tawny. **Similar species** Clamorous Reed-warbler has whiter throat without streaking, buffier underparts, no pale tips on tail, comparatively longer, slenderer bill, yellow gape, different vocalisations. **Habitat** Freshwater wetlands and paddyfields usually in dense reedbeds and tall grasses, also thickets and overgrown gardens, to 200 m. **Behaviour** Skulking; feeds on insects and aquatic invertebrates in thick vegetation over water; clambers around thick vegetation. **Voice** Call is a powerful *wich wich wich-wich-wich-wich…* with variable number of notes (2.5–3.8 kHz). **Range & status** Siberia, Japan, China, NE India, SE Asia, Sumatra, Philippines, Wallacea. **Borneo** Common non-breeding visitor and passage migrant, generally in coastal areas throughout, September–May.

Adult (fresh)

Adult (worn)

CLAMOROUS REED-WARBLER
Acrocephalus stentoreus

Identification 18–20 cm. Olive-brown warbler with buffish underparts and narrow whitish supercilium. **Adult** *lentecaptus* Upperparts olive-brown, narrow greyish-white supercilium and darker greyish eyestripe, throat white, rest of underparts white with buff wash; iris brown; long slender bill pinkish with grey culmen; gape yellow, legs and feet grey. **Juvenile** As adult but brighter, more rufous upperparts, stronger buffish wash on underparts. **Similar species** See Oriental Reed-warbler. **Habitat** Freshwater wetlands and paddy-fields usually in dense reedbeds and tall grasses, also mangroves and thickets. **Behaviour** Skulking and secretive; feeds on invertebrates and small vertebrates in thick vegetation over water. **Voice** Song is a loud, monotonous chattering and grating, *kirit kirit kirit chrt chrt*; also a short, harsh 'broken stick' *cht*. **Range & status** N Africa, Middle East, Indian Subcontinent, S China, SE Asia, Indonesia, Philippines, New Guinea, Solomon Islands. **Borneo** Uncommon resident S, E and W Kalimantan. **Breeding** Undescribed in Borneo.

First winter (fresh)

Adult (worn)

MEGALURIDAE: Grasshopper warblers, *Bradypterus* bush-warblers, grassbird & allies

Worldwide c.41 species, 5 in Borneo. A rather varied family of small to large warblers with medium to long, graduated tails. The plumage is generally drab brownish and buffish often with streaks on wings and upperparts. Feed on small invertebrates by clambering about in thick, scrubby vegetation.

MIDDENDORFF'S GRASSHOPPER WARBLER
Locustella ochotensis

Identification 13–14 cm. Monotypic. Small, dull-coloured warbler with relatively broad, rounded, white-tipped tail. **Adult** Upperparts olive-brown faintly mottled dark brown, tawnier on rump; buffish-grey supercilium, underparts greyish-white with buffish wash on breast and flanks, graduated tail tipped greyish-white; iris brown, bill grey with pink lower base, legs and feet pink. **Juvenile** Upperparts darker, more distinctly mottled; supercilium and underparts tinged yellow, speckled brown on throat and breast. **Similar species** See Rusty-rumped and Lanceolated Warblers. **Habitat** Freshwater wetlands, paddyfields, to 300 m. **Behaviour** Skulking; favours dense low vegetation. **Voice** Call is a soft *chk chk*; song is a rich repertoire of loud clicks and trills, *cht cht cht-cht wittee-wittee-wittee* (2–6.6 kHz, 2–2.5 s), sometimes followed by a buzzy *zzt-ztt-zzt* like toy spacegun. **Range & status** Siberia, Japan; migrates to Philippines. **Borneo** Rare non-breeding visitor and passage migrant September–May, with few records from Sabah, Brunei, Sarawak and E Kalimantan.

RUSTY-RUMPED WARBLER *Locustella certhiola*

Identification 13–14 cm. Small, rufous-washed and streaked, skulking warbler with prominent supercilium. Also known as Pallas's Grasshopper Warbler. **Adult male *certhiola*** Crown olive-brown streaked dark brown, conspicuous buffish-white supercilium, greyish-brown eyestripe, ear-coverts whitish flecked grey, mantle and back rufous-brown with heavy dark brown streaking, flight feathers dark brown fringed buff, rump rufous, tail dark brown tipped buffish-white, throat and underparts whitish with buff wash on breast and rufous-brown flanks. **Juvenile** More yellowish on underparts with less well-defined markings. **Similar species** See Lanceolated Warbler; Middendorf's Grasshopper Warbler is only faintly mottled on upperparts, has less conspicuous supercilium and whitish tips to tail. **Habitat** Freshwater wetlands, grasslands, paddyfields, generally at sea-level but with records up to 1,300 m. **Behaviour** Skulking; feeds on small invertebrates, usually close to ground in thick vegetation. **Voice** Song is a rapid trilling *rt-rt rrrrrt* followed by a more musical, whistled *rit-tik-tik-tik* (5 kHz), each phrase c.3–4 s; call is a soft *pt*. **Range & status** Siberia, N Asia, Indian Subcontinent, SE Asia, Indonesia. **Borneo** Uncommon non-breeding visitor and passage migrant throughout, sparsely distributed, September–May.

LANCEOLATED WARBLER *Locustella lanceolata*

Identification 12–13 cm. Small, heavily streaked skulking warbler. **Adult** *lanceolata* Crown buffish-brown finely spotted dark brown, narrow buff supercilium, upperparts buffish-brown broadly streaked dark brown, primaries dark brown with broad buff fringes; underparts buffish-white; breast, flanks and undertail-coverts with distinct fine dark brown streaks; rest of underparts buffish-white; iris brown, upper mandible grey, lower mandible pink with grey tip; legs and feet pale pink. **Juvenile** As adult but less distinctly marked. **Similar species** Rusty-rumped Warbler has prominent supercilium and rufous on rump; Middendorf's Grasshopper Warbler has only faint mottles on upperparts, plain underparts and whitish tips to tail. **Habitat** Freshwater wetlands, coastal grasslands, paddyfields, at sea-level. **Behaviour** Highly skulking, usually on ground; eats very small invertebrates. **Voice** Elsewhere, call is a short, sharp grating *chk chk chk*; song is a fairly high-pitched continuous reeling trill (c.6–7 kHz) involving c.18 notes/s. **Range & status** Palearctic, NE India, SE Asia, N Philippines, Sumatra, Java. **Borneo** Rare non-breeding visitor to W Sabah, Brunei and E Sarawak.

FRIENDLY BUSH-WARBLER *Bradypterus accentor*

Identification 15 cm. Monotypic. Small, skulking brownish warbler with whitish throat spotted grey. **Adult** Crown and upperparts chestnut-brown, primaries and tail darker brown, supraloral area and ear-coverts grey, throat greyish-white spotted dark grey fading into dark grey breast, flanks and undertail-coverts chestnut-brown; iris and bill black, legs and feet greyish-brown. **Juvenile** Darker, lacks pale throat. **Similar species** See Sunda Bush-warbler. **Habitat** Primary upper montane forest to tree line, 1,800–3,800 m but commoner above 2,200 m. **Behaviour** Usually solitary or in pairs; forages mouse-like for small invertebrates on ground, often with tail cocked; favours thick undergrowth. **Voice** One song is a distinctive loud ringing *di...dee-di-dee-di-dee*, each note slightly downslurred (4.2–3.8 kHz, c.2 s), sometimes without softer introductory *di*; also a slightly shrill, high *tsee tsee chree-chree...* (5.2 kHz, c.1 s) on level pitch, last notes longer and louder with buzzing quality. **Range & status** Endemic, uncommon resident restricted to highest mountains (G. Kinabalu, Trus Madi and Tambuyukon) of Sabah, N Borneo. **Breeding** Undescribed.

STRIATED GRASSBIRD *Megalurus palustris*

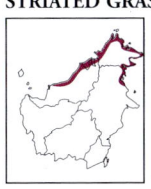

Identification 22–28 cm. Large, streaky warbler with long graduated tail. **Adult** *forbesi* Crown and nape buffish-brown finely streaked blackish-brown, broad buffish supercilium bordered below by dark line behind eye, lores and ear-coverts buffish-brown, underparts whitish with distinct fine blackish-brown streaks on breast and flanks, mantle and back buffish-brown with broad blackish-brown streaks, wing and tail blackish with broad buffish fringes; iris brown, upper mandible grey, lower mandible yellowish, legs and feet yellowish. **Juvenile** More rufous-tinged upperparts less heavily streaked, underparts yellowish and unstreaked. **Habitat** Marshes, swamps, grasslands, paddyfields, at sea-level. **Behaviour** Solitary or in pairs; forages amongst reeds and long grasses for small invertebrates; often sings loudly from conspicuous perch such as fence, powerlines or low bush; flies low with undulating flight. **Voice** One song is a rich bubbling *pit pit pit pri pri pwee-pwee-pwee* (c.4 kHz, 1.5–2 s), first notes softer; also variety of shorter or longer phrases. **Range & status** Himalayas, S China, SE Asia, Philippines, Java and Bali. **Borneo** Uncommon resident Sabah, Brunei, C Sarawak and northern E Kalimantan; recent coloniser from Philippines. **Breeding** Possibly breeds around August but otherwise undescribed in Borneo.

CISTICOLIDAE: Cisticolas, tailorbirds, prinias & allies

Worldwide c.114 species, 5 in Borneo. A large family of tiny to small birds with small slender bill, short rounded wings and rounded or long, graduated tail. Active skulkers in long grass, scrub or thick vegetation. Vocalisations are generally simple but distinctive. Typically sexes similar.

ASHY TAILORBIRD *Orthotomus ruficeps*

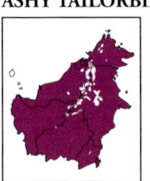

Identification 11–12 cm. Ashy-grey tailorbird with distinctive rufous hood. **Adult male** *borneoensis* (endemic subspecies) Head to chin deep rufous, upperparts dark ashy-grey with wings and tail tinged brown, throat and breast ashy-grey fading to greyish-white on lower belly and undertail-coverts; iris reddish-brown, bill pink with grey culmen, legs and feet pale pink. **Adult female** As male but paler on underparts with grey wash on breast and flanks and white chin and throat. **Juvenile** Upperparts all olive-brown, underparts whitish with grey wash. **Habitat** Primary lowland dipterocarp and riverine forest edges, secondary forest, peatswamp forest, kerangas, mangroves, plantations, gardens, to 1,500 m. **Behaviour** Forages with tail cocked for small invertebrates in dense vegetation from understorey to canopy; very vocal. **Voice** A variety of loud, strident songs and calls including a relatively slow, upwardly inflected *choowit… choowit…* (2–3.5 kHz, 0.4 s), repeated irregularly; also a loud *chi-wit* (4.7 kHz, 0.2 s), first note briefer uttered alone or in couplets, repeated at intervals of c.1–3 s; call is a trilled *prrrrt*. **Range & status** Thai-Malay Peninsula, Sumatra, Java. **Borneo** Common resident throughout including offshore islands. **Breeding** February–September; bird makes tunnel by sewing together long banana or ginger leaf in which nest of grasses and fibres is then made; lays 2–3 eggs.

RUFOUS-TAILED TAILORBIRD *Orthotomus sericeus*

Identification 12 cm. Smart, chestnut-capped tailorbird with relatively short rufous-chestnut tail and long bill. **Adult male** *sericeus* Crown and sides of head bright chestnut contrasting with white ear-coverts and throat, underparts whitish with grey wash on sides of breast, upperparts dark grey, tail bright rufous-chestnut; iris brown, bill pink with grey culmen, legs and feet pink. **Adult female** As male but with subterminal grey spots on tail. **Juvenile** Upperparts all olive, underparts whitish with yellow tinge, tail as female. **Habitat** Forest edges of primary lowland dipterocarp and riverine to lower montane forest, secondary forest with scrubby vegetation, kerangas, plantations, overgrown gardens, mangroves, to 1,200 m. **Behaviour** Skulking but very vocal, so more often seen than heard; forages with tail cocked for small invertebrates in dense vegetation and tangles. **Voice** A variety of loud songs including a rollicking *do-dee do-dee do-dee*, first short note lower-pitched (2 kHz), the higher pitched second note dropping in pitch rapidly (3.2–2.4 kHz), each phrase c.0.5 s; also a rapid *do-dit-do*, first note higher; and a sharp high *dee-dit* (4.5 kHz); all these songs are repeated continuously. **Range & status** Thai-Malay Peninsula, Sumatra, SW Philippines. **Borneo** Common resident throughout including offshore islands. **Breeding** November–June; nest is like that of Dark-necked Tailorbird; lays 3–4 pale pink eggs with purplish-red and brownish markings.

DARK-NECKED TAILORBIRD *Orthotomus atrogularis*

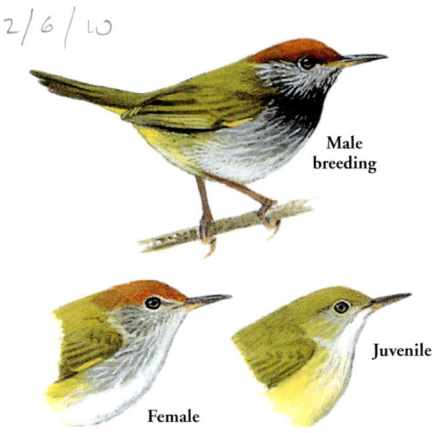

Identification 11–12 cm. Rufous-crowned, greenish tailorbird with broad blackish lower throat and breast (male). **Adult male *atrogularis*** Crown and sides of head rufous, ear-coverts streaky pale grey, throat and upper breast blackish-grey, lower breast streaked grey and white, rest of underparts whitish with yellow undertail-coverts, upperparts olive-green; iris reddish-brown, bill pinkish with grey culmen, legs and feet pinkish-brown. **Adult female** As male but paler rufous on head, paler yellow on undertail-coverts, no dark breast. **Juvenile** Upperparts olive-green, underparts whitish washed yellow. **Adult male *humphreysi*** (endemic subspecies) Much more extensive blackish-grey from chin to lower breast, belly to undertail-coverts pale yellow. **Adult female** As *atrogularis* female but throat and breast white (not grey). **Similar species** Female *humphreysi* differs from Mountain Tailorbird by rufous nape and crown (respectively grey and orange-rufous in latter). **Habitat** Primary and secondary lowland dipterocarp, peatswamp and kerangas forest, favouring areas of disturbance such as roadsides and gaps resulting from tree-falls, to 600 m. **Behaviour** Skulking but active; forages with tail cocked for small invertebrates in dense vegetation and tangles; very vocal and more often seen than heard. **Voice** A jaunty reeling *prreee* (c.4 kHz, 0.7 s) repeated over and over at intervals of 0.1–1.5 s, unlike song of any other tailorbird; call is a squeaky grating *zeetttt*. **Range & status** NE India, SE Asia, Sumatra. **Borneo** Common resident throughout, *humphreysi* NE Borneo, *atrogularis* elsewhere, *anambensis* (similar to nominate) the Anambas and N Natunas. **Breeding** March–August; nest consists of two or more leaves sewn together with cobwebs and lined with fine grass or kapok.

BRIGHT-HEADED CISTICOLA *Cisticola exilis*

Identification 9 cm. **Adult male breeding *lineocapilla*** Crown, nape and face orangey-rufous, mantle and back buffish-brown heavily streaked dark brown, plain rufous rump, wings brown with buffish fringes, tail brown with buffish tips, underparts white with orange wash on breast and flanks; iris and bill brown, legs and feet pink. **Adult male non-breeding** Upperparts more heavily streaked including on crown and rump. **Adult female** Like non-breeding male but duller and paler. **Juvenile** Browner above, pale yellowish underparts with buffish flanks. **Habitat** Grasslands, paddyfields, at sea-level. **Voice** A distinctive, buzzing *zzzt zzzt zzt-zzt* followed by a bubbly *p-prrp*. **Range & status** S and NE India, China, SE Asia, Indonesia, Philippines, New Guinea, Australia. **Borneo** Status uncertain, probably vagrant, SW Borneo (W Kalimantan).

YELLOW-BELLIED PRINIA *Prinia flaviventris*

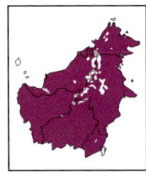

Identification 12–14 cm. **Adult male *latrunculus*** (endemic subspecies) Crown to nape and sides of neck dark grey grading into olive-brown upperparts, short supercilium white, throat white, rest of underparts buffish-white with pale yellow wash on belly and flanks; iris dark red, bill black, legs and feet pink. **Juvenile** Paler with more yellow on underparts. **Habitat** Freshwater wetlands, grasslands, paddyfields, roadside scrub, to 1,550 m. **Behaviour** Feeds on small invertebrates in thick vegetation close to ground; sings from low bushes and tops of tall grass stems. **Voice** A complex but repetitive burbling warble, *wit-wit weety-weety-weet* (c.3.5–5 kHz), each phrase c.0.7 s, repeated at 1–2 s intervals; call is a loud, very nasal *cheet cheet*. **Range & status** Himalayas, S China, Taiwan, SE Asia, Sumatra, Java. **Borneo** Common resident throughout. **Breeding** December–August; lays 2–3 brick-red eggs in domed oval nest of grasses located close to ground in thick vegetation; one was decorated on outside with cobwebs and yellow cocoons.

REFERENCES

Ahlquist, J. E., Sheldon, F. H. and Sibley, C. G. (1984) The relationships of the Bornean Bristlehead (*Pityriasis gymnocephala*) and the Black-collared Thrush (*Chlamydochaera jefferyi*). *Journal of Ornithology* 125: 129-140.

Bakewell, D. N. and Kennerley, P. R. (2008) Field characteristics and distribution of an overlooked *Charadrius* plover from South-East Asia. *BirdingASIA* 9 : 46-5.

van Balen, S. (1997) Faunistic notes from Kayan Mentarang, with new records for Kalimantan. *Kukila* 9: 108-113.

van Balen, S. (1999) Note on the distribution of the Kinabalu Serpent-eagle with a first record from Kalimantan. *Kukila* 10: 154-156.

van Balen, S. (1999) First record of Grey Heron in Kalimantan. *Kukila* 10: 156-157.

van Balen, S. (1999) Note on a sighting of Striated Grassbird in Kalimantan. *Kukila* 10: 157-158.

van Balen S. (2000) A record of Long-tailed Broadbill from Kalimantan. *Kukila* 11: 146.

van Balen, S., Adikerana, A. and Boeadi. (1994) Schrenck's Bittern in Barito Ulu, Central Kalimantan. *Kukila* 7(1): 77.

van Balen, S. and Aspinall, S. (1996) First record of Grey-streaked Flycatcher in Kalimantan. *Kukila* 8: 142-144.

van Balen, S. and Hedges, S. (2000) First sighting of Oriental Plover on mainland Kalimantan. *Kukila* 11: 145.

van Balen, S. and Nurwatha, P. F. (1999) Eastern Marsh-harrier in Kalimantan. *Kukila* 10: 152-153.

van Balen, S. and Prentice, C. (1997) Birds of the Negara River Basin, South Kalimantan, Indonesia. *Kukila* 9: 81-107.

Banks, E. (1952) Mammals and birds from the Maga Mountains in Borneo. *Bulletin of the Raffles Museum* 24: 160-163.

Banks, E. (1961) Review: An annotated checklist of the birds of Borneo. By B. E. Smythies. Sarawak Museum Journal. No. 24 Old Series (Vol. 7, pt 3, New Series), June 1957. pp 523-818. *Bulletin of the Raffles Museum* 26: 197-203.

Bartlett, W. J. (1896) Egg of *Pityriasis gymnocephala*. *Ibis* 38: 158-159.

BirdLife International (2001) *Threatened Birds of Asia: the BirdLife International Red Data Book*. Cambridge, UK: BirdLife International.

Biun, A., Lakim, M. B. and Davison, G. W. H. (2006) Spread of *Tyto capensis* (Smith) 1834 to Borneo. *Sabah Parks Nature Journal* 7: 45-48.

Blaber, S. J. M. and Milton, D. A. (1995) The distribution of nests of the Black-and-red Broadbill, *Cymbirhynchus macrorhynchus*, along a river in Sarawak. *Forktail* 10: 182.

Boden-Kloss, C. (1930) The birds of Mangalum and Matanani Islands off the West Coast of British North Borneo. *Bulletin of the Raffles Museum* 4: 117-123.

Boden-Kloss, C. (1931) A contribution to the zoology of Mangalum Island, North West Borneo: (i). Introduction, mammals, birds, reptiles, amphibians, molluscs. *Bulletin of the Raffles Museum* 5: 87-89.

Brooks, T. (1996) A record of Yellow-rumped Flycatcher from Kalimantan. *Kukila* 8: 151-152.

Carter, C. (1998) Identification of large *Acrocephalus* warblers at Candaba Swamp, Luzon, Philippines. *Oriental Bird Club Bulletin* 27: 51-54.

Chasen, F. N. and Boden-Kloss, C. (1930) On a collection of birds from the lowlands and islands of North Borneo. *Bulletin of the Raffles Museum* 4: 1-112.

Chasen, F. N. and Boden-Kloss, C. (1930) A list of the birds of Banguey, Balambangan, Mallewalle Islands, British North Borneo. *Bulletin of the Raffles Museum* 4: 113-116.

Chasen, F. N. and Boden-Kloss, C. (1930) Additions to the list of Bornean birds. *Bulletin of the Raffles Museum* 4: 124.

Chasen, F. N. and Boden-Kloss, C. (1931) Notes on Malaysian birds. *Bulletin of the Raffles Museum* 5: 80-82.

Chasen, F. N. and Boden-Kloss, C. (1931) Five new Malaysian birds. *Bulletin of the Raffles Museum* 5: 82-86

Cibois, A., Kalyakin, M. V., Han, L. X. and Pasquet, E. (2002) Molecular phylogenetics of babblers (Timaliidae): revaluation of the genera *Yuhina* and *Stachyris*. *Journal of Avian Biology* 33: 380-390.

Colenutt S. (2002) Little known Oriental bird: Bornean Bristlehead. *Oriental Bird Club Bulletin* 35.

Davies, G. and Payne, J. (1982) *A faunal survey of Sabah*. Kuala Lumpur, Malaysia: WWF Malaysia.

Davison, G. W. H. (1997) Bird observations in the Muratus Mountains, South Kalimantan. *Kukila* 9: 114-121.

Davison, G. W. H. (1997) Bird observations on Pulau Laut, South Kalimantan. *Kukila* 9: 122-125.

Davison, G. W. H. (2008) Records of *Rhizothera (longirostris) dulitensis* in Sabah. *Forktail* 24: 125-127.

Davison, G. W. H. and Fook, C. Y. (2008) *A Photographic Guide to the Birds of Borneo*. London, UK: New Holland.

Duckworth, W. and Kelsh, R. (1988) A Bird Inventory of Similajau National Park. *ICBP Study Report* No.31.

Duckworth, J. W., Wilkinson, R. J., Tizard, R. J., Kelsh, R. H., Irvin, S. A., Evans, M. I. and Orrell, T. D. (1997) Bird records from Similajau National Park, Sarawak. *Forktail* 12: 159-196.

duPont, J. E. (1971) *Philippine Birds*. Greenville, USA: Delaware Museum of Natural History.

Dutson, G. (1990) Birds of Barito Ulu in Borneo. *Oriental Bird Club Bulletin* 12: 16.

Dutson. G., Wilkinson, R. and Sheldon, B. (1991) Hook-Billed Bulbul, *Setornis criniger*, and Grey-Breasted Babbler, *Malacopteron albogulare*, at Barito Ulu, Kalimantan. *Forktail* 6: 78.

Dymond, N. (1999) Two records of Black-headed Bunting, *Emberiza melanocephala*, in Sabah – the first

definite occurrences in Malaysia and Borneo. *Forktail* 15: 102.
Eames, J. C. (2005) A preliminary ornithological assessment and conservation evaluation of the PT Daisy logging concession, Beraudistrict, East Kalimantan, Indonesia. *Forktail* 21: 51.
Elkin, J. A. (1993) Japanese Night-Heron *Gorsachius goisagi*: a new species for Borneo. *Forktail* 8: 154.
Elkin J. A., Mann, C. F. and Ozog, C. (1993) Black-collared Starling *Sturnus nigricollis*: a new species for Borneo. *Forktail* 8: 155.
Enticott, J. and Tipling, D. (1997) *Seabirds of the World*. London, UK: New Holland.
Fogden. M. P. L. (1972) The seasonality and population dynamics of equatorial forest birds in Sarawak. *Ibis* 114: 307-343.
Galdikas, B. M. F. and King, B. (1989) Lesser Adjutant nests in SW Kalimantan. *Kukila* 4: 151-152.
Gönner, C. (2000) Birds of Lake Jempang and the Middle Mahakam Wetlands, East Kalimantan. *Kukila* 11: 13.
Gore, M. E. J. (1968) A checklist of the birds of Sabah, Borneo. *Ibis* 10: 165-196.
Gregory-Smith, R. (1999) 'Birds of Sarawak: A Digital Annotated Checklist', www.arbec.com.my/bos (Version 1999), Kuala Lumpur, Malaysia: MIMCED 1999.
Harrison, P. (1983) *Seabirds: an identification guide*. Boston, USA: Houghton Mifflin.
Harrisson, T. (1950) Bird notes from Borneo. *Bulletin of the Raffles Museum* 23: 328-335.
Harvey, W. G. and Holmes, D. A. (1976) Additions to the avifauna of Sumatra and Kalimantan, Indonesia. *Bulletin of the British Ornithologists' Club* 96: 90-92.
Hayman, P., Marchant, J. and Prater, T. (1986) *Shorebirds: an Identification guide*. Helm, London.
Holmes, D. A. (1990) Note on the status of the White-shouldered Ibis in Kalimantan. *Kukila* 5(2): 145-148.
Holmes, D. A. (1997) Kalimantan Bird Report 2. *Kukila* 9: 141-169.
Holmes, D. A. and Burton, K. (1987) Recent notes on the avifauna of Kalimantan. *Kukila* 3: 2-32.
Hood. I. (1995) A sighting of Storm's Stork at Danau Sentarum, West Kalimantan. *Kukila* 7: 157.
Hose, C. (1929) *The Field-Book of a Jungle Wallah*. Singapore: Oxford in Asia.
del Hoyo, J., Elliot, A. and Sargata, G. eds. (1996) *Handbook of the birds of the world. Volume 3: Hoatzin to auks*. Barcelona, Spain: Lynx Edicions.
bin Jalan, B. and Galdikas, B. M. F. (1987) Birds of Tanjung Puting National Park, Kalimantan Tengah: a preliminary list. *Kukila* 3(1-2): 33-37.
Kanouchi, T. (2005) *Identification of wild birds with photographs*. Okumura Printing, Japan.
Kabaya, T. and Matsuda, M. (2001) *The songs and calls of 420 birds in Japan*. Tokyo, Japan: Shogakukan.
Kawai, D., Kawasaki, Y., Shimada, A. and Morohashi, J. (2003) *The wild birds of Hokkaido*. Japan.
Kennerley, P. R., Bakewell, D. N. and Round, P. D. (2008). Rediscovery of a long lost *Charadrius* plover from Southeast Asia. *Forktail* 24: 63-79.
Laman, T. G., Burnaford, J. L. and Knott, C. D. (1997) Sunda Ground-cuckoo observations in Gunung Palung National Park, West Kalimantan. *Kukila* 9: 183-185.
Leader P. J. and Carey G. J. (2003) Identification of Pintail Snipe and Swinhoe's Snipe. *British Birds* 96: 178-198.
Lecroy, M. (2003) Type Specimens of Birds in the American Museum of Natural History. Part 5. Passeriformes: Alaudidae, Hirundinidae, Motacillidae, Campephagidae, Pycnonotidae, Irenidae, Laniidae, Vangidae, Bombycillidae, Dulidae, Cinclidae, Troglodytidae and Mimidae. *Bulletin of the American Museum of Natural History* 278(1).
Lekagul, B. and Round, P. D. (1991) *A guide to the birds of Thailand*. Bangkok, Thailand.
Liang, C. T., Chang, C. H. and Fang, W. H. (2000) Little known Oriental bird: discovery of a breeding colony of Chinese Crested Tern. *Oriental Bird Club Bulletin* 32.
Long, A. J. and Collar, N. J. (2002) Distribution, status and natural history of the Bornean Ground Cuckoo *Carpococcyx radiatus*. *Forktail* 18: 101-119.
Mann, C. F. (1987) Notable bird observations from Brunei, Borneo. *Forktail* 3: 51.
Mann, C. F. (1989) More notable bird observations from Brunei, Borneo. *Forktail* 5: 17.
Mann, C. F. and Diskin, D. A. (1993) Northern Shrike, *Lanius excubitor*: a new species for Borneo and South-East Asia. *Forktail* 8: 153.
Marsh, C. W. (1989) *Expedition to Maliau Basin, Sabah, April-May 1988: final report*. Kota Kinabalu, Malaysia: Yayasan Sabah.
Marshall, J. T. (1978) Systematics of smaller Asian nightbirds based on voice. *Ornithological Monographs* 25.
Mayr, E. (1938) Notes on a collection of birds from south Borneo. *Bulletin of the Raffles Museum* 14: 5-46.
Meier, G. (2004) Notebook: Grey Imperial Pigeon: a new record from East Kalimantan, Indonesia. *BirdingASIA* 1: 56.
Meijaard E., van Balen, S. and Nijman, V. (2005) The former status of the White-shouldered Ibis *Pseudibis davisoni* on the Barito and Teweh rivers, in Indonesia, Borneo. *Raffles Bulletin of Zoology* 53(2): 277-279.
Meijaard, E., Sheil, D., Nasi, R., Augeri, D., Rosenbaum, B., Iskandar, D., Setyawati, T., Lammertink, M., Rachmatika, I., Wong, A., Soehartono, T., Stanley, S. and O'Brien, T. (2005) *Life after logging: reconciling wildlife conservation and production forestry in Indonesian Borneo*. CIFOR, Bogor, Indonesia.
Melville, D. S. (1996) Call of the Grey Imperial Pigeon. *Kukila* 9: 72.
Moyle, R. G., Cracraft, J., Lakim, M., Nais, J. and Sheldon, F. H. (2006) Reconsideration of the phylogenetic relationships of the enigmatic Bornean Bristlehead (*Pityriasis gymnocephala*). *Molecular Phylogenetics and Evolution* 39: 893-898.
Nash, S.V. and Nash, A. D. (1988) An annotated checklist of the birds of Tanjung Puting National Park, Central Kalimantan. *Kukila* 3: 93-116.

Nijman, V., Fredriksson, G. M., Usher, G. F. and Gönner, C. (2005) Little Black Shag in East Kalimantan, Indonesia: first confirmation of the species' presence in Borneo in over 150 years. *Waterbirds* 28: 516-518.

Olson, S. L. (1987) More on the affinities of the Black-collared Thrush of Borneo (*Chlamydochaera jefferyi*). *Journal of Ornithology* 128: 246-248.

Oriental Bird Club Images: www.orientalbirdimages.org

Pavlova, A., Zink, R. M., Rohwer, S., Koblik, E. A., Red'kin, Y. A., Fadeev, I. V. and Nesterov, E. V. (2005) Mitochondrial DNA and plumage evolution in the White Wagtail *Motacilla alba*. *Journal of Avian Biology* 36 (4): 322-336.

Petersen, S. (1991) A record of White-shouldered Ibis in East Kalimantan. *Kukila* 5: 144-145.

Prescott, K. W. (1970) A kingfisher new to Borneo. *Auk* 87(3).

Prieme, A. and Heegaard, M. (1988) A visit to Gunung Nyiut in West Kalimantan. *Kukila* 3: 138-140.

Prum, R.O. (1988) Phylogenetic interrelationships of the barbets (Aves: Capitonidae) and toucans (Aves: Ramphastidae) based on morphology with comparisons to DNA-DNA hybridization. *Zoological Journal of the Linnean Society* 92: 313-343.

Rahman, M. A. and Tuen, A. A. (2006) The avifauna. Pp.129-136 in Abang, F. and Das, I. (eds.) *The biodiversity of a peat swamp forest in Sarawak*. Kota Samarahan, Malaysia: Institute of Biodiversity and Environmental Conservation, Universiti Malaysia Sarawak.

Reid, C. (1997) A record of Bornean Treepie from Kalimantan Barat. *Kukila* 9: 179-180.

Rice, C. G. (1989) A further range extension of the Black-breasted Thrush *Chlamydochaera jefferyi* in Kalimantan. *Kukila* 4: 47-48.

Robson, C. (2007) *New Holland Field Guide to the Birds of South-East Asia*. London, UK: New Holland.

Robson, C. (2008) *A Field Guide to the Birds of South-East Asia*. London, UK: New Holland.

Sangster, G. (1998) Purple Swamp-hen is a complex of Species. *Dutch Birding* 20: 13-22.

Scharringa, J. (2006). *Birds of tropical Asia 3.6*. Westernieland, The Netherlands: Bird Songs International.

Shanahan, M. and Debski, I. (2002) Vertebrates of Lambir Hills National Park, Sarawak. *Malayan Nature Journal* 56: 103-118.

Sharpe, R. B. (1887) Notes on a collection of birds made by Mr John Whitehead on the mountain of Kina Balu, in Northern Borneo, with descriptions of new species. *Ibis* (5)5: 435-454.

Sheldon, F. H. (1985) The taxonomy and biogeography of the Thick-billed Flowerpecker complex in Borneo. *Auk* 102: 606-612.

Sheldon, F. H. (1987) Habitat preferences of the Hook-billed Bulbul *Setornis criniger*, and the White-throated Babbler *Malacopteran albogulare*, in Borneo. *Forktail* 3: 17-25.

Sheldon, F. H., Moyle, R. G. and Kennard, J. (2001) Ornithology of Sabah: history, gazetteer, annotated checklist and bibliography. *Ornithological Monographs* 52.

Showler, D. (1992) Danum Valley Conservation Area, Sabah, Malaysia. *Oriental Bird Club Bulletin* 16: 26.

Sibley, C. G. and Monroe, B. L. (1990) *Distribution and taxonomy of birds of the world*. New Haven: Yale University Press.

Sim Lee Kheng and Akira Mizutani (2005) First record of Aleutian Tern for Borneo. *BirdingASIA* 4: 60.

Smythies, B. E. (1999) *The birds of Borneo*. Natural History Publications (Borneo).

Sonobe, K. and Usui, S. eds. (1993) *A field guide to the water birds of Asia*. Wild Bird Society of Japan, Tokyo.

Sözer, R. (1994) A recent sighting of White-shouldered Ibis in Kalimantan. *Kukila* 7: 75.

Sözer, R. and van der Heijden, A. J. W. J. (1997) An overview of the distribution, status and behavioural ecology of the White-shouldered Ibis in East Kalimantan. *Kukila* 9: 126-140.

Sözer, R. and Nijman, V. (2005) Effects of ENSO-induced forest fires and habitat disturbance on the abundance and spatial distribution of an endangered riverine bird in Borneo. *Animal Conservation* 8: 27-31.

Steinheimer F. D. (1999) The Mountain Black-eye, *Cholorocharis emiliae* (Zosteropidae), as a rhododendron flower visitor on Mt Kinabulu, Sabah, Malaysia. *Forktail* 15: 100.

Viney, C., Phillipps, K. and Lam, C. Y. (1996) *Birds of Hong Kong and South China*. Hong Kong.

Vowles, G. A. and Vowles, R. S. (1997) *An annotated checklist of the birds of Brunei*. Newent, UK: Centro de Estudos Ornitologicos no Algarve.

Whitehead, J. (1893) *Exploration of Mount Kina Balu, North Borneo*. London, UK: Gurney and Jackson.

Wilkinson, R., Dutson, G., Sheldon, B., Darjono and Yus Rusila Noor (1991) The avifauna of the Barito Ulu region, Central Kalimantan. *Kukila* 5: 99-116.

Williams, R. S. R. (2002) The rediscovery and doubtful validity of the Blue-wattled Bulbul *Pycnonotus nieuwenhuisii*. *Forktail* 18: 107-109.

Wilson, K. J. (2004) A provisional sighting of the Silvery Pigeon on the Talang Talang Islands, Sarawak, Malaysia. *BirdingASIA* 1: 55-57.

Witt, C. C. and Sheldon, F. H. (1994) A review of the status and distribution of the Bornean Bristlehead. *Kukila* 7: 54-67.

Yong, D., Scriven, K. W. and Johns, A. (1989) Birds. Pp.145-154 in *Expedition to Maliau Basin, Sabah, April-May 1988*. Sabah Information Paper No. 30. Project No. MYS 126/88 (C. W. Marsh, ed.). Kuala Lumpur, Malaysia: Sabah Foundation and World Wildlife Fund (Malaysia).

INDEX

Abroscopus superciliaris 238
Accipiter gularis 53
Accipiter nisus 53
Accipiter soloensis 52
Accipiter trivirgatus 52
Accipiter virgatus 52
Aceros corrugatus 141
Aceros undulatus 141
Acridotheres cristatellus 204
Acridotheres javanicus 204
Acridotheres tristis 204
Acrocephalus orientalis 257
Acrocephalus stentoreus 257
Actenoides concretus 131
Actitis hypoleucos 75
Adjutant, Lesser 28
Aegithina tiphia 173
Aegithina viridissima 173
Aerodramus fuciphaga 125
Aerodramus maximus 125
Aerodramus salangana 125
Aethopyga siparaja 185
Aethopyga temminckii 185
Alauda gulgula 227
Alcedo atthis 135
Alcedo euryzona 135
Alcedo meninting 135
Alcippe brunneicauda 241
Alophoixus bres 234
Alophoixus finschii 234
Alophoixus ochraceus 235
Alophoixus phaeocephalus 234
Amandava amandava 198
Amaurornis phoenicurus 61
Anas acuta 25
Anas clypeata 24
Anas crecca 26
Anas gibberifrons 26
Anas penelope 23
Anas platyrhynchos 24
Anas querquedula 25
Anas superciliosa 24
Anhinga melanogaster 42
Anorrhinus galeritus 138
Anous minutus 86
Anous stolidus 86
Anthracoceros albirostris 138
Anthracoceros malayanus 139
Anthreptes malacensis 183
Anthreptes rhodolaema 183
Anthreptes simplex 183
Anthus cervinus 200
Anthus gustavi 201
Anthus hodgsoni 201
Anthus richardi 201
Anthus rufulus 202
Aplonis panayensis 205
Apus affinis 126
Apus pacificus 127
Arachnothera affinis 186

Arachnothera chrysogenys 188
Arachnothera crassirostris 187
Arachnothera flavigaster 188
Arachnothera juliae 188
Arachnothera longirostra 187
Arachnothera modesta 186
Arachnothera robusta 187
Arborophila charltonii 18
Arborophila hyperythra 18
Ardea alba 36
Ardea cinerea 35
Ardea purpurea 35
Ardea sumatrana 35
Ardeola bacchus 34
Ardeola speciosa 34
Arenaria interpres 82
Argus, Great 22
Argusianus argus 22
Artamus leucorynchus 172
Asio flammeus 118
Avadavat, Red 198
Aviceda jerdoni 45
Avocet, Pied 63
Aythya fuligula 26

Babbler, Abbott's 253
Babbler, Black-browed 254
Babbler, Black-capped 249
Babbler, Black-throated 244
Babbler, Chestnut-rumped 246
Babbler, Chestnut-winged 246
Babbler, Ferruginous 252
Babbler, Grey-breasted 251
Babbler, Grey-headed 245
Babbler, Grey-throated 245
Babbler, Horsfield's 253
Babbler, Moustached 250
Babbler, Rufous-crowned 251
Babbler, Rufous-fronted 247
Babbler, Scaly-crowned 251
Babbler, Short-tailed 253
Babbler, Sooty-capped 250
Babbler, Temminck's 249
Babbler, White-chested 252
Babbler, White-necked 244
Barbet, Blue-eared 144
Barbet, Bornean 144
Barbet, Brown 144
Barbet, Golden-naped 143
Barbet, Gold-whiskered 142
Barbet, Mountain 143
Barbet, Red-crowned 142
Barbet, Red-throated 142
Barbet, Yellow-crowned 143
Barn-owl, Common 113
Batrachostomus affinis 121
Batrachostomus auritus 119
Batrachostomus cornutus 121
Batrachostomus harterti 119
Batrachostomus mixtus 120

Batrachostomus stellatus 120
Baza, Jerdon's 45
Bee-eater, Blue-tailed 136
Bee-eater, Blue-throated 137
Bee-eater, Red-bearded 136
Berenicornus comatus 140
Besra 52
Bittern, Black 31
Bittern, Cinnamon 31
Bittern, Great 30
Bittern, Von Schrenck's 31
Bittern, Yellow 30
Blackeye, Mountain 243
Bluetail, Red-flanked 211
Blythipicus rubiginosus 151
Boobook, Brown 118
Boobook, Northern 118
Booby, Brown 40
Booby, Masked 40
Booby, Red-footed 40
Botaurus stellaris 30
Brachypteryx montana 211
Bradypterus accentor 259
Bristlehead, Bornean 181
Broadbill, Banded 157
Broadbill, Black-and-red 156
Broadbill, Black-and-yellow 157
Broadbill, Dusky 156
Broadbill, Green 154
Broadbill, Hose's 154
Broadbill, Long-tailed 155
Broadbill, Whitehead's 155
Bubo sumatranus 116
Bubulcus coromandus 34
Buceros rhinoceros 139
Bulbul, Black-and-white 229
Bulbul, Black-headed 228
Bulbul, Blue-wattled 230
Bulbul, Bornean 228
Bulbul, Buff-vented 233
Bulbul, Cinereous 235
Bulbul, Cream-vented 232
Bulbul, Finsch's 234
Bulbul, Grey-bellied 229
Bulbul, Grey-cheeked 234
Bulbul, Hairy-backed 233
Bulbul, Hook-billed 233
Bulbul, Ochraceous 235
Bulbul, Olive-winged 231
Bulbul, Pale-faced 231
Bulbul, Puff-backed 230
Bulbul, Red-eyed 232
Bulbul, Scaly-breasted 227
Bulbul, Sooty-headed 230
Bulbul, Spectacled 232
Bulbul, Straw-headed 229
Bulbul, Streaked 235
Bulbul, Yellow-bellied 234
Bulbul, Yellow-vented 231
Bulweria bulwerii 27

265

Bunting, Black-headed 199
Bunting, Little 199
Bunting, Yellow-breasted 200
Bushchat, Pied 213
Bushlark, Australasian 227
— Bush-warbler, Friendly 259
Bush-warbler, Sunda 239
Butastur indicus 56
Buteo burmanicus 56
Butorides striata 32
Buzzard, Grey-faced 56
Buzzard, Himalayan 56

Cacomantis merulinus 106
Cacomantis sepulcralis 107
Cacomantis sonneratii 106
Calidris acuminata 80
Calidris alba 79
Calidris alpina 81
Calidris canutus 78
Calidris ferruginea 81
Calidris minuta 79
Calidris ruficollis 79
Calidris subminuta 80
Calidris temminckii 80
Calidris tenuirostris 78
Caloenas nicobarica 94
Calonectris leucomelas 27
Caloperdix oculea 18
Calorhamphus fuliginosus 144
Calyptomena hosii 154
Calyptomena viridis 154
Calyptomena whiteheadi 155
Canary-flycatcher, Grey-headed 226
Caprimulgus affinis 123
Caprimulgus concretus 123
Caprimulgus jotaka 122
Caprimulgus macrurus 123
Carpococcyx radiatus 109
Cecropis striolata 236
Centropus bengalensis 112
Centropus rectunguis 112
Centropus sinensis 112
Cettia vulcania 239
Ceyx rufidorsa 134
Chalcoparia singalensis 184
Chalcophaps indica 94
Charadrius alexandrinus 66
Charadrius dealbatus 67
Charadrius dubius 65
Charadrius hiaticula 65
Charadrius leschenaultii 67
Charadrius mongolus 66
Charadrius peronii 66
Charadrius placidus 65
Charadrius veredus 67
Chlamydochaera jefferyi 209
Chlidonias hybrida 90
Chlidonias leucopterus 91
Chlorocharis emiliae 243
Chloropsis cochinchinensis 195
Chloropsis cyanopogon 194

Chloropsis kinabaluensis 194
Chloropsis sonnerati 194
Chroicocephalus ridibundus 91
Chrysococcyx basalis 108
Chrysococcyx minutillus 108
Chrysococcyx xanthorhynchus 107
Chrysocolaptes lucidus 150
Chrysophlegma mentalis 148
Chrysophlegma mineaceus 148
Ciconia stormi 28
Cinnyris jugularis 185
Circus cyaneus 50
Circus melanoleucos 51
Circus spilonotus 50
Cissa chinensis 179
Cissa thalassina 179
Cisticola exilis 261
Cisticola, Bright-headed 261
Clamator coromandus 102
Collared-dove, Island 94
Collocalia dodgei 124
Collocalia esculenta 124
Columba argentina 92
Columba livia 92
Columba vitiensis 92
Coot, Common 60
Copsychus malabaricus 214
Copsychus saularis 213
Copsychus stricklandii 214
Coracina fimbriata 167
Coracina larvata 166
Coracina striata 166
Cormorant, Great 41
Cormorant, Little 41
Cormorant, Little Black 41
Corvus enca 178
Corvus macrorhynchos 178
Corvus splendens 178
Corydon sumatranus 156
Coturnix chinensis 17
— Coucal, Greater 112
Coucal, Lesser 112
Coucal, Short-toed 112
Crake, Baillon's 58
Crake, Band-bellied 59
Crake, Red-legged 57
Crake, Ruddy-breasted 58
Crake, White-browed 59
Crow, House 178
— Crow, Slender-billed 178
Crow, Southern Jungle 178
Crypsirina temia 180
Cuckoo, Banded Bay 106
Cuckoo, Chestnut-winged 102
— Cuckoo, Drongo 108
Cuckoo, Himalayan 105
Cuckoo, Horsfield's Bronze 108
Cuckoo, Indian 104
Cuckoo, Little Bronze 108
Cuckoo, Oriental 105
Cuckoo, Plaintive 106
Cuckoo, Rusty-breasted 107

Cuckoo, Sunda 106
Cuckoo, Violet 107
Cuckoo-dove, Little 93
Cuckoo-dove, Ruddy 93
Cuckooshrike, Bar-bellied 166
— Cuckooshrike, Lesser 167
Cuckooshrike, Sunda 166
Cuculus horsfieldi 105
Cuculus lepidus 106
Cuculus micropterus 104
Cuculus saturatus 105
Culicicapa ceylonensis 226
— Curlew, Eurasian 73
Curlew, Far Eastern 73
Curlew, Little 74
Cyanoptila cyanomelana 218
Cymbirhynchus macrorhynchos 156
Cyornis banyumas 217
Cyornis caerulatus 217
Cyornis concretus 218
Cyornis rufigastra 218
Cyornis superbus 216
Cyornis turcosus 216
Cyornis unicolor 216
Cypsiurus balasiensis 125

— Darter, Oriental 42
Delichon dasypus 236
Dendrocitta cinerascens 180
Dendrocopos canicapillus 146
Dendrocopos moluccensis 146
Dendrocygna arcuata 22
Dendrocygna javanica 23
Dendronanthus indicus 202
Dicaeum agile 189
Dicaeum chrysorrheum 192
Dicaeum cruentatum 193
Dicaeum everetti 189
Dicaeum minullum 192
Dicaeum monticolum 192
Dicaeum thoracicus 191
Dicaeum trigonostigma 191
Dicaeum trochileum 193
Dicrurus aeneus 177
Dicrurus annectans 176
Dicrurus hottentottus 177
Dicrurus leucophaeus 176
Dicrurus macrocercus 176
Dicrurus paradiseus 177
Dinopium javanense 150
Dinopium rafflesii 149
— Dollarbird 131
— Dove, Emerald 94
— Dove, Spotted 93
— Dove, Zebra 95
Dowitcher, Asian 71
Dowitcher, Long-billed 71
Drongo, Ashy 176
Drongo, Black 176
Drongo, Bronzed 177
Drongo, Crow-billed 176
Drongo, Greater Racket-tailed 177

Drongo, Hair-crested 177
Dryocopus javensis 147
Duck, Pacific Black 24
Duck, Tufted 26
Ducula aenea 98
Ducula badia 99
Ducula bicolor 99
Ducula pickeringii 98
Dunlin 81
Dupetor flavicollis 31

Eagle, Black 54
Eagle, Rufous-bellied 56
Eagle-owl, Barred 116
Eared-nightjar, Malaysian 122
— Egret, Chinese 37
— Egret, Eastern Cattle 34
— Egret, Great 36
— Egret, Intermediate 36
— Egret, Little 37
Egretta eulophotes 37
Egretta garzetta 37
Egretta sacra 37
Elanus caeruleus 47
Emberiza aureola 200
Emberiza melanocephala 199
Emberiza pusilla 199
Enicurus borneensis 215
Enicurus leschenaultia 215
Enicurus ruficapillus 215
Erpornis zantholeuca 163
Erpornis, White-bellied 163
Erythrura hyperythra 198
Erythrura prasina 198
Esacus neglectus 61
Eudynamys scolopacea 109
Eumyias indigo 219
Eumyias thalassina 219
Eupetes macrocerus 164
Eurostopodus temminckii 122
Eurylaimus javanicus 157
Eurylaimus ochromalus 157
Eurystomus orientalis 131

Fairy-bluebird, Asian 195
Falco moluccensis 43
Falco peregrinus 44
Falco severus 44
Falco subbuteo 44
Falco tinnunculus 42
Falcon, Peregrine 44
Falconet, Black-thighed 43
Falconet, White-fronted 43
Fantail, Pied 173
— Fantail, Spotted 174
— Fantail, White-throated 174
Ficedula albicilla 222
Ficedula dumetoria 220
Ficedula hyperythra 221
Ficedula mugimaki 221
Ficedula narcissina 220
Ficedula westermanni 222

Ficedula zanthopygia 220
Fireback, Crested 20
Fireback, Crestless 20
Fish-eagle, Grey-headed 48
Fish-eagle, Lesser 49
Fish-owl, Buffy 116
Flameback, Common 150
Flameback, Greater 150
Flowerpecker, Black-sided 192
Flowerpecker, Brown-backed 189
Flowerpecker, Crimson-breasted 190
— Flowerpecker, Orange-bellied 191
Flowerpecker, Plain 192
— Flowerpecker, Scarlet-backed 193
Flowerpecker, Scarlet-breasted 191
Flowerpecker, Scarlet-headed 193
Flowerpecker, Thick-billed 189
Flowerpecker, Yellow-breasted 189
Flowerpecker, Yellow-rumped 190
Flowerpecker, Yellow-vented 192
Flycatcher, Asian Brown 223
Flycatcher, Blue-and-white 218
Flycatcher, Bornean Blue 216
Flycatcher, Brown-streaked 223
Flycatcher, Dark-sided 223
Flycatcher, Ferruginous 224
Flycatcher, Grey-streaked 222
Flycatcher, Hill Blue 217
— Flycatcher, Indigo 219
Flycatcher, Large-billed Blue 217
— Flycatcher, Little Pied 222
Flycatcher, Malaysian Blue 216
Flycatcher, Mangrove Blue 218
Flycatcher, Mugimaki 221
Flycatcher, Narcissus 220
Flycatcher, Pale Blue 216
Flycatcher, Pygmy Blue 219
Flycatcher, Rufous-chested 220
Flycatcher, Snowy-browed 221
Flycatcher, Taiga 222
Flycatcher, Verditer 219
Flycatcher, White-tailed 218
Flycatcher, Yellow-rumped 220
Flycatcher-shrike, Bar-winged 171
— Flycatcher-shrike, Black-winged 171
Forktail, Bornean 215
Forktail, Chestnut-naped 215
Forktail, White-crowned 215
Fregata andrewsi 38
Fregata ariel 39
Fregata minor 39
Frigatebird, Christmas Island 38
Frigatebird, Great 39
Frigatebird, Lesser 39
Frogmouth, Blyth's 121
Frogmouth, Bornean 120
Frogmouth, Dulit 119
Frogmouth, Gould's 120
Frogmouth, Large 119
Frogmouth, Sunda 121
Fruit-dove, Black-naped 95

Fruit-dove, Jambu 95
Fruit-hunter 209
Fulica atra 60
Fulvetta, Brown 241

Gallicrex cinerea 59
Gallinago gallinago 70
Gallinago megala 70
Gallinago stenura 70
Gallinula chloropus 60
Gallinula tenebrosa 61
Gallirallus philippensis 57
Gallirallus striatus 57
Garganey 25
Garrulax palliatus 255
Gelochelidon nilotica 88
Geopelia striata 95
Gerygone sulphurea 164
Gerygone, Golden-bellied 164
Glareola maldivarum 84
Glaucidium brodiei 117
Godwit, Bar-tailed 72
Godwit. Black-tailed 72
Gorsachius goisagi 32
Gorsachius melanolophus 32
Goshawk, Crested 52
Gracula religiosa 205
Gracupica nigricollis 205
Grassbird, Striated 259
Grass-owl, Eastern 113
Grebe, Little 28
Green-pigeon, Cinnamon-headed 96
Green-pigeon, Large 97
Green-pigeon, Little 96
— Green-pigeon, Pink-necked 97
— Green-pigeon, Thick-billed 97
Greenshank, Common 77
Greenshank, Nordmann's 77
Ground-babbler, Bornean 252
Ground-cuckoo, Bornean 109
Gull, Black-headed 91
Gyps bengalensis 51

Haematortyx sanguiniceps 19
Halcyon coromanda 133
Halcyon pileata 133
Haliaeetus leucogaster 48
Haliastur indus 47
Hanging-parrot, Blue-crowned 100
Harpactes diardii 128
Harpactes duvaucelii 130
Harpactes kasumba 128
Harpactes oreskios 130
Harpactes orrhophaeus 129
Harpactes whiteheadi 129
Harrier, Hen 50
Harrier, Pied 51
— Hawk, Bat 46
Hawk-cuckoo, Dark 103
Hawk-cuckoo, Hodgson's 104
Hawk-cuckoo, Large 102

Hawk-cuckoo, Malaysian 103
Hawk-cuckoo, Moustached 103
Hawk-cuckoo, Northern 104
Hawk-eagle, Blyth's 55
— Hawk-eagle, Changeable 54
Hawk-eagle, Wallace's 55
Hemicircus concretus 153
Hemiprocne comata 127
Hemiprocne longipennis 127
Hemipus hirundinaceus 171
Hemipus picatus 171
Hemixos cinereus 235
Heron, Great-billed 35
Heron, Grey 35
— Heron, Little 32
— Heron, Purple 35
Hierococcyx bocki 103
Hierococcyx fugax 103
Hierococcyx hyperythrus 104
Hierococcyx nisicolor 104
Hierococcyx sparverioides 102
Hierococcyx vagans 103
Hill-myna, Common 205
Himantopus himantopus 62
Himantopus leucocephalus 62
Honey-buzzard, Oriental 46
Honeyguide, Malaysian 145
Hoopoe, Common 137
— Hornbill, Black 139
— Hornbill, Bushy-crested 138
Hornbill, Helmeted 140
— Hornbill, Oriental Pied 138
Hornbill, Rhinoceros 139
Hornbill, White-crowned 140
Hornbill, Wreathed 141
— Hornbill, Wrinkled 141
House-martin, Asian 236
Hydrochrous gigas 124
Hydrophasianus chirurgus 68
Hydroprogne caspia 86
Hypogramma hypogrammicum 186
Hypothymis azurea 174

Ibis, Black-headed 29
Ibis, Glossy 29
Ibis, White-shouldered 29
Ichthyophaga humilis 49
Ichthyophaga ichthyaetus 48
Ictinaetus malayensis 54
— Imperial-pigeon, Green 98
Imperial-pigeon, Grey 98
Imperial-pigeon, Mountain 99
Imperial-pigeon, Pied 99
Indicator archipelagicus 145
Iole olivacea 233
— Iora, Common 173

Iora, Green 173
Irediparra gallinacea 68
Irena puella 195
Ixobrychus cinnamomeus 31
Ixobrychus eurhythmus 31
Ixobrychus sinensis 30
Ixos malaccensis 235

Jacana, Comb-crested 68
Jacana, Pheasant-tailed 68
Jaeger, Parasitic 85
Jaeger, Pomarine 85
Jay, Crested 180
Jungle-flycatcher, Brown-chested 224
Jungle-flycatcher, Eyebrowed 225
Jungle-flycatcher, Fulvous-chested 224
Jungle-flycatcher, Grey-chested 225
Jungle-flycatcher, Rufous-tailed 225

Kenopia striata 254
Kestrel, Common 42
Kestrel, Spotted 43
Ketupa ketupu 116
Kingfisher, Banded 132
Kingfisher, Black-capped 133
Kingfisher, Blue-banded 135
— Kingfisher, Blue-eared 135
— Kingfisher, Collared 134
Kingfisher, Common 135
Kingfisher, Ruddy 133
Kingfisher, Rufous-backed 134
Kingfisher, Rufous-collared 131
Kingfisher, Sacred 134
Kingfisher, Stork-billed 132
Kite, Black-eared 47
Kite, Black-shouldered 47
— Kite, Brahminy 47
Knot, Great 78
Knot, Red 78
Koel, Asian 109

Lacedo pulchella 132
Lalage nigra 167
Lanius cristatus 182
Lanius meridionalis 182
Lanius schach 182
Lanius tigrinus 181
Lapwing, Grey-headed 63
Lapwing, Northern 63
Laughingthrush, Bare-headed 256
— Laughingthrush, Chestnut-hooded 256
Laughingthrush, Sunda 255
Leafbird, Blue-winged 195
Leafbird, Bornean 194
Leafbird, Greater Green 194
Leafbird, Lesser Green 194
— Leaf-warbler, Mountain 240
Leptocoma brasiliana 184
Leptocoma calcostetha 184
Leptoptilos javanicus 28
Limicola falcinellus 81

Limnodromus scolopaceus 71
Limnodromus semipalmatus 71
Limosa lapponica 72
Limosa limosa 72
Locustella certhiola 258
Locustella lanceolata 259
Locustella ochotensis 258
Lonchura atricapilla 197
Lonchura fuscans 196
Lonchura leucogastra 197
Lonchura punctulata 197
Lophotriorchis kienerii 56
Lophura bulweri 21
Lophura erythrophthalma 20
Lophura ignita 20
Loriculus galgulus 100
Luscinia calliope 212
Luscinia cyane 211

Macheiramphus alcinus 46
Macronous bornensis 248
Macronous ptilosus 248
Macropygia emiliana 93
Macropygia ruficeps 93
Magpie, Bornean Black 179
Magpie, Common Green 179
Magpie, Short-tailed Green 179
— Magpie-robin, Oriental 213
Malacocincla abbotti 253
Malacocincla malaccensis 253
Malacocincla perspicillata 254
Malacocincla sepiaria 253
Malacopteron affine 250
Malacopteron cinereum 251
Malacopteron magnirostre 250
Malacopteron magnum 251
Malkoha, Black-bellied 110
Malkoha, Chestnut-bellied 110
Malkoha, Chestnut-breasted 111
Malkoha, Raffles's 111
Malkoha, Red-billed 110
Mallard 24
Marsh-harrier, Eastern 50
Megalaima australis 144
Megalaima chrysopogon 142
Megalaima eximia 144
Megalaima henricii 143
Megalaima monticola 143
Megalaima mystacophanos 142
Megalaima pulcherrima 143
Megalaima rafflesii 142
Megalurus palustris 259
Megapodius cumingii 16
Meiglyptes tristis 152
Meiglyptes tukki 152
Melanocichla calva 256
Melanoperdix nigra 17
Merops philippinus 136
Merops viridis 137
Mesophoyx intermedia 36
Microhierax fringillarius 43
Microhierax latifrons 43

268

Micropternus brachyurus 147
Milvus lineatus 47
Minivet, Ashy 167
Minivet, Fiery 168
— Minivet, Grey-chinned 168
— Minivet, Scarlet 168
Mirafra javanica 227
— Monarch, Black-naped 174
Monticola solitarius 210
Moorhen, Common 60
Moorhen, Dusky 61
Motacilla alba 203
Motacilla cinerea 202
Motacilla tschutschensis 203
Mulleripicus pulverulentus 153
— Munia, Chestnut 197
— Munia, Dusky 196
— Munia, Scaly-breasted 197
— Munia, White-bellied 197
Muscicapa dauurica 223
Muscicapa ferruginea 224
Muscicapa griseisticta 222
Muscicapa sibirica 223
Muscicapa williamsoni 223
Muscicapella hodgsoni 219
— Myna, Common 204
Myna, Javan 204
Myna, White-vented 204
Myophonus borneensis 210

Napothera crassa 255
Napothera epilepidota 255
— Needletail, Brown-backed 126
Needletail, Silver-rumped 126
Needletail, White-throated 126
Nettapus coromandelianus 23
Night-heron, Black-crowned 33
Night-heron, Japanese 32
Night-heron, Malaysian 32
Night-heron, Rufous 33
Nightjar, Bonaparte's 123
Nightjar, Grey 122
— Nightjar, Large-tailed 123
Nightjar, Savanna 123
Ninox japonica 118
Ninox scutulata 118
Nisaetus alboniger 55
Nisaetus limnaeetus 54
Nisaetus nanus 55
Noddy, Black 86
— Noddy, Brown 86
Numenius arquata 73
Numenius madagascariensis 73
Numenius minutus 74
Numenius phaeopus 73
Nuthatch, Velvet-fronted 196
Nycticorax caledonicus 33
Nycticorax nycticorax 33
Nyctyornis amictus 136

Oceanodroma monorhis 27
Oculocincta squamifrons 243

Oenanthe oenanthe 212
Onychoprion aleuticus 90
Onychoprion anaethetus 89
Onychoprion fuscatus 89
Ophrydornis albogularis 251
Oriole, Black 169
Oriole, Black-and-crimson 169
Oriole, Black-hooded 170
Oriole, Black-naped 169
Oriole, Dark-throated 170
Oriolus chinensis 169
Oriolus cruentus 169
Oriolus hosii 169
Oriolus xanthonotus 170
Oriolus xanthornus 170
Orthotomus atrogularis 261
Orthotomus ruficeps 260
Orthotomus sericeus 260
Osprey 45
Otus brookii 115
Otus lempiji 115
Otus mantananensis 115
Otus rufescens 114
Otus spilocephalus 114
Owl, Oriental Bay 113
Owl, Short-eared 118
Owlet, Collared 117

Pachycephala cinerea 165
Pachycephala homeyeri 165
Pachycephala hypoxantha 165
Padda oryzivora 196
Painted-snipe, Greater 69
— Palm-swift, Asian 125
Pandion haliaetus 45
Paradise-flycatcher, Asian 175
Paradise-flycatcher, Japanese 175
— Parakeet, Long-tailed 101
Parakeet, Red-breasted 101
Parrot, Blue-naped 101
Parrot, Blue-rumped 100
Parrotfinch, Pin-tailed 198
Parrotfinch, Tawny-breasted 198
Partridge, Black 17
Partridge, Chestnut-necklaced 18
Partridge, Crested 19
Partridge, Crimson-headed 19
Partridge, Dulit 17
Partridge, Ferruginous 18
Partridge, Long-billed 16
Partridge, Red-breasted 18
Parus cinereus 226
Passer montanus 199
Peacock-pheasant, Bornean 21
Pelargopsis capensis 132
Pellorneum capistratum 249
Pellorneum pyrrogenys 249
Pericrocotus divaricatus 167
Pericrocotus igneus 168
Pericrocotus solaris 168
Pericrocotus speciosus 168
Pernis ptilorhynchus 46

Petrel, Bulwer's 27
Phaethon lepturus 38
Phalacrocorax carbo 41
Phalacrocorax niger 41
Phalacrocorax sulcirostris 41
Phalarope, Red 83
Phalarope, Red-necked 83
Phalaropus fulicarius 83
Phalaropus lobatus 83
Pheasant, Bulwer's 21
Philentoma pyrhoptera 172
Philentoma velata 172
Philentoma, Maroon-breasted 172
Philentoma, Rufous-winged 172
Philomachus pugnax 82
Phodilus badius 113
Phyllergates cucullatus 238
Phylloscopus borealis 240
Phylloscopus inornatus 240
Phylloscopus trivirgatus 240
Piculet, Rufous 145
Piculet, Speckled 146
Picumnus innominatus 146
Picus puniceus 149
Pigeon, Metallic 94
Pigeon, Nicobar 94
— Pigeon, Rock 92
Pintail, Northern 25
Pipit, Olive-backed 201
— Pipit, Paddyfield 202
Pipit, Pechora 201
Pipit, Red-throated 200
Pipit, Richard's 201
Pitta arquata 160
Pitta baudii 160
Pitta caerulea 162
Pitta granatina 161
Pitta guajana 162
Pitta megarhyncha 159
Pitta moluccensis 159
Pitta nympha 158
Pitta sordida 158
Pitta ussheri 161
Pitta, Banded 162
Pitta, Black-and-crimson 161
Pitta, Blue-banded 160
Pitta, Blue-headed 160
Pitta, Blue-winged 159
Pitta, Fairy 158
Pitta, Garnet 161
Pitta, Giant 162
Pitta, Hooded 158
Pitta, Mangrove 159
Pityriasis gymnocephala 181
Platalea minor 30
Platylophus galericulatus 180
Platysmurus aterrimus 179
Plegadis falcinellus 29
Plover, Common Ringed 65
Plover, Grey 64
Plover, Kentish 66
Plover, Little Ringed 65

269

Plover, Long-billed 65
Plover, Malaysian 66
Plover, Oriental 67
Plover, Pacific Golden 64
Plover, White-faced 67
Pluvialis fulva 64
Pluvialis squatarola 64
Polyplectron schleiermacheri 21
Pomatorhinus montanus 247
Pond-heron, Chinese 34
Pond-heron, Javan 34
Porphyrio indicus 60
Porzana cinerea 59
Porzana fusca 58
Porzana paykullii 59
Porzana pusilla 58
Pratincole, Australian 84
Pratincole, Oriental 84
Prinia flaviventris 261
Prinia, Yellow-bellied 261
Prionochilus maculatus 189
Prionochilus percussus 190
Prionochilus xanthopygius 190
Psarisomus dalhousiae 155
Pseudibis davisoni 29
Psittacula alexandri 101
Psittacula longicauda 101
Psittinus cyanurus 100
Pteruthius flaviscapis 163
Ptilinopus jambu 95
Ptilinopus melanospila 95
Ptilocichla leucogrammica 252
Puffinus pacificus 27
Pycnonotus atriceps 228
Pycnonotus aurigaster 230
Pycnonotus brunneus 232
Pycnonotus cyaniventris 229
Pycnonotus erythropthalmos 232
Pycnonotus eutilotus 230
Pycnonotus goiavier 231
Pycnonotus leucops 231
Pycnonotus melanoleucos 229
Pycnonotus montis 228
Pycnonotus nieuwenhuisii 230
Pycnonotus plumosus 231
Pycnonotus simplex 232
Pycnonotus squamatus 227
Pycnonotus zeylanicus 229
Pygmy-goose, Cotton 23

Quail, Blue-breasted 17

Rail, Buff-banded 57
Rail, Eastern Water 58
Rail, Slaty-breasted 57
Rail-babbler 164
Rallina fasciata 57
Rallus indicus 58
Recurvirostra avosetta 63
Redshank, Common 76
Redshank, Spotted 76
Reed-warbler, Clamorous 257

Reed-warbler, Oriental 257
Reef-egret, Pacific 37
Reinwardtipicus validus 151
Rhaphidura leucopygialis 126
Rhinocichla treachery 256
Rhinomyias brunneatus 224
Rhinomyias gularis 225
Rhinomyias olivacea 224
Rhinomyias ruficauda 225
Rhinomyias umbratilis 225
Rhinoplax vigil 140
Rhinortha chlorophaeus 111
Rhipidura albicollis 174
Rhipidura javanica 173
Rhipidura perlata 174
Rhizothera dulitensis 17
Rhizothera longirostris 16
Rhopodytes diardi 110
Rhopodytes sumatranus 110
Riparia riparia 236
Robin, Siberian Blue 211
Rock-thrush, Blue 210
Rollulus rouloul 19
Rostratula benghalensis 69
Rubythroat, Siberian 212
Ruff 82

Sanderling 79
Sand-martin, Common 236
Sandpiper, Broad-billed 81
Sandpiper, Common 75
Sandpiper, Curlew 81
Sandpiper, Green 75
Sandpiper, Marsh 77
Sandpiper, Sharp-tailed 80
Sandpiper, Terek 74
Sandpiper, Wood 75
Sand-plover, Greater 67
Sand-plover, Lesser 66
Sasia abnormis 145
Saxicola caprata 213
Saxicola maurus 212
Scimitar-babbler, Chestnut-backed 247
Scolopax rusticola 69
Scops-owl, Mantanani 115
Scops-owl, Mountain 114
Scops-owl, Rajah 115
Scops-owl, Reddish 114
Scops-owl, Sunda 115
Scrubfowl, Tabon 16
Sea-eagle, White-bellied 48
Seicercus montis 239
Serpent-eagle, Crested 49
Serpent-eagle, Mountain 49
Setornis criniger 233
Shama, Rufous-tailed 214
Shama, White-crowned 214
Shama, White-rumped 214
Shearwater, Streaked 27
Shearwater, Wedge-tailed 27
Shortwing, White-browed 211
Shoveler, Northern 24

Shrike, Brown 182
Shrike, Long-tailed 182
Shrike, Southern Grey 182
Shrike, Tiger 181
Shrike-babbler, White-browed 163
Sitta frontalis 196
Skylark, Oriental 227
Snipe, Common 70
Snipe, Pintail 70
Snipe, Swinhoe's 70
Sparrow, Java 196
Sparrowhawk, Chinese 52
Sparrowhawk, Eurasian 53
Sparrowhawk, Japanese 53
Spiderhunter, Grey-breasted 186
Spiderhunter, Little 187
Spiderhunter, Long-billed 187
Spiderhunter, Spectacled 188
Spiderhunter, Streaky-breasted 186
Spiderhunter, Thick-billed 187
Spiderhunter, Whitehead's 188
Spiderhunter, Yellow-eared 188
Spilornis cheela 49
Spilornis kinabaluensis 49
Spoonbill, Black-faced 30
Stachyridopsis rufifrons 247
Stachyris erythroptera 246
Stachyris leucotis 244
Stachyris maculata 246
Stachyris nigriceps 245
Stachyris nigricollis 244
Stachyris poliocephala 245
Staphida everetti 241
Starling, Asian Glossy 205
Starling, Black-collared 205
Starling, Chestnut-cheeked 206
Starling, Purple-backed 206
Starling, Rosy 207
Starling, White-shouldered 206
Stercorarius parasiticus 85
Stercorarius pomarinus 85
Sterna dougallii 88
Sterna hirundo 89
Sterna sumatrana 88
Sternula albifrons 90
Stilt, Black-winged 62
Stilt, White-headed 62
Stiltia isabella 84
Stint, Little 79
Stint, Long-toed 80
Stint, Red-necked 79
Stint, Temminck's 80
Stonechat, Eastern 212
Stork, Storm's 28
Storm-petrel, Swinhoe's 27
Streptopelia bitorquata 94
Streptopelia chinensis 93
Strix leptogrammica 117
Stubtail, Bornean 238
Sturnus philippensis 206
Sturnus roseus 207
Sturnus sinensis 206